INEQUALITY, MOBILITY AND SEGREGATION: ESSAYS IN HONOR OF JACQUES SILBER

RESEARCH ON ECONOMIC INEQUALITY

Series Editors: John A. Bishop and Juan Gabriel Rodriguez

RESEARCH ON ECONOMIC INEQUALITY VOLUME 20

INEQUALITY, MOBILITY AND SEGREGATION: ESSAYS IN HONOR OF JACQUES SILBER

EDITED BY

JOHN A. BISHOP
East Carolina University, USA

RAFAEL SALAS
Universidad Complutense de Madrid, Spain

United Kingdom – North America – Japan
India – Malaysia – China

Emerald Group Publishing Limited
Howard House, Wagon Lane, Bingley BD16 1WA, UK

First edition 2012

British Library Cataloguing in Publication Data
A catalogue record for this book is available from the British Library

ISBN: 978-1-78190-170-0
ISSN: 1049-2585 (Series)

CONTENTS

LIST OF CONTRIBUTORS

Olga Alonso-Villar	Department of Applied Economics, University of Vigo, Vigo, Spain
Francesco Andreoli	Department of Economics, University of Verona, Verona, Italy; THEMA, University of Cergy-Pontoise and ESSEC Business School, Cergy, France
Sanghamitra Bandyopadhyay	Department of Economics, Queen Mary University of London, and London School of Economics, London, UK
Wail Benaabdelaali	National Authority of Evaluation (INE), Higher Education Council, Morocco; Laboratory for Applied Economics for Development (LEAD), University of South Toulon-Var, France
Andrea Brandolini	Department for Structural Economic Analysis, Bank of Italy, Rome, Italy
Michael J. Camasso	Department of Agricultural, Food & Resource Economics, School of Environmental & Biological Sciences, Rutgers, The State University of New Jersey, New Brunswick, NJ, USA
Mª Casilda Lasso de la Vega	Departamento de Economía Aplicada IV and BRIDGE Research Group, University of the Basque Country, UPV/EHU, Spain
Coral del Río	Department of Applied Economics, University of Vigo, Vigo, Spain
Veronika V. Eberharter	Department of Economics, University of Innsbruck, Innsbruck, Austria

B. Essama-Nssah	DevTech Systems, Inc., Arlington, VA, USA
Jürgen Faik	FaMa – Neue Frankfurter Sozialforschung, Frankfurt/Main, Germany
Alessio Fusco	CEPS/INSTEAD, Luxembourg
Carlos Gradín	Department of Applied Economics, University of Vigo, Vigo, Spain
Saîd Hanchane	National Authority of Evaluation (INE), Higher Education Council, Morocco; Laboratory for Applied Economics for Development (LEAD), University of South Toulon-Var, France
Nizamul Islam	CEPS/INSTEAD, Luxembourg
Radha Jagannathan	Bloustein School of Planning & Public Policy, Rutgers, The State University of New Jersey, New Brunswick, NJ, USA
Abdelhak Kamal	National Authority of Evaluation (INE), Higher Education Council, Morocco; Laboratory for Applied Economics for Development (LEAD), University of South Toulon-Var, France
Serge Kolm	Ecole des Hautes Etudes en Sciences Sociales, France
Peter J. Lambert	Economics Department, University of Oregon, Eugene, OR, USA
Cathal O'Donoghue	Teagasc Rural Economy and Development Programme, Ireland
Alfonso Rosolia	Department for Structural Economic Analysis, Bank of Italy, Rome, Italy
Jacques Silber	Department of Economic, Bar Ilan University, Ramat Gan, Israel

Denisa Maria Sologon	CEPS/INSTEAD, Luxembourg
Roberto Torrini	Department for Structural Economic Analysis, Bank of Italy, Rome; ANVUR–National Agency for the Evaluation of Universities and Research Institutes, Rome, Italy
Ana Urrutia	Departamento de Economia Aplicada IV and BRIDGE Research Group, University of the Basque Country, UPV/EHU, Spain

INTRODUCTION

It is our pleasure as editors to dedicate *Research on Economic Inequality*, Volume 20 to Professor Jacques Silber. Jacques is a long-time friend of the series and has kindly functioned as a mentor and advisor to us.

When one begins to take the measure of Jacques' contributions to the economics profession one thinks of Jacques' early interest in, and definitive works upon inequality, and especially the Gini coefficient. On the Gini itself one finds a half-dozen influential papers beginning in 1985 and continuing until the present. Other areas where Jacques has made definitive contributions include tax progressivity decomposition, positional social evaluation functions, and other distributional concepts such as segregation and polarization. Even this impressive list fails to recognize important contributions to the field of human development and the quality of life, mobility and opportunity, health inequality, labor market discrimination, unemployment and low wage labor markets, as well as macro policy and inequality. Although Jacques will formally "retire" this year he currently has five papers under review and at least a dozen different projects in progress.

Jacques has also edited or coedited some much-valued and widely cited books, including the *Handbook on Income Inequality Measurement*. Recent projects include editing the (currently seven volume) series, *Economics Studies in Inequality, Social Exclusion, and Well-Being*. Jacques is the founding editor of the *Journal of Economic Inequality*, which has thrived from its inception. Jacques has sat on distinguished expert panels and conducted numerous funded research projects. He is the current President of the *Society for the Study of Economic Inequality*.

The above is an incomplete listing of Jacques' contributions. His teaching contributions include the chairing and jury membership for many Ph.D. and MA candidates both in Israel and abroad, memberships on editorial boards, countless scholarly paper reviews, and the organization of many conference sessions. Jacques has eagerly embraced young scholars, often collaborating with them to help them establish their research agendas. Above all Jacques is a "gentleman-scholar," always honest in his opinion, always respectful of others. In addition to his commitment to his profession, he would be pleased to also be recognized for his devotion to his family and friends, and particularly, to his wife Fanny.

Volume 20 of *Research on Economic Inequality* contains 15 chapters. In the opening chapter Jacques Silber presents a survey on segregation, where he demonstrates that both the cardinal and ordinal approaches to measuring dual group occupational segregation borrow many ideas from the income inequality measurement literature. Furthermore, he also shows that the more recent advances in multigroup segregation measurement and ordinal segregation could be the basis for additional approaches to the measurement of economic inequality, in particular inequality in life chances, health and happiness, and eventually to the study of polarization.

Following Silber's essay on "Measuring Segregation" are three chapters that evaluate occupation and residential segregation. In Chapter 2 Coral del Río and Olga Alonso-Villar begin by pointing out that standard indices of occupational segregation "do not take into account whether demographic groups tend to occupy high or low status jobs." To tackle this problem they propose an axiomatic framework in which one can measure the segregation of any population subgroup while taking into account the status of occupations in a cardinal way. Status-sensitive segregation curves (and their dominance principles) consistent with their axioms are derived. The authors then contrast U.S. ethnic segregation levels to those obtained using status-sensitive methods. They find that when status of occupation is considered "the performance of African-Americans and Hispanics worsens with respect to Asians."

In Chapter 3 Carlos Gradín documents the extent of occupational segregation among Afro-descendants and whites in five Latin American countries. He then measures *conditional* segregation, or the degree to which occupational segregation can be explained by pre-market factors such as workers' education, location, migration status, and age. He finds that a large proportion of occupational segregation in Brazil and Ecuador can be explained by differences in education. In Costa Rica and Cuba, Gradín finds that taking in to account geographic concentration of Afro-Latinos in certain areas of the country increases the degree of segregation.

Francesco Andreoli's paper, "Multi-group Segregation Patterns and Determinants: The Case of Immigrants in an Italian City" (Chapter 4) investigates residential segregation in the Verona Municipality. In particular, he is concerned with the spatial segregation of six immigrant groups. The paper contributes in two areas, it measures the degree of immigrant concentration, and it investigates the determinants of residential segregation. The author finds that housing structure and local public goods correlate with immigrants' segregation under substantial within city immigrants' mobility.

In Chapter 5 Serge Kolm contributes a paper entitled "Equal-Equivalents for Inequality, Welfare and Liberty: Concepts and Policy." Kolm's work extends the classical concept of equal-equivalent values, originally defined for one-dimensional inequality, to equal-equivalent manifolds appropriate for multidimensional inequality, welfare, and liberty. The welfare framework is discussed ethically, starting from *classical welfare* or *full welfare* (from classical utilitarianism) and moving to what is called *individual welfare* or *strict welfare*. By defining the equal-equivalents in both settings, the author is able to define certain inequality measures. The contribution is that these measures are also extended to a multidimensional framework.

B. Essama-Nssah and Peter J. Lambert in Chapter 6 carefully define and catalog the influence functions and recentered influence functions for a wide range of distributional statistics, including measures of central tendency, inequality, and poverty and also measures of the degree of pro-poorness of the shock or policy-induced change in income levels They provide an extensive catalog of inequality and poverty measures including the mean, *p*th quantile point, variance, Gini coefficient, Atkinson inequality index, (generalized) Lorenz ordinates, FTG index, Watts index, Sen poverty index, Ravallion and Chen growth incidence curve ordinate, TIP curve ordinates, headcount elasticity ratio, and pro-poorness measures for the FGT.

M[a] Casilda Lasso de la Vega and Ana Urrutia in Chapter 7 explore multidimensional generalizations of two axioms that capture the distribution sensitivity among the poor: the *monotonicity sensitivity axiom* and the *minimal transfer axiom* and show that the two generalizations proposed are also identical in the multidimensional setting although offering different interpretations. Relationships between the new properties and those existing in the literature are analyzed.

In "Convergence Club Empirics: Evidence from Indian States" (Chapter 8), Sanghamitra Bandyopadhyay examines the dynamics of income across the entire income distribution. She finds existence of two convergence clusters, or clubs, "one at 50% and another at 125% of national income." Next she employs conditioning exercises to uncover macroeconomics factors that encourage convergence club formation. In particular, fiscal deficits, capital expenditures, and educational expenditures are found to be associated with the formation of the upper convergence club.

In Chapter 9 Andrea Brandolini, Alfonso Rossolia, and Roberto Torrini discuss the advantages and drawbacks of using the Community Statistics on Income and Living Conditions (EU_SILC) to study earnings distributions. They note that only gross earnings are truly comparable across countries.

They make three suggestions to improve the SILC's comparability across countries: improve the comparability across countries of the items subtracted from gross income, add more detail on how imputed items are estimated, and provide additional documentation on instructional features of earnings components. Some results on the distribution of gross earnings across ECU countries are also provided.

Chapter 10 contains "Earnings Mobility, Earnings Inequality, and Labor Market Institutions." The authors, Denisa Maria Sologon and Cathal O'Donoghue use data from the European Community Household Panel to explore earnings mobility and inequality across Europe. They find that the growth in earnings during the 1990s had an equalizing effect on earnings in most countries of Europe. Furthermore, they find that the country ranking in "long-term earning inequality is similar with the country ranking in annual inequality." This supports a limited equalizing role for mobility in countries with high levels of annual inequality. Finally, they find that deregulation in labor and product markets, degree of unionization and corporatism, and spending on active labor market policies increase mobility.

Veronika V. Eberharter's paper (Chapter 11), "Intergenerational Education Mobility and Social Exclusion in Germany and the United States," analyzes the impact of family background on the intergenerational transmission of educational attainment and income positions. She finds that intergenerational educational mobility is significantly higher in Germany. This result is driven by the higher educational mobility in the "less than high school" educational category. Like earlier researchers she finds that the highest intergenerational income persistence at the tails of the distribution. In Germany, low-income positions are significantly less mobile than in the United States, whereas in Germany there is more income mobility at the top of the distribution.

In Chapter 12, Jürgen Faik considers "Variable Equivalence Scales and Trends in German Income Inequality." Faik provides several explanations for why equivalence scales should vary: high accommodation costs for high income households lower the marginal cost of an additional child, prices of commodities vary by income groups, and credit constraints among poor lowers expectations of high economies of scale durables. In Germany, he finds that the use of variable equivalence scales causes an increase in income inequality relative to constant equivalence scales.

Benaabdelaali Wail, Hanchane Said, and Kamal Abdelhak (Chapter 13) use Barro and Lee's (2010) schooling data to present "Educational Inequality in the World, 1950–2010: Estimates from a New Data Set." Their motivation for generating this data is the widely recognized notion that the distribution of income alone is not sufficient for adequately characterizing "inequality." Several interesting finds emerge from their study; from 1950 to 2010, education inequality fell rapidly, and the Gini index of education declines with an increase in the average level of education. However, when educational inequality is measured by the standard deviation of schooling, the relationship with average level of schooling follows a bell shaped curve.

Chapter 14 presents "Understanding the Drivers of Low Income Transitions in Luxembourg." In this chapter Alessio Fusco and Nizamul Islam employ the method of Cappellari and Jenkins (2004). The advantage of this approach is that it corrects for state dependence, initial conditions bias, and non-random attrition. They find a high level of aggregate state dependence, with 60 percent of the aggregate state dependence accounted for by genuine state dependence. Employment is found to protect against both entering poverty and remaining poor.

In the final chapter, Michael J. Camasso and Radha Jagannathan consider the impact of President Clinton's welfare reform on poverty. While widely criticized at the time of adoption, the authors find that the sanctions built into the legislation were more effective at reducing poverty than the positive economic conditions of the late 1990s and early 2000s. Related efforts to increase child support collections were also an important factor in determining poverty rates. The authors use a latent trajectory model that varies across states in both their initial mean poverty level as well as in their poverty trajectories.

John A. Bishop
Series and Volume Coeditor

Rafael Salas
Volume Coeditor

REFERENCES

Barro, R. J., & Lee, J. W. (2010). *A new data set of educational attainment in the world, 1950–2010*. NBER Working Paper No. 15902. National Bureau of Economic Research, Cambridge, MA.

Cappellari, L., & Jenkins, S. P. (2004). Modelling low income transitions. *Journal of Applied Econometrics*, *19*(5), 593–610.

CHAPTER 1

MEASURING SEGREGATION: BASIC CONCEPTS AND EXTENSIONS TO OTHER DOMAINS☆

Jacques Silber

INTRODUCTION: ON "LATERAL THINKING"

In a recent paper entitled "On Lateral Thinking," Atkinson (2011) argued that Economics has benefited not only from borrowing ideas from other disciplines such as physics (e.g., Samuelson's *Foundations of Economic Analysis*, 1947) or psychology (e.g., the growing importance of behavioral economics) but also from applying ideas that appeared in one subfield of Economics to another domain of Economics. As examples of such a cross-fertilization, Atkinson cites duality theory where cost functions were applied to consumer theory or Harberger's (1962) model of tax incidence that was borrowed from international trade theory. Atkinson in fact cited a sentence from his famous 1970 (Atkinson, 1970) article: "My interest in

☆This paper is based on my Presidential address given at the fourth meeting of the Society for the Study of Economic Inequality (ECINEQ) in Catania (Italy), July 18, 2011. It was written while I was visiting the Department of Economic Sciences of the University of Geneva, Switzerland, which I thank for its very warm hospitality. I am also grateful to the editors of this volume who suggested I transform my lecture into a regular paper.

Inequality, Mobility and Segregation: Essays in Honor of Jacques Silber
Research on Economic Inequality, Volume 20, 1–35

ISSN: 1049-2585/doi:10.1108/S1049-2585(2012)0000020004

the question of measuring inequality was originally stimulated by reading an early version of the paper by Rotschild and Stiglitz (1970, 1971)" The same parallelism between uncertainty and inequality had been drawn previously by Serge Kolm in his well-known presentation at the meeting of the International Economic Association in Biarritz, France (see Kolm, 1969), which was inspired by his previous work on uncertainty (Kolm, 1966). Atkinson, however, stressed also the need for care in drawing parallels.

Though attempting to present the main concepts used in measuring segregation, this chapter does not aim at being an exhaustive survey.[1] Its goal is first to show that the cardinal as well as the ordinal approach to the measurement of occupational segregation, when only two groups are considered (generally men and women) borrowed many ideas from the income inequality measurement literature. This paper aims, however, also at showing that more recent advances in segregation measurement, which were the consequence of an extension of segregation measures to the case of multigroup segregation and more recently to the analysis of ordinal segregation, could be the basis for additional approaches to the measurement of economic inequality, in particular inequality in life chances, health, and happiness, and eventually also to the study of polarization. Finally because the measurement of spatial segregation is a field in itself, this chapter will only marginally mention concepts that have been introduced in this no less fascinating domain.[2]

The present chapter is organized as follows. The next section introduces the reader to the concept of "Segregation curve" and defines the Duncan and Duncan, Gini, "generalized Gini," and entropy-related indices of segregation. It also reviews the desirable properties of a measure of segregation. The second section looks then at the measurement of multidimensional segregation and shows first that there are at least four ways of apprehending this issue since an index of multidimensional segregation may be considered as measuring the degree of dependence between the population categories analyzed and, say, their occupations, the disproportionality in group proportions, the extent of diversity in the population, or, when the emphasis is on income segregation, the relative importance of between groups income inequality. The last part of the second section is devoted to the comparison over time (or across geographic units) in the degree of segregation, the idea being to make a distinction between differences (changes) in the marginal distributions (of, say, the shares of the various occupations and different population subgroups examined) and variations in the "pure" (net of differences in the margins) joint distribution of, say, occupations and population subgroups. The third and fourth sections examine the case where an additional dimension is introduced in the analysis. The third section applies this idea to the measurement of spatial segregation and shows how it is possible to incorporate space in the measurement of segregation. Whereas traditional indices of segregation would usually compare the racial composition of the different neighborhoods with the average racial composition in the geographic area under study, spatial segregation indices have been proposed that take into account the spatial pattern of segregation, the emphasis being, for example, on the clustering of ethnic groups in separate geographical areas. The fourth section investigates another case where an additional dimension is introduced in the measurement of segregation, where one assumes, for instance, that occupations may be ranked via, say, some occupational prestige scale. The fifth section finally shows how these recent advances in the measurement of segregation could be the basis for new ways of measuring inequality in life chances, health, or happiness, and eventually social polarization. The chapter ends with some remarks on the respective advantages and shortcomings of specialization in research in the social sciences.

BASIC CONCEPTS: MEASURING SEGREGATION WHEN THERE ARE ONLY TWO GROUPS

The Concept of Segregation Curve

This tool was introduced by Duncan and Duncan (1955). It is derived as follows from the traditional Lorenz curve. Assume, for example, that the distribution of males among various occupations is given by a vector $\vec{M} = [(M_1/M), \ldots, (M_k/M), \ldots, (M_K/M)]$, where M_k is the number of male workers in occupation k, M the total number of male workers in the labor force, and K the total number of occupations. Similarly let the distribution of females among the various occupations be represented by the vector $\vec{F} = [(F_1/F), \ldots, (F_k/F), \ldots, (F_K/F)]$, where F_k is the number of female workers in occupation k and F the total number of female workers in the labor force. Let us now rank the occupations k by increasing ratios (F_k/M_k) and plot on the horizontal axis the cumulative values of the shares (M_k/M) and on the vertical axis the cumulative values of the shares (F_k/F). The curve obtained is what Duncan and Duncan (1955) called a segregation curve.[3]

Indices of Segregation

Two indices of segregation are easily derived from the segregation curve: the Duncan and Duncan index I_{D} and the Gini segregation index I_{G}.

The Duncan and Duncan Index I_D

It was introduced by Duncan and Duncan (1955) and remains the most popular measure of segregation. It is also called "dissimilarity index" and may be expressed, using the notations introduced previously, as

$$I_D = \frac{1}{2}\sum_{k=1}^{K}\left|\left(\frac{M_k}{M}\right) - \left(\frac{F_k}{F}\right)\right| \tag{1}$$

An intuitive interpretation can be given to the Duncan index: it gives the percentage of the male (female) labor force that has to shift occupations so that the share of the male labor force employed in a given occupation will be equal to that of the females employed in this same occupation. It can be shown that the Duncan index corresponds to the greatest vertical distance between the segregation curve and the diagonal. Note that I_{D} may be also written as

$$I_{\mathrm{D}} = \frac{1}{2}\sum_{k=1}^{K}\left(\frac{M_k}{M}\right)\left|\frac{(F_k/M_k) - (F/M)}{(F/M)}\right| \tag{2}$$

or as

$$I_{\mathrm{D}} = \frac{1}{2}\sum_{k=1}^{K}\left(\frac{F_k}{F}\right)\left|\frac{(M_k/F_k) - (M/F)}{(M/F)}\right| \tag{3}$$

The Duncan index I_{D} is therefore a weighted relative mean deviation of the gender ratios (F_k/M_k) or (M_k/F_k).

The Gini Segregation Index

This index was originally proposed by Jahn, Schmid, and Schrag (1947) and Duncan and Duncan (1955). It can be shown that the value of this index corresponds to twice the area lying between the segregation curve and the diagonal. This Gini segregation index can be expressed as

$$I_{\mathrm{G}} = \sum_{h=1}^{K}\sum_{k=1}^{K}\left(\frac{M_h}{M}\right)\left(\frac{M_k}{M}\right)\left|\frac{(F_h/M_h) - (F_k/M_k)}{(F/M)}\right| \tag{4}$$

or as

$$I_G = (1/2)\sum_{h=1}^{K}\sum_{k=1}^{K}\left(\frac{F_h}{F}\right)\left(\frac{F_k}{F}\right)\left|\frac{(M_h/F_h) - (M_k/F_k)}{(M/F)}\right| \quad (5)$$

The Gini segregation index is hence also a measure of the inequality of the gender ratios in the various occupations. One can see here again the parallelism between the measurement of income inequality and that of occupational segregation, the gender ratio playing the role that the relative income of individual i, say, $(y_i/\bar{y})$, where y_i is the income of individual i and $\bar{y}$ the average income in the population, plays when computing the Gini index of income inequality.

The Gini segregation index may be also expressed in a different way (Silber, 1989b) and written as

$$I_G = \vec{M}G\vec{F} \quad (6)$$

where $\vec{M}$ is a row vector of the shares of the male workers in the various occupations and $\vec{F}$ a column vector of the shares of the female workers in the various occupations. Note that the shares in $\vec{M}$ and $\vec{F}$ have to be ranked by decreasing values of the ratios (F_k/M_k). Finally, G, called the G-matrix, is expressed as

$$\begin{matrix} 0 & -1 & -1 & \cdots\cdots & -1 & -1 \\ 1 & 0 & -1 & \cdots\cdots & -1 & -1 \\ \cdots & \cdots & \cdots & \cdots\cdots & \cdots & \cdots \\ 1 & 1 & 1 & \cdots\cdots & 0 & -1 \\ 1 & 1 & 1 & \cdots\cdots & 1 & 0 \end{matrix}$$

In other words the typical element g_{ij} of the matrix G is equal to 0 if $i=j$, to -1 if $j>i$, and to 1 if $i>j$.

The Concept of Generalized Gini and the Measure of Segregation[4]

Using Atkinson's (1970) concept of "equally distributed equivalent level of income" and following earlier work by Blackorby and Donaldson (1978), Donaldson and Weymark (1980) defined a generalized Gini index I_{GG} as

$$I_{GG} = \left[\sum_{i=1}^{n}\frac{\{(((i^{\delta}) - (i-1)^{\delta})/(n^{\delta}))y_i\}}{\bar{y}}\right] \quad (7)$$

where y_i is the income of individual i with $y_1 >> \ldots >> y_i >> \ldots >> y_n$, n being the number of individuals, and $\delta > 1$, while $\bar{y}$ is the arithmetic mean of the various incomes y_i. It can be shown (see Donaldson & Weymark, 1980) that when $\delta = 2$, I_{GG} is equal to the Gini index. Note that, following Atkinson (1970), the numerator of the expression within square brackets in Eq. (7) represents the "equally distributed equivalent level of income" corresponding to the social welfare function defined by Donaldson and Weymark (1980).

It can also be proven that if there is more than one individual with income x_i expression (7) will be written as

$$I_{GG} = 1 - \left\{ \left[\sum_{i=1}^{I} \left(\left(\left(\sum_{j=1}^{i} n_j \right)^{\delta} - \left(\sum_{j=1}^{i-1} n_j \right)^{\delta} \right) \Big/ (n^{\delta}) \right) y_i \right] / \bar{y} \right\} \quad (8)$$

where n_i refers to the number of individuals with income y_i, I is the total number of income categories, and $\sum_{j=1}^{I} n_j = n$.

If we now call q_i the relative frequency (n_i/n) and define a coefficient α_i as

$$\alpha_i = \frac{\left\{ \left[\left(\sum_{j=1}^{i} n_j \right)^{\delta} \right] - \left[\left(\sum_{j=1}^{i-1} n_j \right)^{\delta} \right] \right\}}{n^{\delta}} = \left[\left(\sum_{j=1}^{i} q_j \right)^{\delta} - \left(\sum_{j=1}^{i-1} q_j \right)^{\delta} \right] \quad (9)$$

expression (9) may then be written as

$$I_{GG} = 1 - \left\{ \frac{\sum_{i=1}^{I} \alpha_i y_i}{\bar{y}} \right\} \quad (10)$$

Call now $s_i = (n_i y_i)/(n\bar{y})$ the share of income y_i in total income. It is then easy to derive

$$I_{GG} = 1 - \left[\sum_{i=1}^{I} \alpha_i \left(\frac{s_i}{q_i} \right) \right] \quad (11)$$

so that (11) shows that computing a "generalized Gini" amounts to "transforming" population shares q_i into income shares s_i via the use of an operator α_i.

In such a "transformation" the population shares could be considered as "a priori shares" and the income shares as "a posteriori shares."

Expression (11) may be easily extended to the measurement of occupational segregation by gender. The "a priori shares" q_k could, for example, be the shares $m_k = (M_k/M)$ of the males in the various occupations and the "a posteriori shares" s_k the shares $f_k = (F_k/F)$ of the females in these occupations. In such a case we would define a coefficient α_k as

$$\alpha_k = \left\{\left[\left(\sum_{j=1}^{k} m_j\right)^{\delta}\right] - \left[\left(\sum_{j=1}^{k-1} m_j\right)^{\delta}\right]\right\} \tag{12}$$

Note that in (12) the occupations j should be ranked by decreasing values of the ratios (f_i/m_j) in the same way that in Donaldson and Weymark's (1980) original paper, the (relative) incomes were ranked by decreasing values.

The "generalized Gini index of occupational segregation" I_{GGS} will therefore be expressed, combining (10), (11), and (12) as

$$I_{\mathrm{GGS}} = 1 - \left[\sum_{k=1}^{K} \alpha_k \left(\frac{f_k}{m_k}\right)\right] \tag{13}$$

It can be shown that when $\delta = 2$, the index I_{GG} in (13) is identical to the index I_{G} defined in Eqs. (4), (5), or (6). Note also that if $\delta = 2$ the index I_{GGS} would have been the same, had we assumed that the "a priori shares" are the shares f_k and the "a posteriori shares" the shares m_k.

However when $\delta \neq 2$, the index I_{GGS} will be different if it is assumed that the "a priori shares" are the shares m_k or the shares f_k. In the former case (when the "a priori shares" are the shares m_k), the higher δ, the greater the weight given to the occupations with low ratios (F_k/M_k) (these are hence "male-intensive" occupations). In the latter case, however (when the "a priori shares" are the shares f_k), the higher the value of the parameter δ, the greater the weight given to the occupations with low ratios (M_k/F_k) (these are the "female-intensive" occupations).

The choice of "a priori" and "a posteriori" shares (as well as the selection of the parameter δ) introduces therefore normative elements in the computation of the degree of occupational segregation when using the index I_{GGS}.

Finally note that, since in expression (12) the sum $(\sum_{j=1}^{k} m_j)^{\delta} < 1$ whenever $k < K$, while $(\sum_{j=1}^{K} m_j)^{\delta} = 1$, we may conclude that when $\delta \to \infty$, the sum $(\sum_{j=1}^{k} m_j)^{\delta} \to 0$ for any $k \neq K$ while it is equal to 1 when $k = K$. As a consequence when $\delta \to \infty$, expression (13) will be written as

$$I_{\mathrm{GSS}} = 1 - \left(\frac{f_K}{m_K}\right) \tag{14}$$

This implies that when the "a priori" shares are those of the male workers and if $\delta \to \infty$, the generalized Gini segregation index is equal to the complement to one of the ratio of the percentage of women employed in the occupation with the lowest gender ratio (F_K/M_K) over the percentage of men employed in this same occupation. In other words, when the "a priori shares" are the male shares, the higher the value of the parameter δ, the greater the weight given to the most "male-intensive" occupations.

It is easy to show that in the converse case, when the "a prior shares" are the female shares, the higher the value of the parameter δ, the greater the weight given to the most "female-intensive" occupations.

Measures of Segregation Related to the Concept of Entropy
It is also possible to derive indices of segregation on the basis of concepts introduced in economics by Theil (1967). More precisely, following Theil and Finizza (1971) and Mora and Ruiz-Castillo (2003), the expected information of the message that transforms the proportions $[(F/(F+M)), (M/(F+M))]$ into the proportions $[(F_k/(F_k+M_k)), (M_k/(F_k+M_k))]$ is defined as

$$I_k = \left(\frac{F_k}{(F_k+M_k)}\right)\log\frac{(F_k/(F_k+M_k))}{(F/M)} + \left(\frac{M_k}{(F_k+M_k)}\right)\log\frac{(M_k/(F_k+M_k))}{(M/(F+M))} \tag{15}$$

It is easy to observe that the value of this expected information is 0 whenever the two sets of proportions are identical. This expected information takes larger and larger positive values when the two sets are more different. Note that I_k may be interpreted as an index of local segregation in occupation k. A weighted average of these K indices of local segregation will then constitute an additive index of segregation. Such an index could, for example, be an index I_E, the weighted average of the information expectations, with weights proportional to the number of people in the occupations, that is, to $((F_k+M_k)/(F+M))$, so that

$$I_E = \sum_{k=1}^{K}\frac{(F_k+M_k)}{(F+M)}I_k \tag{16}$$

The Desirable Properties of a Segregation Index

Desirable axioms for an index of occupational segregation have been proposed, for example, by James and Taeuber (1985), Siltanen, Jarman, and Blackburn (1995), Kakwani (1994), Hutchens (1991, 2001), and Mora and Ruiz-Castillo (2005).

Here is a list of some of the most common axioms that appeared in the literature.

Axiom 1. Size Invariance
As before, let $\vec{F}$ and $\vec{M}$ represent, respectively, the vectors $[(F_1/F),\ldots,(F_k/F),\ldots,(F_K/F)]$ and $[(M_1/M),\ldots,(M_k/M),\ldots(M_K/M)]$ and let σ be a segregation index with $\sigma = \sigma(\vec{F}, \vec{M}, F \cdot M)$
Then if, $\forall k$, $F'_k = \gamma F_k$, $M'_k = \gamma M_k$ so that $F = \gamma F$ and $M' = \gamma M$, we will have $\sigma' = \sigma$.

Axiom 2. Complete Integration
If $(F_k/F) = (M_k/M)\ \forall k$, then $\sigma = 0$.

Axiom 3. Complete Segregation
If $F_k(M_k) > 0$ implies $M_k(F_k) = 0\ \forall k$, then $\sigma = 1$.

Axiom 4. Symmetry in Groups
Let $\vec{F}'$ and $\vec{M}'$ be two permutations of $\vec{F}$ and $\vec{M}$, respectively. Then $\sigma(\vec{F}, F, \vec{M}, M) = \sigma(\vec{F}', F, \vec{M}', M)$.

Axiom 5. Symmetry in Types

$$\sigma(\vec{F}, F, \vec{M}, M) = \sigma(\vec{M}, M, \vec{F}, F)$$

Axiom 6. Principle of Transfers
If there is a small shift in the female (male) labor force from a female- (male-) dominated occupation to a male- (female-) dominated occupation, the segregation index must decrease.

Axiom 7. Increasing Returns to a Movement Between Groups
This notion is analogous to the property of *decreasing returns of inequality in proximity* in Kolm (1999), or the *transfer sensitivity* property in Foster and Shorrocks (1987) in the income inequality literature.

Therefore, if there is a small shift in the female (male) labor force from a female- (male-) dominated occupation to a male- (female-) dominated occupation, the segregation index will decrease more, the more male- (female-) dominated the "receiving" occupation is.

Axiom 8. Organizational Equivalence
This axiom was originally proposed by James and Taeuber (1985). It has been called *Insensitivity to Proportional Divisions by* Hutchens (2001).

The idea here is that an index of segregation should be unaffected by the division of an occupation into units with identical segregation patterns. Note that this axiom allows the comparison of economies with a different number of occupations by artificially equalizing those numbers with the help of a suitable division or combination of occupations.

Axiom 9. Additive Decomposability
Assume that the set of K occupations is partitioned into I groups, indexed by $i = 1,\ldots, I$, and denote by G_i the number of occupations in group i, so that $\sum_{i=1}^{I} G_I = K$.

This could, for example, be the case of a one- versus a two-digit classification of the occupations.

We can then make a distinction between an *overall* measure of segregation $\sigma(\vec{F}, F, \vec{M}, M)$, a *within-group* measure of segregation $\sigma_i(\vec{F}_i, F_i, \vec{M}_i, M_i)$ for each i, and a *between-group* measure σ_{BET} of segregation computed as if every occupation j had the mean number of males and females of the group i to which it belongs.

The axiom of *Additive Decomposability*[5] then says that if there exists $\eta_i \geq 0$ for all i with $\Sigma_i \eta_i = 1$, then $\sigma(\vec{F}, F, \vec{M}, M) = \Sigma_i \eta_i \sigma_i(\vec{F}_i, F_i, \vec{M}_i, M_i) + \sigma_{\text{BET}}$

On the basis of at least some of these axioms, several papers have derived axiomatically indices of segregation (e.g., Chakravarty, D'Ambrosio, & Silber, 2009; Chakravarty & Silber, 1994, 2007; Frankel & Volij, 2011; Hutchens, 2001, 2004). There are also papers taking an ordinal approach and deriving conditions for the dominance of a segregation curve over another (e.g., Hutchens, 1991).

THE MULTIDIMENSIONAL ANALYSIS OF SEGREGATION[6]

Segregation as a Measure of the Degree of Dependence

Assume we want to measure occupational (or residential) segregation by ethnic groups, when there are more than two ethnic groups.

To derive such a generalization let us first go back to the formulation of the Duncan index, but rather than comparing the shares of males (M_i/M) with the shares of the females (F_i/F), let us compare the shares (M_i/M) (or the shares (F_i/F)) with the shares of the various occupations i in the total labor force, that is, with the shares (T_i/T) where $T_i = M_i + F_i$ and $T = M + F$.

Moir and Selby-Smith (1979) and Lewis (1982) suggested then using, respectively, the following segregation measures:

$$I_{\mathrm{MSS}} = \frac{1}{2}\sum_{k=1}^{K}\left|\left(\frac{F_k}{F}\right) - \left(\frac{T_k}{T}\right)\right| \tag{17}$$

$$I_{\mathrm{L}} = \frac{1}{2}\sum_{k=1}^{K}\left|\left(\frac{M_k}{M}\right) - \left(\frac{T_k}{T}\right)\right| \tag{18}$$

Karmel and MacLachlan (1988) proposed a kind of mixture of these two formulas and Silber (1992) then proved that their proposition amounted to comparing the "actual" shares (M_k/T) (or (F_k/T)) of individuals of a given gender in a given occupation, in the total labor force, with the "expected" shares $(T_k/T)(M/T)$ (or $(T_k/T)(F/T)$).

These are the expected shares because if there was complete independence between the lines (occupations) and the columns (the gender) one would have expected the share of a given gender in a given occupation in the total labor force to be equal to the product of the share of this occupation and the share of this gender in the total labor force.

In other words, the index proposed by Karmel and MacLachlan (1988) may be expressed as

$$I_{\mathrm{KM}} = \sum_{k=1}^{K}\left|\left(\frac{M_k}{T}\right) - \left(\frac{M}{T}\right)\left(\frac{T_k}{T}\right)\right| \tag{19}$$

This interpretation shows clearly that measuring segregation amounts to measuring the degree of "dependence" between the occupations and the gender. But such an interpretation opens the way to a more generalized measure of segregation which does not have to be limited to two categories (genders). Assume you have K occupations and J categories (e.g., ethnic groups). Call T_{kj} the number of workers of category j working in occupation k. We can then generalize the Karmel and MacLachlan index as

$$I_{\mathrm{KMG}} = \sum_{k=1}^{K}\sum_{j=1}^{J}\left|\left(\frac{T_{kj}}{T}\right) - \left(\frac{T_{k.}}{T}\right)\left(\frac{T_{.j}}{T}\right)\right| \tag{20}$$

where $T_{k.} = \sum_{j=1}^{J} T_{kj}$ and $T_{.j} = \sum_{k=1}^{K} T_{kj}$. We could also call the index I_{KMG} a "generalized Duncan index."

Once we interpret segregation as the comparison of "a priori" shares $(T_{k\cdot}/T)\,(T_{\cdot j}/T)$ with "a posteriori" shares (T_{kj}/T), we are however not limited to using an extension of the Duncan index. We can also apply this idea to the Theil or Gini indices, for example.

One of Theil's two indices (see Theil, 1967) could thus be expressed as

$$T^1_{\mathrm{SEG}} = \sum_{k=1}^{K}\sum_{j=1}^{J}\left[\left(\frac{T_{k.}}{T}\right)\left(\frac{T_{.j}}{T}\right)\right]\log\frac{[(T_{k.}/T)(T_{.j}/T)]}{[(T_{kj}/T)]} \tag{21}$$

while the second Theil index would be written as

$$T^2_{\mathrm{SEG}} = \sum_{k=1}^{K}\sum_{j=1}^{J}\left[\left(\frac{T_{kj}}{T}\right)\right]\log\frac{[(T_{kj}/T)]}{[(T_{k.}/T)(T_{.j}/T)]} \tag{22}$$

The multidimensional generalization $I_{\mathrm{G,MULTI}}$ of the Gini segregation index (see Boisso, Hayes, Hirschberg, & Silber, 1994) would be expressed, using Eq. (6), as

$$I_{\mathrm{G,MULTI}} = \left\{\cdots\left[\left(\frac{T_{k.}}{T}\right)\left(\frac{T_{.j}}{T}\right)\right]\cdots\right\}' G\left\{\cdots\left[\left(\frac{T_{kj}}{T}\right)\right]\cdots\right\}$$

where $\{\ldots[(T_{k\cdot}/T)(T_{\cdot j}/T)]\ldots\}'$ is a row vector of the "a priori" shares $(T_{k\cdot}/T)(T_{\cdot j}/T)$, $\{\ldots[(T_{kj}/T)]\ldots\}$ is a column vector of the "a posteriori" shares (T_{kj}/T), G is a $(K \times J)$ by $(K \times J)$ G-matrix, and the $(K \times J)$ elements of the row and column vectors are classified by decreasing ratios $[T_{kj}/T]/[(T_{k\cdot}/T)(T_{\cdot j}/T)]$.

We can also define a "generalized segregation curve" as follows. Put the cumulative values of the "a priori" shares $(T_{k\cdot}/T)(T_{\cdot j}/T)$ on the horizontal axis and the cumulative shares of the "a posteriori" shares (T_{kj}/T) on the vertical axis, both sets of cumulative shares being ranked by increasing values of the ratios $(T_{kj}/T)/(T_{k\cdot}/T)(T_{\cdot j}/T)$. Note that this "generalized segregation curve" is what is often called a "relative concentration curve."

It is then easy to prove that the multidimensional generalization $I_{\mathrm{G,MULTI}}$ of the Gini segregation index is equal to twice the area lying between the "generalized segregation curve" which has just been defined and the diagonal. Note also that the Karmel and MacLachlan generalized index I_{KMG} will be equal to the maximum distance between the diagonal and this "generalized segregation curve."

Segregation as Disproportionality in Group Proportions

To simplify the notations let us define t_{ij} as $t_{ij} = (T_{ij}/T)$ so that t_{ij} is a typical element of a matrix whose lines i refer, for example, to the various occupations and whose columns j define, say, ethnic groups. So t_{ij} represents the share in the total labor force (all occupations and ethnic groups included) of individuals employed in occupation i and belonging to ethnic group j.

Let also $t_{i\cdot}$ and $t_{\cdot j}$ be respectively equal to $\Sigma_j t_{ij}$ (so that $t_{i\cdot} = (T_{i.}/T)$) and $\Sigma_i t_{ij}$ (so that $t_{\cdot j} = (T_{\cdot i}/T)$). Note that we evidently assume that $\Sigma_i \Sigma_j \, t_{ij} = 1$.

Call now φ_{ij} the ratio $(t_{ij}/t_{i\cdot})$ (the share in occupation i of those individuals belonging to ethnic group j) and call $\varphi_{\cdot j}$ the share $(t_{\cdot j}/1)$ of ethnic group j in the whole labor force. Define also the ratio ρ_{ij} as being equal to $(\varphi_{ij}/\varphi_{\cdot j})$. Clearly if $\varphi_{ij} > 1$ $(\varphi_{ij} < 1)$ ethnic group j is overrepresented (underrepresented) in occupation i since we can also express ρ_{ij} as $\rho_{ij} = (t_{ij}/t_{i\cdot})/(t_{\cdot j}/1)$. The ratio ρ_{ij} reflects therefore the extent to which ethnic group j is disproportionately represented in occupation i.

Occupational segregation can then be considered as the mean disproportionality across groups and occupations.

To measure disproportionality, Reardon and Firebaugh (2002) use[7] a function $f(\rho_{ij})$ such that $f(1) = 0$ and define the weighted average disproportionality D_W as the average value of $f(\rho_{ij})$ across all occupations and ethnic groups, the weights being the shares of the occupations and of the ethnic groups in the total labor force. More precisely we express D_W as

$$D_W = \sum_{i=1}^{I} t_{i.} \sum_{j=1}^{J} t_{.j} f(\rho_{ij}) \tag{23}$$

Example 1. Using an index derived from the relative mean deviation. Assume that $f(\rho_{ij}) = (1/2)|\rho_{ij} - 1|$. Then $D_W = (1/2)\sum_{i=1}^{I} t_{i.} \sum_{j=1}^{J} t_{.j} |\rho_{ij} - 1|$. Given the definition of ρ_{ij} we then derive that

$$D_W = \frac{1}{2} \sum_{i=1}^{I} \sum_{j=1}^{J} |t_{ij} - (t_{i.} t_{.j})| \tag{24}$$

and this clearly amounts to saying that D_W measures the degree of dependence between the lines i and the columns j.

Example 2. An index derived from the Gini index. Assume we defined the function $f(\rho_{ij})$ as $f(\rho_{ij}) = |\rho_i - \rho_j|$. Then the disproportionality measure D_W will be expressed as

$$D_W = \frac{1}{2} \sum_{i=1}^{I} t_{i.} \sum_{h=1}^{J} \sum_{k=1}^{J} (t_{.h} t_{.k}) |\rho_{ih} - \rho_{ik}| \tag{25}$$

so that

$$D_W = \frac{1}{2}\sum_{i=1}^{I}\sum_{h=1}^{J}\sum_{k=1}^{J} t_{i.}t_{.h}t_{.k}\left|\frac{t_{ih}}{(t_{i.}t_{.h})} - \frac{t_{ik}}{(t_{i.}t_{.k})}\right| \tag{26}$$

It is then easy to observe that here again the measure of disproportionality D_W amounts to checking for independence between the lines and the columns.

Example 3. An index derived from the concept of entropy (Theil index). Assume now that we define the function $f(\rho_{ij})$ as $f(\rho_{ij}) = \rho_i \ln(\rho_{ij})$. The disproportionality measure D_W will then be expressed as

$$D_W = \sum_{I=1}^{I} t_{i.} \sum_{j=1}^{J} t_{.j}\rho_{ij}\ln(\rho_{ij}) \tag{27}$$

and this clearly amounts again to checking for the independence between the lines i and the columns j.

Example 4. An index linked to the variance.
Assume finally that the function $f(\rho_{ij})$ is defined as $(\rho_{ij}-1)^2$. The measure of disproportionality D_W will then be written as

$$D_W = \sum_{i=1}^{I} t_{i.} \sum_{j=1}^{J} t_{.j}(\rho_{ij} - 1)^2 \tag{28}$$

which again amounts to checking for the independence between the lines i and the columns j.

Segregation as a Measure Related to the Concept of Diversity

Using the notations defined previously, we define the degree of diversity DIV in the whole labor force as

$$\text{DIV} = \sum_{j=1}^{J} t_{.j}(1 - t_{.j}) \tag{29}$$

The measure DIV is in fact equal to the probability that two individuals, taken randomly in the labor force, belong to two different ethnic groups.

We can similarly define the degree of diversity in occupation i as

$$\text{DIV}_{i.} = \sum_{j=1}^{J}\left(\frac{t_{ij}}{t_{i.}}\right)\left(1 - \left(\frac{t_{ij}}{t_{i.}}\right)\right) \tag{30}$$

The average degree $\overline{\text{DIV}_{i.}}$ of diversity across all occupations may then be expressed as

$$\overline{\text{DIV}_{i.}} = \sum_{i=1}^{I} t_{i.} \sum_{j=1}^{J} \frac{t_{ij}}{t_{i.}} \left(1 - \frac{t_{ij}}{t_{i.}}\right) \tag{31}$$

so that

$$1 - \left(\frac{\overline{\text{DIV}_{i.}}}{\text{DIV}}\right) = 1 - \frac{\sum_{i=1}^{I} t_{i.} \sum_{j=1}^{J} (t_{ij}/t_{i.})(1 - (t_{ij}/t_{i.}))}{\sum_{j=1}^{J} t_{.j}(1 - t_{.j})} \tag{32}$$

This is known as the Goodman and Kruskal (1954) τ_B and is equal to 1 minus the probability that two individuals from the same occupation belong to different ethnic groups over the probability that any two individuals in the labor force belong to different ethnic groups. The previous measure may therefore be interpreted as the average difference between overall and within occupations diversity, divided by the overall diversity.

Such a residual diversity can be attributed only to between occupations differences in ethnic group proportions. It may therefore be interpreted as a measure of the proportion of total diversity attributable to between occupations differences. As expected this residual diversity will be equal to 0 if each occupation has the same ethnic group proportions as the whole labor force and to 1 when each occupation has no diversity whatsoever.

Segregation as the Ratio of Inequality Between Groups of Individuals to Inequality Among Individuals[8]

This emphasis on the relative importance of between occupations differences appears also in a recent article by Jargowsky and Kim (2009). These authors start their analysis from Shannon's (1948) famous article on "A Mathematical Theory of Communication" stating that "the fundamental problem of communication is that of reproducing at one point … a message selected at another point." The reason for the existence of such a problem is evidently the possibility of a noisy transmission process over a medium that has a limited capacity (e.g., a telephone cable). Shannon characterized the *information value* of a source as a function of the number of potential messages that the source could produce. If all individuals are identical, then choosing an individual at random will produce the same message every time. In Shannon's terms the information value of the message is 0 because there is no uncertainty about the message. But if there is a lot of variation among individuals, many possible messages may have been sent so that the information value of the source of the message is high.

Jargowsky and Kim (2009) take as illustration the case of "income segregation." In other words they wanted to know to which extent there are poor and rich neighborhoods.

Call y_i the income of individual i, $\bar{y}$ the average income in the population, and n the number of individuals.

The Gini index of income inequality (see Kendall & Stuart, 1961) in the population will then be expressed as

$$G_{\mathrm{TOTAL}} = \left(\frac{1}{2}\right)\left(\frac{1}{\bar{y}}\right)\left(\frac{1}{n^2}\right)\sum_{h=1}^{n}\sum_{k=1}^{n}|y_h - y_k| \tag{33}$$

Call now $\bar{y}_j$ and $\bar{y}_l$ the mean incomes in areas j and l, n_j and n_l the number of individuals in areas j, and l and J the total number of areas.

If every individual in a given area is assumed to receive the average income prevailing in the area, the Gini index for the whole population would then be expressed as

$$G_{\mathrm{BETWEEN}} = \left(\frac{1}{2}\right)\left(\frac{1}{\bar{y}}\right)\left(\frac{1}{n^2}\right)\sum_{j=1}^{J}\sum_{l=1}^{J}|\bar{y}_j - \bar{y}_l| \tag{34}$$

Jargowsky and Kim (2009) suggest then to measure income segregation via the ratio of G_{BETWEEN} over G_{TOTAL}. In other words segregation is defined as the retention of information about inequality when comparing the group- and the individual-level information.

Comparing Degrees of Segregation

Let us now assume that we want to compare occupational segregation by ethnic groups at two different time periods. In other words we want to compare two matrices like those whose typical element was defined previously as t_{ij}. Karmel and MacLachlan (1988) and later on Watts (1998) have argued that it is not possible to directly compare these two matrices by computing a segregation index in each of the two cases. The reason is that the occupational structure by ethnic groups in a given country at two different points in times may have varied because

- the occupational structure changed,
- the "ethnic structure" changed,

- the "pure" degree of independence between occupations and ethnic groups (the essence of segregation) varied over time.

This is why Karmel and MacLachlan (1988) as well as Watts (1998) have argued that it is essential to make a difference between variations in the margins and what they called a change in the "internal structure" of the matrix. To solve this problem they suggested borrowing a technique originally proposed by Deming and Stephan (1940). A simple illustration of the technique proposed by Deming and Stephan (which is not the only technique available) is presented here. Let us assume we start with an "original" matrix t_{ij} and a "final" matrix v_{ij}. Both matrices are given below.

Original matrix t_{ij}.	
0.05	0.35
0.20	0.40

Final matrix, say v_{ij}.	
0.10	0.25
0.40	0.25

Stage 1: Multiply all the elements of the matrix t_{ij} by the ratios $(v_{i\cdot}/t_{i\cdot})$ and call x_{ij} the new matrix which is then

Matrix x_{ij}.	
0.04375	0.30625
0.21666	0.40000

Stage 2: Multiply all the elements of the matrix x_{ij} by the ratios $(v_{\cdot j}/x_{\cdot j})$ and call y_{ij} the matrix just derived which is then

Matrix y_{ij}.	
0.08509	0.21681
0.42139	0.28319

Stage 3: Multiply all the elements of the matrix y_{ij} by the ratios $(v_{i\cdot}/y_{i\cdot})$ and call z_{ij} the matrix just derived which is then

Matrix z_{ij}.

0.09865	0.25135
0.38875	0.26125

Stage 4: Multiply all the elements of the matrix z_{ij} by the ratios $(v_{\cdot j}/z_{\cdot j})$ and call w_{ij} the matrix just derived which is then

Matrix w_{ij}.

0.10120	0.24517
0.39880	0.25483

Note that already at this stage the horizontal margins of the matrix w_{ij} are, respectively, 0.34637 and 0.65363 whereas the horizontal margins of the matrix v_{ij} are 0.35 and 0.65. The vertical margins of the matrix w_{ij} are, as expected at this stage, identical to those of the matrix v_{ij}, that is, 0.5 and 0.5. Assuming, for simplicity, that the matrix w_{ij} corresponds to the final stage of the iteration, we will say that this matrix w_{ij} has the "internal structure" of the original matrix t_{ij} but the margins of the matrix v_{ij}.

The Deming and Stephan (1940) technique allows us therefore making a distinction between variations over time in the "internal structure" and in the margins of the occupations by ethnic groups matrix. The technique that was just presented assumed that one started from an "original" matrix t_{ij} and ended with a "final" matrix v_{ij}. It would, however, have been also possible to start with an "original" matrix v_{ij} and end with a "final" matrix t_{ij}. This is a standard "index number problem" which can be solved using what is called a "Shapley decomposition" (see Chantreuil & Trannoy, 2012; Sastre & Trannoy, 2002; Shorrocks, 2012).

An Empirical Illustration: Changes in Occupational Segregation in Switzerland Between 1970 and 2000

As an illustration of the application of the Deming and Stephan (1940) technique, we report here results that appeared in Deutsch, Flückiger, and Silber (2009). Using the Swiss Censuses for the years 1970 and 2000, the authors analyzed the changes over time in occupational segregation by

Table 1. Decomposition of the Change in Switzerland Between 1970 and 2000 in the Generalized Duncan Index (Occupational Segregation by Gender, Nationality, and Age)[a].

Criterion of Comparison of Populations	Value of the Index in 1970	Value of the Index in 2000	Change Observed Between 1970 and 2000	Component of the Change due to a Variation in the "Internal Structure" of the Matrix	Component of the Change due to a Variation in the Margins of the Matrix	Component of the Change due to a Variation in the Occupational Structure	Component of the Change due to a Variation in the Shares of the Subpopulations Distinguished
Gender	0.4787	0.4875	0.0088	−0.0216	0.0304	−0.0237	0.0542
Nationality (Swiss vs. foreigners)	0.2449	0.1446	−0.1003	−0.0524	−0.0479	−0.0224	−0.0255
Age (below and above age 50)	0.1325	0.0651	−0.0673	−0.0691	0.0017	0.0036	−0.0019

[a]Deutsch, Flückiger, and Silber (2009) give for each number in the table confidence intervals based on the bootstrap approach.

gender, nationality, and age. Table 1 gives the results of the decomposition they obtained.

This illustration shows clearly that there are cases where "gross segregation" seems to have increased while "net segregation" in fact decreased. There are also cases where the impacts of changes in the margins are in opposite directions (impact of changes in the occupational structure vs. impact of changes in the relative shares of the genders). Deutsch et al. (2009) used here the generalized Duncan index but they could have used in a similar way the generalized Gini segregation index or an entropy-related index.

MEASURING SPATIAL SEGREGATION

Spatial Segregation is a good illustration of the case where an additional dimension has to be introduced to measure multidimensional segregation. Assume data are available on the distribution of ethnic groups across different geographical units (e.g., census tracts) which are part of a bigger geographical area (e.g., a metropolitan area). The measures of multi-dimensional segregation introduced previously section would not correctly measure the degree of spatial segregation because these indices would amount to comparing the ethnic composition of the different geographical units with the average ethnic composition in the bigger geographical area under study. A good measure of spatial segregation should, however, take into account the "geographical component" of the distribution of the ethnic groups across the geographical units. One might want to know, for example, whether the ethnic groups are evenly dispersed across the various geo-graphical units or on the contrary clustered in a few specific areas. Another issue of interest may concern the location of the various ethnic groups with respect to the "center" of the bigger geographical area: does some ethnic group, for example, live in the suburbs of the metropolitan area and some other in the center of the city?

Massey and Denton (1988) considered, thus, five aspects of residential segregation: evenness, exposure, concentration, centralization, and cluster-ing. For them "evenness refers to the differential distribution of two social groups among areal units in a city" while "residential exposure refers to the degree of potential contact, or the possibility of interaction, between minority and majority group members within geographic areas of a city." "Concentration refers to the amount of physical space occupied by a minority group in the urban environment … Centralization is the degree to which a group is spatially located near the center of an urban area … ." Finally, the degree of spatial clustering exhibited by a minority group "is the extent to which areal units inhabited by minority groups adjoin one another, or cluster, in space" (Massey & Denton, 1988). These authors then surveyed 20 potential measures of segregation and checked which of these 5 aspects each segregation index was measuring. Massey and Denton (1988) in fact argued that evenness and exposure are "aspatial dimensions," while concentration, centralization, and clustering are "spatial dimensions" of residential segregation. Reardon and O'Sullivan (2004) criticized these distinctions and suggested an alternative classification. They recommended making a distinction between only two aspects of residential segregation: spatial exposure (as opposed to spatial isolation) and spatial evenness (the contrary of spatial clustering). "Spatial exposure refers to the extent that members of one group encounter members of another group … in their local spatial environments. Spatial evenness … refers to the extent to which groups are similarly distributed in the residential space" (Reardon & O'Sullivan, 2004). These authors reviewed then existing measures of spatial segregation and checked which (desirable) properties they had. They then proposed new indices of spatial segregation.

Since the present paper does not aim at offering also a survey of indices of spatial segregation, only one index of spatial segregation will be presented. It has been proposed by Dawkins (2004) and is a simple extension of the Gini index of segregation I_G defined in Eq. (6).

Assume there are only two ethnic groups, B and W, and that data are available on the number B_k and W_k of individuals belonging to groups B and W in each area k (e.g., census tract). Using Eq. (6) the Gini segregation index may then be expressed as

$$I_{G,SEG} = \vec{w}' G \vec{b} \tag{35}$$

where $\vec{w}'$ is a row vector of the shares (W_k/W) of ethnic group W in the various areas k and $\vec{b}$ is a column vector of the corresponding shares (B_k/B) for ethnic group B, both set of shares being ranked by decreasing ratios (B_k/W_k). The operator G in (35) is naturally the G-matrix that was previously defined. Assume, for example, a city with nine neighborhoods and in each neighborhood there are either blacks or whites. Figs. 1 and 2 draw two such cases with five black neighborhoods and four white neighborhoods.

Let us compute the Gini segregation index I_G for Case 1. Table 2 gives the "blacks/whites" ratios in each neighborhood in Case 1. One possible ordering[9] of the "black/white" ratios will then be given by Table 3.

Fig. 1. Case 1.

Fig. 2. Case 2.

Table 2. Black–White Ratios in Each Neighborhood (Case 1).

∞	0	∞
0	∞	0
∞	0	∞

Table 3. Ordering of the Neighborhoods According to the Black–White Ratios (Case 1).

2	7	1
8	5	6
3	9	4

The traditional Gini segregation index will then be expressed as $\vec{w}'G\vec{b}$ where the row vectors $\vec{w}'$ and $\vec{b}'$ are $\vec{w}' = (0\ 0\ 0\ 0\ 0\ .25\ .25\ .25\ .25)'$ and $\vec{b}' = (.2\ .2\ .2\ .2\ 0\ 0\ 0\ 0\ 0)$. It is easy to derive that in this case $\vec{w}'G\vec{b} = 1$ so that residential segregation is maximal. Note that in Case 2 a similar computation would show that the Gini segregation index I_G is also equal to 1. This is not surprising since the Gini index I_G does not take into account the respective location of the two ethnic groups. It, thus, ignores the degree of clustering of these ethnic groups.

Assume now that we order the neighborhoods according to the order of the closest neighborhood. If, for example, the closest neighborhood to a black neighborhood is a white neighborhood, we will assume that the black neighborhood is not really segregated. A similar assumption will evidently be made for white neighborhoods.

Let us go back to Case 1 and assume, as a simple illustration, that the closest neighborhood is the one below and for the neighborhoods in the bottom line, we assume it is the one above. For Case 1 the relevant "black–white" ratios are then given in Table 4 so that the ordering of the neighborhoods becomes the one given in Table 5.

In such a case we do not compute any more a Gini segregation index but a "pseudo-Gini" segregation index[10] which is expressed as $\tilde{w}' G \tilde{b}$ with $\tilde{w}' = (.25\ .25\ .25\ .25\ 0\ 0\ 0\ 0\ 0)$ and $\tilde{b}' = (0\ 0\ 0\ 0\ .2\ .2\ .2\ .2\ .2)$ so that the

Table 4. New Black–White Ratios in Each Neighborhood (Case 1).

0	∞	0
∞	0	∞
0	∞	0

Table 5. New Ordering of the Neighborhoods According to the Black–White Ratios (Case 1).

6	1	5
2	9	4
7	3	8

"pseudo-Gini" segregation index is equal to −1. Since "pseudo-Ginis" vary between −1 and +1, we can conclude that the level of segregation obtained is now the lowest possible (no segregation). This should be clear because in Case 1, the neighborhood closest to one's neighborhood (the one below) is one with the opposite race, and hence integration is now assumed to be maximal.

The computation of the "pseudo-Gini" for Case 2 will, however, give different results. Here also we will assume that the closest neighborhood is the one below and for the neighborhoods in the bottom line, we assume it is the one above. The "black–white" ratios in Case 2 are given in Table 6 and the ordering of the neighborhoods appears in Table 7.

The "pseudo-Gini" segregation index will as before be expressed as $\tilde{w}' G \tilde{b}$ but now $\tilde{w}' = (0\ 0\ 0\ 0\ 0\ .25\ .25\ .25\ .25)$ while $\tilde{b}' = (.2\ .2\ .2\ .2\ .2\ 0\ 0\ 0\ 0)$ so that now the pseudo-Gini segregation index is equal to 1. We thus find that, as expected, there is much less integration than in Case 1. In fact there is maximal segregation in Case 2. Naturally segregation can be computed in a similar way on the basis of other criteria. We could, for example, rank the neighborhoods on the basis of their distance from the center of the city.

Table 6. New Black–White Ratios in Each Neighborhood (Case 2).

∞	∞	0
∞	0	0
∞	∞	0

Table 7. New Ordering of the Neighborhoods According to the Black–White Ratios (Case 2).

1	2	7
3	6	8
4	5	9

MEASURES OF ORDINAL SEGREGATION

Neither the binary nor the multiple group measures of segregation are appropriate when either the groups or the units have inherent orderings. This is another case where an additional dimension has to be introduced to correctly measure segregation. Assume, for example, that the goal is to measure occupational segregation by gender, taking into account the fact that there is an ordering of the occupations (e.g., there is a prestige scale for the various occupations). Another illustration would be the case where one wants to analyze residential segregation by educational level when there is an ordering of the educational levels.

Let us take the case of occupational segregation by gender and imagine two possibilities (see scenario A and scenario B in Table 8).

In scenario A males are concentrated in prestigious occupations (3 and 4) and females in nonprestigious occupations (1 and 2). In scenario B the data of occupations 3 and 4 were swapped as well as those of occupations 1 and 2. A traditional segregation index (e.g., the Duncan index) would give the same value in scenario A and scenario B, while intuition tells us that there should be more segregation in scenario A. Reardon (2009) proposed indices of segregation that would give different answers for these two scenarios:

Assume that the variable j denotes ordered categories (e.g., occupations), with $j = 1$ to J, while i refers to the unordered categories (here gender or ethnic groups) with $i = 1$ to I.
Let n, $n_{i\cdot}$, $n_{\cdot j}$, and n_{ij} refer, respectively, to the total population, that in group i, that in ordered category j, and that in the cell (i, j).

Table 8. Ordinal Segregation.

	Occupation 1	Occupation 2	Occupation 3	Occupation 4	Total
Scenario A					
Males	10	20	30	40	100
Females	40	30	20	10	100
Total	50	50	50	50	200
Scenario B					
Males	20	10	40	30	100
Females	30	40	10	20	100
Total	50	50	50	50	200

Within each group (unordered category) i call π_{ij} the cumulative proportion of the population in i in ordered category j, that is,

$$\pi_{ij} = \sum_{h=1}^{j} \left(\frac{n_{ih}}{n_{i.}}\right) \tag{36}$$

In fact it is enough to characterize such a distribution by the $[J-1]$-tuple $\pi_i = (\pi_{i1}, \ldots, \pi_{ij}, \ldots, \pi_{i,J-1})$ since, J being the total number of categories, $\pi_{i,J}$ is always equal to 1.

Clearly segregation will be maximal if within each group (unordered category) i all individuals occupy a single ordered category,[11] in which case π_{ij} is always either equal to 0 or to 1. Conversely, segregation will be minimal if within each unordered category i the distribution of the individuals is equal to that of the population (in which case $\pi_{ij} = \pi_{.j}$ $\forall$ i and j).

Following the work of Reardon and Firebaugh (2002) on multigroup (unordered) segregation, Reardon proposes then to measure ordinal segregation as

$$\Psi = \sum_{i=1}^{I} \left(\frac{n_{i.}}{n}\right) \frac{(\xi - \xi_i)}{\xi} \tag{37}$$

where ξ_i and ξ refer, respectively, to a measure of variation (dispersion) in unit i and in the total population.

How shall one measure variation? Variation will be assumed to be maximal when half of the population is located in the first column and half in the last column, that is, half the population belongs to the least prestigious occupation and half to the most prestigious one. Obviously, variation will be minimal when all the observations are in the same column, that is, when all the individuals belong to the same occupation j with $j = 1$, $2\ldots$, or J.

In other words there will be maximal variation when the $[K-1]$-tuple π is written as $\pi_{MAX} = (0.5\ 0.5\ 0.5\ \ldots\ .0.5)$ and there will be minimal variation when π is written as $\pi_{MIN} = (0\ 0\ 0.0\ \ldots, 1\ 1\ 1\ \ldots\ 1)$.

The idea is then to measure variation as an inverse function of the distance from π to π_{MAX}. In other words we will write

$$\xi = (1/(J-1)) \sum_{j=1}^{J-1} f(\pi_j) \tag{38}$$

where $f(\pi)$ is a continuous function on the interval [0,1] such that $f(\pi)$ is increasing for $\pi \in (0,0.5)$ and decreasing for $\pi \in (0.5,1)$. Note that $f(\pi)$ is maximal at $\pi = (1/2)$, that is, $f(1/2) = 1$ and minimal at $\pi = 0$ and $\pi = 1$, that is, $f(0) = f(1) = 0$.

Reardon (2009) suggested then four possible functional forms for f:

$$f_1(\pi) = -[(\pi \log_2 \pi) + ((1 - \pi)\log_2(1 - \pi)] \quad (39)$$

$$f_2(\pi) = 4\pi(1 - \pi) \quad (40)$$

$$f_3(\pi) = 2\sqrt[2]{\pi(1 - \pi)} \quad (41)$$

$$f_4(\pi) = 1 - |2\pi - 1| \quad (42)$$

Substituting these four functions in ξ yields four potential measures of ordinal variation:

$$\Omega_h = \sum_{i=1}^{I} \left(\frac{n_{i.}}{n}\right)\left(\frac{\xi_h - \xi_{hi}}{\xi_h}\right) \quad (43)$$

with $h = 1$–4, each h referring to one of the four functional forms which have just been described.

Note that Ω_1 is an ordinal generalization of the information theory index H and was called by Reardon the *ordinal information theory index*.

Similarly, Ω_2 is an ordinal generalization of the diversity index DIV and was called by Reardon the *ordinal variation ratio index*.

EXTENSIONS TO OTHER DOMAINS: SEGREGATION AND INEQUALITY IN LIFE CHANCES

This section aims at showing that the concepts used in measuring multidimensional segregation may be applied to several other domains.

Inequality in Life Chances: The Case of Cardinal Variables

In a recent paper entitled "Inequality in Life Chances and the Measurement of Social Immobility" Silber and Spadaro (2011), in a book in honor of Serge Kolm, used as database a matrix whose lines correspond to the social category (e.g., occupation or educational level) of the parents and the columns to the income distribution of the children.

They then borrowed the concept of generalized segregation curve which was presented previously, to define what they called social immobility curves. More precisely they plotted on the horizontal axis the cumulative values of the "a priori" probability for an individual to belong to social origin i and income group j, this "a priori" probability being equal to the product of the probability to belong to social origin i and of the probability to belong to income group j. On the vertical axis they plotted cumulative values of the "a posteriori" probabilities, that is, of the actual probability to belong to social origin i and to income group j. On both axes the individuals were classified by increasing values of the ratio of the "a posteriori" over the "a priori" probabilities.

The empirical illustration given by Silber and Spadaro (2011) was in part based on a survey of 2000 individuals conducted in France by Thomas Piketty in the year 1998. To measure the social origin of the parents the authors used information on the profession of either the father or the mother. Eight professions were distinguished (farmer, businessman, store owner or "artisan," manager or independent professional, technician or middle rank manager, employee, blue collar worker, including salaried persons working in agriculture, not working outside the household and retired). The social status of the children's generation was measured via their monthly income classified in eight income categories (see Silber & Spadaro, 2011, for more details).

The authors first computed what they called a "Gini index of social immobility" defined as being equal to twice the area lying between the generalized social immobility curve and the diagonal. They then applied the algorithm proposed by Deming and Stephan (1940) which allowed them to break down into three components the difference between, for example, the degree of social immobility from fathers to sons and that from mothers to daughters. In such an illustration the first component would reflect the impact of differences between the occupational distributions of the fathers and mothers. The second component would correspond to the impact of differences between the income distribution of sons and daughters. Finally, the third element of the breakdown would actually measure differences between the two cases examined in the "pure degree" of social immobility, that is, differences that remain even after differences between the margins of the two cases under study are neutralized. Not surprisingly the authors often found that differences in "gross social immobility" (before "neutralizing" differences in the margins) were often of opposite sign to differences in "net social immobility" (in "pure" social immobility).

Note that in this illustration the fact that the income groups are ordered was not taken into account. The goal of the authors was simply to estimate the degree of independence between the social origin of the parents and the income group to which they belonged. It is, however, possible to extend such an analysis by taking into account the ranking of the income groups, as will now be shown.

Inequality in Life Chances: The Case of Ordinal Variables

In a recent paper Silber and Yalonetzky (2011) suggested that the four indices that Reardon (2009) had proposed to measure ordinal segregation could also be used to measure inequality in life chances when one deals with ordinal variables. Although the paper of Silber and Yalonetzky (2011) does not include any empirical illustration, one could, for example, apply their approach to the case of a matrix whose lines would refer to the unordered social origin of the parents (e.g., occupational category) and the columns to the (ordered) income group to which the individuals belong. Note that in addition to the four indices proposed by Reardon (2009), Silber and Yalonetzky (2011) also suggested two new indices to measure inequality in life chances. Needless to say, these indices could also be applied to the measurement of ordinal segregation.

Extensions to Other Domains: Segregation and Health Inequality

In a very important paper Allison and Foster (2004) showed that cardinal measures of inequality could not be used when attempting to measure the degree of inequality of the distribution of ordinal variable. They then defined a partial inequality ordering allowing one to decide whether a distribution was more "spread out" than another. Abul Naga and Yalcin (2008) then characterized the entire class of continuous inequality indices founded on the Allison and Foster ordering and proposed a parametric family of inequality indices that could be used with Self-Rated Health Status data. More recently Lazar and Silber (forthcoming) showed that the indices of ordinal segregation recently proposed by Reardon (2009) could be also applied to the measurement of health inequality since they satisfied the four axioms specified by Abul Naga and Yalcin (2008). They also suggested an extension of the family of indices proposed by Abul Naga and Yalcin (2008) and Reardon (2009) and gave an empirical illustration.

Segregation and Inequality in Happiness

It should be clear that concepts used to measure ordinal segregation may also be used to measure inequality in happiness. Dutta and Foster (2011) have thus applied the approaches of Allison and Foster (2004) and Abul

Naga and Yalcin (2008) to the analysis of inequality in happiness in the United States during the 1972–2008 period.

Segregation and Polarization

Finally in an unpublished paper entitled "Ordinal Variables and the Measurement of Polarization," Fusco and Silber (2011) suggested applying Reardon's indices to the measurement of income polarization when only ordinal information was available on the income. Their basic idea is that the measurement of polarization, in particular bipolarization, is based, as stressed already by Zhang and Kanbur (2001), on two basic principles:

- polarization increases with between groups inequality,
- polarization decreases with within groups inequality.

These two properties clearly show up in the cardinal indices of polarization proposed by Foster and Wolfson (2010). Since the denominator of the Reardon (2009) ordinal segregation indices refers to overall inequality ("variation") while the numerator is equal to the complement to one of the weighted within groups inequality, Fusco and Silber (2011) suggested that the Reardon indices could be also applied to the measurement of polarization when only ordinal information on income is available. Fusco and Silber (2011) based their empirical illustration on the 2008 cross-sectional data from the *European Union-Statistics on Income and Living Conditions* (EU-SILC). As ordinal variable they took the answers to the question where households' respondents are asked whether they are able to make ends meet. Six possible answers were proposed: (1) with great difficulty, (2) with difficulty, (3) with some difficulty, (4) fairly easily, (5) easily, (6) very easily. The unordered categories refer to the citizenship of the household member who answered the household questionnaire (local vs. foreigners).

CONCLUDING COMMENTS

In her book entitled *How to Be Human, Though an Economist*, Deirdre McCloskey (2000) writes that "In the 1960s the sociologist of science Derek Price used the phrase Invisible College to describe the old-boy network of Big Science. Since then the rest of academic life has caught up to the social structure of physics, scattering old boys and old girls around the globe in each special field. The result has been damaging to the visible college and, in the end, damaging to science and scholarship. The experiment since the 1950s with turning intellectual life over to specialists has not worked, at least in the fields I know, especially economics … . The odd thing about the way the advice has worked out in practice is that it has yielded a drearily uniform economics … . The Kelly green golfing shoe of economics, on which all the best shoemakers agree, is microfoundations of overlapping generations in a game theoretic model with human capital and informational asymmetry … Good economics knows that specialization is not in itself good. The blessed Adam Smith (not to speak of Marx) was eloquent about the damage that specialization per se does to human spirit … . What is good about specialization is that it allows more consumption, through trade … ."

The lesson to be drawn is that although we have no choice but specialize, we should be aware of the usefulness of lateral thinking, as stressed by Atkinson (2011). Clearly those working on the measurement of segregation have greatly benefited from borrowing ideas from the field of income inequality measurement. However, the extension of their analysis to multidimensional segregation is likely to be of great relevance to fields such as the inequality of opportunity, health, and happiness, or to that of social polarization. There is, thus, room for a greater level of interaction between those attempting to measure segregation and those focusing their interest on the measurement of income and more generally economic inequality.

NOTES

1. For a survey of the measurement of segregation in the labor force, published more than 12 years ago, see Flückiger and Silber (1999).
2. For an excellent recent survey of the measurement of spatial segregation, see Reardon and O'Sullivan (2004).
3. We could also rank the occupations by increasing ratios (M_k/F_k) and plot the cumulative values of the shares (F_k/F) on the horizontal axis and the cumulative values of the shares (M_k/M) on the vertical axis. The curve obtained would evidently be the same segregation curve as that defined earlier.
4. This section is based on Deutsch and Silber (2005).
5. The Gini index of segregation I_G cannot be decomposed into the sum of a between and within groups segregation. Such a breakdown includes generally a residual which can be interpreted as measuring the degree of overlap between the group-specific distributions of the gender ratios (F_k/M_k) or (M_k/F_k). For an

illustration of the decomposition of the Gini segregation index, see Deutsch, Flückiger, and Silber (1994).

6. The subsections on disproportionality and diversity were mainly inspired by the nice survey of Reardon and Firebaugh (2002).

7. Reardon and Firebaugh (2002) were more concerned by residential than occupational segregation.

8. This section was inspired by ideas that appear in Jargowsky and Kim (2009).

9. Since there are five areas where the ratio is equal to ∞, we can order these five areas as we wish. Similarly, there are four cases where the ratio is equal to 0 and here again we can order these four areas as we want.

10. For an exact definition of the concept of Pseudo-Gini, see Silber (1989a).

11. Naturally the ordered category should be different for each unordered category.

REFERENCES

Abul Naga, R. H., & Yalcin, T. (2008). Inequality measurement for ordered response health data. *Journal of Health Economics*, *27*(6), 1614–1625.

Allison, R. A., & Foster, J. (2004). Measuring health inequalities using qualitative data. *Journal of Health Economics*, *23*, 505–524.

Atkinson, A. B. (1970). On the measurement of inequality. *Journal of Economic Theory*, *2*, 244–263.

Atkinson, A. B. (2011). On lateral thinking. *Journal of Economic Inequality*, *9*(3), 319–328.

Blackorby, C., & Donaldson, D. (1978). Measures of relative equality and their meaning in terms of social welfare. *Journal of Economic Theory*, *18*, 59–80.

Boisso, D., Hayes, K., Hirschberg, J., & Silber, J. (1994). Occupational segregation in the multidimensional case. *Journal of Econometrics*, *61*, 161–171.

Chakravarty, S., D'Ambrosio, C., & Silber, J. (2009). Generalized Gini occupational segregation indices. In Y. Flückiger, S. Reardon, & J. Silber (Eds.), *Occupational and residential segregation* (Vol. 17, pp. 71–95). Research on Economic Inequality. Bingley, UK: Emerald.

Chakravarty, S., & Silber, J. (1994). Employment segregation indices: An axiomatic characterization. In W. Eichhorn (Ed.), *Models and measurement of welfare and inequality* (pp. 912–920). Berlin: Springer-Verlag.

Chakravarty, S., & Silber, J. (2007). A generalized index of employment segregation. *Mathematical Social Sciences*, *53*(2), 185–195.

Chantreuil, F., & Trannoy, A. (2012). Inequality decomposition values: The trade-off between marginality and consistency. *Journal of Economic Inequality*. Available at http://www.springerlink.com/content/lmj431pg3776l717/fulltext.pdf

Dawkins, C. J. (2004). Measuring the spatial pattern of residential segregation. *Urban Studies*, *41*(4), 833–851.

Deming, W. E., & Stephan, F. F. (1940). On a least squares adjustment of a sampled frequency table when the expected marginals are known. *Annals of Mathematical Statistics*, *11*, 427–444.

Deutsch, J., Flückiger, Y., & Silber, J. (1994). Measuring occupational segregation. Summary statistics and the impact of classification errors and aggregation. *Journal of Econometrics, 61*, 133–146.

Deutsch, J., Flückiger, Y., & Silber, J. (2009). Analyzing changes in occupational segregation: The case of Switzerland (1970–2000). In Y. Flückiger, S. Reardon, & J. Silber (Eds.), *Occupational and residential segregation* (Vol. 17, pp. 171–202). Research on Economic Inequality. Bingley, UK: Emerald.

Deutsch, J., & Silber, J. (2005). Comparing segregation by gender in the labor force across ten European countries in the 1990s. An analysis based on the use of normative segregation indices, with J. Deutsch. *International Journal of Manpower, 26*(3), 237–264.

Donaldson, D., & Weymark, J. (1980). A single parameter generalization of the Gini indices of inequality. *Journal of Economic Theory, 22*, 67–87.

Duncan, O. D., & Duncan, B. (1955). A methodological analysis of segregation indices. *American Sociological Review, 20*(2), 210–217.

Dutta, I., & Foster, J. (2011). *Inequality of happiness in the US: 1972–2008*. School of Economics Discussion paper Series 1110. The University of Manchester.

Flückiger, Y., & Silber, J. (1999). *The measurement of segregation in the labor force*. Heidelberg: Physica Verlag.

Foster, J. E., & Shorrocks, A. F. (1987). Transfer sensitive inequality measures. *Review of Economic Studies, LIV*, 485–497.

Foster, J. E., & Wolfson, M. C. (2010). Polarization and the decline of the middle class: Canada and the US. *Journal of Economic Inequality, 8*, 247–273.

Frankel, D., & Volij, O. (2011). Measuring school segregation. *Journal of Economic Theory, 146*, 1–38.

Fusco, A., & Silber, J. (2011). *Quantifying social polarization when variables are ordinal*. Mimeo.

Goodman, L. A., & Kruskal, W. H. (1954). Measures of association for cross classifications. *Journal of the American Statistical Association, 49*, 732–764.

Harberger, A. C. (1962). The incidence of the corporate income tax. *Journal of Political Economy, 70*(3), 215–240.

Hutchens, R. M. (1991). Segregation curves, Lorenz curves and inequality in the distribution of people across occupations. *Mathematical Social Sciences, 21*(1), 31–51.

Hutchens, R. M. (2001). Numerical measures of segregation: Desirable properties and their implications. *Mathematical Social Sciences, 42*(1), 13–29.

Hutchens, R. M. (2004). One measure of segregation. *International Economic Review, 45*(2), 555–578.

Jahn, J., Schmid, C. F., & Schrag, C. (1947). The measurement of ecological segregation. *American Sociological Review, 12*(3), 293–303.

James, D. R., & Taeuber, K. E. (1985). Measures of segregation. *Sociological Methodology, 15*, 1–32.

Jargowsky, P. A., & Kim, J. (2009). The information theory of segregation: Uniting segregation and inequality in a common framework. In Y. Flückiger, S. F. Reardon, & J. Silber (Eds.), *Occupational and residential segregation* (Vol. 17). Research on Economic Inequality. Bingley, UK: Emerald.

Kakwani, N. C. (1994). Segregation by sex: Measurement and hypothesis testing. In S. Neuman & J. Silber (Eds.), *The economics of labor market segregation and discrimination* (pp. 1–26). Greenwich: JAI Press.

Karmel, T., & MacLachlan, M. (1988). Occupational sex segregation – Increasing or decreasing? *Economic Record*, *64*(186), 187–195.

Kendall, M. G., & Stuart, A. (1961). *The advanced theory of statistics*. London: Griffin & Company.

Kolm, S. C. (1966). *Monetary and financial choices (in French)*. Paris: Dunod.

Kolm, S. C. (1969). The optimal production of social justice. In H. Guitton & J. Margolis (Eds.), *Public economics*. London: Macmillan.

Kolm, S. C. (1999). The rational foundations of income inequality measures. In J. Silber (Ed.), *Handbook on income inequality measurement*. Dordrecht: Kluwer Academic Publishers.

Lazar, A., & Silber, J. (forthcoming). On the cardinal measurement of health inequality when only ordinal information is available on individual health status. *Health Economics*. Available at http://dx.doi.org/10.1002/hec.1821

Lewis, D. E. (1982). The measurement of the occupational and industrial segregation of Women. *Journal of Industrial Relations*, *24*, 406–423.

Massey, D. S., & Denton, N. A. (1988). The dimensions of residential segregation. *Social Forces*, *67*(2), 281–315.

McCloskey, D. (2000). *How to be human though an economist*. Ann Arbor, MI: University of Michigan Press.

Moir, H., & Selby-Smith, J. (1979). Industrial segregation in the Australian labor market. *Journal of Industrial Relations*, *21*, 281–291.

Mora, R., & Ruiz-Castillo, J. (2003). Additive decomposable segregation indexes. The case of gender segregation by occupations and human capital levels in Spain. *Journal of Economic Inequality*, *1*, 147–179.

Mora, R., & Ruiz-Castillo, J. (2005). *An evaluation of an entropy based index of segregation*. Mimeo.

Reardon, S. F. (2009). Measures of ordinal segregation. In Y. Flückiger, S. F. Reardon & J. Silber (Eds.), *Occupational and residential segregation* (Vol. 17, pp. 129–155). Research on Economic Inequality. Bingley, UK: Emerald.

Reardon, S. F., & Firebaugh, G. (2002). Measures of multi-group segregation. *Sociological Methodology*, *32*, 33–67.

Reardon, S. F., & O'Sullivan, D. (2004). Measures of spatial segregation. *Sociological Methodology*, *34*(1), 121–162.

Rotschild, M., & Stiglitz, J. E. (1970). Increasing risk: I. A definition. *Journal of Economic Theory*, *2*(3), 225–243.

Rotschild, M., & Stiglitz, J. E. (1971). Increasing risk: II. Its economic consequences. *Journal of Economic Theory*, *3*(1), 66–84.

Samuelson, P. (1947). *Foundations of economic analysis*. Cambridge, MA: Harvard University Press.

Sastre, M., & Trannoy A. (2002). Shapley inequality decomposition by factor components: Some methodological issues. *Journal of Economics*, (Suppl. 9), 51–89.

Shannon, C. E. (1948). A mathematical theory of communication. *Bell System Technical Journal*, *27*, pp. 379–423, 623–656.

Shorrocks, A. F. (2012). Decomposition procedures for distributional analysis: A unified framework based on the Shapley value. *Journal of Economic Inequality*, forthcoming. Available at http://www.springerlink.com/content/a65m427547227w25/fulltext.pdf

Silber, J. (1989a). Factors components, population subgroups and the computation of the Gini index of inequality. *The Review of Economics and Statistics*, *LXXI*, 107–115.

Silber, J. (1989b). On the measurement of employment segregation. *Economics Letters, 30*(3), 237–243.

Silber, J. (1992). Occupational segregation indices in the multidimensional case: A note. *Economic Record, 68*, 276–277.

Silber, J., & Spadaro, A. (2011). Inequality of life chances and the measurement of social immobility. In M. Fleurbaey, M. Salles, & J. Weymark (Eds.), *Social ethics and normative economics, Essays in honour of Serge-Christophe Kolm* (pp. 129–154). Heidelberg, Germany: Studies in Social Choice and Welfare. Springer Verlag.

Silber, J., & Yalonetzky, G. (2011). On measuring inequality in life chances when a variable is ordinal. In J. G. Rodríguez (Ed.), *Inequality of opportunity: Theory and measurement* (Chapter 4, Vol. 19, pp. 77–98). Research on Economic Inequality. Bingley, UK: Emerald.

Siltanen, J., Jarman, J., & Blackburn, R. M. (1995). *Gender inequality in the labour market. Occupational concentration and segregation. A manual on methodology*. Geneva: International Labour Office.

Theil, H. (1967). *Economics and information theory*. Amsterdam: North-Holland.

Theil, H., & Finizza, S. A. J. (1971). A note on the measurement of racial integration of schools by means of information concepts. *Journal of Mathematical Sociology, 1*, 187–194.

Watts, M. (1998). Occupational gender segregation: Index measurement and econometric modelling. *Demography, 35*(4), 489–496.

Zhang, X., & Kanbur, R. (2001). What differences do polarization measures make? An application to China. *Journal of Development Studies, 37*, 85–98.

CHAPTER 2

OCCUPATIONAL SEGREGATION MEASURES: A ROLE FOR STATUS

Coral del Río and Olga Alonso-Villar

ABSTRACT

This paper defines local segregation measures that are sensitive to status differences among organizational units. So far as we know, this is the first time that status-sensitive segregation measures have been offered in a multigroup context with a cardinal measure of status. These measures allow researchers to aggregate employment gaps of a target group by penalizing its concentration in low-status occupations. They are intended to complement rather than substitute for previous local segregation measures. The usefulness of these tools is illustrated in the case of occupational segregation by race and ethnicity in the United States.

Keywords: Segregation measures; occupations; status; United States

JEL classifications: D63; J0; J15; J71

INTRODUCTION

The literature on segregation devotes a great deal of attention to analyzing segregation in the case of two population subgroups (blacks–whites,

Inequality, Mobility and Segregation: Essays in Honor of Jacques Silber
Research on Economic Inequality, Volume 20, 37–62

ISSN: 1049-2585/doi:10.1108/S1049-2585(2012)0000020005

high–low social position, and women–men).[1] The study of segregation in a multigroup context does not have a long tradition, even though in recent years this topic has received increasing attention among scholars (Boisso, Hayes, Hirschberg, & Silber, 1994; Frankel & Volij, 2011; Reardon & Firebaugh, 2002; Silber, 1992). These multigroup measures allow researchers to quantify the disparities among the population subgroups into which the economy can be partitioned and provide an aggregate or overall segregation value (Iceland, 2004).

Nevertheless, one may be interested in measuring not only overall segregation, which involves simultaneous comparisons among all groups, but also the segregation of a target population subgroup, a topic that gains special relevance in a multigroup context. To address this issue, the literature mainly opts to undertake pairwise comparisons. Thus, in ethnic/racial analyses, for example, studies often contrast Hispanics with whites as well as Hispanics with blacks, Asians, or non-Hispanics in general by using two-group measures (Albelda, 1986; Cutler, Glaeser, & Vigdor, 2008; Hellerstein & Neumark, 2008; King, 1992; Reardon & Yun, 2001). Alternatively, Alonso-Villar and Del Río (2010a) offer an axiomatic set-up within which the segregation of a target group (labeled as local segregation as opposed to overall segregation) can be addressed. In this framework, the distribution of a target group across organizational units is contrasted with the distribution of the total population. This approach places emphasis on how the different demographic groups fill the units, and it allows easy comparisons among groups.[2] These local segregation measures are naturally related to overall measures because they add up to the whole segregation when they are aggregated according to the demographic weights of the mutually exclusive subgroups into which the population can be partitioned.

None of these works, however, consider that organizational units might have different statuses. In particular, in measures of occupational segregation, standard indexes do not take into account whether demographic groups tend to occupy high or low status jobs, even though wage earnings vary considerably among occupations.[3] A segregation measure that takes into account the status of occupations should explicitly assume that it is important not only to determine how uneven the distribution of a group across occupations is with respect to others but also to identify the direction of these differences. In order to illustrate the relevance of these questions in the case of local segregation, consider the following economy with three demographic groups (*A*, *B*, and *C*) of equal size and two occupations (*j* and *k*). Table 1 presents the distribution of these groups between occupations together with the corresponding wages.

Table 1. Example.

	Group A	Group B	Group C	Wage
Occupation *j*	20	80	50	3
Occupation *k*	80	20	50	7

Any of the local segregation measures proposed by Alonso-Villar and Del Río (2010a) would suggest that demographic groups *A* and *B* share identical segregation levels since the discrepancy between the distribution of each of them and that of total employment (150,150) is of the same magnitude. However, some researchers would agree that the segregation suffered by group *B* is of a different nature and more disturbing than that of group *A*, since its employment is strongly concentrated in the low-paid occupation. In this regard, one might reasonably wonder whether it is possible to develop measures that allow one to include the status of organizational units (occupations, branches of activity, etc.) in the segregation measurement of a demographic group. These tools should give a higher segregation value to group $B \equiv (80,20)$ than to $A \equiv (20,80)$. Considering the salary level of occupations in the segregation measurement of a target group means placing emphasis on individuals' well-being.

This paper extends the local measures proposed by Alonso-Villar and Del Río (2010a) by incorporating the status of organizational units (in our case, occupations) in a cardinal way. To our knowledge, this is the first time that any study has offered status-sensitive segregation measures, either local or overall, in a multigroup context by invoking a cardinal measure of status. The few studies that do include the status of occupations in their proposals have focused on overall segregation by considering either an ordinal categorization of occupations in a multigroup context or a cardinal (and ordinal) categorization in a two-group context (Hutchens, 2006, 2009a; Reardon, 2009). Our measures can be used to assess the occupational segregation of a target group, the distribution of which departs from the occupational structure of the economy, by penalizing its concentration in low-status occupations. These measures should be used to complement rather than substitute for previous measures, since they are aimed at aggregating the employment gaps of a target group by taking into account the occupational wage distribution.

For that purpose, Section "Background and discussion" presents the existing discussion in the literature regarding the inclusion of status in segregation measurement. Section "Local segregation measures: the status of occupations" explains that any local segregation measure that takes into account the status of organizational units should satisfy certain properties and then this section presents several measures consistent with those properties. In addition, it proposes status-sensitive segregation curves and establishes the relationship between the corresponding dominance criterion and the mentioned indexes. These tools are used in Section "An illustration: occupational segregation by race and ethnicity in the United States" to analyze occupational segregation according to race and ethnicity in the United States. This illustration shows the potential of this approach, which offers useful hints for distinguishing between occupational distributions that are similar in terms of shares but differ in terms of assessment of those shares. Finally, Section "Conclusions" offers the main conclusions.

BACKGROUND AND DISCUSSION

Three recent papers tackle the inclusion of status or prestige in the measurement of overall segregation. Reardon (2009) offers ordinal overall measures in a multigroup context, which are useful when organizational units can be defined by ordered categories. In doing so, he establishes a set of desirable properties that any ordinal segregation measure should satisfy and then develops a general procedure with which to build these kinds of measures.[4] By following an approach more closely related to that of the literature on inequality, Hutchens (2006, 2009a) proposes overall segregation measures in the binary case, which take into account differences in the prestige of organizational units. In some cases, these measures use ordinal classifications of units, while in others, disparities are addressed with a cardinal scale of prestige. This allows Hutchens to distinguish between the effect of changes in the distribution of employment across occupations and the effect of changes in the status of the occupations.

These studies have opened the axiomatic debate, offering valued proposals for empirical research. However, none of them attempts to include status in local segregation measurement, which is a context where this approach appears particularly relevant. To close that gap somewhat, this paper aims to extend previous local segregation measures to incorporate this new dimension. Its objective is to offer new measures with which to compare the situation of various demographic groups. These measures attend not only to the group's distributions across occupations but also to the consequences of this phenomenon in economic terms.

There is no consensus in the literature regarding the convenience of including status in the analysis of segregation, as the debate between

Jargowsky (2009) and Hutchens (2009b) shows. Jargowsky's criticism addresses two main problems. Firstly, he considers that "the consequences of segregation should not be equated with the phenomenon itself" (p. 121), and secondly, he states that this inclusion involves "an implicit assumption about the causal link between the two dimensions", since status is "stated a priori" (p. 123). However, these criticisms do not seem conclusive. With respect to the former, it seems legitimate to wonder why important characteristics of the segregation phenomenon must be ignored when measuring segregation. In empirical analyses, it seems helpful to distinguish between the performances of two or more demographic groups that share a similar concentration level but that tend to fill occupations with very different economic or social statuses. This allows one to discriminate among similar concentration levels in terms of well-being. Certainly, it seems convenient to use different labels for each phenomenon since they are not exactly the same. Thus, in this paper, we use the term "status-sensitive segregation" to distinguish it from standard segregation. Regarding the second criticism, Hutchens sustains that "an index can combine different kinds of information without implying causality" (p. 127). Jointly analyzing two variables does not necessarily imply a causal relationship between them. In fact, one can find many examples in the literature of multidimensional inequality and poverty.

To address the issue of combining the distribution of status across occupations and that of employment, one could think of using bi-dimensional inequality measures and adapt them to our context. The advantage of these measures is that they have been analyzed from an axiomatic point of view, showing the roles played by the correlation between both variables and the inequality of each of them in measuring aggregate inequality (Atkinson & Bourguignon, 1982; Kolm, 1977; Tsui, 1999). However, we cannot follow this approach to extend local segregation measurement, since the effect of increasing status inequality should depend on the kind of occupations in which the target group tends to concentrate, and this requirement does not suit inequality measurement. If the target group is concentrated in low-status occupations and these occupations lose status as compared to the remaining, it seems reasonable to call for an increase in status-sensitive segregation. On the contrary, status-sensitive segregation should decrease if the group is concentrated in high-status occupations that improve their status. But these requirements are incompatible with some of the basic principles that the literature applies to multidimensional inequality, such as the *Pigou-Dalton bundle principle* (Fleurbaey & Trannoy, 2003) and the *correlation increasing principle* (Tsui, 1999). These principles imply that the researcher should take into account inequalities in the distributions of two variables across occupations (employment of the target group and occupational status), whereas we want to assess the inequality in the distribution of the target group across occupations in a different way, depending on whether the group concentrates in low or high status occupations. We will explain this in more detail after we present our basic properties.

Given our goal, this paper does not follow the multidimensional inequality approach but uses the approaches of Alonso-Villar and Del Río (2010a) and Hutchens (2006) as a starting point and adapts them to incorporate the status of occupations in local segregation measurement. For this purpose, the next section presents several basic properties and offers several status-sensitive local segregation measures that verify them.

LOCAL SEGREGATION MEASURES: THE STATUS OF OCCUPATIONS

This paper considers an economy with $J>1$ occupations among which the total population, denoted by T, is distributed according to distribution $t \equiv (t_1, t_2, \ldots, t_J)$, where $T = \Sigma_j t_j$. Assume that the statuses of occupations are represented by the distribution $s = (s_1, \ldots, s_J)$, where each s_j is a cardinal measure of the status of occupation j and $\Sigma_j (t_j/T) s_j = 1$. The distribution of target group g is denoted by $c^g \equiv (c_1^g, c_2^g, \ldots, c_J^g)$, where $c_j^g \leq t_j \, (g = 1, \ldots, G)$. c^g could represent, for example, the number of individuals of a given ethnic/racial group in each occupation. Therefore, the economy can be summarized by status vector s and matrix E, which represents the number of individuals of each population subgroup in each occupation, where rows and columns correspond to population subgroups and occupations, respectively. Therefore, the total number of individuals in occupation j is $t_j = \Sigma_g c_j^g$, and the total number of individuals in target group g is $C^g = \Sigma_j c_j^g$.

$$G \text{ subgroups} \times J \text{ occupations}$$

$$E = \begin{bmatrix} c_1^1 & \cdots & c_J^1 \\ \vdots & & \vdots \\ c_1^G & \cdots & c_J^G \end{bmatrix} \rightarrow \begin{bmatrix} \sum_j c_j^1 = C^1 \\ \vdots \\ \sum_j c_j^G = C^G \end{bmatrix}$$

$$\downarrow$$

$$\begin{bmatrix} \sum_g c_1^g = t_1 & \cdots & \sum_g c_J^g = t_J \end{bmatrix}$$

A measure of local segregation that takes status into account is a function, Φ_s, that allocates a real number to each vector (c^g; t; s) by measuring the differences between the distribution of target group g among occupations, c^g, and the distribution of reference, t, taking into account the status of occupations and considering that both distributions are expressed in proportions. In other words, distribution $((c_1^g/C^g), \ldots, (c_J^g/C^g))$ is compared with $((t_1/T), \ldots, (t_J/T))$ according to distribution $(s_1, \ldots, s_J)$. Namely, $\Phi_s : D \to \mathbb{R}$, where $D = \cup_{J>1}\{(c^g; t; s) \in \mathbb{R}_+^J \times \mathbb{R}_{++}^J \times \mathbb{R}_{++}^J : c_j^g \leq t_j \forall j\}$.

Basic Properties

We propose the following four basic properties for measuring local segregation in a hierarchical context.

Property 1. *Scale invariance*: Let α and β be two positive scalars such that when $(c^g; t; s) \in D$ vector $(\alpha c^g; \beta t; s) \in D$, then $\Phi_s(\alpha c^g; \beta t; s) = \Phi_s(c^g; t; s)$.[5]

Property 2. *Symmetry in groups*: If $(\Pi(1), \ldots, \Pi(J))$ represents a permutation of occupations (1,…,J) and (c^g; t; s)$\in D$, then $\Phi_s(c^g\Pi; t\Pi; s\Pi) = \Phi_s(c^g; t; s)$, where $c^g\Pi = (c^g_{\Pi(1)}, \ldots, c^g_{\Pi(J)})$, $t\Pi = (t_{\Pi(1)}, \ldots, t_{\Pi(J)})$, and $s\Pi = (s_{\Pi(1)}, \ldots, s_{\Pi(J)})$.

Property 3. *Insensitivity to proportional divisions*: If vector $(c^{g\prime}; t'; s') \in D$ is obtained from vector $(c^g; t; s) \in D$ in such a way that (a) $c_j^{g\prime} = c_j^g$, $t_j' = t_j$, $s_j' = s_j$ for any $j = 1, \ldots, J-1$ and (b) $c_j^{g\prime} = c_J^g/M$, $t_j' = t_J/M$ and $s_j' = s_J$, for any $j = J, \ldots, J+M-1$, then $\Phi_s(c^{g\prime}; t'; s') = \Phi_s(c^g; t; s)$.

The first property means that the segregation index does not change when the total number of jobs in the economy and/or the total number of individuals of target group g vary so long as their respective shares in each occupation remain unaltered. In other words, only employment shares matter, not employment levels. The second property means that the "occupation's name" is irrelevant so that if we enumerate occupations in a different order, the segregation level remains unchanged. The third property states that subdividing an occupation into several categories of equal size, both in terms of total employment and in terms of individuals of the target group, does not affect the segregation measurement as long as the status of the new categories coincides with that of the original occupation.

Property 4. *Sensitivity to disequalizing movements between organizational units*: Consider two occupations, i and h, satisfying $(c_i^g/t_is_i) < (c_h^g/t_hs_h)$.

If vector $(c^{g\prime}; t'; s') \in D$ is obtained from vector $(c^g; t; s) \in D$ in such a way that either (a) $c_i^{g\prime} = c_i^g - d$ and $c_h^{g\prime} = c_h^g + d$ $(0 < d \leq c_i^g)$, other things being equal (i.e., $c_j^{g\prime} = c_j^g \quad \forall j \neq i, h$ and $t_j' = t_j$ and $s_j' = s_j \quad \forall j$), or (b) $t_i' = t_i + e$ and $t_h' = t_h - e$ $(0 < e < t_h; s_i = s_h)$, other things being equal (i.e., $s_j' = s_j$ and $c_j^{g\prime} = c_j^g \; \forall j$ and $t_j' = t_j \; \forall j \neq i, h$), or (c) $s_i' = s_i + f$ and $s_h' = s_h - f$ $(0 < f < s_h;\ t_i = t_h)$, other things being equal (i.e., $t_j' = t_j$ and $c_j^{g\prime} = c_j^g \; \forall j$ and $s_j' = s_j \; \forall j \neq i, h$), then $\Phi_s(c^{g\prime}; t'; s') > \Phi_s(c^g; t; s)$.

This property requires the local segregation to increase when there are disequalizing movements between occupations (being a consequence of changes in either employment or status). It implies, for example, that if occupation i has the same number of jobs and the same status as occupation h (i.e., $t_i = t_h$ and $s_i = s_h$) but has a lower number of positions for the target group than occupation h has (i.e., $c_i^g < c_h^g$), then a movement of target individuals from i to h would result in a disequalizing movement that fosters the segregation of that group. In this case, there would be no difference between this property and the "movement between groups" property proposed by Alonso-Villar and Del Río (2010a) (henceforth AV–DR), since both occupations are considered to have the same status and, therefore, the target group has a lower presence in occupation i in terms of not only employment in that occupation, t_i, but also employment weighted by status, $t_i s_i$.

However, Property 4 also refers to disequalizing movements between occupations with different statuses and these movements are not considered in AV–DR. Thus, for example, if there is a movement of target individuals from i to h, segregation increases when occupation i has the same number of jobs as occupation h (i.e., $t_i = t_h$) but a higher status and lower (or equal) number of positions for the target group than occupation h has (i.e., $s_i > s_h$ and $c_i^g \leq c_h^g$). In addition, a disequalizing movement between two occupations can be found if the employment structure of the economy changes in such a way that the number of jobs increases in occupation i and decreases in h (in the same amount), the former having lower employment positions for the target group and a higher (or equal) employment level weighed by status (i.e., $c_i^g < c_h^g$ and $t_i s_i \geq t_h s_h$).

One might consider it necessary to include an additional property to compare the disequalizing movements of employment that differ in the status of the "receiving" occupation. It seems reasonable that a disequalizing movement of employment toward an occupation with a lower status fosters segregation to a higher extent than a movement toward an occupation with the same status. By following the property of "movements between groups with different prestige" established by Hutchens (2006) to measure overall segregation in a binary context, we can define the next property in our context.

Property 5. *Sensitivity to disequalizing movements between organizational units with different statuses*: Consider three occupations, i, h, and k, such that $(c_i^g/t_i)<(c_h^g/t_h)=(c_k^g/t_k)$ and $s_i=s_h>s_k$. If vectors $(c^{g'};t;s)$, $(c^{g''};t;s)\in D$ are obtained from vector $(c^g;t;s)\in D$ in such a way that $c_i^{g'}=c_i^g-d$ and $c_h^{g'}=c_h^g+d$, and $c_i^{g''}=c_i^g-d$ and $c_k^{g''}=c_k^g+d$ with $(0<d\leq c_i^g)$, other things being equal, then $\Phi_s(c^{g''};t;s)-\Phi_s(c^g;t;s)>\Phi_s(c^{g'};t;s)-\Phi_s(c^g;t;s)>0$.

Note, however, that Property 5 is a particular case of Property 4; therefore, if Property 4 is required, then there is no need for Property 5.

Regarding the performance of Φ_s under changes in the correlation between the distribution of status across occupations and that of the employment of the target group, we find it convenient to propose the next property.

Property 6. *Correlation decreasing principle*: Consider two occupations, i and h, with $t_i=t_h$, satisfying $c_i^g<c_h^g$ and $s_i>s_h$. If vector $(c^g;t;s')\in D$ is obtained from vector $(c^g;t;s)\in D$ in such a way that $s'_i=s_h$ and $s'_h=s_i$, other things being equal (i.e., $s'_j=s_j\ \forall j\neq i,h$), then $\Phi_s(c^g;t;s')<\Phi_s(c^g;t;s)$.

Note, however, that we do not need to add Property 6 to the list of properties that we will require for our measures, since it is a consequence of Properties 2 and 4 taken together.

This sixth property has the opposite effect of the *correlation increasing principle* proposed by Tsui (1999) to measure multidimensional inequality. According to this principle, an increase in the correlation between two variables must lead to an increase in bi-dimensional inequality. On the contrary, in our case, an increase in the correlation between the distribution of a group across occupations and the distribution of status (other things being equal) has to lead to a decrease in the status-sensitive segregation of that group since it involves a higher concentration of the group in high-paid occupations. For the same reason, the *Pigou-Dalton bundle principle* does not apply here, either. Consider, for simplicity, that all occupations have the same number of workers. According to this principle, a movement of target workers from an occupation where this group has fewer workers and lower status toward another occupation would increase inequality. However, we want the status-sensitive segregation of the target group to decrease after this movement.

Status-Sensitive Local Segregation Curves

Keeping Properties 1–4 in mind, we first define local segregation curves that are sensitive to differences among occupations' statuses. The dominance criterion of these curves is later shown to be consistent with these properties. In order to propose measures that can be easily implemented, we use wage as a proxy for occupational status. Namely, we assume that the distribution of status across occupations is equal to $s \equiv (w_1/\bar{w}, \ldots, w_J/\bar{w})$, where w_j is the wage of occupation j and $\bar{w} = \Sigma_j(t_j w_j/T)$.

To build these new curves, we use the local segregation curves proposed in AV–DR but modify the distribution of reference. Thus, the weight of each occupation in the new distribution of reference is equal to its employment level, t_j, weighted by its relative wage $(w_j/\bar{w})$. Consequently, if occupation j has a wage above the average $(w_j > \bar{w})$, it has a high status (>1), and, therefore, the benchmark gains relevance $(t_j(w_j/\bar{w}) > t_j)$. In this way, the discrepancies between the distribution of the target group and the occupational structure of the economy have a larger impact on high-paid occupations than on low-paid ones. Later on, we will see that this change allows the new local measures to satisfy the mentioned four basic properties.

To define a status-sensitive segregation curve for target group g, we propose to compare the distribution of that group, $(c_1^g/C^g, \ldots, c_J^g/C^g)$, with distribution $((t_1/T)(w_1/\bar{w}), \ldots, (t_J/T)(w_J/\bar{w}))$. Then, we plot the cumulative proportion of employment, $\Sigma_{i \leq j}(t_i(w_i/\bar{w}))/T$, on the horizontal axis and the cumulative proportion of individuals of the target group, $\Sigma_{i \leq j}(c_i^g/C^g)$, on the vertical axis.[6] In order to do so, we must arrange the occupations in ascending order of the ratio $(c_j^g/C^g)/((t_j(w_j/\bar{w}))/T)$, which is equivalent to the ranking according to $(c_j^g/(t_j(w_j/\bar{w})))$. Given that $(t_i/T)(w_i/\bar{w}) = (t_i w_i)/(\Sigma_i t_i w_i)$, the interpretation of this curve is simple: it shows the cumulative discrepancy between the employment distribution of the target group and the distribution the group would have if it followed the distribution of salaries, $t_i w_i$, across occupations (assuming there is no wage differences within each occupation).

Definition. We say that the status-sensitive local segregation curve of $(c^g; t; (w/\bar{w})) \in D$ *dominates that of* $(c^{g'}; t'; (w'/\bar{w}')) \in D$, where $w \equiv (w_1, \ldots, w_J)$, as long as the status-sensitive segregation curve of the former lies at no point below the latter yet lies at some point above the latter.

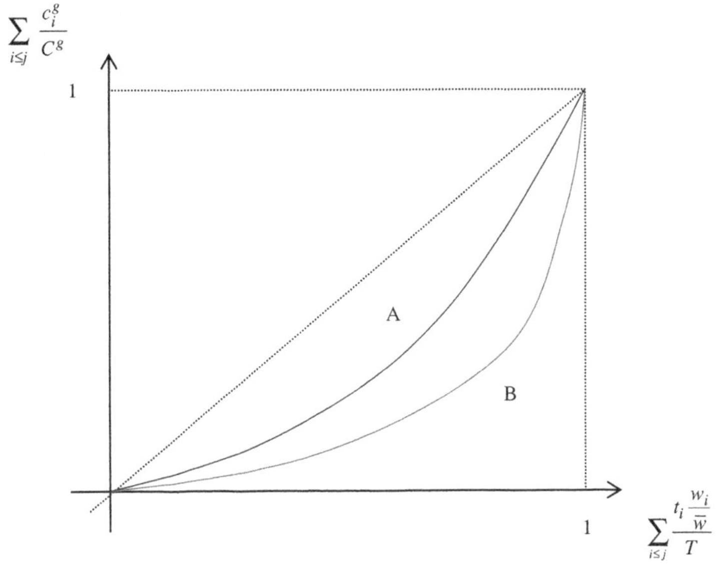

Fig. 1. Status-Sensitive Local Segregation Curves.

Fig. 1 shows the status-sensitive local segregation curves for two demographic groups, *A* and *B*, where the former dominates the latter, that is, *B* has higher status-sensitive segregation than *A*.

Note that, on the one hand, the status-sensitive local segregation curve generalizes the curve previously proposed by AV–DR, since the latter can be obtained as a particular case when all occupations offer the same wage. On the other hand, assuming for simplicity that $t_i = t_h \ \forall i, h$, it is easy to see that the higher the wage inequality across occupations (according to the Lorenz criterion), the larger the difference between this curve and the curve with no wage inequality. It is important to note, however, that the direction of these changes does depend on the correlation between the distributions of wages and the employment distribution of the target group across occupations. Thus, an augmentation in wage inequality reduces status-sensitive segregation when the relationship between both variables is perfectly linear and positive (since the new curve dominates the former). In fact, the curve coincides with the 45° line when the wage of each occupation is equal to the corresponding employment of the group multiplied by a constant. On the contrary, an increment in wage inequality leads to higher status-sensitive segregation levels when the rank correlation between both variables is −1.

Next, we show the relationship between our segregation curves and the segregation indexes that satisfy our basic properties.

Proposition 1. Given vectors $(c^g; t; (w/\bar{w})), (c^{g\prime}; t'; (w'/\bar{w}')) \in D$, the status-sensitive local segregation curve of $(c^g; t; (w/\bar{w}))$ dominates that of $(c^{g\prime}; t'; (w'/\bar{w}'))$ if and only if $\Phi_s(c^g; t; (w/\bar{w})) < \Phi_s(c^{g\prime}; t'; (w'/\bar{w}'))$ for any status-sensitive local segregation index Φ_s that satisfies Properties 1–4.

Proof. See Appendix A

This result shows the robustness of the dominance criterion for measuring the segregation of a demographic group when taking into account the status of occupations, since when a status-sensitive curve dominates another curve, any local segregation index satisfying the above properties will be necessarily consistent with this criterion. This makes the use of these curves a powerful procedure for empirical analysis. However, the indexes that satisfy the basic properties seem most appropriate when the curves cross or when a researcher is interested in quantifying the extent of status-sensitive segregation.

Status-Sensitive Local Segregation Indexes

In what follows, we extend several local segregation measures existing in the literature by incorporating the status of occupations. Thus, the status-sensitive local segregation Gini index of a target group (G_s^g) can be written as the weighted sum of the employment differences between pairs of occupations according to the relative presence of the target group – all ratios being expressed in terms of weighted-status employment – divided by twice the demographic weight of the group:

$$G_s^g = \frac{\sum_{i,j} \frac{t_i}{T}\frac{t_j}{T}\frac{w_i}{\bar{w}}\frac{w_j}{\bar{w}}\left|\frac{c_i^g}{t_i\frac{w_i}{\bar{w}}} - \frac{c_j^g}{t_j\frac{w_j}{\bar{w}}}\right|}{2\frac{C^g}{T}}. \tag{1}$$

Given the parallelism between the classical Gini index and the Lorenz curve, one can easily observe that this measure is equal to twice the area between the above status-sensitive local segregation curve and the 45° line.

The generalized entropy family of local segregation indexes proposed by AV–DR can also be conveniently modified in order to take into account the status of occupations (the generalized entropy family of status-sensitive local segregation indexes, $\Phi^g_{s,\alpha}$):

$$\Phi^g_{s,\alpha} \equiv \Phi_\alpha\left(c^g; t; \frac{w}{\bar{w}}\right) = \begin{cases} \frac{1}{\alpha(\alpha-1)} \sum_j \frac{t_j(w_j/\bar{w})}{T} \left[\left(\frac{c^g_j/C^g}{(t_j(w_j/\bar{w}))/T}\right)^\alpha - 1\right] & \text{if } \alpha \neq 0, 1 \\ \sum_j \frac{c^g_j}{C^g} \ln\left(\frac{c^g_j/C^g}{(t_j(w_j/\bar{w}))/T}\right) & \text{if } \alpha = 1 \end{cases} \tag{2}$$

where α is a parameter.[7] Note that when $\alpha = 0.5$, the above index is $\Phi^g_{s,0.5} = (1/4)\,(1 - \Sigma_j \sqrt{w_j/\bar{w}}\sqrt{(c^g_j/C^g)(t_j/T)})$, which can be interpreted as the local version of the square root index proposed by Hutchens (2006) to measure overall segregation in the binary case when taking the prestige of occupations into account.[8]

Moreover, the popular index of dissimilarity proposed by Duncan and Duncan (1955) can also be conveniently adapted to measure the segregation of target group g when taking status into account (the status-sensitive local dissimilarity index, D^g_s):

$$D^g_s = \frac{1}{2} \sum_j \left| \frac{c^g_j}{C^g} - \frac{t_j}{T} \frac{w_j}{\bar{w}} \right|. \tag{3}$$

Given the parallelism between the status-sensitive local segregation curve of vector $(c^g; t; w/\bar{w})$ and the Lorenz curve of fictitious distribution

$$\left(\underbrace{\frac{c^g_1}{t_1 \frac{w_1}{\bar{w}}}, \ldots, \frac{c^g_1}{t_1 \frac{w_1}{\bar{w}}}}_{t_1 \frac{w_1}{\bar{w}}}, \ldots, \underbrace{\frac{c^g_J}{t_J \frac{w_J}{\bar{w}}}, \ldots, \frac{c^g_J}{t_J \frac{w_J}{\bar{w}}}}_{t_J \frac{w_J}{\bar{w}}} \right)$$

defined in the proof of the above proposition, it is easy to see that the status-sensitive Gini index of target group g, G^g_s, and the family of indexes $\Phi^g_{s,\alpha}$ satisfy Properties 1–4. For the same reason, it follows that local index D^g_s only satisfies Properties 1–3, since the classical index of dissimilarity is not consistent with the Lorenz dominance criterion. It is also straightforward to prove that all these status-sensitive measures satisfy the following property.

Property 7. *Status-Sensitive normalization*: $\Phi_s(c^g; t; s) = 0$ if $c_j^g/C^g = (t_j(w_j/\bar{w})/T)\ \forall j$.

This property has two implications. First, if $w_j = w_h \forall j, h$ and $c_j^g/C^g = (t_j/T)\ \forall j$, then $\Phi_s(c^g; t; s) = 0$. In other words, when all wages are equal, the index is zero as long as there is no local segregation. In fact, if there is no wage dispersion, then these status-sensitive local segregation measures coincide with the local segregation measures proposed by AV–DR. Second, if $w_j \neq w_h$ for occupations j and h and $c_j^g/C^g = (t_j/T)\ \forall j$, then $\Phi_s(c^g; t; s) \neq 0$, because these measures take into account not only the distribution of individuals across occupations but also salary dispersion across occupations. When a demographic group is distributed according to the occupational structure of the economy, these indexes depart from zero when there is heterogeneity in occupations' wages since they measure segregation with respect to the distribution of salaries, $t_i w_i$. Therefore, these status-sensitive measures do not satisfy the following normalization property, which focuses on segregation alone.

Property 8. *Normalization*: $\Phi_s(c^g; t; s) = 0$ if $c_j^g/C^g = (t_j/T)\ \forall j$.

Consequently, given that the use of status-sensitive measures may lead to counterintuitive results when the employment distribution of a group across occupations is equal to that of total employment, some researchers may consider it reasonable to restrict the set over which our indexes are defined as follows: $\tilde{D} = \cup_{J>1}\{(c^g; t; s) \in \mathbb{R}_+^J \times \mathbb{R}_{++}^J \times \mathbb{R}_{++}^J : c_j^g \leq t_j \forall j \text{ and } (c_j^g/C^g) \neq (t_j/T) \text{ for some } j\}$, so that $\Phi_s : \tilde{D} \subset D \to \mathbb{R}$. Within set $\tilde{D}$, our status-sensitive local segregation measures work more properly. Thus, the status-sensitive segregation of a demographic group increases with its concentration in a few occupations. The lower the status of these occupations as compared with the rest, the larger this increase.

Our segregation measures are intended to complement rather than substitute for local segregation measures previously proposed by the literature. They should be mainly used when one finds that the occupational distribution of a group departs from that of the economy as a whole. Our measures will allow one to assess the extent of the segregation of that group by taking status into consideration. Thus, we can compare the performance of a group with the performances of the remaining groups according to the status of occupations in which each of the groups tends to concentrate. These comparisons allow researchers to identify disparities among groups that standard segregation measures do not reveal.

To compare the status-sensitive segregation of groups that face different distributions of status across occupations – as in the case of comparisons among countries and comparisons across time – one should keep in mind that part of the observed differences can be a consequence of disparities in the occupation's status structure. Thus, a group concentrated in low-paid occupations will tend to have a higher status-sensitive segregation level, other things being equal, as the wage inequality of the economy to which the group belongs increases. Note that to analyze the evolution of a group across time, changes in segregation ($\Phi_s(c^g; t; s) - \Phi_s(c^{g'}; t'; s')$) can be decomposed into three components: one due to changes in the distribution of the target group across occupations (c^g), another due to changes in the occupational structure of the economy (t), and a third factor due to changes in the occupational status (s). These contributions can be obtained through Shapley decomposition (Chantreuil & Trannoy, 2012; Sastre & Trannoy, 2002; Shorrocks, 2012). This technique, widely used in income distribution analyses, implies measuring the change in segregation when only one factor varies (either c^g, t, or s) and then averaging over all possible sequences of the change, which brings path independence to this decomposition.[9]

AN ILLUSTRATION: OCCUPATIONAL SEGREGATION BY RACE AND ETHNICITY IN THE UNITED STATES

To illustrate the usefulness of the above measures, we analyze occupational segregation according to ethnicity/race in the United States by paying special attention to the status of occupations.[10] The uneven distribution of a minority across occupations has important consequences on the group's well-being as long as the group concentrates in occupations with low wages and/or bad labor conditions. It seems therefore interesting to wonder not only which minority groups experience higher segregation levels in the U.S. labor market but also how the wage distribution across occupations affects each of them.

The data used in this section are from the 2007 Public Use Microdata Sample (PUMS) files of the American Community Survey (ACS) conducted by the U.S. Census Bureau. After selecting people who were employed, the sample included 1,399,724 observations. For this survey, people were asked to choose the race or races with which they most closely identify and to answer whether they possess Spanish/Hispanic/Latino origin. Based on this self-reported identity, we produce six mutually exclusive groups of workers comprising the four major single race groups that do not have a Hispanic origin, plus Hispanics of any race, and others: whites; African Americans or blacks; Asians; American Indian, Alaskan, Hawaiian or Pacific Islander natives (here referred to as Native Americans for simplicity); Hispanics; and other races (non-Hispanics who report some other race or more than one race). Occupations are considered at a three-digit level of the Census recode classification, which includes 469 occupations based on the 2000 Standard Occupational Classification (SOC) System. To obtain the status-sensitive measures, we used the average hourly wage of each occupation.[11]

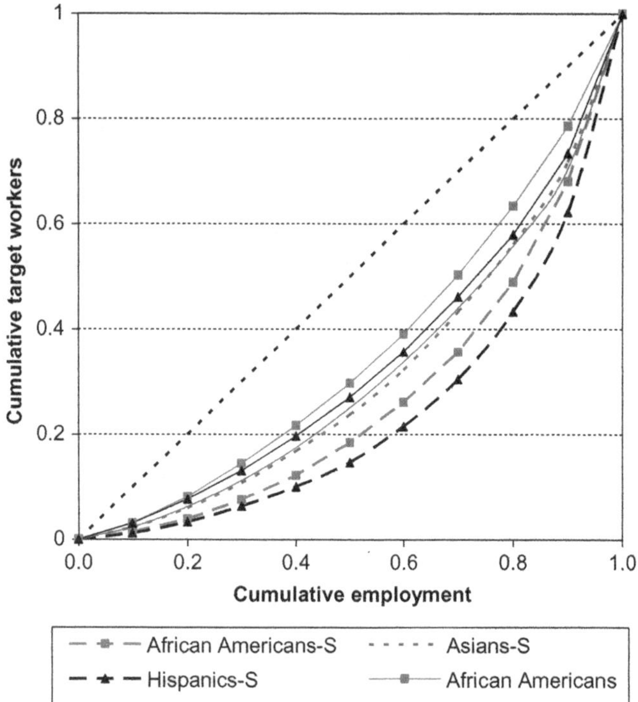

Fig. 2. Segregation Curves and Status-Sensitive Segregation Curves (-S) for the Three Largest Minorities.

Using this survey, Alonso-Villar, Del Río, and Gradín (2012) analyzed the segregation patterns of these six ethnic/racial groups. They showed that Asians and Hispanics are the demographic groups with the highest segregation, while Native and African Americans have an intermediate position between the former and whites and workers of "other races."

In order to assess the segregation of each target group by penalizing its concentration in low-paid occupations, we now use our status-sensitive local segregation measures. The segregation curves and the status-sensitive segregation curves for African Americans, Asians, and Hispanics are shown in Fig. 2, and the corresponding indexes are given in Table 2.

The analysis reveals that the segregation curves for African Americans and Hispanics do substantially change departing from the 45° line when taking wages into account, while the curve for Asians remains almost unaltered. This indicates that as far as the status of occupations is considered, the performance of African Americans and Hispanics worsens with respect to that of Asians. Consequently, without considering the differences between the kinds of occupations in which each demographic group tends to work, one would conclude that Hispanics and Asians are rather similar in terms of segregation, since their curves are rather close. However, despite their sharing a recent immigration profile and a high internal heterogeneity,[12] the performances of both groups clearly depart from each other when taking into account the status of occupations.[13] We find that the relative economic success of advantaged Hispanics does not seem to offset the lower position of the disadvantaged, while the asymmetries between Asians do offset.

Table 2. Local Segregation Indexes and Status-Sensitive Local Segregation Indexes for the Three Largest Minorities.

Local segregation: ethnicity/race	$\Phi^g_{0.1}$	$\Phi^g_{0.5}$	Φ^g_1	Φ^g_2	D^g	G^g
Hispanics	0.185	0.185	0.191	0.231	0.243	0.338
African Americans	0.145	0.139	0.136	0.147	0.209	0.289
Asians	0.264	0.247	0.260	0.371	0.264	0.377
Status-sensitive local segregation: ethnicity/race	$\Phi^g_{s,0.1}$	$\Phi^g_{s,0.5}$	$\Phi^g_{s,1}$	$\Phi^g_{s,2}$	D^g_s	G^g_s
Hispanics	0.490	0.468	0.480	0.670	0.396	0.525
African Americans	0.388	0.363	0.359	0.436	0.345	0.464
Asians	0.268	0.249	0.260	0.398	0.278	0.383

CONCLUSIONS

Segregation analyses mainly focus on measuring the disparities among the occupational distributions of the demographic groups into which total population is partitioned (overall segregation). However, one might be interested not only in this matter but also in exploring the segregation of a target group (local segregation). In this context, the introduction of occupational status into the analysis becomes especially relevant, since the tendency of some demographic groups to concentrate in low pay/status jobs has an important impact on their well-being levels. This paper has tackled this topic in a multigroup context by proposing an axiomatic framework in which one can study the segregation of any population subgroup while taking into account the status of occupations in a cardinal way. This allows one to determine differences among demographic groups in terms of not only employment shares in each occupation but also status. In doing so, this paper has generalized the local segregation curves and indexes proposed by Alonso-Villar and Del Río (2010a).

The usefulness of these measures has been illustrated in our study of occupational segregation in the United States, where we used these tools to analyze disparities in the distributive patterns of workers by race and ethnicity. Even though the segregation levels of Asians and Hispanics are rather similar and higher than the segregation level of African Americans, when taking into account the wages of the occupations in which each major minority group tends to concentrate, the status-sensitive segregation of Hispanics and African Americans turns out to be more severe than that of Asians.

NOTES

1. See classical works by Duncan and Duncan (1955), Karmel and MacLachlan (1988), and Silber (1989). For more recent proposals, see Hutchens (1991, 2004) and Chakravarty and Silber (2007).

2. Recent studies using this approach to analyze the occupational segregation of several demographic groups are Alonso-Villar and Del Río (2010b) and Del Río and Alonso-Villar (2010, 2012).

3. This study focuses on occupational segregation even though it also works for other types of segregation. For simplicity, we use wage as a proxy for status, although a set of relevant dimensions of job status also can be used and then summarized into a one-dimensional variable.

4. This paper also offers a reflection on previous proposals existing in the literature regarding ordinal segregation, which follow alternative approaches, as is

the case of Meng, Hall, and Roberts (2006). Silber and Yalonetzky (2011) and Lazar and Silber (2012) apply Reardon's approach to the measurement of inequality in life chances and health inequality, respectively.

5. We do not require an invariance scale with respect to status because occupational prestige or status can be measured in rather different ways. For some of those ways, this condition may be inappropriate. Thus, status might involve bounded variables. For example, scores are between 0 and 100 in the Australian Socio-economic Index 2006 (see McMillan, Beavis, & Jones, 2009). In our proposal (see Section "Status-sensitive Local Segregation Curves"), the status is measured by the ratio between the wage in each occupation and the average wage of occupations. Therefore, our status-sensitive segregation measures are scale invariant with respect to wages, not with respect to status.

6. Note that considering $s \equiv (w_1/\bar{w}, \ldots, w_J/\bar{w})$ warrants that $\sum_j t_j s_j = \sum_j t_j (w_j/\bar{w}) = \sum t_j = T$.

7. If we had considered local segregation indexes defined on the space of distributions (c^g; t; s) where all components of vector c^g are strictly positive rather than positive, then another index could have been defined: $\Phi^g_{s,\alpha} = \Phi_\alpha(c^g; t; (w/\bar{w})) = \sum_j (t_j(w_j/\bar{w})/T) \ln((t_j(w_j/\bar{w})/T)/(c^g_j/C^g))$ if $\alpha = 0$.

8. The index proposed by Hutchens considers two groups of individuals (women and men, for example) and has the following expression, $O(c^f; c^m; s) = 1 - \sum_j s_j \sqrt{(c^f_j/C^f)(c^m_j/C^m)}$, where f denotes females and m males.

9. Thus, for example, if one is interested in quantifying the effect of a change from c^g to $c^{g'}$, one would have to consider not only the case where t and s remained unaltered but also those where t and/or s have changed.

10. Race/ethnicity disparities in the labor market may emerge from several sources. According to the human capital theory, segregation arises from differences in skills among race/ethnic groups. Language and cultural differences are also likely to be a cause of segregation when minorities are newly arrived. Moreover, the job opportunities of newly arrived immigrants are likely to depend on migrant networks, and the lack of legal status of many of them also strongly determines their employment opportunities. Apart from these factors, the literature has also pointed to discriminatory practices regarding the types of jobs and promotions that minorities are offered.

11. To prevent data contamination from outliers, we compute the trimmed average in each occupation, eliminating all workers whose wage is either zero or is situated below the first or above the 99th percentile of positive values in that occupation.

12. Asians include Southeast Asians and Indians/Chinese. Hispanics include relatively low-educated Puerto Ricans and Mexicans (some of the latter being undocumented) as well as Cubans, who enjoy higher education as well as the sociopolitical support of the United States.

13. Hispanics tend to concentrate in the low-paid occupations to a larger extent than Asians while the latter are markedly bipolarized between some low-paid occupations (such as "miscellaneous personal appearance workers," "tailors, dress-makers, and sewers," and "sewing machine operators") and highly-paid occupations linked to scientific, medical, and computer engineering jobs.

14. Given two income distributions with the same dimension and ranked in ascending order, one is said to majorize the other if and only if both distributions have the same total income, and the cumulative income level of the former, up to next to last individual, is lower than that of the latter.

15. Note that Φ_s also satisfies the property of sensitivity to disequalizing movements between organizational units with different status since a movement of target individuals from occupation i to k involves a sequence of transfers in the fictitious distribution that are more regressive than those corresponding to the movement between occupations i and h (observe that $(c_i^g/C^g)/(t_i(w_i/\bar{w}))< (c_h^g/C^g)/(t_h(w_h/\bar{w}))<(c_k^g/C^g)/(t_k(w_k/\bar{w}))$.

ACKNOWLEDGMENTS

We gratefully acknowledge the financial support from the *Ministerio de Ciencia e Innovación* (ECO2010-21668-C03-03 and ECO2011-23460), *Xunta de Galicia* (10SEC300023PR), and from FEDER. We also want to thank a referee for helpful comments.

REFERENCES

Albelda, R. (1986). Occupational segregation by race and gender, 1958–1981. *Industrial and Labor Relations Review*, *39*(3), 404–411.

Alonso-Villar, O., & Del Río, C. (2010a). Local versus overall segregation measures. *Mathematical Social Sciences*, *60*(1), 30–38.

Alonso-Villar, O., & Del Río, C. (2010b). Segregation of female and male workers in Spain: Occupations and industries. *Hacienda Pública Española/Revista de Economía Pública*, *194*(3), 91–121.

Alonso-Villar, O., Del Río, C., & Gradín, C. (2012). The extent of occupational segregation in the US: Differences by race, ethnicity, and gender. *Industrial Relations*, *51*(2), 179–212.

Atkinson, A. B., & Bourguignon, F. (1982). The comparison of multi-dimensioned distributions of economic status. *Review of Economic Studies*, *12*, 183–201.

Boisso, D., Hayes, K., Hirschberg, J., & Silber, J. (1994). Occupational segregation in the multidimensional case. Decomposition and tests of significance. *Journal of Econometrics*, *61*, 161–171.

Chakravarty, S. R., & Silber, J. (2007). A generalized index of employment segregation. *Mathematical Social Sciences*, *53*, 185–195.

Chantreuil, F., & Trannoy, A. (2012). *Inequality decomposition values: The trade-off between marginality and consistency. Journal of Economic Inequality*, forthcoming, doi:10.1007/s10888-011-9207-y

Cutler, D. M., Glaeser, E. L., & Vigdor, J. L. (2008). Is the melting pot still hot? Explaining the resurgence of immigrant segregation. *The Review of Economics and Statistics*, *90*(3), 478–497.

Del Río, C., & Alonso-Villar, O. (2010). Gender segregation in the Spanish labor market: An alternative approach. *Social Indicators Research*, *98*(2), 337–362.

Del Río, C., & Alonso-Villar, O. (2012). Occupational segregation of immigrant women in Spain. *Feminist Economics*, *18*(2), forthcoming, doi:10.1080/13545701.2012.701014

Duncan, O. D., & Duncan, B. (1955). A methodological analysis of segregation indexes. *American Sociological Review*, *20*(2), 210–217.

Fleurbaey, M., & Trannoy, A. (2003). The impossibility of a Paretian egalitarian. *Social Choice and Welfare*, *21*, 243–263.

Foster, J. E. (1985). Inequality measurement. In H. P. Young (Ed.), *Fair allocation*. Proceedings of Simposia in Applied Mathematics, American Mathematical Society, Providence (Vol. 33, pp. 31–68).

Frankel, D. M., & Volij, O. (2011). Measuring school segregation. *Journal of Economic Theory*, *146*(1), 1–38.

Hellerstein, J. K., & Neumark, D. (2008). Workplace segregation in the United States: Race, ethnicity, and skill. *The Review of Economics and Statistics*, *90*(3), 459–477.

Hutchens, R. M. (1991). Segregation curves, Lorenz curves, and inequality in the distribution of people across occupations. *Mathematical Social Sciences*, *21*, 31–51.

Hutchens, R. M. (2004). One measure of segregation. *International Economic Review*, *45*(2), 555–578.

Hutchens, R. M. (2006). *Measuring segregation when hierarchy matters*. Mimeo: ILR School, Cornell University.

Hutchens, R. M. (2009a). Occupational segregation with economic disadvantage: An investigation of decomposable indexes. *Research on Economic Inequality*, *17*, 99–120.

Hutchens, R. M. (2009b). A response to Paul Jargowsky's comment. *Research on Economic Inequality*, *17*, 125–128.

Iceland, J. (2004). Beyond black and white. Metropolitan residential segregation in multi-ethnic America. *Social Science Research*, *33*, 248–271.

Jargowsky, P. A. (2009). Comment on robert hutchens, occupational segregation with economic disadvantage: An investigation of decomposable indices. *Research on Economic Inequality*, *17*, 121–124.

Karmel, T., & MacLachlan, M. (1988). Occupational sex segregation—increasing or decreasing? *The Economic Record*, *64*, 187–195.

King, M. C. (1992). Occupational segregation by race and sex, 1940–88. *Monthly Labor Review*, *115*, 30–37.

Kolm, S. (1977). Multidimensional equalitarianisms. *Quarterly Journal of Economics*, *91*, 1–13.

Lazar, A., & Silber, J. (2012). On the cardinal measurement of health inequality when only ordinal information is available on individual health status. *Health Economics*, forthcoming, doi:10.1002/hec.1821

McMillan, J., Beavis, A., & Jones, F. L. (2009). The AUSEI06: A new socioeconomic index for Australia. *Journal of Sociology*, *45*(2), 123–149.

Meng, G., Hall, G. B., & Roberts, S. (2006). Multi-group segregation indices for measuring ordinal classes. *Computers, Environment and Urban Systems*, *30*, 275–299.

Reardon, S. F. (2009). Measures of ordinal segregation. *Research on Economic Inequality*, *17*, 129–155.

Reardon, S. F., & Firebaugh, G. (2002). Measures of multigroup segregation. *Sociological Methodology*, *32*, 33–76.

Reardon, S. F., & Yun, J. T. (2001). Suburban racial change and suburban school segregation, 1987–95. *Sociology of Education*, *74*(2), 79–101.

Sastre, M., & Trannoy, A. (2002). Shapley inequality decomposition by factor components: Some methodological issues. *Journal of Economics*, *9*, 51–89.

Shorrocks, A. (2012). Decomposition procedures for distributional analysis: A unified framework based on the shapley value. *Journal of Economic Inequality*, forthcoming, doi:10.1007/s10888-011-9214-z

Silber, J. (1989). On the measurement of employment segregation. *Economics Letters*, *30*, 237–243.

Silber, J. (1992). Occupational segregation indices in the multidimensional case: A note. *The Economic Record*, *68*, 276–277.

Silber, J., & Yalonetzky, G. (2011). Measuring inequality in life chances with ordinal variables. *Research on Economic Inequality*, *19*, 77–98.

Tsui, K.-Y. (1999). Multidimensional inequality and multidimensional generalized entropy measures: An axiomatic derivation. *Social Choice and Welfare*, *16*, 145–157.

APPENDIX A: PROOF OF PROPOSITION 1

First Implication

Assume that Φ_s satisfies Properties 1–4 and consider distributions $(c^g; t; w/\bar{w})$, $(c^{g'}; t'; w/\bar{w}') \in D$, where $\bar{w} = \Sigma_j (t_j/T) w_j$ and $\bar{w}' = \Sigma_j (t'_j/T') w_j$. In what follows, we first transform vector $(c^g; t; w/\bar{w})$ into a fictitious "income" distribution whose Lorenz curve is equal to the segregation curve corresponding to $(c^g; t; w/\bar{w})$, which allows us to use some well-known results from the literature on income distribution. Next, by following steps analogous to those followed by Foster (1985) in a context of income distribution, we multiply distributions $(c^g; t; w/\bar{w})$ and $(c^{g'}; t'; w/\bar{w}')$ by positive scalars in such a way that their corresponding fictitious distributions share the same dimension and mean, while keeping segregation unaltered.

It is easy to verify that the local segregation curve corresponding to $(c^g; t; w/\bar{w})$ is equal to the Lorenz curve corresponding to fictitious distribution

$$\left(\underbrace{\frac{c_1^g}{t_1 \frac{w_1}{\bar{w}}}, \ldots, \frac{c_1^g}{t_1 \frac{w_1}{\bar{w}}}}_{t_1 \frac{w_1}{\bar{w}}}, \ldots, \underbrace{\frac{c_J^g}{t_J \frac{w_J}{\bar{w}}}, \ldots, \frac{c_J^g}{t_J \frac{w_J}{\bar{w}}}}_{t_J \frac{w_J}{\bar{w}}} \right).$$

The same relationship can be established between $(Tc^{g'}; Tt'; w/\bar{w}')$ and

$$y \equiv \left(\underbrace{\frac{Tc_1^{g'}}{Tt'_1 \frac{w_1}{\bar{w}'}}, \ldots, \frac{Tc_1^{g'}}{Tt'_1 \frac{w_1}{\bar{w}'}}}_{Tt'_1 \frac{w_1}{\bar{w}'}}, \ldots, \underbrace{\frac{Tc_J^{g'}}{Tt'_J \frac{w_J}{\bar{w}'}}, \ldots, \frac{Tc_J^{g'}}{Tt'_J \frac{w_J}{\bar{w}'}}}_{Tt'_J \frac{w_J}{\bar{w}'}} \right),$$

and between $(T'((C^{g'}/T')/(C^g/T))c^g;\ T't; w/\bar{w})$ and

$$z \equiv \left(\underbrace{T\frac{C^{g'}}{C^g} \frac{c_1^g}{T't_1 \frac{w_1}{\bar{w}}}, \ldots, T\frac{C^{g'}}{C^g} \frac{c_1^g}{T't_1 \frac{w_1}{\bar{w}}}}_{T't_1 \frac{w_1}{\bar{w}}}, \ldots, \underbrace{T\frac{C^{g'}}{C^g} \frac{c_J^g}{T't_J \frac{w_J}{\bar{w}}}, \ldots, T\frac{C^{g'}}{C^g} \frac{c_J^g}{T't_J \frac{w_J}{\bar{w}}}}_{T't_J \frac{w_J}{\bar{w}}} \right).$$

Note that y and z have the same number of "individuals" (TT') and "income" mean ($C^{g'}/T'$). Without loss of generality in what follows, we assume that $C^g/T > C^{g'}/T'$.

By using Lemma 2 proposed in Foster (1985), the Lorenz curves of the fictitious distributions corresponding to $(c^g; t; w/\bar{w})$ and $(T'((C^{g'}/T')/(C^g/T))c^g; T't; w/\bar{w})$ coincide, since the latter is a (T' times) replication of the former multiplied by a positive scalar $((C^{g'}/C^g)(T/T'))$. The same applies to distributions $(c^{g'}; t'; w/\bar{w}')$ and $(Tc^{g'}; Tt'; w/\bar{w}')$. Consequently, the local segregation curves of $(c^g; t; w/\bar{w})$ and $(T''((C^{g'}/T')/(C^g/T))c^g; T't; w/\bar{w})$ coincide, and also the ones corresponding to $(c^{g'}; t'; w/\bar{w}')$ and $(Tc^{g'}; Tt'; w/\bar{w}')$ do.

Assuming that the local segregation curve of $(c^g; t; w/\bar{w})$ dominates that of $(c^{g'}; t'; w/\bar{w}')$ (i.e., the local segregation curve of the former is at no point below that of the latter), two cases can be distinguished:

(a) The local segregation curve of $(c^g; t; w/\bar{w})$ coincides with that of $(c^{g'}; t'; w/\bar{w}')$. Consequently, the local segregation curve of $(T'((C^{g'}/T')/(C^g/T))c^g; T't; w/\bar{w})$ coincides with that of $(Tc^{g'}; Tt'; w/\bar{w}')$. By using Lemma 1 proposed in Foster (1985), it follows that the ordered distribution (from low to high values) corresponding to y, labeled $\hat{y}$, majorizes that of z, labeled $\hat{z}$, and vice versa.[14] In other words, distributions $\hat{y}$ and $\hat{z}$ are identical, which implies that $\Phi_s(z; e; s) = \Phi_s(y; e'; s')$, where

$$e \equiv \Bigg(\underbrace{\frac{\bar{w}}{w_1}, \ldots, \frac{\bar{w}}{w_1}}_{Tt_1\frac{w_1}{\bar{w}}}, \ldots, \underbrace{\frac{\bar{w}}{w_J}, \ldots, \frac{\bar{w}}{w_J}}_{Tt_J\frac{w_J}{\bar{w}}}\Bigg) \quad \text{and} \quad s \equiv \Bigg(\underbrace{\frac{w_1}{\bar{w}}, \ldots, \frac{w_1}{\bar{w}}}_{Tt_1\frac{w_1}{\bar{w}}}, \ldots, \underbrace{\frac{w_J}{\bar{w}}, \ldots, \frac{w_J}{\bar{w}}}_{Tt_J\frac{w_J}{\bar{w}}}\Bigg).$$

Note that, on one hand, Φ_s satisfies the properties of symmetry, insensitivity to proportional subdivisions, and scale invariance, which implies that $\Phi_s(y; e'; s') = \Phi_s(Tc^{g'}; Tt'; w/\bar{w}')$ and $\Phi_s(z; e; s) = \Phi_s(T'((C^{g'}/T')/(C^g/T))c^g; T't; w/\bar{w})$. On the other hand, by using the scale invariance property, $\Phi_s(Tc^{g'}; Tt'; (w/\bar{w}')) = \Phi_s(c^{g'}; t'; w/\bar{w}')$ and $\Phi_s(T'((C^{g'}/T')/(C^g/T))c^g; T't; w/\bar{w}) = \Phi_s(c^g; t; w/\bar{w})$ (since $C^g/T > C^{g'}/T'$). Consequently, $\Phi_s(c^g; t; w/\bar{w}) = \Phi_s(c^{g'}; t'; w/\bar{w}')$.

(b) The local segregation curve of $(c^g; t; w/\bar{w})$ is at no point below that of $(c^{g'}; t'; w/\bar{w}')$ and at some above. By following analogous steps to those in case (a), it follows that the local segregation curve of distribution $(T'((C^{g'}/T')/(C^g/T))c^g; T't; w/\bar{w})$ also dominates that of $(Tc^{g'}; Tt'; w/\bar{w}')$, which implies, by Lemma 3 in Foster (1985), that $\hat{y}$ is obtained from $\hat{z}$ by a finite sequence of regressive transfers. Therefore, since Φ_s

satisfies the property of symmetry and that of movement between locations, $\Phi_s(y;e';s') > \Phi_s(z;e;s)$. In addition, the properties of insensitivity to proportional subdivisions of locations and scale invariance mean that $\Phi_s(y;e';s') = \Phi_s(Tc^{g'};Tt';w/\bar{w}') = \Phi_s(c^{g'};t';w/\bar{w}')$ and $\Phi_s(z;e;s) = \Phi_s\left(T'((C^{g'}/T')/(C^g/T))c^g;T't;w/\bar{w}\right) = \Phi_s(c^g;t;w/\bar{w})$. Therefore, $\Phi_s(c^{g'};t';w/\bar{w}') > \Phi_s(c^g;t;w/\bar{w})$.

Second Implication

Assume now that Φ_s is consistent with the local segregation criterion. As mentioned above, the local segregation curve corresponding to distribution $(c^g;t;w/\bar{w})$ coincides with the Lorenz curve of the corresponding fictitious distribution

$$\left(\underbrace{\frac{c_1^g}{t_1\frac{w_1}{\bar{w}}},\ldots,\frac{c_1^g}{t_1\frac{w_1}{\bar{w}}}}_{t_1\frac{w_1}{\bar{w}}},\ldots,\underbrace{\frac{c_J^g}{t_J\frac{w_J}{\bar{w}}},\ldots,\frac{c_J^g}{t_J\frac{w_J}{\bar{w}}}}_{t_J\frac{w_J}{\bar{w}}}\right).$$

Therefore, when comparing two occupational distributions, there is consistency between the conclusions reached by using the local segregation curves and those attained with the Lorenz curves of the fictitious distributions. In what follows, we show that index Φ_s satisfies the four basic properties.

(a) Φ_s satisfies scale invariance, since the Lorenz curve of the fictitious distribution

$$\left(\underbrace{\frac{\alpha c_1^g}{\beta t_1\frac{w_1}{\bar{w}}},\ldots,\frac{\alpha c_1^g}{\beta t_1\frac{w_1}{\bar{w}}}}_{\beta t_1\frac{w_1}{\bar{w}}},\ldots,\underbrace{\frac{\alpha c_J^g}{\beta t_J\frac{w_J}{\bar{w}}},\ldots,\frac{\alpha c_J^g}{\beta t_J\frac{w_J}{\bar{w}}}}_{\beta t_J\frac{w_J}{\bar{w}}}\right)$$

coincides with that of

$$\left(\underbrace{\frac{c_1^g}{t_1\frac{w_1}{\bar{w}}},\ldots,\frac{c_1^g}{t_1\frac{w_1}{\bar{w}}}}_{t_1\frac{w_1}{\bar{w}}},\ldots,\underbrace{\frac{c_J^g}{t_J\frac{w_J}{\bar{w}}},\ldots,\frac{c_J^g}{t_J\frac{w_J}{\bar{w}}}}_{t_J\frac{w_J}{\bar{w}}}\right).$$

(b) Φ_s satisfies symmetry, since "individuals" of the fictitious distribution play symmetric roles in the Lorenz curves.

(c) Φ_s satisfies insensitivity to proportional subdivisions because when an occupation j is subdivided into two occupations (j' and j'') such that $c_{j'}^g = c_{j''}^g = c_j^g/2$ and $t_{j'} = t_{j''} = t_j/2$, the Lorenz curve of the fictitious distribution does not change.

(d) Φ_s satisfies the property of sensitivity to disequalizing movements between organizational units, since any movement from occupation i to h of the types mentioned in Property 4 leads to a sequence of regressive transfers in the fictitious distribution, which results in an increase in inequality according to the Lorenz criterion. As a consequence, the local segregation index Φ_s also increases.[15]

CHAPTER 3

OCCUPATIONAL SEGREGATION OF AFRO-LATINOS

Carlos Gradín

ABSTRACT

The goal of this study was to use census information to measure the level of occupational segregation of workers of African descent with respect to whites in various Latin American countries. I further investigated the extent to which segregation levels can be accounted for by different workers' characteristics. The results show that Afro-Latinos are generally highly segregated across occupations but with high heterogeneity across countries. A large proportion of this segregation would not exist if Afro-Latinos had attained the same education as whites in Brazil and Ecuador, where most segregation occurs across major occupational categories. However, the proportion of occupational segregation explained by educational inequalities is much lower in other countries, where most segregation occurs within the major occupational groups. Further, occupational segregation would be even higher, especially in Costa Rica, if the geographical distribution of black and white populations were similar across these countries.

Keywords: occupational segregation; conditional segregation; education; race and ethnicity; Afro-Latinos

JEL Classification: D63; J15; J16; J71; J82

Inequality, Mobility and Segregation: Essays in Honor of Jacques Silber
Research on Economic Inequality, Volume 20, 63–90

ISSN: 1049-2585/doi:10.1108/S1049-2585(2012)0000020006

INTRODUCTION

Latin America is a region with a remarkably diverse population made up of people with indigenous, European, African, and Asian origins. In particular, the development of sugar and coffee plantations during the European colonization brought several million slaves captured in sub-Saharan countries to Latin America. Later, several internal migrations of people of African descent within or between countries in response to new economic activities helped to shape the current demography of this group. The most salient case is Brazil where, according to the 2010 Census, 51 percent of its 191 million people reported that they were either black or of mixed race, officially outnumbering whites for the first time in many years and comprising the largest black population outside of Africa. Communities of African ancestry are also important in many other countries, especially in the Caribbean region, although their reports about their numbers are often controversial due to the lack of reliable sources.[1]

Slavery was officially abolished in these countries during the 19th century, with Cuba and Brazil being the last to ban the practice in the 1880s, and there was no segregation of the type imposed in the U.S. South.[2] However, a legacy of racial inequality across several dimensions lingers today all over the region. Racial inequalities have extended to people's living conditions, especially with regard to higher poverty and deprivation rates, unequal access to quality education, lack of political representation, and generally worse labor market outcomes. According to a recent report by the Inter-American Commission on Human Rights: "[...] the Afro-descendant population – either constituting the minority or majority percentage of the population – is affected by structural discrimination in all aspects and levels, which deprives them from enjoying and exercising their human rights" (IACHR, 2011, p. 23).[3] One of the most important racial inequalities is related to the way blacks and whites enter the labor market, which constrains the opportunities available to Afro-Latinos to earn a living and fulfill their personal aspirations. According to the previous report, "the statistics indicate that the Afro-descendant population occupies the lowest positions in the job hierarchy and mostly perform informal-sector and low-grade tasks or work that is poorly remunerated – even when comparing wages of non-Afro-descendants who perform the same tasks – they lack the social security benefits, and the rate of unemployment of this community is greater than for the population as a whole" (IACHR, 2011, p. 18). Indeed, as can be derived from our analysis below, in several countries with a significant black population, there is a tendency for blacks to be overrepresented in some occupations, typically those that are more informal, provide lower pay, and demand lower-skills, which directly affects the social inclusion of nonwhites and may undermine social cohesion in these countries.[4]

Despite its relevance, segregation of Afro-descendants by occupations has not been extensively analyzed in Latin America. An important exception was an analysis by King (2009), who recently documented the segregation of Afro-Brazilians in the period from 1976 to 2001.[5] Using the dissimilarity index, she found evidence that segregation was decreasing for women but not for men. She also highlighted the relevance of education because segregation was lower for black workers with an educational level similar to that of whites, and that segregation increased with years of schooling. To our best knowledge, even less attention has been paid to the segregation of people of African descent in other Latin American countries.[6]

Segregation by occupation based on race can be explained in various ways. It could be the consequence of discrimination in the labor market induced by racial prejudices held by employers, customers, or coworkers. It could also reflect the existence of inequality in human capital accumulation across races, providing access to a different set of available jobs depending on workers' skills. As a matter of fact, a high level of segregation among blacks may be partly due to premarket inequalities, such as blacks dropping out of school earlier than whites or the fact that they are generally younger or migrants and thus have less experience in the local market. When segregation is measured at the national level, it may also be possible that it is the consequence of blacks and whites living in different areas of the country with different levels of economic development or regional specialization, so their occupational structures differ.

As a matter of fact, in the case of the United States, Alonso-Villar, del Río, and Gradín (2012) and Gradín (2010), using different methodologies, showed that a large share of the segregation of Hispanic and Asian workers can be attributed to differences in initial endowments, mainly the result of recent immigration to the United States and the lack of English proficiency. However, in the case of blacks, the proportion that is explained by these characteristics is smaller, between 9 and 17 percent, depending on the index used (Gradín, 2010). Blacks' lower level of education is responsible for between 14 and 30 percent of observed segregation, but the geographical distribution of blacks counteracts that effect.

The aim of this chapter is to document the extent of segregation among Afro-descendants and whites by occupations in some Latin American countries and then to measure how much of this segregation is explained by factors such as workers' education, location, migration status, and age in order to better understand where and how segregation is actually produced. The level of segregation across occupations that cannot be explained by workers' characteristics is *conditional segregation*, which is a measurement of the segregation of blacks and whites that would prevail if they had the same characteristics, a more genuine measure of occupational dissimilarity. In order to separate explained and unexplained or conditional segregation and to attribute each factor's contribution to explaining segregation, I constructed counterfactual occupational distributions in which blacks are given the characteristics of whites using a reweighting technique developed by Gradín (2010), who extended DiNardo, Fortin, and Lemieux's (1996) approach originally proposed to the analysis of wage differentials.

The structure of the chapter is as follows. The next section describes the available data, and the following one describes the methodology used. The last two sections provide the results and the main conclusions.

DATA

The empirical analysis was based on microdata samples extracted from censuses conducted in 2000 in Brazil, Puerto Rico, and Costa Rica, in 2001 in Ecuador, and in 2002 in Cuba. The figures were obtained from the *Integrated Public Use Microdata Series International* (IPUMS-I) available at the Minnesota Population Center at the University of Minnesota.[7] This institution collected and harmonized censuses from all over the world. I have chosen those in the Latin American region with the relevant information available around 2000.[8] The use of census data guarantees larger samples from which to analyze segregation across a more detailed classification of occupations of groups that are not large enough in some countries, thus overcoming the problem of small units bias.

All these datasets provide the required information related to workers' characteristics. There are some comparability issues, however. The definition of race (or skin color) is self-reported in all countries, thus reflecting self-identification, except in Cuba where it is reported by the census enumerator except in specific cases in which the target person was absent and the color could not be inferred. Whites in Costa Rica are defined by exclusion as those not claiming to be members of any other ethnic group (Indigenous, Afro-Costa Rican, or Asian-Chinese), which could cause an overestimation of people included in this group. Blacks and people who are of mixed black and white races are all considered part of one group called Afro-Latinos due to the well-known potential endogeneity problems of self-identification. That is, those who are black and brown (*preto*) in Brazil or black and mulatto in Ecuador or Cuba are all regarded as Afro-Latino.[9,10] As a result, the proportion of Afro-Latino workers ranges from only around 2 percent of both sexes in Costa Rica to 45 (41) percent of men (women) in Brazil (see Table A.1).

Regarding occupations, I used two different classifications. The most aggregated one has nine major categories, following the International Standard Classification of Occupations (ISCO) at one digit, after excluding the armed forces and unknown or other occupations that are too small or nonexistent in some countries. This classification scheme has the advantage of being standardized, so it is comparable across all datasets, but if the occupations' boundaries are too wide, a big share of segregation remains hidden. For that reason, I also used the most disaggregated classification of occupations in each dataset, the equivalent at three digits, allowing a more accurate measure of the level of segregation, but this made a direct comparison across countries harder because segregation indices are very sensitive to the classification used, and this one is country specific. In this case, the number of categories goes from 103 in Costa Rica to 509 in Brazil. The other workers' characteristics are generally comparable. Education was measured as years of schooling and literacy (Brazil, Costa Rica, and Ecuador). If the information was not available, I used the level of education attained (Cuba and Puerto Rico). Age and age squared were also included in order to measure potential experience. Several variables available in each dataset account for migration status, including internal migration, time of residence, or citizenship.[11] Geographical location is measured at the state level (Brazil) or provincial level (Costa Rica, Cuba, and Ecuador), and it also takes into account whether the area of residence was rural or urban (Brazil, Costa Rica, and Ecuador). In the case of Puerto Rico, the metropolitan areas were used instead, with a category for nonmetropolitan areas.

The analysis of segregation is based on the sample of workers, but it should be noted that employment rates (as well as activity or unemployment rates) of Afro-Latinos differ by country. The proportion of workers ranges from 52 percent of men at least 16 years old in Puerto Rico to 76 percent in Ecuador, and from 31 percent of women in the same age range in Ecuador to around 38 percent in Cuba and Brazil. Employment rates are larger among Afro-Latino men than among whites in Ecuador and Puerto Rico, lower in Costa Rica and Brazil, and similar in Cuba. In the case of women, the racial differentials are larger, showing higher rates for Afro-Latinas, compared with those of whites, in Puerto Rico, Cuba and Costa Rica and lower rates in Ecuador and Brazil (see Table A.2 for details).

METHODOLOGY

Measuring Unconditional Segregation

I adopted here the standard convention of approaching the racial segregation by occupations of blacks compared with the reference group, whites, in each country.[12] Several indices can be found in the literature to account for segregation levels, with the dissimilarity index (Duncan & Duncan, 1955) being, by far, the most popular in empirical analysis despite its well-known limitations. Other indices have been proposed verifying better properties, most of them borrowed from measurements of income inequality. Examples of these are the Gini index or the Generalized Entropy family of indices, which embrace the Theil index or the Hutchens square root as particular cases (Duncan & Duncan, 1955; Hutchens, 1991, 2004; Jahn, Schmid, & Schrag, 1947). For the sake of robustness but wanting to keep things simple, in this empirical analysis I report the Hutchens and dissimilarity indices.[13]

Let us consider a population of N workers divided into two groups: N^0, Afro-Latinos, and N^1, whites. We are interested in measuring the segregation of this population across T occupations in the economy. Let us denote by $n^i = (n_1^i, \ldots, n_T^i)$ the distribution for one group across occupations so that $N^i = \sum_{j=1}^{T} n_j^i,\ i = \{0, 1\}$. Then, based on the proportions of whites and blacks in each occupation, we define the following two segregation indices:

$$D(n^0, n^1) = \frac{1}{2}\sum_{j=1}^{T}\left|\frac{n_j^1}{N^1} - \frac{n_j^0}{N^0}\right|; \quad H(n^0, n^1) = 1 - \sum_{j=1}^{T}\sqrt{\frac{n_j^0}{N^0}\frac{n_j^1}{N^1}} \qquad (1)$$

D is the dissimilarity index proposed by Duncan and Duncan (1955). H is the Hutchens square root index, which has appealing properties that were well-described in Hutchens (1991, 2004). Note that D and H are bounded between 0, when there is no segregation because whites and Afro-Latinos have the same distribution across occupations, and 1, when segregation is at its maximum because there is no overlap between the two distributions (whites and Afro-Latinos work in different occupations).

Measuring Conditional Segregation

In this section, we follow the methodology outlined by Gradín (2010), who adapted the reweighting approach provided by DiNardo et al. (1996) for measuring occupational segregation. This propensity score technique was initially used in the context of decomposing the wage differential between two given populations across the entire distribution. In presenting the procedure, we first need to reformulate the notation. Each individual observation belongs to a joint distribution $F(e, z, W)$ of occupations $e \in \{1, 2, \ldots, T\}$, (continuous or discrete) individual characteristics $z = (z_1, z_2, \ldots, z_k, \ldots, z_K)$ defined over the domain Ω_z, and a dummy W indicating group membership. The joint distribution of occupations and attributes of each group is the conditional distribution $F(e, z|W)$. The discrete density function of occupations for each group, $f^i(e)$, can be expressed as the product of two conditional distributions:

$$f^i(e) \equiv f(e|W = i) = \int_z dF(e, z|W = i)\, dz = \int_z f(e|z, W = i) \cdot f(z|W = i)\, dz \tag{2}$$

where $i = 0$ for Afro-Latinos and 1 for whites.

Then, under the general assumption that the structure of occupations of Afro-Latinos, represented by the conditional density $F(e|z, W = 0)$, does not depend on the distribution of attributes, we can define the hypothetical counterfactual distribution $f_z(e)$:

$$\begin{aligned} f_z(e) = \int_z f(e|z, W = 0) \cdot f(z|W = 1)\, dz = \int_z f(e|z, W = 0) \cdot \psi_z \\ \cdot f(z|W = 0)\, dz = \int_z \psi_z f(e, z|W = 0)\, dz \end{aligned} \tag{3}$$

as the density that would prevail if the population of Afro-Latinos kept its own conditional probability of being in a given occupation, $f(e|z, W = 0)$, but had the same characteristics of whites given by their marginal distribution $f(z|W = 1)$. Expression (3) shows that this counterfactual distribution can be produced by properly reweighting the original distribution of the target group. The reweighting scheme ψ_z can be obtained, after using Bayes' theorem, as the product of two probability ratios:

$$\psi_z = \frac{f(z|W = 1)}{f(z|W = 0)} = \frac{\Pr(W = 0)}{\Pr(W = 1)} \frac{\Pr(W = 1|z)}{\Pr(W = 0|z)} \tag{4}$$

The first ratio is given by the unconditional probabilities of group membership and is a constant. The second ratio is given by conditional probabilities and can be obtained by pooling the samples for whites and

Afro-Latinos and estimating a logit (or probit) model for the probability of being white conditional on z. I estimated the following logit model:

$$\Pr(W = 1|z) = \frac{\exp(z\hat{\beta})}{1 + \exp(z\hat{\beta})} \tag{5}$$

where $\hat{\beta}$ is the associated vector of estimated coefficients. Alternatively, one could think in terms of using a nonparametric approach, estimating the weights based on the empirical distribution of characteristics in both groups, that is, by computing the proportion of both populations in each cell that result from crossing all discrete characteristics (e.g., the proportion of native-born whites and Afro-Latinos with a university degree). However, this approach could be difficult to implement when a large number of covariates are involved (many cells will be zero or will have a small number of observations), or when some factors are approached by continuous covariates. The approach used in this study overcomes these problems and makes it easy to identify the individual contribution of each factor.

For any given segregation index S, we can measure unconditional segregation defined over the distributions of occupations for whites and blacks, $S(e) \equiv S(f(e|W=1), f(e|W=0))$, and define segregation conditional on z to be the same index computed after replacing the density of Afro-Latinos by the counterfactual: $S(e|z) \equiv S(f(e|W=1), f_z(e))$. This is the amount of (unexplained) segregation that remains after controlling for characteristics. The change in segregation after conditioning on characteristics $S(e|z)-S(e)$ provides a measure of segregation that is actually explained by our covariates z. This is in line with how wage differentials are usually decomposed into their characteristics (explained) and coefficients (unexplained) effects.

Furthermore, the change in segregation after conditioning on characteristics (explained part) can be additionally disaggregated into the detailed contribution of each covariate (or subset of covariates) z_k in order to identify which factors are more explicative (explaining a larger reduction in segregation after conditioning). With $s(z_k)$ being the relative contribution of covariate k,

$$S(e|z) - S(e) = \sum_k s(z_k)[S(e|z) - S(e)] \tag{6}$$

In order to obtain this detailed decomposition, we could compute a new counterfactual distribution $f_{z_k}(e)$ in which the corresponding reweighting factor ψ_{z_k} is obtained, setting all of the other logit coefficients but this one to zero (Lemieux, 2002). The problem with this approach is that it assumes that each factor is the only one that changes and the sum of the contributions do not total one. Alternatively, we can shift all of the coefficients following a specific sequence (i.e., first location, then immigration, schooling, etc.), computing the contribution of each factor as the result of changing its associated coefficients. This recalls the well-known path-dependency problem in inequality decomposition because the contribution of a factor to the overall change in segregation will depend on the order in which we consider them. This difficulty was overcome in the empirical analysis by computing the Shapley decomposition that results from averaging over all possible sequences (Chantreuil & Trannoy, 2011; Shorrocks, 2012). Thus, the contribution of a given factor (i.e., education) will be the average of the contribution of education for all possible paths when education coefficients are changed in the first case, in the second, and so on.[14] In this way, the contribution of each factor is path independent, and the contributions of all factors add up to one.

OCCUPATIONAL SEGREGATION OF AFRO-LATINOS IN SELECTED COUNTRIES

It is a matter of fact that Afro-Latinos generally work in different occupations than whites in their countries. Given that men and women also work in different occupations (and have different employment rates), the analysis was done separately for each sex in order to allow identifying different racial patterns by sex. Table 1 shows the distribution of male and female workers in each country by race across major ISCO occupational categories.

Indeed, Afro-Latino male workers are more likely than whites to work in elementary occupations and in jobs that demand fewer skills, like trade workers (in all countries except Costa Rica) and farmers/fishermen (in Ecuador and Brazil). On the other hand, they are less likely to be found working as managers, professionals, and plant operators in all countries or as technicians and clerks in Ecuador, Brazil, and Puerto Rico. The largest black–white gaps in the proportion of male workers, however, vary across countries. The proportion of blacks working in elementary occupations is 11 percentage points larger than whites in Ecuador, 5 in Costa Rica, but about 2 in the rest of the target countries. The black–white differential in the proportion of farmers/fishermen is 10 percentage points in Brazil and 7 in Ecuador, while it is negative in the other countries. Similarly, the proportion

Table 1. Distribution of Afro-Latino and White Workers by Country, Sex, and Major Occupational Categories.

	Costa Rica		Cuba		Ecuador		Puerto Rico		Brazil	
	Afro-Latinos	White	Afro-Latinos	White	Afro-Latinos	White	Afro-Latinos	White	Afro-Latinos	White
Men										
Legislators, senior officials and managers	1.9	3.0	9.9	11.9	1.1	5.5	7.2	10.9	2.3	6.9
Professionals	5.3	6.1	5.3	6.5	2.2	8.6	7.7	10.5	2.3	6.4
Technicians and associate professionals	14.7	12.9	8.2	8.0	1.4	3.8	5.3	6.5	4.7	8.0
Clerks	6.1	4.9	1.7	2.0	3.4	5.6	11.7	13.6	4.3	6.4
Service workers and shop and market sales	12.5	11.8	11.7	11.7	13.3	17.9	13.6	12.0	14.4	14.7
Skilled agricultural and fishery workers	4.8	7.7	18.7	20.4	16.8	9.4	2.0	2.6	28.3	18.1
Crafts and related trades workers	11.4	15.0	20.9	15.6	24.5	20.7	30.8	23.8	26.0	21.9
Plant and machine operators and assemblers	11.4	12.3	10.0	12.4	7.6	9.7	8.1	8.8	9.6	11.4
Elementary occupations	32.0	26.4	13.6	11.5	29.7	18.8	13.8	11.5	8.1	6.1
Total	100	100	100	100	100	100	100	100	100	100
Women										
Legislators, senior officials and managers	2.6	2.4	7.1	8.6	2.1	5.7	5.4	7.3	1.6	4.9
Professionals	21.3	15.6	14.4	17.1	6.2	12.1	14.0	17.6	3.9	10.6
Technicians and associate professionals	11.0	12.7	23.8	24.1	2.9	5.5	12.7	11.8	9.4	11.5
Clerks	18.6	14.6	10.6	13.6	6.2	14.3	33.4	35.7	9.5	15.5
Service workers and shop and market sales	18.3	19.2	17.3	16.7	25.2	27.8	13.6	10.1	43.7	32.2
Skilled agricultural and fishery workers	0.4	0.5	5.5	3.1	5.3	3.5	0.4	0.3	13.0	8.2
Crafts and related trades workers	3.0	2.6	6.1	5.6	7.6	10.0	4.0	4.5	2.2	2.7
Plant and machine operators and assemblers	2.9	7.1	1.7	1.4	1.1	1.0	5.5	5.9	6.3	7.1
Elementary occupations	21.9	25.4	13.6	9.9	43.5	20.2	10.9	6.8	10.3	7.4
Total	100	100	100	100	100	100	100	100	100	100

ISCO classification of occupations (nine categories).
Source: Own construction based on IPUMS-I Censuses around 2000.

of white managers (professionals) is about 5 (4) percentage points higher than among blacks in Brazil, 4 (6) in Ecuador, 4 (3) in Puerto Rico, but 2 (1) in Cuba, and 1 (1) in Costa Rica.

Afro-Latino women also have different jobs than whites. The former generally work in less-skilled occupations, except for the outstanding case of Costa Ricans. There is a larger concentration of black women in elementary occupations that is especially evident in Ecuador (23 percent larger than whites) but also important in Puerto Rico (4), Cuba (4), and Brazil (3), and among service workers in Brazil (11 percent higher) and Puerto Rico (3). To a lesser extent, black women are also more likely to work as famers/fisherpersons in Brazil (5), Cuba, and Ecuador (2). On the other hand, they are also less likely to work as technicians (except in Puerto Rico) and as managers, professionals, or clerks, with the remarkable exception of Costa Rica where the situation is reversed.

Based on the distribution of workers by race and sex across occupations, Table 2 reports segregation levels of Afro-Latinos and whites computed separately for each sex in each country using both occupational classifications, along with the ISCO's nine major categories in the first four columns and the country-specific one in the other four columns. Indices *H* and *D* are

Table 2. Afro-Latino/White Occupational Segregation by Country and Sex.

Country	Segregation	Harmonized ISCO (Nine Categories)				National Classification			
		Men		Women		Men		Women	
		D	*H*	*D*	*H*	*D*	*H*	*D*	*H*
Brazil	Unconditional	0.162	0.022	0.193	0.025	0.202	0.035	0.228	0.039
	Conditional	0.060	0.004	0.085	0.006	0.136	0.013	0.143	0.016
Costa Rica	Unconditional	0.094	0.006	0.104	0.009	0.173	0.034	0.200	0.043
	Conditional	0.089	0.007	0.144	0.012	0.196	0.042	0.199	0.064
Cuba	Unconditional	0.075	0.004	0.076	0.005	0.108	0.010	0.133	0.050
	Conditional	0.082	0.004	0.055	0.003	0.114	0.011	0.126	0.042
Ecuador	Unconditional	0.221	0.038	0.252	0.044	0.231	0.048	0.281	0.060
	Conditional	0.129	0.013	0.140	0.014	0.158	0.022	0.188	0.029
Puerto Rico	Unconditional	0.109	0.007	0.087	0.006	0.172	0.032	0.164	0.034
	Conditional	0.058	0.002	0.050	0.001	0.147	0.028	0.136	0.028

Using two classifications of occupation: Duncan (*D*) and Hutchens (*H*) indices.
Source: Own construction based on IPUMS-I Censuses around 2000.

both reported. The first row for each country shows the observed or unconditional level of segregation, while the second row provides the level of these two indices after conditioning on workers' characteristics.

According to standardized data, segregation of Afro-Latinos seems to be unsurprisingly high in Ecuador and in Brazil and much lower in Cuba, Puerto Rico, and Costa Rica. Segregation based on these major categories is also higher among women than among men in Brazil, Ecuador, and Costa Rica, while in Cuba and Puerto Rico, they look fairly similar (except for *D* in Puerto Rico, which is lower for women). Regarding welfare considerations, it is important to keep in mind that the segregation of blacks generally occurs in less-prestigious occupations, except for Costa Rican women, as previously shown.

The observed levels of segregation may be at least partially the result of the different characteristics by race in each country. In order to distinguish what part of segregation is due to black–white inequality in factors such as geographical location, attained education, age, or migration, conditional levels of both indices are also reported in Table 2. It becomes clear that after conditioning on characteristics, segregation is substantially reduced in those two countries with the highest observed levels: Brazil and Ecuador. However, while Ecuador keeps its position as the most segregated country after conditioning by characteristics, Brazil is no longer the second one. Segregation is also reduced in Puerto Rico and in Cuba for women, remains at a similar level for men in Cuba, and is actually increased in Costa Rica.

As a consequence, the proportion of segregation that is explained by workers' characteristics that differ by race is substantial for both sexes in Brazil (80 percent for men/78 percent for women), Puerto Rico (71/75 percent), and Ecuador (66/68 percent), and, to a much lower extent, it is also important for women in Cuba (50 percent). This is according to results for index *H* in Table 3 that reports the percentage of change in segregation induced by controlling for characteristics (for *D* the percentages are smaller). However, segregation among both sexes would increase in Costa Rica (18/32 percent) if blacks are given whites' characteristics, as well as in Cuba for men (12 percent).

In all those cases in which a big share of segregation is explained, the main reason for the reduction was compensating for inequalities in education. This seems to be especially important in the cases of women and men in Brazil, consistently with King's, 1992 results (explaining 95 and 82 percent of observed segregation measured by *H* index), Ecuador (78 and 50 percent), Puerto Rico (52/55 percent), and in Cuba, especially for women (62 percent). Even in the case of men in Cuba, in which there was actually an increase in

Table 3. Factors Explaining Afro-Latino/White Occupational Segregation by Country and Sex.

Country	Characteristics (% Change)	Harmonized ISCO (Nine Categories)				National Classification			
		Men		Women		Men		Women	
		D	*H*	*D*	*H*	*D*	*H*	*D*	*H*
Brazil	All	−63.3	−80.0	−55.8	−77.7	−32.6	−61.2	−37.4	−60.0
	Geographical Location	−1.5	1.8	6.6	15.2	3.5	2.2	9.1	12.7
	Education	−63.0	−81.5	−63.4	−94.7	−34.8	−60.2	−48.2	−74.4
	Migration	−0.9	−1.3	−0.2	−0.4	−0.6	−1.2	−0.2	−0.4
	Age	2.0	1.0	1.2	2.2	−0.7	−2.0	1.9	2.0
Costa Rica	All	−4.5	17.8	38.3	32.1	13.8	22.9	−0.3	48.0
	Geographical location	−23.0	−21.2	13.4	12.0	0.1	16.8	13.8	44.6
	Education	7.7	7.7	25.9	17.1	7.2	0.3	−9.6	5.0
	Migration	7.3	21.7	−0.5	5.5	4.5	2.6	−6.4	−4.8
	Age	3.5	9.6	−0.5	−2.5	2.0	3.1	1.9	3.2
Cuba	All	9.6	11.8	−27.9	−50.0	5.1	6.0	−5.1	−15.5
	Geographical location	17.4	32.3	9.3	12.5	12.4	20.0	9.5	14.8
	Education	−6.0	−16.1	−37.2	−61.9	−5.3	−11.3	−14.3	−29.8
	Migration	0.9	1.6	−0.8	−2.0	1.5	4.2	−0.8	−1.1
	Age	−2.7	−5.9	0.9	1.4	−3.5	−6.9	0.4	0.6
Ecuador	All	−41.6	−66.3	−44.5	−67.6	−31.4	−53.7	−33.1	−51.8
	Geographical location	−11.4	−12.9	4.0	8.1	−9.0	−14.1	−1.2	−1.6
	Education	−28.6	−49.5	−50.5	−77.5	−20.2	−35.5	−33.2	−51.9
	Migration	−1.3	−3.0	−1.8	−3.2	−1.5	−2.6	−1.1	−2.2
	Age	−0.3	−0.9	3.8	4.9	−0.6	−1.5	2.4	3.8
Puerto Rico	All	−47.0	−70.8	−42.2	−75.1	−14.5	−14.5	−17.2	−18.0
	Geographical location	−1.1	−3.4	−0.1	−2.6	−1.6	−1.4	−1.7	−1.3
	Education	−38.5	−55.3	−31.4	−52.3	−12.2	−13.3	−10.7	−11.5
	Migration	−4.4	−6.3	−14.1	−23.2	−0.6	0.7	−6.0	−6.7
	Age	−3.0	−5.8	3.4	3.0	−0.1	−0.6	1.3	1.5

Percentage of change in unconditional segregation due to each set of characteristics (Shapley decomposition). Using two classifications of occupation: Duncan (*D*) and Hutchens (*H*) indices.
Source: Own construction based on IPUMS-I Censuses around 2000.

segregation after conditioning on characteristics, education plays a role (16 percent), but its impact is offset by the opposite side effect of equalizing the geographical location (that would increase segregation by 32 percent).

The role of education in explaining segregation becomes clear when one looks at Table 4, which reports the distribution of workers by years of schooling in Brazil, Costa Rica, and Ecuador. The proportion of black male workers with 15 or more years of schooling is lower than that of whites in these three countries but with a different magnitude, 15 percentage points in Ecuador, 7 in Brazil, and 2 in Costa Rica. The differential among females is similar in Ecuador and a bit higher in Brazil (9), and it is reversed in Costa Rica (−2), which is the reason they work in the best occupations and thus segregation increases rather than decreases after equalizing education for blacks and whites. Similarly, Table 5 demonstrates the distribution of attained education for people in Cuba and Puerto Rico. Whites are more likely to have higher levels of education in Puerto Rico, especially Bachelor's degrees (9 percentage points among women and 7 among men), and in Cuba (4 and 3 percentage points higher, respectively, in post-secondary education).

Among the other observed factors, inequalities in migration status explain an additional 23 percent of segregation for Puerto-Rican women (6 percent for men) and 3 percent for both sexes in Ecuador.[15] Compensating for inequalities in the geographical location of blacks and whites across the country would substantially reduce segregation across major occupations among men in Costa Rica (21 percent) and Ecuador (13 percent), and to a smaller extent in Puerto Rico (about 3 percent). In the rest of cases, segregation would actually increase rather than decrease after conditioning on this characteristic, especially in Cuba (32 percent increase for men, 12 percent for women) and for females in Brazil (15 percent), Costa Rica (12 percent), and Ecuador (8 percent).[16]

Costa Rica turned out to be a special case, given that compensating for inequalities in all characteristics (including education) except for age[17] for women and location for men increased segregation by an overall amount of 18 percent for men and 32 percent for women.

The second part of Tables 2 and 3 reports the results using the national-specific classifications, which is more accurate but less comparable across countries. However, some features are qualitatively similar to those highlighted earlier. As expected, segregation increases with the narrower definition of occupations in all countries, and it is generally larger among women than among men, unlike what happens with racial minorities in the United States (Gradín, 2010) where segregation was larger among most male minorities. Additionally, the share of segregation that is explained is reduced,

Table 4. Distribution of Afro-Latino and White Workers by Sex and Years of Schooling.

	Women						Men					
	Brazil		Costa Rica		Ecuador		Brazil		Costa Rica		Ecuador	
	Afro-Latinos	White	Afro-Latinos	White	Afro-Latinos	White	Afro-Latinos	White	Afro-Latinos	White	Afro-Latinos	White
Unknown	1.1	0.7	–	–	0.6	0.2	1.2	0.7	–	–	0.7	0.3
None	9.6	3.5	2.0	1.9	9.1	3.2	14.5	5.6	3.7	4.0	10.0	4.3
1–3	16.6	8.8	3.9	5.1	12.4	6.4	22.2	12.6	8.4	10.0	14.5	8.4
4–7	30.6	25.2	22.2	31.4	27.0	16.4	33.1	31.7	38.7	44.6	32.5	24.4
8–10	16.4	17.1	15.7	14.5	15.1	11.8	14.4	17.9	20.1	14.5	14.6	13.4
11–14	21.8	31.3	35.4	28.8	15.2	25.8	12.5	22.4	21.8	17.8	12.4	18.8
15+	3.9	13.4	20.8	18.4	20.7	36.1	2.0	9.1	7.3	9.2	15.4	30.3
Total	100	100	100	100	100	100	100	100	100	100	100	100

Source: Own construction based on IPUMS-I Censuses around 2000.

Table 5. Distribution of Afro-Latino and White Workers by Sex and Attained Education.

Country	Level of Attained Education	Women		Men	
		Afro-Latinos	White	Afro-Latinos	White
Cuba	Unknown	0.45	0.29	1.38	1.14
	None	2.2	1.8	4.6	4.5
	Primary	7.1	6.1	11.9	12.2
	Lower secondary: basic	22.1	20.3	31.6	31.0
	Lower secondary: skilled manual	1.4	0.9	4.5	3.2
	Upper secondary: pre-university	21.4	20.8	18.9	18.0
	Upper secondary: mid-level technical	25.5	26.5	17.6	17.6
	Upper secondary: mid-level teaching	2.2	1.9	0.6	0.6
	Postsecondary	17.5	21.3	9.0	11.7
	Total	100	100	100	100
Puerto Rico	None	1.0	0.9	2.5	1.5
	Primary, grade 1–4	2.0	1.0	3.4	2.4
	Primary, grade 5–8	7.5	4.3	12.5	9.8
	High school (9–12)	11.7	8.8	18.4	15.5
	High school graduate	22.8	20.4	27.0	26.4
	Some college, associate degree	31.3	32.1	23.4	25.0
	Bachelor's degree or higher	23.8	32.6	12.8	19.4
	Total	100	100	100	100

Source: Own construction based on IPUMS-I Censuses around 2000.

but a large share of segregation is still associated with racial inequality in the distribution of workers' characteristics in Brazil[18] (about 60 percent) and Ecuador (more than 50 percent), but it remains mainly unexplained in the other cases. These percentages are significantly larger than those found for African Americans (15–17 percent) in the United States and closer to those found regarding other minorities in that country (Gradín, 2010). Further, education is also responsible here for most of the explained segregation. As in the aggregated case, segregation after controlling for workers' characteristics increases in Costa Rica (48 percent for women and 23 percent for men) and in Cuba among men (6 percent).

The use of the more detailed classification highlights a few features that would remain unclear with the major occupational groups. First, it is particularly interesting to note the large increase in segregation among Cuban,

Puerto Rican, and Costa Rican Afro-Latinos, especially women, in the detailed classification with respect to ISCO, indicating that segregation in these countries mostly occurs within major occupational groups and not across them. Second, in these countries, most of the high segregation across the detailed classification of occupations remains unexplained after controlling for characteristics, unlike what was shown in Brazil and Ecuador. Indeed, they only explained 15–18 percent of observed segregation in Puerto Rico (both sexes) and Cuba (men), while segregation increased in the other cases (Costa Rica for both sexes and Cuba for women). Third, the uneven geographical distribution of Afro-Latinos and whites explained most of the increase in segregation in Costa Rica after controlling for characteristics when using the detailed classification of occupations, with education playing a much more modest role than in the aggregate case.

GEOGRAPHICAL DISTRIBUTION OF OCCUPATIONAL SEGREGATION IN BRAZIL

Brazil stands out for being the country with the largest Afro-Latino community. It is also remarkable as the case in which a large share of the observed level of segregation can be explained by workers' characteristics. For this reason, I extended the analysis for this country, looking at the geographical dimension of the phenomenon, to find out to what extent blacks are uniformly segregated across the country.

Table 6 reports segregation results, both conditional and unconditional, across the main metropolitan areas using the 2000 Census. This exercise allows us to discuss segregation at local markets, where some of the heterogeneity of workers linked to geographical variation of development, regional specialization, demographics, etc. in a large country like Brazil is already gone. It becomes clear that occupational segregation of blacks is generalized all across metropolitan areas in the country but not with the same intensity. Segregation for men and women is much larger in Salvador (northeast) and in the southeastern sector of the country, especially in Belo Horizonte but also in the other metropolitan areas (Rio de Janeiro, São Paulo, Porto Alegre, and Curitiba), and further north, in Belém, Recife, and Fortaleza. After controlling for characteristics, in all metropolitan areas there is a substantial reduction of segregation among men driven by the compensation of education inequalities. The figures go from 20 percent in Porto Alegre and about a third in Curitiba and Belém to about 50 percent or more in the rest, with the largest proportional reduction in Belo Horizonte (60 percent). There

Table 6. Afro-Latino/White Occupational Segregation (*H*) in Brazil by Sex and Main Metropolitan Area.

Hutchens Index	Men						Women					
	Unconditional	Conditional	Change in segregation after conditioning				Unconditional	Conditional	Change in segregation after conditioning			
			All (%)	Education (%)	Migration (%)	Age (%)			All (%)	Education (%)	Migration (%)	Age (%)
Belém	0.043	0.028	−35.5	−34.5	−0.7	−0.4	0.036	0.022	−39.5	−40.2	0.0	0.6
Fortaleza	0.040	0.020	−49.1	−47.4	−1.1	−0.6	0.038	0.017	−55.9	−56.1	0.4	−0.2
Recife	0.047	0.022	−54.1	−50.8	−1.0	−2.3	0.049	0.021	−56.1	−56.5	−0.6	0.9
Salvador	0.087	0.037	−57.6	−52.0	−3.0	−2.6	0.082	0.031	−62.0	−61.2	−1.5	0.7
Belo Horizonte	0.060	0.022	−63.1	−59.7	−0.6	−2.8	0.068	0.024	−64.0	−66.2	−0.2	2.4
Rio de Janeiro	0.055	0.023	−57.4	−54.4	−1.5	−1.5	0.070	0.024	−65.2	−66.1	−0.7	1.6
São Paulo	0.055	0.020	−63.1	−57.4	−5.6	−0.1	0.067	0.024	−64.1	−63.5	−3.2	2.5
Curitiba	0.057	0.038	−33.9	−33.4	0.5	−1.0	0.074	0.044	−40.9	−42.7	0.1	1.7
Porto Alegre	0.065	0.052	−19.7	−19.4	−0.6	0.3	0.083	0.058	−30.7	−30.1	−0.2	−0.4
Unweig. average	0.057	0.029	−48.2	−45.4	−1.5	−1.2	0.063	0.029	−53.2	−53.6	−0.7	1.1

Detailed occupations (509 categories).
Source: Own construction based on IPUMS-I Census 2000.

is a similar pattern in segregation among women but with even higher reductions (the largest being Rio de Janeiro, 65 percent). As a consequence, the risk of blacks facing segregation even with the same characteristics of local whites (segregation conditional on characteristics) is largest in Porto Alegre and Curitiba in the southeast and Salvador in the northeast.

CONCLUSIONS

This study has demonstrated that workers of African descent are generally segregated in several Latin American countries, typically into less-skilled occupations. Segregation is particularly higher in Ecuador and in Brazil across major occupational categories, but it is also important in other countries within the major occupations. Occupational segregation is largely explained by lower educational levels among African descendents in Brazil and to a lesser extent in Ecuador or among women in Cuba, but this is much less so in the other cases. Indeed, after conditioning on workers' characteristics, Brazil turned out to have lower segregation than other countries while Ecuador remained the most highly segregated country. This means that Afro-Ecuadorians face both high inequality in access to education and a higher risk of being segregated even when they reach the same amount of schooling as whites do. On the other hand, the geographical concentration of Afro-Latinos in certain areas of their countries generally contributes to reducing or hiding the observed level of segregation, which is especially important in Costa Rica and Cuba. The level of segregation tends to be larger among women than among men, mainly due to larger inequalities in education attainment. In any case, in all countries a substantial factor related to segregation is that it cannot be attributed to pre-labor market conditions, even across major occupational groups. This could be the result of discrimination against blacks in some labor markets across the Latin American and Caribbean region. In addition, it reflects the different quality of education attained by this group. However, it is noteworthy that the segregation of Afro-Costa Ricans is not only generally lower, at least across major occupational groups, but it reflects that blacks, especially women, who have attained higher levels of education and are highly concentrated geographically tend to work in more-skilled occupations.

Finally, in the case of Brazil, this study showed that the level of segregation of Afro-Latinos varies across metropolitan areas, with Salvador and Porto Alegre showing higher levels both before and after conditioning on characteristics.

NOTES

1. For a documented history of Afro-Latinos, see Andrews (2004).

2. An important exception was the geographical confinement of Afro-Costa Ricans in the province of Limón who lacked citizenship and other rights until 1948. Afro-Costa Rican communities were the result of the immigration of blacks from the British Indies to do railway construction work who later worked on plantations.

3. These social inequalities are also documented in country reports. See, for example, those from the Observatory of Racial Discrimination in Colombia (Rodríguez, Alfonso, & Cavelier, 2009) or from LAESER in Brazil (Paixão, Rossetto, Montovanele, & Carvano, 2011).

4. Regarding wage differentials between Afro-descendants and whites in Brazil, Arcand and D'Hombres (2004) concluded that wage discrimination accounted for 36 (23) percent of the racial wage discrepancy for blacks (browns), while occupational segregation explained an additional 8 (5) percent. Campante, Crespo, and Leite (2004) reported 26 percent of wage discrimination among Afro-Brazilians, while Leite (2005) found a lower value of 11 percent after controlling for differences in the mother's education, pointing to the role played by intergenerational transmission of education in the observed race-based pay gap.

5. Additionally, Lovell (1999) previously analyzed trends in racial inequalities among women in the Brazilian labor market, while Arcand and D'Hombres (2004) investigated the relationship between occupational segregation and wage differentials in Brazil. The latter found no significant effect of "pure" segregation (after controlling for endowments) across seven major occupations on the racial wage differential in 1998.

6. By contrast, several studies have addressed the issue of occupational segregation by race in the United States. See, among others, Albelda (1986), King (1992), Spriggs and Williams (1996), Rawlston and Spriggs (2002), Queneau (2009), Alonso-Villar et al. (2012), or Gradín (2010).

7. These databases covered 10 percent of the population in Costa Rica, Cuba, and Ecuador, 6 percent in Brazil, and 5 percent in Puerto Rico. See Table A.1 for a detailed description of the samples used.

8. In particular, Colombia, 2005, and Venezuela, 2001, were excluded because the former lacks the variable for occupation and the latter has no variable for race.

9. Browns in Brazil could also include a minority of those of mixed white and indigenous ancestry.

10. Telles (2002), for example, supports this view because it is less ambiguous. After comparing the consistency in a specific survey between interviewer and respondent categorizations, he showed that a racial classification of black and brown people in Brazil is influenced by characteristics, such as education, gender, age, and local racial composition.

11. Citizenship was used in all countries. Time of residence since a person immigrated and migration status according to whether the worker lived in the same administrative unit or abroad five years ago were used in all countries except Puerto Rico.

12. Alternatively, I could have considered the measurement of multigroup segregation instead (see, among others, Alonso-Villar & del Río, 2010; Chakravarty, D'Ambrosio, & Silber, 2009; Reardon & Firebaugh, 2002; Frankel & Volij, 2011;

Silber, 1992). However, I adopted the binary approach because I am interested in comparing the employment distribution of blacks and that of the affluent whites, and because of the fact that the number and size of groups vary across countries.

13. Other indices such as Gini or those from the Generalized Entropy family behave very similarly to *D* and *H*, respectively, and for that reason those results are omitted for simplicity.

14. See Sastre and Trannoy (2002) for a formalization of this procedure.

15. In Puerto Rico, the proportion of foreign-born workers was 13 (11) percent among female (male) whites, compared with 18 (16) percent among Afro-Latinos. In the case of Ecuador, foreign-born workers were 4 percent among whites of both sexes, which contrasted with less than 2 percent among Afro-Latinos. In Costa Rica, the proportion of foreign-born workers was also larger among whites, 12 (10) percent for women (men), compared to 8 percent among Afro-Latinos. In Cuba and Brazil, the proportions were very small (less than 1 percent) for both races (see Table A.3).

16. Afro-Latinos are relatively overrepresented in certain areas of their countries: northeastern states of Brazil (such as Bahía, Pará, and Maranhão); Havana and most western provinces of Cuba (Santiago de Cuba, Guantánamo, Gramma); Limón on the Caribbean coast of Costa Rica; Esmeraldas in the north of Ecuador; and the metropolitan area of San Juan-Bayamón in Puerto Rico (see Table A.4 for details).

17. Costa Rica is the only case studied in which Afro-Latinos are older on average than whites: 35.3 (36.4) years old for women (men) compared with 34.1 (35.7). In the other cases, either both groups have similar ages (Cuban and Puerto-Rican women), or Afro-Latinos are younger (see Table A.5).

18. A similar analysis using the *Pesquisa Nacional por Amostra de Domicílios* (PNAD) collected by the Instituto Brasileiro de Geografía e Estatística (IBGE) shows that segregation was reduced for the 2002–2009 period, driven by a reduction in conditional or unexplained segregation, with the explained segregation remaining stable.

ACKNOWLEDGMENT

I acknowledge financial support from the Spanish *Ministerio de Ciencia e Innovación* (grant ECO2010-21668-C03-03/ECON) and *Xunta de Galicia* (grant 10SEC300023PR).

REFERENCES

Albelda, R. (1986). Occupational segregation by race and gender, 1958–1981. *Industrial and Labor Relations Review*, *39*(3), 404–411.

Alonso-Villar, O., & del Río, C. (2010). Local versus overall segregation measures. *Mathematical Social Sciences*, *60*(1), 30–38.

Alonso-Villar, O., del Río, C., & Gradín, C. (2012). The extent of occupational segregation in the US: Differences by race, ethnicity, and gender. *Industrial Relations, 51*(2), 1–34.
Andrews, G. R. (2004). *Afro-Latin America 1800–2000*. New York: Oxford University Press.
Arcand, J.-L., & D'Hombres, B. (2004). Racial discrimination in the Brazilian labour market: Wage, employment and segregation effects. *Journal of International Development, 16*(8), 1053–1066.
Campante, F. R., Crespo, A. R. V., & Leite, P. G. P. G. (2004). Desigualdade salarial entre raç as no mercado de trabalho urbano brasileiro: Aspectos regionais. *Revista Brasileira de Economia, 58*(2), 185–210.
Chakravarty, S., D'Ambrosio, C., & Silber, J. (2009). Generalized Gini occupational segregation indices. *Research on Economic Inequality, 17*, 71–95.
Chantreuil, F., & Trannoy, A. (2011). Inequality decomposition values: The trade-off between marginality and consistency. *Journal of Economic Inequality*. doi:10.1007/s10888-011-9207-y
DiNardo, J., Fortin, N. M., & Lemieux, T. (1996). Labor market institutions and the distribution of wages, 1973–1992: A semiparametric approach. *Econometrica, 64*, 1001–1044.
Duncan, O. D., & Duncan, B. (1955). A methodological analysis of segregation indexes. *American Sociological Review, 20*(2), 210–217.
Frankel, D. M., & Volij, O. (2011). Measuring school segregation. *Journal of Economic Theory, 146*(1), 1–38.
Gradín, C. (2010). *Conditional occupational segregation of minorities in the US*. ECINEQ Working Paper Series, No. 185.
Hutchens, R. M. (1991). Segregation curves, Lorenz curves, and inequality in the distribution of people across occupations. *Mathematical Social Sciences, 21*, 31–51.
Hutchens, R. M. (2004). One measure of segregation. *International Economic Review, 45*(2), 555–578.
Jahn, J., Schmid, C. F., & Schrag, C. (1947). The measurement of ecological segregation. *American Sociological Review, 12*(3), 293–303.
King, M. C. (1992). Occupational segregation by race and sex, 1940–88. *Monthly Labor Review, 115*, 30–37.
King, M. C. (2009). Occupational segregation by race and sex in Brazil, 1989–2001. *The Review of Black Political Economy, 36*(2), 113–125.
IACHR. (2011). The situation of people of African descent in the Americas. Inter-American Commission on Human Rights (IACHR), *Organization of American States*. Available at http://www.oas.org/en/iachr/afro-descendants/docs/pdf/AFROS_2011_ENG.pdf
Leite, P. G. (2005). *Race discrimination or inequality of opportunities: The Brazilian case*. Discussion Paper, No. 118, Ibero-America Institute for Economic Research, Georg-August-Universität Göttingen, Göttingen.
Lemieux, T. (2002). Decomposing wage distributions: A unified approach. *Canadian Journal of Economics, 35*(4), 646–688.
Lovell, P. (1999). Women and racial inequality at work in Brazil. In M. Hanchard (Ed.), *Racial politics in contemporary Brazil* (pp. 138–153). Durham, UK: Duke University Press.
Paixão, M., Rossetto, I., Montovanele, F., & Carvano, L. M. (2011). *Relatório Anual das Desigualdades Raciais no Brasil; 2009-2010*. Laboratorio de Análisis Económicos, Históricos, Sociales y Estadísticos de las Relaciones Raciales (LAESER), Instituto de Economía, Universidad Federal de Río de Janeiro, Brazil.

Queneau, H. (2009). Trends in occupational segregation by race and ethnicity in the USA: Evidence from detailed data. *Applied Economics Letters*, *16*(13), 1347–1350.

Rawlston, V., & Spriggs, W. E. (2002). A logit decomposition analysis of occupational segregation: An Update for the 1990s of Spriggs and Williams. *Review of Black Political Economy*, *29*(4), 91–96.

Reardon, S. F., & Firebaugh, G. (2002). Measures of multigroup segregation. *Sociological Methodology*, *32*(1), 33–67.

Rodríguez, C., Alfonso, T., & Cavelier, I. (2009). *Raza y derechos humanos en Colombia*. Observatorio de Discriminación Racial, Bogotá, Colombia.

Sastre, M., & Trannoy, A. (2002). Shapley inequality decomposition by factor components: Some methodological issues. *Journal of Economics*, *9*(suppl. 1), 51–89.

Shorrocks, A. (2012). Decomposition procedures for distributional analysis: A unified framework based on the Shapley value. *Journal of Economic Inequality*. doi:10.1007/s10888-011-9214-z

Silber, J. (1992). Occupational segregation indices in the multidimensional case: A note. *Economic Record*, *68*, 276–277.

Spriggs, W. E., & Williams, R. M. (1996). A logit decomposition analysis of occupational segregation: results for the 1970s and 1980s. *Review of Economics and Statistics*, *78*, 348–355.

Telles, E. E. (2002). Racial ambiguity among the Brazilian population. *Ethnic and Racial Studies*, *25*(3), 415–441.

APPENDIX

Table A.1. Proportion of Afro-Latinos, Size, and (Nonempty) Occupational Categories by Sample.

IPUMS-I Censuses	ISCO Nine Categories				National Classifications					
	Men		Women		Men			Women		
	% Afro-Latinos	Size	% Afro-Latinos	Size	% Afro-Latinos	Size	Category	% Afro-Latinos	Size	Category
Costa Rica, 2000	1.9	88,353	2,2	36,163	1.9	88,353	103	2,2	36,163	100
Cuba, 2002	34.6	268,216	37.0	150,900	35.1	276,797	117	37.0	152,750	117
Ecuador, 2001	34.9	44,389	27.6	23,639	35.2	49,060	115	27.7	26,110	111
Puerto Rico, 2000	14.1	38,528	13.4	31,056	14	38,598	452	13.4	31,068	398
Brazil, 2000	45.1	2,353,537	40.8	1,397,616	45.1	2,419,759	509	40.8	1,414,767	506
Belém					70.3	18,703	369	67.1	12,722	242
Fortaleza					62.2	32,060	405	56.9	22,151	285
Recife					59	32,579	408	54	22,335	288
Salvador					77.2	31,225	396	74.7	24,304	295
Belo Horizonte					52.3	53,069	440	48.6	38,558	340
Rio de Janeiro					46.2	122,808	472	44.7	86,150	396
São Paulo					33.3	208,409	488	30.7	143,773	434
Curitiba					18.5	35,752	422	15.1	24,185	309
Porto Alegre					12.7	45,818	450	13.4	32,902	358
Brazil, PNAD 2002					46.8	100,924	476	43.6	71,471	382
Brazil, PNAD 2009					52.1	108,991	476	48.5	81,611	404

Table A.2. Activity, Employment, and Unemployment Rates of Afro-Latino and White Workers by Country and Sex.

Sex	Country	Activity Rate (% 16+ Population)		Employment Rate (% 16+ Population)		Unemployment Rate (% Active Population)	
		Afro-Latinos	White	Afro-Latinos	White	Afro-Latinos	White
Male	Costa Rica	75.9	77.2	70.6	73.2	6.9	5.2
	Cuba	66.5	66.1	63.8	63.7	4.0	3.5
	Ecuador	79.7	76.5	76.4	73.9	4.1	3.4
	Puerto Rico	62.2	56.6	51.8	49.1	16.6	13.2
	Brazil	79.9	79.7	69.2	71.6	13.3	10.2
Female	Costa Rica	35.2	30.0	34.0	29.4	3.6	2.3
	Cuba	38.6	33.8	37.9	33.2	1.8	1.5
	Ecuador	32.5	35.7	31.2	34.6	3.9	3.0
	Puerto Rico	48.0	39.2	37.3	33.0	22.4	15.8
	Brazil	49.5	50.6	38.5	41.9	22.2	17.2

Source: Own construction based on IPUMS-I Censuses around 2000.

Table A.3. Proportion of Foreign-Born Afro-Latino and White Workers by Country and Sex.

	Women		Men	
	Afro-Latinos	Whites	Afro-Latinos	Whites
Brazil	0.1	0.4	0.1	0.7
Costa Rica	8.2	12.5	7.6	10.0
Cuba	0.1	0.2	0.1	0.1
Ecuador	1.7	4.3	1.2	3.9
Puerto Rico	18.0	12.8	15.6	11.3

Source: Own construction based on IPUMS-I Censuses around 2000.

Table A.4. Geographical Distribution of Afro-Latino and White Workers by Country and Sex.

	Women		Men			Women		Men	
	Afro-Latinos	Whites	Afro-Latinos	Whites		Afro-Latinos	Whites	Afro-Latinos	Whites
Brazil (States)					*Costa Rica (provinces)*				
Rondônia	0.9	0.6	1.2	0.7	San José	24.2	45.6	16.4	36.6
Acre	0.4	0.1	0.5	0.2	Alajuela	2.3	16.4	4.2	19.5
Amazonas	2.1	0.6	2.2	0.6	Cartago	1.6	11.4	2.4	12.2
Roraima	0.3	0.1	0.3	0.1	Heredia	5.0	11.2	4.6	9.8
Pará	4.7	1.3	5.7	1.6	Guanacaste	1.3	4.9	1.4	6.1
Amapá	0.4	0.1	0.4	0.1	Puntarenas	0.8	6.1	1.8	8.9
Tocantins	0.9	0.3	1.1	0.4	Limón	64.9	4.5	69.1	7.0
Maranhão	4.6	1.3	5.2	1.4	*Ecuador (provinces)*				
Piauí	2.5	0.7	2.8	0.8	Azuay	1.6	4.3	1.5	3.7
Ceará	5.6	2.6	5.8	2.6	Bolívar	0.4	1.2	0.4	1.2
Rio Grande do Norte	1.8	1.1	1.9	1.1	Cañar	0.4	0.7	0.6	0.7
Paraíba	2.4	1.3	2.5	1.4	Carchi	1.0	0.7	1.3	0.7
Pernambuco	5.5	3.1	5.4	2.9	Cotopaxi	0.6	1.8	0.5	1.4
Alagoas	2.0	0.8	2.1	0.8	Chimborazo	0.6	1.9	0.5	1.4
Sergipe	1.5	0.5	1.5	0.5	El Oro	3.6	4.4	5.0	5.2
Bahía	12.1	3.1	11.8	3.2	Esmeraldas	24.0	2.3	21.7	3.5
Minas Gerais	11.5	10.4	11.3	10.9	Guayas	36.3	38.3	37.1	39.4
Espírito Santo	2.3	1.8	2.2	1.8	Imbabura	3.6	1.7	2.4	1.3

Rio de Janeiro	9.6	8.8	8.1	8.2
São Paulo	15.3	29.3	14.2	29.0
Paraná	2.9	8.4	3.1	8.6
Santa Catarina	0.7	6.0	0.8	5.9
Rio Grande do Sul	2.0	11.3	1.8	10.7
Mato Grosso do Sul	1.2	1.2	1.3	1.3
Mato Grosso	1.6	1.1	2.0	1.4
Goiás	3.5	2.7	3.6	2.9
Distrito Federal	1.8	1.3	1.4	1.0
Cuba (provinces)				
Pinar del Rio	4.3	7.4	4.1	8.5
La Habana	4.3	7.4	3.9	7.9
Ciudad de la Habana	29.2	21.5	23.1	16.9
Matanzas	4.9	7.1	4.6	7.3
Villa Clara	3.9	9.3	3.5	9.7
Cienfuegos	2.7	4.3	2.6	4.4
Sancti Spiritus	2.0	5.4	2.0	6.0
Ciego de Ávila	2.3	4.9	2.4	4.9
Camagüey	5.0	8.3	5.3	8.4
Las Tunas	2.7	4.6	3.6	5.4
Holguín	4.3	9.0	5.2	10.9
Granma	8.3	4.4	12.4	4.1
Santiago de Cuba	16.7	4.0	17.4	3.4
Guantánamo	8.2	1.6	9.0	1.4
Isla de la Juventud	1.1	0.9	1.0	0.7

Loja	0.4	0.9	0.6	0.9
Los Ríos	2.8	2.6	5.3	4.6
Manabí	2.6	4.4	4.5	5.9
Morona Santiago	0.1	0.4	0.1	0.5
Napo	0.2	0.4	0.2	0.4
Pastaza	0.1	0.3	0.2	0.4
Pichincha	18.4	28.5	14.3	23.1
Tungurahua	1.0	3.9	0.9	3.1
Zamora Chinchipe	0.1	0.1	0.1	0.3
Galápagos	0.2	0.2	0.1	0.2
Sucumbíos	1.0	0.5	1.4	0.9
Orellana	0.5	0.3	0.5	0.6
Disputed Zones	0.5	0.4	0.8	0.7
Puerto Rico (MAs)				
Non-MA	29.1	37.4	32.6	40.6
Aguadilla	2.3	3.6	2.5	4.2
Arecibo	1.5	2.6	1.6	3.0
Caguas	2.4	4.4	2.5	3.9
Ponce	3.7	4.5	4.2	4.8
San Juan-Bayamón	61.1	47.6	56.7	43.5

Source: Own construction based on IPUMS-I Censuses around 2000.

Table A.5. Average Age of Afro-Latino and White Workers by Country.

	Women		Men	
	Afro-Latinos	Whites	Afro-Latinos	Whites
Brazil	34.1	34.7	34.3	35.9
Costa Rica	35.3	34.1	36.4	35.7
Cuba	38.7	38.5	38.9	39.9
Ecuador	34.3	37.0	35.1	37.8
Puerto Rico	37.9	38.2	38.8	39.6

Source: Own construction based on IPUMS-I Censuses around 2000.

CHAPTER 4

MULTIGROUP SEGREGATION PATTERNS AND DETERMINANTS: THE CASE OF IMMIGRANTS IN AN ITALIAN CITY

Francesco Andreoli

ABSTRACT

Models of race-based segregation establish that individual characteristics or housing market attributes are complementary causes of the observed level of races' concentration inside an urban space. The goal of this work is to establish which variables, and in which order of magnitude, among individual characteristics, housing features, and local amenities correlate with immigrants' segregation, in the case of consistent within-city immigrants' mobility. We capture the degree of segregation for different immigration groups by a local concentration statistics that is directly obtained from segregation curves, and we use data on the Verona Municipality as a case study. We find strong evidence in favor of the role of the housing market and housing ownership distribution across city areas.

Keywords: Segregation measures; local sorting; immigrants segregation; housing

JEL classifications: J15; R23; I31

Inequality, Mobility and Segregation: Essays in Honor of Jacques Silber
Research on Economic Inequality, Volume 20, 91–116

ISSN: 1049-2585/doi:10.1108/S1049-2585(2012)0000020007

INTRODUCTION

Residential segregation is a particular *pattern of spatial distribution* of *social groups* in a *geographical environment*. The extent of segregation can be measured in different ways, accounting for a-spatial or spatial dimensions, as pointed out by Massey and Denton (1988) and Reardon and O'Sullivan (2004). A-spatial dimensions capture, for instance, the evenness in distribution of groups in an urban area, or the probability of interaction between members of different social groups. Spatial analysis also takes into account the distance between locations. In this paper we analyze segregation patterns of different groups of immigrants in exogenously partitioned subareas of Verona urban space, using a-spatial measures. The analysis of segregation measures suggests that a concentration statistics, identifying the slope of the segregation curve at a given point, should be considered a good *local* measure of immigrants' segregation.

The goal of this work is to establish which variables, and in which order of importance, among individual characteristics, housing structure, and local public goods correlate with immigrants' segregation, under substantial within-city immigrants' mobility. We capture the degree of segregation for different immigration groups by a local concentration statistics that derives from segregation curves, and we use data on the Verona Municipality as a case study. In the Italian panorama, Verona has behaved in the last two decades as a central attraction pole for immigration, although recently urban congestion has dramatically shortened the immigration flows from outside the city.[1] As a result, we find evidence in favor of housing market effect and housing ownership distribution across areas as the major sources of covariance with local immigrants' concentration.

The result fits the predictions of the *Space Stratification Models* (Charles, 2003) in the case of *decentralized* discrimination (Cutler, Glaeser, & Vigdor, 2008a). The model posits that segregation is a result of the free individual behavior in social and market interactions. For instance, natives may pay a premium to move away from a neighborhood where they observe increasing concentration of individuals belonging to different immigration groups (see Saiz & Wachter (2011) for a discussion and an empirical application on US data).[2] Conversely, *centralized* segregation is the consequence of individual- and institutional-level actions explicitly hindering immigrants' freedom in location choice (screening of new people entering in a neighborhood by neighbors or racial laws neglecting equality in access to certain locations). Other types of models are often advocated in the literature: the *Spatial Assimilation Model*[3] and the *Tiebout-type Sorting Models*,[4] although none of them can be directly tested, since the phenomenon of individual discrimination is not observable in the Italian case, and there is not enough variation across urban areas in terms of tax schedules to generate sorting incentives based on preferences over public good provision and financing.

The paper contributes in two directions. Firstly, we analyze the informative content of segregation curves, and we derive a local concentration statistics that measures the degree of concentration of one immigration group that lives in a given urban section compared to the remaining population in the same section. This statistic is nicely related to the majority of a-spatial indices and by studying its changes across time we can spot urban section that behaves as sources of immigrants segregation, in the sense of the segregation curve. Using data on Verona municipality, we identify immigrants location choice variation between 2000 and 2005 and we spot some clusters of urban sections that behave as attraction poles for immigrants concentration.

The second contribution of the paper is to exploit the determinants of immigrants segregation inside the city, by looking at the separated effect of housing features and population characteristics. We exploit the statistical information given by a very detailed micro-level census database on the resident population in Verona in one given year. A preliminary analysis on the segregation patterns in the period from 2000 to 2005 is reproduced, such that we can pin down the direction of the changes in segregation and spot the areas of the city that are more interested in immigrants concentration phenomena.

Our empirical strategy consists in regressing, for each immigration group separately, a concentration index computed at section level (which is the slopes of the *segregation curve* for a given group computed in correspondence to the urban section analyzed) on the characteristics of the whole population living in that area and the characteristics of the buildings of the same urban region. Cautiously, we prefer to interpret our results only in terms of association rather than causation, as segregation may of course determine the spatial distribution of several variables used in estimation, which are indeed related to individual economic outcomes (Cutler, Glaeser, & Vigdor, 2008b). The econometric model tries to reproduce for immigrants groups the results for race-based segregation in (Bayer, McMillan, & Rueben, 2004).

We stress here a few empirical issues. Firstly, in our regression analysis we use microdata at family level for the whole population living in the city, and for each family we collect information on the attributes, rather than outcomes, of both families heads and for the houses where households are located. Two factors may convince the reader that the issue of reverse causation (the fact that immigrants concentration explains the distribution of family head or household attributes) is not as important as in Bayer et al. (2004) for the scope of our analysis. On the one hand, many characteristics are predetermined, such as household head education, family composition, or housing features, and they would be better explained by past, rather than current, immigrants' segregation patterns. On the other hand, the aggregated statistics show that the massive immigration flows in the city have occurred in the last decade of the twentieth century, thus suggesting that in the city there is no significant phenomenon of past segregation that may affect recent immigrants' urban segregation patterns.

Secondly, our work is differentiated from the strand of literature on the effects of segregation on outcomes, well summarized in Cutler et al. (2008b). Our scope is to determine whether (and which type of) demographic and housing market information observable to the city planner may explain (or should be considered as a reliable indicator for) unobservable immigrants' location patterns in an environment characterized by high immigration flows. This can be done by exploiting information at the household level or averaged at census tract level. We use the former setting in the optic of the central planner who is interested in understanding how individual location choices and the relative distribution of attributes may explain the degree of immigrants' concentration.

Finally, we regress each of the six immigration group-specific models on the whole population of household heads, rather than on the corresponding immigrants' subgroup population under analysis. This is motivated by the fact that the concentration statistics of a given immigration group captures the information about the distribution of that group versus the distribution of the remaining population.

The organization of the paper is as the following: in Section "Data: immigrants in Verona" we describe the type of microdata we use; in Section "A model for segregation patterns" we motivate the use of a concentration statistic directly connected to the segregation curve and the econometric strategy that we adopt; in Section "Results" we present the results of our analysis, while Section "Conclusions" concludes.

DATA: IMMIGRANTS IN VERONA

The analysis of the paper is based on a dynamic comparison of the patterns of segregation of immigrants inside the city and a static regression model on a variety of population measures. We use two different databases, both published by ISTAT, the Italian Bureau of Statistics. The first type of questions is addressed with the analysis of vital statistics of the resident population in the city, while the econometric analysis exploits census data for the year 2001.

We exploit immigration segregation changes by using vital statistics for the years 2000 and 2005. The dataset provides information on nationality, family affiliation, and other demographic attributes of each inhabitant in the municipality of Verona. Information about individual spatial location is available for different partitions of the urban space: an individual can be associated either to one of the 1940 "Census Sections" (CS) or, alternatively, to one of the 80 "Homogeneous Territorial Zones" (HTZ) in which the municipality territory is partitioned (each HTZ gathers together, on average, 130 census sections).[5] We partition the immigrants' population into six groups using nationality codes, making use of the World Bank definition[6]: East Europe, UE 2001, Africa (North and Middle East, Sub-Saharan Africa), Asia, Latin America, and a remaining group that collects all individual with non-Italian citizenship. For Asia, two groups for China and Sri Lanka are also formed, given their relative importance in Verona urban space. Table 1 reports the absolute and relative presence of the selected groups in Verona in the years 2000 and 2005. The illegal immigration is not considered in the analysis.[7]

Table 1. Immigrants in Verona in 2000 and 2005 with Regard to Group Distinction.

Groups	2000		2005	
	a	*b*	*a*	*b*
Immigrants (total)	4.91	100	8.91	100
UE 2001	0.58	11.93	0.89	10
East Europe	0.83	16.98	2.38	26.7
Africa	2.06	42.4	2.52	28.39
North Africa	*0.76*	*15.5*	*1.04*	*11.7*
Sub-Saharian Africa	*1.3*	*26.9*	*1.48*	*16.6*
Asia	0.99	20.2	2.3	25.7
China	*0.17*	*3.58*	*0.33*	*3.78*
Sri Lanka	*0.66*	*13.58*	*1.64*	*18.44*
Latin America	0.34	7	0.76	8.6
Other	0.12	1.27	0.5	2.21

Note: Shares (in %) of the overall population (a) and of the total number of immigrants (b). No statistical significance indicator is reported. The data merely represent population counts from census data.

Table 2. Mean Levels and Range of Variation of Family Head and House Characteristics.

Observations	Italians	Immigrants						Range
		Total	East Europe	North Africa	Sub-Saharan Africa	Asia	Latin America	
	102,025	6,152	1,003	857	1,544	1,421	490	
House features								
(1) Conservation								
Very good	0.308	0.198	0.232	0.16	0.151	0.193	0.247	{0, 1}
Good	0.557	0.545	0.55	0.502	0.552	0.556	0.602	{0, 1}
Bad	0.126	0.22	0.196	0.248	0.261	0.213	0.141	{0, 1}
Very bad	0.009	0.036	0.022	0.09	0.035	0.037	0.01	{0, 1}
(2) Age								
<1919	0.116	0.195	0.19	0.16	0.191	0.237	0.145	{0, 1}
1919–1945	0.088	0.117	0.102	0.138	0.114	0.116	0.112	{0, 1}
1946–1961	0.201	0.26	0.23	0.308	0.285	0.259	0.235	{0, 1}
1962–1971	0.251	0.241	0.242	0.204	0.264	0.237	0.288	{0, 1}
1972–1981	0.157	0.104	0.117	0.1	0.095	0.093	0.116	{0, 1}
1982–1991	0.112	0.049	0.066	0.054	0.028	0.037	0.057	{0, 1}
>1981	0.076	0.035	0.053	0.037	0.023	0.021	0.047	{0, 1}
(3) Title of enjoyment								
Owner	0.653	0.125	0.131	0.104	0.064	0.124	0.148	{0, 1}
Rent	0.285	0.835	0.8	0.87	0.923	0.817	0.819	{0, 1}
Other	0.062	0.04	0.069	0.026	0.013	0.059	0.033	{0, 1}
(4) Property								
Natural person	0.909	0.934	0.919	0.865	0.946	0.968	0.953	{0, 1}
Firm	0.015	0.019	0.029	0.016	0.012	0.015	0.018	{0, 1}
Co-op	0.005	0.005	0.001	0.02	0.005	0.001	0.002	{0, 1}
Public	0.004	0.001	0.001	0.002	0	0	0	{0, 1}

Municipality	0.025	0.016	0.02	0.046	0.011	0.003	0.012	{0, 1}
Welfare institution	0.006	0	0	0	0.001	0	0.002	{0, 1}
Housing projects	0.023	0.008	0.009	0.022	0.008	0.004	0.002	{0, 1}
Other	0.013	0.017	0.022	0.029	0.017	0.01	0.01	{0, 1}
(5) Floors	4.199	4.065	4.209	3.761	3.822	4.203	4.431	[1, 17]
(6) Internals	20.081	19.233	22.027	17.991	16.459	19.474	23.118	[1, 351]
(7) Rooms	3.417	2.664	2.693	2.477	2.543	2.749	2.713	[1, 28]
Sqm	95.789	78.851	79.635	73.433	72.727	83.837	80.563	[14, 929]
(8) Kitchen	0.737	0.662	0.635	0.642	0.676	0.675	0.65	[0, 2]
Household head characteristics								
(9) Sex F	0.324	0.293	0.354	0.099	0.338	0.193	0.514	{0, 1}
(10) Age	56.303	36.452	35.625	36.895	34.612	35.89	36.132	[17, 102]
(11) Education (years degree)								
0	0.025	0.047	0.016	0.121	0.042	0.051	0.039	{0, 1}
5	0.271	0.084	0.043	0.143	0.103	0.089	0.073	{0, 1}
8	0.284	0.438	0.315	0.478	0.485	0.594	0.4	{0, 1}
11	0.079	0.109	0.203	0.068	0.111	0.06	0.102	{0, 1}
13	0.205	0.19	0.264	0.14	0.17	0.128	0.25	{0, 1}
16	0.013	0.028	0.035	0.011	0.02	0.017	0.049	{0, 1}
18	0.092	0.081	0.108	0.033	0.062	0.043	0.075	{0, 1}
>18	0.03	0.022	0.016	0.006	0.006	0.019	0.012	{0, 1}
(12) Job								
Employed	0.336	0.676	0.674	0.703	0.752	0.713	0.574	{0, 1}
Self-employed	0.153	0.167	0.184	0.159	0.113	0.178	0.223	{0, 1}
Unemployed	0.511	0.158	0.142	0.138	0.135	0.109	0.202	{0, 1}
Household characteristics								
(13) No. of underage	0.335	0.468	0.511	0.543	0.466	0.462	0.413	[0, 9]
(14) No. family members	1.232	1.047	1.057	1.175	0.879	1.226	0.941	[0, 12]
(15) Partner works	0.534	0.336	0.336	0.346	0.257	0.451	0.226	{0, 1}

Notes: Mean values for household head and house characteristics from Census Data 2001, Verona Municipality. Mean values are conditioned to immigration group and for Italians. The range of variation is also reported for each variable.

The econometric analysis exploits ISTAT Census microdata for the year 2001. The Census database provides information about buildings, households, and individuals living in 2001 in the Verona municipality. We use a restricted access version of database that provides the full census survey of the 253,208 inhabitants of the Verona municipality, organized in 109,786 families with 2.27 individuals per family, while more than 4,000 individuals live in communities. Moreover, we are able to link observations to the census section (and HTZ) where they live in, up to the civic number level.

Table 2 highlights the differences between immigrants and Italians, and among immigration groups. Concerning the housing structure, no substantial variability is observed between immigration groups. Compared to Italians, immigrants live in older buildings (31.2% lives in a house built before 1946, while the corresponding figure for Italians lowers down to 19%) of lower quality (26% of immigrants versus 13% of Italians) and smaller size (the difference is of the magnitude of 17 sqm), and they face a lower accessibility to housing projects (0.8%). Buildings ownership rate ranges between 6% and 13% among immigrants, while it grows up to 65% among natives. The demographic characteristics of the population follow the same pattern across groups. Immigrants are younger, less educated and more active in labor market than natives. We will exploit these differences, and their variability in space, in our econometric model.

A MODEL FOR SEGREGATION PATTERNS

Let a metropolitan area be partitioned into T sections and the city population comprising K mutually exclusive groups with $k=1, \ldots, K$. A two-dimensional study of residential segregation is developed. The distribution of each group is analyzed and compared with the distributions of the remaining $K-1$ groups. Let x_k^j be the number of individuals belonging to group k living in section j, with $j=1, \ldots, T$; then $X_k := \sum_{j=1}^{T} x_k^j$ is the total number of individuals in group k, while X defines the total population in the city and $X_{-k} := X-X_k$ denotes the number of individuals who do not belong to group k. We also define $X_j := \sum_{k=1}^{K} x_k^j$ as the total population that lives in section j. Let $s_k^j := x_k^j/X_k$ denote the proportion of all individuals belonging to group k living in section j. A similar definition holds for group $-k$.

Given the K vectors of $2T+2$ dimensions $[s_k^j, s_{-k}^j, X_k, X_{-k}; j=1, \ldots, T]$, containing the shares s_k^j and s_{-k}^j for all T sections and the total number of persons belonging to groups k and $-k$, it is possible to obtain a first measure of residential segregation, the *Concentration Index* Q_k^j, which measures the relative concentration of group k with respect to group $-k$ for every urban section j. It is expressed as:

$$Q_k^j := \frac{s_k^j}{s_{-k}^j}$$

and takes values $0 \leq Q_k^j < 1$ if in section j the group k is underrepresented or absent; while $Q_k^j = 1$ if the presence of group k in the section perfectly reflects its presence in the city; $Q_k^j > 1$ if the group is concentrated in the section.

As a local measure of segregation, this index has a variety of properties and potential applications:

- The local concentration for urban area j varies across time and between immigration groups. We can therefore assess which group is more concentrated in j as well as in which sections the statistic grows fastly over time.
- The concentration statistic is not sensitive to the absolute size of the groups: if every group k is replicated ρ_k times in every section j, the index does not change. If the population in a section is replicated for a factor that is constant across groups, the concentration index does not vary. Moreover, it is not additive with respect to urban space decomposition, so it must be computed independently for every different partition.[8]
- Once sections have been ranked in increasing order of magnitude of Q_k^j, for every group k it is possible to derive the relative *segregation curve* (see Duncan & Duncan, 1955; Flückiger & Silber, 1999; Hutchens, 1991, 2001; Reardon & Firebaugh, 2002). The curve starts from the (0,0) origin and ends in (1,1) and it connects all the points whose coordinates are the cumulative sum of s_k^j on the horizontal axis and the cumulative sum of s_{-k}^j on the vertical axis. By construction Q_k^j is the slope of the segregation curve in the point corresponding to section j.

If the segregation curve associated to the distribution Y lies no point above and some point below the segregation curve associated to distribution Z, then any measure of segregation consistent with the Transfer Principle[9] will record higher segregation for Y than for Z. Conversely, when segregation curves intersect, unanimity in ranking distributions is lost and the choice should be made according to a cardinal comparison of segregation indices. In our analysis, we make use of the *Dissimilarity Index*, the *Gini Segregation Index*, and the *Entropy Index* as well as a-spatial *Interaction (Isolation) Indices* (see, for instance, Hutchens, 2001).

We construct the segregation curves using the CS partition to model the segregation patterns of the total immigrants group and other immigration subgroups, each compared with the remaining population. We propose a robustness check by comparing the two distributions under the courser HTZ partition.[10] Moreover, the analysis of the dynamic across time of the concentration statistics allows us to pinpoint the macroareas of the city that behave as attractors for immigrant's concentration.

The empirical analysis serves as an introductory description for the econometric model. We consider the finer partition given by census sections. For each CS j, we compute the concentration statistics Q_k^j for a set of population groups defined by nationality: total immigrants, East Europe, North Africans, South Africans, Asians, and South Americans. For each of the six groups indexed by k (five immigration groups plus the total immigrants), we construct a regression model where the variability of Q_k^j is regressed on a set of characteristics of the households residing in section j.

We do not restrict model k to be estimated on the subpopulation of group k, but rather on the population as a whole. This choice is motivated by the fact that segregation is a global phenomenon that involves the location choices of individuals in group k as well as the remaining population. The joint variability of the two subpopulations is captured by the statistic Q_k^j in the form of a ratio of two distribution functions of group k and $-k$ across regions. The variability of Q_k^j across the j sections is therefore jointly explained by the variability in the overall population living in the area and not by just a subgroup.

In the model we face three dimensions to control for: households, groups, and sections. For the i-th household living in section j and for each immigration group $k = 1, \ldots, 6$ separately, we specify our model in a linear additive form as:

$$Q_k^j = \alpha_k + \beta_k X_i^j + \delta_k Y_i^j + \gamma_k Z_i^j + \lambda_k W_i^j + \pi_k S^j + \varepsilon_{k,i}^j$$

where Q_k^j is our local concentration index, specific for each census section of the urban environment and repeated for each observation living in the area j. We capture its mean variability by a linear function defined on X_i^j, the set of dummies for the residential area in which the family lives; Y_i^j, the vector of structural characteristics of the houses (quality, age, property, rent, housing project, number of rooms, dimension, kitchen); Z_i^j, the vector of socioeconomic characteristics of the household head (sex, age, education, working status) and family (number of children, head partner works); W_i^j, a set of dummies for the group of immigration to which the observed family head belongs and S^j is the vector of section-specific characteristics, common to all families living in the same section (the percentage of commercial buildings, the share of buildings used for community purposes). The term $\varepsilon^j_{k,i}$ is the individual- and group-specific residual.

RESULTS

In Fig. 1 we report segregation curves for the years 2000 and 2005 associated to distributions of resident immigrant groups in Verona, compared according to the CS partition. In Fig. 2 we perform the same analysis according to the HTZ partition of the urban space. In both cases we consider the following groups: (a) total immigrants, (b) East Europe, (c) Africa, and (d) Asia, which represent the most important communities in the city (see Table 1). As a first result, the curves suggest an uneven distribution of immigrants in Verona in both years. Considering the CS partition, segregation curves of all groups considered are nonintersecting, identifying for each immigration group a slight increase in evenness in 2005 with respect to 2000, though the population of immigrants (total and for each group) remains segregated.

The segregation curves reported in Fig. 2 intersect in at least one point for all groups. The test on the coarser HTZ partition is a robustness check against spatial clustering. In fact, if the segregation ordering obtained under the CS partition were preserved under the HTZ space partition, then it would have been the case that some census sections, similar in terms of immigrants composition, were also clustered in space. Aggregation in HTZ would have preserved the section ranking, thus smoothing segregation curves while still validating dominance. The curves constructed on the HTZ partition also signal that the segregation ranking is preserved for the section with relative low immigrants groups' concentration, while it should be rejected (or it is reversed) at the top of the curves, corresponding to HTZ with higher immigrants' concentration.

This phenomenon is not captured by the segregation indices reported in Table 3, which point in the direction of decreasing segregation in the city. This assessment is robust to the choice of the index. For instance, the Dissimilarity index D_k and the Gini segregation index G_k are related to the segregation curve. They correspond, respectively, to the highest vertical distance between the segregation curve and the diagonal, and to double the area between the segregation curve and the diagonal (see Duncan & Duncan, 1955; Hutchens, 2001). Both indexes describe a similar picture:

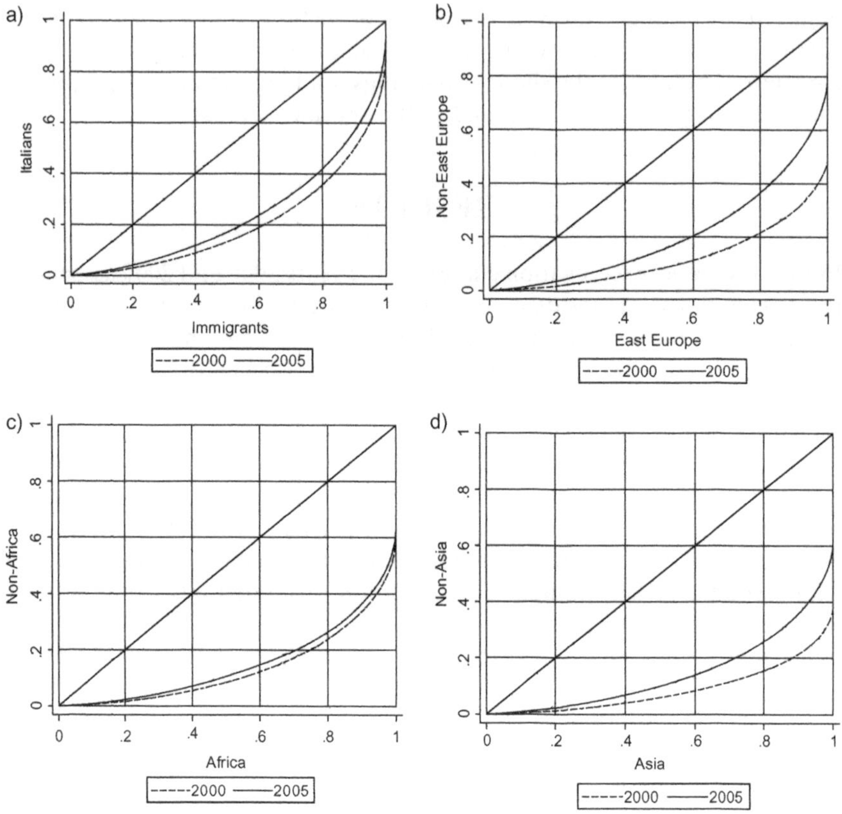

Fig. 1. Segregation Curves for 2000 and 2005 of Four Immigration Groups Living in Verona: (a) Total Immigrants, (b) East Europe, (c) Africa, and (d) Asia. Census Sections Partition.

segregation decreases substantially across years for all groups, independently of the partition of the urban space, thus providing evidence against the clustering phenomenon (at HTZ level). The patterns of segregation identified by the entropy index H_k, which measure the diversity in neighborhoods' social composition, are substantially identical.

We now analyze the information given by the local concentration index Q_k^j in order to detect the spatial units that mostly contribute in determining the variation across periods in immigrants' segregation patterns. We compare index values for different HTZs in the city and extend the analysis in both years considered. Then, we select areas that show particular patterns

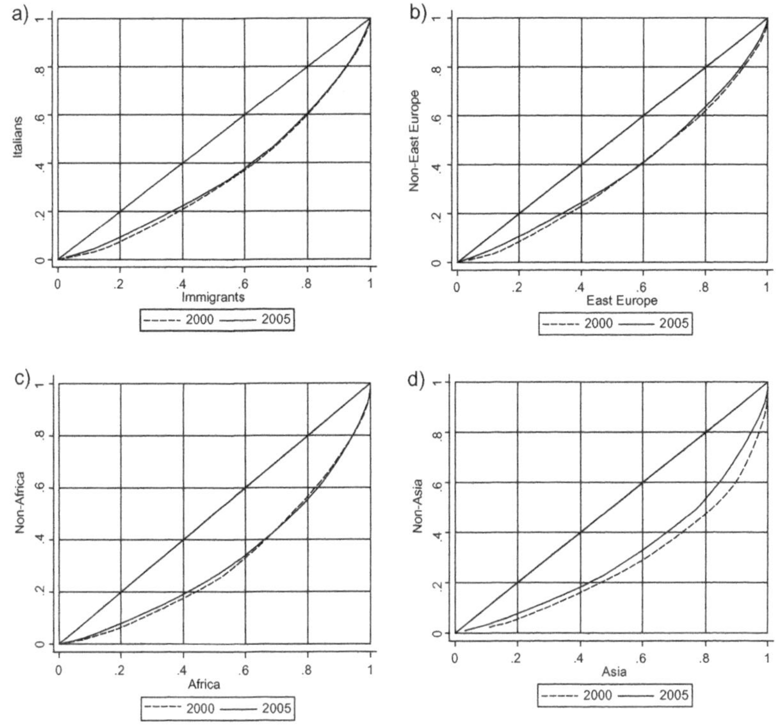

Fig. 2. Segregation Curves for 2000 and 2005 of Four Immigration Groups Living in Verona: (a) Total Immigrants, (b) East Europe, (c) Africa, and (d) Asia. HTZ partition.

of this local statistic. For each year, we detect two areas in the central part of the city that exhibit sustained high levels of immigrant concentration: the tourist city center area (hereafter identified as CC) characterized also by an intensive presence of tertiary activities, and an area of mainly housing land, Veronetta (see Fig. 3). Comparing the level of $Q_{k,j}$ for 2000 and 2005, we identify also the HTZs that show an increasing immigrant concentration, as captured by the local statistic used. By examining the spatial position on a map of the HTZs characterized by high attractiveness to immigration, we, furthermore, find that these urban units are also spatially concentrated. We name South Area (SA) this new cluster of HTZs.[11]

In Table 4 we report the average and maximum values of the concentration statistics associated to each group, space partition, and year. As

Table 3. Three Indices for A-Spatial Segregation of Different Immigration Groups: Evenness.

K	Census Tracts (1940)						HTZ (80)					
	D_k		G_k		H_k		D_k		G_k		H_k	
	2000	2005	2000	2005	2000	2005	2000	2005	2000	2005	2000	2005
Immigrants (total)	0.445	0.384	0.60	0.527	0.157	0.131	0.233	0.222	0.32	0.299	0.042	0.038
East Europe	0.6	0.435	0.76	0.59	0.203	0.131	0.189	0.192	0.282	0.258	0.026	0.022
Africa	0.56	0.542	0.738	0.703	0.22	0.201	0.27	0.261	0.374	0.36	0.049	0.045
North Africa	*0.68*	*0.63*	*0.832*	*0.78*	*0.258*	*0.227*	*0.283*	*0.268*	*0.398*	*0.367*	*0.047*	*0.042*
Sub-Saharian Africa	*0.64*	*0.61*	*0.802*	*0.771*	*0.257*	*0.235*	*0.291*	*0.296*	*0.405*	*0.398*	*0.054*	*0.05*
Asia	0.68	0.546	0.827	0.71	0.263	0.199	0.324	0.276	0.452	0.377	0.062	0.048
China	*0.9*	*0.843*	*0.954*	*0.924*	*0.388*	*0.35*	*0.478*	*0.41*	*0.619*	*0.566*	*0.095*	*0.089*
Sri Lanka	*0.77*	*0.59*	*0.884*	*0.751*	*0.323*	*0.218*	*0.35*	*0.268*	*0.493*	*0.376*	*0.074*	*0.046*
Latin America	0.69	0.56	0.832	0.723	0.239	0.174	0.315	0.263	0.435	0.36	0.052	0.036
UE 2001	0.62	0.556	0.746	0.718	0.182	0.176	0.258	0.241	0.354	0.33	0.033	0.03
Other	0.65	0.54	0.803	0.71	0.22	0.168	0.293	0.257	0.412	0.348	0.047	0.034

Notes: Dissimilarity index, Gini index, and Entropy index are reported in order, for years 2000 and 2005 separately for two different partitions of urban space (Census Tracts partition is finer than HTZ one). All indices are significantly different from zero at 1% level (bootstrapped standard errors).

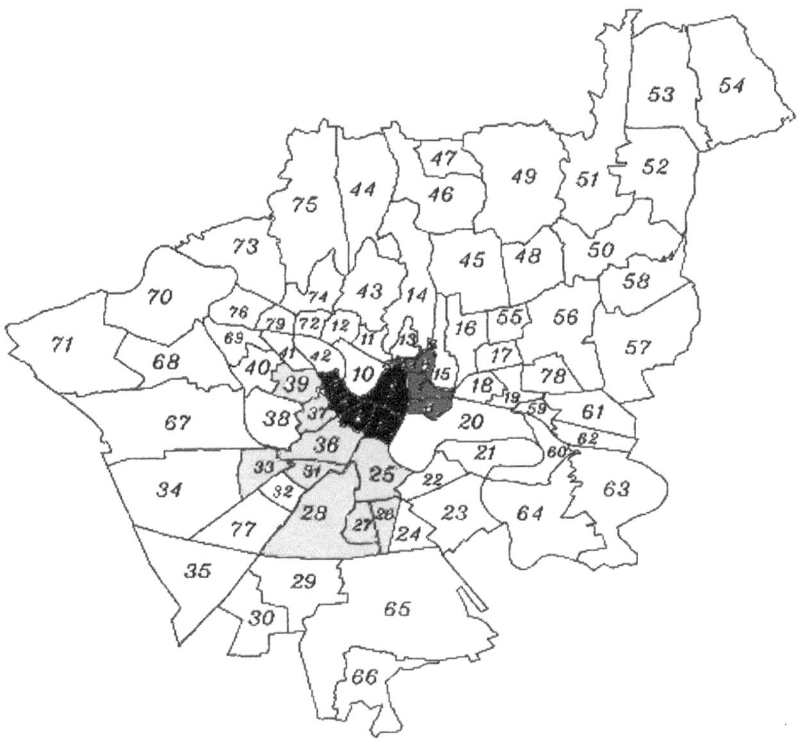

Fig. 3. The Spatial Partition of Verona Municipality in HTZ with the Three Areas of Interest. *Note*: The three areas represented are South Area SA ■ Central City CC ■ Veronetta.

shown in the table, CC and Veronetta exhibit high levels of concentration, which decreased substantially in 2005, both in average and for the extreme values. For instance, in 2000 the concentration of all immigrants groups was, on average, between two and three times larger than the expected one, while this figure lowered significantly in 2005. Although the two sections slowly moved toward a balanced composition in the period considered, this is in contrast to what it happened in SA and in the rest of the city. In SA, the immigrants' concentration grew up, on average, well above the expected values in 2005. This phenomenon is not only driven by reallocation of people living in CC and Veronetta, but also by the shift in the composition of the remaining areas of the city (marked as Other in Table 4)

Table 4. Mean and Max Values for Concentration Statistic for Seven Immigration Groups, by Area and Years.

Group	Central City Area				Veronetta Area			
	2000		2005		2000		2005	
	Mean	Max	Mean	Max	Mean	Max	Mean	Max
Immigrants (total)	1.330	1.944	1.195	1.465	2.742	4.022	1.938	2.992
UE 2001	1.758	2.736	1.540	2.037	2.205	3.735	2.099	3.679
East Europe	1.162	1.637	0.968	1.303	2.286	3.605	1.225	1.715
Africa	0.801	1.310	0.939	1.782	2.516	4.023	1.748	2.807
Asia	1.902	2.221	1.518	2.232	3.054	4.784	2.101	3.138
Latin America	2.119	7.100	1.069	1.579	2.660	3.866	2.381	4.072
Other	2.128	6.315	1.202	1.630	2.556	3.681	2.361	3.817
Group	**South Area**				**Other**			
	2000		2005		2000		2005	
	Mean	Max	Mean	Max	Mean	Max	Mean	Max
Immigrants (total)	1.411	2.305	1.779	2.646	0.821	4.987	0.700	2.497
UE 2001	1.173	1.725	1.207	2.045	0.758	2.302	0.699	3.323
East Europe	1.302	1.998	1.703	2.298	0.838	3.026	0.706	3.108
Africa	1.571	2.938	1.905	3.065	1.038	9.026	0.978	8.179
Asia	1.302	1.820	1.632	2.541	0.496	3.096	0.517	2.716
Latin America	1.286	2.257	1.669	2.651	0.525	3.907	0.487	2.024
Other	1.164	1.997	1.604	2.484	0.572	3.869	0.492	1.950

Notes: The statistics has been computed for each HTZ that is part of the four areas reported. The mean and the max value by area are calculated for years 2000 and 2005.

toward natives' concentration (for the area Other, figures are decreasing and below unit in both 2000 and 2005). Hence, SA is relevant for our analysis because it is an attraction pole for immigrant groups.

The changes in the concentration statistics values are mainly generated by internal flows of natives and immigrant groups as well as by new immigrants' arrivals in the city. Table 5 reports the demographic movements of both Italians and immigrants (separately) for the period 2000–2005, between the four areas previously identified. The table reports in the central block (for both groups) the relative number of movements from one area in 2000 (row) to another area (column) in 2005, computed as a share of the total population that decided to relocate *within* the city. The cells identified by the same area in 2000 (row) and 2005 (column) contains the share of people

Table 5. Natives' and Immigrants' Flows Distinctly from 2000 to 2005 as a Share of Total Flows.

Natives						
Within-City Areas 2000	Within-City Areas 2005					Outside
	Center	Veronetta	South	Other	*Total*	
Center	3.41	0.68	1.54	3.65	*9.29*	4.85
Veronetta	0.67	0.89	0.89	2.46	*4.90*	2.59
South	0.76	0.28	10.52	8.81	*20.36*	10.90
Other	2.00	1.04	5.70	56.72	*65.45*	27.95
Total	*6.84*	*2.88*	*18.64*	*71.64*	*100.00*	*46.29*
Outside	5.60	3.48	13.34	31.28	*53.70*	
Immigrants						
Within-City Areas 2000	Within-City Areas 2005					Outside
	Center	Veronetta	South	Other	*Total*	
Center	1.89	1.08	2.45	5.81	*11.24*	1.09
Veronetta	1.06	0.90	1.41	3.92	*7.30*	1.23
South	1.21	0.44	8.43	14.01	*24.09*	2.69
Other	3.19	1.65	9.07	43.47	*57.37*	4.62
Total	*7.35*	*4.08*	*21.36*	*67.21*	*100.00*	*9.63*
Outside	9.43	5.86	22.45	52.64	*90.38*	

Notes: Figures report the within-city flows of natives and immigrants separately from one area to another one or inside the same area, and are defined as the share (in %) of the total within city movements from 2000 to 2005. Row "Outside" reports movements by 2000 from outside the city into the different areas; column "Outside" movements from the different areas away from the city till 2005. Both values expressed as a percentage share of total outside-city movements.

moving inside the same section. The row and column named "Outside" contain the relative shares of people leaving (by row) and entering (by column) the specified areas of the city, obtained as a fraction of the total of movements to/from *outside* the city. Due to data shortage, we cannot observe whether individuals leave the city definitively or if they decide to move to suburban areas (not considered here), nor we can address the causes (job shifts, the decision to commute, housing decisions and so on). We can, nevertheless, highlight some patterns of within-city movements by comparing the two periods under analysis.

First, a remarkable difference in the dynamic of people moving into/out of the city from abroad depends on their group of nationality. While immigrants are only 5% of the population remaining in the city between 2000 and 2005, the group represents 14% of within-city movers in the same period. More interestingly, immigrants correspond to the 29% of newcomers till 2005 and only 10% of leavers by 2000. Moreover, the shares of Italian leavers and comers are roughly equal in total (54% and 46% respectively) and with respect to areas, while we observe a strong displacement for immigrants: only 9.6% of immigrant movements are due to people leaving the city from 2000 to 2005, while the 90.4% are due to new arrivals, manifesting a strong tendency to spatial stabilization.

Looking at within-city flows, we immediately see that relative movements inside the same area are less sustained for immigrants, denoting a natural tendency to stabilize in the initial space, giving support to the global results of increased exposure to natives as captured by the indices. These results do not translate in a dramatic shift of immigrants from the Veronetta area to SA, but rather in a new composition of the social structure of the areas due to joint location decisions of all groups considered.

Table 6 reports the estimated marginal effects of the census variables considered in our regression analysis on the variability of the concentration statistic, estimated by OLS. Since the dependent variable is a function of simultaneous presence of the group k and $-k$ members in the same section, its variability must be explained jointly considering population from both groups. We use standardized coefficients in order to make marginal effects comparable in magnitude across regressors. The constant terms of each group represent the average population concentration for the reference category living outside the three critical urban subregions: CC, Veronetta, and SA. In this way, we can identify and measure the marginal impact on concentration of family-level differences attributable to groups living in other areas of the city. By controlling for the macroarea of residence identified in the previous analysis (CC, Veronetta, and SA), we account for the unobservable dynamic component of the segregation pattern in the city.

Living in Veronetta has clearly a high positive impact on average concentration, twice as much as the effect of SA. This relation is similar for each group, except for East Europe group. This is mainly due to the incisive presence of the East Europe group in various areas of the city. Differently, the concentration statistics in CC does not vary uniformly between immigrants' groups. Once we control for the effects of other covariates, its trend seems not to differ from what observed in other areas of the city. We immediately notice that the area SA in 2001 does not show a particularly high level of concentration (in fact, the relevance of this area emerges from

Table 6. Regression Results of House and Household Head Characteristics on Concentration Statistic for Six Immigration Groups.

	(1) Immigrants	(2) East Europe	(3) North Africa	(4) Sub Saharan Africa	(5) Asia	(6) Latin America
Area: CC	−0.033	−0.145	−0.497	−0.917	0.588	0.631
	(0.019)*	(0.024)***	(0.041)***	(0.037)***	(0.030)***	(0.084)***
Area: Veronetta	2.055	1.311	1.282	1.571	3.097	2.447
	(0.046)***	(0.034)***	(0.097)***	(0.059)***	(0.060)***	(0.116)***
Area: SA	0.507	0.524	0.400	0.320	0.758	0.656
	(0.010)***	(0.012)***	(0.022)***	(0.021)***	(0.016)***	(0.028)***
House characteristics						
Quality: good	0.041	0.072	0.257	−0.053	0.350	−0.598
	(0.032)	(0.047)	(0.094)***	(0.060)	(0.058)***	(0.080)***
Quality: bad	1.005	1.051	1.730	0.965	0.444	−0.820
	(0.314)***	(0.168)***	(0.228)***	(0.305)***	(0.229)*	(0.126)***
Quality: very bad	0.889	0.547	2.712	−0.443	2.853	−1.059
	(0.244)***	(0.603)	(0.754)***	(0.093)***	(0.663)***	(0.104)***
Age: <1919	0.532	0.379	0.144	0.783	0.755	−0.345
	(0.034)***	(0.039)***	(0.058)**	(0.055)***	(0.067)***	(0.112)***
Age: 1920 – 1945	0.396	0.253	0.489	0.770	0.540	−0.156
	(0.035)***	(0.041)***	(0.069)***	(0.067)***	(0.060)***	(0.127)
Age: 1946 – 1970	0.368	0.292	0.126	0.767	0.512	−0.350
	(0.017)***	(0.023)***	(0.034)***	(0.038)***	(0.030)***	(0.054)***
Age: 1971–1991	−0.009	−0.019	−0.176	0.110	0.089	−0.413
	(0.013)	(0.020)	(0.028)***	(0.022)***	(0.023)***	(0.046)***
Rent	0.125	0.166	0.204	0.309	0.262	0.187
	(0.012)***	(0.013)***	(0.038)***	(0.024)***	(0.017)***	(0.034)***
Housing project	−0.431	−0.348	0.060	−0.569	−0.769	−0.946
	(0.021)***	(0.019)***	(0.043)	(0.061)***	(0.026)***	(0.042)***

Table 6. *(Continued)*

	(1) Immigrants	(2) East Europe	(3) North Africa	(4) Sub Saharan Africa	(5) Asia	(6) Latin America
Immigration group						
East Europe	0.928	–	0.298	0.018	0.158	0.502
	(0.109)***		(0.363)	(0.103)	(0.070)**	(0.170)***
North Africa	2.405	0.094	–	0.308	0.112	−0.040
	(0.383)***	(0.067)		(0.203)	(0.086)	(0.150)
Sub Saharan Africa	2.034	0.242	0.282	–	0.362	0.513
	(0.099)***	(0.053)***	(0.141)**		(0.081)***	(0.131)***
Asia	1.114	0.174	−0.421	0.038	–	0.179
	(0.065)***	(0.059)***	(0.141)***	(0.101)		(0.139)
Latin America	0.441	0.093	−0.274	−0.130	0.201	–
	(0.163)***	(0.177)	(0.260)	(0.267)	(0.273)	
CS average attributes						
% of industrial buildings	1.582	1.198	1.992	3.773	0.538	−1.201
	(0.123)***	(0.114)***	(0.191)***	(0.327)***	(0.145)***	(0.170)***
% of public use buildings	2.139	7.366	−11.874	3.237	8.750	−2.267
	(0.873)**	(0.961)***	(2.425)***	(1.578)**	(0.840)***	(1.968)
Constant	1.145	1.058	1.984	2.123	0.887	1.255
	(0.061)***	(0.056)***	(0.187)***	(0.126)***	(0.070)***	(0.137)***
Observations	109242	109243	109243	109243	109242	109243
R-squared	0.17	0.08	0.05	0.06	0.15	0.03

Notes: Robust standard errors in brackets (***, **, * indicate statistical significance at 1%, 5% and 10% respectively). The benchmark family characteristics are: very good house conservation, age >1991, owner; household head is man, with average education level with unemployed partner. Unit of analysis is household head. Regressions also control for interaction between age and global quality of the house, number of rooms, dimension; family had attributes: sex, age, education, job position, and number of sons.

an intertemporal comparison) but already incorporates some attractiveness components with respect to the reference area.

We also introduce dummy variables for immigration groups in order to capture interaction between groups. Among all immigrants, Africans show a significantly positive effect on the concentration of all other immigrant groups. This result confirms previous findings of a sustained level of interaction of Africans with other immigrants, but less intensive interaction with natives.

In the analysis, we also control for the spatial variability in the typology of buildings. For all groups, the model predicts a significantly positive effect of the share of commercial buildings and a moderately lower, but still positive, effect of the share of schools and community buildings on immigrants concentration. This effect is, nevertheless, negative for the concentration of North Africans, more inclined to live in housing projects (see Table 2). An immediate interpretation is that housing prices in more industrialized areas are likely to be lower than the average price level in the city (even conditional on housing attributes), thus making such residential units attractive for immigrants. Conversely, the lower percentage of commercial buildings in residential areas, jointly with a widespread housing ownership, imply the lower level of concentration in such areas.

The space stratification model posits that household characteristics are good predictor of immigrants' concentration across areas. Our results indicate, for the total immigrants group, that individual characteristics like gender, education, or job position of the family head, have a negligible and statistically insignificant marginal impact on immigrants' concentration variability across spatial units. Moreover, the F-test indicates that the lack of joint significance of marginal effects for total immigrant group cannot be rejected. On the contrary, the joint effect of household head characteristics is significant, when the analysis moves to single immigration groups' concentration patterns. Our interpretation is that single family attributes lose explicative power when we combine together different immigrants' sorting patterns, while they have a consistent joint effect for each immigrant group separately. This fact is surprising if we observe Table 2 and other average statistics. For example, the average immigrant is 20 years younger than the average Italian, explaining why only 15% of immigrants are currently not working. Although the proportion of self-employed is greater for each group of immigrants than it is for Italians, the disproportion is even more sensible looking at employees. Differences in such covariates are significant between immigrants and natives, but they reduce or disappear within immigrants of different groups.

A different picture emerges by looking at house characteristics. We find that housing features, like age, preservation,[12] number of rooms, dimension, presence of a kitchen, have a predominant (and significant) role in explaining the variability of Q_k^j. The patterns, dimensions, and signs of the marginal effects are the ones expected. For example, we expect that houses with more rooms are inhabited by larger families, which are more likely to occur in the native group, as Table 2 reports. As a consequence, an increasing number of rooms are associated with a significant negative effect on immigrants concentration, since a lower number of immigrants are expected in the sections with larger houses. Moreover, living in a housing project significantly decreases expected concentration, since the number of immigrants having access to the program is very limited, compared to natives, and houses are likely to be evenly distributed in the territory. Since prevalently Italian families live in housing projects (incidence is three times higher for Italians than it is for immigrants), it is expected a higher degree of concentrations of natives in those sections were housing project buildings are concentrated. The North Africa groups are an exception: since North Africans have the same access rate of natives to housing projects (2.2% versus 2.3% for the Italian), it is expected that the housing project participation does not lead to significant changes in this group concentration, as reported in Table 6.

Is there a possible new interpretation for these estimation results, and in particular for unusual findings on individual family characteristics? We assert that, in general, it is not the single attribute of a resident family that has the power to explain immigrants' concentration, but rather a combination of different attributes. OLS coefficients show that section averaged estimations lead to nonsignificant marginal effects. This can happen if the aggregation of information by section (we used the mean) does not account for some unobservable relations between variables. In this sense, we can read stereotyping not in terms of single attributes, but rather in terms of households types, each corresponding to a particular combination of attributes. If families sort in space according to their type (rather than according to single attributes), then only a combination of their characteristics may be a good predictor of the level of segregation observed. A similar result is also supported by the study of Bayer et al. (2004) on American data.[13]

We find another interesting issue related to housing characteristics, especially relevant in environments characterized by increasing immigration flows: the concentration of home-ownership matters. For all groups and on a homogeneous scale, we find positive and significant effects of renting on the local concentration of immigrant groups. Looking at the data, we find a disproportionally high share of rented houses in our selected areas, from 40% of SA to more than 50% in Veronetta, double the average value observed in the other areas. As a possible future research issue, we state that areas where renting – and natives' renting – is more common,[14] are good candidates for attracting immigrants. As a policy issue, major integration through other channels than working place or linguistic homogeneity is needed. High polarization in housing property, some opportunistic behavior of renters, and lack of controls leave room for the formation of heterogeneous communities inside the same city environment, transforming some areas in potential traps for immigrants' concentration.

CONCLUSIONS

Census data suggest that immigrants sort themselves in poor-quality housing units with low rate of housing ownership, thus hindering sustained internal mobility within the city. We control for macroareas fixed effect to take into consideration not only the dynamic patterns of immigrants' segregation but also the fixed unobservable characteristics of such areas. We find that characteristics of housing markets have strong predicting power over the concentration of different immigrant groups: ownership and characteristics of the houses' marginal correlation with the CS-level variability of the concentration statistic largely overcome the effect of household characteristics.

The result is a first attempt to relate variability of a concentration statistics, which constitute the basic information exploited in the construction of the segregation curve, with microdata on the characteristics of individuals and houses. A promising direction of research would consist in exploiting the housing market information (prices, rents) to obtain measures of local quality of life and relate them with population groups' relative concentration. Moreover, the study clearly points where the local policy maker should intervene or monitor in an environment characterized by strong immigration flows and rapidly changing immigrants' segregation patterns.

NOTES

1. In recent years, the immigration flow to the city has been sustained: from 2000 to 2011 the share of immigrants almost triplet and currently represents the 13.8% of

the resident population in Verona, compared to a share of 7.5% at national level (ISTAT). Although the demographic balance of the immigrant (foreign) population is still positive in the city (the arrivals over departure rate of registered immigrants is 1.32 in 2010 and the annual immigrants growth rate is 4%), the new flow seems to be directed toward other regions of Italy (where immigrants population grew by 8% in 2010), thus signaling that population congestion phenomena seem to take place in Verona. A proof of that is also confirmed by natives' flow from the city: the natives' net migration flow (relative to overall population) has steadily decreased from 1.2% in 2002 to −0.05% in 2010, while the residents flow to other municipalities has increased from 1.7% in 2002 to 2.3% in 2010. A projection by the local office for immigration studies, CESTIM (Center for Studies on Immigration), reveals that the share will rise to 20% of the total urban population before the year 2020. This feature allows us to treat Verona as a research field where to study immigrant location choices and segregation patterns.

2. See Yinger (1995) for a review of the main empirical results based on audit studies.

3. The *Spatial Assimilation Models* posit that cultural, linguistic, and social differences between immigrants and natives can be good predictors of segregation outcomes observed at the citywide level. The closer is the ability of immigrants to speak the local language and integrate in the labor market, the higher the probability to share the same urban space with the native community. Cultural differences also matter for informal insurance models, which consider segregation as the result of immigrants' cost-minimizing behavior (where costs are mainly related to specific ethnic goods or access to host country-specific information on housing and job opportunities).

4. In recent empirical works on US data, Hoyt and Rosenthal (1997) and Rhode and Strumpf (2003) show the importance of public good provision in determining the sorting paths of different communities, assuming that a racial component is embedded in preferences toward public goods and relying on some sustainable Tiebout's assumptions (i.e., people sort in space according to preferences toward quantity and quality of public goods consumption, spatial heterogeneity in public goods provision, and limited movement costs). Cutler et al. (2008a, 2008b) find significant association between spatial dissimilarity in public transit supply and increasing segregation. Our analysis is unfortunately not related to local public finance, as in the restricted geographical environment under analysis we do not observe significant spatial differences in levels or quality of public goods provision.

5. On average we count 137 individuals and nearly 70 households living in each census section. However, the demographic dimension of the sections is highly variable in the urban space, from 5 to more than 1,000 individuals.

6. The reference is to the system of classification of countries used by World Bank for geographical aggregates. See, for example, "WB, World Development Indicators, 2004."

7. For our empirical analysis based on a-spatial indices, we are forced to impose partitions exogenously and we therefore face two potential problems: the *Modifiable Areal Units Problem (MAUP)* and the so-called *Checkerboard Problem*. The first problem arises since the definition of spatial units of the urban area is imposed exogenously and does not necessarily correspond with a meaningful definition of the urban organizational units. The checkerboard problem arises because, using a-spatial measures, the proximity between neighborhoods is neglected and we

cannot measure spatial correlation between observed group frequencies across sections. In order to verify the robustness of our findings, we compare the results of indices under (the finer) CS or (the coarser) HTZ partitions.

8. Although this may seem a problem, in fact it represents a desirable property, as the statistic is not sensitive to the density of residents and the dimension of the sections considered. In alternative to Q_k^j one could use another location index as the *location quotient* $LQ_k^k := p_k^j/p_k$. However, notice that when the focus of the analysis is on comparisons between sections of the concentration of each group, then for every two sections j and i, the following condition holds: $Q_k^j \geq Q_k^i$ if and only if $LQ_k^j \geq LQ_k^i$. Thus, the two indices convey the same ordinal information. This is not in general the case when we compare different groups k and h belonging to the same section, unless $p_k = p_h$.

9. The Pigou–Dalton Transfer Principle (P7 in Hutchens (2001)) takes place when the distribution of a group k across urban sections is obtained by another through a "regressive transfer" such that, for any two areas i and j with $Q_k^i < Q_k^j$, we move group k members from i to j.

10. We expect that the ranking produced by segregation curves changes when moving from the CS to the HTZ partition, since the coarser HTZ partition is obtained from the finer CS partition by aggregating the CS-level group counts within each HTZ into a single population count associated to the corresponding HTZ. If groups are uniformly distributed within HTZ, this operation preserves the segregation curves (and therefore the ranking of distributions). Otherwise, the ranking may vary according to the compositional similarity of the census sections which belong to the same HTZ.

11. In Fig. 3, a map of the city and the spatial position of the three areas to figure out the dimensions of the space portion considered is given.

12. Interaction between age and preservation is also considered. In fact, we argue that the effect of increasing preservation on the value of a house increases with the age of the building, so we also expect fewer immigrants to live in such kinds of houses. Though we still find positive but decreasing effects of both condition and age on concentration, the interaction of the two variables gives significantly negative marginal effects for all groups.

13. Using micro data at family level, the authors find that *together* income, education, language, and immigration status explain high shares of different immigrant groups' segregation, whereas these variables have a much lower explanatory power for race-based segregation phenomena. We suggest that the spatial stratification assumption must be reformulated in the immigration framework by incorporating the role of family types.

14. For example, in SA area 40% of Italians live in a rented house, though this percentage decreases dramatically to 24% in the rest of the city.

ACKNOWLEDGMENTS

I would like to thank John Bishop, Eugenio Peluso, Claudio Zoli, and an anonymous referee for extremely valuable insights. This paper also benefitted from the comments of the participants to the fourth ECINEQ

Meeting in Catania and the IT2009 Winter School (Canazei). The financial support from the Università Italo-Francese (UIF/UFI), Bando Vinci 2010, is kindly acknowledged. All errors remain mine.

REFERENCES

Bayer, P., McMillan, R., & Rueben, K. S. (2004). What drives racial segregation? New evidence using Census microdata. *Journal of Urban Economics*, *56*(3), 514–535.

Charles, C. (2003). The dynamics of racial residential segregation. *Annual Review of Sociology*, *29*, 167–207.

Cutler, D. M., Glaeser, E. L., & Vigdor, J. L. (2008a). Is the meting pot still hot? Explaining the resurgence of immigrant segregation. *The Review of Economics and Statistics*, *90*, 478–497.

Cutler, D. M., Glaeser, E. L., & Vigdor, J. L. (2008b). When are ghettos bad? Lessons from immigrant segregation in the United States. *Journal of Urban Economics*, *63*(3), 759–774.

Duncan, O. D., & Duncan, B. (1955). A methodological analysis of segregation indexes. *American Sociological Review*, *20*(2), 210–217.

Flückiger, Y., & Silber, J. (1999). *The measurement of segregation in the labour force*. Heidelberg: Physica-Verlag.

Hoyt, W. H., & Rosenthal, S. S. (1997). Housold location and tiebout: Do famlilies sort according to preferences for local amenities? *Journal of Urban Economics*, *42*, 159–178.

Hutchens, R. M. (1991). Segregation curves, Lorenz curves, and inequality in the distribution of people across occupations. *Mathematical Social Sciences*, *21*(1), 31–51.

Hutchens, R. M. (2001). Numerical measures of segregation: Desirable properties and their implications. *Mathematical Social Sciences*, *42*(1), 13–29.

Massey, D., & Denton, N. (1988). The dimensions of residential segregation. *Social Forces*, *67*(2), 281–315.

Reardon, S. F., & Firebaugh, G. (2002). Measures of multigroup segregation. *Sociological Methodology*, *32*, 33–67.

Reardon, S. F., & O'Sullivan, D. (2004). Measures of spatial segregation. *Sociological Methodology*, *34*(1), 121–162.

Rhode, P. W., & Strumpf, K. S. (2003). Assessing the importance of Tiebout sorting: Local heterogeneity from 1850 to 1990. *The American Economic Review*, *93*(5), 1648–1677.

Saiz, A., & Wachter, S. (2011). Immigration and the neighborhood. *American Economic Journal: Economic Policy*, *3*(2), 169–188.

Yinger, J. (1995). *Closed doors, opportunities lost: The continuing costs of housing discrimination*. New York, NY: Russel Sage Found.

CHAPTER 5

EQUAL-EQUIVALENTS FOR INEQUALITY, WELFARE, AND LIBERTY: CONCEPTS AND POLICY

Serge Kolm

ABSTRACT

The concepts of the "equal-equivalents" permit the definition of one-dimensional and multidimensional inequalities, of individual "welfare" (the same function for all individuals) and, as a result, of classical inequality properties and of the optimal allocation in "macrojustice" (optimum income taxation and transfers, amounting in particular to equal liberty of choice in different domains).

SUMMARY

If an equality is the object of moral judgment – for instance, it could be an injustice – comparisons and measures of this inequality may be derived from an overall evaluation of the social situation. Two characteristics of this judgment are relevant. First, the judgment often takes the form of an ordering, for instance with a maximand function. Then, indexes of inequality can be derived from comparisons between averages and "equal-equivalents" (Kolm, 1966b), that is individual allocations such that, if every "individual"

Inequality, Mobility and Segregation: Essays in Honor of Jacques Silber
Research on Economic Inequality, Volume 20, 117–134

ISSN: 1049-2585/doi:10.1108/S1049-2585(2012)0000020008

had the same, the overall allocation would be as good as the one under consideration. For multidimensional inequalities in bundles of quantities of several goods, the equal-equivalent allocations are those of the "equal-equivalent manifold." The second aspect refers to the "substance" that motivates the judgment. This substance often refers to the concept of welfare or of freedom. "Welfare," a descent from classical utilitarianism, was a common reference in economics and in political philosophy. In 1971, Rawls argued both that this criterion is never used in actual social choices of "social justice" ("macrojustice") and that it should not be used there. However, a closer analysis shows that what is convincingly objected to is not the reference to individuals' happiness but only inter-individual *differences* in hedonic capacities (capacities to enjoy) and in tastes. Actually, the concept of individual *welfare* is commonly used in distributive judgments, with the implicit (or explicit) assumption that an individual's welfare is a concave function of this individual consumption, the same function for all. The classical technical concept is the individual's "utility function." The individual utility functions can be cleaned of inter-individual differences in hedonic capacities and tastes in order to provide the relevant individual welfare function thanks to the basic concept of the "equal-equivalent utility function." This permits both to make sense of classical properties of inequality analysis and to determine the optimum macrojustice allocation, and income transfers, taxes, and subsidies. The result (ELIE for equal-labor income equalization) has a number of ethically and logically meaningful definitions and properties, including equal liberty of choice (with different domains). This outcome divides individual hedonic and productive or earning capacities into two parts, one that is self-owned and the other the benefits from which in welfare or income are equally distributed.

SITUATION

Welfare?

If some inequality is injustice, comparisons and measures of this inequality can be derived from an overall social ethical evaluation. From social metaethics, this has two consequences:

1. A standard such evaluation, particularly in economics, is *classical welfarism*: max $W[\{u_i(x_i)\}]$. This implies two structures:
   (a) It is an *ordering*, with a maximand $U\{x_i\} = U(X)$. $U[\{x_i\}]$ is written as $U\{x_i\}$.

(b) It uses "*welfare*," u_i : what does this mean?

The validity of this principle raised the central modern debate. John Rawls writes in 1971 that it is never used in actual choices and that it should not be used.

If not, which value should we use? Is it freedom?

2. Social ethics demands that its principles be judged according to *all their aspects*: all their properties, axioms, and consequences (see, for instance, Plato's "dialectics" in *Republic* or Rawls' "reflective equilibrium" for applications).

Notations

There are n comparable "individuals" (more generally "justiciables") indexed by i. An "allocation" for i is denoted as $x_i \in D$ $\{x_i\} = X \in D^n$ Particular cases $D = \Re^m$.

case $m = 1$	$x_i = y_i$	income
$m > 1$	multi dimensional inequality	
$m = 2$	important for "optimum income tax":	
$x_i = y_i$,	ℓ_i *or*	$\lambda_i = 1 - \ell_i$
disposable imcome	labor	leisure

Domains of Justice

(1) *Levels of justice*
- *Macrojustice*: overall income distribution from main social resources: main ones are human (capacities) for production or earning and for consumption or enjoyment. Rawls calls his topic: "social justice," which is macrojustice (he says "macro" and "not micro").
- *Microjustice*: multifarious situations, specific for circumstances, goods, and people.
- *Mesojustice*: important goods that concern everybody, for example, health and education are mostly "being goods" or "ontological goods," which contrast with "having goods" (and "doing goods," which are means, freedoms).

(2) *"Spheres of justice"*: Max Weber (1962) says that people want equality for each specific type of good. This induces Michael Walzer's (1983) concept of "spheres of justice." He forgets that one sphere is particularly large: income in a market setting. "Spheres" are separated by lack of

substitutability or compensatability: what is the income value of living one year longer? Health and education are largely "sphered goods."
Notations (continuation)

$$e = n\text{-duplication} : e\alpha = \alpha, \alpha, \alpha \ldots \alpha \quad n \text{ times}$$
$$X = ex\text{: equal allocations}(x_i = x, \forall i)$$
$$x_i \in P_i = P \subset D$$
$$X = \{x_i\} \in Q \subset \Pi P_i = P^n \subset D^n$$
$$q = \{x\text{: } ex \in \mathrm{Q}\} \text{ possible equalities}$$

Multi-meaning properties (continuation)

Most famous example: the twenty or so mathematically equivalent properties, one of which is the "transfer principle" (T.P.) for $m = 1$ (y).

$n = 2$: y' is "inclusion more equal" than y when $[y'_1, y'_2] \subset [y_1, y_2] \Rightarrow$ progressive transfers (P.T.) inclusion-reduce inequality.

$n > 2$: small P.T. inclusion-increase pairwise inequalities between the lower, receiving income and other incomes equal and lower, and between the higher, yielding income and other incomes as high and higher: The overall effect on inequality is ambiguous. There are two solutions.

1. Consider other properties for $n \geq 2$ that become the T.P. for $n = 2$ Notably:
   (1) *Concentration* (linear uniform concentration toward the mean):

$$y'_i = ay_i + (1 - a)\bar{y} \quad a \in [0, 1[$$

   (2) (Balanced bi-) *Truncations* $y'_i = a$ if $y_i \leq a$, b if $y_i \geq b$, y_i if $a < y_i < b$, with $a \leq b$ and $\Sigma y'_i = \Sigma y_i$.
2. Consider other properties equivalent to a sequence of P.T. in particular: welfare:

$$\text{compare } \Sigma u(y_i) \text{ for all concave } u \qquad (1)$$

Meaning?
$\Sigma u_i(y_i) =$ utilitarianism. But what is u without i?

There are two classical answers, both based on uncertainty and von Neumann-Morgenstern (VNM) theory, but mistakenly applied.

(1) *Lerner (repeated by Leontief, Samuelson, and Sen at the Biarritz conference)*: u_i uncertain, stochastic $\tilde{u}_i$ i.i.d. $E\tilde{u}_i = u$.
But VNM theory says: max $EF(\Sigma\tilde{u}_i)$, for some function F, which has no reason to be an affine function.

(2) *Allocation original position*: Any individual with a concave $u(y)$ receives any of the actual y_i with equal probabilities. $Eu(y) = (1/n)\Sigma u(y_i)$

But

(a) VNM theory says that if u = welfare, the risk-relevant utility is not u but $v = f[u(y)]$ for some f: $f' > 0$.

$v' = f'u'$.
$v'' = f'u'' + f''u'$: u concave does not imply v concave.

(b) Theories of original position take individual evaluation in uncertainty as social ethical value. But the social ethical value refers to social ethics, society, and others (not egoism in uncertainty).

Condition (1) assumes: $\exists$ meaningful function $u(y)$ increasing concave, same for all individuals. This would denote "individual welfare." Meaning? Relation with the u_i?

ORDERING, EQUAL-EQUIVALENTS

$U(X)$ maximand

Denote $U(ex) = V(x)$

$\bar{x} = (1/n)\Sigma xi \quad \text{if } D = \Re^m$ average

define $\bar{\bar{x}}$: $U(X) = V(\bar{\bar{x}}) = U(e\bar{\bar{x}})$ equal-equivalent (2)

Case $D = \Re$: y_i income. U increasing: $\bar{\bar{y}}$ is well defined (Fig. 1).
Inequality indexes I from $\bar{y}$ and $\bar{\bar{y}}$. Six are useful for specific questions:

$$\underset{\text{absolute}}{I^a = \bar{y} - \bar{\bar{y}}}, \quad \underset{\text{relative}}{I^Y = I^a/\bar{y}}, \quad \underset{\text{total}}{I^t = nI^a}, \quad \underset{\text{yield}}{\eta = \bar{y}/\bar{\bar{y}} = 1 - I^r},$$

$$\underset{\text{unit cost}}{\gamma = \bar{y}/\bar{\bar{y}} = 1/\eta}, \quad \underset{\text{excess unit cost, unit loss}}{I^a/\bar{\bar{y}} = \gamma - 1}$$

Case $D = \Re^m$: $m > 1$ multidimensional. x_i^j = dimension (e.g., quantity) j for individual i. $x_i = \{x_i^j\}_i$ (a m-vector).

(Eq. (2)): $\bar{\bar{x}} \in E$ *equal-equivalent manifold* ((m–1) – manifold, hypersurface) (Fig. 2).

Measures of multidimensional inequality

$U(X) = V[(1 - I)\bar{x}]$ overall relative inequality.
$U(X) = V(\bar{x} - aJ_a)$ absolute. Case $a = \bar{x}$: $J_{\bar{x}} = I$.

$$a \in \Re^m \text{ case } a \in \Re \text{ numéraire}$$

Choice of vector a: importance of goods; and social ethical choice, dialogue, etc. as for coefficients of a price index.

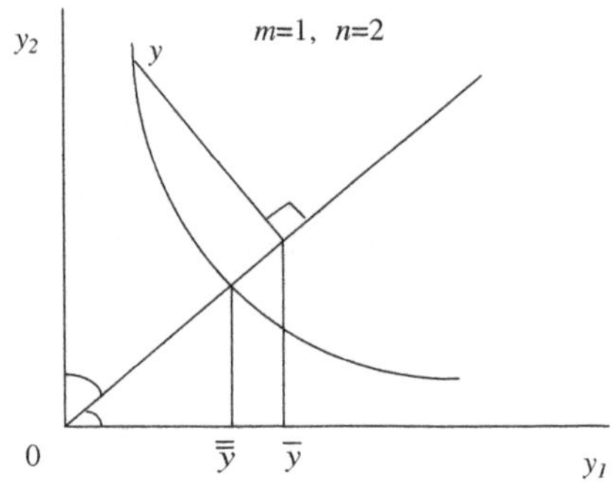

Fig. 1. One-Dimensional Inequality.

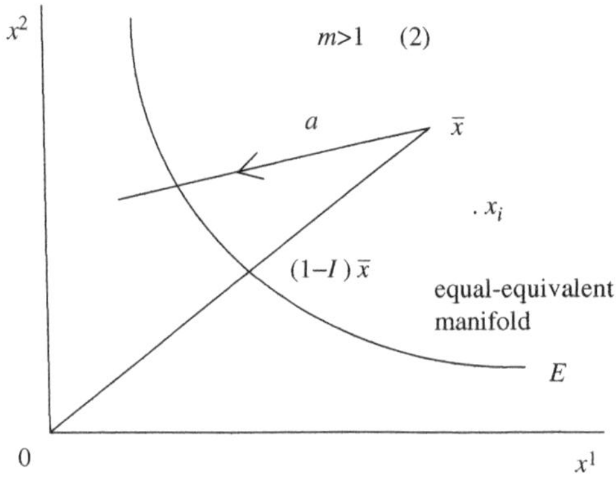

Fig. 2. Multidimensional Inequality.

WELFARE Case $U(X) = W[\{u_i(x_i)\}]$

The Ethical Value of "Welfarism"

Our moral intuition about the relevance of the criterion of "welfare" can be tested by a few questions.

(1) *Macrojustice, income tax.* Should you pay a higher income tax than someone else because she likes dollars more than you do, notably those taken away and one is utilitarian, or less than you do, notably the remaining ones and one is egalitarian (in utility)? Should you pay more or less than the other because the other (or you) has a cheerful character (which may lead one to enjoy a euro more or to regret its absence less – opposite effects again)? Or are these psychological characteristics or differences thought to be irrelevant for this issue, that is, people would be deemed entitled to their benefits and accountable for their shortcomings (as enforcing money transfers or modulating the income tax to compensate for differences in physical beauty is neither practiced nor – it seems – advocated)?
(2) *Tastes.* Should you finance someone else's beverage because she only likes expensive wines? This classical "expensive tastes" argument extends in two ways. The other person may have to compensate you for your inability to experience such delicate gastronomic pleasures. And utilitarians meet "cheap tastes": should you finance the other's beverage because she likes cheap beer and hence generates low-cost utility? Differences in tastes raising "different kinds of problems" are precisely the reason Mirrlees gives in 1971 for taking identical individual utility functions for determining the income tax.
(3) *Desires.* Rawls (1982) takes up still another possible meaning of "utility" when he notes that, for "social justice" (the present macrojustice), "Desires and wants, however intense, are not by themselves reasons in matters of justice. The fact that we have a compelling desire does not argue for its satisfaction any more than the strength of a conviction argues for its truth."
(4) *Liberal, earning.* Finally, since income is mostly earned, should I take the 10 dollars you just earned because I like them more than you do (or more than you dislike the labor with which you earned them)?

From reflexions of the type of the first ones, Rawls concludes that individual utility functions $u_i(\ )$ are irrelevant for macrojustice ("social justice"). However, what these questions actually show is that what is irrelevant for macrojustice are the *differences* in the individual functions $u_i(\ )$ rather than these functions themselves.

Therefore, if a social ethic, and in particular a conception of distributive justice, wants to be "welfarist," it has to consider a concept of inter-individually comparable individual "welfare." This has to be defined by derivation from individual "utility functions" by erasing differences in these functions. These differences are then due to other causes of individual "utility" or preferences, in particular the differences in capacities to enjoy and in tastes that the above questions have suggested to be morally irrelevant for the evaluation of the distributions under consideration. The theory of the "equal-equivalent utility function" provides the technical solution to this problem and, hence, the required definition of the "individual welfare."

The Equal-Equivalent Utility Function

Consider an equal allocation *ex*.

$$\text{Define function } u(x) \text{ by: } W\{u_i(x)\} = W[eu(x)] = \underset{\text{def of } w}{w[u(x)]} \qquad (3)$$

W increasing $\Rightarrow u(x)$ is well defined.
u is the *equal-equivalent utility function.*

u is utility minus specific	hedonic capacities $u_i(\ )$ and tastes	which are averaged away, thanks to W as averaging function.

It is *individual "welfare," the same function for all.*

$$(3) \Rightarrow u(x) = w^{-1} \circ W\{u_i(x)\} \qquad (3')$$

For balance, W has to be symmetrical. This requires that the u_i are comparable by $>$ or $=$ (They are "fundamental utility," at least co-ordinal).

This u, which gives individuals' $u(x_i)$, which can be compared and evaluated by the social ethical function W and are "in between" utilities u_i and goods or income x_i, also seems to be a proper definition of the *midfare* that Cohen (1989) seeks as the ethically relevant "currency of justice."

Two Equal-Equivalent Allocations

Therefore, there are two possible definitions of *equal-equivalent allocations* with utilities or welfares.

$$\begin{array}{lllll} & \text{def } \bar{\bar{x}} & \text{def } u & & \\ W\{u_i(x_i)\} = & W\{u_i(\bar{\bar{x}}_u)\} = & W[eu(\bar{\bar{x}}_u)] & \bar{\bar{x}}_u \in E_u & \text{utility} \\ W\{u(x_i)\} = & W[eu(\bar{\bar{x}}_w)] = & W\{u_i(\bar{\bar{x}}_w)\} & \bar{\bar{x}}_w \in E_w & \text{welfare} \end{array}$$

Cases $D = \Re^m$.

Case $m = 1$: $\bar{\bar{y}}_u$ and $\bar{\bar{y}}_w \Rightarrow$ 6 more indices of inequality I_w ...

Case $m > 1$ (Fig. 3).

E_u and E_w are both iso-u loci $\Rightarrow$ hence they do not intersect. For all defined I, they provide the same ranking.

Comparison: $W\{u_i(x_i)\} > W\{u(x_i)\}$ if there is a positive correlation between allocations and taste preferences.

There are two limiting forms

equity-"no-envy"	$u_i(x_i) \geq u_i(x_j), \forall i, j$	|
		| Plus 1 strict>
"adequacy"	$u_i(x_i) \geq u_j(x_i), \forall i, j$	|

Case $m = 1$, $\bar{\bar{y}}_w < \bar{\bar{y}}_u$. $I_w > I_u$ for I^a, I^r, I^t, η.

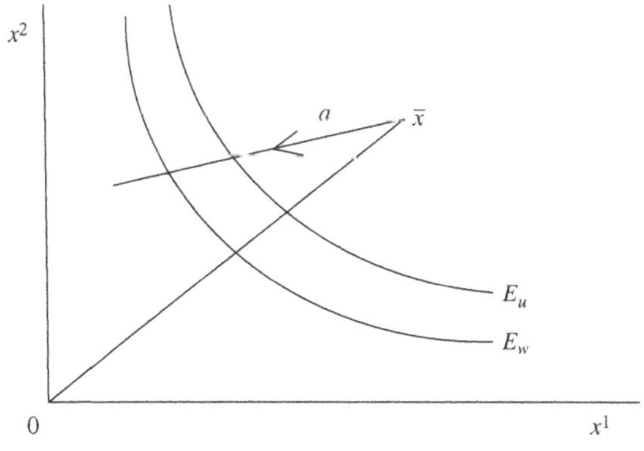

Fig. 3. The Two Equal-Equivalent Manifolds.

From Eq. (3): u_i increasing in x^k $\forall i \Rightarrow$ idem u.

The equal-equivalent utility function will be put here to two uses: define the welfarist "equivalent property" and, more importantly, determine the optimum distribution in macrojustice.

The Welfarist "Equivalent Property"

Consider the case $W=\Sigma$ (utilitarianism),

$$W\{u_i(x)\} = nu(x), u = (1/n)\Sigma u_i$$

$$W\{u(x_i)\} = \Sigma u(x_i) = (1/n)\Sigma_{i,j} u_i(x_j)$$

For the case $x_i = y_i$, $D = \Re$ $(m=1)$

u_i concave $\forall i \Rightarrow u$ concave. Information u_i concave $\forall i$, hence u concave. *For* $\forall$ u concave: this is the property.

MACROJUSTICE

A case $m = 2 : x_i = y_i$, ℓ_i or $\lambda_i = 1 - \ell_i$. Only one good is transferable, y.
labour leisure

Classical "optimum income tax" theory uses max W $\{u(x_i)\}$ with concave functions.

(Mirrlees: "u because differences in tastes are irrelevant for this issue.")

This amounts to minimize a bidimensional inequality.

$$W\{u(x_i)\} < W[en^{-1}\Sigma u(x_i)]$$

$$W\{u(x_i)\} \leq W[en^{-1}\Sigma u(x_i)] < W[en^{-1}u(\bar{x})]$$

= for case Σ
(utilitarianism)

The ethical end-value is the equalizand (that which should ideally be equalized). Hence this is x_i rather than $u(x_i)$ (equal $x_i \Rightarrow$ equal $u(x_i)$, not converse).

Hence the "first-best" is equal x_i.

Rawls' ideal is equality in "primary goods"

His economic primary goods are in 1971: y_i
in 1974 (post Musgrave (1974)):
2: y_i and λ_i.

Consider equal x_i. But which equal allocation?

$$x_i = x, \forall_i$$
$$W\{u_i(x)\} = w \circ u(x). \quad \text{Max } W \Leftrightarrow \text{Max } u.$$

Note $y_i = y, \ell_i = \ell, \forall i.$ $\max u(y, \ell)$ |
constraint $\Sigma y_i = \Sigma \ell_i w_i \Rightarrow y = \ell \bar{w}$ | $\ell = k$
| $\Rightarrow$ K(see Fig. 4)
| $y = k\bar{w}$

This best egalitarian solution has *three vices*:

there is no | freedom: each i prefers other (y_i, ℓ_i) to K
| Pareto-efficiency: idem.
| Partial self-ownership (see question 4 of Section The ethical value of welfarism).

Remedy to all these three issues: free (action, exchange, labor) from K (Fig. 4).

i chooses ℓ_i, earns extra income $(\ell_i - k)w_i$ (if $\ell_i > k$, see below), untaxed.

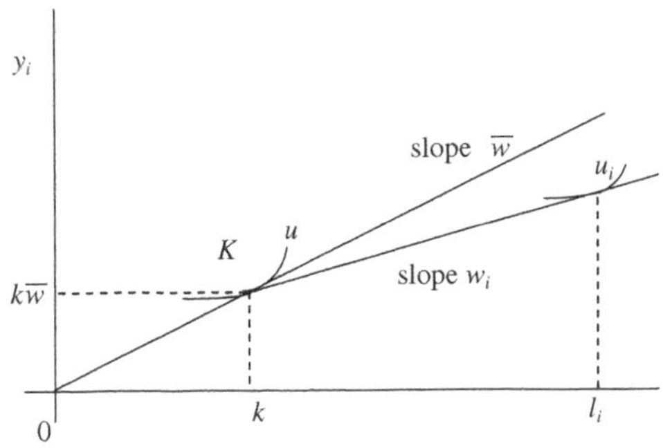

Fig. 4. Equal-Labor Income Equalization.

This result has the following meanings, structures and properties:

1. *The two-part income*

$$yi = k\bar{w} \quad + \quad (\ell_i - k)w_i \tag{4}$$

egalitarian (equal income for equal labour) — liberal

according to: *desert* — *merit* (labor and capacity w_i).

2.

$$y_i = w_i\ell_i \quad + \quad k \cdot (\bar{w} - w_i) \tag{4'}$$

earned — transfers $= t_i = -T_i$

3. t_i = ELIE (Equal-Labour Income Equalization).

4. Policy not based on ℓ_i: *no disincentive effect*. Pareto-efficient.

5. = each yields to each other the product of the same labor $(k/n)w_i$: *general equal-labor reciprocity*.
Promotes reciprocitarian sentiments (voluntary).

6. *Productivity-progressive transfers: Ea*ch *i* yields to each *j* less productive ($w_j < w_i$) the same fraction of the difference in productivities, (k/n) $(w_i - w_j)$.

7. = *equal universal basic income* ($k\bar{w}$) *financed by an equal labor* (k) *of each*.

8. *Total income*: earned plus leisure.

value of leisure: $w_i\lambda_i$ From (Eq. (4′)) (with $l_i + \lambda_i = 1$),

$$Y_i = y_i + w_i\lambda_i = (1-k)w_i + k\bar{w} = P_i \underset{\text{def}}{=} P(1, w_i) \tag{5}$$

(equal uniform) *concentration* (to the mean) of total productivities. (generalizable transfer principle).

9. Eq. (5): $P_i = P(1, w_i)$ = price index of prices of income/goods (1) and labor/leisure (w_i) with coefficients $k\bar{w}$ and (1–k).
From (Eq. (5)), Y_i / P_i is the same for all i.
This means equal real income, purchasing power, freedom of choice.

10. Also *equal free exchange* (labor) *from an equal allocation* (K).
Note: $k \leq \ell_i$, $\forall i$.
(1) *De facto*: actual redistributions produce the same decrease in inequality as ELIE with k from 1 (US) to 2 (Scandinavia) days/week.
(2) *Ethics*: if $k > \ell_i$, $k - \ell_i$ is a part of leisure

- taxed at value of labor if $w_i > \bar{w}$: is rejected;
- receiving wage complement $w_i - \bar{w}$ for hours that produce no wage if $w_i < \bar{w}$: is absurd.

If involuntary unemployment: there is an extension of the theory (Kolm, 2004).

11. There is a minimum income $k\bar{w}$ (from Eq. (4)).

Implementation

(1) *Incentive compatible*

i chooses type and amount of labor ℓ_i. Capacity w_i = most remunerative possible labor.

max $u_i(y_i, \ell_i)$ on (Eq. (4)) $\Rightarrow$ chooses the highest w_i for $\ell_i - k > 0$.

This reveals productive capacities.

(2) wage labor = 9/10 of labor in modern economies.

Firms cannot hide $\{w_i\}$.

(3) Tax w_i. For instance: exempt overtime income over rather low benchmark.

$$T_i = k \cdot (w_i - \bar{w}) = (k/\ell^o)w_i\ell^o - k\bar{w}$$

Applied in France since 2007. ℓ^o = 35 hours/week or idem in days/year for executives. And a uniform tax rebate. (And for partial labor ℓ_i: exempt "supplementary hours" from the labor contract).

Actually, an individual productivity is due in part to her natural capacities and to education, which comes from her own effort, her family effort and influence, and public education. In the detailed analysis (Kolm, 2004), the individual learning effort is a part of her labor, public education financed by a tax on earned income is distributionally neutral, and the given resources w_i reduce to natural talents and family influence and support.

CONCLUSION

The Four Nodes of Income Justice

Fig. 5 summarizes the main stages and reasons of the foregoing discussion.

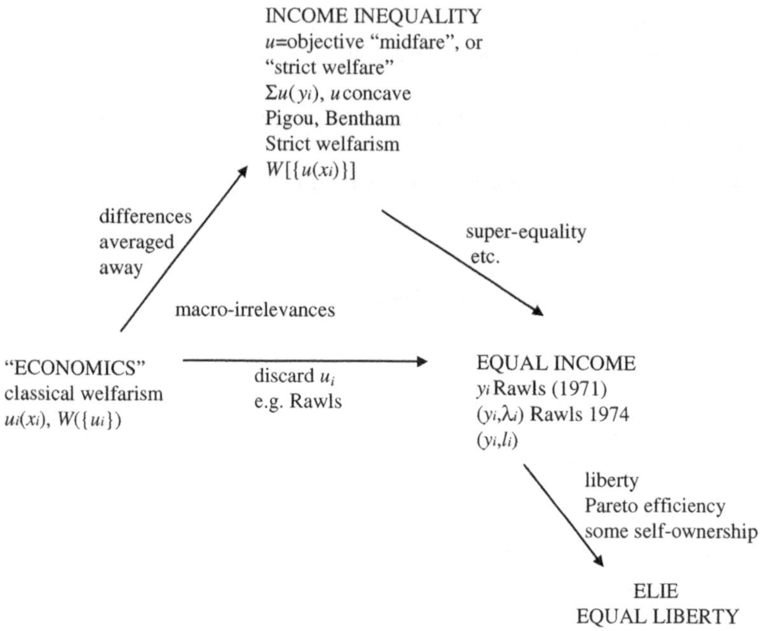

Fig. 5. The Four Nodes of Income Justice.

Distribution of Benefits from Capacities: The Entitlement-Accountability Cut

The main resources of a society are the human resources or *capacities* of its members. They are of two kinds and each piece or the benefits from it can be allocated according to two alternative principles. There are the *productive* or *earning capacities*, of value w_i for individual i, and which produce income (and consumption). And there are the *hedonic capacities*, individuals' capacities to enjoy, represented by the utility functions $u_i(\ )$ for each individual i. Since a capacity is held by an individual, its holder, a piece of it or the benefit from this piece can be a priori allocated to its holder who then is *entitled* to this piece or benefit, and also *ipso facto* is *accountable* for any corresponding shortcoming of this capacity. This is *self-ownership*. The other *prima facie* alternative is *equal sharing* of this benefit (and of this accountability) between the members of the society, or some criterion referring to some tangible equality.

The great classical ethical theories of distributive justice define themselves along these lines (Fig. 6). *Classical liberalism* is *full self-ownership* of all capacities, productive and hedonic. Classical welfarism takes as end-values individuals' happiness, say the u_i , by maximizing some aggregate "social welfare function" $W(\{u_i\})$. This can be some ideal highest equality in the u_i, perhaps maximin or leximin in the u_i, or the effect of a symmetrical strictly quasi-concave (or concave) function W. This objective is the aim of the policy allocating the allocations x_i. Rawls (1971), Dworkin (1981), and others deny relevance of the utility functions $u_i(x_i)$ in this process. Rawls's ideal is a basic equality in "primary goods," with, in 1971, income as the economic primary good and a second-best egalitarian solution as $\text{maxmin}_i\ y_i$ (the "difference principle"). This implies self-ownership for hedonic capacities.

The obtained ELIE solution cuts across both types of capacities for defining the domains of self-ownership and equal allocation. These two cuts correspond to one another. Labor k is a fraction of productive or earning capacities if total time is measured as 1. The corresponding products are equally shared by the ELIE policy. The complement $1-k$ is self-owned, but individuals i who freely choose to work ℓ_i do not put all this resource to earning use if $\ell_i < 1$ ($\lambda_i > 0$); the rest is leisure λ_i. As for the hedonic part, welfare u only is the same function for all, and the individuals are entitled to or accountable for its difference with their own utility functions u_i. These two capacity "cuts" are related since coefficient or equalization labor k has been obtained from the maximization of $u(\ell\bar{w}, \ell)$ for ℓ. Since function $W(\{u_i\})$ determines the equal-equivalent utility function u, it determines the value of k. Classical liberalism is ELIE with $k=0$. However, this simple and richly meaningful index k of the policy is bound to be a direct object of the social ethical and political debate and choice.

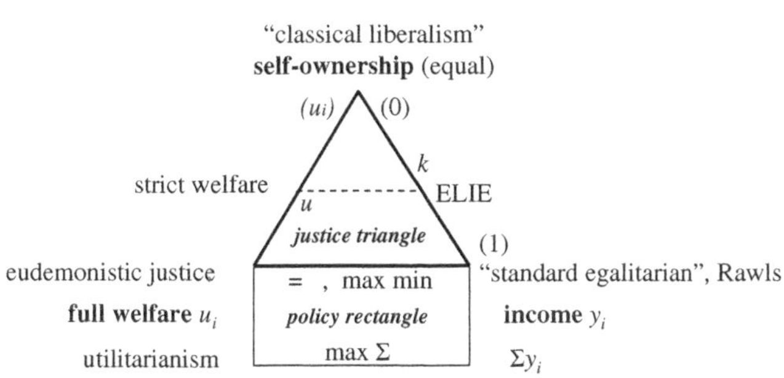

Fig. 6. The Justice Triangle.

In addition to this sharing of the various capacities, the policy requires a principle concerning the comparison and aggregation of the chosen individual end-values (for instance, the u_i or the y_i). Equality in these variables is a possibility, with the highest possible equal value. When equality is not possible or is dominated by unequal sets of these variables, which give more to each i, the second-best egalitarian solution can be maximin or leximin (for instance, Rawls' "difference principle" for incomes, or "practical justice" as leximin in comparable u_i – "fundamental utility" – in *Justice and Equity* (Kolm, 1971). The solution can be a maximand $W(\{u_i\})$ or $M(\{y_i\})$, with an egalitarian preference for symmetrical concave functions. The case opposite to equality is the highest sum, Σu_i (utilitarianism) or Σy_i (highest social income). Then, equality refers to comparisons of variations of the variables (see Fig. 6).

This result concerns macrojustice. In addition, there can be policies – including solidaristic public transfers, social insurances, and free or controlled ordinary insurances – for issues of mesojustice (notably health care and education) and microjustice for exceptional needs, situations, or accidents.

Finally, the concept of equal-equivalence, applied to any allocation, notably one-dimensional or multidimensional, or to utility functions, permits one to derive, from the overall ethical evaluation, comparisons and measures of the ethical wrongness of inequality – notably of its injustice –, the morally relevant interpersonally comparable concept of "welfare," and the general meaning-rich structure of optimum income distribution, transfers, and taxation.

The obtained rational ethical equalities are bound to be morally accepted or required as just by all citizens, thus permitting a society of peace, good social relations, and efficient cooperation.

REFERENCES

Cohen, G. A. (1989). On the currency of egalitarian justice. *Ethics*, *99*, 906–944.

Dworkin, R. (1981). What is equality? Part I: Equality of welfare; Part II: Equality of resources. *Philosophy and Public Affairs*, *10*, 185–246, 283–345.

Kolm, S.-Ch. (1966b). *The optimal production of social justice*. In H. Guitton & J. Margolis (Eds.), Proceedings of the International Economic Association Conference on Public Economics, Biarritz. Economie Publique (1968) (pp. 109–177), Paris: CNRS; Public Economics (1969) (pp. 145–200), London: Macmillan. Reprinted in Landmark Papers in

General Equilibrium Theory, Social Choice and Welfare. The Foundations of 20th Century Economics, selected by K.J. Arrow and G. Debreu (2001), Edward Elgar, Cheltenham, pp. 606–663.
Kolm, S.-Ch. (1972[1971]). *Justice et Equité* [*Justice and equity* (1997). Cambridge, MA: MIT Press]. Paris: Cepremap (Reprinted Paris: CNRS).
Kolm, S.-Ch. (2004). *Macrojustice, the political economy of fairness*. New York, NY: Cambridge University Press.
Mirrlees, J. (1971). An exploration in the theory of optimum income taxation. *Review of Economic Studies*, *38*, 175–208.
Rawls, J. (1971[1999]). *A theory of justice* (Revised ed.), Cambridge, MA: Harvard University Press.
Rawls, J. (1982). Social unity and primary goods. In A. Sen & B. Williams (Eds.), *Utilitarianism and beyond* (pp. 159–185). Cambridge, MA: Cambridge University Press.
Walzer, M. (1983). *Spheres of justice*. Oxford: Blackwell.
Weber, M. (1962). *Basic concepts in sociology*. New York, NY: Citadel Press.

FURTHER READING

Atkinson, A. B. (1995). *Public economics in action: The basic income/flat tax proposal*. Oxford: Oxford University Press.
Bentham, J. (1961[1789]). An introduction to the principles of morals and legislation. New York, NY: Delphin Books.
Bourguignon, F., & Spadaro, A. (2008). *Tax-benefit revealed social preferences*. Working Paper No. 2008-37, PSE, Paris.
Dasgupta, P., & Hammond, P. J. (1980). Fully progressive taxation. *Journal of Public Economics*, *13*, 141–154.
Fleurbaey, M., Salles, M., & Weymark, J. A. (2011). *Social ethics and normative economics. Essays in Honour of Serge-Christophe Kolm*. Heidelberg: Springer.
Hicks, J. (1959). *Essays in world economy*. Oxford: Basil Blackwell.
Kolm, S.-Ch. (1966a). *Les Choix Financiers et Monétaires (Théories et Techniques Modernes)*. Paris: Dunod.
Kolm, S.-Ch. (1974). Sur les conséquences économiques des principes de justice et de justice pratique. *Revue d'Economie Politique*, *84*(1), 80–107.
Kolm, S.-Ch. (1996). *Modern theories of justice*. Cambridge, MA: MIT Press.
Kolm, S. Ch. (1999). Rational foundations of income inequality measurement. In J. Silber (Ed.), *Handbook of income inequality measurement* (pp. 19–100). Dordrecht: Kluwer.
Kolm, S.-Ch. (2008). *Reciprocity, an economics of social relations*. Cambridge: Cambridge University Press.
Kolm, S.-Ch. (2011a). Equality. In B. Badie, D. Berg-Schlosser & L. Morlino (Eds.), *International encyclopedia of political science*. London: Sage.
Kolm, S.-Ch. (2011b). In C. Gamel & M. Lubrano (Eds.), *On Kolm's theory of macrojustice*. Heidelberg: Springer (Chapter 2, General Presentation (pp. 35–68); Chapter 3, Economic Macrojustice: Fair Optimum Income Distribution, Taxation and Transfers (pp. 69–132); Macrojustice in Normative Economics and Social Ethics (pp. 341–370).

Locke, J. (1960[1689]). *Second treatise of government*. Cambridge: Cambridge University Press.
Maniquet, F. (1998). An equal right solution to the compensation/responsibility dilemma. *Mathematical Social Sciences*, *35*, 185–202.
Mill, J. (1957[1861]). *Utilitarianism*. New York, NY: Bobbs-Merrill.
Musgrave, R. (1959). *The theory of public finance*. New York, NY: McGraw-Hill.
Musgrave, R. (1974). Maximin, uncertainty, and the leisure trade-off. *Quarterly Journal of Economics*, *88*(4), 625–632.
Phelps, E. (1973). *Economic justice*. Hammondsworth: Penguin Education.
Pigou, A. (1912). *Wealth and welfare*. London: Macmillan.
Rawls, J. (1974). Reply to Alexander and Musgrave. *Quarterly Journal of Economics*, *88*, 633–655.
Schokkaert, E. (1999). Monsieur tout-le-monde est post-welfariste. *Revue Economique*, *50*(4), 811–831.
Schokkaert, E., & Overlaet, B. (1989). Moral intuitions and economic models of distributive justice. *Social Choice and Welfare*, *6*, 19–31.
Van Parijs, P. (1995). *Real freedom for all*. Oxford: Oxford University Press.

CHAPTER 6

INFLUENCE FUNCTIONS FOR POLICY IMPACT ANALYSIS

B. Essama-Nssah and Peter J. Lambert

ABSTRACT

Social evaluation functions used in policy impact analysis can be viewed as real-valued functionals of the underlying outcome distributions. Influence functions may be used to identify the sources of variation in social outcomes in terms of individual or household characteristics. This chapter sets forth in clear terms the definition of the influence function and recentered influence function, and catalogs these functions for a wide range of distributional statistics, including measures of central tendency, inequality, and poverty and also measures of the degree of pro-poorness of a shock- or policy-induced change in income levels.

INTRODUCTION

Distributional considerations play a crucial role in public policymaking. Indeed policy implementation entails a redistribution of socioeconomic burdens and advantages, and policymakers are particularly interested in knowing whether or not an intervention had (or is likely to have) the intended effects on policy-relevant socioeconomic groups, and why. Policy

Inequality, Mobility and Segregation: Essays in Honor of Jacques Silber
Research on Economic Inequality, Volume 20, 135–159

ISSN: 1049-2585/doi:10.1108/S1049-2585(2012)0000020009

impact analysis is therefore an exercise in *social impact evaluation* understood as an assessment of variation in individual and social outcomes attributable to a socioeconomic shock or the implementation of public policy. Sen (1995) explains that any evaluative approach is characterized by its informational basis which clearly identifies the information required in passing judgments within the chosen approach. Two key elements underpin the informational basis. The focal space defines individual advantage (desirable outcome at the individual level), while the focal combination is used to assess social progress (desirable social outcome). The focal combination is essentially a rule for combining individual outcomes into an aggregative indicator of the prevailing social state. In other words, the focal combination is a social evaluation function (e.g., a social welfare function or a poverty measure) used to rank social states represented by distributions of individual outcomes.

The above considerations suggest that social evaluation functions used in policy impact analysis are nothing but distributional statistics, which can be viewed as real-valued and continuous functionals of the relevant outcome distributions. In the context of robust statistics, a distributional statistic that is continuous is said to be qualitatively robust (Wilcox, 2005). If this statistic is also differentiable, then it is said to be infinitesimally robust. Its first-order directional derivative is known as its *influence function* (Hampel, 1974). In other words, the influence function of a distributional statistic (and hence of a social evaluation function) measures the relative effect of a small perturbation in the underlying outcome distribution on the statistic of interest. One can therefore build an infinitesimal approach to policy impact analysis on the notion of the influence function. Within that approach and under the assumption that the distributional change in question is due to policy implementation, the influence function of a social evaluation criterion may be viewed as a local measure of the distributional impact of policy. This is analogous to what Rothe (2010) calls a *distributional policy effect*.[1]

For policymaking purposes, it is not enough to measure the impact of policy on the outcome distribution; policymakers are also interested in identifying the forces that drive the observed outcomes. Individual outcomes from participation in a policy intervention ultimately depend on individual endowments, behavior, and the circumstances that determine the returns to those endowments in any socioeconomic transaction. This perspective creates a need for linking social evaluation functions to individual (or household) characteristics depending on the unit of analysis. Recent work of Firpo, Fortin, and Lemieux (2009) has developed a regression technique using the *recentered influence function* (RIF), as a straightforward way to establish such a link. These authors define the RIF as the first two leading terms of the von Mises (1947) linear approximation of the corresponding social evaluation function. Assuming that the outcome variable is observed along with relevant covariates representing individual characteristics, they use the fact that the expected value of the influence function is equal to zero and the law of iterated expectations to express the social evaluation function of interest as the conditional expectation of the RIF given the covariates. This conditional expectation is what they call RIF regression.

Within the RIF regression framework, Firpo et al. (2009) define two very useful parameters in policy analysis, the marginal effect of a ceteris paribus change in the distribution of covariates and the unconditional partial effect. If the conditional outcome distribution given the covariates does not change following a small perturbation of the distribution of those covariates, then the marginal effect of this distributional change on the social outcome can be computed on the basis of the RIF regression. Furthermore, the same regression model can be used to compute the partial effect of a small location shift in the distribution of a continuous covariate on the social outcome. Under the assumption that the RIF regression is linear, these effects can be computed using standard OLS. Rothe (2011) proposes a parameter analogous to the unconditional partial effect which he calls the partial distributional policy effect. This parameter is a measure of the effect of a ceteris paribus change in the unconditional distribution of a single covariate on some functional of the unconditional distribution of the outcome variable. In contrast to Firpo et al. (2009), this author presents a fully non-parametric framework for the identification and estimation of this parameter for general changes in the covariate distribution including location shifts.

Declaring a policy outcome socially desirable on the basis of some social evaluation function is a result of aggregate judgment that may hide more than it reveals about the heterogeneity of impacts underlying the aggregate outcome. The possibility to link social evaluation criteria to individual characteristics via RIF regression offers an opportunity to understand this heterogeneity and to design targeted interventions that might enhance the effectiveness of public policy. Furthermore, attribution of outcomes to policy is the hallmark of policy impact evaluation. Variations in individual and social outcomes associated with policy implementation could be driven at least in part by changes in confounding factors in the socioeconomic environment. Looking at the individual outcome as a function of policy and type (base on characteristics), one can resort to counterfactual decomposition of observed distributional change *à la* Oaxaca–Blinder to sort out the part that is due to policy and the part due to confounding factors. RIF regression makes it possible to extend this type of decomposition to variation in social outcomes. However, a key limitation of this approach stems from the fact that RIF regression coefficients provide only a local approximation for the effect of changes in the relevant covariates on the distributional statistic of interest. Nonetheless, the approach based on linearization, which is of course widespread throughout economics, is very attractive in an operational environment.[2]

In this paper, we carefully define and catalog the influence functions and RIFs for a wide range of distributional statistics, including measures of central tendency, inequality and poverty and also measures of the degree of pro-poorness of the shock- or policy-induced change in income levels. We include the mean, *p*th quantile point, variance, Gini coefficient, Atkinson (1970) inequality index, Lorenz curve ordinate, generalized Lorenz curve ordinate (Shorrocks, 1983), Foster, Greer, and Thorbecke (1984) poverty index (henceforth the FGT index), Watts (1968) poverty index, Sen (1976) poverty index, growth incidence curve ordinate (Ravallion & Chen, 2003), TIP curve ordinate (Jenkins & Lambert, 1997), poverty elasticity of the headcount ratio, and pro-poorness measures for the FGT, Watts, and headcount indices (Essama-Nssah & Lambert, 2009). Such a catalog has not been available in the literature heretofore.

The organization of the remainder of the paper is as follows. In the second section, directional derivatives are defined, and are determined for each of the distributional statistics just listed. In the third section, influence functions and RIFs are determined for each of these distributional statistics. Appendix A contains proofs of all claimed results. For the reader's convenience, Appendix B contains a table in which the definitions of the distributional statistics we have covered, and their RIFs, are summarized using a simplified notation.

DIRECTIONAL DERIVATIVES OF DISTRIBUTIONAL STATISTICS

Suppose that, at the individual or household level, the outcome y we are interested in is income. Let $F(y)$ be an outcome distribution, for which we may assume without loss of generality that the frequencies $F'(y) = f(y)$ and support are bounded. Now let $T(\cdot)$ be a distributional statistic (e.g., a social evaluation function or indicator of a social outcome) that is qualitatively and infinitesimally robust. The influence function is the directional derivative of $T(F)$ at F and it measures the effect of a small perturbation in

F on $T(F)$, as follows. Let H be some distribution other than F. When the data does not follow F exactly, but a slightly different distribution, one that is "going toward" H, the effect is revealed by the *directional derivative of T at F in the direction of H*:

$$\nabla T_{F\to H} = \frac{d}{dt} T(tH + (1-t)F)\bigg|_{t=0} = \lim_{t\to 0} \frac{T(tH + (1-t)F) - T(F)}{t} \tag{1}$$

(see Wilcox, 2005).

The following proposition both defines the notation used in the rest of the paper, and determines the directional derivatives for the distributional statistics we have listed. The density functions associated with $F(x)$ and $H(x)$ are $f(x)$ and $h(x)$, and z is an exogenous poverty line. Some explanatory comments follow the statement of the proposition.

Proposition 1. For each of the following distributional statistics $T(\cdot)$, the directional derivative $\nabla T_{F\to H}$ is as shown:

(a) The mean, $\mu_F = T_\mu(F) = \int xf(x)\,dx$: $\nabla T_{\mu,F\to H} = \mu_H - \mu_F$

(b) The pth quantile point, $v_p = T_{vp}(F) = F^{-1}(p)$: $\nabla T_{vp,F\to H} = [p - H(v_p)]/f(v_p)$

(c) The variance, $\sigma_F^2 = T_{\sigma^2}(F) = \int (x-\mu)^2 f(x)\,dx$: $\nabla T_{\sigma^2,F\to H} = \sigma_H^2 - \sigma_F^2 + (\mu_H - \mu_F)^2$

(d) The Gini coefficient, $G_F = T_G(F) = (1/\mu_F)\int F(x)[1-F(x)]\,dx$:

$$\nabla T_{G,F\to H} = \frac{\mu_F - \mu_H}{\mu_F} G_F + \frac{1}{\mu_F}\int [H(x) - F(x)][1 - 2F(x)]\,dx$$

(e) The Atkinson inequality index $I_F(e) = T_{\text{ATK}}(F) = 1 - (\xi/\mu_F), e > 0$, where

$$U(x) = \begin{cases} x^{1-e}/(1-e) & 0 < e \neq 1 \\ \ln(x) & e = 1 \end{cases}$$

and $U(\xi) = \int U(x) f(x)\,dx$:

$$\nabla T_{\text{ATK},F\to H}(F) = \begin{cases} \left\{\frac{e}{1-e} + \frac{\mu_H}{\mu_F}\right\}[1 - I_F] - \frac{[1-I_F]^e \int x^{1-e} h(x)\,dx}{(1-e)\mu_F^{1-e}} & 0 < e \neq 1 \\ (1 - I_F)\left\{\ln\{\mu_F(1 - I_F)\} - \int \ln(x) h(x)\,dx + \left(\frac{\mu_H}{\mu_F} - 1\right)\right\} & e = 1 \end{cases}$$

(f) The generalized Lorenz ordinate at $p \in [0, 1]$, $\mathrm{GL}_F(p) = T_{\mathrm{GL}_p}(F) = \int_0^{v_p} xf(x)\,dx$:

$$\nabla T_{\mathrm{GL}_p,F\to H} = \int_0^{v_p} xh(x)\,dx + v_p[p - H(v_p)] - T_{\mathrm{GL}_p}(F)$$

(g) The Lorenz ordinate at $p \in [0, 1]$, $L_F(p) = T_{\mathrm{L}_p}(F) = (1/\mu_F) \int_0^{v_p} xf(x)\,dx$:

$$\nabla T_{\mathrm{L}_p,F\to H} = \frac{\int_0^{v_p} xh(x)\,dx + v_p[p - H(v_p)]}{\mu_F} - T_{\mathrm{L}_p}(F).\frac{\mu_H}{\mu_F}$$

(h) The FGT index for poverty line z, $T_{\mathrm{FGT}\alpha}(F) = \int_0^z (1 - (x/z))^\alpha f(x)\,dx \quad (\alpha \geq 0)$:

$$\nabla T_{\mathrm{FGT}\alpha,F\to H} = \int_0^z \left(1 - \frac{x}{z}\right)^\alpha h(x)\,dx - T_{\mathrm{FGT}\alpha}(F)$$

(i) The Watts index for poverty line z, $T_{\mathrm{W}}(F) = \int_0^z \ln(z/x) f(x)\,dx$:

$$\nabla T_{\mathrm{W},F\to H} = \int_0^z \ln\left(\frac{z}{x}\right) h(x)\,dx - T_{\mathrm{W}}(F)$$

(j) The Sen index for poverty line z, $T_{\mathrm{S}}(F) = \{2/zF(z)\} \int_0^z (z - x)[F(z) - F(x)] f(x)\,dx$:

$$\nabla T_{\mathrm{S},F\to H} = -\left(1 + \frac{H(z)}{F(z)}\right) T_S(F) - \frac{2}{zF(z)}\left\{\int_0^z (H(z) - H(x))(F(z) - F(x))\,dx\right\} + 2H(z)$$

(k) The TIP curve ordinate for poverty line z at $p \in [0, 1]$, $\mathrm{TIP}_F(p) = T_{\mathrm{TIP}_p}(F) = \begin{cases} \int_0^{v_p} (z - x) f(x)\,dx & v_p \leq z \\ \int_0^z (z - x) f(x)\,dx & v_p \geq z \end{cases}$

$$\nabla T_{\mathrm{TIP}_p,F\to H}(F) = \begin{cases} \int_0^{v_p} (z - x)h(x)\,dx + (z - v_p)\left[p - H(v_p)\right] \\ \quad - T_{\mathrm{TIP}_p}(F) & v_p \leq z \\ \int_0^z (z - x)h(x)\,dx - T_{\mathrm{TIP}_p}(F) & v_p \geq z \end{cases}$$

(l) The growth incidence curve ordinate at p, $\mathrm{GIC}_F(p) = T_{\mathrm{GIC}_p}(F) = \gamma q(v_p)$, where γ is the aggregate growth rate (also in parts (*m*)–(*p*) to follow):

$$\Delta T_{\mathrm{GIC}_p, F \to H} = \frac{\mu_H}{\mu_F} T_{\mathrm{GIC}_p}(F) + \gamma q'(v_p) \cdot \left[\frac{p - H(v_p)}{f(v_p)}\right]$$

(m) Pro-poorness for the FGT index, $T_{\mathrm{ppFGT}\alpha}(F) = (\alpha/z) \int_0^z x(1-(x/z))^{\alpha-1}[q(x)-1]f(x)\,dx \quad (\alpha \geq 1)$:

$$\nabla T_{\mathrm{ppFGT}\alpha, F \to H} = \frac{\alpha}{z}\int_0^z x\left(1-\frac{x}{z}\right)^{\alpha-1}\{\gamma q(x)[q(x)+xq'(x)]-1\}h(x)\,dx - \left[1+\frac{\mu_H}{\mu_F}\right] T_{\mathrm{ppFGT}\alpha}(F)$$

(n) Pro-poorness for the Watts index, $T_{\mathrm{ppW}}(F) = \int_0^z [q(x)-1]f(x)\,dx$:

$$\nabla T_{\mathrm{ppW}, F \to H}(F) = \int_0^z \{\gamma q(x)[q(x)+xq'(x)]-1\}h(x)\,dx - \left[1+\frac{\mu_H}{\mu_F}\right] T_{\mathrm{ppW}}(F)$$

(o) Pro-poorness for the headcount ratio: $T_{\mathrm{ppHC}}(F) = z(q(z)-1)f(z)$:

$$\nabla T_{\mathrm{ppHC}, F \to H} = -zh(z)\{1+\gamma q(z)(q(z)+zq'(z))\} - \left[1+\frac{\mu_H}{\mu_F}\right] T_{\mathrm{ppHC}}(F) - zf(z)\frac{\mu_H}{\mu_F}$$

(p) The poverty elasticity of the headcount ratio, $T_{\mathrm{EHC}}(F) = -(zq(z) \times f(z)/F(z))$:

$$\nabla T_{\mathrm{EHC}, F \to H} = -T_{\mathrm{EHC}}(F)\left[\frac{H(z)}{F(z)} + \frac{\mu_H}{\mu_F} + \frac{\gamma h(z)}{f(z)}[q(z)+zq'(z)]\right]$$

All of these results follow using calculus and/or limiting arguments. Each is proven in Appendix A, Part I. Note that the median income value is case (*b*) with $p = 1/2$. For the growth incidence curve and pro-poorness measures, $q(x)$ is the income growth pattern, an elasticity function telling by what percentage income x grows when the overall income growth is 1%, as in Essama-Nssah and Lambert (2009), where pro-poorness for an additively separable poverty index $P = \int_0^z \psi(x|z)f(x)\,dx$, in which the poverty contribution function $\psi(x|z)$ is convex, decreasing and equals zero for $x \geq z$, is defined as $T_{\text{PPP}}(F) = \int_0^z \{-x\psi'(x|z)\}[q(x) - 1]f(x)\,dx$ (and pro-poorness for the headcount ratio $F(z)$ is separately defined as in (p)).

INFLUENCE FUNCTIONS AND RECENTERED INFLUENCE FUNCTIONS

For y in the domain of F, let $H = \Delta_y$ be the cumulative distribution function for a probability measure which gives mass 1 to y. That is, $H(x) = \Delta_y(x) = \begin{cases} 0 & x<y \\ 1 & x \geq y \end{cases}$. The density function $h(x)$ is zero everywhere except for an infinite spike at $x=y$. In particular, $\int_0^\infty \Delta_y(x)f(y)\,dy = \int_0^x f(y)\,dy = F(x)$. The influence function for an estimator $T(\cdot)$ is defined as

$$IF(y;T;F) = \nabla T_{F\to\Delta y} \tag{2}$$

It describes the effect of an infinitesimal "contamination" at the point y on the estimator: in the mixed distribution $tH + (1-t)F$, it is as if an observation is randomly sampled from distribution F with probability $(1–t)$ and from Δ_y with probability t. The influence function is also known as the *Gâteaux derivative*, following Gâteaux (1913). It has become a key tool in robust statistics.

An important property of the influence function is that, in all cases in which the frequencies and range of the y-values are bounded,

$$\int_0^\infty \text{IF}(y;T;F)f(y)\,dy = 0 \tag{3}$$

See Part II of Appendix A for the proof of this result, whose significance will become apparent.

The recentered influence function is defined by adding the influence function to the functional itself:

$$\text{RIF}(y;T;F) = T(F) + \text{IF}(y;T;F) \tag{4}$$

Because of (3) we have

$$\int_0^\infty \text{RIF}(y;T;F)f(y)\,dy = T(F) \tag{5}$$

The following proposition determines the influence functions and RIFs for the distributional statistics whose directional derivatives are given in Proposition 1. Again, some comments follow the statement of this proposition.

Proposition 2. For the following distributional statistics $T(\cdot)$, the influence functions $\text{IF}(y;T;F)$ and recentered influence functions $\text{RIF}(y;T;F)$ are as shown:

(a) The mean: $\text{IF}(y;T_\mu;F) = y - \mu_F$ and $\text{RIF}(y;T_\mu;F) = y$

(b) The pth quantile point:

$$\text{IF}(y;T_{vp};F) = \begin{cases} \dfrac{p}{f(v_p)} & y > v_p \\ \dfrac{-(1-p)}{f(v_p)} & y < v_p \end{cases}$$

and

$$\text{RIF}(y;T_{vp};F) = \begin{cases} v_p + p/f(v_p) & y > v_p \\ v_p - (1-p)/f(v_p) & y < v_p \end{cases}$$

(c) The variance: $\text{IF}(y;T_{\sigma^2};F) = -\sigma_F^2 + (y-\mu_F)^2$ and $\text{RIF}(y;T_{\sigma^2};F) = (y-\mu_F)^2$

(d) The Gini coefficient:

$$\text{IF}(y;T_G;F) = -\frac{\mu_F + y}{\mu_F} G_F + 1 - \frac{y}{\mu_F} + \frac{2}{\mu_F}\int_0^y F(x)\,dx$$

and

$$\text{RIF}(y;T_G;F) = -\frac{y}{\mu_F} G_F + 1 - \frac{y}{\mu_F} + \frac{2}{\mu_F}\int_0^y F(x)\,dx$$

(e) The Atkinson index:

$$\text{IF}(y;T_{\text{ATK}};F) = \begin{cases} \left\{\dfrac{e}{1-e} + \dfrac{y}{\mu_F}\right\}[1-I_F] - \dfrac{[1-I_F]^e y^{1-e}}{(1-e)\mu_F^{1-e}} & 0 < e \neq 1 \\ (1-I_F)\left\{\ln\{\mu_F(1-I_F)\} - \ln(y) + \left(\dfrac{y}{\mu_F} - 1\right)\right\} & e = 1 \end{cases}$$

and

$$\mathrm{RIF}(y; T_{\mathrm{ATK}}; F) = I_F + \begin{cases} \left\{\dfrac{e}{1-e} + \dfrac{y}{\mu_F}\right\}[1 - I_F] - \dfrac{[1 - I_F]^e y^{1-e}}{(1-e)\mu_F^{1-e}} & 0 < e \neq 1 \\ (1 - I_F)\left\{\ln\{\mu_F(1 - I_F)\} - \ln(y) + \left(\dfrac{y}{\mu_F} - 1\right)\right\} & e = 1 \end{cases}$$

(f) The generalized Lorenz ordinate:

$$\mathrm{IF}(y; T_{\mathrm{GL}_p}; F) = \begin{cases} y - (1-p)v_p - T_{\mathrm{GL}_p}(F) & y < v_p \\ pv_p - T_{\mathrm{GL}_p}(F) & y \geq v_p \end{cases}$$

and

$$\mathrm{RIF}(y; T_{\mathrm{GL}_p}; F) = \begin{cases} y - (1-p)v_p & y < v_p \\ pv_p & y \geq v_p \end{cases}$$

(g) The Lorenz ordinate:

$$\mathrm{IF}(y; T_{\mathrm{L}_p}; F) = \begin{cases} \dfrac{y - (1-p)v_p}{\mu_F} - T_{\mathrm{L}_p}(F).\dfrac{y}{\mu_F} & y < v_p \\ \dfrac{pv_p}{\mu_F} - T_{\mathrm{L}_p}(F).\dfrac{y}{\mu_F} & y \geq v_p \end{cases}$$

and

$$\mathrm{RIF}(y; T_{\mathrm{L}_p}; F) = \begin{cases} \dfrac{y - (1-p)v_p}{\mu_F} + T_{\mathrm{L}_p}(F) \cdot \left(1 - \dfrac{y}{\mu_F}\right) & y < v_p \\ \dfrac{pv_p}{\mu_F} + T_{\mathrm{L}_p}(F) \cdot \left(1 - \dfrac{y}{\mu_F}\right) & y \geq v_p \end{cases}$$

(h) The FGT index ($\alpha \geq 0$):

$$\mathrm{IF}(y; T_{\mathrm{FGT}\alpha}; F) = \begin{cases} \left(1 - \dfrac{y}{z}\right)^{\alpha} - T_{\mathrm{FGT}\alpha}(F) & y < z \\ -T_{\mathrm{FGT}\alpha}(F) & y > z \end{cases}$$

and

$$\mathrm{RIF}(y; T_{\mathrm{FGT}\alpha}; F) = \begin{cases} \left(1 - \dfrac{y}{z}\right)^{\alpha} & y < z \\ 0 & y > z \end{cases} \quad (\alpha \geq 0)$$

(i) The Watts index:

$$\mathrm{IF}(y; T_{\mathrm{W}}; F) = \begin{cases} \ln\left(\dfrac{z}{y}\right) - T_{\mathrm{W}}(F) & y < z \\ -T_{\mathrm{W}}(F) & y > z \end{cases}$$

and

$$\mathrm{RIF}(y; T_{\mathrm{W}}; F) = \begin{cases} \ln\left(\dfrac{z}{y}\right) & y < z \\ 0 & y > z \end{cases}$$

(j) The Sen index:

$$\mathrm{IF}(y; T_{\mathrm{S}}; F) = \begin{cases} -\left(1 + \dfrac{1}{F(z)}\right) T_{\mathrm{S}}(F) - \dfrac{2}{zF(z)} \displaystyle\int_0^y (F(z) - F(x))\, dx + 2 & \\ & y < z \\ -T_{\mathrm{S}}(F) & y > z \end{cases}$$

and

$$\mathrm{RIF}(y; T_{\mathrm{S}}; F) = \begin{cases} -\left(\dfrac{1}{F(z)}\right) T_{\mathrm{S}}(F) - \dfrac{2}{zF(z)} \displaystyle\int_0^y (F(z) & \\ \quad -F(x))\, dx + 2 & y < z \\ 0 & y > z \end{cases}$$

(k) The TIP curve ordinate at $p \in [0, 1]$:

$$\mathrm{IF}(y; T_{\mathrm{TIP}_p}; F) = -T_{\mathrm{TIP}_p}(F) + \begin{cases} z - y \quad y < z & \\ 0 \quad\quad\;\; y > z & z < v_p \\ pz + (1-p)v_p - y \quad y < v_p & \\ p(z - v_p) \quad\quad\quad\quad y > v_p & z > v_p \end{cases}$$

and

$$\mathrm{RIF}(y; T_{\mathrm{TIP}_p}; F) = \begin{cases} z - y & y < z \\ 0 & y > z \end{cases} \quad z < v_p \qquad \begin{cases} pz + (1-p)v_p - y & y < v_p \\ p(z - v_p) & y > v_p \end{cases} \quad z > v_p$$

(l) The growth incidence curve ordinate at p:

$$\mathrm{IF}(y; T_{\mathrm{GIC}_p}; F) = \frac{y}{\mu_F} T_{\mathrm{GIC}_p}(F) + \begin{cases} \dfrac{\gamma p q'(v_p)}{f(v_p)} & y > v_p \\ \dfrac{-\gamma(1-p)q'(v_p)}{f(v_p)} & y < v_p \end{cases}$$

and

$$\mathrm{RIF}(y; T_{\mathrm{GIC}_p}; F) = \begin{cases} \gamma\left\{\left[\dfrac{y}{\mu_F} + 1\right] q(v_p) + \dfrac{pq'(v_p)}{f(v_p)}\right\} & y > v_p \\ \gamma\left\{\left[\dfrac{y}{\mu_F} + 1\right] q(v_p) - \dfrac{(1-p)q'(v_p)}{f(v_p)}\right\} & y < v_p \end{cases}$$

(m) Pro-poorness for the FGT index ($\alpha \geq 1$):

$$\mathrm{IF}(y; T_{\mathrm{ppFGT}\alpha}, F) = \begin{cases} \dfrac{\alpha y}{z}\left(1 - \dfrac{y}{z}\right)^{\alpha - 1} \{\gamma q(y)[q(y) + yq'(y)] - 1\} \\ \qquad - \left[1 + \dfrac{y}{\mu_F}\right] T_{\mathrm{ppFGT}\alpha}(F) & y < z \\ -\left[1 + \dfrac{y}{\mu_F}\right] T_{\mathrm{ppFGT}\alpha}(F) & y > z \end{cases}$$

and

$$\mathrm{RIF}(y; T_{\mathrm{ppFGT}\alpha}, F) = \begin{cases} \dfrac{\alpha y}{z}\left(1 - \dfrac{y}{z}\right)^{\alpha - 1} \{\gamma q(y)[q(y) + yq'(y)] - 1\} \\ \qquad - \left[\dfrac{y}{\mu_F}\right] T_{\mathrm{ppFGT}\alpha}(F) & y < z \\ -\left[\dfrac{y}{\mu_F}\right] T_{\mathrm{ppFGT}\alpha}(F) & y > z \end{cases}$$

(n) Pro-poorness for the Watts index:

$$\mathrm{IF}(y;T_{\mathrm{ppW}},F)=\begin{cases}\{\gamma q(y)[q(y)+yq'(y)]-1\} \\ \qquad -\left[1+\dfrac{y}{\mu_F}\right]T_{\mathrm{ppW}}(F) & y<z\\ -\left[1+\dfrac{y}{\mu_F}\right]T_{\mathrm{ppW}}(F) & y>z\end{cases}$$

and

$$\mathrm{RIF}(y;T_{\mathrm{ppW}},F)=\begin{cases}\{\gamma q(y)[q(y)+yq'(y)]-1\}-\left[\dfrac{y}{\mu_F}\right]T_{\mathrm{ppW}}(F) & y<z\\ -\left[\dfrac{y}{\mu_F}\right]T_{\mathrm{ppW}}(F) & y>z\end{cases}$$

(o) Pro-poorness for the headcount ratio:

$$\mathrm{IF}(y;T_{\mathrm{ppHC}};F)=-\left[1+\frac{y}{\mu_F}\right]T_{\mathrm{ppHC}}(F)-zf(z)\frac{y}{\mu_F}\quad (y\neq z)$$

and

$$\mathrm{RIF}(y;T_{\mathrm{ppHC}};F)=-\left[\frac{y}{\mu_F}\right]T_{\mathrm{ppHC}}(F)-zf(z)\frac{y}{\mu_F}\quad (y\neq z)$$

(p) Poverty elasticity of the headcount ratio:

$$\mathrm{IF}(y;T_{\mathrm{PEHC}};F)=\begin{cases}-T_{\mathrm{EHC}}(F)\left[\dfrac{1}{F(z)}+\dfrac{y}{\mu_F}\right] & y<z\\ -T_{\mathrm{EHC}}(F)\left[\dfrac{y}{\mu_F}\right] & y>z\end{cases}$$

and

$$\mathrm{RIF}(y;T_{\mathrm{PEHC}};F)=\begin{cases}-T_{\mathrm{EHC}}(F)\left[\dfrac{1-F(z)}{F(z)}+\dfrac{y}{\mu_F}\right] & y<z\\ T_{\mathrm{EHC}}(F)\left[1-\dfrac{y}{\mu_F}\right] & y>z\end{cases}$$

The proofs of these result are immediate from those in Proposition 1, simply substituting the general distribution $H(x)$ by $\Delta_y(x) = \begin{cases} 0 & x<y \\ 1 & x \geq y \end{cases}$ throughout. Other notations may be used for some of these expressions. For example, Firpo et al. (2009) write the influence function for the pth quantile point $v_p = T_{vp}(F) = F^{-1}(p)$ as $\text{IF}(y; T_{vp}; F) = (\mathbf{I}(y > v_p) - (1-p))/f(v_p)$ where $\mathbf{I}$ is an indicator function. Their expression for the Gini influence function (given in an unpublished companion paper) is $\text{IF}(y; T_G; F) = A_2(F) + B_2(F)y + C_2(y, F)$ where $A_2(F) = (2/\mu)R(F)$, $B_2(F) = (2/\mu^2)R(F)$ and $C_2(y, F) = -(2/\mu)\{y[1 - p(y)] + \text{GL}(p(y), F)\}$ in which, in our terms, $\text{GL}(p(y), F) = \int_{-\infty}^{y} x dF(x) = -\int_{-\infty}^{y} F(x)\,dx + yF(y)$ and $R(F) = (1/2)\mu_F(1 - G_F)$: in fact this expression is equivalent to ours.[3] In Cowell and Victoria-Feser (1996b), influence functions are derived generally for additively separable poverty indices, of the form $T_P(F) = \int_0^z p(x, z)f(x)\,dx$, and are of the form $\text{IF}(y;\ T_P;\ F) = p(y,\ z) - T_P(F)$ (so that $\text{RIF}(y;\ T_P;\ F) = p(y,\ z)$). The authors describe this as "the (p, P) rule" (p. 1764). This rule covers cases (h) and (i) for the FGT and Watts indices (and also accounts for (a) and (c), for the mean and variance, in fact). The authors extend their rule to the class of quasi additively separable poverty indices, which take the form $T_P(F) = \int_0^z p(x, F(x), z)f(x)\,dx$. Here, the result is more complicated: see their Eq. (11). In Dadson (2012), an expression for the RIF of the Sen index is derived from this using an indicator function, which is equivalent to the measure in part (j) of Proposition 2. The reader will notice that for the poverty-related measures, we have not defined influence functions at the poverty line value $y = z$. This is because these influence functions may be infinite at $y = z$. Properties (3) and (5) can be verified in all cases, although we must interpret $\text{IF}(z; T; F)f(z)dz$ and $\text{RIF}(z; T; F)f(z)dz$ as each equal to $T(F)$ in the poverty-related cases.

RIF regression offers a simple way of establishing a direct link between a social evaluation function and individual or household characteristics x, because of (5), which says that the expected value of the RIF is equal to the corresponding distributional statistic, $T(F) = E_F[\text{RIF}(y; T, F)]$. By the law of iterated expectations, the distributional statistic can thus be written as the conditional expectation of $\text{RIF}(y; T, F)$, given observable covariates, and is determined in a RIF regression, as shown in Firpo et al. (2009).

CONCLUSION

In this paper, we have laid out a catalog of influence functions and associated RIFs for a range of social evaluation functions widely used in assessing the distributional and poverty impacts of public policy. These social evaluation functions are distributional statistics, whose RIFs can be used in regression analysis to link social outcomes to individual characteristics, and hence to assess the heterogeneity of impacts underlying the social outcomes. A stumbling block may until now have been the computation of the relevant influence function(s). It is our hope that this paper will help distributional analysts to overcome that difficulty.

NOTES

1. The influence function has also been used to quantify the impact of data contamination upon various distributional statistics, see Cowell and Victoria-Feser (1996a, 1996b).
2. This limitation of the RIF regression approach is well recognized. Chernozhukov, Fernández-Val, and Melly (2009) directly estimate an exact effect without approximation error. See also Rothe (2010, 2011) in which no shape restriction is imposed on the conditional distribution of the outcome given explanatory variables.
3. In Cowell and Victoria-Feser (1996a, p. 87), an influence function is derived for the Gini coefficient in the special case that the mean is unchanged by the introduction of the perturbation H (i.e., when $\mu_{\mathrm{H}} = \mu_F$).

ACKNOWLEDGMENTS

The authors wish to thank Daniel Dugger and Phillipe Van Kerm for assistance in the preparation of this paper. Much of the work was undertaken while Essama-Nssah was Senior Economist in the Poverty Reduction and Equity Group at the World Bank.

REFERENCES

Atkinson, A. B. (1970). On the measurement of inequality. *Journal of Economic Theory*, *2*, 244–263.

Chernozhukov, V., Fernández-Val, I., & Melly, B. (2009). *Inference on counterfactual distributions*. Working Paper No. 08-16. Department of Economics, Massachusetts Institute of Technology, Cambridge, MA.

Cowell, F. A., & Victoria-Feser, M.-P. (1996a). Robustness properties of inequality measures: The influence function and the principle of transfers. *Econometrica, 64*, 77–101.

Cowell, F., & Victoria-Feser, M.-P. (1996b). Poverty measurement with contaminated data: A robust approach. *European Economic Review, 40*, 1761–1771.

Dadson, N. (2012). *Poverty recentered influence function regressions and decompositions*. Mimeo. Burnaby BC, Canada: Simon Fraser University.

Essama-Nssah, B., & Lambert, P. J. (2009). Measuring pro-poorness: A unifying approach with new results. *Review of Income and Wealth, 55*, 752–778.

Firpo, S., Fortin, N. M., & Lemieux, T. (2009). Unconditional quantile regressions. *Econometrica, 77*, 953–973.

Foster, J. E., Greer, J., & Thorbecke, E. (1984). A class of decomposable poverty measures. *Econometrica, 52*, 761–766.

Gâteaux, R. (1913). Sur les fonctionnelles continues et les fonctionnelles analytiques. *Comptes Rendus de l'Académie des Sciences-Series I – Mathematics, 157*, 325–327.

Hampel, F. R. (1974). The influence curve and its role in robust estimation. *Journal of the American Statistical Association, 60*, 383–393.

Jenkins, S. P., & Lambert, P. J. (1997). Three 'I's of poverty curves, with an analysis of U.K. poverty trends. *Oxford Economic Papers, 49*, 317–327.

Ravallion, M., & Chen, S. (2003). Measuring pro-poor growth. *Economics Letters, 78*, 93–99.

Rothe, C. (2010). Nonparametric estimation of distributional policy effects. *Journal of Econometrics, 155*, 56–70.

Rothe, C. (2011). *Partial distributional policy effects*. Mimeo. Toulouse, France: Toulouse School of Economics.

Sen, A. (1976). Poverty: An ordinal approach to measurement. *Econometrica, 44*, 219–231.

Sen, A. (1995). *Inequality reexamined*. Cambridge, MA: Harvard University Press.

Shorrocks, A. F. (1983). Ranking income distributions. *Economica, 50*, 3–17.

von Mises, R. (1947). On the asymptotic distribution of differentiable statistical functions. *Annals of Mathematical Statistics, 18*, 309–348.

Watts, H. (1968). An economic definition of poverty. In D. P. Moynihan (Ed.), *On understanding poverty: Perspectives from the social sciences* (pp. 316–329). New York, NY: Basic Books.

Wilcox, R. R. (2005). *Introduction to robust estimation and hypothesis testing* (2nd ed). Amsterdam: Elsevier.

APPENDIX A

Part I: Proof of results stated in Proposition 1.

(a) $\nabla T_{\mu,F\to H} = \frac{d}{dt}\left[\int x(th(x)+(1-t)f(x))\,dx\right]\Big|_{t=0} = \frac{d}{dt}\left[t\mu_H+(1-t)\mu_F\right]\Big|_{t=0}$
$= \mu_H - \mu_F$

(b) Let $w(t)$ be the pth quantile point of $tH+(1-t)F$, so that $tH(w(t)) + (1-t)F(w(t)) = p$ and $w(0) = v_p$. Then

$$\frac{\partial p}{dt} = 0 = H(w(t)) - F(w(t)) + w'(t)[th(w(t)) + (1-t)f(w(t))]$$

that is,

$$w'(t) = \frac{F(w(t)) - H(w(t))}{th(w(t)) + (1-t)f(w(t))}$$

Now

$$\nabla T_{vp,F\to H} = w'(0) = \frac{F(w(0)) - H(w(0))}{f(w(0))} = \frac{F(v_p) - H(v_p)}{f(v_p)} = \frac{p - H(v_p)}{f(v_p)}$$

as claimed.

(c) $\nabla T_{\sigma^2,F\to H} = \frac{d}{dt}\int(x - t\mu_H - (1-t)\mu_F)^2\,(th(x)+(1-t)f(x))\,dx|_{t=0} = \int(x-\mu_F)^2(dH - dF) + \int 2(x-\mu_F)(\mu_F - \mu_H)\,dF = -\sigma_F^2 + \int(x-\mu_F)^2\,dH = \sigma_H^2 - \sigma_F^2 + (\mu_H - \mu_F)^2$ as claimed.

(d) $\mu_F G_F = \int F(x)[1-F(x)]\,dx \Rightarrow \mu_{tH+(1-t)F}G_{tH+(1-t)F} = \int[tH(x)+(1-t)F(x)][1 - tH(x) - (1-t)F(x)]\,dx \Rightarrow \frac{d}{dt}[\mu_{tH+(1-t)F}G_{tH+(1-t)F}]|_{t=0} = \int[H(x) - F(x)][1-2F(x)]\,dx$. Since $\frac{d}{dt}[\mu_{tH+(1-t)F}] = \mu_H - \mu_F$, $\int[H(x)-F(x)][1-2F(x)]\,dx = (\mu_H - \mu_F)G_F + \mu_F\nabla T_{G,F\to H}$ implying the result.

(e) Let ξ_0 be the equally distributed equivalent (EDE) income for F, and let $\xi(t)$ be the EDE income for $tH+(1-t)F$. Then $I_F = 1-(\xi_0/\mu_F)$ and $I_{tH+(1-t)F} = 1-(\xi(t)/\mu_{tH+(1-t)F})$, where $U(\xi_0) = \int U(x)f(x)\,dx$ and $U(\xi(t)) = t\int U(x)h(x)\,dx + (1-t)U(\xi_0)$. Differentiating and setting $t=0$, $U'(\xi_0)\xi'(0) = \int U(x)h(x)\,dx - U(\xi_0)$ and

$$\nabla T_{\text{ATK},F\to H}(F) = \frac{d}{dt}I_{tH+(1-t)F}\Big|_{t=0} = \frac{-\xi'(0)\mu_F + \xi_0(\mu_H - \mu_F)}{\mu_F^2}$$
$$= \left\{\frac{U(\xi_0) - \int U(x)h(x)\,dx}{\mu_F U'(\xi_0)}\right\} + \frac{\xi_0(\mu_H - \mu_F)}{\mu_F^2}$$

Setting $U(x) = x^{(\frac{1-e}{1-e})}$ for the case $0 < e \neq 1$ and then $U(x) = \ln(x)$ for the case $e = 1$, and substituting, the cited values for $\nabla T_{\text{ATK},F\to H}(F)$ follow after some manipulation.

(f) Let $p = tH(w(t)) + (1-t)F(w(t))$ as in (b), so that

$$\text{GL}_{tH+(1-t)F}(p) = \int_0^{w(t)} x[th(x) + (1-t)f(x)]\,dx, \quad w(0) = v_p$$

and

$$\nabla T_{\text{GL}_p,F\to H} = \frac{d}{dt}\left[\int_0^{w(t)} x[th(x) + (1-t)f(x)]\,dx\right]\Bigg|_{t=0}$$
$$= \int_0^{v_p} x[h(x) - f(x)]\,dx + w'(0)v_p f(v_p)$$

and

$$w'(0) = \frac{p - H(v_p)}{f(v_p)}$$

So

$$\nabla T_{\text{GL}_p,F\to H} = \int_0^{v_p} xh(x)\,dx + v_p[p - H(v_p)] - T_{\text{GL}_p}(F)$$

as claimed.

(g) $\frac{d}{dt}\left[\mu_{tH+(1-t)F}L_{tH+(1-t)F}(p)\right]\big|_{t=0} = \nabla_{\text{GL}_p,F\to H}$ and $\frac{d}{dt}\left[\mu_{tH+(1-t)F}\right]\big|_{t=0} = \mu_H - \mu_F$ whence $(\mu_H - \mu_F)L_F(p) + \mu_F \nabla_{\text{L}_p,F\to H} = \nabla_{\text{GL}_p,F\to H} \Rightarrow \nabla_{\text{L}_p,F\to H} = \frac{1}{\mu_F}\nabla_{\text{GL}_p,F\to H} + \left(1 - \frac{\mu_H}{\mu_F}\right)L_F(p)$ which is as claimed.

(h), (i), (j) These follow by applying the operator $\frac{d}{dt}\big|_{t=0}$ to the three expressions:

$$T_{\text{FGT}\alpha}(tH + (1-t)F) = \int_0^z \left(1 - \frac{x}{z}\right)^\alpha [th(x) + (1-t)f(x)]\,dx$$

$$T_{\text{W}}(tH + (1-t)F) = \int_0^z \ln\left(\frac{z}{x}\right)[th(x) + (1-t)f(x)]\,dx$$

$$[tH(z) + (1-t)F(z)]T_S(tH + (1-t)F)$$
$$= \frac{2}{z}\int_0^z (z - x)[(tH(z) + (1-t)F(z)) - (tH(x)$$
$$+ (1-t)F(x))](th(x) + (1-t)f(x))\,dx$$

In the last of these cases, some extra manipulations involving integration by parts are needed.

(k) As for (*b*) and (*f*), let $p = tH(w(t)) + (1-t)F(w(t))$ so that $w'(0) = (p - H(v_p))/(f(v_p))$. Now

$$\mathrm{TIP}_{tH+(1-t)F}(p) = \begin{cases} \int_0^{w(t)} (z-x)[th(x) + (1-t)f(x)]\,dx & w(t) < z \\ \int_0^{z} (z-x)[th(x) + (1-t)f(x)]\,dx & w(t) > z \end{cases}$$

and

$$\nabla T_{\mathrm{TIP}_p, F\to H}(F) = \frac{d}{dt}\mathrm{TIP}_{tH+(1-t)F}(p)\Big|_{t=0}$$

Differentiating, we have

$$\frac{d}{dt}\mathrm{TIP}_{tH+(1-t)F}(p) = \begin{cases} \int_0^{w(t)} (z-x)[h(x) - f(x)]\,dx + w'(t)(z - w(t)) & \\ \quad \times [th(w(t)) + (1-t)f(w(t))] & w(t) < z \\ \int_0^{z} (z-x)[h(x) - f(x)]\,dx & w(t) > z \end{cases}$$

and setting $t = 0$,

$$\nabla T_{\mathrm{TIP}_p, F\to H}(F) = -T_{\mathrm{TIP}_p}(F) + \begin{cases} \int_0^{v_p} (z-x)[h(x) - f(x)]\,dx & \\ \quad + [p - H(v_p)](z - v_p) & v_p < z \\ \int_0^{z} (z-x)[h(x) - f(x)]\,dx & v_p > z \end{cases}$$

which is as claimed since

$$T_{\mathrm{TIP}_p}(F) = \begin{cases} \int_0^{v_p} (z-x)f(x)\,dx & v_p \le z \\ \int_0^{z} (z-x)f(x)\,dx & v_p \ge z \end{cases}$$

(l)–(p) For these results, we need to allow for changing income growth patterns in computing the directional derivatives. Let the income distributions at times 0 and 1 be F and $\tilde{F}$ respectively, where $\mu_{\tilde{F}} = (1+\gamma)\mu_F$. An income x at time 0 increases to $x[1 + \gamma q(x)]$ at time 1. For $t \in [0, 1]$, consider distributions $tH + (1-t)F$ at time 0 and $tH + (1-t)\tilde{F}$ at time 1, that is, H stays unchanged as F experiences growth. The mean is $t\mu_H + (1-t)\mu_F$ at time 0 and $t\mu_H + (1-t)(1+\gamma)\mu_F$ at time 1, that is, the aggregate growth rate is $\gamma(t) = ((1-t)\gamma\mu_F)/(t\mu_H + (1-t)\mu_F)$, whence

$$\gamma(0) = \gamma,\ \gamma'(0) = \gamma\frac{\mu_H}{\mu_F} \tag{A.1}$$

Let $q_t(x)$ be the growth elasticity of x in the distribution $tH + (1-t)F$ (so that $q_0(x) \equiv q(x)$). An income of x in period 0 grows to $x[1 + \gamma(t)q_t(x)]$ in period 1. If there are no rank changes from one period to the next, as we shall assume, then

$$tH(x) + (1-t)F(x) = tH(x[1+\gamma(t)q_t(x)]) + (1-t)\tilde{F}(x[1+\gamma(t)q_t(x)])\,\forall x \tag{A.2}$$

For $t=0$, this says that

$$F(x) = \tilde{F}(x[1+\gamma q(x)])\,\forall x \tag{A.3}$$

that is, that income growth in F involves no rank changes; also, differentiating, that

$$f(x) = \tilde{f}(x[1+\gamma q(x)])\cdot[1+\gamma q(x) + x\gamma q'(x)]\,\forall x \tag{A.4}$$

Differentiating with respect to t in (A.2) and setting $t=0$, we have

$$\begin{aligned} H(x) - F(x) &= H(x[1+\gamma q(x)]) - \tilde{F}(x[1+\gamma q(x)]) \\ &\quad + x\tilde{f}(x[1+\gamma q(x)])\cdot\left[\left\{\frac{d}{dt}\gamma(t)q_t(x)\big|_{t=0}\right\}\right] \end{aligned}$$

Using (A.1), (A.3) and (A.4), this reduces to

$$\frac{d}{dt}q_t(x)\big|_{t=0} = -\frac{q(x)h(x)[1+\gamma q(x)+x\gamma q'(x)]}{f(x)} - \left\{q(x)\frac{\mu_H}{\mu_F}\right\} \tag{A.5}$$

which will be important for what follows. Finally, among these general results for income growth scenarios, note that if $q_t(x)$ is continuously differentiable, then $q_t'(x) \to q'(x)\,\forall x$ as $t \to 0$.

(l) We have $T_{\mathrm{GIC}_p}(tH + (1-t)F) = \gamma(t)q_t(w(t))$ in this case, where $w(t)$ is the pth quantile point of $tH + (1-t)F$, where $w(0) = v_p$ and $w'(0) = (p - H(v_p))/(f(v_p))$ as in cases (*b*), (*f*) and (*j*). Now $(d/dt)\left[\gamma(t)q_t(w(t))\right] = \gamma'(t)q_t(w(t)) + \gamma(t)q_t'(w(t))w'(t)$ and so, at $t=0$, we have $\nabla T_{\mathrm{GIC}_p,F\to H} = \gamma'(0)q(v_p) + \gamma(0)q'(v_p)w'(0) = \gamma q(v_p)\frac{\mu_H}{\mu_F} + \gamma q'(v_p)[p - (H(v_p)/f(v_p))]$ as claimed.

(m)–(n) In each of these cases, the distributional statistic is of the form $T(F) = \int_0^z xu'(x)[q(x)-1]f(x)\,dx$, where z is the poverty line and $u(x)$ is the poverty contribution function. For the FGT index, $u(x) = (1-(x/z))^\alpha$ $(\alpha \geq 0)$ and for the Watts index, $u(x) = \ln(z/x)$. Generically,

$$T(tH + (1-t)F) = \int_0^z xu'(x)[q_t(x) - 1]\{th(x) + (1-t)f(x)\}\,dx$$

and

$$\begin{aligned}\nabla T_{F\to H} &= \frac{d}{dt}[T(tH + (1-t)F)]|_{t=0} \\ &= \int xu'(x)\left\{[q(x) - 1]\{h(x) - f(x)\} + \left[\frac{d}{dt}q_t(x)|_{t=0}\right]f(x)\right\}dx\end{aligned}$$

Using (A.5), we find that

$$\nabla T_{F\to H} = -\left[1 + \frac{\mu_H}{\mu_F}\right]T(F) - \int xu'(x)\{\gamma q(x)[q(x) + xq'(x)] - 1\}h(x)\,dx$$

The cited results follow.

(o) In this case, we have $T_{\text{ppHC}}(tH + (1-t)F) = z(q_t(z) - 1)\{th(z) + (1-t)f(z)\}$ and so

$$\begin{aligned}\nabla T_{\text{ppHC},F\to H} &= \frac{d}{dt}T_{\text{ppHC}}(tH + (1-t)F)|_{t=0} \\ &= z(q(z) - 1)\{h(z) - f(z)\} + zf(z)\frac{d}{dt}q_t(z)|_{t=0}\end{aligned}$$

Using (A.5), this reduces to

$$\begin{aligned}\nabla T_{\text{ppHC},F\to H} = &-zh(z)\{1 + \gamma q(z)(q(z) + zq'(z))\} \\ &- \left[1 + \frac{\mu_H}{\mu_F}\right]T_{\text{ppHC}}(F) - zf(z)\frac{\mu_H}{\mu_F}\end{aligned}$$

(p) Here

$$T_{EHC}(tH + (1-t)F) = -zq_t(z)\left(\frac{th(z) + (1-t)f(z)}{tH(z) + (1-t)F(z)}\right)$$

and therefore

$$\begin{aligned}\nabla T_{\text{EHC},F\to H} &= \frac{d}{dt}T_{\text{ppHC}}(tH + (1-t)F)|_{t=0} \\ &= -zq(z)\left(\frac{h(z)F(z) - f(z)H(z)}{F(z)^2}\right) - \frac{zf(z)}{F(z)}\frac{d}{dt}q_t(z)|_{t=0}\end{aligned}$$

that is,

$$\nabla T_{\mathrm{EHC},F\to H} = -T_{\mathrm{EHC}}(F)\left[\frac{H(z)}{F(z)} + \frac{\mu_H}{\mu_F} + \frac{\gamma h(z)}{f(z)}[q(z) + zq'(z)]\right]$$

using (A.5).

Part II: Proof of property (3)

From (1), $T((1-t)F + tH) \approx T(F) + t\nabla T_{F\to H} + o(t^2)$ which can be extended: if

$$t = \sum_{i=1}^{n} t_i$$

then

$$T\left((1-t)F + \sum_{i=1}^{n} t_i H_i\right) \approx T(F) + \sum_{i=1}^{n} t_i \nabla T_{F\to H_i} + o(t^2)$$

Let the distribution F comprise values $y_1, y_2, \ldots y_n$ with frequencies $f(y_1), f(y_2), \ldots f(y_n)$ and let $t_i = tf(y_i)$ and $H_i = \Delta y_i$, $1 \le i \le n$. Then

$$\sum_{i=1}^{n} t_i \nabla T_{F\to H_i} = t\int_{-\infty}^{\infty} \mathrm{IF}(y;T;F)f(y)\,dy$$

and

$$\sum_{i=1}^{n} t_i H_i = t\int \Delta y f(y)\,dy = tF$$

Thus, $T((1-t)F + tF) \approx T(F) + t\int_{-\infty}^{\infty} \mathrm{IF}(y;T;F)f(y)\,dy + o(t^2)$ proving the result.

APPENDIX B: DISTRIBUTIONAL STATISTICS AND THEIR RECENTERED INFLUENCE FUNCTIONS IN TABULAR FORM

Distributional Statistic	Recentered Influence Function
Mean $\mu = \int xf(x)\,dx$	$\mathrm{RIF}(y;\mu;F) = y$
pth quantile point $v_p = F^{-1}(p)$	$\mathrm{RIF}(y;v_p;F) = \begin{cases} v_p + p/f(v_p) & y > v_p \\ v_p - (1-p)/f(v_p) & y < v_p \end{cases}$
Variance $\sigma^2 = \int (x-\mu)^2 f(x)\,dx$	$\mathrm{RIF}(y;\sigma^2;F) = (y-\mu_F)^2$
Gini coefficient $G = (1/\mu_F)\int F(x)[1-F(x)]\,dx$	$\mathrm{RIF}(y;G;F) = -\frac{y}{\mu_F}G_F + 1 - \frac{y}{\mu_F} + \frac{2}{\mu_F}\int_0^y F(x)\,dx$
Atkinson inequality index $I(e) = 1 - \frac{\xi}{\mu}, e > 0,$ (here, $U(x) = \begin{cases} x^{1-e}/(1-e) & 0 < e \neq 1 \\ \ln(x) & e = 1 \end{cases}$ and $U(\xi) = \int U(x) f(x)\,dx$)	$\mathrm{RIF}(y;I(e);F) = I_F + \begin{cases} \left\{\frac{e}{1-e} + \frac{y}{\mu_F}\right\}[1-I_F] - \frac{[1-I_F]^e y^{1-e}}{(1-e)\mu_F^{1-e}} & 0 < e \neq 1 \\ (1-I_F)\left\{\ln\{\mu_F(1-I_F)\} - \ln(y) + \left(\frac{y}{\mu_F} - 1\right)\right\} & e = 1 \end{cases}$

Generalized Lorenz ordinate at p $GL(p) = \int_0^{v_p} xf(x)\,dx$	$RIF(y; GL(p); F) = \begin{cases} y-(1-p)v_p & y<v_p \\ pv_p & y \geq v_p \end{cases}$
Lorenz ordinate at p $L(p) = \frac{1}{\mu}\int_0^{v_p} xf(x)\,dx$	$RIF(y; L(p); F) = \begin{cases} \frac{y-(1-p)v_p}{\mu_F} + T_{L_p}(F)\cdot\left(1-\frac{y}{\mu_F}\right) & y<v_p \\ \frac{pv_p}{\mu_F} + T_{L_p}(F)\cdot\left(1-\frac{y}{\mu_F}\right) & y \geq v_p \end{cases}$
FGT index for poverty line z $FGT_\alpha = \int_0^z \left(1-\frac{x}{z}\right)^\alpha f(x)\,dx$	$RIF(y; FGT_\alpha; F) = \begin{cases} \left(1-\frac{y}{z}\right)^\alpha & y<z \\ 0 & y>z \end{cases} \quad (\alpha \geq 0)$
Watts index for poverty line z $W = \int_0^z \ln\left(\frac{z}{x}\right) f(x)\,dx$	$RIF(y; W; F) = \begin{cases} \ln\left(\frac{z}{y}\right) & y<z \\ 0 & y>z \end{cases}$
Sen index for poverty line z $S = \frac{2}{zF(z)}\int_0^z (z-x)[F(z)-F(x)]f(x)\,dx$	$RIF(y; T_S; F) = \begin{cases} -\left(\frac{1}{F(z)}\right) T_S(F) - \frac{2}{zF(z)}\int_0^y (F(z)-F(x))\,dx + 2 & y<z \\ 0 & y>z \end{cases}$
TIP curve ordinate for poverty line z at p $TIP(p) = \begin{cases} \int_0^{v_p}(z-x)f(x)\,dx & v_p \leq z \\ \int_0^z (z-x)f(x)\,dx & v_p \geq z \end{cases}$	$RIF(y; TIP(p); F) = \begin{cases} \begin{cases} z-y & y<z \\ 0 & y>z \end{cases} & z<v_p \\ \begin{cases} pz+(1-p)v_p-y & y<v_p \\ p(z-v_p) & y>v_p \end{cases} & z>v_p \end{cases}$

Growth incidence curve ordinate at p $GIC(p) = \gamma q(v_p)$ (here and henceforth, γ is the aggregate growth rate and $q(x)$ is the growth pattern)	$RIF(y; GIC(p); F) = \begin{cases} \gamma\left\{\left[\frac{y}{\mu_F}+1\right]q(v_p) + \frac{pq'(v_p)}{f(v_p)}\right\} & y > v_p \\ \gamma\left\{\left[\frac{y}{\mu_F}+1\right]q(v_p) - \frac{(1-p)q'(v_p)}{f(v_p)}\right\} & y < v_p \end{cases}$
Pro-poorness for the FGT index $PP_\alpha^{FGT}(F) = \frac{\alpha}{z}\int_0^z x\left(1-\frac{x}{z}\right)^{\alpha-1} \times [q(x)-1]f(x)\,dx$ $(\alpha \geq 1)$	$RIF(y; PP_\alpha^{FGT}, F) = \begin{cases} \frac{\alpha y}{z}\left(1-\frac{y}{z}\right)^{\alpha-1}\{\gamma q(y)[q(y)+yq'(y)]-1\} - \left[\frac{y}{\mu_F}\right]T_{ppFGT\alpha}(F) & y<z \\ -\left[\frac{y}{\mu_F}\right]T_{ppFGT\alpha}(F) & y>z \end{cases}$
Pro-poorness for the Watts index $PP^W(F) = \int_0^z [q(x)-1]f(x)\,dx$	$RIF(y; PP^W, F) = \begin{cases} \{\gamma q(y)[q(y)+yq'(y)]-1\} - \left[\frac{y}{\mu_F}\right]T_{ppW}(F) & y<z \\ -\left[\frac{y}{\mu_F}\right]T_{ppW}(F) & y>z \end{cases}$
Pro-poorness for the headcount ratio $PP^{HC}(F) = z(q(z)-1)f(z)$	$RIF(y; PP^{HC}; F) = -\left[\frac{y}{\mu_F}\right]T_{ppHC}(F) - zf(z)\frac{y}{\mu_F}, \quad (y \neq z)$
Poverty elasticity of the headcount ratio, $PEHC(F) = -(zq(z)f(z)/F(z))$	$RIF(y; PEHC; F) = \begin{cases} -T_{EHC}(F)\left[\frac{1-F(z)}{F(z)}+\frac{y}{\mu_F}\right] & y<z \\ T_{EHC}(F)\left[1-\frac{y}{\mu_F}\right] & y>z \end{cases}$

CHAPTER 7

A NOTE ON MULTIDIMENSIONAL DISTRIBUTION-SENSITIVE POVERTY AXIOMS

Mª Casilda Lasso de la Vega and Ana Urrutia

ABSTRACT

In the unidimensional poverty field, a number of axioms capture the distribution sensitivity among the poor. One of them is the monotonicity sensitivity axiom that demands that a poverty measure should be more sensitive to a reduction in the income of a poor person, the poorer that person is. On the other hand, the minimal transfer axiom requires poverty to decrease when a transfer of income is made from a poor person to a poorer one. These axioms turn out to be identical, but they provide different and interesting interpretations. Both of them rely deeply on the income-ranking of the poor.

Some generalizations of the minimal transfer axiom and its variations have been proposed in the multidimensional framework. In none of them the partial ordering of the poor is taken into account. No counterpart of the monotonicity sensitivity axiom exists.

This note introduces multidimensional generalizations of the two mentioned axioms, keeping the crucial assumption that only when the poor involved are unambiguously ranked are the axioms uncontroversial.

Inequality, Mobility and Segregation: Essays in Honor of Jacques Silber
Research on Economic Inequality, Volume 20, 161–173

ISSN: 1049-2585/doi:10.1108/S1049-2585(2012)0000020010

We show that the two generalizations proposed are also identical in the multidimensional setting although offering different interpretations. Relationships between the new properties and those existing in the literature are analyzed.

INTRODUCTION

This paper focuses on two axioms that have been proposed following Sen's (1976) suggestion that a poverty measure should capture the exact pattern of the distribution among the poor. On the one hand Donaldson and Weymark (1986) introduce the minimal transfer axiom that demands that poverty should decrease when a transfer of income is made from a poor person to a poorer one.[1] On the other hand, the monotonicity sensitivity axiom proposed by Kakwani (1980) requires a poverty measure to be more sensitive to a drop in a poor person's income the poorer the person happens to be.

Since the transfers from one individual to a poorer one reduce inequality, the transfer axiom makes clear that a poverty measure should be sensitive to the inequality among the poor: the lower the inequality among the poor, the lower the poverty level. However, it is not so clear how this property could help policy makers in the alleviation of poverty when additional resources can be distributed among the poor. Now the monotonicity sensitivity axiom shows its interest. When interventions take place, this latter axiom reveals that targeting the poorest group achieves a maximum reduction in poverty levels.

What is more interesting is that the minimal transfer axiom and the monotonicity sensitivity axiom impose the same restrictions on the functional form of the poverty measure (Kakwani, 1980; Zheng, 1997).

The equivalence between the above axioms is well known to many theorists and will be formally proved in Section "The multidimensional monotonicity sensitivity and minimal transfer axioms" in the multidimensional setting. Actually the intuition behind it is quite simple. Imagine that an additional amount of income is given to a poor individual q. Poverty is bound to decrease. Now imagine that individual q transfers the extra amount to a poorer individual p. If the minimal transfer axiom is assumed, then poverty decreases. Notice that the final result is an increment in the income of individual p. Thus, the poorer the individual receiving an extra amount of income is, the higher the decrease in poverty. Conversely, imagine that individual q transfers an amount of income to a poorer individual p. At first the situation can be seen as individual q receiving the extra amount, whereas in the final stage individual p is the receiver. Since monotonicity sensitivity holds, poverty is lower in the second situation, and thus, the minimal transfer axiom is now fulfilled.

We would like to stress that both the minimal transfer and the monotonicity sensitivity axioms rely deeply on the income-ranking of the poor, that is, the two individuals p and q involved are unambiguously ordered. Then, the two axioms come down to the same property.

The need for a multidimensional approach to the measurement of poverty has already been emphasized in the literature, and a number of axioms have been introduced trying to capture multidimensional poverty.[2] Some of them attempt to generalize those existing in the unidimensional framework. In this respect, multidimensional generalizations of the minimal transfer axiom have been proposed. The multidimensional transfer axiom, henceforth MTP,[3] explored by Tsui (2002) and Bourguignon and Chakravarty (2003), is one of the most widely used in the derivation of multidimensional poverty indices.[4] However, some difficulties arise when MTP is used to order distributions, since poverty comparisons are allowed only when one distribution is obtained from another by transferring between two poor individuals the same proportions of all the attributes. Firstly, the reasons for transferring all the dimensions in the same proportions are not clear. Secondly, the idea of a transfer is not necessarily meaningful for all the attributes, for instance education or health. Finally, if the transfers are made between any two poor people, where one is not necessarily poorer than the other, the motivations for considering that the new distribution shows less poverty are not evident.

Although MTP coincides with the minimal transfer axiom when only one attribute is considered, when more dimensions are taken into consideration, in our view, MTP does not maintain the rationale behind this axiom. The reason is that MTP considers transfers between any two poor individuals, not necessarily one poorer than the other. Moreover, it is clear that the alternative interpretation provided by the monotonicity sensitivity axiom is completely lost in the multidimensional framework.

In addition, it is worth noting that none of the existing generalizations manage to extend the notion given by the monotonicity sensitivity axiom. Indeed, no multidimensional counterpart of the monotonicity sensitivity axiom exists, and it is not obvious how to design such a property. In this paper, we develop multidimensional generalizations of both the monotonicity sensitivity axiom and the minimal transfer axiom, which bear a similar relationship to each other as in the unidimensional case. We also prove that they are identical in the multidimensional framework, although keeping the different interpretations.

Specifically, the generalization of the monotonicity sensitivity axiom proposed in this paper, henceforth MS, demands that in a multidimensional context too, a poverty measure should be more sensitive to a decrease in any attribute of a poor individual, the poorer the person is. This note proves that it is equivalent for a poverty measure to fulfill MS or to satisfy that the poverty level diminishes under a transfer of any attribute from a poor individual to a poorer one. This latter property is the poverty counterpart of the Pigou–Dalton bundle principle introduced by Fleurbaey and Trannoy (2003) and explored in Diez, Lasso de la Vega, de Sarachu, and Urrutia (2007) and Lasso de la Vega, Urrutia, and de Sarachu (2010). We will refer to this axiom as MT. As a consequence, MS and MT may be considered straightforward generalizations of the monotonicity sensitivity axiom, and of the minimal transfer axiom, since they extend the original idea behind both axioms. The new concepts MS and MT have much to offer over the axioms commonly used in the multidimensional poverty literature. In fact, MT gets over the difficulties that MTP presents. First of all, transfers take place only between two poor people, one unambiguously poorer than the other. Second, it is not necessary to transfer all the attributes in the same proportions. And finally, the attributes considered as transferable can be selected. Although this appealing axiom seems to lead to one of the coarsest poverty orderings, not all the poverty indices, not even those fulfilling MTP, as we will show in this note, are consistent with it. We will show in Section "The multidimensional monotonicity sensitivity and minimal transfer axioms" that the families derived by Chakravarty, Mukherjee, and Ranade (1998), Chakravarty and Silber (2008), and Tsui (2002) fulfill the new axiom. By contrast, the indices in Maasoumi and Lugo (2008) fail the requirement. Finally, as regards the class introduced by Bourguignon and Chakravarty (2003), we will identify the subfamily consistent with MS and the subfamily that violates the axiom.

Some other specific issues in the multidimensional context have also been analyzed in the literature. Taking into account the sensitivity of poverty to the correlation between distributions of attributes, Tsui (2002) introduces the poverty nondecreasing rearrangement, PNR.[5]

In order to be sensitive to attribute dispersion and attribute correlation, most of the existing multidimensional poverty measures have been derived assuming MTP along with PNR. In this paper, we prove that for subgroup decomposable poverty families, invoking MTP and PNR is more demanding than MS, or equivalently, than MT.

The rest of this paper is structured as follows. Section "Notation and basic definitions" begins with a brief introduction of the notation and basic definitions, and reviews some multidimensional axioms concerned with the distribution among the poor. In Section "The multidimensional monotonicity sensitivity and minimal transfer axioms" we propose and analyze the multidimensional monotonicity sensitivity axiom, and the multidimensional minimal transfer axiom, MT, and show that they are in fact equivalent. Finally, Section "Conclusions" offers some conclusions.

NOTATION AND BASIC DEFINITIONS

We consider a population of $n \geq 3$ individuals endowed with a bundle of $k \geq 2$ attributes, where k is given and fixed. We assume that each attribute is represented by a continuous variable that is measurable on a ratio scale.[6] A multidimensional distribution is represented by an $n \times k$ real matrix X. The ijth entry of X, denoted by x_{ij}, represents the ith individual's amount of the jth attribute. The ith row of X, denoted by x_i, is individual i's vector of attributes. We denote $M(n)$ the class of all $n \times k$ real matrices over the non-negative real elements. Let D be the set of all such matrices, that is, $D = \underset{n \in N}{\cup} M(n)$. Comparisons of vectors of attributes are denoted as follows: $x_q \geq x_p$ if $x_{qj} \geq x_{pj}$ for all $j = 1, \ldots, k$, $x_q > x_p$ if $x_{qj} \geq x_{pj}$ and $x_p \neq x_q$.

For any given poverty line $z_j > 0$, individual i is deprived as regards attribute j if $x_{ij} < z_j$. Let $z = (z_1, z_2, \ldots, z_k) \in \mathbb{R}^k_{++}$ be the vector of poverty lines for all $j = 1, \ldots, k$. A number of different approaches may be used to identify the multidimensional poor in the society.[7] Nevertheless the axioms proposed in this paper and the results obtained do not depend on the identification method selected.

In this paper a multidimensional poverty index is a real value function $P : D \times \mathbb{R}^k_{++} \to \mathbb{R}$ satisfying the following six properties:

(i) *Focus*: For any $(X, z) \in D \times \mathbb{R}^k_{++}$, any person i and attribute j such that $x_{ij} \geq z_j$, an increase in x_{ij} does not change the poverty level $P(X, z)$.
(ii) *Monotonicity*: For any $(X, z) \in D \times \mathbb{R}^k_{++}$, any poor person i and attribute j such that $x_{ij} < z_j$, a decrease in x_{ij} increases the poverty level $P(X, z)$.
(iii) *Continuity*: For any $z \in \mathbb{R}^k_{++}$, P is a continuous function in $X \in D$.
(iv) *Normalization*: For any $(X, z) \in D \times \mathbb{R}^k_{++}$ if $x_{ij} \geq z_j$ for all i and j, then $P(X, z) = 0$.
(v) *Symmetry*: For any $(X, z) \in D \times \mathbb{R}^k_{++}$, $P(X, z) = P(\Pi X, z)$ where Π is a permutation matrix.
(vi) *Replication invariance*: For any $(X, z) \in D \times \mathbb{R}^k_{++}$, $P(X, z) = P(X^{(l)}, z)$, where $X^{(l)}$ is a l-fold replication of X.

Most of the indices proposed in the literature are subgroup decomposable according to the following definition:

- *Subgroup decomposability*: There exists a function $\phi : \mathbb{R}^k_+ \times \mathbb{R}^k_{++} \to \mathbb{R}$ such that:

$$P(X,z) = \frac{1}{n} \sum_{1 \le i \le n} \phi(x_i, z) \qquad \text{for all } X \in D \tag{1}$$

The function ϕ is the same for all the individuals and it is usually interpreted as individual i's multidimensional poverty level.

The next axiom reduces to the minimal transfer axiom when only one attribute is considered. It is proposed by Tsui (2002) and Bourguignon and Chakravarty (2003) in order to capture dispersion of attribute distributions.

- *Multidimensional transfer axiom*, MTP: For any $z \in \mathbb{R}^k_{++}$ and for any $X, Y \in D$ if $Y = BX$ for some bistochastic matrix B, where the transfers are among the poor, then $P(Y,z) \le P(X;z)$.

MTP involves transfers that replace the original bundles of any pair of poor individuals by some convex combination of all their attributes. Notice that these poor individuals do not have to be ordered. Tsui (2002) and Bourguignon and Chakravarty (2003) analyze the implications of MTP for subgroup decomposable poverty measures, and prove that MTP is equivalent to requiring that the function ϕ in Eq. (1) be convex.

The following axiom introduced by Tsui (2002) is concerned with poverty change when the bundles of attributes of two poor individuals are rearranged so that one receives at least as much of every attribute as the other, and more of at least one attribute. As a consequence, one becomes unambiguously poorer than the other.

Definition 2. Let $X, Y \in D$. Distribution X may be derived from distribution Y by a *correlation increasing transfer* if there exist two individuals p and q such that (i) $x_{pj} = \min\{y_{pj}, y_{qj}\}$ for all $j = 1, \ldots, k$, (ii) $x_{qj} = \max\{y_{pj}, y_{qj}\}$ for all $j = 1, \ldots, k$ and (iii) $x_m = y_m$ for all $m \neq p,q$.

- *Poverty nondecreasing rearrangement, PNR*: For any $(Y,z) \in D \times \mathbb{R}^k_{++}$, if $X \in D$ is derived from Y by a correlation increasing transfers between two poor individuals, with no one becoming nonpoor due to the transfers, then $P(Y,z) \le P(X;z)$.

THE MULTIDIMENSIONAL MONOTONICITY SENSITIVITY AND MINIMAL TRANSFER AXIOMS

In this section, we propose two multidimensional distribution-sensitive poverty axioms that are straightforward generalizations of the monotonicity sensitivity axiom proposed by Kakwani (1980) and the minimal transfer axiom proposed by Donaldson and Weymark (1986).

Let us consider two poor individuals, p and q, such that p is unambiguously poorer than q, that is, the respective vectors of attributes fulfill that $x_p < x_q$. Let us assume that a certain amount of one attribute is decreased for either individual p or individual q. Monotonicity demands that the poverty level increases under the two transformations. Nevertheless, the axiom we propose goes beyond monotonicity and, similarly to its unidimensional version, demands that the increase in poverty under the former decrement, that affecting the poorer individual, should be higher than under the latter. Formally, the axiom is formulated as follows:

Definition 3. Let $X, Y \in D$. Distribution Y is derived from X by a decrement δ to individual i if:

(i) $y_m = x_m$ for all $m \neq i$
(ii) $y_i = x_i - \delta$ where $\delta = (\delta_1, \ldots, \delta_k) \in \mathbb{R}^k_+$ with at least one $\delta_j > 0$.

- *Multidimensional monotonicity sensitivity axiom*, MS: For any $(X, z) \in D \times \mathbb{R}^k_{++}$, if $Y \in D$ is derived from X by a decrement δ to poor individual p, and $Y' \in D$ is derived from X by a decrement δ to poor individual q , such that $x_p < x_q - \delta$, then $P(Y; z) - P(X; z) \geq P(Y'; z) - P(X; z)$.

Note that individual p is unambiguously poorer than individual q. Then the axiom demands that a decrease in one attribute of a poorer person should count for more than the same decrease experienced by a less poor person. This axiom is of great interest for policy makers. Monotonicity sensitivity measures guarantee that targeting the poorest groups is the most efficient intervention in the alleviation of the poverty.

A Pigou–Dalton bundle transfer, PDB transfer, according to Fleurbaey and Trannoy (2003) is a progressive transfer of some attributes from one individual to a poorer one. We propose a direct multidimensional generalization of the minimal transfer axiom, MT, demanding that poverty should not increase under a PDB transfer as long as the individuals involved are poor.[8]

Definition 4. Let $X, Y \in D$. Distribution Y is derived from X by a *PDB transfer* from individual q to individual p if:

(i) $y_m = x_m$ for all $m \neq p,q$
(ii) $y_q = x_q - \delta$ and $y_p = x_p + \delta$ where $\delta = (\delta_1, \ldots, \delta_k) \in \mathbb{R}^k_+$ with at least one $\delta_j > 0$.
(iii) $y_q \geq y_p$

Note that conditions (ii) and (iii) imply that, in both the initial and the final distributions, individual p is poorer than individual q in all the attributes.

- *Multidimensional minimal transfer axiom*, MT: For any $(X, z) \in D \times \mathbb{R}^k_{++}$, if $Y \in D$ is derived from X by a PDB transfer from poor individual q to poor individual p, then $P(Y; z) \leq P(X; z)$.

As already mentioned, the monotonicity sensitivity axiom and the minimal transfer axiom impose the same restrictions on a poverty measure in the unidimensional field. The next proposition shows that the same happens with MS and MT.

Proposition 1. A poverty measure $P : D \times \mathbb{R}^k_{++} \to \mathbb{R}$ satisfies MS if and only if it satisfies MT.

Proof. Let $(X, z) \in D \times \mathbb{R}^k_{++}$ and Y be derived from X by a PDB transfer from poor individual q to poor individual p with $x_p < x_q$. Lets define $W \in D$ as $w_i = y_i$ if $i \neq q$ and $w_q = x_q$. Then Y is derived from W by a decrement to individual q and X is derived from W by a decrement to individual p. By MS $P(Y; z) \leq P(X; z)$. The converse of the proposition follows with a similar reasoning. Consider that Y and W are derived from X by decrements to individuals p and q, respectively, with $x_p < x_q$. Then W can be considered as derived from Y by a PDB transfer from individual q to individual p, and by MT $P(W; z) \leq P(Y; z)$. Hence MS holds. ■

Although, as proved in this proposition, MS and MT impose the same restrictions on the functional form of a poverty measure, the different interpretations of these two axioms shed light on the behavior of these measures.

If we add structure upon the poverty index, MS and MTP turn our not to be independent. Our next proposition shows that requiring validity of MTP and PNR for a subgroup decomposable function is more demanding than invoking MS.

Proposition 2. If a subgroup decomposable poverty measure $P : D \times \mathbb{R}^k_{++} \to \mathbb{R}$ satisfies MTP and PNR, then it fulfills MS.

Proof. Let x_p and x_q be the two poor individuals' bundles involved in a PDB transfer according to Definition 4. Lets assume that they only transfer an amount δ_1 of the first attribute and let $\delta = (\delta_1, 0, \ldots, 0)$. Given that P is a subgroup decomposable poverty measure, taking into account Proposition 1, it suffices to prove that $\phi(x_p) + \phi(x_q) \geq \phi(x_q - \delta) + \phi(x_p + \delta)$ where $x_q - \delta$ and $x_p - \delta$ are the two individuals' bundles after the transfer, and $x_p + \delta \leq x_q - \delta$. Lets consider $u = (x_{q1}, x_{p2}, \ldots, x_{pk})$ the bundle of an additional poor individual. Then $\phi(x_p) + \phi(x_q) + \phi(u) \geq \phi(x_q) + \phi(x_p + \delta) + \phi(u - \delta)$ by subgroup decomposability and MTP, $\geq \phi(x_q - \delta) + \phi(x_p + \delta) + \phi(u)$ by PNR. Again by subgroup decomposability we get the result. ■

This Proposition 2 makes a simple but important observation about the relationships of these criteria for subgroup decomposable poverty functions. Most of the poverty classes in the literature, such as Chakravarty et al. (1998), Chakravarty and Silber (2008), and Tsui (2002) families, are subgroup decomposable functions fulfilling MTP and PNR. Then, Proposition 2 ensures that all of them satisfy MS.

However, not all the poverty indices, not even those fulfilling MTP, are consistent with MS. Some examples can be found in the Bourguignon and Chakravarty (2003) poverty family. The members of this family fulfilling MTP are given by

$$P_{\text{BC}}(X; z) = \frac{1}{n} \sum_{i=1}^{n} \left(\sum_{j=1}^{k} w_j \left(\max\left(1 - \left(\frac{x_{ij}}{z_j}\right); 0\right)\right)^{\theta} \right)^{\alpha/\theta}$$

where θ is greater than 1, and α is greater than or equal to 1. Moreover, the relationship between α and θ determines whether PNR is satisfied or not. It is proved that when α is greater than or equal to θ, PNR is also fulfilled; and consequently, from Proposition 2, MS holds. Nevertheless, when α is smaller than θ the corresponding subfamily does not fulfill PNR. As regards this subfamily, examples can be found to prove that MS is not fulfilled. To see this, let us consider a society with two individuals p and q, whose bundles of attributes are (5,4) and (7,11), respectively, and suppose that the vector of thresholds for both dimensions is $z = (9,12)$. Notice that both individuals are deprived in both attributes. Let us assume two different transformations leading to two different social situations, A and B. In the first case, only the first attribute of the poorer individual p is decreased by 1 unit, and the bundles of attributes become (4,4) and (7,11) (social situation A). In the second case, only the first attribute of the richer individual q is decreased by the same amount and the bundles of attributes come to be (5,4) and (6,11) (social situation B). According to MS the increase in poverty in the first case should not be smaller than in the second. However, we get that the poverty level in social situation A is 0.3977, whereas in social situation B it is 0.4214 if the Bourguignon and Chakravarty poverty index for $\alpha=1$, $\theta=3$, and $w_1=w_2=0.5$ is considered.

Another example of not MS consistent indices can be found in the Maasoumi and Lugo (2008) poverty family, which is derived following an interesting approach based on the information theory. If the following index of the Maasoumi and Lugo family

$$P_{\mathrm{ML}}(X;z)=\frac{1}{n}\sum_{i=1}^{n}\left(\max\left(1-\frac{(\Sigma_{j=1}^{k}w_j x_{ij}^{\theta})^{1/\theta}}{(\Sigma_{j=1}^{k}w_j z_j^{\theta})^{1/\theta}};0\right)\right)^{\alpha}$$

with $\alpha=0.5$, $\theta=-10$, and $w_1=w_2=0.5$ considered, it is straightforward to see that in the above example the poverty level in social situation B, 0.6605, is higher than that in social situation A, 0.6156; therefore, MS is not satisfied. More examples can be found for the rest of members of the family to show that MS is violated.

CONCLUSIONS

This paper introduces a multidimensional generalization of the monotonicity sensitivity axiom and also a new multidimensional version of the minimal transfer axiom. Two main features characterize this proposal. On the one hand, and similar to their one-dimensional counterparts, the proposed generalizations are shown to be equivalent. Second, they keep the crucial assumption that only when the poor affected are unambiguously ranked the axioms are uncontroversial.

Although as proved, these two properties impose the same functional restriction to the poverty measure, they allow for different interpretations. The MTP demands that decreases in the inequality among the poor diminish the poverty. However, there are attributes for which transfers make no sense. In addition, sometimes policy makers can target specific groups. In these circumstances, the MS reveals that it is more efficient to focus on the poorest individuals.

Although there exist some indices that violate the new axioms, we have shown that the multidimensional poverty families that fulfill MTP and PNR preserve the underlying motivations behind the monotonicity sensitivity and the minimal transfer axioms.

This note is restricted to attributes represented by ratio-scale variables. Monotonicity sensitivity compares the effect in the poverty level when the "same amount" of one attribute is reduced for two poor people. When we deal with ratio-scale variables the meaning of the "same" amount is quite clear. This is not the case for categorical or ordinal variables. Thus, work in greater depth would be interesting in order to seek similar properties when these types of dimensions are considered.

The axioms introduced in this note have a simplifying function in the literature on multivariate poverty, and on links with unidimensional poverty. Moreover, taking into account the rationales behind them we think that it would be meaningful to consider measures consistent with them when poverty needs to be examined and analyzed.

NOTES

1. For a comprehensive discussion about the different transfer sensitivity axioms and their relationships see for instance Zheng (1997).
2. Thorough surveys of the literature on multidimensional poverty are provided by Chakravarty (2009) and Kakwani and Silber (2008).
3. MTP, which will be formally defined in Section "Notation and basic definitions", is the poverty counterpart to the uniform majorization criterion proposed by Kolm (1977) in the inequality field. Tsui (2002) refers to it as the poverty nonincreasing minimal transfer axiom with respect to uniform majorization criterion.
4. Another more demanding multidimensional generalization of the minimal transfer principle is the one-dimensional transfer principle, OTP, introduced by Bourguignon and Chakravarty (2003). They show that the poverty measures possessing first-order partial derivatives and satisfying OTP are additive across individuals and across attribute components.
5. PNR, which will be formally defined in Section "Notation and basic definitions", is the poverty counterpart to the correlation increasing majorization of multidimensional inequality indices proposed by Tsui (1999). Bourguignon and Chakravarty (2003) suggest a stronger axiom, the nondecreasing poverty under a correlation increasing switch axiom, NDCIS, when the attributes are substitutes. When the attributes are complements, they propose an axiom that requires poverty not to increase under a correlation increasing switch.

6. Our framework rules out the possibility of including a dimension that is represented by an ordinal or categorical variable.
7. See for instance, Atkinson (2003), Bourguignon and Chakravarty (2003), Gordon, Nandy, Pantazis, Pemberton, and Townsend (2003), Lasso de la Vega (2010), and Alkire and Foster (2011).
8. Diez et al. (2007) analyze the relationships between the corresponding inequality axiom and others already introduced in the literature. Lasso de la Vega et al. (2010) examine the implications of this new axiom for an aggregative inequality measure.

ACKNOWLEDGMENTS

This research has been partially supported by the Spanish Ministerio de Educación y Ciencia under project SEJ2009-11213, cofunded by FEDER, and by the Basque Government under the project GIC07/146-IT-377-07.

REFERENCES

Alkire, S., & Foster, J. (2011). Counting and multidimensional poverty measurement. *Journal of Public Economics*, *95*(7–8), 476–487.

Atkinson, A. B. (2003). Multidimensional deprivation: Contrasting social welfare and counting approaches. *Journal of Economic Inequality*, *1*, 51–65.

Bourguignon, F., & Chakravarty, S. R. (2003). The measurement of multidimensional poverty. *Journal of Economic Inequality*, *1*, 25–49.

Chakravarty, S. R. (2009). Inequality, polarization and poverty: Advances in distributional analysis. In J. Silber (Ed.), *Economic studies in inequality, social exclusion and well-being* (Vol. 6). New York, NY: Springer.

Chakravarty, S. R., Mukherjee, D., & Ranade, R. (1998). The family of subgroup and factor decomposable measures of multidimensional poverty. *Research on Economic Inequality*, *8*, 175–194.

Chakravarty, S. R., & Silber, J. (2008). Measuring multidimensional poverty: The axiomatic approach. In N. Kakwani & J. Silber (Eds.), *Quantitative approaches to multidimensional poverty measurement* (pp. 192–209). New York, NY: Palgrave Macmillan.

Diez, H., Lasso de la Vega, M. C., de Sarachu, A., & Urrutia, A. (2007). A consistent multidimensional generalization of the Pigou-Dalton transfer principle: An analysis. *The B.E. Journal of Theoretical Economics*, *7*(1), Art. 45, 1–15.

Donaldson, D., & Weymark, J. A. (1986). Properties of fixed-population poverty indices. *International Economic Review*, *27*, 667–688.

Fleurbaey, M., & Trannoy, A. (2003). The impossibility of a Paretian egalitarian. *Social Choice and Welfare*, *21*, 243–263.

Gordon, D., Nandy, S., Pantazis, C., Pemberton, S., & Townsend, T. (2003). *Child poverty in the developing world*. Bristol: The Policy Press.

Kakwani, N. (1980). On a class of poverty measures. *Econometrica*, *48*, 437–446.

Kakwani, N., & Silber, J. (2008). *Quantitative approaches to multidimensional poverty measurement*. New York, NY: Palgrave Macmillan.

Kolm, S. C. (1977). Multidimensional egalitarianism. *Quarterly Journal of Economics*, *91*, 1–13.

Lasso de la Vega, C. (2010). Counting poverty orderings and deprivation curves. Studies in applied welfare analysis. *Research on Economic Inequality*, *18*, 153–172.

Lasso de la Vega, C., Urrutia, A., & de Sarachu, A. (2010). Characterizing multidimensional inequality measures which fulfil the Pigou-Dalton bundle principle. *Social Choice and Welfare*, *35*, 319–329.

Maasoumi, E., & Lugo, M. A. (2008). The information basis of multivariate poverty assessment. In N. Kakwani & J. Silber (Eds.), *Quantitative approaches to multidimensional poverty measurement* (pp. 1–29). New York, NY: Palgrave Macmillan.

Sen, A. K. (1976). Poverty: An ordinal approach to measurement. *Econometrica*, *44*, 219–231.

Tsui, K. Y. (1999). Multidimensional inequality and multidimensional generalized entropy measures: An axiomatic derivation. *Social Choice and Welfare*, *16*(1), 145–157.

Tsui, K. Y. (2002). Multidimensional poverty indices. *Social Choice and Welfare*, *19*, 69–93.

Zheng, B. (1997). Aggregate poverty measures. *Journal of Economic Surveys*, *11*(2), 123–162.

CHAPTER 8

CONVERGENCE CLUB EMPIRICS: EVIDENCE FROM INDIAN STATES

Sanghamitra Bandyopadhyay

ABSTRACT

The distribution dynamics of incomes across Indian states are examined using the entire income distribution. Unlike standard regression approaches, this approach allows us to identify specific distributional characteristics such as polarisation and stratification. The period between 1965 and 1997 exhibits the formation of two convergence clubs: one at 50% and another at 125% of the national average income. Income disparities across the states declined over the sixties and then increased from the seventies to the nineties. Conditioning exercises reveal that the formation of the convergence clubs is associated with the disparate distribution of macro-economic factors such as capital expenditure and fiscal deficits. In particular, capital expenditure, fiscal deficits and education expenditures are found to be associated with the formation of the upper convergence club.

Keywords: Convergence clubs; distribution dynamics; fiscal deficits; capital expenditure; panel data; India

JEL Classification: C23; E62; O23

Inequality, Mobility and Segregation: Essays in Honor of Jacques Silber
Research on Economic Inequality, Volume 20, 175–203

ISSN: 1049-2585/doi:10.1108/S1049-2585(2012)0000020011

INTRODUCTION

One of the paradoxes of our times is the co-existence of extreme economic affluence amidst enormous pockets of poverty. This phenomenon holds across countries and even more so within countries and across regions. Cross-country and cross-regional distributions of per capita income seem quite volatile. The extremes seem to be diverging away from each other – with the poor becoming poorer and the rich richer. This paper documents the dynamics of income across Indian states over three decades (1965–1997), and provides some explanations of the observed income dynamics.

Explaining why some countries or regions grow faster than others is important – persistent disparities in income across countries and across regions lead to wide disparities in welfare and are often a source of social and political tension, particularly so within national boundaries. Over the last five decades, India's population has risen by almost three-fold, and its GDP has increased almost 30-fold. This growth experience has not been evenly distributed – some of the richest states in India, like Gujarat and Maharashtra, are similar to middle-income countries such as Brazil and Poland in their levels of development, whereas the poorest states such as Bihar and Orissa are more akin to that of some of the poorest Sub-Saharan African countries.

In the recent empirical growth literature on the convergence of GDPs across regions and countries, the 'growth regression' approach (Barro & Sala-i-Martin, 1992) is popularly used to establish empirics of convergence (and divergence). In this paper, however, I observe the distributional dynamics rather than just beta or sigma convergence. This approach moves away from establishing simply empirics of convergence and divergence; it describes the evolution of state-level income distribution over time. In doing so, one can identify the empirics of catch-up more accurately and the presence of long-run cohesive tendencies, polarisation, stratification or the emergence of convergence clubs. I then provide some explanations of the observed dynamics: I find several macro-economic indicators to be significantly associated with the evolution of the income distribution and the formation of convergence clubs.

The paper reveals the existence of two convergence clubs: in the late 1960s I observe that there were some tendencies of cohesion, but from the 1970s to the 1990s the income distribution spreads significantly and I observe the formation of two convergence clubs. The paper focuses in particular on the role of a set of macro-economic indicators in explaining the observed polarisation. The results suggest that some macro-economic indicators, namely capital expenditures, education expenditures and fiscal deficits are robustly associated with the upper-income convergence club.

This exercise follows from the new wave of empirical growth analyses across Indian states. Studies which use the popular cross-section regression approach, namely Bajpai and Sachs (1996), Cashin and Sahay (1996), Nagaraj, Varoukadis, and Venganzones (1997), Aiyar (2000) and Trivedi (2003) uncover diverging distributional characteristics but are unable to describe intra-distributional mobility. Convergence as an empirical concept, as defined by Solow (1957), is understood as a single economy approaching its theoretically derived steady state growth path. Standard empirical analyses only study the behaviour of the representative economy. While such an empirical methodology can accurately uncover tendencies of divergence, it does not uncover the distributional patterns (of polarisation or stratification) that I wish to expose. Similarly, time series approaches as used by Carlino and Mills (1993) that estimate the univariate dynamics of income also remain incomplete in describing the dynamics of the entire cross-section. Several country studies have highlighted the emergence of such convergence clubs, such as for China (Maasoumi & Le Wang, 2008), Greece (Fotopolos, 2006), the European Union (Grazia-Pittau, Zelli, & Johnson, 2010; Pittau & Zelli, 2006) and Brazil (Andrade, Madalozzo, & Valls Pereira, 2004).

A large literature discusses what drives such income disparities (see Durlauf & Quah, 1999, for an overview), though it is only recently that studies have emphasised the non-linear relationship of the many drivers of economic growth with growth outcomes. Kalaitzidakis, Mamuneas, Sawides, and Stengos (2001) and Fiaschi and Lavezzi (2003), for instance, focus on the non-linear impact of education on economic growth. Standard empirical tools of panel or cross-section regression are not designed to explain or even detect the presence of convergence clubs at different parts of the income distribution. The presence of these convergence clubs corresponds to the existence of multiple equilibria, as is conceived in the theoretical contributions of Bernaud and Durlauf (1994), Durlauf and Johnson (1995), Esteban and Ray (1994), Ben-David (1994), De Long (1988) and Galor and Zeira (1993). These models allow for explicit patterns of cross-economy interaction, where economies cluster together into groups to emerge endogenously. The focus of this literature is that economies do not evolve in isolation, but in clubs and groups. These distributional characteristics cannot be exposed under standard empirical techniques of panel regression or time series analyses for studying convergence. The analysis in this paper adopts this approach empirically.

Bianchi (1995), Jones (1997), Desdoigts (1994), Fiaschi and Lavezzi (2003) and Grazia-Pittau et al. (2010) like the analysis undertaken in this paper, use non-parametric methods to track the distribution dynamics. In this paper I use the distribution dynamics approach as presented in Quah (1997). It encompasses both time series and cross-section properties of the data simultaneously where the intra-distribution dynamics information is encoded in a transition probability matrix, and the ergodic distribution associated with this matrix describes the long-term behaviour of the income distribution. I find evidence of two convergence clubs, namely a low-income (poor) club of states and a high-income club of states. There is also little evidence of mobility of states between the two clubs. This method can also be extended to identify factors governing the formation of these convergence clubs, and I focus on the non-linear effects of some macro-economic factors on the distribution dynamics. I find that several macro-economic factors, such as capital expenditure patterns, fiscal deficits and education expenditures, explain the formation of the upper-income convergence clubs.

The rest of the paper is organised as follows. Section 'Some basic statistics' presents some statewise basic statistics. Section 'The distribution dynamics approach' describes the observed distribution dynamics and polarisation, and Section 'What explains polarisation? The role of macro-economic factors' presents a number of explanatory macro-economic factors which are associated with the observed distribution dynamics. Section 'Interpretation of results' presents a brief discussion of the results and Section 'Conclusions' concludes.

SOME BASIC STATISTICS

Let us have an initial look at the state-wise income distribution across Indian states. Some simple estimations clearly demarcate the rich states from the poorer states. GDP per capita and price data used for this paper have been obtained from Ozler, Dutt, and Ravallion (1996). GDP per capita data for 1989–1998 has also been obtained from the World Bank, compiled as a separate dataset, and from Government of India sources.[1]

Fig. 1 highlights the states as 'rich' or 'poor' in 1965 and 1995 on the basis of GDP. One can see that there has been a lot of persistence for both the rich and the poor states. There are some changes in the 1995 map: in particular, the rich states' group has seen the addition of Karnataka and Tamil Nadu but the loss of West Bengal. Therefore, some upward mobility has taken place.

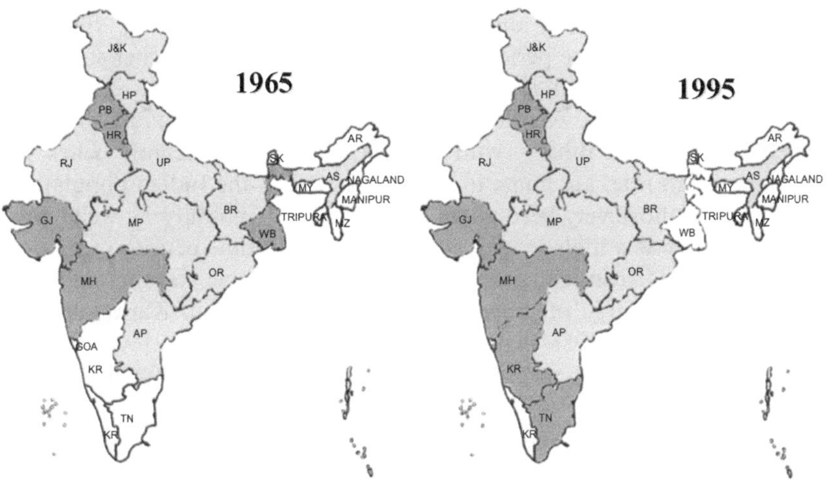

Fig. 1. AS Assam, BR Bihar, GJ Gujarat, HP Himachal Pradesh, J&K Jammu and Kashmir, KR Karnataka, MH Maharashtra, MP Madhya Pradesh, OR Orissa, PB Punjab, RJ Rajasthan, TN Tamil Nadu, UP Uttar Pradesh, WB West Bengal. Indian states: Rich (light grey), Poor (dark grey).

Let us take a look at some simple statistics of these states. The richest state, Punjab, experienced a rise in GDP per capita of 34% between 1965 and 1988, reflecting an increase of 34% over the period, followed by another 21% rise by 1997. Similarly Gujarat's and Maharashtra's per capita income increased by 20% and 27%, respectively, and by another staggering 40% and 51% by 1997, respectively. This is starkly against the fact that the Indian average per capita GDP rose by only 27% between 1965 and 1988, and increased by another 33% by 1997. Thus Punjab was already almost twice as rich as the Indian average in 1965, while Maharashtra, Gujarat and Haryana's per capita GDP was also almost twice the Indian average in 1965, and remained so in 1997. Averaging, Punjab, Haryana, Gujarat and Maharashtra were at 123% of the national average in 1965 and over 152% in 1988, and grew a further 36% as a group from 1988 to 1997.

The low-income club states are mostly clustered in north India, namely Bihar and Orissa in the east, Rajasthan in the west, and Uttar Pradesh in the north. States of Bihar, Orissa, Uttar Pradesh and Rajasthan have had their GDPs per capita at 85% in 1965 and 80% in 1988 of the Indian average, respectively, and grew by only another 19% as a group by 1997. To summarise, over the time period studied, the income of the richer states has been almost three times that of the poor states. It is interesting to note that the six poorest states – Madhya Pradesh, Assam, Andhra Pradesh, Uttar Pradesh, Orissa, and Bihar – with average incomes significantly below the national growth rate, are home to more than half of the Indian population.

There have, however, been some experiences of mobility as well. West Bengal, which was a high-growth state in the earlier time periods examined, notably, dropped from being the second highest income state to eighth by 1988. Again, the surge of growth in the 1980s pushed up Karnataka and Tamil Nadu, whose 1988 per capita income increased by 21% and 36% between 1980 and 1988, respectively, and by a further 45% for both states by 1997.

To further summarise the income dynamics, between 1965 and 1997 the standard deviation (SD) of per capita income increased by 192%, while the inter-quartile range (IQR) increased by 137%. With the SD almost double that of the IQR, the increase in spread is clearly evident. However, with the IQR accounting for the middle 50% of the distribution, the fact that the SD is significantly larger than the IQR implies that the rise in SD is attributable to some high performers outperforming the rest of the intermediate and poor states.

To summarise these basic statistics of the dynamic spatial patterns of Indian regional growth,

- There is evidence of both persistence and mobility.
- While some rich states have remained rich, and the poor have remained poor, there have been some instances of high performers who have declined in their performance over the period, such as West Bengal, while others have picked up over the period, for example Karnataka and Tamil Nadu.
- Thus, apart from those consistent performers, there is plenty of evidence of relative success and failure all across India.

THE DISTRIBUTION DYNAMICS APPROACH

So far I have only taken a look at several snap-shots of how different Indian states have grown or fallen behind over time. For a more informative picture, I will now track the evolution of the entire income distribution over time; this will reveal the intra-distributional dynamics of GDP growth of the Indian states over the given period of time. Markov chains are used to approximate and estimate the laws of motion of the evolving distribution[2]. The intra-distribution dynamics information is then encoded in a transition probability matrix.

To set up the transition probability matrix, the income distribution is divided into a number of 'income states'; each spatial unit (i.e., Indian state) is then located within this income space. For example, in the lowest income state the poorest Indian states are included, whereas in the highest income state the richest Indian states are included. The transition probability matrix then describes the probabilities with which the Indian states would transit from one income state to another. If the probabilities of transition from one income state to another are non-zero, then one deduces mobility. If these probabilities are small, or almost zero, one deduces persistence.

There are, however, some drawbacks to the discretised approach. The most significant drawback is that the selection of income states is arbitrary. Such arbitrary sets of discretisations may lead to different results. The stochastic kernel improves on the transition probability matrix by allowing the space of income values to be a continuum of states[3]. Using the stochastic kernel removes the arbitrariness in the discretisation of the states. One now has an infinite number of rows and columns replacing the transition probability matrix and observes a probability mass (the sloping surface) recording the probabilities of persistence and mobility.[4]

One can interpret the stochastic kernels as follows. Fig. 2 presents two benchmark stochastic kernel contours. The vertical axis measures the time *t*

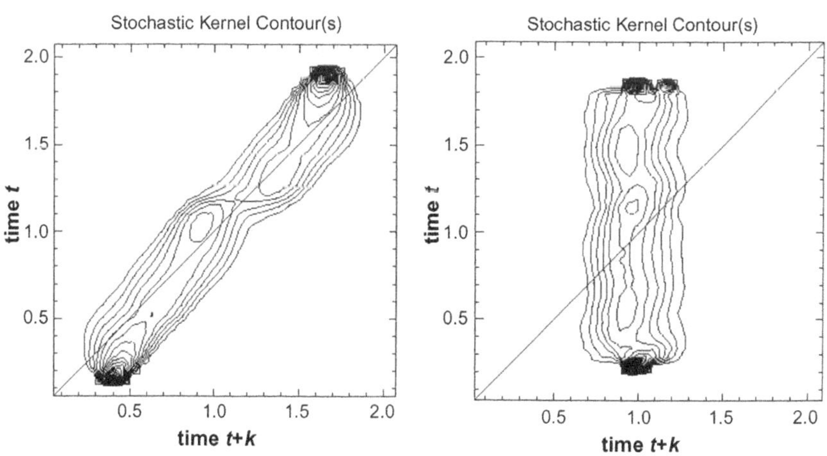

Fig. 2. Benchmark Stochastic Kernels.

income distribution, and the horizontal axis measures the time $t+k$ income distribution. If the probability mass runs along the diagonal, as in the first panel in Fig. 2, it indicates persistence in the Indian states' relative positions and therefore exhibits low tendencies of mobility. Convergence is indicated when the probability mass runs parallel to the t axis in the second panel of Fig. 2. If the probability mass were to run along the negative slope, it would imply overtaking of the economies in their rankings (not in figure). If the probability mass runs parallel to the $t+k$ axis, it indicates that the probability of being in any income state at period $t+k$ is independent of their position in period t; this, then, is evidence of low persistence (not in figure).

We can now present the salient distribution dynamics over time periods 1965–1970, 1971–1980, 1981–88 and 1990–97. Figs. 3–6 present the stochastic kernels for relative per capita income of 1-year transitions for four sub-periods 1965–1970, 1971–1980, 1981–1988 and 1990–1997.

Observation of the stochastic kernels and the contour plots reveal that the later years provide increasing evidence of persistence and low probabilities of changing their relative position. The most salient feature is that of the existence of two convergence clubs in all time periods. Over the periods 1965–1970, 1971–1980, 1981–1988 and 1989–1997 we observe in Figs. 3–6 the probability mass lengthening and shifting totally in line with the positive diagonal, the two peaks still at the two ends of the mass. The cluster of States at the two peaks: one of which consists of low income economies at around 50% of the all India average, while the other peak consists of States

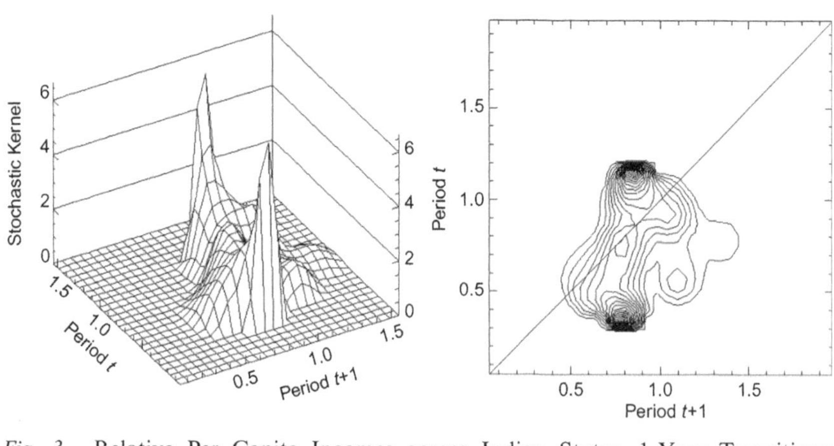

Fig. 3. Relative Per Capita Incomes across Indian States, 1-Year Transitions. 1965–1970.

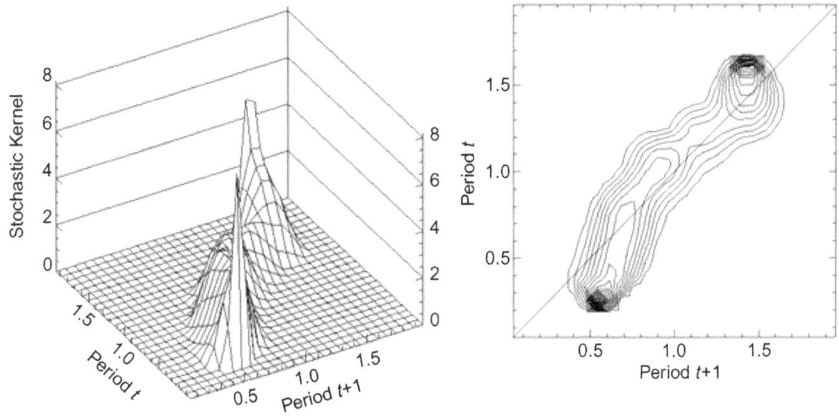

Fig. 4. Relative Per Capita Incomes across Indian States, 1-Year Transitions. 1971–1980.

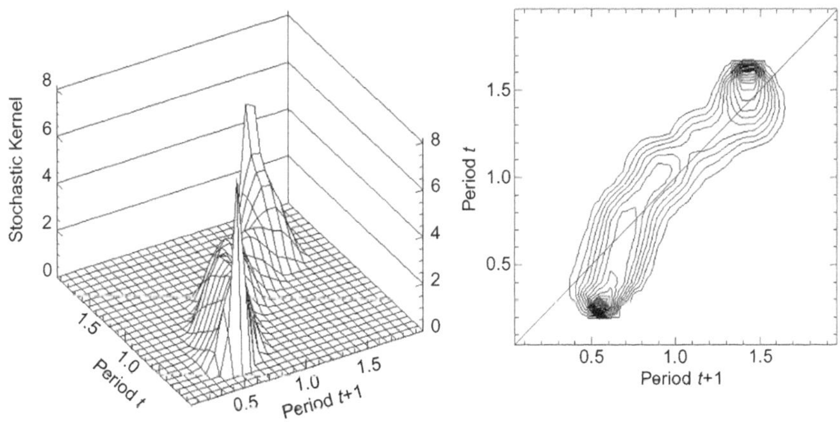

Fig. 5. Relative Per Capita Incomes across Indian States, 1-Year Transitions. 1981–1988.

at 150% of the all India average. The period 1965–1970 shows some signs of cohesion: as is clearly revealed in the contour plot, the two clubs are aligned parallel to the original axis (vertical axis). This indicates some tendencies of convergence. The following time periods, particularly during the later years, have shown the cohesive forces substantially dissipating in influence.[5]

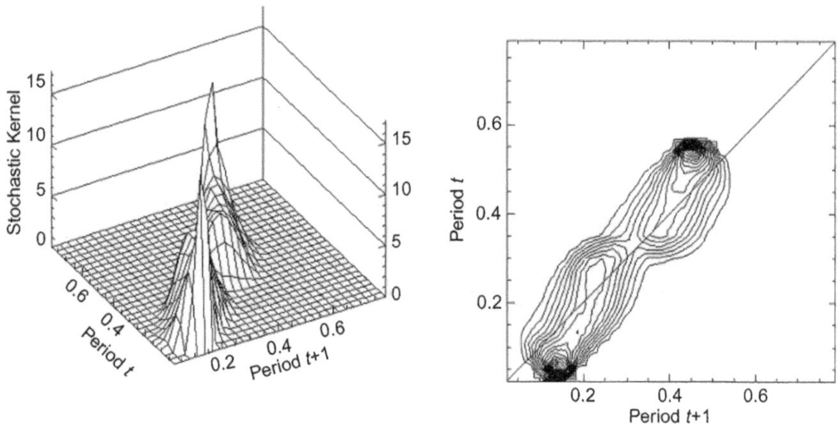

Fig. 6. Relative Per Capita Incomes across Indian States, 1-Year Transitions. 1991–1997.

For robustness, I estimate stochastic kernels over the different sub-periods and over 5- and 10-year periods. The results obtained (not presented for brevity and obtainable from the author) reveal the same results as above: there has been convergence over the late 1960s, with increasing divergence over the 1970s, 1980s and 1990s. To summarise our findings,

- I obtain evidence of two convergence clubs – a low-income club and a high-income club – one at 50% of the national average and another at 125% of the national average. I also obtain some tendencies of convergence in the time period 1965–1970.
- The periods from 1970s to the 1990s reveal evidence of persistence and increasing divergence. Some evidence is also obtained of intra-distributional mobility over the late 1960s.
- The stochastic kernels also suggest that disparities have been widening. Robustness statistics (such as bootstrapped standard errors for the probabilities) are statistically irrelevant here and are therefore not presented.

We also observe that the composition of the two income convergence clubs does not drastically differ over the time periods. The Indian states at 50% of the national average are Assam, Bihar, Jammu and Kashmir, Orissa, Madhya Pradesh, Rajasthan and Uttar Pradesh for all the four time periods examined, with the exception of Kerala. Kerala started in the 1960s in the low-income club and has moved in and out of it over the time periods examined. For the high-income club membership has changed over the four decades: while Delhi, Punjab, Haryana, Gujarat and Maharashtra have dominated the top five ranks for all four decades examined, West Bengal moved out of the high-income club in the mid-1970s. Andhra Pradesh and Tamil Nadu have been the most recent entrants (1990s) into the high-income club.

These results are in agreement with those of Trivedi (2003) where similar clubs are revealed with kernel estimates of the densities of the Indian state income distribution between 1960 and 1992.[6] The stochastic kernels improve over these estimates by providing the intra-distribution dynamics of how these clubs evolve over time.

WHAT EXPLAINS POLARISATION? THE ROLE OF MACRO-ECONOMIC FACTORS

It is widely accepted that a stable macro-economic environment is required (though not sufficient) for sustainable economic growth. That taxation, public investment, inflation and other aspects of fiscal policy can determine an economy's growth trajectory has been articulated in the growth literature for the last three decades. Endogenous growth models have also stressed the long-run role of fiscal policy as a key determinant of growth. Many cross-country studies also provide evidence that the causation runs in good measure from good macro-economic policy to growth (Barro, 1991; Easterly & Rebelo, 1993; Fischer, 1991, 1993; Perotti, 2011; Romer & Romer, 2010).

The link between short-run macro-economic management and long-run growth, however, remains one of the most controversial areas in the cross-country literature. A number of studies estimating regressions show significant correlations, with the expected signs, though it has been perniciously difficult to isolate any particular policy variable and demonstrate a robust correlation with growth, irrespective of endogeneity concerns and other variables. Endogeneity proves to be the hardest of problems to deal with as economic crises do not occur in isolation–inflation typically accompanies bad fiscal discipline, political instability and exchange rate crises.

The recent cross-country literature deals with much of establishing such correlations, revealing the complexity of the relationships. Levine and Renelt (1992) show that high-growth countries are with lower inflation, have smaller governments and have lower black market premia. While their results show that the relationship between growth and every other macro-economic indicator (other than investment ratio) is fragile, Fischer (1991) extends the basic Levine and Renelt regression to show that growth is significantly negatively associated with inflation and positively with budget surplus as a ratio of GDP. Easterly and Rebelo (1993) also present convincing evidence of fiscal deficits being negatively related to growth. Recent studies also highlight the non-linear effects of fiscal deficits on economic growth outcomes. Adam and Bevan (2005) show for a panel of 45 developing countries that a contraction in fiscal deficit is positively associated with growth outcomes up to a threshold of 1.5% as a percentage of GDP. For further fiscal contraction below 1.5% the effect is reversed. Similar evidence is also presented in Giavazzi, Tullio, and Pagano (2000) highlighting the non-linear effects of fiscal deficits on economic growth for a panel of industrial and developing countries. Links between inflation and growth are particularly controversial. Levine and Zervos (1994) show that inflation is significant, though not robust, and relates to only high-inflation countries. Their composite indicator of macro-economic performance, a function of inflation and fiscal deficit, is shown to be positively related with growth performance (lower inflation, lower fiscal deficit). Bruno and Easterly (1998) also take a short-run approach and find that high-inflation crises are associated with output losses, but that output returns to the same long-run growth path once inflation has been reduced. This may be the reason for the weak inflation and growth relationship. Some empirical studies highlight the non-linear nature of the relationship between inflation and growth: Sarel (1996) highlights that for inflation below 8%, it has no effect (or possibly positive effect) on economic growth; for values above 8%, its negative effect is strong and robust.

In the following section I discuss the macro-economic crisis that has been faced by the Indian states over the late 1980s into the 1990s which may have perpetuated uneven growth experiences.[7]

The Macro-Economic Crisis in India in the late 1980s and 1990s

Recent years have seen fundamental economic transformation in India which has resulted in improved aggregate and state-wise economic growth. India's trend of growth rate of 5.8% per annum since 1980 is the highest outside South East and East Asia among large developing countries. However, while the short-term outlook has improved, current policies have been deemed as insufficient to sustain the 7–8% growth rate that the Indian government considers necessary for poverty reduction. Recent estimates suggest that every third person in India lives below the poverty line (Ozler et al., 1996). Further, this growth trajectory is accounted for by agriculture growing at an average rate of 7%, while growth in all other major sectors has been on the decline.

One of the biggest problems facing policy makers has been the unsustainable fiscal deficits generated at both the centre and state levels. Gross fiscal deficit to GDP ratio of all state governments touched a high of 4.2% in 1998–1999 – the highest in Indian fiscal history. The fiscal performance of the individual states varied widely over the 1990s, with the most marked deterioration observed in some of the poorer states. In Uttar Pradesh, the fiscal deficit rose from 4.5% of GDP in 1993–1994 to 8.6% in 1997–1998; in Bihar, from 4.0% to 6.2%; and in Orissa from 5.7% to 6.3%. Fiscal turbulence was not limited to only the poorer states – Kerala and Rajasthan, which are middle-income states, also observed the fiscal deficit deteriorating to 7.3% and 4.6%. The central government's deficit of 1998–1999 was 6.5% of GDP – the same as that of the crisis year of 1990–1991. To add to that the revenue deficit, at 6.2% of GDP, is substantially higher than that of 1990–1991, the worst of the decade, continuing the long-run trend of increased government dis-saving to finance consumption.

As an immediate fall-out of such deficits, the poorer states, in particular, have become highly indebted; in Uttar Pradesh the debt-GDP ratio rose from 26% to 31%; in Bihar it increased from 35% to 42%, while in Orissa, from 41% to 43%. Financing such large deficits has meant increased borrowings and issuing state government guarantees. The states are constitutionally prohibited from borrowing internationally and have tight limits on overdrafts from the Reserve Bank of India (the central bank of India). Thus, Indian states face a relatively hard budget constraint. The state government guarantees have often been used as a convenient means to circumvent the ceiling imposed on borrowing (of the central government on its behalf) from the RBI. This, however, has led to a huge debt bill – total outstanding guarantees now account for about 9–10% of states' combined GDP. Variation among states is large – as a percentage of GDP, state guarantees range from 4% in Uttar Pradesh to 14% in Punjab.

Such high deficits, thus, have a telling effect on macro-economic management. They crowd out private sector borrowing by keeping interest rates higher than they would otherwise be, and crowd out public development spending within government budgets due to high-interest costs of the government debt. The real cost of such interest repayments was realised particularly after financial liberalisation in the early 1990s. With financial liberalisation, the interest costs of central and state governments have risen by over 1% of GDP since 1990–1991.

On the other hand, investors' and rating agencies' concerns over the high fiscal deficits tend to increase international risk premia and lower the bond ratings that India faces, pushing up real interest costs, even if one were to maintain macro-economic stability.

Much of this deterioration in the fiscal performance in recent years is attributed to the unstable nature of the governments at both the state level and the centre. Unstable coalition governments at the centre resulting from the elections of 1996 and 1998 have resulted in four offices with four prime ministers and finance ministers. Though all offices have followed in line with the 1991 reforms of the Congress office, internal disagreement over policy due to unstable political coalitions has resulted in many withdrawals of various ongoing reforms. This has been accompanied by the frequent changes of offices in the state governments themselves. For example, states of Bihar, Uttar Pradesh and Himachal Pradesh have seen changes of up to three times in one year, during the volatile years of the 1990s. Curiously, much of the instability in local governments has been observed in some of the poorest states, for example, that of Bihar, Orissa and Uttar Pradesh. Such weak and unstable governments are also characterised by endemic corruption and a general lack of social and political governance. Such corruption is known to discourage investment, limit economic growth and even alter the composition of government spending, often to the detriment of future economic growth.

The 1991 reforms changed the policy environment significantly after the central government's liberalisation of trade and investment. These reforms and other policy changes allowed the states a larger role in determining their development paths and attracting investment. Gujarat, Maharashtra and other middle-income states were able to take greater advantage of the new conditions, because of better initial conditions, infrastructure and human resources, than other low-income states. The poorer states on the other hand, with the exception of Orissa, failed to improve state policies to off-set their initial disadvantage in attracting new investment.

In light of the factors discussed above, I will empirically investigate the role of a number of macro-economic indicators in the following section for the period 1986–1998. I will be using panel data for indicators of capital expenditure, education expenditure, fiscal deficit, inflation and interest expenditure.

Conditioning with Indicators of Macro-economic Stability

Recent studies have already sought to identify such non-linear relationships using non-parametric methods, for example, Kalaitzidakis et al. (2001) and Fiaschi and Lavezzi (2003). The distribution dynamics method is an appropriate method to explore non-linear relationships. The conditioning methodology in the distribution dynamics approach is similar to that of traditional panel or cross-section regression approaches. While with standard methods of panel regression one compares E(Y) and E(Y|X) to deduce conditional convergence, the distribution dynamics approach compares the entire distributions of Y to Y|X. When no change in the conditioned and unconditioned distributions is observed, one concludes that the conditioning variable does not explain the distribution dynamics. Quah (1997) shows that just as stochastic kernels can provide information about how distributions evolve over time, they can also describe how a set of conditioning factors alter the mapping between any two distributions. Hence, in order to understand if a hypothesised set of factors explains a given distribution one can estimate a stochastic kernel mapping the unconditioned distribution to the conditioned one. If one then obtains convergence, one deduces conditional convergence.

In the next section the data used for the conditioning analysis is described and then the results of the conditioning exercise are presented. To test for associations of macro-economic stability with the observed convergence dynamics, I will use the following macro-economic variables, for the period 1986–1997, obtained from the World Bank (2000):

- Fiscal deficit as a ratio to state GDP
- Interest and administrative expenditure as a ratio to state GDP
- Capital expenditure as a ratio to state GDP
- Expenditure on education and other social services as a ratio to state GDP
- Inflation.

To construct the conditioned distribution with the variables discussed above, it is first important to ascertain the exogeneity/endogeneity of the variables. Granger causality tests confirm the endogeneity of the capital expenditure. To allow the conditioned distribution to be free from feedback effects (or bi-directional causality), it is estimated by regressing state GDPs on a two-sided distributed lag of the time-varying conditioning variables. I then extract the fitted residuals for subsequent analysis. This will result in

Table 1. Lead-Lag Regressions of Growth Rates on Capital Expenditures.

Capital Expenditure	Co-Efficients in Two-Sided Projections		
Lead			
4			−0.00 (0.003)
3		0.01 (0.008)	0.012 (0.009)
2	0.013 (0.008)	−0.018 (0.01)	−0.019 (0.016)
1	0.020 (0.01)	0.021 (0.012)	0.024 (0.019)
0	−0.022 (0.016)	−0.024 (0.018)	−.0.029 (0.019)
Lag			
1	−0.021 (0.014)	−0.02 (0.016)	−0.022 (0.015)
2	−0.01(0.010)	−0.01 (0.011)	−0.01 (0.011)
3		−0.00 (0.007)	−0.00 (0.010)
4			−0.005 (0.004)
Sum of co-efficients	−0.02	−0.051	−0.034
R^2	0.17	0.13	0.11

a conditioned distribution free from feedback effects irrespective of the exogeneity of the right-hand side variables. The method derives from Sims (1972), implemented in Quah (1996), where endogeneity (or the lack of it) is determined by regressing the endogenous variable on the past, current and future values of the exogenous variables and observing whether the future values of the exogenous variables have significant zero co-efficients. If they are zero, then one deduces that there exists no 'feedback' or bi-directional causality. The residuals constitute the variation of the dependent variable unexplained by the set of exogenous variables, irrespective of endogeneity. The results for these two-sided regressions are tabulated in Table 1.

All projections in Table 1 suggest that capital expenditure at lead 1 though lag 2 is significant for predicting GDP, but not consistently for other leads and lags. Fit does not improve with increasing lags (or leads). There is a fairly stable set of co-efficients of the two-sided projections. The residuals of the second lead–lag projections are used as the conditioned distribution of GDP on capital expenditure, though the final results are unaltered by using residuals from other projections.

What is observable in all projections is that capital expenditure at lead 1 though lag 2 appears significant for predicting growth, but other leads and lags, not so consistently. Fit does not seem to improve with increasing lags (or leads). We seem to have a fairly stable set of co-efficients of the two-sided projections. The residuals of the second lead–lag projections are saved for the conditional distribution of growth on capital expenditure. Conditioning two-sided projections is also derived for the other auxiliary variables, namely, capital expenditure, and education expenditure, fiscal deficits, interest expenditure and inflation. We discuss the results for each of these variables in turn.

Figs. 7–9 present the stochastic kernels mapping the unconditioned to conditioned distributions, for capital expenditure, fiscal deficits and

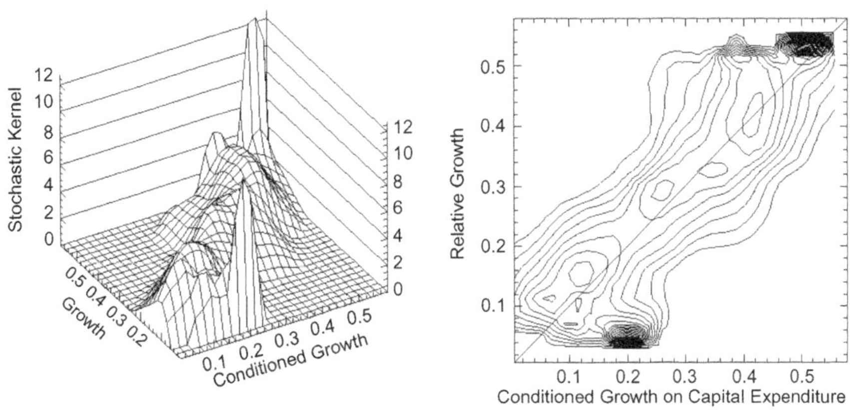

Fig. 7. Relative Per Capita Incomes across Indian States: Capital Expenditure Conditioning.

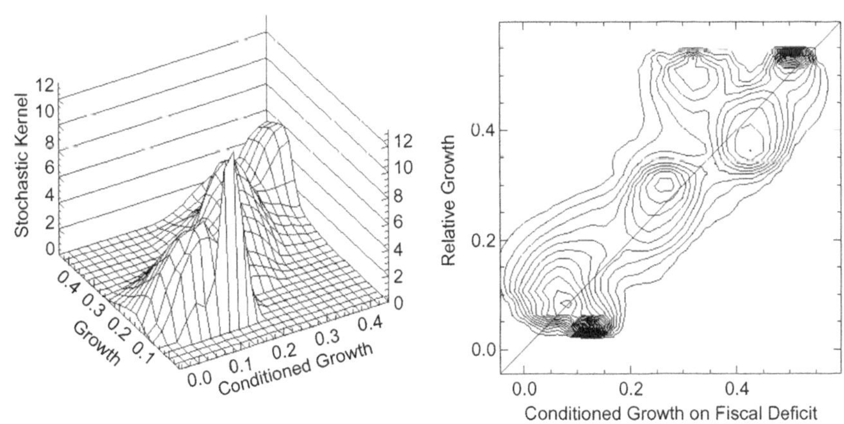

Fig. 8. Relative Per Capita Incomes across Indian States: Fiscal Deficit Conditioning.

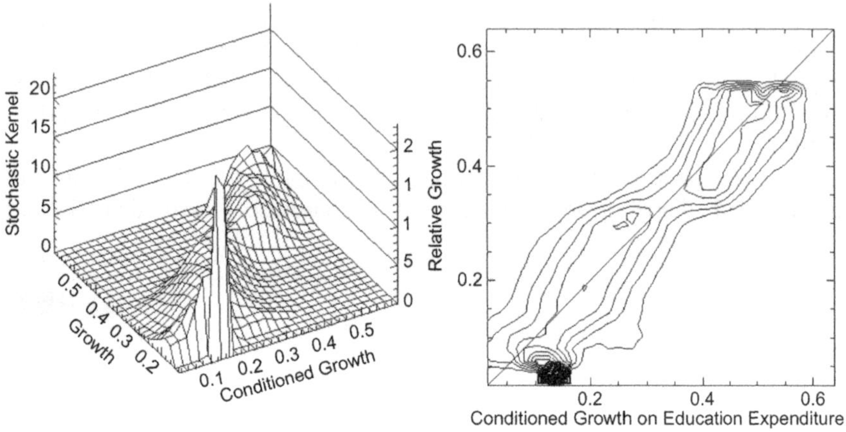

Fig. 9. Relative Per Capita Incomes across Indian States: Education Expenditure Conditioning.

education expenditures. Fig. 7 presents the stochastic kernel representing conditioning with capital expenditure. The appropriate conditioned distribution has been derived by extracting the residuals from our earlier two-sided regressions. The probability mass lies predominantly on the diagonal, though one can observe some local clusters running off the diagonal at the very low and high ends of the distribution. These clusters are more clearly revealed in the contour plot. In particular, one can observe a local cluster at the bottom end of the stochastic kernel running parallel to the vertical axis. This is also the case at the upper end of the distribution, where two individual clusters – one at 0.4 of the national average and another at 0.5 of the national average – are parallel to the vertical axis.

Fig. 8 maps the conditioning stochastic kernel with fiscal deficit. The appropriate conditioned distribution has been derived by extracting the residuals from the two-sided lead–lag regressions[8].

Here I find that there are several convergence clubs. Of the five identifiable convergence clubs, one can observe that one of the clusters at the upper end of the distribution lies off the diagonal, aligned parallel to the original axis. The club lying at 0.4 of the national average, while predominantly lying on the diagonal, is twisted such that it is parallel to the original axis. Similar dynamics are also observed with respect to the lowest convergence club – it twists such that it is parallel. The middle convergence club also while lying mostly on the diagonal has tendencies to lie to parallel to the original axis. In short, all five convergence clubs exhibit tendencies to run parallel to the original axis, with the upper two clubs most clearly lying parallel to it. These results suggest that fiscal deficits are associated with individual convergence clubs at several parts of the income distribution, mostly clearly with clubs at the upper end of the distribution.[9]

Fig. 9 maps the conditioning stochastic kernel with education expenditure as auxilliary variable. The appropriate conditioned distribution has been derived by extracting the residuals from the two-sided lead–lag regressions, as in earlier exercises.[10] In this case I observe that the stochastic kernel runs mainly along the diagonal, with the upper and lower tails tending to run off parallel to the unconditioned axis. In particular, I observe in the contour plot that the stochastic kernel is clearly divided into two clubs, with the upper club parallel to the original axis. The lower convergence club also shows tendencies to run parallel to the original axis. In short, I find the two convergence clubs to be associated with education expenditure, in particular the upper convergence club.

I also undertake similar conditioning exercises with inflation and interest expenditure, both results presented in Fig. A.1. Here the effects of these auxilliary factors do not reveal significant insights of the convergence clubs being associated with specific convergence clubs. I observe that most of the stochastic kernel lies mainly on the diagonal, with none of the convergence clubs showing any tendencies to align themselves parallel to the original axis.[11]

To summarise:

- I observe tendencies for conditional convergence for the upper-income club when conditioning with the capital expenditure index.
- Several convergence clubs are obtained when conditioning with fiscal deficits. I observe instances of conditional convergence for the two upper convergence clubs, and with tendencies for conditional covergence at the lower end of the income distribution.
- I also observe similar tendencies when conditioning with education expenditure. Both convergence clubs exhibit tendencies of conditional convergence, particularly at the upper end of the income distribution.
- The results obtained depart from those found by earlier empirical studies by isolating conditional convergence at specific parts of the income distribution. These results would go uncovered by using standard methods of estimating conditional convergence with regression analysis. I have uncovered specific factors (fiscal deficits, capital expenditure and education expenditure) which are associated with GDP outcomes at different parts

of the income distribution. In particular, I find that these factors are associated GDP outcomes at the upper end of the income distribution.[12]

Interpretation of Results

The results on the association of capital expenditures with the higher income clubs is strongly suggestive of the successful high investment strategy undertaken in the high-growth states. The high-income states of Gujarat, Maharashtra, Tamil Nadu and Andhra Pradesh are characterised by heavy industries, mostly in iron and steel-based, and derivative industries. Karnataka in recent years has also seen a surge in growth rates, due to the development of the service sector-based industries and in software consulting. States of Punjab and Haryana, which are also rich-income states, are not driven by industry, but by agriculture. The two states combined constitute a significant part of the aggregate agricultural GDP in India (contributing to almost 100% of India's wheat produce and the second largest contributor to rice production, after West Bengal). Capital expenditures, therefore, in these two states are mostly devoted to infrastructures in the agricultural sector and not in capital-based industries as in the other states belonging to the high-income club.

The second result worth noting is that of the association of fiscal deficits with the high-income convergence club. Indeed, the result conforms with recent findings of the non-linear relationship of fiscal deficits with economic growth outcomes. Adam and Bevan (2005) identify that the effects of fiscal contraction are positive for fiscal deficits up to 1.5%, and negative thereafter. The respective sizes of the fiscal deficits of the states concerned are all above 1.5% (an average of 4–5% for the period concerned). That these high-income states are associated with high level of fiscal deficits, and lesser so for the low-income club of states, also alludes to the recent studies on the expansionary effects of fiscal deficits – Romer and Romer (2010) and Perotti (2011) provide empirical evidence using US tax data of the expansionary effects of fiscal shocks. Christiano, Eichenbaum, and Rebelo (2009) in their recent paper also highlight specific conditions under which an expansionary fiscal policy may result in large multiplier effects.[13] In short, the evidence is telling of the non-linear relationship that fiscal deficits have with economic growth, though economists are not unified on the conditions under which the non-linearity rests. That high-growth outcomes are found to be associated with large fiscal deficits and capital expenditures is an important finding, given that the size of the fiscal deficits (in particular) of the richer states and poorer states are not significantly different from each other. The results in the paper could be suggestive that the state-level fiscal policies may determine growth outcomes of these states, though further research is required to ascertain any particular policy recommendation that may positively impact upon the growth outcomes of these states.

CONCLUSION

In this paper I have examined the convergence of growth and incomes across the Indian states using an empirical model of dynamically evolving distributions, and present some explanations of the observed dynamics. The model reveals "twin peaks" dynamics, or polarisation across the Indian states, over 1965–1997 – empirics who would not be revealed under standard empirical methods of cross-section, panel data and time series econometrics. I find that the dominant cross-state income dynamics are that of persistence, immobility and polarisation, with some cohesive tendencies in the 1960s, only to dissipate over the following three decades. These findings contrast starkly with those emphasised in the works of Bajpai and Sachs (1996), Nagaraj et al. (1997), Rao, Shand, and Kalirajan (1999) and Kalra and Sodsriwiboon (2010).

A conditioning methodology using the same empirical tools further reveals that such income dynamics are associated with the disparate distribution of capital expenditure, fiscal deficit and education expenditure patterns. Unlike standard methods, this model allows us observe the income dynamics at different levels of the distribution. I obtain conditional convergence for the upper convergence club with capital expenditure, fiscal deficits and education expenditure. Capital expenditure is found to be strongly associated with the formation of the upper convergence club; fiscal deficits are associated with the upper-income club, and with some smaller convergence clubs at the upper end of the income distribution. Similar results are also observed with education expenditure: it is again found to be associated with the upper-income club, though not as clearly as with the case of capital expenditure and fiscal deficits. These stylised facts are interesting for policy purposes in tracking the forces which govern growth dynamics across the Indian states.

The empirical results suggest that the association between these macroeconomic factors and growth outcomes across Indian states is significant.

The associations identified are prominent for the upper income club of states. The findings are suggestive that there may be policy implications for these macro-economic indicators of these states: while the upper-income group states have experienced high levels of economic growth and development, they are also characterised by macro-economic imbalances. On the other hand, that capital expenditures are found to be associated with the upper-income club is suggestive of the specific investment strategies that have been successful in catapulting these states into high-growth states. This is also reflected in education expenditure being associated with the upper-income club as well. It is interesting to note that these factors do not yield conditional convergence for the lower income group of states.

The results with respect to capital expenditure for the upper-income clubs suggest that similar potential expenditure strategies can be emulated by the low-growth states; further research is required to ascertain whether there are some institutional pre-requisites for such a strategy to be successful. The particular results with fiscal deficits are also strongly suggestive of the non-linear nature of the relationship of fiscal deficits with growth outcomes. Indeed, the Indian government (and the respective state governments) has undertaken relevant strategies in reduction of the fiscal deficits, but the empirics in this paper suggest that their efforts have not yet been fully successful.

NOTES

1. Comparability of GDP estimates of the two separate datasets has been ascertained by merging the two sets of income estimates via normalisation. Both sets of income data in their raw form were highly comparable to start with, and therefore did not pose any problems in being able to merge both datasets.

2. The distribution dynamics approach (Quah, 1997) is based on treating a single income distribution as a random element in a field of income distributions, called the random field. The density function of the income distribution is estimated at each point in time and is then observed how it evolves over time. A transition probability matrix records the probabilities of persistence and mobility across the income distribution. Stochastic kernels and transition matrices provide an estimate of intra-distribution mobility taking place. An economy (in our case, an Indian state) over a given time period (say, one year or five years) either remains in the same position, or changes its position in the income distribution. The transition probabilities are then encoded in the transition probability matrix for transitions over the income distribution. Low probabilities of transition indicate persistence, while higher probabilities indicate mobility.

3. For further refinements proposed in discretising a continuous state-space Markov chain in the distribution dynamics context, see Bulli (2001).

4. There are some other problems with the discretised approach. With the estimates being based on time stationary transition matrices, they are not reliable for long time periods for economic structural changes. Also, the number of states with the Indian example is small, thereby I cannot make inferential statements by bootstrapped p-values associated with the probabilities. For further methods highlighting how more information may be obtained from such transition matrices, see Fiaschi and Lavezzi (2003).

5. The income distribution dynamics results are also established in Bandyopadhyay (2004).

6. There are no studies beyond that of the author and of Trivedi's (2003) for the Indian case that explicitly test for the existence of multiple convergence clubs. Most recently Kalra and Sodsriwiboon (2010) test for convergence across Indian states using panel data techniques and find no tendencies of convergence, similar to the findings in this paper.

7. A robust macroeconomic framework as a potential mechanism associated with the emergence of income convergence clubs is just one out of several potential associations that are discussed in the convergence literature. Inequality in opportunities that lead to "inequality traps" such as discussed in Bourguignon, Ferriera, and Walton (2007) and Marrero and Rodreguez (2010) is another association popularly studied in the convergence club literature, and directly relates to models proposed in Galor and Zeira (1993).

8. The table of results for the lead–lag regressions for fiscal deficits is not presented for brevity and is obtainable from the author. The projections suggest that fiscal deficits at lead 1 though lag 2 is significant for predicting GDP, but not consistently for other leads and lags. Fit again does not improve with increasing lags (or leads). The residuals of the second lead–lag projections are used as the conditioned distribution of GDP on fiscal deficits, though the final results are unaltered by using residuals from other projections.

9. All these 'explanatory factors' were also tested using standard panel regression methods, that is, standard 'growth regressions', where each one of these factors was found to be significantly associated with the state-level growth rates and no conditional convergence. The distribution-specific effects of these variables cannot be identified using the panel regression method, but these are highlighted using the distribution dynamics method.

10. Results again are not presented to maintain brevity and are obtainable from the author.

11. The analysis does not include years following 1997. There is precious little work done in the area of testing for convergence clubs in India beyond the author's and Trivedi (2003)'s, and almost none that use non-parametric methods to identify causal mechanisms underpinning these convergence clubs beyond the late 1990s. Preiliminary work by the author for the late 1990s–2007 is suggestive that there still exists two convergence clubs, consisting of low- and high-income states, and there is some evidence of a middle-income group of states emerging. Results for this period are available with the author. Conditioning analysis has not been undertaken for this time period, and remains a topic of future research.

12. These results complement the results that are obtained using standard panel regression and pooled OLS analysis. Fiscal deficits are significantly and negatively correlated with growth, as is also the case for the effects of inflation on growth. Expenditure on education is observed to have a positive impact on growth, especially in the later years of the 1990s. Interest expenditure, in our short-run OLS regressions, has a negative effect on growth – this is one of the results most robust to the different specifications used.

13. Giavazzi and Pagano (1990) on the other hand have shown the reverse – they use the example of Denmark and Ireland in the 1980s whereby fiscal expansion has a contractionary effect on the economy.

REFERENCES

Adam, C. S., & Bevan, D. L. (2005). Fiscal deficits and growth in developing countries. *Journal of Public Economics*, *89*, 571–597.

Aiyar, S. (2000). Growth theory and convergence across Indian states: A panel study. In T. Callen, P. Reynolds & C. Towe (Eds.), *India at the crossroads: Sustaining growth and reducing poverty* (pp. 143–169). Washington, DC: International Monetary Fund.

Andrade, M., Madalozzo, R., & Valls Pereira, P. L. (2004). Convergence clubs among Brazilian municipalities. *Economics Letters*, *83*, 179–184.

Bajpai, N., & Sachs, J. D. (1996, May). *Trends in inter-state inequalities of income in India.* Discussion Paper No. 528, Harvard Institute for International Development, Cambridge, MA.

Bandyopadhyay, S. (2004). Twin peaks-distribution dynamics of economic growth across Indian states. In A. Shorrocks & R. van der Hoeven (Eds.), *Growth, inequality and poverty: Prospects for pro-poor growth* (pp. 176–196). Oxford: Oxford University Press.

Barro, R. J. (1991). *Inflation and growth.* NBER Working Paper No. 5326.

Barro, R. J., & Sala-i-Martin, X. (1992). Convergence. *Journal of Political Economy*, *100*, 223–251.

Ben-David, B. (1994). *Converging clubs or diverging economies.* Working Paper No. 922, CEPR, London.

Bernaud, A., & Durlauf, S. (1994). *Interpreting tests of the convergence hypothesis.* NBER Technical Working Paper No. 159.

Bianchi, M. (1995). Testing for convergence: A bootstrap test for multimodality. *Journal of Applied Econometrics*, *12*, 393–409.

Bourguignon, F., Ferriera, F., & Walton, M. (2007). Equity, efficiency and inequality traps: A research agenda. *Journal of Economic Inequality*, *5*, 235–256.

Bruno, W., & Easterly, W. (1998). Inflation crises and long-run growth. *Journal of Monetary Economics*, *41*, 3–26.

Bulli, S. (2001). Distribution dynamics and cross-country convergence: A new approach. *Scottish Journal of Political Economy*, *48*, 226–243.

Carlino, G., & Mills, L. (1993). Are US regional incomes converging? A time series analysis. *Journal of Monetary Economics*, *32*, 335–346.

Cashin, P., & Sahay, R. (1996). Internal migration, centre-state grants, and economic growth in the states of India. *IMF Staff Papers*, *43*, 123–171.

Christiano, L., Eichenbaum, M., & Rebelo, S. (2009). *When is the government spending multiplier large*? NBER Discussion Paper No. 15394, Northwestern University.

De Long, J. B. (1988). Productivity growth, convergence, and welfare: Comment. *American Economic Review*, *78*, 1138–1154.

Desdoigts, A. (1994). *Changes in the world income distribution: A non-parametric approach to challenge the neo-classical convergence argument*. PhD dissertation, European University Institute, Florence.

Durlauf, S. N., & Johnson, P. (1995). Multiple regimes and cross country growth behaviour. *Journal of Applied Econometrics*, *10*, 365–384.

Durlauf, S. N., & Quah, D. (1999). The new empirics of economic growth. In J. B. Taylor & M. Woodford (Eds.), *Handbook of macroeconomics* (1st ed., Vol. 1, pp. 235–308). Amsterdam: Elsevier.

Easterly, W., & Rebelo, S. (1993). Fiscal policy and economic growth: An empirical investigation. *Journal of Monetary Economics*, *32*, 417–458.

Esteban, J., & Ray, D. (1994). On the measurement of polarisation. *Econometrica*, *62*, 819–851.

Fiaschi, D., & Lavezzi, A. M. (2003). Distribution dynamics and nonlinear growth. *Journal of Economic Growth*, *8*, 379–401.

Fischer, S. (1991). Growth, macroeconomics and development. *NBER Macroeconomics Annual*, *6*, 329–364.

Fischer, S. (1993). Macro-economic factors in growth. *Journal of Monetary Economics*, *32*, 485–512.

Fotopolos, G. (2006). Nonparametric analysis of regional income dynamics: The case of Greece. *Economics Letters*, *91*, 450–457.

Galor, O., & Zeira, J. (1993). Income distribution and macroeconomics. *Review of Economic Studies*, *60*, 35–52.

Giavazzi, F., & Pagano, M. (1990). Can severe fiscal contractions be expansionary? Tales of two small European countries. *NBER Macroeconomics Annual 1990*, *5*, 75–122.

Giavazzi, F., Tullio, J., & Pagano, M. (2000). Searching for non-linear effects of fiscal policy: Evidence from industrial and developing countries. *European Economic Review*, *44*, 1259–1289.

Grazia-Pittau, M., Zelli, R., & Johnson, P. A. (2010). Mixture models, convergence clubs and polarization. *Review of Income and Wealth*, *56*, 102–122.

Jones, C. I. (1997). On the evolution of the world income distribution. *Journal of Economic Perspectives*, *11*, 19–36.

Kalaitzidakis, P., Mamuneas, T., Sawides, A., & Stengos, T. (2001). Measures of human capital and nonlinearities in economic growth. *Journal of Economic Growth*, *6*, 229–254.

Kalra, S., & Sodsriwiboon, P. (2010). *Growth convergence and spillovers among Indian states: What matters? What does not?* IMF Working Papers No. WP/10/96.

Levine, R., & Renelt, D. (1992). A sensitivity analysis of cross country growth regressions. *American Economic Review*, *76*, 808–819.

Levine, R., & Zervos, S. (1994). Looking at the facts: What we know about policy and growth from cross sectional analysis. In R. Solow & L. Pasinetti (Eds.), *Economic growth and the structure of long-term development* (pp. 22–44). UK: Macmillan Press.

Maasoumi, E., & Wang, L. (2008). Economic reform, growth and convergence in China. *Econometrics Journal*, *11*, 128–154.

Marrero, G., & Rodriguez, J. (2010). *Inequality of opportunity and growth*. ECINEQ Working Paper No. 154.

Nagaraj, R., Varoukadis, A., & Venganzones, M. (1997). *Long run growth trends and convergence across Indian states*. Technical Paper No. 131, OECD Development Centre, Paris.

Ozler, B., Dutt, G., & Ravallion, M. (1996). *A database on poverty and growth in India*. Working Paper. Poverty and Human Resources Division, Policy Research Department, World Bank.

Perotti, R. (2011). *The effects of tax shocks on output: Not so large, but not small either*. NBER Working Paper 16786.

Pittau, M. G., & Zelli, R. (2006). Empirical evidence of income dynamics across EU regions. *Journal of Applied Econometrics, 21*, 605–628.

Quah, D. (1996). Convergence empirics across economies with (some) capital mobility. *Journal of Economic Growth, 1*, 95–124.

Quah, D. (1997). Twin peaks: Growth and convergence in models of distribution dynamics. *Economic Journal, 106*, 1045–1055.

Rao, G., Shand, R. T., & Kalirajan, K. P. (1999). Convergence of incomes across Indian states: A divergent view. *Economic and Political Weekly, 17*, 769–778.

Romer, C. D., & Romer, D. H. (2010). The macroeconomic effects of tax changes: Estimates based on a new measure of fiscal shocks. *American Economic Review, 100*, 763–801.

Sarel, M. (1996). Non-linear effects of inflation on economic growth. *IMF Staff Papers, 43*, 199–215.

Sims, C. A. (1972). Money, income and causality. *American Economic Review, 62*, 540–552.

Solow, R. (1957). Technical change and the aggregate production. *Review of Economics and Statistics, 39*, 312–320.

Trivedi, K. (2003). *Regional convergence and catch-up in India between 1960 and 1992*. Technical Report, Oxford University Economics Department Working Paper.

World Bank (2000). *India: Policies to reduce poverty and accelerate sustainable development – A World Bank report*.

APPENDIX A: STATES USED IN THE STUDY

Andhra Pradesh
Assam
Bihar
Delhi
Gujarat
Haryana
Jammu and Kashmir
Karnataka
Kerala
Madhya Pradesh
Maharashtra
Orissa
Punjab
Rajasthan
Tamil Nadu
Uttar Pradesh
West Bengal

Other states were excluded from the study due to the incomplete data available over the given period. These states together constitute for over 80% of the national population.

Price data that has been used to deflate the nominal GDPs has also been obtained from the above mentioned dataset, and is the adjusted CPIAL index.

APPENDIX B: THE DISTRIBUTION DYNAMICS APPROACH

Quah (1997) exploits a duality property from Markov process theory to provide a model of distribution dynamics. To model the distribution dynamics, one observes a scalar stochastic process, and then derives the implied unobservable sequence of distributions associated with this process. This hypothesised distribution sequence is then defined to be the dual to the observed scalar stochastic process. The property is reversed (the mathematics involved, however, remaining unaffected) to track the distribution dynamics as follows: while the sequence of distributions is observed, its dual, the scalar stochastic process, is implied, though unobserved. The dynamics of the scalar process is described in a transition probability matrix, while the dual to this, the stochastic kernel, describes the "law of motion" of the sequence of distributions. These will serve as models which describe the distribution dynamics across the Indian states.

The following clarifies the concepts discussed above. Let F_t be the measure corresponding to the cross-country income distribution at time t. The stochastic kernel which measures the evolution from F_t to F_{t+1} is a mapping M_t from the Cartesian product of income values and Borel measurable sets to [0; 1], such that

$$\nabla \text{Borel} - \text{measurable } A,\ F_{t+1}(A) \int M(A, y) dF_t(y) \tag{A.1}$$

It is M_t which encodes all the information about the evolution, or the law of motion of the sequence of distributions over time periods t and $t+1$. It contains information of the intra-distributional dynamics, hence revealing specific external shapes of the distribution, unrevealed in standard empirical proceed. M_t is assumed to be time-invariant, (and in this case, leaving out an error term, inclusion of which would render the model as analogous to a first order vector auto-regression in distributions rather than scalars or finite dimensional vectors), one can re-write the above expression as

$$F_{t+1} = MF_t \tag{A.2}$$

$$F_{t+s} = M^s F_t \tag{A.3}$$

As $s \rightarrow \infty$ it is possible to characterise the long-run distribution – this is called the ergodic distribution and it predicts the long-term behaviour of the underlying distribution. If F_{t+s} degenerates to a point mass one can conclude that there is a tendency towards global convergence. If F_{t+s} tends towards a bi-modal distribution (the case with the Indian states), one can conclude that there is tendency to polarisation, with the rich and the poor being pulled apart. Different variants of Eq. (A.1) allow the researcher to derive the various spectral characteristics of M_t, such as intra-distributional mobility and the speed of convergence.

APPENDIX C: CONDITIONING RESULTS

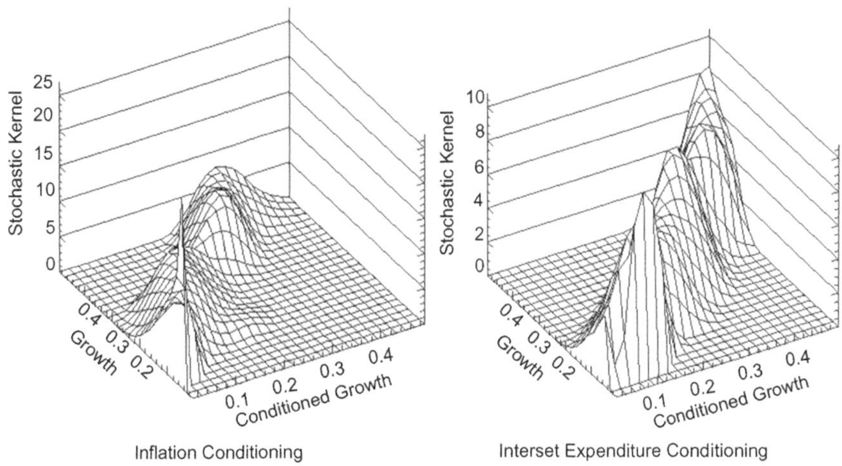

Fig. A.1. Relative Per Capita Incomes across Indian States: Inflation Conditioning and Interest Expenditure Conditioning.

CHAPTER 9

THE EU-WIDE EARNINGS DISTRIBUTION

Andrea Brandolini, Alfonso Rosolia and Roberto Torrini

ABSTRACT

This chapter studies the distribution of labour earnings among employees within the EU using data from Wave 2007-1 of the EU-SILC. The ranking of countries by median full-time equivalent monthly gross earnings shows Eastern European nations at the bottom and Luxembourg at the top; earnings differences are sizeable, both across and within countries. Taking the euro area and the EU-25 as a whole, inequality is higher when earnings are measured in euro at market exchange rates than at purchasing power parities. Unsurprisingly, the wage distribution is narrower in the euro area than in the EU-25, which includes the poorer Eastern European countries joining the Union in 2004. The higher inequality observed for the EU-25 is largely attributable to between-country differences, which in turn reflect differences in returns to individual attributes more than in workforce composition.

Keywords: Wage inequality; EU and euro area labour markets

JEL classifications: J31; D33

Inequality, Mobility and Segregation: Essays in Honor of Jacques Silber
Research on Economic Inequality, Volume 20, 205–235

ISSN: 1049-2585/doi:10.1108/S1049-2585(2012)0000020012

INTRODUCTION

Creating an integrated labour market is a long-standing aim of Europe's unification process, recently reaffirmed by the European Union's (EU) strategy 'Europe 2020' (European Commission, 2010). Yet, we only have a limited knowledge of the microeconomic structure of the EU-wide earnings distribution. Information on how entry pay levels, tenure-related wage progression, returns to education and other personal characteristics vary across EU member states is scarce, notwithstanding the importance of these questions for assessing the actual integration of European labour markets and for understanding the factors behind people's decision to move within the Union. While the area-wide distribution of household incomes is a thriving research topic,[1] little attention has been paid so far to the wage distribution in the EU as a whole.

In this chapter we try to fill this gap using data from the EU Statistics on Income and Living Conditions (EU-SILC) (Clemenceau & Museux, 2007) to estimate the EU-wide distribution of labour earnings among employees in 2006 (excluding Malta, for which data are unavailable).[2] We exclude the self-employed, as the information on their labour income tends to be less reliable than that on wages and salaries. While common in the labour literature, we must bear in mind that this choice leads to a picture which is necessarily incomplete and possibly biased by the varying importance of self-employment across EU countries.[3] As regards labour income, we consider three alternatives definitions: *total compensation*, the overall cost incurred by employers; *gross earnings*, the total compensation net of social security contributions paid by employers; *net earnings*, the take-home pay or the part of labour remuneration that employees can actually spend after income taxes and social insurance contributions are paid out of their earnings.[4] The first concept is the most pertinent in the analysis of labour demand, for instance to assess the comparative cost of hiring people across EU countries, whereas the last concept has obvious bearings on the decision of people to move within the Union. We examine all three earnings definitions in the assessment of the EU-SILC data and show how measured inequality is lower for net earnings than for total compensations or gross earnings, as a consequence of tax progressivity. In the analysis of the EU-wide wage distribution we focus only on the intermediate, and conceptually less satisfactory, concept of gross earnings, as it is the only one available for all countries. To derive the overall wage distribution we express wages in a common unit by using either the market exchange rates for countries outside the euro area or a purchasing power parity index which corrects for cross-national differences in the cost of living.

Our estimated statistics for the national earnings distributions show that there are sizeable differences, both across and within EU countries. The aggregation of the EU-25 countries into a single entity gives rise, however, to an overall wage distribution which is at most as dispersed as that of the most unequal country; for the more homogeneous euro area, measured inequality is even lower. To investigate the factors shaping the EU-wide wage distribution, we decompose the overall variance of the logarithms of full-time equivalent earnings and find that differences in wage schedules are far more important than differences in the composition of the labour force. The impact on the overall wage distribution of small changes in the employee composition by sex, age, education and country of birth is explored by using a novel methodology proposed by Firpo, Fortin, and Lemieux (2009).

The chapter is organised as follows. In the second section we review the relevant EU-SILC data, we compare them with external information from the national accounts and we discuss the time unit of earnings (annual vs. monthly) and the conversion from national currencies into euro. In the third section we present statistics for the wage distribution in EU countries and show their sensitivity to the three concepts of labour earnings. In the fourth section we present the estimates of the EU-wide wage distribution and a first analysis of its determinants. We draw our conclusions in the fifth section.

THE EU-SILC DATA ON EARNINGS

The paucity of suitable earnings data has hindered the analysis of the EU-wide distribution.[5] The collection of wages and salaries in the Labour Force Survey (LFS) is mandatory only since 2007 and data have not been released yet. Every four years, the Structure of Earnings Survey (SES) provides harmonised data on gross earnings and hours paid, which are used by Eurostat to estimate statistics on the distribution of earnings (e.g. Casali & Alvarez Gonzalez, 2010). However, the SES coverage of sectors and firms is partial and the access to microdata is highly restricted (Eurostat, 2012).[6] The only suitable sources are the EU-SILC, since the late 2000s, and its predecessor European Community Household Panel (ECHP), for the EU15 countries in the 1990s.[7]

In this chapter we use Wave 2007-1 of the EU-SILC users' database. This database contains information on three different concepts of annual earnings:[8] net and gross employee cash or near cash income (PY010N and PY010G), where gross and net refer to taxes and social contributions deducted at source, and employer's social insurance contribution made to public and private insurers on a mandatory or optional basis (PY030G).[9] The cash income is the compensation of employees, and includes wages and salaries and any other payment in cash (holiday, overtime and piece-rate payments, tips and gratuities, 13th month payment, bonuses and performance *premia*, allowances for transport and working in remote locations), with the exception of reimbursements for business travel, severance, termination and redundancy payments, and union strike pay. Gross earnings are available for all countries, but net earnings are missing in eight countries (CY, DE, DK, FI, HU, NL, SK, UK). Employers' social insurance contributions are virtually unavailable in two countries (DE, UK) and are equal to zero in a suspiciously large number of cases in seven other countries (CY, ES, FR, IE, LT, PL, SI). In spite of the efforts by Eurostat and the national statistical institutes, definitions are not fully homogenous across countries, as discussed in detail by Brandolini, Rosolia, and Torrini (2010). All statistics are calculated using personal cross-sectional weights (PB040) which sum to the country population of household members aged 16 and over and ensure that grossed-up values and area-wide aggregation are meaningful.

How does the EU-SILC Compare to Other Sources?

At the aggregate level, national accounts provide the natural benchmark for assessing the information collected in the EU-SILC. In Table 1, we compare the grossed-up EU-SILC values for gross wages and salaries and the compensation of employees with the corresponding amounts in the annual sector accounts.[10] The latter are the most comparable aggregates, as they refer to the amounts received by the household sector and are net of compensations paid to non-residents; on the other hand, they include the labour earnings of people living permanently in institutions (hostels, boarding houses, prisons, military installations, etc.) as well as of illegal immigrants, which are not covered by the EU-SILC. As generally found in similar comparisons (e.g. Atkinson & Micklewright, 1983, for the UK; Brandolini, 1999, for Italy), the matching between the two sources tends to be fairly good: the discrepancy is around 10 per cent or less in 15 (out of 23) countries for gross wages and salaries and in 10 (out of 20) countries for the compensation of employees. Yet, some discrepancies are worrying: gross earnings appear to be between a

Table 1. Earnings in the EU-SILC and in National Accounts in 2006 (Millions of Euro and Per Cent).

Country	Country Acronym	Wages and Salaries			Compensation of Employees		
		EU-SILC [1]	National Accounts [2]	Ratio (%) [3]=[1]:[2]	EU-SILC [4]	National Accounts [5]	Ratio (%) [6]=[4]:[5]
Belgium	BE	119,793	122,499	97.8	163,457	163,944	99.7
Czech Republic	CZ	30,888	37,021	83.4	41,600	48,943	85.0
Denmark	DK	97,861	105,998	92.3	109,048	116,187	93.9
Germany	DE	897,097	926,210	96.9	–	1,148,990	–
Estonia	EE	4,577	4,770	96.0	6,017	6,194	97.1
Ireland	IE	51,612	67,392	76.6	57,530	71,955	80.0
Greece	EL	56,580	56,027	101.0	72,571	71,910	100.9
Spain	ES	325,009	360,220	90.2	405,164	464,266	87.3
France	FR	557,621	695,771	80.1	739,743	944,904	78.3
Italy	IT	446,592	444,766	100.4	575,211	608,547	94.5
Cyprus	CY	6,593	5,648	116.7	7,413	6,455	114.8
Latvia	LV	5,488	6,299	87.1	6,545	7,417	88.2
Lithuania	LT	8,027	8,289	96.8	8,027	10,432	76.9
Luxembourg	LU	9,051	–	–	10,300	–	–
Hungary	HU	21,605	32,989	65.5	27,838	42,327	65.8
Netherlands	NL	216,255	206,548	104.7	265,790	263,652	100.8
Austria	AT	90,579	101,338	89.4	108,151	125,508	86.2
Poland	PL	84,230	87,357	96.4	92,729	100,427	92.3
Portugal	PT	54,277	60,524	89.7	56,433	77,630	72.7
Slovenia	SI	12,056	13,823	87.2	14,631	15,783	92.7
Slovakia	SK	12,033	13,941	86.3	15,741	17,669	89.1
Finland	FI	64,259	64,864	99.1	80,274	80,944	99.2
Sweden	SE	118,684	124,932	95.0	146,538	168,134	87.2
United Kingdom	UK	885,562	919,280	96.3	–	1,089,590	–

Notes: The EU-SILC totals include cash and non-cash components of wages and salaries. The national accounts figures refer to incomes received by the household sector; those for the UK refer to 2007 instead of 2006 in order to improve comparability with the EU-SILC totals.
Sources: Authors' elaboration on EU-SILC users' database (Version 2007-1, March 2009) and Eurostat data (http://epp.eurostat.ec.europa.eu/portal/page/portal/national_accounts/data/database, accessed on 24 June 2010).

1/5 and 1/3 lower in the EU-SILC than in national accounts in Hungary, Ireland and France; the shortfall for the compensation of employees exceeds 20 per cent in the same three countries and in Lithuania and Portugal; conversely, Cyprus exhibits EU-SILC values well above the corresponding national accounts aggregates. This comparison warns us that the picture drawn from the EU-SILC may deviate from that derived from national accounts: for instance, France accounts for 16 per cent of gross earnings in national accounts, but for only 13 per cent in the EU-SILC aggregates, while the Italian share goes up from 10 to 11 per cent.

A second instructive exercise is to compare the tax wedge as estimated from the EU-SILC data with that computed by Eurostat on the basis of a well-established methodology developed by the Organisation for Economic Co-Operation and Development (OECD, 2008). While the former relates to the actual amount of taxes and social contributions paid by people, the latter refers to the amount that a representative taxpayer would pay under existing legislation. The tax wedge on labour costs is defined by Eurostat (2010) as the percentage ratio of the sum of the income tax on gross wage earnings and the employee's and the employer's social security contributions to the total compensation of the earner (excluding in-kind payments). Eurostat computes this indicator only for single persons without children earning 67 per cent of the average wage.[11] To match as closely as possible these estimates, we restrict the EU-SILC sample to full-time wage-earners employed throughout the year, whose earnings are within a ± 15 per cent band around the average value utilised by Eurostat, and who do not have a partner, a child or a dependent cohabiting relative. For the 15 countries where this computation is possible, Fig. 1 compares the Eurostat figures in 2006 with the EU-SILC medians, 1st quartiles and 3rd quartiles. There is considerable variation in the level of the tax wedge, from around 50 per cent in Belgium to below 20 per cent in Ireland. This is consistently brought out by both Eurostat figures and EU-SILC medians, which are highly correlated (the Pearson correlation coefficient is 0.88). In nine countries (BE, CZ, EE, EL, ES, IE, IT, LU, SI) the EU-SILC values are narrowly distributed around the median and close to Eurostat estimates. In two countries (FR, LV) the tax wedge is for a sizeable proportion of employees well below that calculated by Eurostat: this could signal a problem in the data, but could also follow from employment subsidies entailing a reduction of social security contributions. The EU-SILC values appear to underestimate the Eurostat tax wedge by somewhat more than 4 percentage points in three countries (AT, PL, SE) and, rather more worryingly, by as much as 14 points in one country (PT).

The comparisons with national accounts aggregates and with independently calculated tax wedges help to detect areas needing further investigation in the EU-SILC data: for instance, the French data are somewhat at variance with external sources, whereas social security contributions paid by employers appear to be substantially understated in Portugal. Although

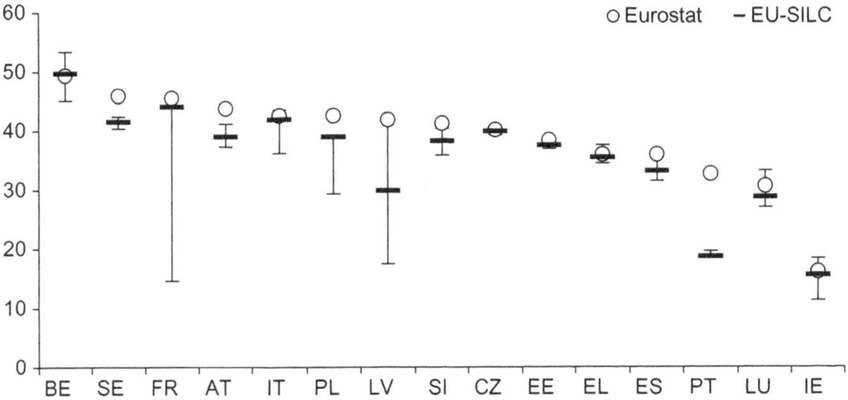

Fig. 1. Tax Wedge on Labour Costs for Low Wage Earners in 15 EU Countries in 2006 (per cent). *Notes*: The tax wedge is defined as the percentage ratio of the sum of the income tax on gross wage earnings and the employee's and the employer's social security contributions to the total compensation of the employee; low wage earners are single persons without children earning 67 per cent of the average wage. The EU-SILC figures refer to median values; vertical bars around the median indicate the first and third quartiles. Countries are ranked in descending order of the Eurostat tax wedge from left to right. *Sources*: Authors' elaboration on EU-SILC users' database (Version 2007-1, March 2009) and Eurostat data (http://appsso.eurostat.ec.europa.eu/nui/show.do?dataset=earn_nt_taxwedge&lang=en, accessed on 31 May 2010).

more work is necessary to validate the data and to document legitimate discrepancies from external sources, overall these comparisons provide some reassuring evidence on the quality of the EU-SILC information on earnings.

Time Unit

As seen, annual (cash) gross earnings are the only variable which is available for all EU countries. Annual earnings are useful to study the contribution of labour income to total household income, but are an imperfect measure of the remuneration of labour as they reflect both the wage rate and the amount of time spent at work. To have a better indication of the variation of the price of labour across countries, we compute full-time equivalent monthly earnings by dividing the annual value (PY010G) by the number of months worked in full-time jobs (PL070) plus the number of months worked in part-time jobs (PL071) scaled down by a country-sex specific factor equal to the ratio of median hours of work (PL060) in part-time jobs to median hours of work in full-time jobs (PL030). (A month is spent at work if the respondent worked for two or more weeks.) For both annual and monthly earnings, we restrict our attention to employees who report positive values. Our sample is consequently larger for annual wages, as 9 per cent of monthly wages cannot be calculated because the number of months in work is missing. Lost observations range from 1 per cent (EL, ES, LT, LU, PT) to around 20 per cent (DK, SI). The overwhelming majority of these cases correspond to observations where both the number of months worked in full-time jobs and the number of months worked in part-time jobs are coded as zero. It is conceivable that gross earnings are positive while no or limited work was made (e.g. arrears, very short temporary contracts), but the joint occurrence of positive earnings and no month spent in work is suspiciously frequent (11–13 per cent of cases in FI, IT, LV, NL, SE, UK). We do not make any adjustment for this difference in the samples, but it should be borne in mind that it is bound to affect the observed discrepancies between annual and monthly values.

Conversion Rates

Earnings are expressed, as all other EU-SILC income variables, in euro. For the 14 countries which were not part of the monetary union in 2006, the values collected in national currency are converted into euro at the average market exchange rates. As these rates do not reflect the price structures that prevail in the various countries, we also use Purchasing Power Parities (PPP), which provide the relative values, in national currencies, of a fixed bundle of goods and services. PPP convert all values into a common standard (denominated Purchasing Power Standard, PPS, in Eurostat statistics) adjusted for differences in price levels.

For European countries, annual PPP indices are available for gross domestic product (GDP) and for a number of expenditure components of GDP (Eurostat and Organisation for Economic Co-Operation and Development, 2006). The choice of the index matters. By deflating nominal wages by the PPP index for household final consumption expenditure (HFCE) rather than the PPP index for GDP (both normalised to 1 for the EU-27), in 2006 real wages are 5–8 per cent lower in five poorer countries (EE, LT, LV, PL, SK) and 2–3 per cent higher in five richer countries (AT, FR, NL, SE, UK).

The use of the PPP–GDP index tends to narrow international differences in real wages relative to the PPP–HFCE index. The PPP–HFCE index (applied to net earnings) is preferable for the EU distribution of 'consumer' wages, as it measures purchasing power in terms of consumption goods and services, but the PPP–GDP index (applied to total compensations) is more appropriate for the distribution of 'producer' wages, as it refers to the whole value added. Note that the PPP–GDP index is generally applied to derive all national accounts variables expressed in PPS.

EARNINGS DISTRIBUTIONS IN EU COUNTRIES

The distribution of real monthly full-time equivalent gross earnings in 2006 in all EU-25 member countries (except for Malta) is shown in Fig. 2. Gross earnings are here expressed in thousands of PPS using the PPP–HFCE index. The graph shows for each country the average value (the thick horizontal mark), the median value (the light horizontal line), the distance between the 20th and the 80th percentiles (the vertical box) and the 5th and 95th percentiles (the two extremes of the thin vertical bar). Countries are ranked in ascending order of median earnings from left to right. As expected, Eastern European nations precede Southern European countries and then the remaining EU countries, which are rather close to each other except for the outlier Luxembourg. Earnings differences are sizeable, both across and within countries. The Slovak median is only 18 per cent of the Luxembourger median, a gap that widens to 23 per cent if the comparison is made at the 5th percentile. For almost 80 per cent of Eastern Europeans labour incomes are below or at most comparable to those of the poorest 20 per cent of Europeans living in the richer Central and Nordic countries.

The variable lengths of the vertical bars reveal some noticeable differences in within-country earnings dispersion, such as that between Belgium or Denmark and the United Kingdom, three countries which share similar median values. On the other hand, there are unexpected similarities among countries as different as France, Finland and Italy, which exhibit remarkably close values of the mean, the median, and the 20th and 80th percentiles. It should be noted that these bars show *absolute* and not *relative* differences. If percentiles were expressed as percentages of national medians, as customary in cross-national inequality comparisons, earnings differences in Eastern Europe would not look so small compared to those in the EU-15. Indeed, as shown in Table 2, Latvia and Lithuania would exhibit, together with

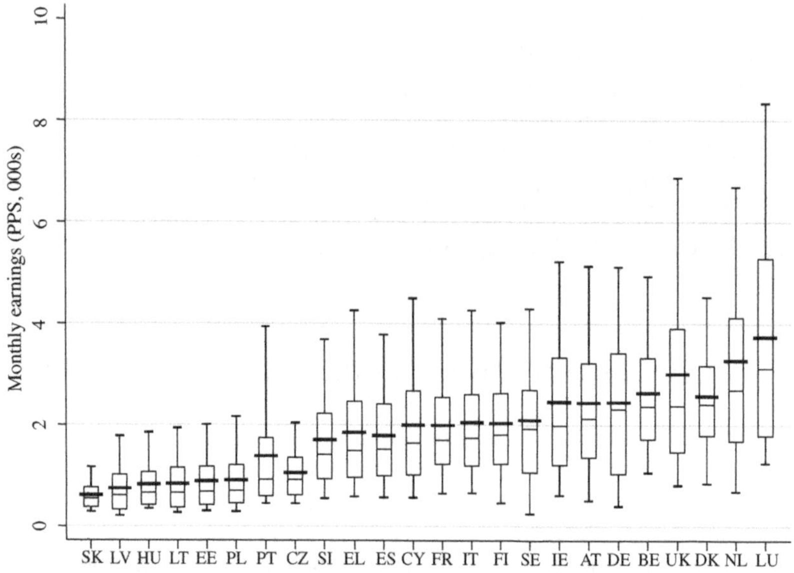

Fig. 2. Distribution of Real Monthly Full-Time Equivalent Gross Earnings in EU Countries in 2006 (thousands of euro in PPS-HFCE). *Notes*: Boxes span 20th to 80th percentiles; vertical bars span 5th to 95th percentile; light horizontal lines are median earnings; thick horizontal lines are average earnings. Countries are ranked in ascending order of median earnings from left to right. *Sources*: Authors' elaboration on EU-SILC users' database (Version 2007-1, March 2009) and Eurostat PPP data (http://epp.eurostat.ec.europa.eu/portal/page/portal/purchasing_power_parities/introduction, accessed on 3 June 2010).

Luxembourg, the second largest value of the quintile ratio (the ratio of the 80th percentile to the 20th percentile) after Germany.

Table 2 also reports the decile ratio (the ratio of the 90th percentile to the 10th percentile) together with the mean logarithmic deviation, the Theil index and the Gini index. The country ranking does not coincide across these inequality measures: for monthly full-time equivalent gross earnings, Germany shows the highest decile and quintile ratios but the 11th highest value of the Theil index; Sweden shows the highest value for the mean logarithmic deviation but the 13th highest value for the Gini index; movements are less extreme for most of the other countries. By and large, there is however a substantial agreement across all five inequality measures, as testified by values of Spearman's rank correlation coefficients in excess of

Table 2. Statistics for the Distribution of Gross Earnings in EU Countries in 2006.

Country	Sample Size	No. of Employees (000)	Mean (Euro)	Median (Euro)	Mean (PPS-HFCE)	Median (PPS-HFCE)	Mean Logarithmic Deviation	Theil Index	Gini Index	Quintile Ratio	Decile Ratio
					Monthly full-time equivalent gross earnings						
BE	5,648	3,862	2,848	2,560	2,644	2,377	0,124	0,121	0.255	1.9	2.9
CZ	8,979	4,043	654	576	1,066	939	0,135	0,145	0.279	2.2	3.2
DK	6,945	2,319	3,573	3,339	2,582	2,413	0,147	0,119	0.243	1.8	2.8
DE	12,288	33,385	2,525	2,381	2,461	2,320	0,253	0,212	0.346	3.3	6.8
EE	6,493	651	613	472	895	689	0,208	0,244	0.353	2.8	4.8
IE	4,593	1,677	3,025	2,462	2,430	1,977	0,231	0,254	0.357	2.7	5.1
EL	3,725	3,059	1,657	1,331	1,862	1,496	0,197	0,207	0.337	2.5	4.1
ES	12,959	18,255	1,648	1,400	1,795	1,525	0,179	0,175	0.313	2.4	4.1
FR	10,159	23,760	2,171	1,853	2,001	1,708	0,173	0,168	0.296	2.1	3.5
IT	15,867	18,199	2,140	1,826	2,054	1,752	0,186	0,183	0.307	2.2	3.6
CY	4,146	327	1,779	1,469	2,004	1,654	0,202	0,219	0.340	2.6	4.4
LV	4,690	1,020	460	379	757	623	0,234	0,235	0.367	3.0	5.4
LT	5,254	1,483	483	388	842	676	0,218	0,222	0.359	3.0	5.0
LU	4,533	200	4,176	3,480	3,752	3,127	0,202	0,204	0.344	3.0	4.9
HU	8,155	3,782	507	408	836	673	0,187	0,205	0.329	2.5	3.7
NL	11,584	6,748	3,421	2,810	3,289	2,702	0,274	0,325	0.364	2.4	4.6
AT	6,776	3,467	2,495	2,171	2,449	2,131	0,220	0,199	0.327	2.4	4.9
PL	12,625	13,262	573	447	917	716	0,212	0,233	0.354	2.7	4.5
PT	4,087	4,024	1,183	793	1,394	934	0,284	0,335	0.414	2.9	5.3
SI	11,836	786	1,314	1,093	1,713	1,424	0,195	0,206	0.325	2.4	3.9
SK	6,174	2,247	446	403	623	562	0,126	0,127	0.260	2.0	3.1
FI	12,409	2,447	2,505	2,219	2,042	1,809	0,215	0,183	0.301	2.1	3.9
SE	8,988	4,395	2,494	2,298	2,106	1,940	0,294	0,225	0.336	2.5	6.2
UK	7,912	22,720	3,259	2,581	2,947	2,334	0,241	0,256	0.365	2.7	4.6

Table 2. *(Continued)*

Country	Sample Size	No. of Employees (000)	Mean (Euro)	Median (Euro)	Mean (PPS-HFCE)	Median (PPS-HFCE)	Mean Logarithmic Deviation	Theil Index	Gini Index	Quintile Ratio	Decile Ratio
					Yearly gross earnings						
BE	5,877	4,022	29,159	27,278	27,074	25,327	0,254	0,187	0.319	2.4	5.8
CZ	9,283	4,179	7,252	6,605	11,825	10,770	0,232	0,195	0.326	2.5	5.2
DK	8,497	2,899	33,549	34,246	24,246	24,750	0,415	0,247	0.361	4.3	14.5
DE	13,241	36,067	24,611	22,328	23,987	21,762	0,444	0,312	0.424	6.5	15.3
EE	6,691	666	6,692	5,369	9,767	7,836	0,298	0,293	0.392	3.2	6.3
IE	4,836	1,790	28,286	22,665	22,720	18,204	0,503	0,368	0.460	5.9	19.9
EL	3,764	3,092	18,197	14,493	20,446	16,284	0,290	0,262	0.384	3.2	6.8
ES	13,146	18,524	17,311	15,220	18,857	16,580	0,293	0,229	0.365	3.2	7.7
FR	10,925	25,497	21,851	19,682	20,139	18,140	0,325	0,252	0.364	3.0	8.1
IT	18,072	20,524	21,442	19,419	20,578	18,636	0,393	0,265	0.381	3.4	10.7
CY	4,340	341	19,248	16,121	21,675	18,154	0,356	0,301	0.403	3.5	10.5
LV	5,305	1,131	4,813	3,812	7,922	6,275	0,414	0,321	0.427	4.0	11.7
LT	5,290	1,493	5,346	4,210	9,322	7,341	0,297	0,271	0.395	3.4	6.7
LU	4,563	202	44,366	35,100	39,861	31,536	0,310	0,268	0.392	3.4	7.1
HU	8,710	4,027	5,337	4,371	8,801	7,208	0,326	0,280	0.393	3.0	8.3
NL	13,263	7,934	27,257	24,069	26,209	23,143	0,524	0,354	0.440	5.8	21.2
AT	7,012	3,589	25,235	22,376	24,765	21,959	0,349	0,274	0.392	3.7	10.4
PL	13,708	13,288	6,258	5,013	10,020	8,028	0,318	0,290	0.400	3.2	7.7
PT	4,112	4,050	13,266	9,070	15,625	10,684	0,351	0,366	0.439	3.0	7.0
SI	15,039	970	12,367	10,825	16,124	14,113	0,509	0,334	0.430	5.4	22.4
SK	6,685	2,426	4,734	4,351	6,602	6,068	0,295	0,199	0.328	2.4	6.6
FI	13,901	2,691	23,574	22,758	19,213	18,548	0,549	0,324	0.414	5.7	24.3
SE	10,211	4,975	23,525	23,526	19,860	19,861	0,529	0,294	0.396	5.1	24.6
UK	8,979	25,874	32,929	26,332	29,773	23,808	0,309	0,284	0.393	3.1	7.1

Sources: Authors' elaboration on EU-SILC users' database (Version 2007-1, March 2009) and Eurostat PPP data (http://epp.eurostat.ec.europa.eu/portal/page/portal/purchasing_power_parities/introduction, accessed on 3 June 2010).

0.8 in most of the pair-wise comparisons. These differences aside, the country ranking shown in Table 2 is partly surprising. It is somewhat unusual to observe the highest values of the decile ratio in Germany and Sweden, and much lower values in the United Kingdom and especially Italy. This ordering is the opposite of that usually found for household equivalent incomes (e.g. Wolff, 2010). It is beyond the scope of this chapter to study the factors that help to explain such a difference (e.g. employment rates, other sources of income, welfare unit; see Atkinson & Brandolini, 2007). Here, suffice it to say that comparing the EU-SILC with the SES results provides reassuring evidence. The correlation of the decile ratios for monthly full-time equivalent gross earnings in Table 2 with the corresponding SES figures reported by Casali and Alvarez Gonzalez (2010, p. 4, Table 2) is positive but moderate (correlation coefficient equal to 0.42), also for the impact of two outliers, Germany and Sweden (left panel of Fig. 3); when the EU-SILC sample is restricted to full-time workers employed throughout the year, in order to better match the SES definition, the relationship becomes much stronger (correlation coefficient equal to 0.84) (right panel of Fig. 3). The contrast between the two panels of Fig. 3 shows that the spreading of temporary occupations and jobs lasting for less than the whole year has a considerable impact on measured wage inequality. This observation is further confirmed by the much higher dispersion of annual earnings relative to that of monthly full-time equivalent earnings (compare the top and bottom panels in Table 2).

Before examining the EU-wide distribution, it is useful to assess the importance of the earnings definition. The three panels of Fig. 4 report the median, the decile ratio and the Gini index for the distributions of net earnings, gross earnings and total compensations in 14 countries where all three variables are available. All three variables are expressed on a monthly basis after adjusting for part-time and are deflated by the PPP–HFCE index; the sample is restricted to observations that have a positive value for all definitions. Countries are ranked in ascending order of median net earnings. The absolute gap between net and gross earnings tends to widen as countries become richer, with the exception of Ireland. Latvia and Poland together with Ireland and Luxembourg show narrow differences between gross earnings and total compensations, whereas Belgium stands out for the largest difference. In all countries but France, Latvia, Poland and Spain, dispersion decreases substantially considering net rather than gross earnings, as a consequence of the progressive structure of labour income taxation. Conversely, there is little difference, on average, between the dispersion of the labour cost and that of gross earnings. This follows from the fact that the difference

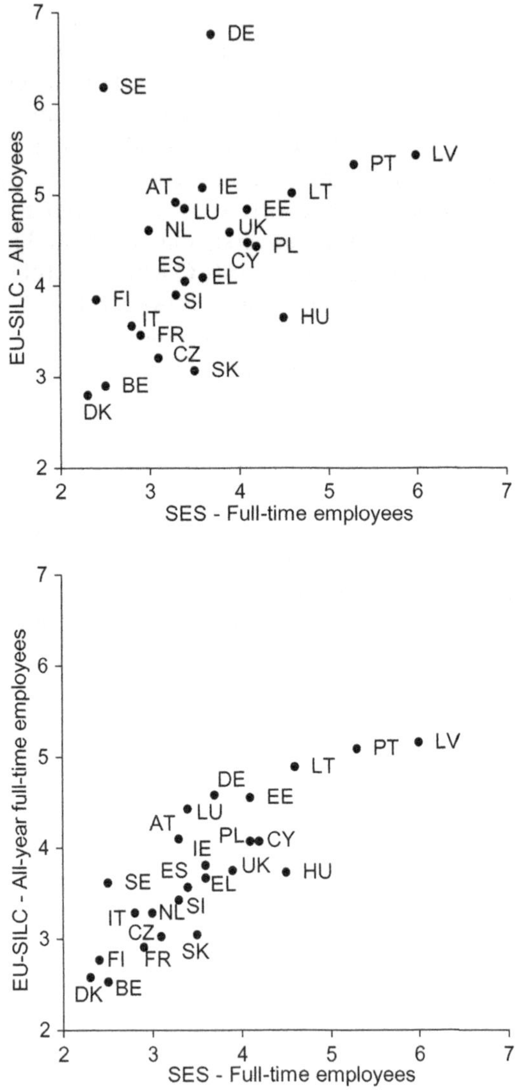

Fig. 3. Decile Ratio of Gross Earnings in EU Countries in 2006. *Notes*: The SES figures are for the annual earnings of full-time employees in the sectors covered by the survey; the EU-SILC figures are for monthly full-time equivalent gross earnings of all employees in the left panel and of full-time workers employed throughout the year in the right panel. *Sources*: Authors' elaboration on EU-SILC users' database (Version 2007-1, March 2009) and SES data drawn from Casali and Alvarez Gonzalez (2010, p. 4, Table 2).

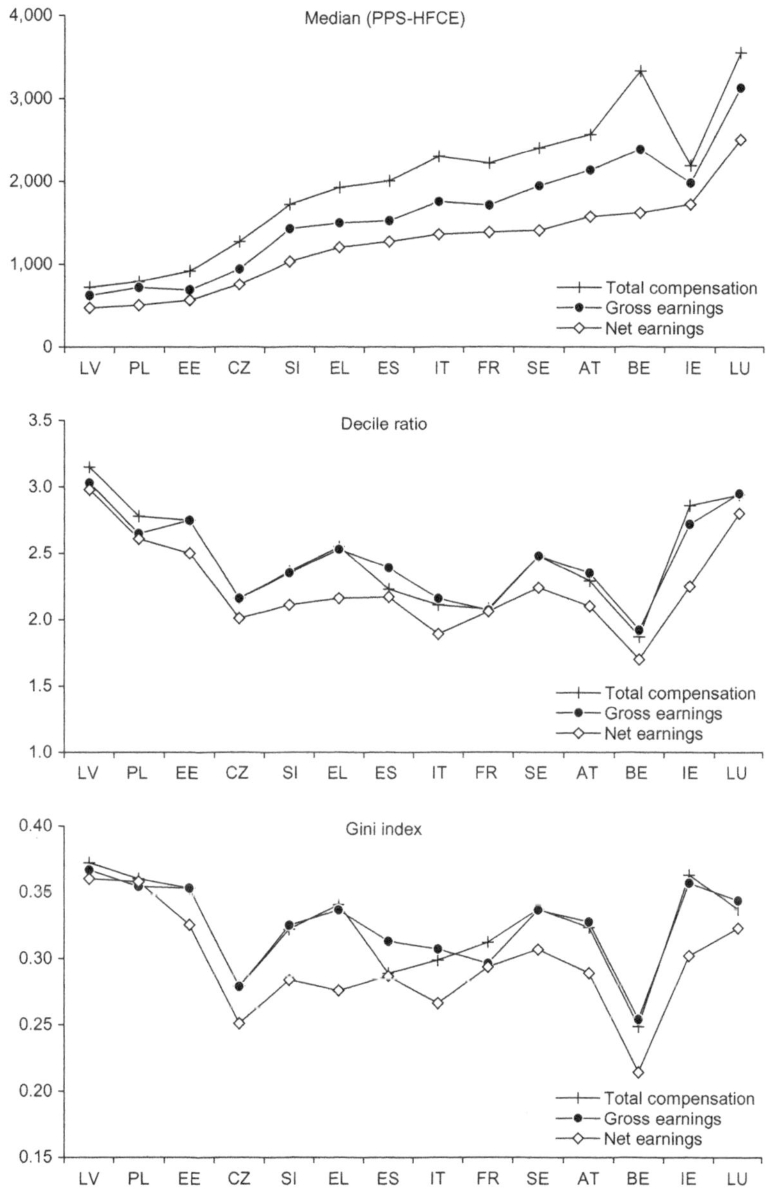

Fig. 4. Distribution of Real Monthly Full-Time Equivalent Earnings in Selected EU Countries by Different Definitions of Earnings in 2006 (PPS-HFCE).

Sources: Authors' elaboration on EU-SILC users' database (Version 2007-1, March 2009) and Eurostat PPP data (http://epp.eurostat.ec.europa.eu/portal/page/portal/purchasing_power_parities/introduction, accessed on 3 June 2010).

is generally small and in either direction, as employers' social security contributions tend to be roughly proportional and sometimes mildly regressive (especially in Spain, apparently).[12]

Taking the 14 countries as a whole, median net earnings are 69 per cent of median gross earnings, and 62 per cent of median labour cost. The Gini index falls slightly from 0.354 for total compensations to 0.350 for gross earnings, and more significantly to 0.330 for net earnings. A similar picture is provided by the mean logarithmic deviation which has the advantage of being decomposable into a between- and within-country component. The fall in dispersion from gross to net earnings is entirely due to a decline in the within-country component: the progressivity of income taxes and employees' social contributions reduces the degree of inequality in each country without affecting countries' relative rankings. The fall in dispersion from total compensations to gross earnings is instead driven by the between-country component, following from the high cross-country variability of employers' social security contributions levied at approximately proportional rates. This evidence confirms that the earnings definition may affect the comparison of national distributions and, hence, the construction of area-wide statistics. Gross earnings are the only measure available for all countries in the EU-SILC users' database, but are possibly the least suited, as they do not account for the different structure of income taxes across countries and depend on the composition of social contributions.[13]

THE EU-WIDE DISTRIBUTION OF GROSS EARNINGS

Statistics for the distribution of monthly (full-time equivalent) and annual earnings for both the euro area and the EU-25 taken as a whole are reported in Table 3. Since the conversion factor affects mean country earnings and thus distributive measures for groups of countries, Table 3 contains statistics based on market exchange rates as well as the two PPP indices for GDP and HFCE. Using unadjusted figures parallels the standard practice in national reports of ignoring territorial differences in price levels, a sensible exercise particularly in the analysis of the wage distribution in the monetary union.[14]

In the euro area, the average employee earns 2,263 euro per month, gross of taxes and social contributions and after adjusting for part-time, while the median employee earns 15 per cent less, or 1,918 euro per month. These values fall by 5 and 7 per cent to 2,153 and 1,786 euro per month, respectively, when the whole EU-25 is considered.

Table 3. Statistics for the EU-Wide Distribution of Gross Earnings in 2006.

Gross Earnings Definition	Sample Size	No. of Employees (000)	Mean	Median	Mean Logarithmic Deviation	Theil Index	Gini Index	Quintile Ratio	Decile Ratio
					Euro area				
Monthly full-time equivalent									
PPS-HFCE	104,628	119,083	2,199	1,857	0.226	0.219	0.343	2.7	5.0
PPS-GDP	104,628	119,083	2,200	1,860	0.224	0.218	0.342	2.7	4.9
Euro at market rates	104,628	119,083	2,263	1,918	0.234	0.226	0.349	2.8	5.3
Yearly									
PPS-HFCE	112,712	127,982	21,745	18,722	0.390	0.290	0.405	4.2	11.7
PPS-GDP	112,712	127,982	21,760	18,736	0.389	0.288	0.404	4.1	11.7
Euro at market rates	112,712	127,982	22,368	19,246	0.396	0.295	0.409	4.3	11.8
					EU-25				
Monthly full-time equivalent									
PPS-HFCE	196,825	176,118	2,099	1,732	0.276	0.267	0.381	3.3	6.5
PPS-GDP	196,825	176,118	2,099	1,734	0.269	0.261	0.377	3.2	6.3
Euro at market rates	196,825	176,118	2,153	1,786	0.338	0.306	0.410	4.1	9.2
Yearly									
PPS-HFCE	215,450	190,252	21,071	17,443	0.417	0.324	0.428	4.6	11.7
PPS-GDP	215,450	190,252	21,072	17,510	0.412	0.320	0.425	4.5	11.5
Euro at market rates	215,450	190,252	21,613	17,684	0.473	0.362	0.453	5.9	14.4

Sources: Authors' elaboration on EU-SILC users' database (Version 2007-1, March 2009) and Eurostat PPP data (http://epp.eurostat.ec.europa.eu/portal/page/portal/purchasing_power_parities/introduction, accessed on 3 June 2010).

Inequality is always higher when earnings are measured in euros at market rates than in PPS with either index; it is always lower if earnings are converted using the PPP–GDP index (but differences are generally small, especially in the euro area). The much greater dispersion observed for annual than monthly earnings indicate that labour supply does not offset lower wage rates. Lastly, inequality is larger when measured for the EU-25 than for the euro area, which is not surprising given that the latter does not include the poorer Eastern European countries that joined the Union in 2004.

The aggregation of the EU-25 countries into a single entity yields an overall distribution of monthly full-time equivalent earnings which is no more dispersed than that of the most unequal country: for instance, taking earnings converted by the PPP–HFCE index, the Gini index is 0.381 in the EU-25 vis-à-vis 0.414 in Portugal and 0.367 in Latvia; at 3.3 the quintile ratio is the same as that measured for Germany. The more homogeneous euro area would be much further down in the country ranking by earnings inequality.

Decomposition of the Variance of Logarithms

The distribution of earnings in the euro area and in the EU-25 can be traced back to the distribution of the observable characteristics of the underlying populations. By denoting by y_{jc} the (natural logarithm of) earnings of person j in country c, the overall variance can be decomposed as follows:

$$\mathrm{Var}(y_{jc}) = \frac{1}{N}\sum_{c}\sum_{j}(y_{jc} - y_{\mathrm{EU}})^2 = \sum_{c}\sigma_c n_c + \sum_{c} n_c(y_c - y_{\mathrm{EU}})^2$$

where n_c is the share of EU population in country c, σ_c is the variance in country c, and y_c and y_{EU} are the average earnings of country c and the EU as a whole, respectively.[15] The first term on the right-hand side is the within-country component of the total variance while the second term is the between-country component. These components can be linked to the observable (X) and unobservable (u) individual characteristics by assuming that (log) earnings are a linear function of them, or $y_{jc} = X_{jc}b_c + u_{jc}$.

Country differences may stem from differences in the characteristics of workers (such as education) and differences in the way these characteristics are valued in the labour market (returns). To disentangle these two factors we make use of the Oaxaca–Blinder decomposition (Blinder, 1973; Oaxaca, 1973), which allows us to decompose the term $(y_c - y_{\mathrm{EU}})$ into a part explained by population differences between country c and the whole EU and a part due to differences in returns to specific individual attributes:

$$(y_c - y_{EU}) = X_c b_c - X_{EU} b_{EU} = (X_c - X_{EU}) b_{EU} + X_c(b_c - b_{EU})$$

Since this decomposition applies to the difference in means, while we are interested in the effects of these two components on the between-country variance, we compute $CBV = \sum_c n_c[(X_c - X_{EU})b_{EU}]^2$. CBV can be interpreted as the counterfactual between-country variance that would arise if all countries displayed the same EU-wide returns to given observable attributes (i.e. the same wage schedule). As our calculations below include a set of dummy variables for the interaction of sex, education, age and birth in the survey country, the above quantity can also be seen as the pure effect of country composition on between-country differences. Within-country variance σ_c reflects both the heterogeneity of the underlying population, $\text{Var}(X_{jc})$, and the returns to unobservable characteristics. We compute the explained within-country variance as $\text{Var}(X_{jc} b_c)$, where b_c is the OLS estimate of the vector of parameters of the country wage equation. The residual is the unexplained component.

Table 4 shows the results of this decomposition for the distribution among employees aged 20–64 of the logarithm of monthly full-time equivalent gross earnings, both in euro and PPS–HFCE, in the euro area and the EU-25. The earnings equation includes a dummy for birth in survey country (PB210 = LOC), two dummies for education (High School, if PE040 = 3; College, if PE040 = 4,5), with 'at most ISCED3' (PE040 = 1,2,3) as the residual category, and nine age classes (20–24, 25–29, 30–34, 35–39, 40–44, 45–49, 50–54, 55–59, 60–64). Column [1] of Table 4 reports the total variance, which is the sum of the between-countries component, in column [2], and the within-countries component, in column [4]; the latter is in turn decomposed into the part explained by observable characteristics, in column [5], and the residual unexplained part, in column [6]. Differences among countries in average monthly earnings explain a small part, less than 1/10, of total dispersion in the euro area, but are much more important in the EU-25 (24 per cent with PPS–HFCE, 41 per cent with euro). Conversely, the within-country component accounts for more than 90 per cent of total variance in the euro area, but for only 59 (euro) or 76 (PPS–HFCE) per cent in the EU-25: in both areas, however, no more than a quarter of the within-country component is attributable to observable characteristics, the rest being unexplained by the empirical model. Lastly, the counterfactual between-country variance, reported in column [3], is virtually nil in all cases, suggesting that the between-country component is essentially due to

Table 4. Variance Decomposition of the Logarithm of Monthly Full-Time Equivalent Earnings in 2006 (Absolute Values and Percentage Shares in Italics).

Gross Earnings Unit of Account	Total	Between-Countries		Within-Countries		
		Actual	Counter-factual	Total	Explained	Unexplained
	[1] = [2] + [4]	[2]	[3]	[4] = [5] + [6]	[5]	[6]
			Euro area			
PPS-HFCE	0.498	0.029	0.004	0.469	0.116	0.353
	100.0	*5.9*	*0.8*	*94.1*	*23.3*	70.9
Euro at market rates	0.517	0.049	0.005	0.469	0.116	0.353
	100.0	*9.4*	*0.9*	*90.6*	*22.4*	*68.2*
			EU-25			
PPS-HFCE	0.611	0.147	0.002	0.463	0.107	0.357
	100.0	*24.1*	*0.3*	*75.9*	*17.5*	*58.4*
Euro at market rates	0.789	0.326	0.002	0.463	0.107	0.357
	100.0	*41.3*	*0.3*	*58.7*	*13.5*	*45.2*

Notes: The total variance in column [1] is equal to the sum of the between-countries component in column [2] and the within-countries component in column [4]; the latter component is decomposed into the part explained by observable characteristics in column [5] and the residual unexplained part in column [6]. The counterfactual between-countries variance in column [3] is obtained by imposing the same EU-wide returns to given observable attributes in all countries.
Source: Authors' elaboration on EU-SILC users' database (Version 2007-1, March 2009) and Eurostat PPP data (http://epp.eurostat.ec.europa.eu/portal/page/portal/purchasing_power_parities/introduction, accessed on 3 June 2010).

heterogeneous returns to individual attributes rather than to a different demographic composition of employees. A similar conclusion is reached for the EU-15 countries by Behr and Pötter (2010) using ECHP data.

A First Look into the Determinants of the EU-Wide Distribution of Gross Earnings

The previous decomposition is silent about the extent to which the variance of (log) earnings hinges on the distribution of each characteristic. For example, would the variance increase or decrease, should the educational composition of the workforce change, holding all else constant? In order to address this question, we apply here the regression-based method recently developed by Firpo et al. (2009), which allows us to isolate the effect of each characteristic on the variance more straightforwardly than the alternative procedures devised by Machado and Mata (2005) and Melly (2005).

Firpo, Fortin and Lemieux's method replaces the dependent variable of interest (in our case, log earnings) with the recentered influence function (RIF) for the distributional statistic of interest (in our case, the variance). The influence function (IF), a widely used and easy-to-compute concept in robust statistics, measures the robustness of a given functional g of a specific distribution F, $g(F)$, to outlier data and is defined by:

$$\mathrm{IF}(y; g, F) = \frac{\lim_{e \to 0}[g(F_e) - g(F)]}{e}$$

where $F_e(y) = (1 - e)F + e\delta_y$, $0 \leq e \leq 1$, and δ_y is a distribution that only puts mass at y. For the variance, $g(F) = \int(s - \mu)^2 dF(s)$ and

$$\begin{aligned}
\mathrm{IF}(y; g, F) &= \frac{\lim_{e \to 0}\left[\int(s - \mu)^2 dF_e(s) - \int(s - \mu)^2 dF(s)\right]}{e} \\
&= \frac{\lim_{e \to 0}\left[(1 - e)\int(s - \mu)^2 dF(s) + e(y - \mu)^2 - \int(s - \mu)^2 dF(s)\right]}{e} \\
&= \frac{\lim_{e \to 0}\left[e(y - \mu)^2 - e\int(s - \mu)^2 dF(s)\right]}{e} = (y - \mu)^2 - \sigma^2
\end{aligned}$$

The RIF is simply obtained by adding the statistic of interest to IF, $\mathrm{RIF}(y; g, F) = g(F) + \mathrm{IF}(y; g, F)$, and is obviously defined for each available observation. It can be shown that $\int \mathrm{IF}(y; g, F) dF(y) = 0$, which implies $\int \mathrm{RIF}(y; g, F) dF(y) = g(F)$. The main contribution of Firpo et al. (2009) is to show that the effect on the statistic of interest of a small location shift in the distribution of a specific covariate, all else constant, can be obtained by estimation by standard methods of the relevant RIF.

This method can be applied to any statistic for which a RIF can be computed: here, we consider the variance and the main percentiles. We focus, as before, on gross monthly earnings in PPS–HFCE of employees aged 20–64, but we restrict the attention to full-time employees in order to obtain more robust estimates. As a term of comparison, we report results also for Germany, the largest EU economy, in addition to those for the euro area and the EU-25 taken as a whole. The results in Table 5 and Fig. 5 show the effects on the distribution of (log) earnings of a small change in the composition of the workforce by sex, birth in the survey country, education and age.[16] (To facilitate comparisons of the effects of different covariates, the same scale is used for the vertical axis in each panel of Fig. 5.) Unlike those obtained from standard conditional quantile regressions, these effects represent the change in the unconditional distribution associated with a change in the characteristic of interest. Thus, the fact that the effect of high school in Germany is larger at the 10th than at the 90th percentile implies that its overall effect is to reduce inequality, as measured by the difference between these two percentiles. In a standard conditional quantile regression this conclusion would apply only to employees sharing the same values of the other covariates; in the case of the unconditional quantile regressions underlying the results of Table 5, the conclusion is more general as the estimation accounts also for the effect of high school achievement across groups.

In all three areas, an increase in the share of female full-time employees would lead to a statistically significant reduction of all percentiles, which confirms the existence of a gender wage gap. The change would be however similarly spread across the entire distribution, and the effect on the overall inequality would be negligible (mildly significant only in the euro area). The objective of raising female labour participation in the EU need not bring about a more unequal wage dispersion.

On the contrary, results for the effect of being born in the survey country are mixed. An increase in the proportion of native born employees would increase the overall variance in Germany, would reduce it in the euro area, and would have no effect in the EU-25. The German result is driven by a strong, and difficult to explain, deterioration at the bottom of the distribution (see top-right panel in Fig. 5), which dominates an otherwise flat profile. In the euro area, a larger share of native employees would instead thicken the middle of the distribution: the effects are small but statistically significant. In the EU-25, there is little action in the middle, while the worsening bottom and very top percentiles offset each other. These results are not easy to interpret, but suggest that an increase of cross-country mobility might increase wage inequality in the euro area, and possibly in the EU-25, as mobile workers polarise at the bottom and the top of the earnings distribution.

To assess the effects of population ageing, we partition employees in three groups: the young, or those aged 20–34, those aged 35–49, and the old, aged 50–64. The age effects are rather consistent across the three areas: an increase

Table 5. Determinants of the Distribution of the Logarithm of Real Monthly Gross Earnings Among Full-Time Employees Aged 20 to 64 in Germany, the Euro Area and the EU-25 in 2006.

Characteristic	Variance	Bottom Decile	2nd Decile	3rd Decile	4th Decile	5th Decile	6th Decile	7th Decile	8th Decile	Top Decile
					Germany					
Female	0.016	−0.237**	−0.270**	−0.213**	−0.175**	−0.152**	−0.166**	−0.170**	−0.183**	−0.254**
	(0.023)	(0.056)	(0.033)	(0.024)	(0.018)	(0.014)	(0.013)	(0.013)	(0.014)	(0.018)
Birth in country	0.107**	−0.201	0.085	0.083	0.089*	0.058	0.001	0.007	0.016	−0.008
	(0.036)	(0.129)	(0.077)	(0.055)	(0.040)	(0.032)	(0.029)	(0.030)	(0.034)	(0.049)
Aged 20–34	0.416**	−1.372**	−0.722**	−0.528**	−0.397**	−0.310**	−0.252**	−0.222**	−0.194**	−0.197**
	(0.025)	(0.069)	(0.038)	(0.028)	(0.021)	(0.016)	(0.014)	(0.014)	(0.016)	(0.020)
Aged 50–64	0.027	0.062	−0.039	−0.013	0.026	0.028	0.031*	0.060**	0.084**	0.121**
	(0.027)	(0.035)	(0.031)	(0.025)	(0.020)	(0.017)	(0.015)	(0.016)	(0.019)	(0.028)
High school	−0.665**	1.368**	0.664**	0.404**	0.282**	0.207**	0.145**	0.094**	0.077**	0.052*
	(0.037)	(0.135)	(0.068)	(0.047)	(0.033)	(0.024)	(0.021)	(0.019)	(0.019)	(0.023)
College	−0.605**	1.688**	0.971**	0.725**	0.595**	0.519**	0.472**	0.466**	0.469**	0.529**
	(0.038)	(0.136)	(0.067)	(0.047)	(0.033)	(0.024)	(0.021)	(0.021)	(0.022)	(0.031)
					Euro area					
Female	−0.023*	−0.328**	−0.253**	−0.219**	−0.229**	−0.235**	−0.243**	−0.259**	−0.253**	−0.292**
	(0.011)	(0.016)	(0.009)	(0.007)	(0.007)	(0.007)	(0.007)	(0.007)	(0.007)	(0.009)
Birth in country	−0.061**	0.071*	0.116**	0.119**	0.119**	0.107**	0.092**	0.055**	0.025	0.009
	(0.019)	(0.034)	(0.019)	(0.015)	(0.014)	(0.015)	(0.014)	(0.015)	(0.015)	(0.021)
Aged 20–34	0.029*	−0.479**	−0.352**	−0.318**	−0.328**	−0.345**	−0.339**	−0.329**	−0.283**	−0.297**
	(0.012)	(0.019)	(0.010)	(0.008)	(0.008)	(0.008)	(0.008)	(0.008)	(0.007)	(0.010)

Table 5. *(Continued)*

Characteristic	Variance	Bottom Decile	2nd Decile	3rd Decile	4th Decile	5th Decile	6th Decile	7th Decile	8th Decile	Top Decile
Aged 50–64	0.068** (0.015)	0.079** (0.014)	0.079** (0.009)	0.068** (0.008)	0.090** (0.008)	0.105** (0.008)	0.132** (0.009)	0.145** (0.009)	0.144** (0.010)	0.161** (0.015)
High school	−0.140** (0.014)	0.565** (0.022)	0.393** (0.012)	0.343** (0.009)	0.349** (0.008)	0.356** (0.008)	0.327** (0.008)	0.286** (0.008)	0.210** (0.007)	0.174** (0.009)
College	−0.006 (0.014)	0.783** (0.022)	0.585** (0.011)	0.548** (0.009)	0.596** (0.008)	0.647** (0.008)	0.657** (0.008)	0.667** (0.008)	0.612** (0.009)	0.671** (0.013)
EU-25										
Female	−0.007 (0.009)	−0.375** (0.012)	−0.379** (0.010)	−0.315** (0.008)	−0.275** (0.006)	−0.285** (0.006)	−0.278** (0.006)	−0.286** (0.006)	−0.268** (0.006)	−0.298** (0.008)
Birth in country	0.000 (0.015)	−0.182** (0.022)	−0.177** (0.021)	−0.062** (0.017)	0.003 (0.014)	0.007 (0.014)	0.023 (0.014)	0.007 (0.014)	−0.028 (0.015)	−0.054* (0.021)
Aged 20–34	−0.007 (0.009)	−0.345** (0.013)	−0.400** (0.012)	−0.344** (0.009)	−0.319** (0.007)	−0.329** (0.007)	−0.329** (0.007)	−0.322** (0.007)	−0.283** (0.007)	−0.286** (0.009)
Aged 50–64	0.069** (0.011)	0.000 (0.011)	0.016 (0.010)	0.042** (0.008)	0.049** (0.007)	0.064** (0.007)	0.076** (0.008)	0.093** (0.008)	0.080** (0.008)	0.085** (0.012)
High school	0.066** (0.011)	−0.010 (0.017)	0.077** (0.015)	0.161** (0.011)	0.228** (0.009)	0.269** (0.008)	0.269** (0.008)	0.265** (0.007)	0.215** (0.006)	0.189** (0.008)
College	0.137** (0.012)	0.436** (0.016)	0.546** (0.015)	0.526** (0.011)	0.556** (0.009)	0.627** (0.008)	0.651** (0.008)	0.687** (0.008)	0.638** (0.008)	0.681** (0.011)

Notes: Standard errors in parentheses; significance $^{**}p<0.01$, $^{*}p<0.05$. There are 8,436 observations for Germany, 80,574 for the euro area, and 161,617 for the EU-25.

Sources: Authors' elaboration on EU-SILC users' database (Version 2007-1, March 2009) and Eurostat PPP data (http://epp.eurostat.ec.europa.eu/portal/page/portal/purchasing_power_parities/introduction, accessed on 3 June 2010).

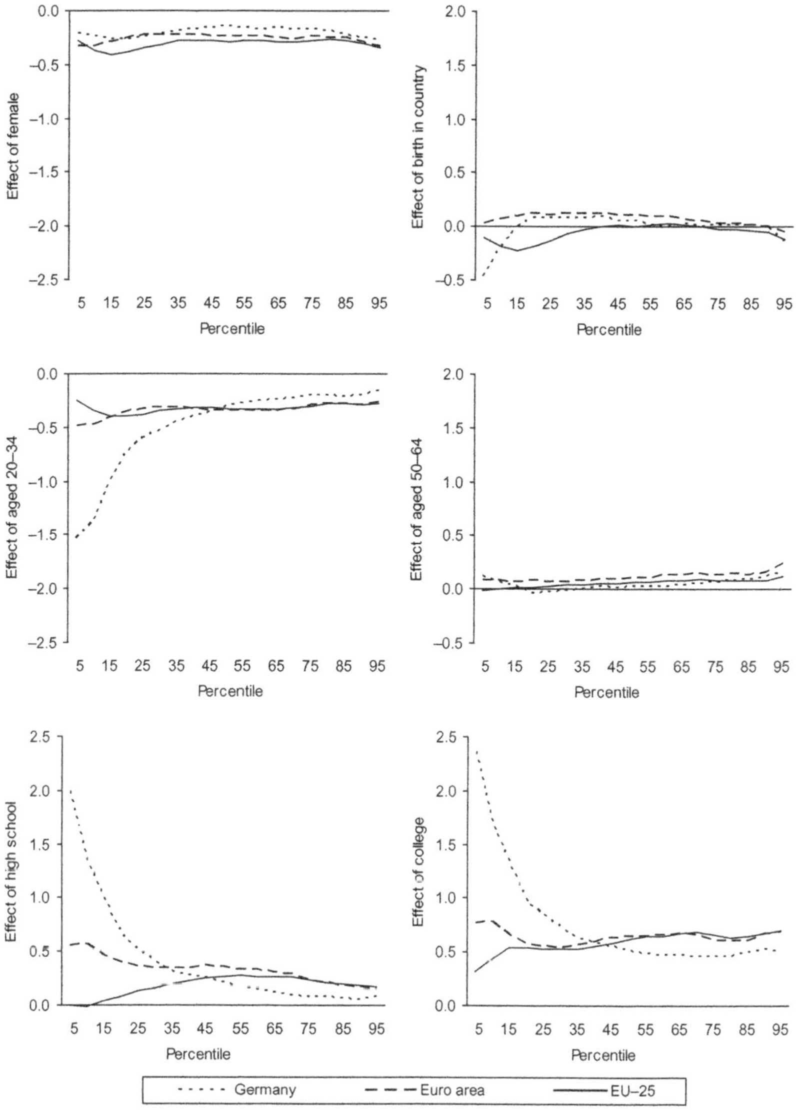

Fig. 5. Determinants of the Distribution of the Logarithm of Real Monthly Gross Earnings among Full-Time Employees Aged 20 to 64 in Germany, The Euro Area and the EU-25 in 2006. *Note*: Effects are shown for all 19 vingtiles. *Sources*: Authors' elaboration on EU-SILC users' database (Version 2007-1, March 2009) and Eurostat PPP data (http://epp.eurostat.ec.europa.eu/portal/page/portal/purchasing_power_parities/introduction, accessed on 3 June 2010).

in the proportion of employees younger than 35 would reduce all percentiles, while a rise in the share of the older employees would tend to increase all percentiles (somewhat less in Germany). The earnings gap of the young appears to be strong in Germany, and the steep percentile profile shown in Fig. 5 implies that the overall variance would significantly go up should their proportion increase. The effect is far smaller in the euro area and the EU-25, where it would rather be a greater presence of older employees to widen the distribution. All in all, these results indicate that, by itself, ageing is likely to make the European earnings distribution more unequal.

The greatest effects are associated with education, but in very different ways. In Germany, a rise in the share of more educated people increases all percentiles, but far more intensively at the bottom: there is a clear egalitarian impact, as measured by the variance or the difference between the 90th and the 10th percentiles. Effects are stronger for college than for high school. The opposite results are found for the EU-25: raising the average educational level has a greater positive influence at the top than at the bottom of the earnings distribution and increases the overall variance. The evidence for euro area falls between these two extremes. As for ageing, improving the educational level of the employees might lead to higher earnings inequality for the EU as a whole. On the other hand, the contrasting results found for Germany and the EU-25 point at the operation of different mechanisms of wage determination.

CONCLUSIONS

The EU-SILC database is a valuable source for comparative analysis of the structure of the labour cost in the EU. We have shown that the comparisons of EU-SILC figures with national accounts, SES data, and external estimates of the tax wedge provide satisfactory results. However, data comparability can be further improved by using more homogeneous definitions and by completing the coverage of the different concepts of labour income. Net earnings are missing in some countries and are not fully comparable in the others, because of differences in the items subtracted from the gross value. Comparisons of the labour cost are limited because employers' social insurance contributions are unavailable in two major countries and puzzlingly characterised by many nil values in several other countries. Gross earnings are available for all countries, but are probably the least suited indicator for cross-country comparisons, as they fail to account for the different structure of income taxes and social security contributions across countries. All in all, however, the EU-SILC data provide a reliable basis for a first assessment of the EU-wide earnings distribution.

Our results for the distribution of full-time equivalent monthly gross earnings show the expected ranking of countries by the median value, with Eastern European nations at the bottom and Luxembourg at the top. Earnings differences are sizeable, both across and within countries. Taking the euro area and the EU-25 as a whole, inequality is higher when earnings are measured in euro at market exchange rates than converted using a PPP index, and using the PPP index for HFCE than that for GDP. Inequality is higher when measured for the EU-25 than for the euro area, which is not surprising given that the former includes the poorer Eastern European countries that joined the Union in 2004. The variance decomposition shows that measured inequality in the EU-25 is higher owing especially to the between-country component. This in turn is essentially due to the returns to individual attributes rather than to a different composition of the employees with respect to these attributes. This suggests that monitoring the evolution of these returns may provide useful insights on the integration of the EU labour markets.

NOTES

1. See Atkinson (1996), Beblo and Knaus (2001), Boix (2004), Morrisson and Murtin (2004), Brandolini (2007), Cobas (2007), Hoffmeister (2009), Beckfield (2009) and Bonesmo Fredriksen (2012). Beckfield (2006, 2009) and Bertola (2010) study the impact of European integration on within-country income inequality.
2. Throughout, we indicate by EU the European Union in general, and by EU-27, EU-25 and EU-15 the current Union comprising 27 members, the Union as of 2006 (even where Malta is missing) and the Union before the enlargement in 2004, respectively. The euro area comprises all 12-member countries of the monetary union in 2006 (AT, BE, DE, EL, ES, FI, FR, IE, IT, LU, NL, PT). See Table 1 for country acronyms.
3. According to LFS statistics, in 2007 the share in total employment of the self-employed (including family workers) ranged from 7–9 per cent in Denmark, Estonia and Luxembourg to 34–36 per cent in Greece and Romania. On the determinants of the self-employment share, see Torrini (2005).
4. In the national accounts, the first two concepts correspond to 'Compensation of employees' and 'Gross wages and salaries', while the third concept has no counterpart.
5. On the cross-country comparability of earnings data, see Atkinson and Brandolini (2007) and Atkinson (2008).
6. The SES generally excludes agriculture, fishing, public administration, private households and extra-territorial organizations as well as enterprises with less than 10

employees. Existing analyses of the wage distribution based on the SES cover less than ten countries (Christopoulou, Jimeno, & Lamo, 2010; Lallemand, Plasman, & Rycx, 2007; Simón, 2005, 2010).

7. See Behr and Pötter (2010) for a study of wage distributions in EU countries using the ECHP.

8. The reference period is the whole calendar year preceding the interview for all countries except Ireland, which takes the twelve months immediately prior the date of interview, and the United Kingdom, which takes the calendar year of the interview. While there is no straightforward solution for the Irish data, the British data could be aligned to those for the other countries by taking the wave of the previous year. Despite the implied inconsistency, we however stick to Eurostat practice of reporting information from the same wave. In the estimation of the EU earnings distribution, however, we adjust nominal values for the increase in the harmonised index of consumer prices, between 2006 and 2007 in the United Kingdom (2.3 per cent) and between 2006 and the 2007 average of the 12-month moving averages of the index in Ireland (1.3 per cent).

9. We do not consider the variable current gross monthly earnings (PY200G) because it is available only for nine countries. In a study of the British household income distribution in the 1990s, Böheim and Jenkins (2006) find that current income measures and annual income measures provide, in practice, similar results.

10. In both cases, we include in-kind payments (PY020N, PY020G) to match the national accounts definitions.

11. The OECD estimates include other categories of employees, but do not cover the EU Member States that are not member of the OECD.

12. For the same reason, estimates of the average returns to education are barely affected by the choice between gross earnings or total compensation, whereas more substantial changes are observed if net instead of gross earnings are used. Labour income taxation affects country ranking: for instance, France moves from the 12th to the 9th position looking at the returns to tertiary education for male full-time workers if net instead of gross earnings are used.

13. Thus, nations with similar levels of labour cost will show different average gross earnings depending on the share of contributions paid by the employee. In some countries, like France, contributions paid by employers are the largest component of the total tax wedge, but in other countries they account for a smaller fraction and the difference between gross earnings and labour cost is narrow. Similar considerations would apply to in-kind payments, which are not considered here.

14. It is, however, potentially inconsistent to correct only for cost-of-living differences across nations, while ignoring those across geographical areas within the same nation. This would be justifiable if the latter were less important than the former, but little is known due to the lack of reliable territorial price indices. Accounting for within-country territorial differences is likely to affect results considerably. Moretti (forthcoming) recently estimated that almost 1/4 of the observed increase in the college premium in the United States between 1980 and 2000 disappears when nominal wages are deflated by a price index that allows for the differences in local housing costs. Whether, more generally, we should use group-specific price indices to transform nominal wages into real wages is an issue beyond the scope of this chapter.

15. For analytical convenience and comparability with the literature in labour economics, we focus here on the variance of logarithms, though it is not a proper inequality measure due to its violation of the Pigou–Dalton transfer principle (Foster & Ok, 1999).
16. The same model estimated with country dummies yields similar results.

ACKNOWLEDGEMENT

This chapter partly draws on Brandolini et al. (2010), a paper prepared for the research project 'Network for the Analysis of EU-SILC' (Net-SILC) coordinated by Eric Marlier. We would like to thank for their valuable comments and suggestions an anonymous referee and Tony Atkinson, Francesco Figari, Eric Marlier, John Micklewright, and participants in the Conference 'Comparative EU Statistics on Income and Living Conditions' (Warsaw, 25–26 March 2010), the 4th Meeting of the Society for the Study of Economic Inequality–ECINEQ (Catania, 18–20 July 2011), and the 8th Joint ECB/CEPR/IFW Labour Market Workshop 'Wages in a time of adjustment and restructuring' (Frankfurt am Main, 13–14 December 2011). The views expressed here are solely ours; in particular, they do not necessarily reflect those of the Bank of Italy.

REFERENCES

Atkinson, A. B. (1996). Income distribution in Europe and the United States. *Oxford Review of Economic Policy*, *12*, 15–28.

Atkinson, A. B. (2008). *The changing distribution of earnings in OECD countries*. Oxford: Oxford University Press.

Atkinson, A. B., & Brandolini, A. (2007). From earnings dispersion to income inequality. In F. Farina & E. Savaglio (Eds.), *Inequality and economic integration* (pp. 35–62). London: Routledge.

Atkinson, A. B., & Micklewright, J. (1983). On the reliability of income data in the family expenditure survey 1970–1977. *Journal of the Royal Statistical Society, Series A*, *146*(Part 1), 33–53.

Beblo, M., & Knaus, T. (2001). Measuring income inequality in Euroland. *Review of Income and Wealth*, *47*, 301–320.

Beckfield, J. (2006). European integration and income inequality. *American Sociological Review*, *71*, 964–985.

Beckfield, J. (2009). Remapping inequality in Europe: The net effect of regional integration on total income inequality in the European Union. *International Journal of Comparative Sociology*, *50*, 486–509.

Behr, A., & Pötter, U. (2010). What determines wage differentials across the EU? *Journal of Economic Inequality*, *8*, 101–120.

Bertola, G. (2010). Inequality, integration, and policy: Issues and evidence from EMU. *Journal of Economic Inequality*, *8*, 345–365.

Blinder, A. (1973). Wage discrimination: Reduced form and structural estimates. *Journal of Human Resources*, *8*, 436–455.

Böheim, R., & Jenkins, S. P. (2006). A comparison of current and annual measures of income in the British household panel survey. *Journal of Official Statistics*, *22*, 733–758.

Boix, C. (2004). The institutional accommodation of an enlarged Europe. *Friedrich Ebert Stiftung, Europäische Politik*, *6*, 1–9.

Bonesmo Fredriksen, K. (2012, April). *Income inequality in the European Union*. Working Paper No. 952. OECD Economics Department, Paris.

Brandolini, A. (1999). The distribution of personal income in post-war Italy: Source description, data quality, and the time pattern of income inequality. *Giornale degli Economisti e Annali di Economia*, *58*(New Series), 183–239.

Brandolini, A. (2007). Measurement of income distribution in supranational entities: The case of the European Union. In S. P. Jenkins & J. Micklewright (Eds.), *Inequality and poverty re-examined* (pp. 62–83). Oxford: Oxford University Press.

Brandolini, A., Rosolia, A., & Torrini, R. (2010). The distribution of employees' labour earnings in the European union: data, concepts and first results. In A. B. Atkinson & E. Marlier (Eds.), *Income and living conditions in Europe* (pp. 265–287). Luxembourg: Publications Office of the European Union.

Casali, S., & Alvarez Gonzalez, V. (2010). 17% of full-time employees in the EU are low-wage earners. *Eurostat. Statistics in focus*, Population and social conditions, No. 3, January.

Christopoulou, R., Jimeno, J. F., & Lamo, A. (2010, May). *Changes in the wage structures in EU countries*. ECB Working Paper No. 1199. ECB, Franfurt am Main.

Clemenceau, A., & Museux, J.-M. (2007). EU-SILC (community statistics on income and living conditions: general presentation of the instrument). In *Comparative EU statistics on Income and Living Conditions: Issues and challenges – Proceedings of the EU-SILC* Conference (Helsinki, 6-8 November 2006) (pp. 13–36). Luxembourg: Office for Official Publications of the European Communities.

Cobas, A. T. (2007). Income inequality in the EU15 and member countries. In J. Bishop & Y. Amiel (Eds.), *Inequality and poverty* (Vol. 14, pp. 119–136). Research on Economic Inequality. Bingley, UK: Emerald.

European Commission. (2010). *Europe 2020: A strategy for smart, sustainable and inclusive growth*. Communication from the Commission, COM(2010) 2020, Brussels. Retrieved from http://ec.europa.eu/eu2020/pdf/COMPLET%20EN%20BARROSO%20%20%20007%20-%20Europe%202020%20-%20EN%20version.pdf

Eurostat. (2010). *Net earnings and tax rates*. Reference Metadata in Euro SDMX Metadata Structure (ESMS). Retrieved from http://epp.eurostat.ec.europa.eu/cache/ITY_SDDS/EN/earn_net_esms.htm. Accessed on 31 May 2010.

Eurostat. (2012). *SES microdata for scientific purposes: How to obtain them?* Retrieved from http://epp.eurostat.ec.europa.eu/portal/page/portal/microdata/documents/EN-SES-MICRODATA.pdf. Accessed on 3 April 2012.

Eurostat and Organisation for Economic Co-Operation and Development. (2006). *Eurostat – OECD methodological manual on purchasing power*. Luxembourg: Office for Official Publications of the European Communities.

Firpo, S., Fortin, N. M., & Lemieux, T. (2009). Unconditional quantile regressions. *Econometrica*, *77*, 953–973.

Foster, J. E., & Ok, E. A. (1999). Lorenz dominance and the variance of logarithms. *Econometrica, 67*, 901–907.

Hoffmeister, O. (2009). The spatial structure of income inequality in the enlarged EU. *Review of Income and Wealth, 55*, 101–127.

Lallemand, T., Plasman, R., & Rycx, F. (2007). The establishment-size wage premium: Evidence from European countries. *Empirica, 34*, 427–451.

Machado, A. F., & Mata, J. (2005). Counterfactual decomposition of changes in wage distributions using quantile regression. *Journal of Applied Econometrics, 20*, 445–465.

Melly, B. (2005). Decomposition of differences in distribution using quantile regression. *Labour Economics, 12*, 577–590.

Moretti, E. (forthcoming). Real wage inequality. *American Economic Journal: Applied Economics.*

Morrisson, C., & Murtin, F. (2004). *History and prospects of inequality among Europeans.* Mimeo.

Oaxaca, R. (1973). Male-female wage differentials in urban labor markets. *International Economic Review, 14*, 693–709.

Organisation for Economic Co-operation and Development. (2008). *Taxing wages 2006/2007.* Edition 2007. Paris: OECD Publications.

Simón, H. (2005). Employer wage differentials from an international perspective. *Economics Letters, 88*, 284–288.

Simón, H. (2010). International differences in wage inequality: A new glance with European matched employer-employee data. *British Journal of Industrial Relations, 48*, 310–346.

Torrini, R. (2005). Cross-country differences in self-employment rates: The role of institutions. *Labour Economics, 12*, 661–683.

Wolff, P. (2010). 17% of EU citizens were at-risk-of-poverty in 2008. *Eurostat. Statistics in focus.* Population and social conditions, No. 9, February.

CHAPTER 10

EARNINGS MOBILITY, EARNINGS INEQUALITY, AND LABOR MARKET INSTITUTIONS IN EUROPE☆

Denisa Maria Sologon and Cathal O'Donoghue

ABSTRACT

The economic reality of the 1990s in Europe forced the labor markets to become more flexible. Using a consistent comparative dataset for 14 countries, the European Community Household Panel (ECHP), we explore the degree of earnings mobility and inequality across Europe, and the role of labor market institutions in understanding the cross-national differences in earnings mobility. We study the degree of rank mobility and the degree of mobility as equalizer of long-term earnings. The country ranking in long-term earnings inequality is similar with the country ranking in annual inequality, which is a sign of limited long-term

☆This research is part of the "Earnings Dynamics and Microsimulation" project supported by the Luxembourg "Fonds National de la Recherche" through an AFR grant (PDR no. 893613) under the Marie Curie Actions of the European Commission (FP7-COFUND). An earlier version of this chapter is registered as Sologon D.M. and O'Donoghue C. (2010a), 'Earnings Mobility in the EU: 1994–2001', CEPS/INSTEAD Working Paper Series, 2010-36, CEPS/INSTEAD.

Inequality, Mobility and Segregation: Essays in Honor of Jacques Silber
Research on Economic Inequality, Volume 20, 237–283

ISSN: 1049-2585/doi:10.1108/S1049-2585(2012)0000020013

equalizing mobility within countries with higher levels of annual inequality. In long-term earnings inequality, Denmark renders the most mobile earnings distribution with the second highest equalizing effect. The only disequalizing mobility in a lifetime perspective is found in Portugal. With respect to the relationship between earnings mobility and earnings inequality, we find a significant negative association both in the short and the long run. Based on the rankings in long-term Fields mobility and long-term inequality, Denmark is expected to have the lowest lifetime earnings inequality in Europe, followed by Finland, Austria, and Belgium. The Mediterranean countries (Spain and Portugal) are expected to have the highest long-term inequality. With respect to the institutional factors that may be related to earnings mobility, we bring evidence that the deregulation in the labor and product markets, the degree of unionization, the degree of corporatism and the spending on ALMPs are positively associated with earnings mobility.

Keywords: Earnings mobility; inequality; distributional change; labor market policies and institutions

JEL classifications: D31; D39; D63; J08; J31; J50; J60

INTRODUCTION

Income inequality has been on the rise in most countries around the world over the past four decades, and was largely driven by changes in the distribution of earnings, which account for 75% of household income (Gottschalk, 1997; Haider, 2001; OECD, 2011). Understanding the increase in cross-sectional earnings inequality has motivated the interest in the underlying dynamics of the earnings distribution, namely in the degree of intragenerational mobility in individual earnings over time (Atkinson, Bourguignon, & Morrisson, 1992).

Earnings mobility and inequality are strongly interrelated. Earnings mobility provides information on the relation between cross-sectional inequalities between periods, and between short-term and long-term inequalities, thereby helping us to gauge the lifetime implications of the change in inequality over time. Some analysts argue that rising annual inequality does not necessarily have negative implications. This statement relies on the "offsetting mobility" argument, which states that if there has been a sufficiently large simultaneous increase in mobility, the inequality of earnings measured over a longer period of time, such as lifetime earnings or "permanent" earnings, can be lower despite the rise in annual inequality, with a positive effect on welfare. This statement, however, holds only under the assumption that individuals are not averse to earnings variability, future risk, or multiperiod inequality (Creedy & Wilhelm, 2002; Gottschalk & Spolaore, 2002). Therefore, there is not a complete agreement in the literature on the value judgment of earnings mobility (Atkinson et al., 1992).

Those that value earnings mobility positively perceive it either as a goal or as an instrument to another end. The goal of having a mobile society is linked to the goal of securing equality of opportunity in the labor market and of having a more flexible and efficient economy (Atkinson et al., 1992; Friedman, 1962). The instrumental justification for mobility takes place in the context of achieving distributional equity: lifetime equity depends on the extent of movement up and down in the earnings distribution over the lifetime (Atkinson et al., 1992). In this line of thought, Friedman (1962) underlined the role of social mobility in reducing lifetime earnings differentials between individuals, by allowing them to change their position in the earnings distribution over time. Thus, earnings mobility is perceived in the literature as a way out of poverty. In the absence of mobility the same individuals remain stuck at the bottom of the earnings distribution; hence, annual earnings differentials are transformed into long-term or lifetime differentials. A cross-sectional snapshot of earnings distribution overstates lifetime inequality to a degree that depends on the degree of earnings mobility. If countries have different mobility levels, then single-year inequality country ranking may lead to a misleading picture of long-term inequality ranking. Thus, earnings mobility studies are an important complement to earnings inequality studies.

The relationship between mobility and inequality is put forward also by the literature on the political economy for redistribution, which views social mobility as a factor shaping the preferences for redistribution (Fong, 2001; Piketty, 1995). Whether social mobility increases or decreases the preferences for redistribution is an unsettled debate as it depends on many factors. Piketty (1995) shows theoretically that past mobility experiences and beliefs about the extent to which earnings depend on effort or on circumstances beyond the individual control affect the preferences for redistribution. In addition, the expectations about future mobility, either upward or downward, affect significantly the preferences for redistribution. The "prospect of upward mobility" is found to reduce the support for redistribution even among the currently poor (Benabou & Ok, 2001a; Ravallion & Lokshin, 2000). The prospect of downward mobility, however, increases the preference for redistribution even among the rich, as the redistributive policies may be perceived as safety nets against adverse circumstances. In addition, if individuals are risk averse, and they are uncertain with respect to future earnings, redistributive policies offer valuable insurance. This calls for an increase in the demand for redistribution, thereby suggesting a negative association between mobility and inequality (Ravallion & Lokshin, 2000). These issues contribute to the ongoing debate about the relationship between earnings mobility and earnings inequality.

Our chapter contributes to the literature by exploring different facets of earnings mobility across Europe. First, we explore the cross-national trends in earnings mobility and the relationship with earnings inequality in order to understand the evolution of the economic inequality and opportunity, and the implications for lifetime inequality. Second, we explore the role of labor market institutions in understanding the cross-national differences in earnings mobility across Europe. Using a consistent comparative dataset for 14 EU countries between 1994 and 2001, the European Community Household Panel (ECHP), this study explores the following questions:

(i) What is the country ranking with respect to earnings inequality and how does the ranking change when the horizon over which inequality is measured increases?
(ii) Did short-term mobility increase over time across the EU? What is the relationship between mobility and inequality in short term?
(iii) Do EU countries differ in the extent to which earnings mobility equalizes long-term earnings relative to cross-sectional inequality? What is the relationship between mobility and inequality long-term?
(iv) What is the country ranking with respect to earnings mobility and what are the implications for the country ranking in lifetime or long-term earnings inequality?
(v) What is the role of labor market institutions in understanding the cross-national differences in earnings mobility across Europe?

The cross-national comparative perspective across Europe is motivated primarily by the increasing country heterogeneity in labor market institutions, which followed the labor market reforms starting in the early 1990s. The economic reality of the 1990s in Europe forced the labor markets to become more flexible, to lower non-wage labor costs, and to allow wages to better reflect productivity and market conditions (OECD, 2004). The trends in the OECD labor market indicators related to the wage-setting mechanism show a deregulation in the labor and product markets, an increase in the labor market state support as active labor market policies and unemployment benefits replacement rates, and a decrease in the tax wedge (most prominently in the Anglo-Saxon countries, followed by the Scandinavian and the Mediterranean countries). The pace of the institutional changes differs across Europe, resulting in a higher institutional heterogeneity across countries (Palier, 2010). The high degree of institutional heterogeneity across Europe is reflected in Fig. 1, which plots the indicators related to the wage-setting mechanism: employment protection legislation (EPL); the level of labor market support as spending for active labor market policies (ALMPs) and average unemployment benefit replacement rates (UBRR); the degree of unionization and corporatism; the tax wedge and product market regulation (PMR).[1] The Anglo-Saxon countries (the United Kingdom and Ireland) have the lowest EPL, the lowest tax wedge, and a medium union density. They differ substantially from one another in the

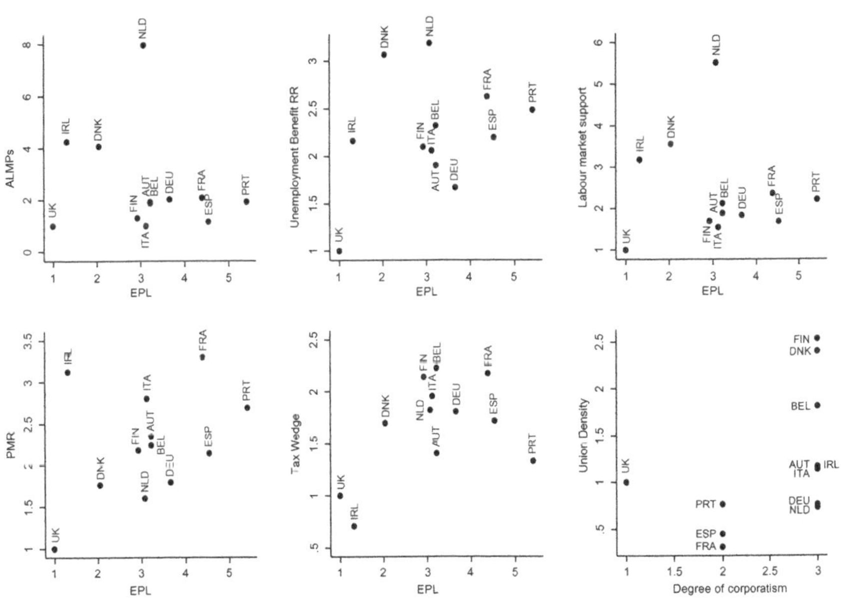

Fig. 1. Labor Market Policies/Institutions in 2001 (Scaled UK = 1).
Notes: EPL = Employment protection legislation; PMR = product market regulation; ALMPs = spending on active labor market policies; labor market support is the arithmetic average between ALMPs and the unemployment benefit replacement rate.
Sources: Based on OECD data on labor market indicators provided by Bassanini and Duval (2006a, 2006b).

labor market support, corporatism, and PMR, with the United Kingdom having the lowest values in Europe. The Northern Flexicurity countries (the Scandinavian countries and the Netherlands) (Boeri, 2002) have among the lowest levels of labor market and PMRs, among the highest levels of labor market support, a high corporatism, and among the highest union densities (except the Netherlands) and tax wedges. The pioneers of "Flexicurity" (Denmark and Netherlands) stand out with the highest labor market support. The Mediterranean countries (Greece, Portugal, and Spain) have among the strictest regulation in the labor and product markets, among the lowest levels of labor market support, among the lowest union densities, an intermediate corporatism, and medium–high tax wedges. Italy differs with a lower EPL and a high corporatism. Germany, France, Belgium, and Austria form the "Rhineland model" (Boeri, 2002) with a relatively strict labor market regulation, a high labor market support, a medium–high unionization and corporatism, and a high tax wedge. This country heterogeneity in labor market institutions has the potential to help us understand the cross-national differences in earnings mobility across Europe.

To the best of our knowledge, no study has explored in a consistent comparative fashion the different facets of earnings mobility and inequality across Europe over a recent period and covering a time frame longer than six years. Most studies focus on the comparison between the United States and a small number of European countries for different periods between the late 1970s and the mid-1990s: Germany (Burkhauser & Poupore, 1997; Burkhauser, Holtz-Eakin, & Rhody (1997)); Germany and the United Kingdom (Schluter, 1998); Germany and the Netherlands (Goodin, Headey, Muffels, & Dirven, 1999); Germany and Belgium (Van Kerm, 2004); Germany and Sweden (Gangl, Palme, & Kenworthy, 2008); the Scandinavian countries (Aaberge et al., 2002; Fritzell, 1990). Several OECD studies compare earnings inequality and mobility across the OECD countries (OECD, 1996, 1997). These studies find similar country rankings for multiperiod income inequality and single-year income inequality. Despite being the most unequal, the United States has similar levels of income mobility with the low income inequality EU countries (e.g., the Nordic countries). This suggests that low-inequality EU countries are not less mobile than the United States. Using only European data, Prieto, Rodríguez, and Salas (2008, 2010) found a positive association between social mobility and household income inequality, which suggest that low-inequality EU countries tend to have low-mobility levels. These findings contribute to the ongoing debate regarding the puzzling relationship between mobility and inequality. Ayala and Sastre (2008) examined the differences in the level and structure of income mobility across five EU countries and found that earnings represent the income source with the largest contribution to short-term mobility. Despite this large contribution, no consistent comparative study on earnings mobility could be identified at the European level. In addition, the literature about the relationship between labor market institutions and earnings mobility is scarce, and extremely needed to shed light on the cross-national distributional differences.[2] By addressing this gap in the literature, our chapter aims to make a substantive contribution to the literature on cross-national comparisons of earnings mobility. Exploring mobility in the income components is relevant, given that the different income components do have different determinants.

We examine the mobility–inequality linkage across Europe using approaches which bring complementary evidence, both short-term and long-term, neglected by previous studies. Our chapter also contributes to the debate on the limitations of the Shorrocks index in capturing the equalizing/disequalizing effect of mobility (Benabou & Ok, 2001b; Fields, 2009). We argue for the need to complement the evidence brought by the Shorrocks index with an alternative measure developed by Fields (2009), in order to bring complementary information that can be used to make inferences about lifetime earnings distributions.

DATA

This study uses the ECHP[3] over the period 1994–2001 for 14 EU countries. Luxembourg and Austria are observed between 1995 and 2001, and Finland between 1996 and 2001. Following the tradition of previous studies, the analysis focuses on men, to avoid the selection bias typically associated with women's earnings. The earnings measure is real net hourly wage adjusted for CPI of male workers aged 20–57, born between 1940 and 1981.[4] The hourly earnings are calculated using the current net monthly wage and the number of hours worked per week. We use hourly earnings as they are a measure of the productivity of the individual. Only observations with hourly wage higher than 1 Euro and lower than 50 Euros are considered. The resulting sample for each country is an unbalanced panel. For more details on the inflows/outflows in the sample, see Sologon and O'Donoghue (2009). Table 1 shows the unweighted sample size with positive earnings for each country.

One of the causes of movements out of the earnings sample is attrition over time. The degree of attrition in ECHP has been explored in several studies. Behr, Bellgardt, and Rendtel (2005) found that the extent and the

Table 1. Sample Statistics of Hourly Earnings[a].

Denmark	Mean	10.89	11.40	11.58	11.61	11.86	11.85	12.02	12.08
	N	1360	1339	1284	1224	1125	1051	1015	997
Finland	Mean			7.89	8.01	8.41	8.45	8.66	8.86
	N			1613	1628	1606	1557	1293	1297
Netherlands	Mean	9.69	9.56	9.59	9.7	10.02	9.88	10.04	9.91
	N	2209	2390	2444	2416	2351	2379	2412	2371
Austria	Mean		9.08	8.33	8.37	8.49	8.55	8.55	8.54
	N		1673	1673	1619	1520	1427	1309	1246
Germany	Mean	9.43	9.49	9.61	9.52	9.57	9.48	9.6	9.72
	N	3010	3147	3106	3025	2815	2802	2700	2550
Belgium	Mean	8.48	8.82	8.71	8.75	8.81	8.83	8.92	9.1
	N	1475	1410	1362	1304	1216	1153	1079	999
France[b]	Mean	10.23	9.92	9.87	10.05	10.33	10.6	10.55	10.87
	N	2960	2845	2865	2673	2146	2066	2030	2114
Luxembourg	Mean		16.18	15.81	16.73	17.39	17.15	17.22	17.1
	N		1712	1436	1597	1475	1516	1363	1407
UK	Mean	8.16	8.11	8.22	8.34	8.68	9.01	9.21	9.68
	N	1859	1882	1967	2059	2076	2066	2065	2021
Ireland	Mean	9.3	9.54	9.76	10.02	10.43	10.84	11.69	12.44
	N	1762	1561	1393	1348	1238	1081	891	764
Italy	Mean	7.16	6.91	6.96	7.05	7.29	7.37	7.28	7.32
	N	3063	3107	3098	2858	2812	2616	2621	2433
Spain	Mean	6.83	6.95	7.09	6.89	7.18	7.37	7.45	7.42
	N	2905	2756	2696	2651	2530	2527	2451	2425
Portugal	Mean	9.08	8.33	8.37	8.49	8.55	8.55	8.54	9.08
	N	1912	2082	2180	2227	2253	2224	2199	2194
Greece	Mean	4.95	5.03	5.23	5.59	5.63	5.85	5.7	5.77
	N	1666	1656	1577	1500	1385	1355	1315	1365

[a]Weighted statistics, except for $N =$ unweighted number of individuals with positive earnings.
[b]The amounts for France are gross.

determinants of panel attrition in ECHP vary between countries and across waves within one country, but these differences do not bias the analysis of income mobility and inequality, or the ranking of national results. Ayala, Navarro, and Sastre (2011) confirm that attrition in ECHP does not significantly affect the aggregated mobility indicators. We correct for attrition by applying the weighting system recommended by Eurostat, namely the "base weights" of the last wave observed for each individual, bounded between 0.25 and 10.

Unlike previous studies that rely on a fully balanced sample to explore mobility as an equalizer of longer-term earnings, we use an unbalanced sample over different subperiods. We explore mobility as an equalizer of longer-term earnings not only for those employed over the entire sample period but also for those that move into and out of employment. Focusing only on the fully balanced sample may bias the estimation of mobility due to the overestimation of earnings persistency. Moreover, besides the employment status, there are other factors determining panel attrition. Although not reported here, we compared the results using a fully balanced panel in order to check for the impact of differential attrition on earnings mobility as an equalizer of longer-term differentials using the Shorrock and the Fields indices. The Fields index is affected to a larger extent by differential attrition than the Shorrocks index. Whereas the overall qualitative conclusions regarding the evolution of mobility over time and across horizons are not affected by using a balanced or an unbalanced sample, more differences are observed for the country rankings (see Sologon & O'Donoghue, 2010a for the results using the balanced sample).

The definitions and summary statistics of the labor market indicators are shown in Tables A.1 and A.2.

METHODOLOGY

The degree of earnings mobility is explored here using three mobility measures introduced over time as improved alternatives.[5] We have in mind two aspects of mobility: mobility as opportunity and mobility as equalizer of longer-term differentials (Friedman, 1962).

Mobility as Opportunity to Change Positions in the Earnings Distributions Between Years

The opportunity to move in the earnings distribution between periods is best reflected by rank measures, which capture positional movements in the distribution of earnings. Traditional rank measures are derived from the transition matrix approach between income groups. This approach to mobility, however, fails to capture the movement within each income group, running the risk of underestimating the degree of mobility. An alternative approach, used in Dickens (2000), is to compute the ranking of the individuals in the wage distribution for each year and examine the degree of movement in percentile ranking from one year to the other. For each mobility comparison only individuals with positive earnings in both periods are considered. The measure of mobility between year t and year s is

$$M_{ts} = 2 \times \frac{\sum_{i=1}^{N} |F^t(w_{it}) - F^S(w_{is})|}{N} \quad (1)$$

where $F(w_{it})$ and $F(w_{is})$ are the cumulative distribution functions for earnings in year t and year s and N the number of individuals with positive earnings in both years. The degree of mobility equals twice the average absolute change in percentile ranking between year t and year s. When there is no mobility $M=0$, people maintain their earnings position from year t to s: the difference between $F^t(w_{it})$ and $F^s(w_{is})$ equals 0 for all individuals. M equals maximum 1 if earnings in the two years are perfectly negatively rank correlated – in the second period there is a complete reversal of ranks – and the value 2/3 if earnings in the two periods are independent. The robustness of this measure of mobility is discussed in Dickens (2000).

We estimate two types of mobility measures:

(i) Short-term mobility or 2-year period mobility $M(t, t+1)$ – defined as mobility between periods one year apart, used to assess the pattern of short-term mobility over time and its link with the evolution of cross-sectional inequality.
(ii) Long-term mobility or 8-year period mobility $M(t, t+7)$ – defined as mobility between periods seven years apart, used to assess the extent to which mobility increases with the time span.[6]

This measure, referred to as "the Dickens index" in the rest of the chapter, however, fails to formalize the relationship between earnings mobility and inequality, a limitation corrected by Shorrocks (1978).

Mobility as Opportunity to Change Positions in the Distribution of Long-Term Earnings Relative to Single-Year Earnings

Shorrocks (1978) introduced a family of mobility measures that incorporates a close relationship between income mobility and income inequality.

Mobility is measured as the relative reduction in the weighted average of single-year inequality when the accounting period is extended.[7] The degree of mobility is computed as $M_T = 1 - R_T$, where R_T is the rigidity index. R_T ranges from 0 (perfect mobility) to 1 (complete rigidity), and has the following specification:[8]

$$0 \leq R_T = \frac{I(\sum_{t=1}^{T} y_{it})}{\sum_{t=1}^{T} w_t I(y_{it})} \leq 1 \tag{2}$$

where y_{it} represents individual earnings in year t; t time $t = 1,\ldots,T$; I is an inequality index that is a strictly convex function of incomes relative to the mean; $I(\sum_{t=1}^{T} y_{it})$ the inequality of lifetime income; w_t the share of earnings in year t of the total earnings over a T-year period; and $I(y_{it})$ the cross-sectional annual inequality. There is complete income rigidity if lifetime inequality is equal to the weighted sum of individual period income inequalities, meaning that everybody holds their position in the income distribution from period to period. Perfect mobility is achieved when everybody has the same average lifetime income, meaning that there is a complete reversal of positions in the income distribution. Shorrocks (1978)'s mobility definition is important from an economic point of view because it provides a way of identifying those countries that exhibit a high annual income inequality, but fare better when a longer period of time is considered. If a country A has both greater annual inequality and greater rigidity than country B, it will be more unequal than B whatever period is chosen for comparison. But if A exhibits more mobility, this may be sufficient to change the rankings when longer periods are considered (Shorrocks, 1978).

In the literature the Shorrocks index is usually classified among the measures of mobility as an equalizer of longer-term differentials. During recent years, however, the criticism that Shorrocks fails to capture the equalizing effect has been gaining momentum. Benabou and Ok (2001b) and Fields (2009) highlighted the main limitation of the Shorrocks measure: it fails to quantify the direction and the extent of the difference between inequality of longer-term income and inequality of base-year income, treating equalizing and disequalizing changes essentially in an identical fashion. Our study brings additional evidence for this criticism, and argues for the need to complement the evidence brought by the Shorrocks index with an alternative measure that is able to capture the equalizing/disequalizing impact of mobility. Thus, we opt for the Shorrocks index as an overall measure of lifetime mobility – conceptualized as the opposite of earnings rigidity, which captures the opportunity to change positions in the distribution of long-term/lifetime earnings relative to the cross-sectional distribution.

Mobility as Equalizer of Longer-Term Differentials – Fields Index[9]

Fields (2009) proposed an alternative index, which circumvents the limitation of the Shorrocks index, capturing mobility as an equalizer/disequalizer of longer-term earnings:

$$\varepsilon = 1 - \left(\frac{I(a)}{I(y_{\text{base year}})} \right) \tag{3}$$

a is a vector of individual average earnings over the horizon measured by the mobility index, $y_{\text{base year}}$ is the vector of base-year earnings, and $I(\cdot)$ is a Lorenz-consistent inequality measure such as the Gini coefficient or the Theil index (GE(1)). A positive/negative value of ε indicates that average earnings (a) are more/less equally distributed than the base-year incomes ($y_{\text{base year}}$), and a 0 value indicates that a and $y_{\text{base year}}$ are distributed equally unequally. For a complete description of the properties of the Fields index, please refer to Fields (2009). Other applications of this index can be found in Fields et al. (2007) and Hungerford (2011).

By applying the Shorrocks and the Fields indices, we first assess the degree of long-term earnings mobility across 14 EU countries, and second we establish whether this mobility is equalizing or disequalizing long-term earnings differentials. We report the mobility measures based on the Theil 1 index. For each approach we estimate two types of mobility measures:

(i) Short-term mobility or 2-year period mobility $M(t, t+1)$ – which for Shorrocks measures the degree to which the relative earnings positions observed on an annual basis are shuffled in the distribution of 2-year earnings, and for Fields measures the extent to which mobility equalizes the inequality measured over a 2-year horizon relative to cross-sectional inequality in base year t.

(ii) Long-term mobility or 8-year[10] period mobility $M(t, t+7)$ – which for Shorrocks measures the degree to which the relative earnings positions observed on an annual basis are shuffled in the distribution of 8-year earnings, and for Fields measures the extent to which mobility equalizes the inequality measured over an 8-year horizon relative to cross-sectional inequality in base year t.

We distinguish between three types of inequality: cross-sectional inequality, short-term inequality (inequality in earnings measured over a 2-year horizon), and long-term inequality (inequality measured over the sample period horizon).

Most studies about mobility as an equalizer of longer-term differentials rely on a fully balanced panel, meaning only individuals recording positive earnings over the entire sample. The main drawback of this approach is the exclusion of individuals with irregular profiles, which increases the risk of overestimating earnings persistency. Therefore, we opted for an "unbalanced" approach: we use unbalanced panels across different subperiods (e.g., the mobility index for 1994–1997 is based on individuals with positive earnings in each year between 1994 and 1997, and not only on individuals with positive earnings over the entire sample period 1994–2001, which would be the case under a fully "balanced" approach).

CHANGES IN EARNINGS INEQUALITY

We start by describing the evolution of the distribution of hourly earnings over time and across time horizons, in order to get a glimpse into the intracountry and intercountry changes.

Changes in the Cross-Sectional Earnings Distribution Over Time

Earnings growth and earnings mobility contribute to changes in the cross-sectional distribution of earnings over time. Table 1 shows that, on average, men got richer over time in most EU countries except Austria. Earnings growth can have an equalizing effect on earnings if the earnings of those at the bottom of the distribution improve to a larger extent than the earnings of those at the top. Plotting the percentage change in mean hourly earnings between the beginning of the sample period and 2001 at each point of the distribution for each country (Fig. 2) reveals a negative and nearly monotonic relationship between the quantile rank and the growth in real earnings in most countries: the higher the rank, the smaller the increase in earnings. This means that hourly earnings of low-paid individuals improved to a larger extent than those of the better-off individuals; thus, the growth in earnings had an equalizing effect on earnings in most countries in Europe. The steepest profile is identified in Ireland, suggesting that across Europe, the Irish low wage individuals improved their wages the most relative

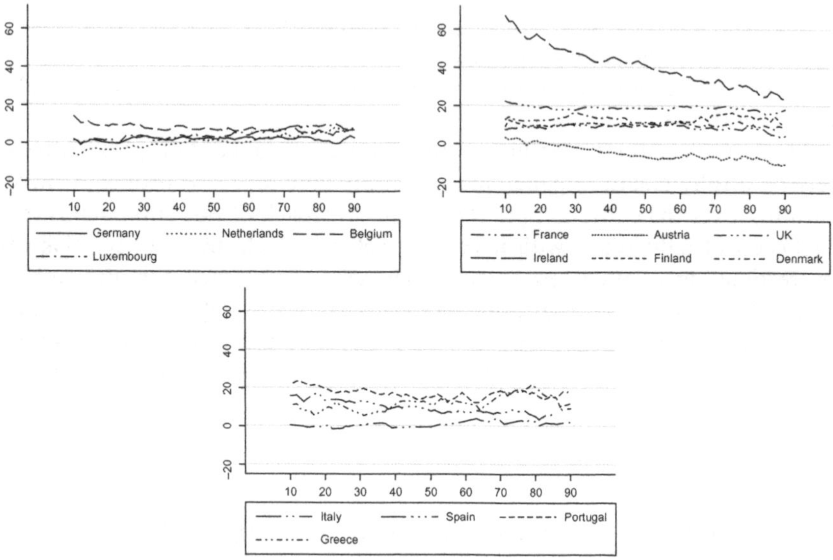

Fig. 2. Percentage Change in Mean Hourly Earnings by Percentiles Over the Sample Period.

to high wage individuals. In Austria, people at the top of the distribution experienced a decrease in mean hourly wage over time, which may have contributed to the decrease in the overall mean. Among the countries with a negative association between the quantile rank and the growth in real earnings, cross-sectional inequality increased only in Luxembourg, Italy, and Portugal, a sign that in these countries mobility may have had a disequalizing effect on earnings inequality which counteracted the equalizing effect of earnings growth. Cross-sectional inequality decreased over time in the remaining countries which display a negative association between the quantile rank and the growth in real earnings.[11]

Finland, Netherlands, Germany, and Greece diverge from the other European countries experiencing a higher relative increase in earnings the higher the rank. More disconcerting is that, in the Netherlands, men at the bottom of the income distribution recorded deterioration in their work pay. This is consistent with recent findings showing increasing low pay and working poverty in the Netherlands in the 1990s (Salverda, 2008). In these countries, the growth in earnings had a disequalizing effect on earnings, which contributed to the increase in cross-sectional inequality over time, as

Table 2. Earnings Inequality (Index*100).

		1994	1995	1996	1997	1998	1999	2000	2001
Denmark	Gini	15.76	15.26	15.52	15.21	14.24	14.68	14.94	14.05
	Theil	4.22	3.92	4.23	4.15	3.37	3.73	3.83	3.35
	A(1)	4.26	3.78	4.10	3.96	3.37	3.76	3.78	3.33
Finland	Gini			17.32	17.80	17.30	17.81	17.10	18.50
	Theil			5.22	5.46	5.23	5.38	5.08	5.98
	A(1)			4.94	5.29	4.83	5.19	4.76	5.53
Netherlands	Gini	18.07	18.37	19.19	18.80	18.93	17.92	18.18	20.67
	Theil	5.63	5.76	6.32	6.07	5.96	5.40	5.56	7.25
	A(1)	5.56	5.77	6.33	5.90	5.65	5.18	5.44	7.08
Austria	Gini		19.49	18.34	18.34	17.39	17.07	16.72	16.85
	Theil		6.67	5.84	5.90	5.27	5.10	4.93	4.97
	A(1)		6.44	5.62	5.52	4.87	4.80	4.67	4.82
Germany	Gini	22.15	22.34	22.04	21.89	22.58	22.81	22.75	22.54
	Theil	8.22	8.61	8.23	8.06	8.85	8.96	8.92	8.72
	A(1)	8.08	8.38	8.04	7.84	8.12	8.53	8.41	8.17
Belgium	Gini	19.10	17.71	17.64	18.13	17.53	17.33	17.13	17.85
	Theil	6.23	5.37	5.35	5.58	5.15	5.11	5.04	5.48
	A(1)	5.92	4.95	5.04	5.24	4.85	4.92	4.69	5.14
Luxembourg	Gini		25.23	24.74	25.41	25.62	26.58	26.50	26.32
	Theil		10.09	9.85	10.24	10.37	11.19	11.15	10.89
	A(1)		9.88	10.00	10.16	10.02	10.95	11.09	10.66
France	Gini	27.62	26.47	26.26	27.23	27.28	27.41	26.83	26.49
	Theil	13.21	12.04	11.63	12.88	12.58	12.65	11.94	11.87
	A(1)	11.64	10.88	10.58	11.41	11.54	11.59	11.17	10.98

Table 2. (*Continued*)

		1994	1995	1996	1997	1998	1999	2000	2001
UK	Gini	24.26	24.22	23.35	23.36	23.54	23.25	23.35	23.51
	Theil	10.08	10.01	9.20	9.05	9.24	9.08	9.16	9.29
	A(1)	9.25	9.19	8.57	8.46	8.55	8.32	8.46	8.51
Ireland	Gini	27.59	26.87	25.76	25.47	25.00	23.39	22.77	21.70
	Theil	12.87	11.97	11.00	10.83	10.60	9.31	8.78	7.85
	A(1)	11.84	11.21	10.50	10.14	9.85	8.66	8.15	7.64
Italy	Gini	19.16	18.47	19.02	18.93	19.85	19.72	19.78	19.90
	Theil	6.51	6.08	6.42	6.29	7.13	7.01	7.08	7.19
	A(1)	5.99	5.58	5.91	5.78	6.41	6.30	6.33	6.39
Greece	Gini	23.62	24.37	23.80	25.55	25.66	26.98	26.51	26.37
	Theil	9.51	9.97	9.44	11.23	11.09	12.20	11.93	12.17
	A(1)	8.77	9.13	8.70	9.97	9.99	10.97	10.68	10.55
Spain	Gini	27.87	28.27	28.19	28.71	28.37	26.99	26.36	26.07
	Theil	13.08	13.22	13.36	13.67	13.47	12.69	12.09	11.47
	A(1)	11.84	12.13	11.94	12.33	12.17	11.07	10.60	10.28
Portugal	Gini	30.05	31.14	30.66	30.85	31.13	30.11	31.32	31.72
	Theil	15.79	16.93	16.76	17.27	18.01	17.21	18.86	19.27
	A(1)	13.23	14.16	13.80	14.05	14.37	13.55	14.60	14.92

revealed by the Gini, Theil (GE(1)), and Atkinson (aversion parameter = 1) indices in Table 2.

These trends shuffled the country ranking in cross-sectional inequality slightly, as shown by the significant rank correlation of 88.13% between the first and the last waves. Portugal and Denmark remain the most and the least unequal in Europe throughout the period. In 2001, in between the two extremes, in ascending order of inequality (Theil) we find Greece, France, Spain, Luxembourg, the United Kingdom, Germany, Ireland, Netherlands, Italy, Finland, Belgium, and Austria. In general, these rankings are consistent across indices.

Changes in Earnings Inequality with the Accounting Period

We complement the earnings distribution picture with the evolution of earnings inequality when we extend the horizon over which inequality is measured, using both an unbalanced and a balanced sample (Table 3). As expected, the longer the horizon the lower the inequality in all countries. One exception is Portugal, where the 8-year inequality is higher than the inequality in 1994 when the balanced sample is used.[12] Even based on average earnings over the sample period, a substantial inequality in the permanent component of earnings is still present in all countries. There is a tendency, however, for the intercountry inequality differences to be smaller when earnings are averaged over several years than in single-year inequality comparisons: the standard deviation for the Theil indices for eight-year average earnings is 13.8% lower than that for single-year earnings.[13] The country ranking in long-term inequality changes slightly compared with single-year inequality, as shown by the significant high rank correlation 95.5%. Denmark and Finland with the lowest inequality and Portugal with the highest inequality maintain their ranks. Austria, Belgium, and Netherlands converge to values close to Finland, followed by Italy, then Germany, the United Kingdom, Luxembourg, Greece, Ireland with similar values, and finally France and Spain. The inequality measures under the unbalanced approach are higher than those under the balanced approach. This is expected, given that people working over the entire sample are expected to have more stable jobs, and thus lower earnings differentials as opposed to the case when we include also those with unstable jobs.

Next, we explore the trends in earnings mobility across Europe between 1994 and 2001.

Table 3. Short- and Long-Term Inequality.

Inequality (Theil)	Dk	Fi	Nl	Au	Ge	Be	Lu	Fr	UK	Ir	It	Gr	Sp	Pt
Unbalanced														
First wave	0.0422	0.0522	0.0563	0.0667	0.0822	0.0623	0.1009	0.1321	0.1008	0.1287	0.0651	0.0951	0.1308	0.1579
First–second wave	0.0316	0.0422	0.0468	0.0514	0.0744	0.0496	0.0869	0.106	0.0866	0.1109	0.054	0.0801	0.1179	0.1524
First–sixth wave	0.0232	0.0346	0.0424	0.0372	0.0623	0.0399	0.0678	0.0915	0.0653	0.0819	0.049	0.0756	0.1046	0.1381
First–eighth wave	0.0205		0.0395		0.06	0.0395		0.0847	0.063	0.0718	0.0494	0.0698	0.0929	0.1423
Balanced														
First wave	0.0329	0.0422	0.0479	0.0500	0.0709	0.0516	0.0797	0.1113	0.0803	0.1163	0.0573	0.0848	0.1092	0.1414
First–second wave	0.0282	0.0373	0.0431	0.0438	0.0655	0.0425	0.0701	0.0971	0.0709	0.1042	0.0520	0.0744	0.0966	0.1340
First–sixth wave	0.0219	0.0346	0.0401	0.0375	0.0611	0.0395	0.0665	0.0871	0.0632	0.0791	0.0487	0.0714	0.0938	0.1382
First–eighth wave	0.0205		0.0395		0.0600	0.0395		0.0847	0.0630	0.0718	0.0494	0.0698	0.0929	0.1423

SHORT-TERM MOBILITY OVER TIME AND ITS LINKS WITH CROSS-SECTIONAL AND SHORT-TERM INEQUALITY

First, we explore the changes in short-term mobility over time and its links with the evolution of inequality over time. Table 4 reveals the Dickens, Shorrocks, and Fields short-term mobility indices for the first–second wave period and 2000–2001. The Dickens index shows that short-term rank mobility decreased in most countries, except in Denmark, Ireland, the United Kingdom, and Spain. The decrease in short-term rank mobility signals that in 2000, men have a lower opportunity to escape low pay from one year to the next than in the first wave. Linking back with the evolution in cross-sectional inequality between the first wave and 2001 (Table 2), we find that in all countries where cross-sectional inequality increased, short-term rank mobility decreased. The opposite holds in most countries where cross-sectional inequality decreased.[14] Based also on what we find in the fourth section, we conclude that, in Finland, Netherlands, Germany, and Greece the decrease in rank mobility and the disequalizing effect of the earnings growth contributed to the increase in cross-sectional inequality. In Luxembourg, Italy, and Portugal, the decrease in rank mobility had a disequalizing effect on cross-sectional inequality, which dominated the equalizing effect of the growth in earnings. In Denmark, Ireland, the United Kingdom, and Spain the increase in rank mobility and the equalizing effect of the earnings growth contributed to the decrease in cross-sectional inequality. In Austria, Belgium, and France, the decrease in inequality is mainly the result of narrowing differentials between income classes rather than re-ranking.

The short-term Shorrocks and Fields indices show that short-term mobility decreased in most countries also in terms of equalizing short-term earnings differentials (Table 4). To recall, short-term inequality is based on average earnings over pairs of adjacent years. Exceptions are Denmark where Shorrocks stagnates, the Netherlands and Finland where Shorrocks increases, Italy and Spain where both indices increase. In the Netherlands, the short-term Fields index turns negative in 2000–2001, indicating that short-term mobility became disequalizing in the early 2000s. This is opposite to what is suggested by the increase in the short-term Shorrocks mobility index. Considering both indices, we conclude that short-term mobility increased in the Netherlands, but it became disequalizing short-term. These differences in findings between the two indices reinforce the limitations of

Table 4. Short-Term Mobility Over Time – Unbalanced.

Mobility Index	Dk	Fi	Nl	Au	Ge	Be	Lu	Fr	UK	Ir	It	Gr	Sp	Pt
Dickens														
First–second wave	0.267	0.264	0.193	0.286	0.189	0.27	0.144	0.225	0.211	0.214	0.255	0.295	0.215	0.206
2000–2001	0.271	0.253	0.19	0.192	0.174	0.207	0.131	0.173	0.217	0.234	0.205	0.187	0.261	0.172
Shorrocks														
First–second wave	0.108	0.111	0.078	0.108	0.053	0.106	0.051	0.107	0.088	0.077	0.085	0.130	0.065	0.048
2000–2001	0.108	0.114	0.082	0.062	0.046	0.057	0.042	0.055	0.073	0.078	0.060	0.058	0.078	0.040
Fields														
First–second wave	0.168	0.104	0.085	0.130	0.067	0.170	0.080	0.153	0.116	0.127	0.094	0.131	0.091	0.057
2000–2001	0.165	0.023	−0.018	0.056	0.053	0.050	0.072	0.067	0.102	0.128	0.051	0.050	0.121	0.028

Note: The Shorrocks and Fields mobility indices are based on the Theil index.

the Shorrocks index and the need to complement the evidence based on Shorrocks with the one based on Fields to understand the complex link between mobility and inequality (Benabou & Ok, 2001b; Fields, 2009).[15]

With respect to the relationship between mobility and inequality in the short run, a preliminary analysis using pairwise correlations and pooled OLS with clustered SE (Table 5a–c, column 4) indicates a strong and significant negative association between short-term mobility and cross-sectional inequality: the higher the short-term mobility ($M_{t,t+1}$), the lower the cross-sectional inequality I_{t+1}.[16] For testing further these associations, we estimate several models where we control for time effects and unobserved country heterogeneity: a random intercept and slope model, a random effects model, and a fixed effects model. The estimates are reported in Table 5a–c (columns 1–3). The significant negative association is confirmed in all models. We also test the relationship between short-term mobility ($M_{t,t+1}$) and short-term inequality defined as inequality in average earnings over years t and $t+1$ ($I_{t,t+1}$) to see whether higher mobility between pairs of adjacent years is associated with lower short-term inequality. Running the same models, the negative association is confirmed. We report the random intercept and random slope estimates in Table A.3. Our findings show that, in Europe, more mobile wage distributions are associated with lower levels of wage inequality in the short run. The negative association is confirmed also in the long run, as we show in the sixth section. Thus, in Europe, earnings mobility does not seem to diminish the social predilections for redistribution. Also, if we consider that high levels of earnings mobility are a sign of "effort," then our findings bring supporting evidence that equal societies do not kill the individual incentives and the "effort" to improve. This shows that the Europeans value earnings mobility, but also safety nets. This makes sense in labor markets which are becoming increasingly flexible, and where workers put high value on redistributive policies as they provide valuable insurance in the event of an adverse shock in earnings. The prospect of increased flexibility may have increased the perception of vulnerability to adverse earnings shocks in the European labor markets, which in turn may have increased the support for redistribution. Risk-averse individuals experiencing a higher mobility will accept paying higher taxes on future earnings, as they represent an insurance against downside earnings risks, independent of their effort.

Using household income instead of individual earnings for the EU countries, Prieto et al. (2008, 2010) found a positive association between cross-sectional household income inequality and social mobility. The difference between findings may stem from the income measure and from the

Table 5. Regression Estimates for Cross-Sectional Inequality.

Dependent: Cross-Sectional Inequality	(1) Random Intercept and Slope b/se	(2) Random Effects b/se	(3) Fixed Effects b/se	(4) OLS b/se
(a)				
Short-term Dickens mobility	−20.484***	−19.209***	−18.139***	−55.118**
	(4.358)	(3.866)	(3.849)	(19.504)
Constant	13.213***	12.905***	12.776***	20.239***
	(1.271)	(1.177)	(0.803)	(4.486)
Time effects	Yes	Yes	Yes	Yes
R^2_{overall}		0.295	0.295	0.300
Wald χ^2	24.859			
Test of parameter constancy χ^2	236.205			
N	94	94	94	94
Number of countries	14	14	14	
(b)				
Short-term Shorrocks mobility	−22.395***	−26.556***	−21.668***	−120.407***
	(6.968)	(7.263)	(6.956)	(30.270)
Constant	10.703***	10.791***	10.540***	17.183***
	(1.058)	(0.890)	(0.504)	(2.674)
Time effects	Yes	Yes	Yes	Yes
R^2_{overall}		0.479	0.475	0.485
Wald χ^2	12.256			
Test of parameter constancy χ^2	194.959			
N	94	94	94	94
Number of countries	14	14	14	14
(c)				
Short-term Fields mobility	−11.376***	−13.037***	−12.615***	−55.739**
	(2.331)	(2.514)	(2.639)	(22.347)
Constant	10.861***	9.864***	9.928***	12.753***
	(1.241)	(0.956)	(0.246)	(2.369)
Time effects	Yes	Yes	Yes	Yes
R^2_{overall}		0.287	0.286	0.295
Wald χ^2	27.571			
Test of parameter constancy χ^2	240.174			
N	94	94	94	94
Number of countries	14	14	14	14

**$p<0.05$, ***$p<0.01$.

measure of mobility. We use male net wages which are affected to a lesser extent by redistributive policies than household income. Wages reflect better individual effort, are more sensitive to labor market shocks, and exhibit a higher mobility compared to household income, which is cushioned by redistribution. The redistributive mechanisms cushion the variability in earnings, resulting in lower levels of household income inequality compared with earnings inequality and lower levels of income mobility compared with earnings mobility. As the redistributive systems vary considerably across Europe, the relationship between household income mobility and household income inequality depends on the differences in the "cushioning" effect between systems. For example, in countries with high levels of earnings mobility and with strong preferences for redistribution illustrated by low levels of inequality (e.g., the Scandinavian countries), the redistributive mechanism may reduce the mobility in income relative to mobility in earnings to a larger extent than in countries with lower levels of mobility and with weaker preferences for redistribution (less redistribution). The former country may end up with a lower income mobility and a lower income inequality than the latter, which in turn suggests a positive association between household income inequality and mobility, despite the negative association between earnings mobility and inequality. Considering the findings of Prieto et al. (2008, 2010), we may conclude that the redistributive mechanisms in Europe affect considerably the relationship between mobility and inequality, especially when different income measures are considered. The findings may differ also because we use different mobility measures: mobility indices that depend on income distances between ranks rather than on ranks tend to display a higher mobility when inequality is higher. This holds for the mobility measures in Prieto et al. (2008, 2010).

LONG-TERM MOBILITY AND ITS LINKS WITH LONG-TERM INEQUALITY

Next, we turn to the comparison of earnings mobility when we extend the period over which mobility is measured (Table 6). In line with previous studies, the longer the period over which rank mobility is measured the higher the earnings mobility. Ireland stands out with the highest relative increase in rank mobility with the time span (almost 80%). Relating back to the strong negative relationship between the quintile rank and the growth in real earnings identified in Fig. 2, we conclude that low wage individuals may

Table 6. Short-Term and Long-Term Mobility.

Mobility Index	Dk	Fi	Nl	Au	Ge	Be	Lu	Fr	UK	Ir	It	Gr	Sp	Pt
Dickens														
First–second wave	0.267	0.264	0.193	0.286	0.189	0.270	0.144	0.225	0.211	0.214	0.255	0.295	0.215	0.206
First–sixth wave	0.385	0.365	0.276	0.360	0.265	0.333	0.205	0.279	0.305	0.335	0.333	0.324	0.275	0.303
First–eighth wave	0.427		0.318		0.305	0.372		0.300	0.351	0.384	0.354	0.378	0.296	0.320
Shorrocks														
First–second wave	0.108	0.111	0.078	0.108	0.053	0.106	0.051	0.107	0.088	0.077	0.085	0.130	0.065	0.048
First–sixth wave	0.235	0.218	0.141	0.193	0.108	0.171	0.100	0.141	0.172	0.160	0.145	0.169	0.109	0.080
First–eighth wave	0.267		0.173		0.124	0.185		0.135	0.186	0.176	0.149	0.180	0.132	0.093
Fields														
First–second wave	0.168	0.104	0.085	0.130	0.067	0.170	0.080	0.153	0.116	0.127	0.094	0.131	0.091	0.057
First–sixth wave	0.309	0.180	0.140	0.239	0.121	0.237	0.161	0.238	0.224	0.374	0.141	0.130	0.140	0.070
First–eighth wave	0.376		0.175		0.153	0.235		0.240	0.216	0.382	0.138	0.177	0.149	−0.007

Note: The Shorrocks and Fields mobility indices are based on the Theil index.

be the main beneficiaries of this increase in mobility over the lifecycle. The ordering of countries in long-term mobility relative to short-term mobility changes substantially as illustrated in Fig. 3.[17] Based on the Dickens index, Luxembourg and Denmark are the least and the most mobile long-term. Long-term mobility is high enough to suggest that people are not stuck at the bottom top of the earnings distribution. But is there enough mobility to wash out the effect of yearly inequality in a lifetime perspective? To answer, we turn to the Shorrocks and the Fields indices.

The increase in mobility with the horizon over which mobility is measured shows that the opportunity to change ones position in the cross-sectional earnings distribution is higher the more years elapse between periods. In this context, the lifetime implications of these trends are of interest. Is there any earnings mobility in a lifetime perspective, meaning are the relative income positions observed on an annual basis shuffled in the distribution of long-term or lifetime earnings?

To answer this question we look at the stability profile which plots the Shorrocks rigidity index across different time horizons. In Fig. 4 the time horizons are expressed in reference to the first wave for each country. In all countries, the rigidity declines monotonically as the time horizon is

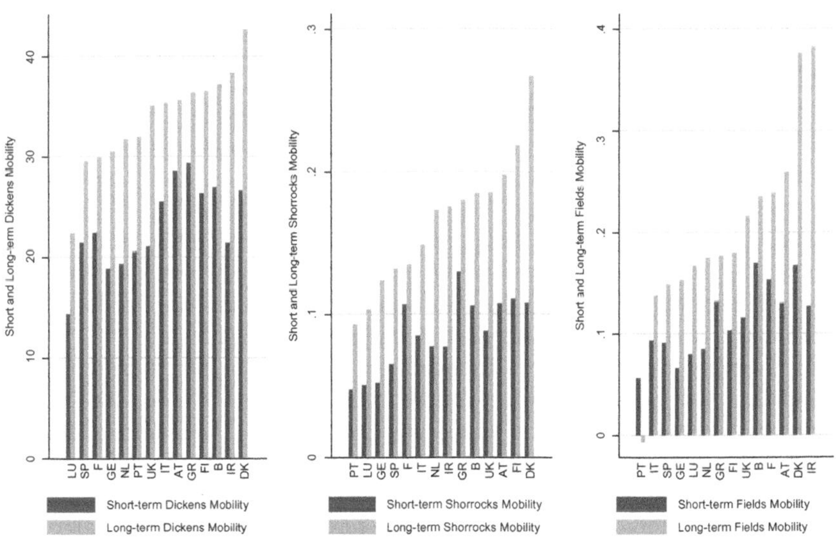

Fig. 3. Short- and Long-Term Mobility. *Note:* Spearman rank correlation: 51.82% (Dickens), 83.30% (Shorrocks), 78.90% (Fields).

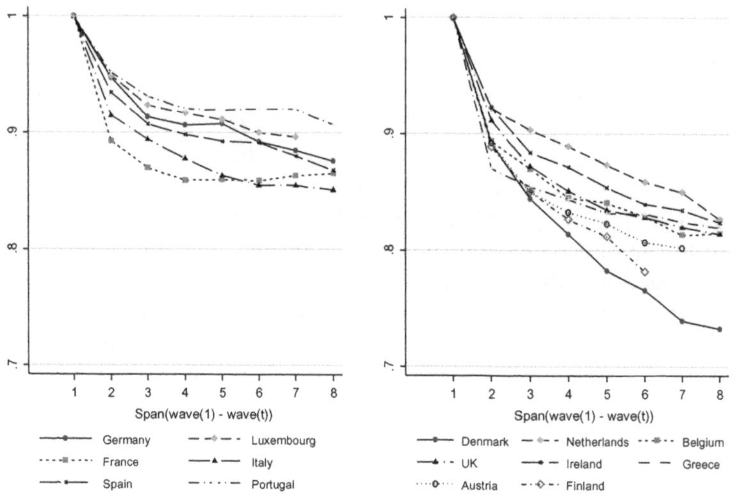

Fig. 4. Stability Profiles for Male Earnings for Selected Countries (Based on Theil) – Unbalanced. *Notes*: The stability profile plots the rigidity index against the horizon over which the index is measured: 1-year rigidity = 1; 2-year rigidity = rigidity index over a horizon of 2 years, span wave (1)–wave (2); 8-year rigidity = rigidity index over a horizon of 8 years, span wave (1)–wave (8).

extended, suggesting that lifetime mobility is present. All EU men have an increasing mobility in the distribution of lifetime earnings as they advance in their career.[18] The ordering of countries in long-term mobility relative to short-term mobility changes slightly (Fig. 3, Shorrocks). Over the sample-span horizon, Denmark has the highest mobility, followed by Finland, Austria, United Kingdom, Belgium, Greece, Ireland, Netherlands, Italy, France, Spain, Germany, Luxembourg, and the lowest, Portugal. Denmark provides the highest opportunity of reducing lifetime earnings differentials relative to cross-sectional ones, and Portugal the lowest.[19]

Is mobility equalizing or disequalizing lifetime earnings differentials compared with annual earnings differentials? The Fields index in Table 6 captures whether mobility is equalizing/disequalizing long-term differentials. Overall, mobility increases with the horizon for all countries, except Portugal. All countries except Portugal record positive values of mobility, showing that mobility is equalizing long-term earnings differentials.[20] In Portugal, mobility turns negative when measured over an 8-year horizon, showing that mobility is exacerbating long-term earning differentials relative

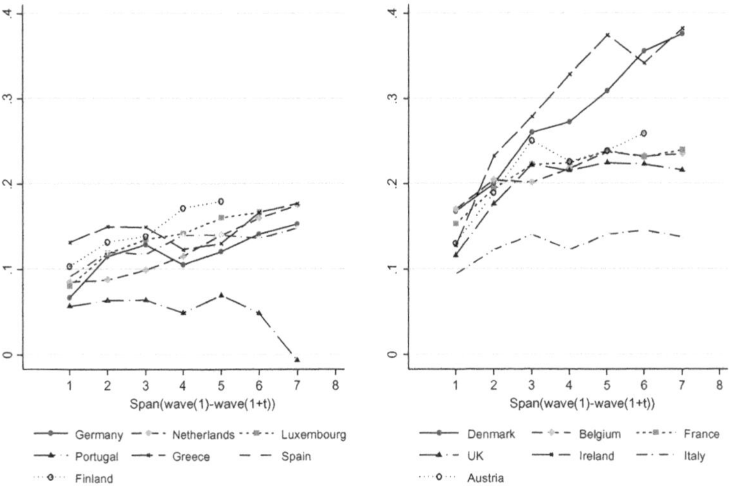

Fig. 5. Mobility Profile Based on the Fields Index – Unbalanced. *Notes*: The mobility profile plots the Fields index against the horizon over which the index is measured: 1-year mobility = 1; 2-year mobility = mobility index over a horizon of 2 years, span wave (1)–wave (2); 8-year mobility = mobility index over a horizon of 8 years, span wave (1)–wave (8).

to cross-sectional differentials. Portugal has the lowest Fields mobility profile, indicating the lowest mobility as equalizer of long-term differentials (Fig. 5). Denmark and Ireland have the steepest profiles and the highest long-term mobility. Some convergence trends emerge as the horizon over which mobility is measured increases. For a horizon of seven to eight years, mobility converges to similar values in Denmark and Ireland, in Belgium and France, in Spain and Germany, and in Luxembourg, Greece, and Netherlands (Fig. 5).[21]

The ordering of countries in long-term Fields mobility relative to short-term mobility changes to a larger extent compared with the Shorrocks index, but to a lesser extent compared with the Dickens index: the Spearman rank correlation is 65.27%. The highest long-term (sample-span) mobility (Fig. 3 and Fig. 6) is recorded in Ireland and Denmark, followed by Austria, France, and Belgium with similar values, then United Kingdom, Finland, Greece, Netherlands, Luxembourg, Germany, Spain, Italy, and Portugal.[22] Assuming that the eight-year mobility is a good approximation for lifetime mobility, Ireland and Denmark have the highest equalizing mobility in a

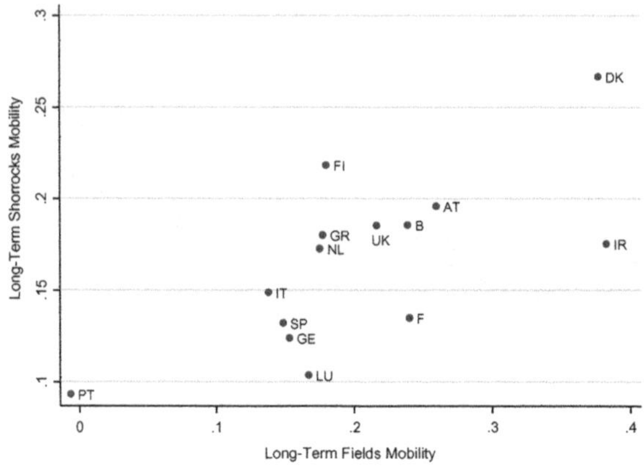

Fig. 6. Scatter Plot of Long-Term (6-Year, 7-Year, and 8-Year) Mobility: Shorrocks versus Fields.

lifetime perspective, and Italy, Spain, and Germany the lowest. Portugal is the only country where mobility acts as a disequalizer of lifetime differentials.[23]

With respect to the relationship between mobility and inequality in the long run, the pairwise correlations reveal a strong negative association between long-term mobility ($M_{t,t+8}$) and long-term inequality ($I_{t,t+8}$): −55.35% for the Dickens index, −78.65% for the Shorrocks index, and −62.70% for the Fields index. For testing these associations while controlling for country unobserved heterogeneity, we use the 5-year period inequality ($I_{t,t+4}$) as the proxy for long-term inequality and the 5-year period mobility ($M_{t,t+4}$) as the proxy for long-term mobility. The random effects, fixed effects, and pooled OLS regression with clustered SE estimates of the 5-year period inequality ($I_{t,t+4}$) against the 5-year period mobility ($M_{t,t+4}$) confirm the negative association between long-term inequality and long-term mobility (Table 7). We conclude that, in Europe, more mobile countries are more equal also in the long run.

Inferences for Lifetime Inequality Ranking

On comparing the rankings in long-term mobility between the Shorrocks and the Fields indices in Fig. 6, it is found that the mobility pictures differ to

Table 7. Regression Estimates for Five-Year Period Inequality Against Five-Year Period Mobility.

Five-Year Period Inequality (I_{t-t+4})	(1) Random Effects b/se	(2) Fixed Effects b/se	(3) OLS b/se	Five-Year Period Inequality (I_{t-t+4})	(1) Random Effects b/se	(2) Fixed Effects b/se	(3) OLS b/se	Five-Year Period Inequality (I_{t-t+4})	(1) Random Effects b/se	(2) Fixed Effects b/se	(3) OLS b/se
Dickens mobility ($M_{t,t+4}$)	−7.252	−5.345	−35.659**	Shorrocks mobility ($M_{t,t+4}$)	−24.310***	−17.839***	−65.479***	Fields mobility ($M_{t,t+4}$)	−3.966**	−3.315*	−24.840*
	(4.788)	(4.863)	(12.847)		(6.187)	(6.230)	(17.365)		(1.967)	(1.922)	(12.723)
Constant	8.983***	8.592***	17.162***	Constant	10.135***	9.401***	15.683***	Constant	7.479***	7.543***	10.751***
	(1.638)	(1.415)	(4.026)		(1.061)	(0.828)	(2.709)		(0.870)	(0.300)	(2.247)
Time effects	No	No	Yes	Time effects	No	No	Yes	Time effects	No	No	Yes
R^2	0.204	0.032	0.209	R^2	0.557	0.181	0.569	R^2	0.267	0.074	0.282
N	52	52	52	N	52	52	52	N	52	52	52

$^*p<0.1$, $^{**}p<0.05$, $^{***}p<0.01$.

a moderate extent, confirmed also by the moderate Spearman rank correlation (70.55%) between the long-term Shorrocks and Fields indices. Portugal records the lowest values based on both indices, with a disequalizing lifetime mobility. The Scandinavian countries, the "Rhineland" Austria and Belgium, and the Anglo-Saxon countries rank among the seven highest in both Shorrocks and Fields lifetime mobility, suggesting that they have the highest lifetime mobility with the highest equalizing impact on lifetime earnings differentials. Denmark scores the highest in lifetime mobility, but the second highest after Ireland in equalizing mobility, suggesting that mobility in Ireland is slightly more equalizing in a lifetime perspective than in Denmark. Compared with the other countries, Denmark has a higher lifetime mobility with a higher lifetime equalizing impact.

Based on these findings, and on the country ranking in long-term inequality (the fourth section), we attempt to make inferences regarding the country ranking in lifetime inequality. Denmark is the least unequal long-term, has the highest Shorrocks mobility, and the most equalizing mobility; thus, it is expected to have the lowest inequality in a lifetime perspective. At the opposite extreme we find unequivocally Portugal. Austria has a higher equalizing mobility than Finland and may become less unequal in a lifetime perspective. Finland and Austria are expected to be among the three least unequal countries in a lifetime perspective after Denmark. For the other countries, we do not always find a consistent ranking in expected lifetime inequality rankings based on the Shorrocks and the Field indices, which indicates that the two indices indeed capture different facets of mobility. Future research is needed to settle this dilemma.

Fig. 7 illustrates the ranking in lifetime inequality relying on the Fields index. Belgium has a lower long-term mobility and a higher equalizing mobility than all countries, except Denmark, Finland, and Austria; thus, it is expected to be the fourth country in lifetime inequality. The Netherlands and the United Kingdom are expected to rank next in lifetime inequality, but we cannot establish their relative ranks, given that the United Kingdom has a more equalizing long-term mobility than the Netherlands. Next we expect to find Italy, Germany, Luxembourg, Greece, Ireland, and France,

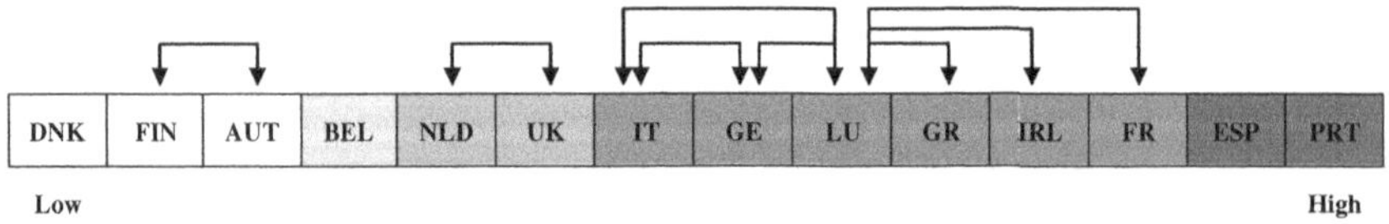

Fig. 7. Lifetime Earnings Inequality Ranking.

with interchanging ranks. Spain and Portugal, with the least equalizing mobility, are expected to have the highest long-term inequality. The "Flexicurity" countries have the lowest expected lifetime inequality and the Mediterranean countries the highest.

EARNINGS MOBILITY AND LABOR MARKET POLICIES AND INSTITUTIONS

Lastly, we explore the role of the labor market policies and institutions in understanding the cross-country differences in earnings mobility across Europe. We consider the OECD labor market indicators linked to the wage-setting mechanism: employment protection legislation (EPL), active labor market policies (ALMPs) and the average unemployment benefit replacement rates (UBRR), the degree of unionization and corporatism, the tax wedge and product market regulation (PMR).[24] For studying the relationship with short-term mobility, we use the moving averages of the labor market indicators over pairs of two years for each country. For studying the relationship with long-term mobility, we use the average indicators over the sample period 1994–2001 for each country.

A preliminary analysis of the pairwise correlations between short-term mobility and labor market policies/institutions reveals significant moderate to strong associations for most factors, except the tax wedge and ALMPs (Table A.4). The signs are consistent across the three mobility indices, but the significance differs. We find evidence of a negative association between short-term mobility and EPL and PMR. A higher union density and corporatism are found to be positively associated with earnings mobility. A positive association is found also for the generosity of the unemployment benefit replacement rates. To test further these associations, we estimate models where we account for time effects and unobserved country heterogeneity. We regress short-term mobility against each factor in turn, allowing for cohort-specific intercepts and slopes (Table 8a–c). Most associations are maintained: EPL is negatively associated with short-term mobility (except for the short-term Dickens mobility); union density and corporatism are positively associated with short-term mobility; PMR is negatively associated with short-term Shorrocks mobility; ALMPs are positively associated with short-term Shorrocks mobility.

The pairwise correlations between long-term mobility and the institutional factors (Table A.5) indicate stronger associations than for short-term

Table 8. Random Intercept and Slope Estimates.

	(1) b/se	(2) b/se	(3) b/se	(4) b/se	(5) b/se	(6) b/se	(7) b/se
(a) Short-Term Dickens Mobility							
EPL	−0.008						
	(0.007)						
Union Density		0.108***					
		(0.034)					
High Corporatism			0.036**				
			(0.016)				
PMR				−0.006			
				(0.008)			
Tax wedge					−0.128		
					(0.083)		
URR						−0.059	
						(0.055)	
ALMPs							0.036
							(0.054)
Constant	0.255***	0.187***	0.209***	0.252***	0.271***	0.246***	0.222***
	(0.019)	(0.016)	(0.013)	(0.033)	(0.026)	(0.018)	(0.012)
Time effects	Yes	Yes	Yes	Yes	Yes	Yes	Yes
Wald χ^2	15.926	26.881	22.604	11.973	14.198	11.336	15.016
Test of parameter constancy χ^2	52.210	54.266	71.761	74.415	77.098	74.208	81.454
Nr groups	12	12	12	12	12	12	12
N	88	94	94	81	81	81	81

(b) Short-Term Dickens Mobility							
EPL	−0.009**						
	(0.004)						
Union Density		0.071***					
		(0.018)					
High Corporatism			0.020**				
			(0.009)				
PMR				−0.010*			
				(0.005)			
Tax wedge					−0.042		
					(0.054)		
URR						−0.004	
						(0.034)	
ALMPs							0.044*
							(0.027)
Constant	0.114***	0.060***	0.077***	0.125***	0.099***	0.085***	0.075***
	(0.012)	(0.008)	(0.007)	(0.021)	(0.017)	(0.010)	(0.008)
Time effects	Yes	Yes	Yes	Yes	Yes	Yes	Yes
Wald χ^2	38.908	51.794	42.332	32.600	28.470	21.900	39.466
Test of parameter constancy χ^2	57.309	43.382	71.620	78.421	84.046	79.012	89.856
Nr groups	12	12	12	12	12	12	12
N	88	94	94	81	81	81	81
(c) Short-Term Dickens Mobility							
EPL	−0.017***						
	(0.005)						
Union Density		0.077***					
		(0.030)					
High Corporatism			0.023*				
			(0.013)				

Table 8. *(Continued)*

	(1) b/se	(2) b/se	(3) b/se	(4) b/se	(5) b/se	(6) b/se	(7) b/se
PMR				−0.010			
				(0.008)			
Tax wedge					−0.127		
					(0.108)		
URR						0.004	
						(0.061)	
ALMPs							0.063
							(0.052)
Constant	0.162***	0.086***	0.102***	0.158***	0.158***	0.112***	0.100***
	(0.017)	(0.015)	(0.012)	(0.036)	(0.039)	(0.021)	(0.012)
Time effects	Yes	Yes	Yes	Yes	Yes	Yes	Yes
Wald χ^2	32.645	30.787	27.737	20.126	20.295	16.934	21.310
Test of parameter constancy χ^2	8.637	17.319	24.887	27.103	29.679	28.124	33.204
Nr groups	12	12	12	12	12	12	12
N	88	94	94	81	81	81	81

$^{*}p<0.1$, $^{**}p<0.05$, $^{***}p<0.01$.

mobility. The pairwise correlations reveal that long-term mobility is negatively associated with EPL and positively associated with union density. To test these associations in a regression setting where we control for unobserved country heterogeneity, we use the 5-period mobility measure as proxy for long-term mobility and regress it against the 5-period moving averages of the labor market factors. In Table 9a–c we report the random effects estimates.[25] Most associations are confirmed also in the long run: EPL is negatively associated with long-term mobility (except Shorrocks); union density and corporatism are positively associated with long-term mobility; ALMPs are positively associated with long-term Dickens mobility.

The negative association between earnings mobility and EPL is consistent with the view that a strict labor market regulation is a source of labor market rigidity (Cazes & Nesporova, 2004). More labor market support as spending on ALMPs (which typically consist of job search, vocational training, or hiring subsidies programs) is found to be positively associated with earnings mobility. These associations show that countries with more flexible labor markets and more labor market support could be expected to have a higher earnings mobility. These findings are consistent with the evidence that more developed ALMPs increase the employability of vulnerable groups, while a low EPL facilitates their reintegration into the labor market (Bassanini & Duval, 2006a, 2006b). Coupling these two policies has the potential to improve the labor market opportunities for more vulnerable groups.

The positive association between earnings mobility and unionization suggests that the union protection increases the opportunity of improving one's position in the earnings distribution. The positive association found for corporatism runs counter the traditional view that corporatist economies are more rigid than decentralized ones, but they are in line with the most recent findings showing that corporatist systems could be more flexible, even more than decentralized economies as they allow the renegotiation of contracts in response to aggregate shocks (Teulings & Hartog, 2008). The negative association between earnings mobility and PMR is consistent with the view that a strict regulation is a source of market rigidity, hindering mobility.

CONCLUDING REMARKS

The economic reality of the 1990s in Europe forced the labor markets to become more flexible. These labor market reforms increased the country

Table 9. Random Effects Estimates for Long-Term Dickens Mobility.

	(1) b/se	(2) b/se	(3) b/se	(4) b/se	(5) b/se	(6) b/se	(7) b/se
(a) Long-term Dickens Mobility ($M_{t,t+4}$)							
EPL	−1.553*						
	(0.942)						
Union Density		15.775***					
		(4.657)					
High Corporatism			5.001**				
			(2.108)				
PMR				−0.616			
				(0.728)			
Tax wedge					0.070		
					(14.461)		
URR						4.028	
						(8.661)	
ALMPs							6.463*
							(3.904)
Constant	33.617***	23.200***	26.289***	31.899***	29.774***	28.348***	27.904***
	(2.458)	(1.976)	(1.592)	(2.729)	(4.881)	(3.309)	(1.614)
R^2	0.162	0.440	0.254	0.032	0.031	0.078	0.051
N	49	52	52	45	45	45	45
(b) Long-term Shorrocks Mobility ($M_{t,t+4}$)							
EPL	−0.010						
	(0.009)						
Union Density		0.167***					
		(0.036)					
High Corporatism			0.042**				
			(0.019)				

PMR				0.008			
				(0.006)			
Tax wedge					0.197		
					(0.124)		
URR						−0.048	
						(0.082)	
ALMPs							0.018
							(0.031)
Constant	0.163***	0.071***	0.110***	0.111***	0.073*	0.155***	0.133***
	(0.023)	(0.015)	(0.015)	(0.022)	(0.042)	(0.032)	(0.015)
R^2	0.322	0.570	0.225	0.137	0.001	0.120	0.088
N	49	52	52	45	45	45	45
(c) Long-term Fields Mobility ($M_{t,t+4}$)							
EPL	−0.054***						
	(0.012)						
Union Density		0.205**					
		(0.082)					
High Corporatism			0.068**				
			(0.032)				
PMR				0.012			
				(0.017)			
Tax wedge					−0.089		
					(0.284)		
URR						0.079	
						(0.166)	
ALMPs							0.058
							(0.086)
Constant	0.286***	0.077**	0.115***	0.122**	0.192**	0.134**	0.146***
	(0.031)	(0.035)	(0.024)	(0.061)	(0.095)	(0.063)	(0.032)
R^2	0.530	0.273	0.199	0.028	0.106	0.041	0.076
N	49	52	52	45	45	45	45

$^{*}p<0.1$, $^{**}p<0.05$, $^{***}p<0.01$

heterogeneity in labor market institutions, which is reflected in the distributional outcomes. This study explores the degree of earnings mobility and inequality in the 1990s across 14 European countries, and the role of labor market intuitions in understanding the cross-national differences in earnings mobility. We study the degree of rank mobility and the degree of mobility as equalizer of longer-term earnings. We argue for the need to complement the Shorrocks index with additional measures that capture mobility as an equalizer of long-term differentials, such as the Fields index, in order to make inferences regarding lifetime earnings distributions.

In the 1990s, the growth in earnings had an equalizing effect on earnings in most European countries, with men at the bottom improving to larger extent relative to the ones at the top. Exceptions are Finland, the Netherlands, Germany, and Greece, where the disequalizing effect of the earnings growth and the decrease in rank mobility contributed to the increase in cross-sectional inequality. In Luxembourg, Italy, and Portugal, the decrease in rank mobility had a disequalizing effect on cross-sectional inequality, which dominated the equalizing effect of the growth in earnings. In Denmark, Ireland, the United Kingdom, and Spain the increase in rank mobility and the equalizing effect of the earnings growth contributed to the decrease in cross-sectional inequality. In Austria, Belgium, and France, the decrease in inequality is mainly the result of narrowing differentials between income classes.

The country ranking in long-term earnings inequality is similar with the country ranking in annual inequality, a sign of limited long-term equalizing mobility within countries with higher levels of annual inequality. During the 1990s, Denmark and Finland have been the most equal countries, and Portugal the most unequal in Europe, and this holds even over an 8-year horizon. Long-term, Denmark renders unequivocally the most mobile earnings distribution with the second highest equalizing effect in Europe. Using the rank measure, men in Luxembourg are found to have the lowest opportunity to improve their position in the distribution of earnings in the long run. In terms of the opportunity to shuffle long-term the relative income positions observed on an annual basis, the lowest values are found in Portugal and Luxembourg. The least equalizing long-term mobility is found in Italy, and the only disequalizing mobility in a lifetime perspective in Portugal. Based on the Shorrocks and Fields indices, Denmark, Finland, Austria, the United Kingdom, Belgium, and Ireland are found to have the highest lifetime mobility with the highest equalizing impact on lifetime earnings differentials.

With respect to the relationship between earnings mobility and earnings inequality, we find a significant negative association both in the short run and in the long run. This suggests that in Europe, low levels of earnings inequality coexist with high levels of earnings mobility. Thus, in Europe, earnings mobility does not seem to diminish the social predilections for redistribution. If we consider that the high levels of mobility are a sign of "effort," then our findings bring supporting evidence that equal societies do not kill the individual incentives to improve. This shows that the Europeans not only value earnings mobility but also safety nets. This makes sense in labor markets which are becoming increasingly flexible, and where workers put high value on redistributive policies as they provide valuable insurance in the event of an adverse shock in earnings. Based jointly on the rankings in long-term Fields mobility and in long-term inequality, Denmark is expected to have the lowest lifetime earnings inequality in Europe, followed by Finland, Austria, and Belgium. The Mediterranean countries (Spain and Portugal) are expected to have the highest long-term inequality.

With respect to the institutional factors, we find that the deregulation in the labor and product markets, the degree of unionization, the degree of corporatism and the spending on ALMPs are positively associated with earnings mobility. Thus low levels of regulation, high levels of activations, and a high unionization and corporatism have the potential to stimulate earnings mobility and reduce lifetime differentials relative to annual ones.

NOTES

1. The indicators are re-scaled by setting the UK as the base. The definition of the OECD indicators and their summary statistics are in Tables A.1 and A.2. For a complete description of the OECD data, please refer to Bassanini and Duval (2006a, 2006b). The data was obtained by email from the authors.
2. Sologon and O'Donoghue (2010b) explore the relationship between earnings immobility measured by the ratio between permanent and transitory inequality, and the labor market institutions and macroeconomic shocks, and reach similar conclusions.
3. The ECHP provided by Eurostat via the Department of Applied Economics at the Université Libre de Bruxelles.
4. For France the wage is in gross amounts.
5. For a review of the methodology regarding mobility, please refer to Fields and Ok (1999); Fields, Leary, and Ok (2003).
6. For Luxembourg and Austria the sample span is of 7 years, and in Finland of 6.
7. The formula applies for a cohort of constant size.

8. To compute this index only individuals that are present in all years are considered.

9. The concept of mobility as an equalizer of longer-term income is an old one, complementing mobility as time independence, positional movement, share movement, nondirectional income movement, and directional income movement (Fields, 2009).

10. For Luxembourg and Austria the longest horizon is of seven years and for Finland of six.

11. The trends for Denmark, UK, Spain, and Germany are consistent with those found by Gregg and Vittori (2008).

12. This trend is confirmed by all three inequality indices, for all countries.

13. The SD for the Theil indices for eight-year average earnings is 0.031 and for single-year earnings is 0.036.

14. Austria, Belgium, and France are exceptions with a decreasing mobility and a decreasing cross-sectional inequality.

15. Although not reported here, most trends are confirmed by the balanced approach. Overall, the Shorrocks index is affected to a lesser extent by differential attrition than the Fields index (see Sologon & O'Donoghue, 2010a for the balanced approach).

16. The pairwise correlations are −52.5% for the Dickens index, −65.6% for the Shorrocks index, and −49.5% for the Fields index.

17. The Spearman rank correlation is moderate 51.82%.

18. Comparing the unbalanced and balanced approaches, although not reported here, we find consistent trends, thus limiting impact of differential attrition (see Sologon & O'Donoghue, 2010a for the balanced approach).

19. The Spearman rank correlation is high 83.3%. Finland has the same ranking when comparing all countries over a six-year horizon. Austria and Luxembourg have the same ranking when comparing all countries over a seven-year or six-year horizon. The ranking between Denmark, UK, Spain, and Germany is consistent with the one found by Gregg and Vittori (2008) using the Shorrocks index based on all indices considered.

20. The story is confirmed also using a fully balanced sample (Sologon & O'Donoghue, 2010a).

21. These trends are in general consistent with the balanced approach, which is not reported but it is available upon request.

22. Austria, Luxembourg, and Finland have the same ranking when comparing all countries over a seven-year or a six-year horizon.

23. Although not reported here, we find that the Fields index is affected to a larger extent by differential attrition than the Shorrocks index. Whereas the overall qualitative conclusions regarding the evolution of mobility over time and across horizons are not affected by using a balanced or an unbalanced sample, more differences are observed for the country rankings (see Sologon & O'Donoghue, 2010a for the results using the balanced sample).

24. The definition and the summary statistics of the OECD labor market indicators are in the appendix.

25. The fixed effects and pooled OLS estimates confirm most significant associations and can be provided upon request.

ACKNOWLEDGMENTS

This research is funded by the Fond National de la Recherche, Luxembourg. The authors would like to thank Philippe Van Kerm, CEPS/INSTEAD, Luxembourg for helpful comments. The usual disclaimer applies.

REFERENCES

Aaberge, R., Bjorklund, A., Jantti, M., Palme, M., Pedersen, P. J., Smith, N., & Wannemo, T. (2002). Income inequality and income mobility in the Scandinavian countries compared to the United States. *Review of Income and Wealth*, *48*(4), 443–469.

Atkinson, A. B., Bourguignon, F., & Morrisson, C. (1992). *Empirical studies of earnings mobility*. Suisse: Harwood Academic Publishers.

Ayala, L., Navarro, C., & Sastre, M. (2011). Cross-country income mobility comparisons under panel attrition: the relevance of weighting schemes. *Applied Economics*, *43*(25), 3495–3521.

Ayala, L., & Sastre, M. (2008). The structure of income mobility: empirical evidence from five EU countries. *Empirical Economics*, *35*, 451–473.

Bassanini, A., & Duval, R. (2006a). *The determinants of unemployment across OECD countries: Reassessing the role of policies and institutions*. OECD Economics Studies, 42, 2006/1.

Bassanini, A., & Duval, R. (2006b). *Employment patterns in OECD countries: Reassessing the role of policies and institutions*. Working Papers No. 486. OECD Economics Department, Paris.

Behr, A., Bellgardt, E., & Rendtel, U. (2005). Extent and determinants of panel attrition in the European Community Household Panel. *European Sociological Review*, *21*(5), 489–512.

Benabou, R., & Ok, E. A. (2001a). Social mobility and the demand for redistribution. The POUM hypothesis. *The Quarterly Journal of Economics*, *116*(2), 447–487.

Benabou, R., & Ok, E. A. (2001b). *Mobility and progressivity: Ranking income processes according to equality of opportunity*. NBER Working Paper No. 8431, National Bureau of Economic Research.

Boeri, T. (2002). *Making social Europe(s) compete*. Mimeo, University of Bocconi and Fondazione Rodolfo Debenedetti. Paper prepared for the conference at Harvard University on Transatlantic perspectives on US-EU Economic relations: Convergence, Conflict, Co-operation, April 11–12 2002.

Burkhauser, R. V., Holtz-Eakin, D., & Rhody, S. E. (1997). Labor earnings mobility and inequality in the United States and Germany during the growth years of the 1980s. *International Economic Review*, *38*, 775–794.

Burkhauser, R. V., & Poupore, J. G. (1997). A cross-national comparison of permanent inequality in the United States and Germany. *Review of Economics and Statistics*, *79*, 10–17.

Cazes, S., & Nesporova, A. (2004). Labor markets in transition: balancing flexibility and security in Central and Eastern Europe. *Revue de l'OFCE*, *5*, 23–54.

Creedy, J., & Wilhelm, M. (2002). Income mobility, inequality and social welfare. *Australian Economic Papers*, *41*(2), 140–150.

Dickens, R. (2000). Caught in a trap? Wage mobility in Great Britain: 1975–1994. *Economica, 67*, 477–497.

Fields, G. S. (2009). Does income mobility equalize longer-term incomes? New measures of an old concept. *Journal of Economic Inequality*, *8*(4), 409–427.

Fields, G. S., Hernández, R. D., Freije, S., Puerta, M. L. S., Arias, O., & Assunção, J. (2007). Intragenerational income mobility in Latin America. *Economía*, *7*(2), 101–154.

Fields, G. S., Leary, J. B., & Ok, E. A. (2003). Stochastic dominance in mobility analysis. *Economic Letters, Elsevier*, *75*(3), 333–339.

Fields, G. S., & Ok, E. A. (1999). Measuring movement of incomes. *Economica*, *66*(264), 455–471.

Fong, C. (2001). Social preferences, self-interest and the demand for redistribution. *Journal of Public Economics*, *82*, 225–246.

Friedman, M. (1962). *Capitalism and freedom*. Chicago, IL: University of Chicago Press.

Fritzell, J. (1990). The dynamics of income distribution: Economic mobility in Sweden in comparison with the United States. *Social Science Research*, *19*(1), 17–46.

Gangl, M., Palme, J., & Kenworthy, L. (2008). *Is high inequality offset by mobility?* Unpublished manuscript.

Gottschalk, P. (1997). Inequality, income growth, and mobility: The basic facts. *Journal of Economic Perspectives*, *11*, 21–40.

Goodin, R. E., Headey, B., Muffels, R., & Dirven, H. (1999). *The real worlds of welfare capitalism*. Cambridge: Cambridge University Press.

Gottschalk, P., & Spolaore, E. (2002). On the evaluation of economic mobility. *Review of Economic Studies*, *68*, 191–208.

Gregg, P., & Vittori, C. (2008). Exploring Shorrocks mobility indices using European data. *The Centre for Market and Public Organisation*, *8*, 206.

Haider, S. (2001). Earnings instability and earnings inequality of males in the United States: 1967–1991. *Journal of Labor Economics*, *19*, 799–836.

Hungerford, T. L. (2011). How income mobility affects income inequality: U.S. evidence in the 1980s and the 1990s. *Journal of Income Distribution*, *20*(1), 83–103.

OECD. (1996). Earnings inequality, low paid employment and earnings mobility. *Employment Outlook*, pp. 59–99. Paris: OECD.

OECD. (1997). Earnings mobility: Taking a longer view. *Employment Outlook*. Paris: OECD.

OECD. (2004). Employment protection regulation and labor market performance. *Employment Outlook*. Paris: OECD.

OECD. (2011). *Divided we stand: Why inequality keeps rising*. Paris: OECD.

Palier, B. (Ed.). (2010). *A long goodbye to Bismark? The politics of welfare reform in continental Europe*. Amsterdam: Amsterdam University Press.

Piketty, T. (1995). Social mobility and redistributive politics. *The Quarterly Journal of Economics*, *CX*(3), 551–584.

Prieto, J., Rodríguez, J. G., & Salas, R. (2008). A study on the relationship between economic inequality and mobility. *Economics Letters*, *99*, 111–114.

Prieto, J., Rodríguez, J. G., & Salas, R. (2010). Income mobility and economic inequality from a regional perspective. *Journal of Applied Economics*, *2*, 335–350.

Ravallion, M., & Lokshin, M. (2000). Who wants to redistribute? The tunnel effect in 1990 Russia. *Journal of Public Economics*, *76*, 87–104.

Salverda, W. (2008). The bite and effects of wage bargaining in the Netherlands. In M. Keune & B. Galgoczi (Eds.), *Wages and wage bargaining in Europe*. Brussels: ETUI-REHS.

Schluter, C. (1998). *Income dynamics in Germany, The USA, and The UK: Evidence from panel data*. STICERD/CASE Discussion Paper 8. London School of Economics, London.

Shorrocks, A. F. (1978). Income inequality and income mobility. *Journal of Economic Theory*, *19*, 376–393.

Sologon, D. M., & O'Donoghue, C. (2009). Increased opportunity to move up the economic ladder? Earnings Mobility in EU: 1994–2001. IZA Discussion Papers, No. 4311(July), Institute for the Study of Labor.

Sologon, D. M., & O'Donoghue, C. (2010a). *Earnings mobility in the EU: 1994–2001*. CEPS/INSTEAD Working Paper Series 2010-36, CEPS/INSTEAD.

Sologon, D. M., & O'Donoghue, C. (2010b). Shaping earnings mobility: Policy and institutional factors. *The European Journal of Comparative Economics*, *8*(2), 175–202.

Teulings, C., & Hartog, J. (2008). *Corporatism or competition? Labor contracts, institutions and wage structures in international comparison*. Cambridge: Cambridge University Press

Van Kerm, P. (2004). What lies behind income mobility? Re-ranking and distributional change in Belgium, Western Germany, and The USA. *Economica*, *71*, 223–239.

APPENDIX

Table A.1. Description of OECD Variables.

OECD Variables	Description
EPL = Employment Protection Legislation	OECD summary indicator of the stringency of Employment Protection Legislation. EPL ranges from 0 to 6.
Union Density	Trade union density rate, i.e., the share of workers affiliated to a trade union, in %.
Degree of Corporatism	Indicator of the degree of centralization/coordination of the wage bargaining processes, which takes values 1 for decentralized and uncoordinated processes, and 2 and 3 for intermediate and high.
Tax Wedge	The tax wedge expresses the sum of personal income tax and all social security contributions as a percentage of total labor cost.
PMR = Product Market Regulation	OECD summary indicator of regulatory impediments to product market competition in seven nonmanufacturing industries. The data used in this paper cover regulations and market conditions in seven energy and service industries. PMR ranges from 0 to 6.
ALMPs = Public expenditures on active labor market policies	Public expenditures on active labor market programs per unemployed worker as a share of GDP per capita, in %.
Average unemployment benefit replacement rate (UBRR)	Average unemployment benefit replacement rate across two income situations (100% and 67% of APW earnings), three family situations (single, with dependent spouse, with spouse in work).

Source: Bassanini and Duval (2006a, 2006b).

Table A.2. OECD Labor Market Indicators – Summary Statistics.

Variable		Mean	Std. Dev.	Min	Max	Observations
EPL	Overall	2.423	0.956	0.600	3.854	$N = 101$
	Between		0.944	0.621	3.739	$n = 13$
	Within		0.251	1.537	3.211	$T = 7.769$
Union Density	Overall	0.371	0.191	0.096	0.794	$N = 108$
	Between		0.201	0.098	0.779	$n = 14$
	Within		0.017	0.302	0.429	$T = 7.714$
Degree of Corporatism	Overall			1	3	$N = 93$
	Between					$n = 12$
	Within					$T = 7.75$
Tax Wedge	Overall	0.326	0.068	0.128	0.449	$N = 93$
	Between		0.067	0.219	0.404	$n = 12$
	Within		0.022	0.234	0.390	$T = 7.75$
PMR	Overall	3.394	1.015	1.133	5.236	$N = 93$
	Between		0.871	1.454	4.415	$n = 12$
	Within		0.563	2.155	4.459	$T = 7.75$
ALMPs	Overall	0.301	0.209	0.048	1.261	$N = 93$
	Between		0.188	0.094	0.750	$n = 12$
	Within		0.101	−0.035	0.812	$T = 7.75$
Unemployment Benefit RR	Overall	0.360	0.117	0.166	0.649	$N = 93$
	Between		0.115	0.174	0.599	$n = 12$
	Within		0.030	0.271	0.451	$T = 7.75$

Source: Own calculations based on the OECD data.

Table A.3. Random Intercept and Slope Estimates of Short-Term Inequality Against Short-Term Mobility.

Inequality $I_{(t,t+1)}$	(1) Random Intercept and Slope b/se	(2) Random Intercept and Slope b/se	(3) Random Intercept and Slope b/se
Dickens mobility $(M_{t,t+1})$	−22.740***		
	(4.420)		
Shorrocks mobility $(M_{t,t+1})$		−27.499***	
		(7.113)	
Fields mobility $(M_{t,t+1})$			−6.559**
			(2.635)
Constant	12.681***	9.874***	8.431***
	(1.400)	(1.017)	(0.947)
Time effects	Yes	Yes	Yes
Wald χ^2	29.704	17.150	9.387
Test of parameter constancy χ^2	256.812	203.813	224.119
Nr groups	14	14	14
N	94	94	94

$^{*}p<0.1$, $^{**}p<0.05$, $^{***}p<0.01$

Table A.4. Correlation Between Short-Term and Labor Market Policies/Institutions.

	Short-Term Dickens Mobility	Short-Term Shorrocks Mobility	Short-Term Fields Mobility
EPL	−0.2934*	−0.4070*	−0.4367*
Union Density	0.5745*	0.6180*	0.3978*
Corporatism	0.3141*	0.2451*	0.1481
PMR	−0.0988	−0.2388*	−0.0524
Tax Wedge	0.0839	0.1415	−0.0681
URR	0.2124	0.2858*	0.1693
ALMPs	0.0147	0.2148	0.1001

Note: *significant at 5% level of confidence.

Table A.5. Correlation Between Long-Term Mobility and Labor Market Policies/Institutions.

	Long-Term Dickens Mobility	Long-Term Shorrocks Mobility	Long-Term Fields Mobility
EPL	−0.5197	−0.5962*	−0.7181*
Union Density	0.6051*	0.7402*	0.4393
Corporatism	0.3841	0.3386	0.2917
PMR	−0.1274	−0.4351	−0.0753
Tax Wedge	−0.1779	−0.0139	−0.2098
URR	0.2384	0.3721	0.2135
ALMPs	0.1975	0.3260	0.2925

Note: *significant at 5% level of confidence.

CHAPTER 11

INTERGENERATIONAL EDUCATIONAL MOBILITY AND SOCIAL EXCLUSION – GERMANY AND THE UNITED STATES COMPARED

Veronika V. Eberharter

ABSTRACT

This paper analyzes the impact of family background characteristics and social exclusion features on the intergenerational transmission of educational attainment and income positions, and the relative poverty risk in Germany and the United States. These countries vary widely by welfare regime, family role patterns, and labor market settings. From these differences we predict higher intergenerational income elasticities in the United States and higher intergenerational educational elasticities in Germany. Using longitudinal data from the Cross-National Equivalent File (CNEF) 1980–2008, we find some empirical support for these hypotheses. In both countries, parental educational attainment stimulates

Inequality, Mobility and Segregation: Essays in Honor of Jacques Silber
Research on Economic Inequality, Volume 20, 285–309

ISSN: 1049-2585/doi:10.1108/S1049-2585(2012)0000020014

intergenerational economic and social mobility, which accentuates the importance of promoting human capital accumulation.

Keywords: Intergenerational educational mobility; intergenerational income mobility; income inequality; poverty; social exclusion

JEL classifications: D90; J24; D3

INTRODUCTION

The increasing social and economic inequalities in many industrialized countries direct attention to the determinants of the intergenerational transmission of low income and social exclusion. The negative correlation between intergenerational mobility and cross-sectional inequality and poverty (OECD, 2008) suggests an increasing intergenerational transmission of social and economic disadvantages, poverty, and social exclusion.

Poverty and social exclusion are dynamic processes limiting a person's future prospects. Poverty is discussed as either a dimension of social exclusion (Marlier & Atkinson, 2010) or a concept very close to it. Social exclusion reflects a combination of interrelated factors resulting from a lack of capabilities (Sen, 1985, 1992) required to participate in economic and social life (poor skills, labor market exclusion, living in a jobless household), service exclusion (public transport, gas, electricity, water, telephone), exclusion from social relations (common activities, social networks), exclusion from support available in normal times and in times of crisis, exclusion from engagement in political and civic activity, poor housing, high-crime environment, disability, health problems, or family breakdown (Saunders, 2008; Saunders, Naidoo, & Griffiths, 2007; Social Exclusion Unit, 1997). If poverty is understood as a low-income situation implying a lack of participation in the key activities in social, political, and cultural life (Burchard, Le Grand, & Piachaud, 2002; Duffy, 1995; Townsend, 1979; United Nations, 1995; Walker & Walker, 1997) or the inability to do things, which are in some sense considered normal by the society as a whole (Howarth, Kenway, Palmer, & Street, 1998), or the insufficiency of different attributes of well-being (e.g., housing, literacy, health, provision of public good, income, etc.), then both the concepts become very close (Bourguignon & Chakravarty, 2003).

The structural hypothesis of the intergenerational transmission of economic and social status can be deduced from the logic of the neoclassical human capital approach (Becker, 1964; Mincer, 1974). This view emphasizes that parental investments increase the children's human capital which in turn affects their earning capacity as adults (Becker & Tomes, 1986; Chadwick & Solon, 2002; Mayer & Lopoo, 2005, 2008; Solon, 1999), their ability to gain nonlabor income, and their success in the marriage market (Pencavel, 1998). The parental position directly affects the economic and social success of the children, but more likely the intervening variables are affected by it and in turn affect economic and social success.

The research of educational mobility encompasses two branches. The empirical results of the analysis of the mobility of different cohorts in their educational choice are country specific and ambiguous. Esping-Andersen (2004), Shavit, Gamoran, and Menahem (2007), and Breen and Jonsson (2007) report little changes in the educational mobility, whereas Breen, Luijkx, Müller, and Pollak (2009) report opposite results using different data. Blanden, Gregg, and Machin (2005) examine educational mobility at both the secondary and the tertiary levels and find first a rise and then a decline in cohort educational inequality at the secondary level but an increase at the tertiary level. They attribute that latter changes to increased financing constraints for higher education. The research focusing on the intergenerational transmission of education concentrates on the correlation between the children's and the parents' educational attainment. D'Addio (2007) found that educational differences tend to persist across generations. Other studies (Cameron & Heckman, 1998; Haveman & Wolfe, 1995; Hertz et al., 2008; Mulligan, 1999) state that among the household background characteristics, the parent's education is the most important factor in explaining the educational attainment of the children.

Most of the empirical research on intergenerational income mobility concedes that individual success is related to the characteristics of the household in which the individual grew up. There is an implicit stress on human capital development with poorer families lacking sufficient resources for the human capital investments in the children (Blanden & Gregg, 2004; Cameron & Heckman, 2001, 2002; Dustmann, 2004). The endowment factors are difficult to unbundle, and no single indicator provides a complete picture of intergenerational mobility. Among the endowment conditions are not only the parental education, employment behavior, and occupational choice, but also the social capital environment, neighborhood and social conditions, ethic origin, and social role norms, the institutional settings in the labor market, the social policy design, and the existing welfare state regime (Finnie & Sweetman, 2003; Stevens, 1999).

The typologies of welfare state regimes are defined on various dimensions (Arts & Gelissen, 2002; Bonoli, 1997; Siaroff, 1994). The Esping-Anderson typology (Esping-Andersen, 1990, 1994, 1999) is based on the level of decommodification and stratification, and clusters democratic industrial societies into liberal, conservative, and social democratic welfare state regimes.

The liberal welfare state regime (United States, Great Britain, Canada, Australia, New Zealand) is characterized by low decommodification and strong individualistic self-reliance. Furthermore it promotes the market, rather than the state, in guaranteeing the welfare needs of its citizens. The labor market policies offer less protection for workers and thus induce a flexible labor market (Couch & Dunn, 1997; Dustmann, 2004). The state reacts only in the case of social failures, the transfers are modest, and the rules for entitlement are very strict. The public philosophy is grounded on the idea of opportunity reflecting individual efforts, which indicates an open, liberal, and dynamic social system.

The conservative-corporatist welfare state regime (Germany, Austria, France, Italy) is typified by a modest level of decommodification. The government protects those who are unable to succeed in the market place. The labor market policy ensures a high degree of employment stability, and social policy is designed to guarantee income equality. Higher education, health care, welfare, social insurance, national assistance, and old age pensions are publicly provided. In countries with traditional family structures (e.g. Germany, Austria), female labor market participation tends to be lower than in countries with a liberal welfare state regime (Dustmann, 2004).

The social democratic welfare state regime (Scandinavian countries) is especially committed to create equal opportunity, to reduce social risks, and to diminish social divisions. These countries have a high level of decommodification, and stratification is directed to achieve a system of highly distributive benefits. Social policy aims at maximizing the capacities of individual independence. Women are encouraged to participate in the labor market.

This paper examines the impact of individual and family background characteristics and social exclusion features on intergenerational educational mobility, intergenerational income mobility, and the relative risk of poverty. The paper aims to produce a better understanding of the mechanisms of transmission of disadvantages across generations and the development of a self-replicating underclass. The value addition of this paper is to evaluate the intergenerational educational and income elasticities, and to compare the contribution of a comprehensive set of family background resources and social exclusion characteristics to these elasticities. Furthermore, we analyze the structural differences of the intergenerational transmission of educational and income status with the help of transition matrices. Additionally, the paper evaluates the impact of family background variables and social exclusion characteristics on the relative risk of poverty. In these points the paper differs from the authors' studies on the intergenerational mobility of earnings (Eberharter, 2003, 2009a), and income (Eberharter, 2002, 2005, 2007, 2009b), and the impact of social exclusion variables on intergenerational income and poverty persistence (Eberharter, 2011) for different cohorts, and observation periods.

The analysis focuses on the situation in Germany and the United States, differing with regard to the institutional labor market settings, the family role patterns, the welfare state regime, and the social policy design. The paper addresses the following questions: (i) Do these countries differ concerning intergenerational income mobility and intergenerational educational mobility? (ii) To what extent does a set of family background and social exclusion attributes determine intergenerational income and educational mobility? (iii) To what extent do family background characteristics and social exclusion attributes determine the relative risk of poverty?

We begin with the hypothesis that the intergenerational link between social stratification and endowment factors works differently according to the welfare state regimes, the family role patterns, and the social policy:

- Due to the liberal welfare state regime and social policy in the United States, we expect lower intergenerational income mobility and higher intergenerational income persistence at the bottom of the income distribution than in Germany.
- In Germany we expect two opposing effects: Due to the traditional family role patterns, we expect a higher influence of individual and family background resources on the intergenerational educational and income elasticities. Due to the publicly financed higher educational system and the redistributive social policy, we expect a higher educational and income mobility than in the United States.
- In both the countries we expect that social disadvantages in childhood as instable family structures, unemployment, and health dissatisfaction boost the intergenerational poverty persistence.

The empirical analysis is based on longitudinal data (CNEF 1980–2008) providing nationally representative socioeconomic data of individuals and households. To study the determinants of intergenerational income and educational mobility, we employ regression approaches (Björklund & Jäntti,

2000; Couch & Lillard, 2004; Grawe, 2004; Hertz, 2005; Solon, 1999, 2002, 2004). To capture the structure of intergenerational economic and social mobility, we examine transition matrices. To analyze the determinants of the risk to be poor, we employ a binomial logit model (Heckman, 1981; Maddala, 1983; McFadden, 1973). The explanatory variables include a set of individual, family background, and social exclusion attributes.

The paper proceeds as follows: Section "Data and sample organization" reports the data and sample selection, Section "Methodology" outlines the methodology of intergenerational income and social mobility, Section "Empirical results" presents the empirical results. Section "Conclusions" concludes with a summary of findings and a discussion of some stylized facts about the intergenerational transmission of economic and social disadvantages, the resulting policy implications, and the directions for further research.

DATA AND SAMPLE ORGANIZATION

The empirical analysis is based on nationally representative data from the German Socio-Economic Panel (SOEP) and the US Panel Study of Income Dynamics (PSID), which were made available by the Cross-National Equivalent File 1980–2008 (CNEF 1980–2008) project at the College of Human Ecology at Cornell University, Ithaca, New York.[1] The SOEP started in 1984 and contains a sample of about 29,000 German individuals, including households in the former East Germany since 1990. The PSID is similar in structure to the SOEP in the way individuals and households are followed and in the type of information that is collected. Starting in 1980, the PSID contains an unbalanced panel of about 40,000 individuals. After 1997 the PSID data are available biyearly. The surveys track socioeconomic attributes of the members of a given household, such as age, gender, marital status, educational level, labor market participation, working hours, employment status, occupational position, income situation, as well as household size and composition. Both the samples are representative of households and individuals in all years of the panel, not accounting for immigration. The income variables are measured on an annual basis and refer to the prior calendar year.

We analyze the economic and social situation of children living in the parental household and as adults in their own households. The data do not provide a sufficiently long-time horizon to observe parents and children at identical life cycle situations, but do cover a sufficiently long period to observe the socioeconomic characteristics of the parents living with their children and to link these data with the children's individual and household socioeconomic characteristics when becoming members of other family units.

We define 'parents' as adults, whose marital status is 'married', or 'living with a partner,' and who are living in households with persons indicated as 'children'. To avoid overrepresentation of children staying at home until a late age, our sample is restricted to children aged 14–20 years, co-resident with their parents in 1987–1993 (United States) or 1988–1994 (Germany). The children are at least 28 years old when we observe their economic and social status in 2002–2008 (Germany) or 2001–2007 (USA) in their own household. The US-sample includes 2,585 persons. We consider 2,128 persons out of the children's generation in the former West Germany, because the SOEP does not cover former East German households until the reunification in 1989.

We use family (household) identifiers and relationship codes to match sons and daughters to their fathers and mothers within each dataset. A major factor that will lead to changes in the quality of mobility data is that response rates tend to decline over time and so the representativeness of mobility tables derived from survey data may worsen. As the income variables highly determine survey-attrition we follow (Fitzgerald, Gottschalk, & Moffit, 1998a, 1998b) to construct a set of sample specific weights to address to the non-random sample attrition bias, which do not account for attrition in general, but for attrition among the particular groups under study, we estimate a probit equation that predicts retention in the sample (i.e., being observed as an adult) as a function of pre-determined variables measured during childhood. Presuming that the samples are representative when the children are still living at home we construct a set of weights

$$w(z,x) = \left[\frac{\Pr(A = 0\vdots z,x)}{\Pr(A = 0\vdots x)}\right]^{-1} \tag{1}$$

where x denotes the parental income as primary regressor, and z is a vector of covariates to predict attrition, indicated by $A = 1$. Thus $w(z, x)$ will take higher values for people whose characteristics z make them more likely to exit the panel before their adult income can be measured. The variables considered in z are the child's gender, the parental age and education, and their squares. We suppose these variables to affect the attrition propensities and to be endogenous to the outcome, that is, to have an effect on the children's income as adults conditional on the parental income. The weights

$w(x, z)$ are multiplied with the parental household weights, which yields a set of weights that apply to the household of the children as adults. The parental household weights are assumed to capture the attrition effects, and the weights $w(z, x)$ compensate for subsequent nonrandom attrition.

METHODOLOGY

Intergenerational Educational Mobility

To quantify the intergenerational educational mobility, we apply ordinary least squares (OLS) to the regression of the educational attainment of the children (EDUC) on the educational attainment of one of their parents (EDUC_P)

$$\text{EDUC} = \beta_0 + \beta_1 \text{EDUC}_\text{P} + \varepsilon \tag{2a}$$

The subscript (P) indicates the family background characteristics. In "two-parent" families, these are the breadwinners (in most of the families the father), and in single-parent families, these are characteristics of either the father or the mother. The educational attainment is captured with the years of education in the last year of the observation period. In the case of missing values the years of education are set equal to the amount reported in the next year.

The constant term β_0 represents the change in the educational status common to the children's generation. The slope coefficient β_1 is used as a measure of intergenerational mobility and expresses the elasticity of the children's education with respect to that of their parents. The larger the β_1, the more likely an individual as an adult will inhabit the same educational position as her parents, which implies a greater intergenerational educational persistence. The random error component ε is usually assumed to be distributed $N(0, \sigma^2)$.

We include a set of individual and family background controls (X_c) to capture the indirect effects of the parental education on the children's education

$$\text{EDUC} = \beta_0 + \beta_1 \text{EDUC}_\text{P} + \sum_{c=2}^{n} \beta_c X_c + \varepsilon \tag{2b}$$

We include gender (GEN, 1 male) to control for gender differences. To analyze whether the household size and structure interfere with equal chances of the children, we include the number of children in the parental household ($CHILD_P$) to capture the effects of higher-investment requirements. To consider the impact of the social class origin, we consider the occupational status of one of the parents (OCC_P). The specification of the occupational status is oriented at the ISCO-88 (International Standard Classification of Occupations). ISCO-88 aggregates the occupations into broadly similar categories in a hierarchical framework according to the degree of complexity of constituent tasks and skill specialization, and essentially the field of knowledge required for competent performance of these tasks. There is a distinctive ranking of the occupational dimensions: lower-numbered categories offer a higher prestige and a higher social status. This is particularly true for countries, where economic and social hierarchies are salient.[2] The analysis includes four aggregated occupational categories: "1 academic/scientific professions/managers, professionals/technicians/associate professionals", "2 trade/personal services", "3 agricultural/fishery workers, craft and related workers", and "4 plant and machine operators/assemblers, elementary occupations". The unemployment situation in the parental household (EMP_P) takes the value 1 if one of the parents was employed less than half the observation period. Finally, we consider social exclusion characteristics: the family disruption ($DISRUPT_P$ 1 if the marital status of one of the parents is "widowed", "divorced", or "separated", 0 else), the disability status ($DISABIL_P$) that takes the value 1 if one of the parents is disabled, and heath status ($HEALTH_P$) that takes the value 1 if one of the parents is in poor health. In general, the variables in (X_c) are observed in the last year of the observation period of each of the samples (Table 1).

Intergenerational Income Elasticity

The most common approach to quantify the intergenerational income mobility is to apply OLS to the regression of a logarithmic measure of the children's income variable (y) on a logarithmic measure of the income variable of the parental household (y_P)

$$y = \beta_0 + \beta_1 y_p + \varepsilon \tag{3a}$$

We use the log of the permanent real equivalent income [2001 = 100] of the parents' and the children's households. We use the post-government household income (pre-government household income plus household public transfers, plus household security pensions, deducting household total

Table 1. Descriptive Statistics.

Variables	Description	Germany		United States	
		Mean/% in 1	SD	Mean/% in 1	SD
y	ln(permanent real equivalent post-government income (2001 = 100, OECD equivalence scale, 5-year average))	9.564	.491	9.835	.930
	Permanent real equivalent post-government income (2001 = 100, OECD equivalence scale, 5-year average)	15,948.8	7,921.9	22.961.5	10,973.3
	40 pct, permanent real equivalent post-government income (2001 = 100, OECD equivalence scale, 5-year average)	12,883.0		17,057.3	
	Gini coefficient, permanent real equivalent post-government income (2001 = 100, OECD equivalence scale, 5-year average)	.2551		.4333	
y_P	ln(permanent real equivalent post-government income (2001 = 100, OECD equivalence scale, 5-year average)), parental household	9.380	.388	9.445	.659
	Permanent real equivalent post-government income (2001 = 100, OECD equivalence scale, 5-year average), parental household	12,751.2	5,111.4	13,714.6	8,985.46
	40 pct of permanent real equivalent post-government income (2001 = 100, OECD equivalence scale, 5-year average), parental household	11,022.7		11,300.1	
	Gini coefficient, permanent real equivalent post-government income (2001 = 100, OECD equivalence scale, 5-year average), parental household	.1968		.3616	
GEN	1 male, 0 female	.5202		.4887	
EDUC	Educational attainment, school years	12.442	2.916	12.807	2.030
$EDUC_P$	Educational attainment parents, average years of education	10.521	1.971	12.446	1.851

Table 1. *(Continued)*

Variables	Description	Germany		United States	
		Mean/% in 1	SD	Mean/% in 1	SD
$CHILD_P$	Number of children in the parental household	1.128	1.052	1.412	1.278
EMP_P	1 Father/mother is employed less than half the observation period, 0 else	.2093		.2830	
OCC	*Occupational categories*				
	1 "1 Academic/scientific professions/managers", 0 else	.4632		.3405	
	1 "2 Professionals/technicians/ associate professionals", 0 else	.2538		.1916	
	1 "3 Trade/personal service", 0 else	.1028		.2211	
	1 "7 Elementary occupations", 0 else	.1802		.1562	
OCC_p	*Occupational categories (father/mother)*				
	1 "1 Academic/scientific professions/managers", 0 else	.3144		.3721	
	1 "2 Professionals/technicians/ associate professionals", 0 else	.2085		.1878	
	1 "3 Trade/personal service", 0 else	.1070		.1259	
	1 "7 Elementary occupations", 0 else	.1572		.2387	
DISRUPT	Family disruption: 1 widowed, divorced, separated, 0 else	.0903		.0952	
$DISRUPT_P$	Family disruption: father/mother 1 widowed, divorced, separated, 0 else	.1775		.2669	
DISABIL	Disability status: 1 disabled, 0 else	.0862		.0712	
$DISABIL_P$	Disability status: father/mother 1 disabled, 0 else	.0519		.0809	
HEALTH	Health status: 1 poor, very poor, 0 else	.1233		.0952	
$HEALTH_P$	Health status, father/mother: 1 poor, very poor, 0 else	.1693		.1358	
N	Number of observations	2,128		2,585	

Source: CNEF 1980–2008, author's calculations.
Note: The subscripts indicate the parental household characteristics in two-parent families; the variable refers to the breadwinner (father), in single-parent households to the father or the mother.

family taxes) from the databases, thus the results make no allowance for the bias of nonresponse imputed values on income inequality and income mobility (Frick & Grabka, 2005). To consider the family structure, we adopt the "old" OECD-equivalence scale (OECD, 1982) made available in the database, which weighs the first adult in the household with 1, each other adult in the household with .7, and the children with .5.[3] The household income per adult equivalent is deflated with the national CPI (2001 = 100) to reflect constant prices. To exclude transitory income shocks and cross-section measurement errors, we use moving averages of the income variable.

The constant term β_0 represents the change in the income status common to the children's generation. The larger the elasticity of the children's income with respect to their parents (β_1) the more likely an individual as an adult will inhabit the same income position as their parents. The random error component ε is usually assumed to be distributed $N(0, \sigma^2)$. The inclusion of a set of individual and family background controls (X_c) into Eq. (3a) allows us to account for the indirect effects of the parental income on the children's income position. To the extent that these variables lower the coefficient β_1 compared to (3a) these other effects "account for" the raw intergenerational income elasticity

$$y = \beta_0 + \beta_1 y_p + \sum_{c=2}^{n} \beta_c X_c + \varepsilon \tag{3b}$$

We control for gender differences (GEN), the individual and parental educational attainment (EDUC, EDUC_p), the number of children (CHILD) living in the household to consider the effects of care requirements, the unemployment situation in the parental household (EMP_P), and the social status of the individual and one of their parents (OCC, OCC_p), which is captured by four aggregate occupational categories. Additionally, we consider social exclusion variables in the own and the parental household that are known to have adverse effects on one's life: family disruption (DISRUPT, DISRUPT_p), disability (DISABIL, DISABIL_p), and poor health status (HEALTH, HEALTH_p) (Table 1).

Intergenerational Income and Educational Transitions

The intergenerational educational and income elasticities measure the average social and economic mobility. To evaluate the probability of the intergenerational movement from one educational or income position to another, which are the key issues from a welfare point of view (Heckman, 1981), we employ transition matrices. The elements $p_{ij} \geq 0$ of the transition matrix indicate the probability (in percent) that a person belongs to the *j*th position of the distribution given that they belong to the *i*th position of the distribution of the variable in the parental household with $\sum_j p_{ij} = \sum_i p_{ij} = 1$ (Formby, Smith, & Zheng, 2004). The elements on the diagonal (p_{ii}) represent the stayers and the off-diagonal term (p_{ij}) represents the movers concerning the intergenerational position. The degree of immobility at the top and at the bottom of the distribution might be exaggerated, for upward mobility is not possible for those performing the highest category and downward mobility is not possible for persons in the lowest category.

To evaluate the intergenerational educational mobility, we cluster the EDUC and the parents into three educational groups: group 1 "less than high school (7–10 years of education)", group 2 "high school level (11–13 years of education)", and group 3 "more than high school (14–18 years of education). To evaluate the intergenerational income mobility, the logarithms of the permanent real equivalent household income [2001 = 100] of the parents and the children are allocated to five equally populated ranked income groups indexed by *i* and *j*. The more independent the educational or income positions of both, the children and the parents, the greater the likelihood that the elements of the transition matrix are close to .33 for education and .2 for income.

To quantify the dimension of the intergenerational mobility, we employ the Bartholomew index (Bartholemew, 1982; Dearden, Machin, & Reed, 1997), which expresses the mobility in terms of average income boundaries crossed over the observation period. The Bartholemew index sums up the moves across the income classes, that is, outside the main diagonal

$$B = \frac{1}{m}\sum_{i=1}^{m}\sum_{j=1}^{m} p_{ij}\left|i - j\right| \tag{4a}$$

where p_{ij} is the proportion of children in income class *j* having parents in the educational or income group *i*. The farther the distance between the children's and the parents' positions, the greater the weight assigned to it. In the case of no mobility, the Bartholomew index takes the value zero. The more the mobility, the higher the value of the index. The value of the Bartholemew index depends on the order of the transition matrix. The values of the index based on a matrix of five groups will be different from those based on a matrix consisting of 10 groups. Hence, this index will not be comparable across countries based on transition matrices of different orders (Björklund & Jäntti, 2000).

The Relative Risk of Poverty

To evaluate the impact of individual and household characteristics on the probability to have an income position at the bottom of the income distribution, we employ a binomial logit model (Heckman, 1981; Maddala, 1983; McFadden, 1973). The dependent variable (pov) takes the value 1 if a person is positioned in the first or the second income quintile of the real (2001 = 100) equivalent post-government household income distribution. The probability that the individual is potentially socially excluded then is estimated to be

$$P(\text{pov} = 1) = \frac{e^Z}{1 + e^Z} \tag{4b}$$

The Z characterizes the linear combination $Z = B_0 + \sum_{c=2}^{n} B_c X_c$ with X_c the independent variable and B_c the regression coefficients. In general, if the probability is less than .5, we predict that the individual is better off. The interpretation of the regression coefficient B_c is based on the odds, that is, the ratio of the probability that the person is in a poverty situation and the probability that the household is well off.

$$\frac{P(\text{pov} = 1)}{P(\text{pov} = 0)} = e^{B_0 + \sum_{c=2}^{n} B_c X_c} \tag{5}$$

The $\exp(B_c)$ values express the relative risk ratio of poverty or social exclusion with a one-unit change in the cth independent variable. The variables in (X_c) contain a set of individual and family background resources as well as a set of social exclusion attributes that are expected to affect the relative poverty risk (Table 1).

EMPIRICAL RESULTS

Intergenerational Educational Mobility

In Germany the intergenerational educational elasticity amounts at .720 and is significantly higher than in the United States (.455). In both the countries, the individual and family background characteristics and social exclusion attributes lower the raw intergenerational educational elasticity by about 13 percentage points. The significantly positive impact of the parental income on the educational mobility corroborates human capital theory that high-income parents are able to invest in the human capital accumulation of their children. The size and income situation of the parental household as well as the father's engagement in professional occupations significantly positively affect the intergenerational educational mobility. The results reveal significant gender effects only in the United States, whereas the father's poor health status exerts a significant effect on the intergenerational educational mobility only in Germany (Table 2).

Table 2. Intergenerational Educational Elasticity.

		Germany		USA	
	Constant	3.573**	1.168	7.075***	4.156***
$EDUC_P$	Years of education, father	.720***	.588***	.455***	.325***
y_P	Post-government income, parental household		.399*		.409**
GEN	Gender, child 1 male		−.137		−.415***
$CHILD_P$	Number of children, parental household		−.561*		−.167**
OCC_P	Occupational status, father				
	1 Academic/scientific/ managers		.489		.386
	1 Professional		.399**		.362*
	1 Trade/personal service		.335		.197
	1 Elementary occupation		−.042		−.145
EMP_P	Employment status, father 1 Unemployed, 0 else		−.0801		.007
$DISRUPT_P$	Family disruption, parents 1 Family disruption, 0 else		−.162		.329
$DISABIL_P$	Disability status, parents 1 Disabled, 0 else		.278		.443
$HEALTH_P$	Health status, parents 1 Poor, very poor, 0 Excellent, good, fair		−.177**		−.109
	N	503	343	1,018	536
	R^2adj	.1091	.136	.254	.310
	RMSE	.3362	.3499	.6958	.4155
	LL	−1,450.6	−984.33	−981.16	−940.22
	Mean VIF	1.26		1.39	

Source: CNEF 1980–2008, author's calculations. *$p<.05$; **$p<.01$; ***$p<.001$.

Intergenerational Income Elasticity

The results of the regression of the real equivalent post-government household income of the children's generation on the real equivalent post-government household income of the parents' generation (Eq. (3a)) corroborates the findings of various studies reporting a range of intergenerational income elasticity of .4 or even higher according to the chosen countries, sample designs, time windows, age cohorts, or income variables (Becker & Tomes, 1986; Eberharter, 2002, 2003, 2005, 2007, 2008, 2009a, 2009b, 2011; Mayer & Lopoo, 2005, 2008; Solon, 1992, 1999, 2002, 2004).

In the United States (.678) the intergenerational income elasticity is significantly higher than in Germany (.483). The countries differ concerning the impact of the family background characteristics and social exclusion features on the intergenerational elasticity. In Germany these variables account for 10.9 percentage points of the intergenerational elasticity compared to 27.9 percentage points in the United States. Being female and a higher number of children significantly entail higher intergenerational income persistence. Educational attainment significantly increases the household's financial well-being, which corroborates the human capital hypothesis. In Germany, the father's educational attainment has a significantly positive effect on the children's income situation. Social origin also matters: the German father's academic occupation has a significantly positive effect on the household's income situation, whereas in the United States the results reveal no significant effect. The effects of social exclusion features on intergenerational income mobility are country specific: In both the countries family disruption in the *children's* household has a significantly negative impact on the disposable income, the influence of a family break-down in the *parental* household is not significant. The German father's disability has a significantly negative effect on the disposable household income; in the United States this effect is not significant (Table 3).

Intergenerational Income and Educational Transitions

The Bartholemew index indicates a significantly higher intergenerational educational mobility in Germany (.3475) than in the United States (.3008). German children experience a higher probability of reaching a higher educational attainment than their parents. The intergenerational educational persistence in the lowest educational category amounts 36.1% compared to

Table 3. Intergenerational Income Elasticity.

		Germany		USA	
	Constant	5.002***	6.192***	3.346***	5.709***
y_P	Post-government income, parental household	.483***	.376***	.678***	.399***
EDUC	Years of education, child		.018***		.076***
$EDUC_P$	Years of education, father		.032*		.008
GEN	Gender, child 1 male		–.123**		–.102*
CHILD	Number of children, children's household		–.161***		–.211***
OCC_P	Occupational status, parents				
	1 Academic/scientific/ managers		.144*		.023
	1 Professional		.096		.043
	1 Trade/personal service		–.016		.056
	1 Elementary occupation		–.115		–.061
EMP_P	Employment status, parents 1 Unemployed, 0 else		–.031		–.034
DISRUPT	Family disruption, children 1 Family disruption, 0 else		–.155**		–.358***
$DISRUPT_P$	Family disruption, parents 1 Family disruption, 0 else		.085		–.161*
$DISABIL_P$	Disability status, parents 1 Disabled, 0 else		–.222*		–.019
HEALTH	Health status, children 1 Poor, very poor, 0 Excellent, good, fair		–.043		–.334**
$HEALTH_P$	Health status, parents 1 Poor, very poor, 0 Excellent, good, fair;		.123		–233
	N	919	341	1,079	698
	R^2adj	.1299	.3935	.229	.362
	RMSE	.4576	.3384	.815	.652
	LL	–584.54	–105.63	–1,309.68	–683.68
	Mean VIF	1.24		1.32	

Source: CNEF 1980–2008, author's calculations. $^{*}p<.05$; $^{**}p<.01$; $^{***}p<.001$.

43.8% in the United States. In the United States, the intergenerational educational persistence is highest in the "high school" educational category (78.2%), whereas the highest intergenerational educational matching in Germany is evident in the "more than high school" category (86%). These results corroborate the findings of Lentz & Laband (1989) (Table 4a).

Table 4. Intergenerational Educational and Income Dynamics.

(a) Intergenerational Educational Dynamics[a]

Education	Children		
Parents	< High school	= High school	> High school
Germany < high school	.3611	.5000	.1389
USA < high school	.4381	.4762	.0857
Germany = high school	.1250	.5478	.3272
USA = high school	.0316	.7816	.1867
Germany > high school	.0200	.1200	.8600
USA > high school	.0076	.3220	.6705

	Pearson Chi^2(4)	Pr	Total immobility (%)	*B*-index
Germany	111.56	.000	52.36	.3475
USA	466.98	.000	71.63	.3008

(b) Intergenerational Income Dynamics[b]

Income Quintiles	Children				
Parents	1	2	3	4	5
Germany 1	.4397	.1986	.1560	.1206	.0851
USA 1	.3756	.3032	.1403	.1267	.0543
Germany 2	.3273	.2545	.1758	.1212	.1212
USA 2	.2081	.2308	.2353	.1674	.1584
Germany 3	.1309	.3037	.2147	.1728	.1780
USA 3	.1131	.2308	.1900	.2398	.2262
Germany 4	.1520	.1324	.2353	.2598	.2298
USA 4	.0888	.1075	.2009	.3364	.2664
Germany 5	.0550	.1330	.2018	.2798	.3303
USA 5	.0248	.1040	.1485	.2624	.4604

	Pearson Chi^2(16)	Pr	Total immobility (%)	*B*-index
Germany	163.99	.000	29.48	1.1486
USA	245.91	.000	32.63	1.1205

[a]*Source*: CNEF 1980–2008, author's calculations.
[b]*Source*: CNEF 1980–2008, author's calculations.

The Bartholomew indices indicate no significant country differences concerning intergenerational income mobility. The transition matrices show country differences in the tails of the income distribution, which counterbalance the Bartholomew indices. In Germany the bottom income quintile is significantly less mobile than in the United States, whereas the intergenerational mobility of the top income quintiles is significantly lower than in United States. The results might reflect higher redistributional effects in Germany, and corroborate the hypothesis that social policy succeeds to contribute to a higher permeability of the social system (Table 4b).

The Relative Poverty Risk

Table 5 presents the relative risk ratios ($\exp(B_c)$) and the significance level for each of the explanatory variables X_c of the binomial logit model to quantify the probability to be poor. In both the countries, being female and a higher number of children significantly increase the relative risk of poverty, and

Table 5. Relative Poverty Risk Ratios.

	Germany	USA
GEN 1 male 0 female	1.757*	2.143**
EDUC	.947	.723***
CHILD	2.633***	1.810***
$EDUC_P$	.679***	.787**
OCC_P		
1 "Academic/scientific/managers", 0 else	1.275*	1.780
1 "Professionals", 0 else	1.624	1.323
1 "Trade/personal service", 0 else	.831	.789*
1 "Elementary occupations", 0 else	.494*	.995
EMP_P 1 unemployed, 0 else	.287**	.658
$DISRUPT_P$ 1 family disruption	.353	.784
DISRUPT 1 family disruption	.482	.451**
HEALTH 1 poor, very poor; 0 excellent, good, fair	.429	.771
$HEALTH_P$ 1 poor, very poor, 0 excellent, good, fair	.381*	.243
L	−142.089	−247.719
χ^2	112.83	123.57
Pseudo-R^2	.2842	.1996
N	340	565

Source: CNEF 1980–2008, author's calculations.
Indicates significance at the 5% level in a two-tailed test ($p<.05$; ** $p<.01$; ***$p<.001$).

well-educated parents lower the relative risk of poverty. In the United States, a higher educational attainment significantly lowers the relative poverty risk. Social class origin matters: in Germany to have parents engaged in academic/scientific/manager occupations results in a significantly lower risk of poverty, whereas persons with parents in elementary occupations are confronted with a significant higher poverty risk. In the United States, children with parents in trade/personal service professions are confronted with a higher relative risk of poverty. Social exclusion works differently: in Germany, an unemployment situation in the parental household and parents in poor health significantly increase the relative risk of poverty in adulthood, and in the United States these effects are not significant. Family disruption significantly increases the relative poverty risk in the United States, whereas this effect is not significant in Germany.

CONCLUSIONS

We started from the hypotheses that family background characteristics and social exclusion features work differently on the intergenerational income and educational mobility, and the relative risk of poverty. The empirical evidence partly supports these hypotheses.

The intergenerational educational elasticity is significantly higher in the United States, contradicting the hypothesis of a mobile society. In both the countries family background characteristics and social exclusion features contribute about 13 percentage points to the intergenerational educational elasticity. Parental income, the number of children in the parental household, and the parental occupational status significantly influence the intergenerational transmission of educational level.

The Gini coefficient indicates significantly higher income variability in the United States. The negative correlation between income inequality and income mobility suggests a higher intergenerational mobility of economic status in Germany. In fact, the results show significant higher intergenerational income elasticity in the United States. The results report country differences concerning the impact of family background characteristics and social exclusion features on intergenerational income mobility. In Germany, these variables lower the raw intergenerational income elasticity by 10.7 percentage points, whereas the contribution of family background variables and social exclusion features to the intergenerational income mobility amounts at 27.9 percentage points. Gender, educational attainment, and the number of children significantly affect intergenerational income mobility and the relative poverty risk. The ambiguous effects of social exclusion attributes on the intergenerational income mobility and the relative poverty risk might partly be traced back to the country differences in the welfare state regimes.

The transition matrices reveal structural differences in the countries' mobility patterns. The Bartholomew index indicates an intergenerational educational persistence of 71.6% in the United States, compared with 52.4% in Germany. In both the countries intergenerational educational improvement is easier to realize for children growing up in financial well-off households. In Germany, the higher intergenerational educational mobility in the 'less than high school' category may be attributed to the publicly financed educational system that allows a higher social permeability.

The highest intergenerational income persistence is evident in the tails of the income distribution. The findings corroborate the results of Corcoran (2001), and supports the 'rags-to-rags' and 'riches-to-riches' picture. The income transition matrices show significant country differences in the mobility structure, which counterbalance the Bartholomew indices: in Germany low-income positions are significantly less mobile than in the United States, whereas in the United States the top income positions are significant less mobile than in Germany.

NOTES

1. For a detailed description of the databases, see Burkhauser, Butrica, Daly, and Lillard (2001).
2. We rearrange the two-digit occupational categories provided by the database into seven categories: "1 academic/scientific professions/managers", "2 professionals/technicians/associate professionals", "3 trade/personal services", "4 agricultural/fishery workers", "5 craft and related workers", "6 plant and machine operators/assemblers", and "7 elementary occupations".
3. The introduction of the modified OECD-equivalence scale (Hagenaars, de Vos, & Zaidi, 1994) weighting the first adult in the household with one, each other adult with 0.5, and the children with 0.3 does not change the sign and the significance level of the coefficients.

ACKNOWLEDGMENTS

The author is grateful to John Bishop and an anonymous referee for their valuable comments and suggestions to clarify the exposition. The shortcomings and errors remain the author's as usual.

REFERENCES

Arts, W., & Gelissen, J. (2002). Three worlds of welfare capitalism or more? A state-of-the-art report. *Journal of European Social Policy, 12*, 137–158.

Bartholemew, D. J. (1982). *Stochastic models for social processes* (3rd ed.). Chichester: Wiley.

Becker, G. S. (1964). *Human capital*. New York, NY: National Bureau of Economic Research.

Becker, G. S., & Tomes, N. (1986). Child endowments and the quantity and quality of children. *Journal of Political Economy, 84*, S143–S1162.

Björklund, A., & Jäntti, M. (2000). Intergenerational mobility of socio-economic status in comparative perspective. *Nordic Journal of Political Economy, 26*, 3–33.

Blanden, J., & Gregg, P. (2004). Family income and educational attainment: A review of approaches and evidence for Britain. *Oxford Review of Economic Policy, 20*, 245–263.

Blanden, J. P., Gregg, P., & Machin, S. (2005). Educational inequality and intergenerational mobility. In S. Machin & A. Vignoles (Eds.), *What's the good of education? The economics of education in the United Kingdom* (pp. 99–114). Princeton, NJ: Princeton University Press.

Bonoli, G. (1997). Classifying welfare states: A two-dimension approach. *Journal of Social Policy, 26*(3), 351–372.

Bourguignon, F., & Chakravarty, S. (2003). The measurement of multidimensional poverty. *Journal of Economic Inequality, 1*, 25–49.

Breen, R., & Jonsson, J. (2007). Explaining change in social fluidity: Educational equalization and educational expansion in twentieth century Sweden. *American Journal of Sociology, 112*, 1775–1810.

Breen, R., Luijkx, R., Müller, W., & Pollak, R. (2009). Non-persistent inequality in educational attainment: Evidence from eight European countries. *American Journal of Sociology, 114*, 1475–1521.

Burchard, T., Le Grand, J., & Piachaud, D. (2002). Social exclusion in Britain 1991–1995. *Social Policy and Administration, 33*(3), 227–244.

Burkhauser, R. V., Butrica, B. A., Daly, M. C., & Lillard, D. R. (2001). The cross-national equivalent file: A product of cross-national research. In I. Becker, N. Ott & G. Rolf (Eds.), *Soziale Sicherung in einer dynamischen Gesellschaft* (pp. 354–376). Frankfurt.

Cameron, S. V., & Heckman, J. J. (1998). Life cycle schooling and dynamic selection bias: Models and evidence for five cohorts of American males. *Journal of Political Economy, 106*, 262–333.

Cameron, S. V., & Heckman, J. J. (2001). The dynamics of educational attainment for black, hispanic and white males. *The Journal of Political Economy, 109*, 455–499.

Carneiro, P., & Heckman, J. J. (2002). The evidence on credit constraints in post-secondary schooling. *Economic Journal, 112*, 989–1018.

Chadwick, L., & Solon, G. (2002). Intergenerational income mobility among daughters. *American Economic Review, 92*(1), 335–344.

Corcoran, M. (2001). Mobility, persistence, and the consequences of poverty for children: Child and adult outcomes. In S. Danziger & R. Haveman (Eds.), *Understanding poverty*. Harvard.

Couch, K. A., & Dunn, T. A. (1997). Intergenerational correlation in labour market status, a comparison of the United States and Germany. *Journal of Human Resources, 32*(4), 210–232.

Couch, K. A., & Lillard, D. R. (2004). Non-linear patterns in Germany and the United States. In M. Corak (Ed.), *Generational income mobility in North America and Europe* (pp. 190–206). Cambridge: Cambridge University Press.
D'Addio, A. C. (2007). Intergenerational transmission of disadvantage: Mobility or immobility across generations? OECD Social, Employment and Migration Working Papers No. 52, OECD Publishing, Paris.
Dearden, L., Machin, S., & Reed, H. (1997). Intergenerational mobility in Britain. *Economic Journal, 107*, 46–66.
Duffy, K. (1995). *Social exclusion and human dignity in Europe*. Strasbourg: Council of Europe.
Dustmann, C. (2004). Parental background, secondary school, track choice, and wages. *Oxford Economic Papers, 56*, 209–230.
Eberharter, V. V. (2002). Poverty inequality and poverty mobility in Germany in the 1990s. *Journal of Income Distribution, 10*(1–2), 13–25.
Eberharter, V. V. (2003). Structural features of female employment status and earnings mobility. The experience in Germany. *Review of Social Economy, 61*(4), 511–533.
Eberharter, V. V. (2005). Low income: Inequality and mobility patterns in the 1990s. Empirical evidence from the United States and Germany. *Journal of Economic and Social Research, 4*(2), 53–70.
Eberharter, V. V. (2007). Traditional Role patterns, family background, and intergenerational income mobility – Germany and the United States compared. *Journal of Applied Social Science Studies, 127*, 1. Special Issue: Proceedings of the 7th International Socio-Economic Panel User Conference (SOEP2006) (pp. 7–20).
Eberharter, V. V. (2008). Intergenerational income inequality, and dynastic poverty persistence-Germany and the United States compared. In J. Bishop & B. Zheng (Eds.), *Research on Economic Inequality, 16*, 157–175.
Eberharter, V. V. (2009a). Redistribution, intergenerational inequality, and poverty transmission – Germany and the United States compared. In J. B. Davis (Ed.), *Global social economy. Development, work and policy* (pp. 164–181). London: Routledge, Taylor & Francis.
Eberharter, V. V. (2009b). Labor supply decisions, occupational segregation, and intergenerational income mobility-Germany and the United States compared. *Journal of Income Distribution, 18*(3 4), 93–109. Special Issue "Income Distribution and the Family".
Eberharter, V. V. (2011). The intergenerational transmission of economic disadvantages and social exclusion – constraints on social mobility. *Journal of Applied Social Science Studies, 131*, 2. Special Issue: Proceedings of the 9th International Socio-Economic Panel User Conference (SOEP2010) (pp. 287–299).
Esping-Andersen, G. (1990). *The three worlds of welfare capitalism*. Cambridge: Polity Press.
Esping-Andersen, G. (1994). Welfare states and the economy. In N. J. Smelser & R. Swedberg (Eds.), *The handbook of economic sociology* (pp. 711–732). Cambridge: Polity Press.
Esping-Andersen, G. (1999). *Social foundations of postindustrial economies*. Oxford: Oxford University Press.
Esping-Andersen, G. (2004). Untying the Gordian knot of social inheritance. *Research in Social Stratification and Mobility, 21*, 115–138.
Finnie, R., & Sweetman, A. (2003). Poverty dynamics: Empirical evidence for Canada. *Canadian Journal of Economics, 36*, 291–325.

Fitzgerald, J., Gottschalk, P., & Moffit, R. (1998a). An analysis of the impact of sample attrition in panel data: The Michigan panel study of income dynamics. *Journal of Human Resources*, *33*, 251–299.
Fitzgerald, J., Gottschalk, P., & Moffit, R. (1998b). An analysis of the impact of sample attrition in panel data: The Michigan panel study of income dynamics. *Journal of Human Resources*, *33*, 300–344.
Formby, J. P., Smith, W. J., & Zheng, B. (2004). Mobility measurement, transition matrices and statistical inference. *Journal of Econometrics*, *120*, 181–205.
Frick, J. R., & Grabka, M. M. (2005). Item-non-response on income questions in panel surveys: Incidence, imputation and the impact on inequality and mobility. *Allgemeines Statistisches Archiv*, *89*, 49–61.
Grawe, N. D. (2004). Reconsidering the use of nonlinearities in intergenerational earnings mobility as a test for credit constraints. *Journal of Human Resources*, *39*, 813–827.
Hagenaars, A., de Vos, K., & Zaidi, M. A. (1994). *Poverty Statistics in the Late 1980s: Research Based on Micro-data*. Luxembourg: Office for Official Publications of the European Communities.
Haveman, R., & Wolfe, B. (1995). The determinants of children's attainments: A review of methods and findings. *Journal of Economic Literature*, *33*, 1829–1878.
Heckman, J. J. (1981). Statistical models for discrete panel data. In C. F. Manski & D. McFadden (Eds.), *Structural analysis of discrete data with econometric applications* (pp. 114–178). Cambridge: MIT Press.
Hertz, T. (2005). Rags, riches and race: The intergenerational economic mobility of black and white families in the United States. In S. Bowles, H. Gintis & M. Osborne (Eds.), *Unequal chances: Family background and economic success* (pp. 165–191). Princeton, NJ: Princeton University Press.
Hertz, T., Jayasundera, T., Piraino, P., Selcuk, S., Smith, N., & Verashchagina, A. (2008). The inheritance of educational inequality: International comparisons and fifty-year trends. *Advances in Economic Analysis & Policy*, *7*(2), Article 10. Berkeley Electronic Press.
Howarth, C., Kenway, P., Palmer, G., & Street, C. (1998). *Monitoring poverty and social exclusion: Labour's inheritance*. York: New Policy Institute, Joseph Rowntree Foundation.
Lentz, B. F., & Laband, D. N. (1989). Why so many children of doctors become doctors: Nepotism vs. human capital transfers. *Journal of Human Resources*, *24*, 396–413.
Maddala, G. S. (1983). *Limited-Dependent and qualitative variables in econometrics*. Cambridge: Cambridge University Press.
Marlier, E., & Atkinson, A. B. (2010). Indicators of poverty and social exclusion in a global context. *Journal of policy analysis and management*, *29*, 285–304.
Mayer, L. M., & Lopoo, S. E. (2005). Has the intergenerational transmission of economic status changed? *The Journal of Human Resources*, *40*(1), 169–185.
Mayer, S. E., & Lopoo, L. M. (2008). Government spending and intergenerational mobility. *Journal of Public Economics*, *92*(1–2), 139–158.
McFadden, D. (1973). Conditional logit analysis of qualitative choice behavior. In P. Zarembka (Ed.), *Frontiers of econometrics* (pp. 105–142). New York, NY: Academic Press.
Mincer, J. (1974). *Schooling, experience and earnings*. New York, NY: NBER.
Mulligan, C. B. (1999). Galton vs the human capital approach to inheritance. *Journal of Political Economy*, *107*, 184–224.
OECD. (1982). *The OECD list of social indicators*. Paris: OECD Publishing.

OECD. (2008). *Growing unequal? Income Distribution and Poverty in OECD Countries.* Paris: OECD Publishing.

Pencavel, J. (1998). Assortative mating by schooling and the work behavior of wives and husbands. *American Economic Review, 88*(2), 326–329.

Saunders, P. (2008). Measuring wellbeing using non-monetary indicators: Deprivation and social exclusion. *Family Matters, 78*, 8–17.

Saunders, P., Naidoo, Y., & Griffiths, M. (2007). *Towards new indicators of disadvantage: Deprivation and social exclusion in Australia.* Sydney: Social Policy Research Centre.

Sen, A. K. (1985). *Commodities and capabilities.* Amsterdam: North-Holland.

Sen, A. K. (1992). *Inequality re-examined.* Oxford: Clarendon Press.

Shavit, Y. A., Gamoran, R., & Menahem, A. G. (2007). *Stratification in higher education: A comparative study.* Stanford: Stanford University Press.

Siaroff, A. (1994). Work, welfare and gender equality: A new typology. In D. Sainsbury (Ed.), *Gendering welfare states* (pp. 82–100). London: Sage.

Social Exclusion Unit (SEU). (1997). *Social exclusion unit: Purpose, work priorities and working methods.* London: Cabinet Office.

Solon, G. (1992). Intergenerational income mobility in the United States. *American Economic Review, 82*(3), 326–329.

Solon, G. (1999). Intergenerational mobility in the labor market. In O. Ashenfelter & D. Card (Eds.), *Handbook of labor economics* (Vol. 3, pp. 1761–1800). Amsterdam: North Holland

Solon, G. (2002). Cross-country differences in intergenerational earnings mobility. *Journal of Economic Perspectives, 16*, 59–66.

Solon, G. (2004). A model of intergenerational mobility variation over time and place. In M. Corak (Ed.), *Generational income mobility in North America and Europe* (pp. 38–47). Cambridge: Cambridge University Press.

Stevens, A. H. (1999). Climbing out of poverty. Falling back in: Measuring the persistence of poverty over multiple spells. *Journal of Human Resources, 34*, 557–588.

Townsend, P. (1979). *Poverty in the United Kingdom.* Harmondsworth: Penguin.

United Nations. (1995). *The Copenhagen declaration and programme of action: World summit for social development*, March 6–12, UN Department of Publications, New York, NY.

Walker, A., & Walker, C. (Eds.). (1997). *Britain divided: The growth of social exclusion in the 1980s and 1990s.* London: CPAG.

CHAPTER 12

VARIABLE EQUIVALENCE SCALES AND TRENDS IN GERMAN INCOME INEQUALITY

Jürgen Faik

ABSTRACT

This paper examines the impact on German personal income distribution of income-dependent (variable) equivalence scales. The use of variable equivalence scales causes distinctive increases in income inequality compared with income-independent, constant equivalence scales. The narrowing of income limits between the upper and lower income regions also leads to an increase in income inequality.

INTRODUCTION

In order to compare incomes for different household types, household net incomes must be divided by "normalizing" values called equivalence scales. The resulting variable is equivalent household net income. Thus, an equivalence scale is used as a "well-being deflator" by dividing, for example, household incomes by such scale values.

Equivalence scales capture different needs (e.g., between children and adults) as well as economies of scale which are the result of household

Inequality, Mobility and Segregation: Essays in Honor of Jacques Silber
Research on Economic Inequality, Volume 20, 311–336

ISSN: 1049-2585/doi:10.1108/S1049-2585(2012)0000020015

members' joint household "consumption activities" (e.g., concerning accommodation costs). The impact on personal income distribution of different equivalence scales with different levels of economies of scale depends on two opposing effects: Assuming a positive correlation between household size and household income, decreasing economies of scale result in a levelling of equivalent household incomes, and measured inequality decreases ("concentration effect"). On the other hand, decreasing economies of scale, producing reductions of larger households' equivalent incomes, may generate changes in equivalent incomes' rankings between the different household types (sizes), and this may cause an increase in the measured inequality at some point ("re-ranking effect").[1,2]

Typically, studies of personal income distribution refer to equivalence scales which hold for the entire income spectrum; these scales are called constant equivalence scales and are based on the assumption that equivalence scales and therefore the needs of different household types are independent of a base level of income or utility (see, e.g., Lewbel, 1989). They contrast to income-dependent, variable equivalence scales which vary with the income level of the different households. There are good reasons for basing distributional analyses on such flexible equivalence scales (e.g., see Koulovatianos, Schröder, & Schmidt, 2005, p. 969; Schröder, 2004, p. 42):

1. In the higher income ranges the underlying consumption levels (e.g., concerning accommodation costs) would be high so that a new household member's appearance (e.g., the "adding" of a child) would increase the corresponding costs only slightly, and this would lead to low *relative* costs, that is, flat equivalence scales for larger households in the upper income range compared with the lower incomes.
2. Prices of commodities can differ from each other across income groups such that members of the upper income classes obtain price advantages.
3. Credit constraints for households in the bottom income range may shift the consumption bundles of these households toward lower expenditure shares of durables which are connected with relatively high economies of scale.

The paper is organized as follows. After discussing the concept of variable equivalence scales theoretically, calculations of such scales for Germany, found in literature, are presented. On this basis, present author's own empirical sensitivity findings for German personal income distribution 1991/1992–2009/2010 are considered.

MICROECONOMIC SPECIFICATIONS OF VARIABLE EQUIVALENCE SCALES

In the context of utility-based, microeconomic estimations of equivalence scales, two methods for functionalizing an equivalence scale by different reference income levels exist: the Barten ("Scaling") and the Translating approach.[3]

In Barten's (1964) approach it is assumed that higher commodity-specific scale values m_j represent higher household needs for the corresponding commodity compared with the reference household type. Thus, the normalized commodity-specific quantities q_j/m_j ($j = 1, 2, \ldots, n$) in the direct utility function have the same amount for the different household types:

$$U = U\left[\frac{q_1}{m_1}, \frac{q_2}{m_2}, \ldots, \frac{q_n}{m_n}\right] \tag{1}$$

The socio-demographic standardizations of the Translating approach result from subtractions of socio-demographically functionalized quantity elements l_j from the overall consumption quantities q_j ($j = 1, 2, \ldots, n$):

$$U = U[q_1 - l_1, q_2 - l_2, \ldots, q_n - l_n] \tag{2}$$

Unlike Barten's approach, the Translating approach can describe a situation in which the reference household does not buy a special commodity in contrast to other households (see Bradbury, 1992, pp. 15–16).

Fig. 1 illustrates, in a general way, the concept of variable equivalence scales which implies a degressive indirect utility function concerning marginal utility rates. In this example, the reference household type R is a smaller household than the other household type h. Thus, at a given utility level the larger household needs more income Y to satisfy needs of additional household members. It is shown that a higher reference income level ($Y_2^{(R)} > Y_1^{(R)}$) implies shrinking equivalence scale values ($Y_2^{(h)}/Y_2^{(R)} < Y_1^{(h)}/Y_1^{(R)}$) which simply is the meaning of variable equivalence scales.[4]

VARIABLE EQUIVALENCE SCALES IN DISTRIBUTIONAL ANALYSES

The incorporation of variable equivalence scales into distributional studies is accompanied by the initial problem of separating the upper and lower ranges of equivalent incomes. In order to do this, a specific equivalence

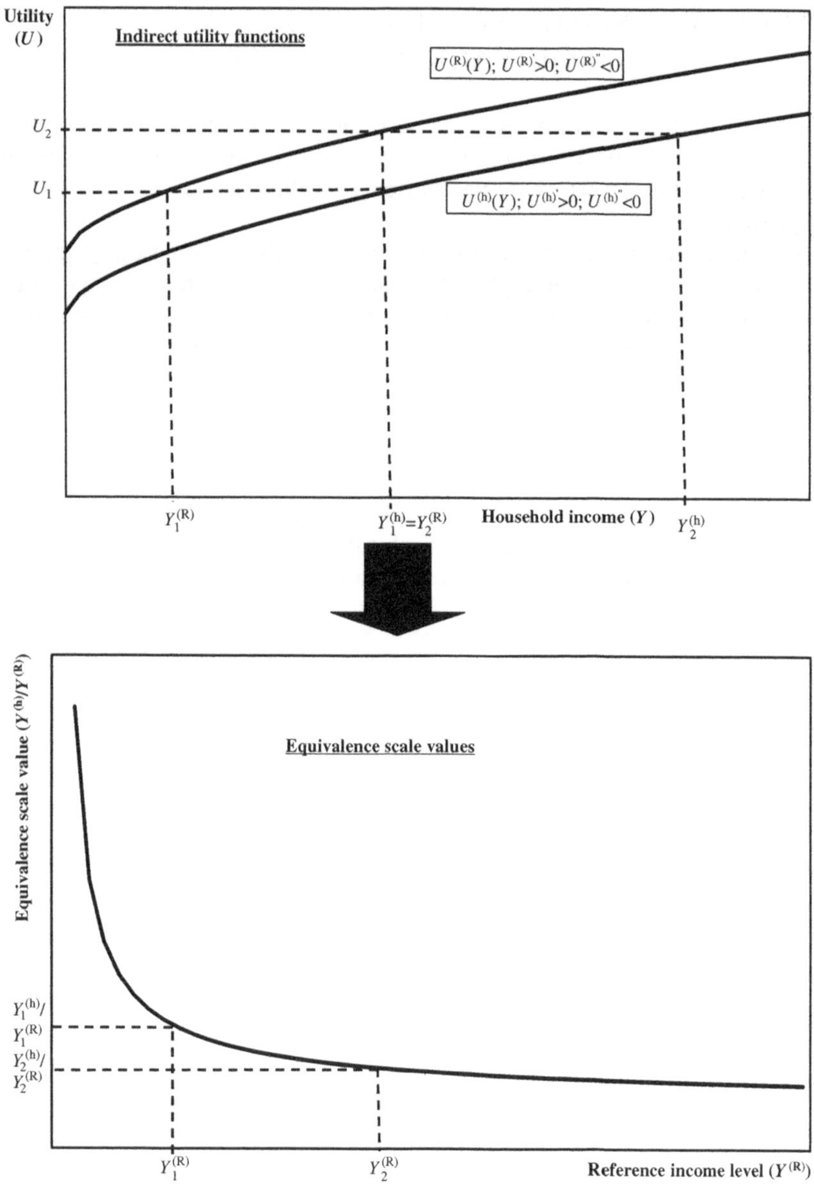

Fig. 1. Microeconomic Foundation of Variable Equivalence Scales.

scale for the whole income range may be assumed as a starting point which would be a normative decision (see Faik, 1995, pp. 286–287).

This normative (identification) problem can be circumvented by a "decomposition approach". Let us assume two or more income regions and that these income regions will be *separately* generated for each household type so that – because of homogeneity of each group – no *overall* equivalence scale must be specified a priori. The latter means an orientation of welfare levels only on the behavior of one's *own* group of households. This assumption follows from sociopsychological approaches like Festinger's theory of social comparisons (see Festinger, 1954). A number of empirical sociopsychological findings point in this direction (see, e.g., Clark & Oswald, 1996, or Frey & Stutzer, 2002, pp. 88–90; contrary: Koulovatianos et al., 2010).

Since such welfare comparisons refer to *household* incomes and since households are (very) different with respect to size and composition, it seems to be a Herculean task for each individual to consider all these aspects in the context of his/her well-being rankings. It is much easier for individuals to compare themselves with household types which are similar to their own type. This implies a kind of bounded rationality (see, e.g., Simon, 1957, or Leibenstein, 1976) since people do not have (or do not want to have) complete information on society's entire income situation.

According to the idea of variable equivalence scales, the scale values in the lowest income region are highest, and those in the upper income region are lowest, that is: The income values in the lowest income region are divided by higher scale values than the incomes in higher income regions. This is sketched in Fig. 2 for three income regions (low-, middle- and high-income region).

If variable equivalence scales with lower values are used for the upper income region, the differences of the equivalent incomes between the bottom and the upper income classes become larger than they would be without using variable equivalence scales. Thus, the measured inequality would increase. In this sense, Fig. 3 compares the application of variable equivalence scales with the alternative method which uses income-independent, constant equivalence scales. For illustrative purposes, both figures are characterized by only two income regions, a bottom and an upper region.

In the upper part of Fig. 3 the overall equivalence scale in the income-independent case is set to the same level as in the upper income region in case with variable equivalence scales. This congruence leads to more inequality because of a more right-skewed income distribution in the latter variant

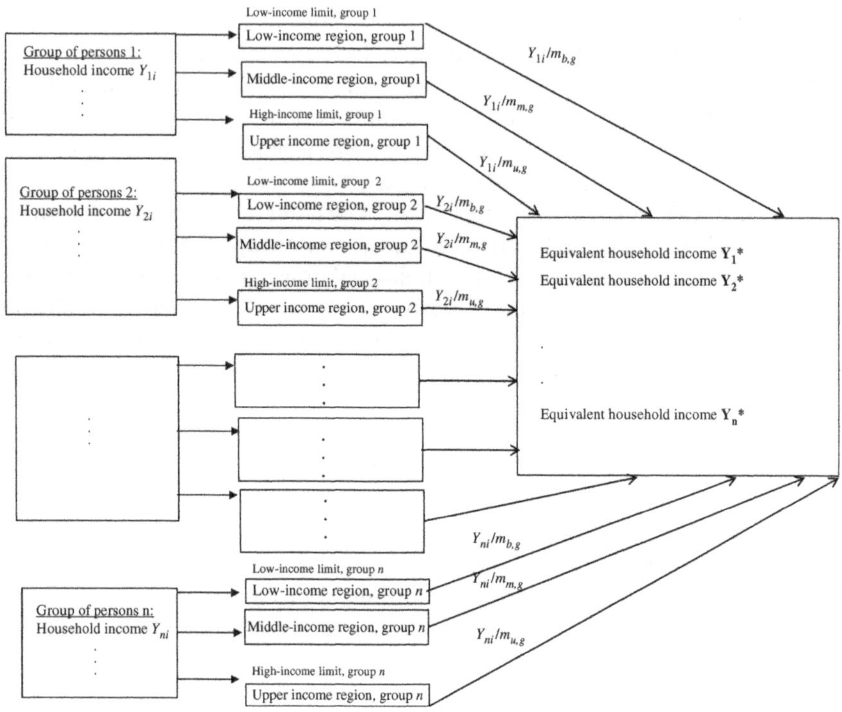

Fig. 2. A "Decomposition Approach" for Measuring Income Inequality. *Notes*: Y_{gi} = income of unit of analysis i in group g ($g = 1, 2, \ldots, n$), $m_{b,g}$ = equivalence scale value of group g in the bottom income region, $m_{m,g}$ = equivalence scale value of group g in the middle-income region, $m_{u,g}$ = equivalence scale value of group g in the upper income region; $m_{b,g} > m_{m,g} > m_{u,g}$; $\mathbf{Y}_\mathbf{g}^*$: vector of equivalent household incomes within group g ($g = 1, 2, \ldots, n$).

of measuring inequality. The reason for this result is that in the variant with variable equivalence scales the incomes of multi-person households in the lower income region are diminished by higher scale values than in the variant with constant equivalence scales.

In the bottom part of Fig. 3 an alternative assumption is made: The equivalence scales in the income-independent case and in the lower income region of the variant with variable equivalence scales shall equal each other. This corresponds with higher equivalent incomes of the multi-person households within the upper income region in the case with variable equivalence scales and, thus, generates a higher degree of income dispersion.

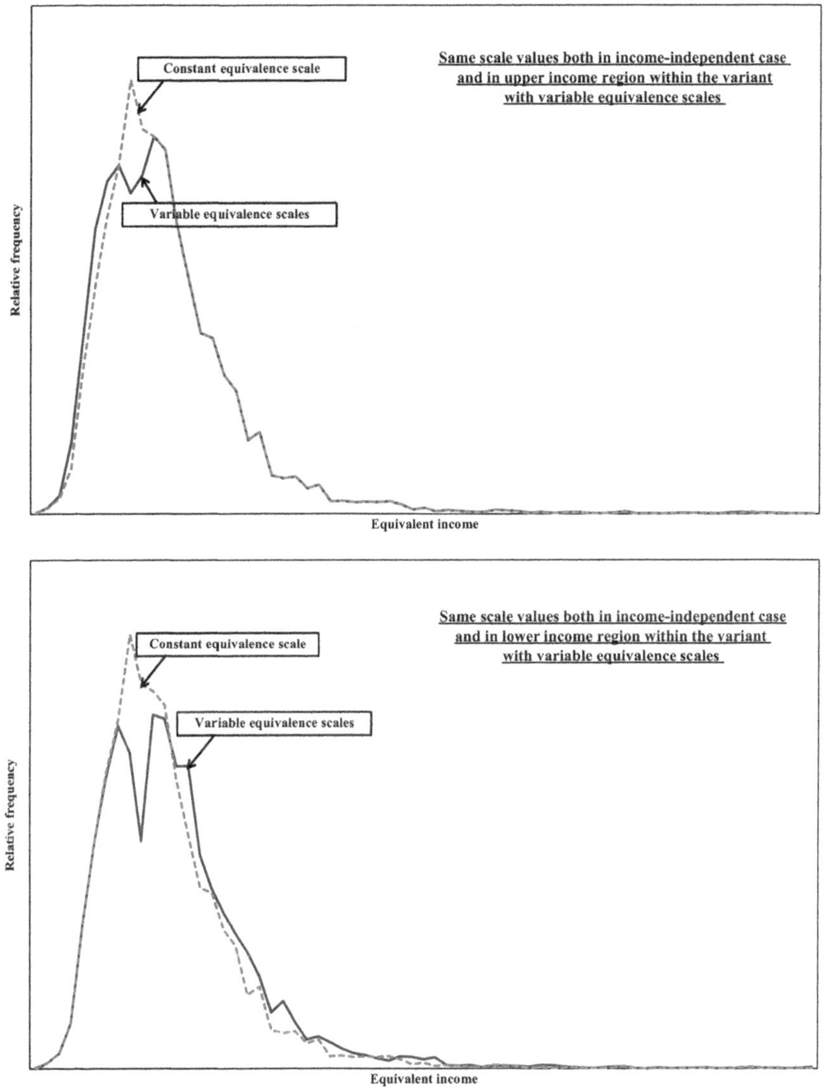

Fig. 3. Constant versus Variable Equivalence Scales and Their Impact on the Distribution of Income. *Note*: Both figures are based on 2010 German Socio-Economic Panel.

ESTIMATES OF VARIABLE EQUIVALENCE SCALES IN GERMANY

Faik (1995, pp. 285–289) estimates income region-dependent equivalence scales on the basis of cross-sectional data from the 1983 German Income and Consumption Survey (so-called *Einkommens- und Verbrauchsstichprobe*; *EVS*). He divides the entire income spectrum into three regions: a low-, a middle-, and a high-income region. Furthermore, he makes use of an expenditure-based method for estimating equivalence scales: the Engel approach. This method requires well-being (utility) levels of different household types to being equal if their budget shares of (bundles of) goods, specified beforehand, are of equal amount.

In order to separate the three income regions from each other (i.e., to solve the identification problem), Faik uses a special equivalence scale. As a starting point he chooses constant equivalence scale values in two variants, one based only on the expenditures for food and the other resting on the expenditures for a bundle of goods consisting of the categories food, housing, clothing and shoes, and body and health; each of these alternative scales is estimated via a linear Engel curve.

In a next step (and in both variants), Faik defines the upper limit of the low-income region as half the arithmetic mean of equivalent incomes and the lower limit of the high-income region as 1.5 times the arithmetic mean of equivalent incomes. For each of the three income regions defined in the way aforementioned, Faik estimates – via Engel curves' (OLS) regressions – iteratively new equivalence scales – up to the point where the scale values converge.

In variant 1 (using food's expenditures as dependent variable in the regressions), relatively small differences between the three income regions emerge across the different household types (household members) considered – especially for adults. This can be seen by the individual scale weights stated in Table 1. These weights (x%) are the differences between the scale values of a two-person household [$(100 + x)$%] and a single-person household (100%) within a specific income region.

For the younger age groups the scale decreases from low- to middle-income region (however, comprising an implausible low value for children in the age until six years). Variant 2 (based on the expenditures for a bundle of goods) reveals a much clearer picture of the income dependence of equivalence scale values: Within all age classes the individual scale weights drop in case of transition from low- to middle-income region (with the

Table 1. Income Region-Dependent Equivalence Scales (Individual Scale Weights, in %; 1st Household Member: 100%) in Germany, 1983 *EVS*[a].

Age Class	Variant[b]	Low-Income Region	Middle-Income Region	High- Income Region
Until 6 years	1	12	0 (−12; −100.0%)	0 (0; 0.0%)
	2	22	14 (−8; −36.4%)	7 (−7; −50.0%)
7–11 years	1	25	16 (−9; −36.0%)	15 (−1; −6.3%)
	2	16	25 (+9; +56.3%)	17 (−8; −32.0%)
12–19 years	1	39	28 (−11; −28.2%)	34 (+6; +21.4%)
	2	36	30 (−6; −16.7%)	25 (−5; −16.7%)
20–59 years	1	44	38 (−6; −13.6%)	42 (+4; +10.5%)
	2	50	22 (−28; −56.0%)	25 (+3; +12.0%)
60 years and older	1	41	37 (−4; −9.8%)	38 (+1; +2.7%)
	2	47	25 (−22; −46.8%)	25 (0; 0.0%)

Source: Faik (1995, pp. 286–287) and present author's own calculations.
[a]The values in parentheses indicate the change of individual scale weights with respect to transitions from low- to middle-income region and from middle- to high-income region in percentage points as well as in percent.
[b]Variant 1: expenditures for food; variant 2: expenditures for food, housing, clothes & shoes, and body & health.

exception of age class 7–11 years). Thus, in this sense there is a tendency toward income (region)-dependent equivalence scales in accordance with the theoretical considerations stated above.

For the transition from middle- to high-income region such a clear tendency does not emerge in variant 1. But in the more plausible variant 2 – that is, basing well-being (utility) levels on a more exhaustive bundle of goods than only using the expenditures for food as a welfare indicator – in three of five cases (age classes) the individual scale weights drop; for both adults' age classes the nonnegative changes are constant (60+ years) or do not vary very substantial (20–59 years).

Thus, conclude that there is some evidence in favor of income-dependent equivalence scales especially for the transition from low- to middle-income region and also, less pronounced, for the transition from middle- to high-income region in Germany.[5]

In contrast to the estimates presented in Table 1, alternative calculations of variable equivalence scales are estimated over the entire income spectrum but under the assumption of different income levels of the reference household type. That means that the definition of these additional variable equivalence scales does not refer to income regions (in the sense of discrete variables) but to (quasi-)continuous variables (like Barten's or Translating approach sketched above). The corresponding estimates are from van Praag and van der Sar (1988), Faik (1995), and Koulovatianos et al. (2005).[6]

Van Praag and van der Sar's estimates are based on a subjective approach, the Income Evaluation Question, and correspond to Germany 1979. Koulovatianos et al. also use a subjective method, the so-called consensual approach, to estimate variable scales for Germany in 1999. In both approaches people are asked for equivalent income levels belonging to their own and/or to other household types.

The results of Table 2 demonstrate that the basic thesis of the concept of variable equivalence scales – that is, declining scale values (as individual scale weights) with increasing reference income levels – is fulfilled in both studies. This finding strengthens the theoretical arguments for variable equivalence scales.

Furthermore, in Table 2 variable scales estimated by Faik (1995) are presented, once more in terms of individual weights which, in this context and according to the chosen reference income levels, are defined as scale differences between two succeeding household sizes. Faik's estimates refer to an expenditure-based, multi-equations approach on the basis of the Functionalized Extended Linear Expenditure System (FELES). He estimates Barten as well as Translating scales: Only in the Translating variant, income dependence becomes evident (but with implausible, negative individual weights for the 6th person).

EMPIRICAL SENSITIVITY ANALYSES

The Data Base

The data used is from the German Socio-Economic Panel (SOEP) for the years 1992–2010. The SOEP of the German Institute for Economic Research (*DIW* Berlin; see, e.g., Wagner, Frick, & Schupp, 2007) has been collected since 1984 in annual intervals. Its sample sizes (from 1992 on) are provided in Table A.1. The participants of the surveys give detailed information on their incomes, household composition, earnings' and family's biographies, health, life satisfaction, etc.

Table 2. Reference Income-Dependent Equivalence Scales (Individual Scale Weights; in %) for Germany[a].

Study	Reference Income Level	3rd Person	4th Person	5th Person	6th Person
van Praag and van der Sar (1988) for Germany 1979	Middle	16	13	10	10
	High	13 (−3; −18.8%)	10 (−3; −23.1%)	8 (−2; −20.0%)	7 (−3; −30.0%)

Study	Reference Income Level	2nd Person	3rd Person	4th Person	5th Person	6th Person
Faik (1995; Barten) for Germany 1983	Low	48	26	16	11	−2
	Middle	48 (0; 0.0%)	25 (−1; −3.8%)	16 (0; 0.0%)	9 (−2; −18.2%)	−5 (−3; −150.0%)
	High	48 (0; 0.0%)	25 (0; 0.0%)	14 (−2; −12.5%)	8 (−1; −11.1%)	−7 (−2; −40.0%)
Faik (1995; Translating) for Germany 1983	Low	48	26	16	11	−2
	Middle	34 (−14; −29.2%)	19 (−7; −26.9%)	11 (−5; −31.3%)	8 (−3; −27.3%)	−1 (1; −50.0%)
	High	22 (−12; −35.3%)	12 (−7; −36.8%)	7 (−4; −36.4%)	7 (−1; −12.5%)	−1 (0; 0.0%)
Koulovatianos et al. (2005) for Germany 1999	Low	75	52	45	45	–
	Middle	50 (−25; −33.3%)	22 (−30; −57.7%)	20 (−25; −55.6%)	20 (−25; −55.6%)	–
	High	39 (−11; −22.0%)	10 (−12: −54.5%)	10 (−10; −50.0%)	9 (−11; −55.0%)	–

Source: Present author's own calculations based on Schulte (2007, p. 41), Koulovatianos et al. (2005, p. 991), and Faik (1995, pp. 244–245).
[a]The values in parentheses indicate the change of individual scale weights with respect to transitions from low- to middle-income level and from middle- to high-income level in percentage points as well as in percent. Reference household types (with scale value = 100%): upper part of Table 2: two-person household, bottom part of Table 2: single-person household (for the dependence of equivalence scales on the chosen reference household type see Ebert and Moyes, 2003).

A number of subsamples have been drawn to capture different subpopulations:

- *Sample A*: German households in the Federal Republic of Germany since 1984;
- *Sample B*: households of foreigners in the Federal Republic of Germany since 1984;
- *Sample C*: private households in eastern Germany (German Democratic Republic) since 1990;
- *Sample D*: households of immigrants in Germany since 1994/1995;
- *Sample E*: complementary sample of households in Germany since 1998;
- *Sample F*: complementary sample of households in Germany since 2000;
- *Sample G*: sample of high-income receivers (households) in Germany since 2002; and
- *Sample H*: complementary sample of households in Germany since 2006.

For distributional analyses two central income variables are available: Monthly household income of the current year and annual household income of the previous year so that the query for the latter variable is retrospective. In this study, I use annual household net income which includes household's income obtained from all sources (including imputed rents) over a one year's period.

The data analysis begins with wave 1992 (with information on annual incomes in 1991) since from this period on SOEP data for unified Germany is available.

Distributional Results on the Basis of Variable Versus Constant Equivalence Scales

In the following analyses, the whole income range is divided into three regions, the bottom, the middle, and the upper income class. Current FELES regression results for Germany (2003 *EVS*) place the low-income line at 70% of average net incomes (see Faik, 2011). Thus, for all household types considered in this paper[7] this line is used (by only referring to "pure" net incomes for the reasons stated above). The high-income lines for the different household types are determined – in accordance with other (German) studies (see, e.g., Grabka, Westerheide, Hauser, & Becker, 2007, pp. 60–61) – as twice the group's arithmetic mean of households' net incomes (see Table A.2).

The basic inequality results for Germany 1992–2010 SOEP[8] are shown in Fig. 4.[9] Between 1992 and 2001 income inequality in Germany did not change very much, but since 2002 it has been at a higher level than before, measured by the normalized coefficient of variation (defined as half the squared coefficient of variation). This may be partly the result of a sampling effect since for the transition from 2001 SOEP to 2002 SOEP high incomes have been captured to a higher degree (by sample G; see above), which, obviously, was not corrected by adequate grossing-up factors within the SOEP samples. Because of the relatively large high-income sensitivity of the normalized coefficient of variation this sampling effect might explain at least part of the notable rise of inequality between 2001 and 2002. Moreover, the increase of income inequality might be partly caused by socioeconomic developments in Germany at the beginning of the 21st century, for example, by the increase of low-paid jobs or by a rise of individual incomes' homogamy (with respect to partner relationships in Germany; in this context see Schröder, 2011). At the end of the observation period, income inequality in Germany as a whole decreased. Perhaps (at least partly) this

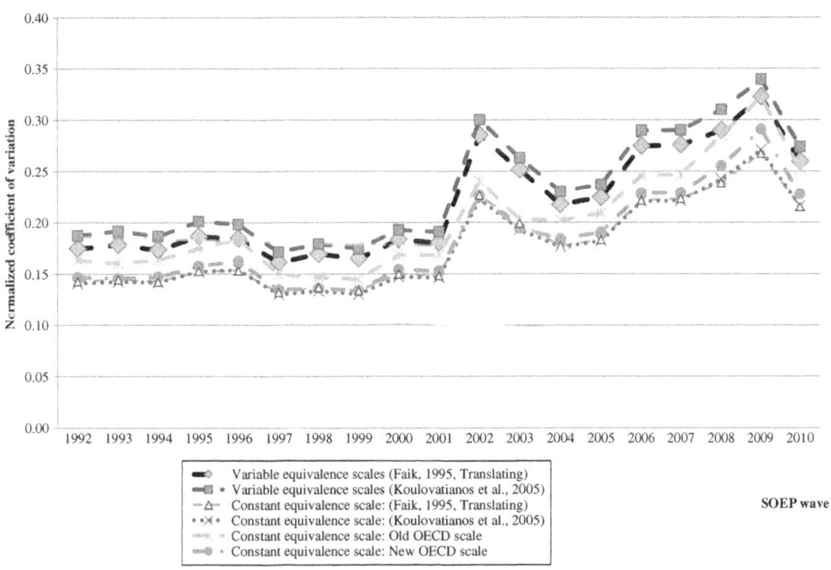

Fig. 4. Variable and Constant Equivalence Scales in Germany as a Whole 1992–2010 SOEP on the Basis of the Normalized Coefficient of Variation (Annual Equivalent Household Net Incomes of the Previous Year).

was a reflection of the diminished unemployment rates in Germany at the end of the first decade of the 21st century.

For the cases with constant equivalence scales, Fig. 4 shows the same pattern of income inequality as in the case with variable equivalence scales but at lower inequality levels which is in accordance with the above theoretical considerations. Referring to the cases with variable equivalence scales, the measured value differences of the normalized coefficients of variation are within the ranges of 21–26% (comparing Faik's 1995 Translating scales with each other) and 25–36% (concerning Koulovatianos et al.'s 2005 scales). It must be stressed that these numerical results rest upon the specification of only three income regions. Assuming more than three income regions would have enlarged those differences. Furthermore, the variable equivalence scales supposed in Fig. 4 also lead to higher inequality values compared to the so-called old and new (constant) OECD scales.[10]

Different Income Limits

Fig. 5 illustrates the consequences of different reference limits for the three income regions in the sense of different fractions or multiples of the different household types' mean net incomes. As variable equivalence scale, Faik's (1995) variable Translating scale is assumed.

It becomes obvious, as a rule, that larger differences in income limits between the upper and the bottom income region cause lower income inequality than smaller differences in income limits. This is because of a larger middle class corresponding with identical scale values over a broader section of the entire income distribution. Despite these findings and on balance, in Fig. 5 the inequality differences between the four variants are relatively small.

Different Inequality Measures

Fig. 6 shows the inequality consequences of different inequality measures (mean logarithmic deviation, Theil's measure of entropy applied in this paper, and normalized coefficient of variation[11]) for Germany 1992–2010 SOEP. These three inequality indicators vary with respect to their sensitivity to changes within different income regions. Compared with the relatively high-income sensitive normalized coefficient of variation, the mean logarithmic deviation and Theil's measure of entropy used here – both not

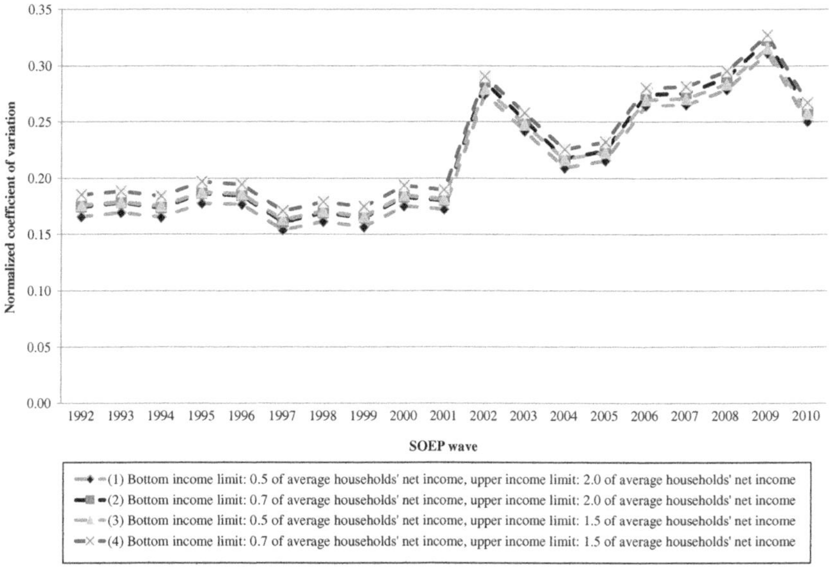

Fig. 5. Different Borders of Income Regions, Variable Equivalence Scales (Faik's 1995 Translating Scales) and Their Consequences for Income Inequality in Germany 1992–2010 SOEP on the Basis of the Normalized Coefficient of Variation (Annual Equivalent Household Net Incomes of the Previous Year).

as sensitive to changes in high-income regions as the normalized coefficient of variation – reveal a rather smoothed "inequality curve" over time.

Especially – and expectedly – this is true for the transition between 2001 and 2002, that is, during the period of time in which the SOEP added many high-income receivers. Additionally, the rise in income inequality between 2004 and 2009 indicated by the normalized coefficient of variation is only weakly revealed by the two other inequality indicators. Thus, the findings of rising inequality between 2001 and 2002 as well as between 2004 and 2009 can primarily be interpreted as a consequence of changes within the upper income range during these periods of time.

CONCLUDING REMARKS

The findings of the paper revealed the sensitivity of distributional results due to different methodical settings.

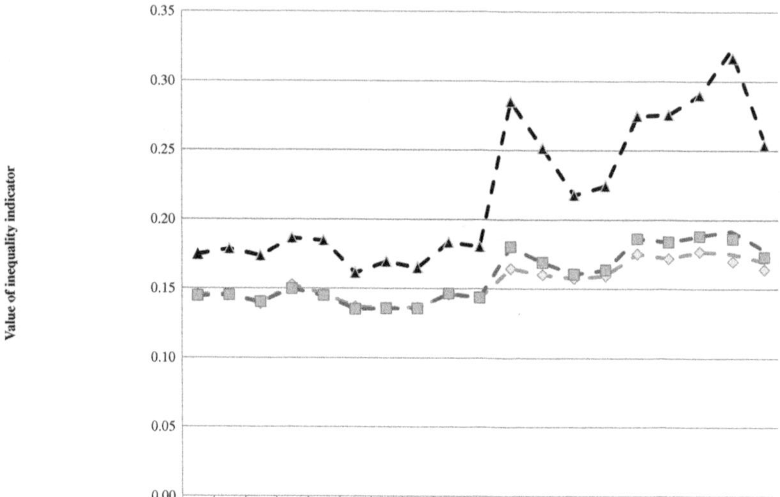

	1992	1993	1994	1995	1996	1997	1998	1999	2000	2001	2002	2003	2004	2005	2006	2007	2008	2009	2010
Mean logarithmic deviation	0.146	0.146	0.139	0.153	0.146	0.137	0.136	0.136	0.146	0.143	0.164	0.160	0.157	0.159	0.175	0.172	0.177	0.175	0.170
Theil's indicator of entropy	0.145	0.145	0.140	0.150	0.145	0.135	0.136	0.136	0.146	0.143	0.180	0.169	0.160	0.163	0.186	0.184	0.188	0.192	0.179
Normalized coefficient of variation	0.175	0.179	0.174	0.187	0.185	0.161	0.170	0.165	0.184	0.180	0.286	0.252	0.218	0.225	0.275	0.276	0.290	0.323	0.260

Fig. 6. Different Inequality Indicators, Variable Equivalence Scales (Faik's 1995 Translating Scales) and Their Consequences for Income Inequality in Germany 1992–2010 SOEP (Annual Equivalent Household Net Incomes of the Previous Year).

The analyses yielded the following conclusions:

1. In the case with variable equivalence scales the measured inequality was substantially higher than in the case with income-independent equivalence scales.
2. A narrowing of income limits between the upper and the bottom income region led to increases in income inequality (within the methodical framework presented here).
3. For Germany the usage of three alternative inequality indicators gave hints toward rising inequality between 2001 and 2002 as well as between 2004 and 2009 especially in the upper (equivalent) income region (but from 2009 to 2010 income inequality decreased, as was indicated by all used inequality measures).

In summary, there appear to be solid theoretical and empirical justifications for using variable equivalence scales in studies of income inequality.

Finally, other applications of variable equivalence scales include tax schemes or benefit programs in order to study horizontal (in)equity aspects (see Ebert & Lambert, 2004; Lambert, 2004; Muellbauer & van de Ven, 2004) and to enlarge the degree of consistency in the design of public policies (see Ayala, Martínez, & Ruiz-Huerta, 2003, p. 599). This indicates the broad scope of variable scales beyond "pure" distributional analyses.

NOTES

1. For a detailed discussion of this issue see especially Cowell and Mercader-Prats (1999, pp. 25–26); see also Coulter, Cowell, and Jenkins (1992), Figini (1998, pp. 7–9), Lancaster, Ray, and Valenzuela (1999), Creedy and Sleeman (2004), and Bönke and Schröder (2008).

2. If a negative correlation between household size and household income occurs, increasing inequality corresponds with decreasing levels of economies of scale since the re-ranking effect does not take place in this case.

3. By the way, a synthesis of Barten's and Translating approach is from Gorman (1976).

4. In practice, the derivation of utility-based equivalence scales, at least partly, suffers from an identification problem which is the consequence of ordinal utility functions and their corresponding robustness concerning cardinal transformations of utility levels.

5. Concerning the estimation of variable equivalence scales see in an international perspective, among others, Fiegehen, Lansley, and Smith (1977, pp. 105–106), van Hoa (1986, pp. 97–98), Aaberge and Melby (1998), or Donaldson and Pendakur (2003), especially pp. 194–197.

6. Schulte (2007, p. 44) also discusses Faik (1995) scale values which refer to the 1969 *EVS* and to the so-called Rothbarth method that is based on typical adults' goods (alcohol) to calculate scale values for children. The corresponding scales vary with (reference) income level negatively but only by construction. Because of this artificiality, they are excluded from Table 2.

7. The paper's calculations are restricted to single- to six-person households since the number of cases for household sizes with seven and more persons is too low for statistical reasons, as can be seen by Table A.1.

8. To avoid largely biased inequality values because of extreme income levels ("outliers"), household net incomes are constrained up to an amount of 1,000,000 € p.a. Each year is related to the corresponding SOEP wave so that, e.g., "1992" expresses income information on the previous year 1991.

9. In the Appendix, additionally, bootstrap estimates (at a 95% level of significance) are documented (for the case of variable equivalence scales).

10. The old OECD scale is characterized by the following individual weights: 1st household member: 1.00, additional adult household member (15 years and older): 0.70, and additional children (until 15 years): 0.50; the weights of the new OECD scale are as follows for the same groups: 1.00, 0.50, and 0.30 (see: http://www.oecd.org/dataoecd/61/52/35411111.pdf, accessed on January 31, 2012). In Fig. 4 approximations of both OECD scales, only with respect to household size, are used.

11. For sensitivity analyses the usage of a general class of inequality indicators is convenient. A very popular class of indicators is the family of Generalized Entropy (GE) measures (in which groups' population shares serve as weighting factors as well as groups' income shares):

$$\mathrm{GE} = \frac{1}{(\lambda^2 - \lambda) \cdot n} \cdot \sum_{i=1}^{n} \left[\left(\frac{Y_i}{\mu} \right)^{\lambda} - 1 \right] \quad \text{for } \lambda \neq 0 \text{ and } \lambda \neq 1$$

$$\mathrm{GE} = \frac{1}{n} \cdot \sum_{i=1}^{n} \ln\left(\frac{\mu}{Y_i} \right) \quad \text{for } \lambda = 0$$

$$\mathrm{GE} = \frac{1}{n} \cdot \sum_{i=1}^{n} \left[\frac{Y_i}{\mu} \cdot \ln\left(\frac{Y_i}{\mu} \right) \right] \quad \text{for } \lambda = 1$$

GE = Generalized Entropy index, λ = parameter with respect to inequality preferences, n = population size, Y_i = income of person i, μ = mean income. The parameter λ reflects the social perceptions of inequality. If λ is greater than 0, the upper income region receives a relatively high weight with respect to inequality (increasingly with higher λ-values at that). The opposite is the case if λ is less 0. For $\lambda = 0$ the GE measure represents the mean logarithmic deviation, for $\lambda = 1$ Theil's measure of entropy used here is the result, and for $\lambda = 2$ the GE measure corresponds with the normalized coefficient of variation. A more comprehensive consideration of the class of GE measures can be found in Shorrocks (1980) or in Mookherjee and Shorrocks (1982).

ACKNOWLEDGMENTS

The author would like to thank Professor Joachim Merz (University of Lueneburg, Germany) and the German Institute for Economic Research *(DIW)*, Berlin, for providing access to SOEP data and both editors of Research on Economic Inequality, Volume 20, Professor John Bishop and Professor Rafael Salas, for very valuable comments on earlier versions of the paper.

REFERENCES

Aaberge, R., & Melby, I. (1998). The sensitivity of income inequality to choice of equivalence scales. *Review of Income and Wealth*, *44*, 565–569.

Ayala, L., Martínez, R., & Ruiz-Huerta, J. (2003). Equivalence scales in tax and transfer policies. *Investigaciones Ecónomicas*, *27*, 593–614.

Barten, A. B. (1964). Family composition, prices and expenditure patterns. In P. E. Hart, G. Mills, & J. K. Whitaker (Eds.), *Econometric analysis for national economic planning* (pp. 277–297). London: Butterworth.

Bönke, T., & Schröder, C. (2008). *Equivalence scales reconsidered – An empirical investigation*, ECINEQ – Society for the Study of Economic Inequality, Working Paper Series, ECINEQ WP 2008-102, Palma de Mallorca.

Bradbury, B. (1992). *Measuring the cost of children*, SPRC Discussion Papers, No. 32, University of New South Wales, Kensington.

Clark, A. E., & Oswald, A. J. (1996). Satisfaction and comparison income. *Journal of Public Economics, 61*, 359–381.

Coulter, F. A. E., Cowell, F. A., & Jenkins, S. P. (1992). Equivalence scale relativities and the extent of inequality and poverty. *Economic Journal, 102*, 1067–1082.

Cowell, F., & Mercader-Prats, M. (1999): *Equivalence scales and inequality*, Distributional Analysis Research Programme, No. DARP 27, London.

Creedy, J., & Sleeman, C. (2004). *Adult equivalence scales, inequality and poverty in New Zealand*, New Zealand Treasury Working Paper No. 04-21, Wellington.

Donaldson, D., & Pendakur, K. (2003). Equivalent-expenditure functions and expenditure-dependent equivalence scales. *Journal of Public Economics, 88*, 175–208.

Ebert, U., & Lambert, P. J. (2004). Horizontal equity and progression when equivalence scales are not constant. *Public Finance Review, 32*, 426–440.

Ebert, U., & Moyes, P. (2003). Equivalence scales reconsidered. *Econometrica, 70*, 319–343.

Faik, J. (1995). *Äquivalenzskalen. Theoretische Erörterung, empirische Herleitung und verteilungsbezogene Anwendung für die Bundesrepublik Deutschland*, Berlin.

Faik, J. (2011). Der Zerlegungs-Ansatz – ein alternativer Vorschlag zur Messung von Armut. *AStA – Wirtschafts- und Sozialstatistisches Archiv, 4*, 293–315.

Festinger, L. (1954). A theory of social comparison processes. *Human Relations, 7*, 117–140.

Fiegehen, G. C., Lansley, P. S., & Smith, A. D. (1977). *Poverty and progress in Britain 1953–1973*. Cambridge: Cambridge University Press.

Figini, P. (1998). *Inequality measures, equivalence scales and adjustment for household size and composition*. Trinity Economic Paper Series, Technical Paper No. 98-8, Dublin.

Frey, B. S., & Stutzer, A. (2002). *Happiness and economics. How the economy and institutions affect human well-being*. Princeton/Oxford: Princeton University Press.

Gorman, W. M. (1976). Tricks with utility functions. In M. J. Artis & A. V. Nobay (Eds.), *Essays in economic analysis* (pp. 211–243). Cambridge: Cambridge University Press.

Grabka, M. M., Westerheide, P., Hauser, R., & Becker, J. (2007). *Integrierte Analyse der Einkommens- und Vermögensverteilung*, Final Report for the German Federal Ministry for Labour and Social Affairs, Berlin et al.

Koulovatianos, C., Schröder, C., & Schmidt, U. (2005). On the income dependence of equivalence scales. *Journal of Public Economics, 89*, 967–996.

Koulovatianos, C., Schröder, C., & Schmidt, U. (2010). *Confronting the representative consumer with household-size heterogeneity*. DIW Berlin Discussion Paper No. 1056, Berlin.

Lambert, P. J. (2004). Equivalence scales, horizontal equity and horizontal inequity. In C. Dagum & G. Ferrari (Eds.), *Household behaviour, equivalence scales, welfare and poverty* (pp. 75–84). Heidelberg: Physica-Verlag.

Lancaster, G., Ray, R., & Valenzuela, M. R. (1999). A cross-country study of equivalence scales and expenditure inequality on unit record household budget data. *Review of Income and Wealth, 45*, 455–482.

Leibenstein, H. (1976). *Beyond economic man: A new foundation for microeconomics*. Cambridge, MA: Harvard University Press.
Lewbel, A. (1989). Household equivalence scales and welfare comparisons. *Journal of Public Economics*, *39*, 377–391.
Mookherjee, D., & Shorrocks, A. F. (1982). A decomposition analysis of the trend in UK income inequality. *Economic Journal*, *92*, 886–902.
Muellbauer, J., & van de Ven, J. (2004). Equivalence scales and taxation: A simulation analysis. In C. Dagum & G. Ferrari (Eds.), *Household behaviour, equivalence scales, welfare and poverty* (pp. 85–106). Heidelberg: Physica-Verlag.
Schröder, C. (2004). *Variable income equivalence scales: An empirical approach*. Heidelberg: Physica-Verlag.
Schröder, Ch. (2011). Einkommensungleichheit und Homogamie. *iw-trends*, *38*, 1–13.
Schulte, J. (2007). *Equivalence scales: Identification and estimation. A cross-sectional analysis of German Data*. Ph.D. thesis, Free University Berlin. Retrieved from http://www.diss.fu-berlin.de/diss/receive/FUDISS_thesis_000000003138. Accessed on February 2, 2012.
Shorrocks, A. F. (1980). The class of additively decomposable inequality measures. *Econometrica*, *48*, 613–625.
Simon, H. A. (1957). *Models of man: Social and rational mathematical essays on rational human behavior in a social setting*. New York, NY: Wiley.
van Hoa, T. (1986). Measuring equivalence scales: A new system-wide method. *Economics Letters*, *20*, 95–99.
van Praag, B. M., & van der Sar, N. L. (1988). Household cost functions and equivalence scales. *The Journal of Human Resources*, *23*, 193–210.
Wagner, G. G., Frick, J. R., & Schupp, J. (2007). The German socio-economic panel study (SOEP) – Scope, evolution and enhancements. *Schmollers Jahrbuch*, *127*, 139–169.

APPENDIX

Table A.1. Unweighted Number of Households in Germany 1992–2010 SOEP Due to Household Size[a].

Wave	1 Person	2 Persons	3 Persons	4 Persons	5 Persons	6 Persons	7 Persons	8 Persons and More	Sum
1992	1,350	2,025	1,472	1,247	393	120	38	18	6,663
1993	1,418	2,040	1,424	1,195	395	110	34	21	6,637
1994	1,450	2,124	1,452	1,210	398	100	37	22	6,793
1995	1,484	2,181	1,467	1,274	401	102	38	20	6,967
1996	1,513	2,195	1,416	1,233	380	101	36	17	6,891
1997	1,488	2,240	1,367	1,205	373	87	33	17	6,810
1998	1,794	2,568	1,500	1,296	359	101	34	13	7,665
1999	1,730	2,536	1,405	1,227	353	95	31	11	7,388
2000	3,399	4,590	2,314	2,074	651	156	39	19	13,242
2001	3,047	4,161	2,073	1,873	601	133	43	14	11,945
2002	3,077	4,592	2,200	1,999	624	144	37	14	12,687
2003	3,026	4,398	2,048	1,839	583	128	34	15	12,071
2004	2,977	4,377	1,978	1,763	545	117	28	13	11,798
2005	3,009	4,253	1,886	1,645	513	107	29	8	11,450
2006	3,391	4,780	2,014	1,690	501	107	23	13	12,519
2007	3,212	4,445	1,902	1,554	463	88	22	10	11,696
2008	3,099	4,270	1,762	1,414	406	88	18	9	11,066
2009	3,357	4,654	1,835	1,503	424	97	22	7	11,899
2010	3,112	4,323	1,591	1,369	347	87	23	5	10,857

Source: Present author's own calculations.

[a]Only households with positive net incomes considered.

Table A.2. Arithmetic Mean Values of Household Net Incomes (€ p.a.) for Germany 1992–2010 SOEP Due to Household Size[a].

Wave	1 Person	2 Persons	3 Persons	4 Persons	5 Persons	6 Persons
1992	13,075	22,762	28,157	31,192	33,068	35,445
1993	13,997	24,569	29,973	33,939	35,412	35,530
1994	14,562	26,125	32,047	34,955	35,579	37,832
1995	14,774	26,435	32,103	34,521	35,898	36,818
1996	15,411	26,949	32,616	35,143	36,840	38,756
1997	15,441	27,460	33,152	35,748	39,449	39,743
1998	15,534	28,251	33,792	36,765	38,063	40,187
1999	16,004	29,263	35,525	37,665	39,491	43,323
2000	16,478	30,464	35,823	39,096	41,611	43,432
2001	17,123	30,886	36,662	40,869	42,152	43,035
2002	17,709	31,653	37,144	42,230	44,060	44,888
2003	18,111	32,319	38,073	42,905	45,491	45,816
2004	17,982	32,595	38,328	42,715	44,572	46,457
2005	18,545	33,219	38,063	43,953	44,232	46,084
2006	18,676	33,778	38,931	44,477	45,347	46,963
2007	18,749	33,775	39,133	46,075	48,040	48,793
2008	19,365	35,022	40,311	47,028	50,054	45,289
2009	19,601	36,078	40,365	48,541	49,744	45,846
2010	19,886	36,356	43,278	48,642	51,963	47,203

Source: Present author's own calculations.

[a]Only households with positive net incomes and up to size of six household members considered.

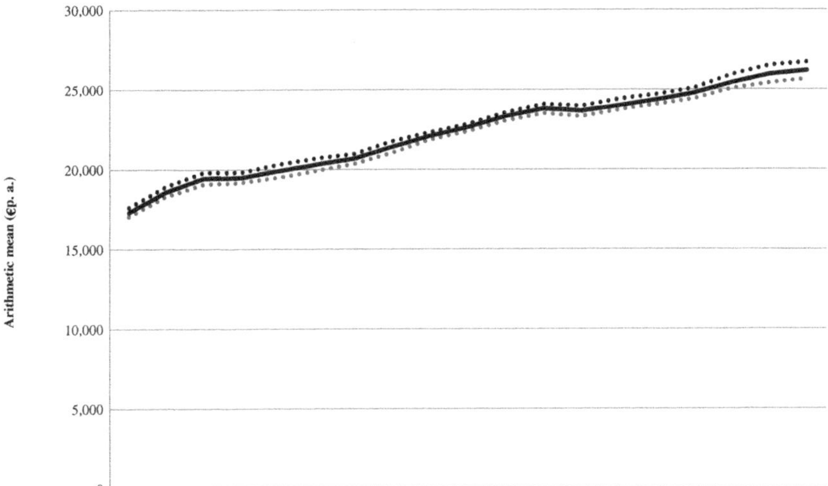

	1992	1993	1994	1995	1996	1997	1998	1999	2000	2001	2002	2003	2004	2005	2006	2007	2008	2009	2010
Bottom Limit	17,064	18,298	19,052	19,180	19,486	19,912	20,337	21,024	21,856	22,372	23,039	23,490	23,302	23,723	24,062	24,409	25,056	25,401	25,660
Estimator	17,341	18,606	19,458	19,504	19,925	20,331	20,686	21,424	22,110	22,649	23,347	23,813	23,670	24,006	24,369	24,783	25,444	25,970	26,206
Upper Limit	17,657	18,964	19,828	19,854	20,346	20,738	20,997	21,791	22,354	22,869	23,595	24,109	23,983	24,443	24,733	25,121	25,966	26,552	26,746

Fig. A.1a. Bootstrap Estimations for Arithmetic Means of Equivalent Household Net Incomes in Germany 1992–2010 SOEP (95% Confidence Intervals; Number of Bootstrap's Cases per Wave: 200 Samples) Based on Faik's (1995) Variable Translating Scales.

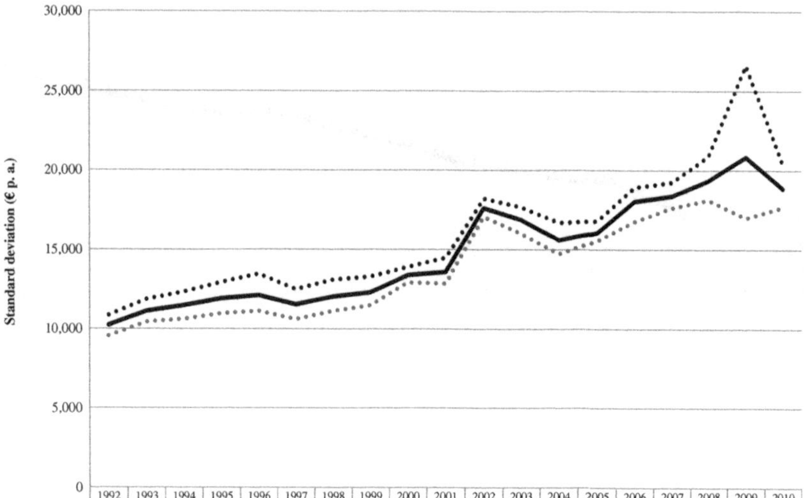

	1992	1993	1994	1995	1996	1997	1998	1999	2000	2001	2002	2003	2004	2005	2006	2007	2008	2009	2010
Bottom Limit	9,560	10,431	10,608	10,959	11,116	10,596	11,123	11,476	12,914	12,851	17,071	16,012	14,724	15,543	16,782	17,641	18,147	17,010	17,697
Estimator	10,254	11,124	11,472	11,921	12,114	11,550	12,047	12,314	13,396	13,607	17,643	16,896	15,623	16,088	18,069	18,407	19,378	20,868	18,893
Upper Limit	10,874	11,878	12,341	12,954	13,480	12,512	13,120	13,312	13,923	14,499	18,257	17,703	16,726	16,831	18,957	19,282	20,906	26,653	20,417

Fig. A.1b. Bootstrap Estimations for Standard Deviations of Equivalent Household Net Incomes in Germany 1992–2010 SOEP (95% Confidence Intervals; Number of Bootstrap's Cases per Wave: 200 Samples) Based on Faik's (1995) Variable Translating Scales.

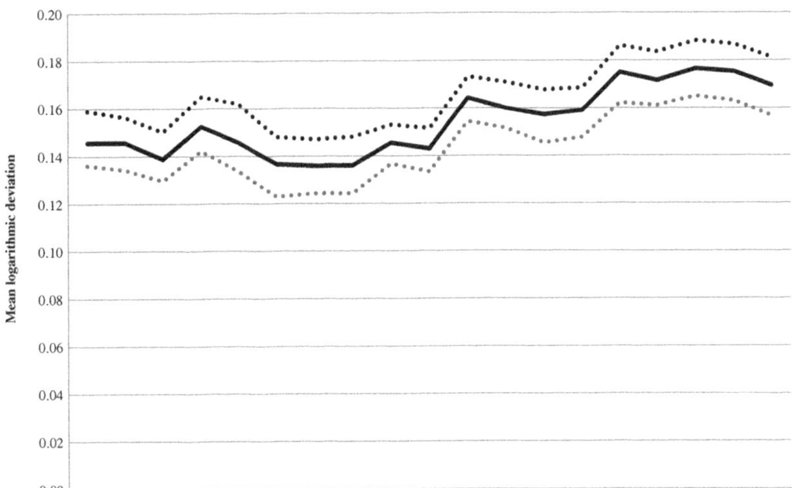

	1992	1993	1994	1995	1996	1997	1998	1999	2000	2001	2002	2003	2004	2005	2006	2007	2008	2009	2010
Bottom Limit	0.1362	0.1343	0.1296	0.1422	0.1337	0.123	0.1244	0.1244	0.1368	0.1334	0.1544	0.1515	0.1454	0.1477	0.1622	0.1612	0.165	0.1631	0.1569
Estimator	0.1458	0.1458	0.139	0.1526	0.1459	0.1368	0.1361	0.1362	0.1457	0.1431	0.1644	0.16	0.1573	0.1592	0.1751	0.1718	0.1766	0.1754	0.1697
Upper Limit	0.1592	0.1565	0.1503	0.1652	0.1621	0.1482	0.1472	0.1482	0.1533	0.1517	0.1735	0.171	0.1679	0.1687	0.1864	0.1838	0.1884	0.1869	0.1815

Fig. A.1c. Bootstrap Estimations for Mean Logarithmic Deviations of Equivalent Household Net Incomes in Germany 1992–2010 SOEP (95% Confidence Intervals; Number of Bootstrap's Cases per Wave: 200 Samples) Based on Faik's (1995) Variable Translating Scales.

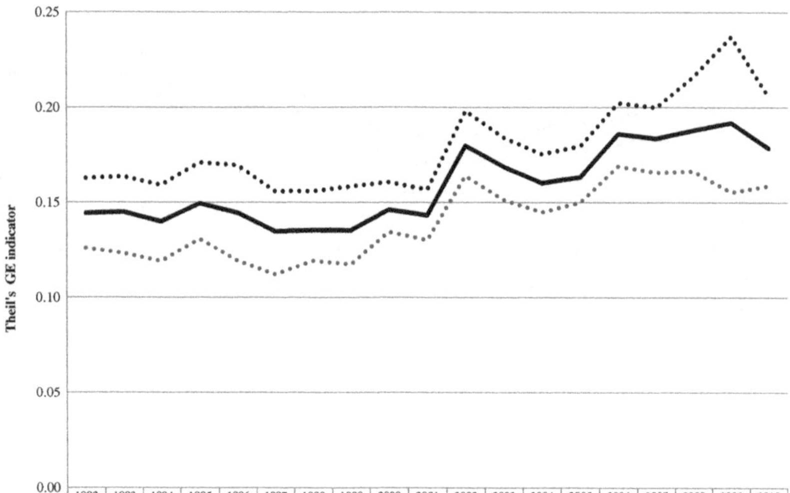

	1992	1993	1994	1995	1996	1997	1998	1999	2000	2001	2002	2003	2004	2005	2006	2007	2008	2009	2010
Bottom Limit	0.126	0.1232	0.1191	0.1308	0.1193	0.1122	0.1192	0.1174	0.1346	0.1303	0.164	0.1514	0.1449	0.1501	0.169	0.1657	0.1665	0.1555	0.1588
Estimator	0.1445	0.1451	0.1402	0.1496	0.1448	0.1350	0.1357	0.1355	0.1463	0.1435	0.1801	0.1689	0.1604	0.1635	0.1862	0.1838	0.1880	0.1920	0.1787
Upper Limit	0.1629	0.1638	0.1593	0.1711	0.1697	0.1561	0.1562	0.1587	0.1608	0.157	0.1984	0.1843	0.1756	0.1797	0.2025	0.2	0.2165	0.2375	0.2059

Fig. A.1d. Bootstrap Estimations for Theil's Entropy Indicator Values of Equivalent Household Net Incomes in Germany 1992–2010 SOEP (95% Confidence Intervals; Number of Bootstrap's Cases per Wave: 200 Samples) Based on Faik's (1995) Variable Translating Scales.

CHAPTER 13

EDUCATIONAL INEQUALITY IN THE WORLD, 1950–2010: ESTIMATES FROM A NEW DATASET☆

Wail Benaabdelaali, Saîd Hanchane and Abdelhak Kamal

ABSTRACT

This paper introduces a new quinquennial dataset of educational inequality disaggregated by age group for 146 countries, from 1950 to 2010, by using the Gini index of education as a measure of the distribution of years of schooling. Based on recent estimates of average years of schooling from Barro and Lee (2010), our calculations take into consideration, for the first time, the changes over time in the duration of educational stages, in each country and for each age group. The

☆The data set of educational inequality measured by the Gini index of education of 146 countries from 1950 to 2010 is availbale in www.education-inequality.com

Inequality, Mobility and Segregation: Essays in Honor of Jacques Silber
Research on Economic Inequality, Volume 20, 337–366

ISSN: 1049-2585/doi:10.1108/S1049-2585(2012)0000020016

downward trends in educational inequality observed during the last decades depend on age group, gender, and development level.

Keywords: Educational inequality; Gini index of education; educational attainment; age group; duration of educational stages

JEL classifications: D63; I21; J24; O15

INTRODUCTION

The analysis of inequality has been the center of interest for scholars in the social sciences. However, most empirical work on inequality uses a unidimensional monetary perspective, which may not be sufficient for adequately characterizing this multidimensional phenomenon. The World Bank's World Development Report of 2006, titled "Equity and Development", moved for the first time beyond the question of income distribution, to emphasizing inequalities in key opportunity dimensions, such as health and education. While many questions about healthcare inequities have raised a lot of concerns for planners and policy makers, little attention has been paid to educational inequality. During the last decades, however, researchers have realized the importance of putting more emphasis on educational inequalities. A recent but rapidly growing literature concerning education inequality has emerged. In fact, several datasets have been created to measure educational inequality (Araujo, Ferreira, & Schady, 2004; Castelló, 2010; Castelló & Doménech, 2002; Checchi, 2004; Földvári & Van Leeuwen, 2011; Lim & Tang, 2008; Meschi & Scervini, 2010; Morrisson & Murtin, 2010; Thomas, Wang, & Fan, 2001, 2003). The most popular and widely used is the one proposed by Thomas et al. (2001) who calculated a Gini index of education of the population aged 15 and over, based on school attainment data.[1] Nevertheless, few studies have explored educational inequalities by age group. This paper introduces a new quinquennial dataset of educational inequality for 146 countries, from 1950 to 2010, and is the first to present a Gini index of education by 5-year intervals and by sex for a broad panel. The Gini index of education is used as a measure of the distribution of years of schooling, with a more in-depth approach compared to existing datasets. After a brief discussion of the empirical literature on the issue – more specifically the existing datasets – we present the data we use in the estimation of the Gini index of education, describe the methodology, and then illustrate some trends in the evolution of inequalities in the world.

LITERATURE REVIEW: A BRIEF DISCUSSION

Research on inequalities in education is important for both political and empirical research. For public policy, it is a tool to assess the progress in educational development of a country. Important disparities in education can compromise the achievement of objectives related to the equality of opportunity. Furthermore, many recent empirical studies highlight the impact of the distributional dimension of human capital on economic growth. The Gini index of education is a measure of the relative inequality of the schooling distribution. It can be calculated using educational resource data, achievement, enrollment, or attainment data.

There have been many attempts to measure educational attainment. Barro and Lee (2010) made the most recent dataset of educational attainment, which includes 146 countries from 1950 to 2010. The data are provided by sex and 5-year age intervals. They have improved the accuracy of estimation – compared to estimates from earlier versions of the Barro-Lee Data Set (1993, 1996, 2001) – by using consistent census data, disaggregated by age group, along with new estimates of mortality rates and completion rates by age and education level. Since Cohen and Soto (2007) and Barro and Lee (2010) are the most commonly used and most accurate datasets, Table 1 is used to present a comparison of both datasets using different criteria. In fact, data sources on educational attainments of Cohen and Soto (2007) are the OECD database and censuses published by UNESCO.[2] Barro and Lee (2001, 2010) argued that there is a significant difference between the OECD data and UNESCO censuses, which can cause inconsistency over time in case of a mix between the two sources. Indeed, OECD data comes mostly from household surveys that are based on samples of labor force and are obviously less robust than censuses. In addition, OECD data are available only for the 1990s, which can lead to underutilization of available information. Barro and Lee (2010) used only UNESCO censuses, with substantially more sources than Cohen and Soto (2007). Indeed, Cohen and Soto's estimation used only 51 UNESCO censuses among 70 data sources for 73 developing countries and 8 UNESCO censuses among 48 data sources for 22 advanced countries, compared to 392 UNESCO censuses for 122 developing countries and 119 for 24 advanced countries in Barro and Lee's (2010) sample. In fact, Cohen and Soto (2007) considered the variation in mortality rates by age groups not by educational levels. They used homogenous duration of schooling stages rather than variations by age groups and over time utilized by Barro and Lee's (2010) estimation. As Barro and Lee (2010) demonstrated, the reliability ratio for their estimation is greater than that of Cohen and Soto (2007), in levels

Table 1. Comparison of Cohen and Soto's (2007) and Barro and Lee's (2010) Datasets.

Criteria	Cohen and Soto (2007)	Barro and Lee (2010)
Data sources on educational attainment	OECD/UNESCO data	UNESCO data
Number of advanced countries (AC)	22	24
Number of UNESCO censuses for the AC	8	119
Number of total data sources for the AC	48	119
Number of developing countries (DC)	73	122
Number of UNESCO censuses for the DC	51	392
Number total data sources for the DC	70	392
Mortality rates	By age group	By age group and by educational level
Duration of educational stages	Homogenous	By age group and over time
Reliability ratio of series in 10-year differences[a]	0.88	1.00
Reliability ratio of series in levels	0.90	0.99

Source: The authors.
[a]As used by Krueger and Lindahl (2001) in checking quality of schooling data, the reliability ratio gauges the fraction of the variability of a (unobserved) true variable in the total variability of the variable measured with error.

and in 10-year differences, in years of schooling for the population aged 15 years and older. Specifically, while the new Barro–Lee dataset has reliability ratios of 0.99 for levels and 1.00 for differences, the reliability ratios of Cohen and Soto (2007) are 0.90 for levels and 0.88 for differences.

Thomas et al. (2001, 2003) were among the first to propose a new dataset of the Gini index of education, based on school attainment data with the focus on the dataset itself. For a chronological overview of existing datasets of inequality in educational attainments, see Table 2. However, several other datasets have been produced in some papers to estimate a Gini index of education with a focus on explaining economic growth, income inequality, or other dependent variables. Although the objectives of these kinds of papers are not the same, the datasets used are still analyzed here thoroughly for the sake of comparison with our dataset.

Moreover, few datasets have explored educational inequalities by age group.[3] Our approach can significantly improve the measurement of inequality in education compared to the existing datasets by producing more realistic and reliable estimates of the Gini index of education,

Table 2. Overview of Datasets on Inequality in Educational Attainments.

Authors	Number of Countries	Data Sources	Number of Levels of Education	Period	Population
López, Thomas, and Wang (1998)	12	BL (1996)	7	1970–1995	15+
Thomas et al. (2001)	85	BL (1996)	7	1960–1990	15+
Castelló and Doménech (2002)	108	BL (2001)	4	1960–2000	15+
Thomas et al. (2003)	140	BL (2001)	7	1960–2000	15+
Checchi (2004)	117	BL (1997)	4	1960–1995	25+
Araujo et al. (2004)	124	Household surveys	–	~2000	ACE
Lim and Tang (2008)	99	BL (2001)	7	1960–2000	25+
Morrisson and Murtin (2010)	78	MM (2009)	7	1870–2010	[15–64]/15+
Meschi and Scervini (2010)	31	International surveys[a]	–	–	25+
Castelló (2010)	83	BL (2010)	4	1960–2000	25+
Földvári and Van Leeuwen (2011)	92/109	CS (2007)/BL (2001)	4	1960–2000	15+

ACE, adults who have completed their education; 15+, population aged 15 and over; 25+, population aged 25 and over; ~2000, 2000 or the closest year; BL, Barro and Lee; CS, Cohen and Soto; MM, Morrison and Murtin.
Source: The authors.
[a]The European Social Survey, the European Union Statistics on Income and Living Conditions, the International Adult Literacy Survey, and the International Social Survey Programme.

especially when it comes to longitudinal and international comparisons. The dataset suggested in this paper gives further insight on educational inequality for many reasons:

- First, as the quality of the estimation of educational attainment levels contributes to the accuracy of the estimation of the Gini index, we use Barro and Lee's (2010) dataset, whose estimation is more accurate and which has specific advantages compared to other datasets. Note that most of previous datasets of educational inequality were based either on Barro and Lee's (1996, 2001) or on Cohen and Soto's (2007) datasets discussed above.
- Second, the dataset is constructed with seven levels of education.[4] All datasets constructed using only four levels of education present a real

limitation. Indeed, the Checchi (2004), Castelló and Doménech (2002), Földvári and Van Leeuwen (2011), and Castelló's (2010) studies have used only four levels of education in their Gini coefficient calculations. These works cannot include the variation within a school stage because they do not differentiate between those who actually completed a level of education and those who did not.

- Third, as we exploit educational attainment data disaggregated by age, we take into account in our calculations the variation of the duration of schooling stages. Indeed, all previous datasets on the Gini index of education included neither the variation of duration of educational stages over time,[5] nor the heterogeneity of age group's duration system; in a given country, different generation groups have different schooling stages' duration for each education stage. In fact, we take into account the heterogeneity of age group duration system over time and educational pathways of different cohorts within a population.[6] Our duration of educational stages' data used in the calculation of the Gini index makes no restriction on our dataset of inequality in educational attainment, contrary to the duration of schooling stages by Thomas et al. (2001, 2003) and Lim and Tang (2008). Thomas et al. (2001, 2003) have used Psacharopoulos and Arriagada (1986) data of duration of school stages, which are fixed in time and present only the duration of a broad secondary phase rather than the lower and upper secondary phases. In fact, the authors have used an approach that does not seem to be compatible with the data they used. Indeed, they hypothesized that the duration of schooling in the lower secondary stage corresponds to the half of the duration of a broad secondary phase. Furthermore, Lim and Tang's (2008) duration of school stages are drawn from the UNESCO Institute for Statistics Database which restricts their dataset to only 99 countries.
- Finally, our dataset is the first to provide an education Gini index by 5-year age intervals and by sex for a broad 146 countries and also for aggregated groups of countries or age intervals, considering the variation and the heterogeneity within these aggregated groups.

METHODOLOGY: ESTIMATION OF THE GINI INDEX OF EDUCATION

The Gini coefficient is widely used to measure inequality in the distribution of income (Lambert, 2001). Analogously, Thomas et al. (2001) developed a Gini coefficient applied to education based on school attainment. Both indicators – income Gini and education Gini – are equal to one half of the mean difference between all pairs of observations, divided by mean. One difference between them is that educational attainment is a discrete variable, whereas income is generally considered as a continuous variable.

Our dataset is about inequality in educational attainments measured by the Gini index of educational attainments. We adopted the formula of Thomas et al. (2001) to calculate a quinquennial Gini index of education of 146 countries by 5-year intervals and by sex and constructed a structural formula of the Gini index of education for aggregated groups, which employs all the abundance of disaggregated data (for a broad age group {15+, 25+, [15, 65], [15, 24], [25, 34] ...} and for groups of countries {The world, Advanced Countries, Developing Countries,[7] Middle East and North Africa, Sub-Saharan Africa, Latin America and the Caribbean, East Asia and the Pacific, South Asia, and Europe and Central Asia}).

Starting from the formula of the income Gini index of the discrete case of Lambert (2001) and assuming there are "*n*" distinct income groups, and that within each income group "*i*" there are a number of individuals earning that income level, we can reconcile this Gini formula with the formula of Thomas et al. (2001):

$$\text{Gini} = \frac{\sum_{\alpha=1}^{N}\sum_{\beta=1}^{N}|y_\alpha - y_\beta|}{2N^2\mu}$$

$$= \frac{\sum_{i=1}^{n}\sum_{j=1}^{n}\left(\frac{1}{N^2}\right)\sum_{h=1}^{n_i}\sum_{k=1}^{n_j}|y_{ih} - y_{jk}|}{2\mu}$$

$$= \frac{\sum_{i=1}^{n}\sum_{j=1}^{n}\left(\frac{n_i}{N}\right)\left(\frac{n_j}{N}\right)|y_i - y_j|}{2\mu}$$

$$= \frac{\sum_{i=1}^{n}\sum_{j=1}^{n}p_i|y_i - y_j|p_j}{2\mu}$$

$$= \frac{1}{\mu}\sum_{i=1}^{n}\sum_{j=1}^{i-1}p_i|y_i - y_j|p_j$$

$$\text{Gini} = \frac{1}{\mu}\sum_{i=1}^{n}\sum_{j=1}^{i-1}p_i|y_i - y_j|p_j \qquad (1)$$

In order to reflect the population size and to standardize the following formulas, we can also rewrite the formula of the Gini index of education as:

$$\text{Gini} = \frac{1}{\mu}\sum_{i=1}^{n}\sum_{j=1}^{i-1} p_i|y_i - y_j|p_j$$

$$= \frac{\sum_{i=1}^{n}\sum_{j=1}^{n} p_i|y_i - y_j|p_j}{2\mu}$$

$$= \frac{\sum_{i=1}^{n}\sum_{j=1}^{n} \left(\frac{n_i}{N}\right)|y_i - y_j|\left(\frac{n_j}{N}\right)}{2\sum_{i=1}^{n}\left(\frac{n_i}{N}\right)y_i}$$

$$= \frac{\sum_{i=1}^{n}\sum_{j=1}^{n} n_i|y_i - y_j|n_j}{2N\sum_{i=1}^{n} n_i y_i}$$

$$\text{Gini} = \frac{\sum_{i=1}^{n}\sum_{j=1}^{n} n_i|y_i - y_j|n_j}{2N\sum_{i=1}^{n} n_i y_i} \tag{2}$$

Note that the value of Gini is sensitive to population size N if the population size is too small. The sensitivity is reflected by a factor of $[N/(N-1)]$. The education Gini formula for a small population is shown in Eq. (3).

$$\text{Gini}_{\text{small population}} = \left(\frac{N}{N-1}\right)\left[\frac{\sum_{i=1}^{n}\sum_{j=1}^{n} n_i|y_i - y_j|n_j}{2N\sum_{i=1}^{n} n_i y_i}\right] = \frac{\sum_{i=1}^{n}\sum_{j=1}^{n} n_i|y_i - y_j|n_j}{2(N-1)\sum_{i=1}^{n} n_i y_i} \tag{3}$$

For all countries, regardless of age group, the population size is quite large, so that the difference between the value of Gini coefficient in Eqs. (2) and (3) is very small.

Gini Index of Education by Age Group

$$\mathrm{Gini}^{a}_{c,t} = \frac{\sum_{i=1}^{n}\sum_{j=1}^{n} n^{a}_{c,i,t}\left|y^{a}_{c,i,t} - y^{a}_{c,j,t}\right| n^{a}_{c,j,t}}{2\ N^{a}_{c,t}\sum_{i=1}^{n} n^{a}_{c,i,t} y^{a}_{c,i,t}} \tag{4}$$

where $\mathrm{Gini}^{a}_{c,t}$, the Gini index of education of age group "a" for the country "c" at the time "t." Age group "a" corresponds to the following: $a=1$ to 15–19, $a=2$ to 20–24 age group, ..., and $a=13$–75, and above. n corresponds to the number of educational levels, which is equal in our study to 7. i and j are educational levels: $i=1$ for no formal education, $i=2$ for incomplete primary, $i=3$ for complete primary, $i=4$ for incomplete secondary, $i=5$ for complete secondary, $i=6$ for incomplete tertiary, and $i=7$ for complete tertiary. $n^{a}_{c,i,t}$ represents the size of the population at the time "t", in the age group "a," and for the country "c" having attained the educational level "i." $N^{a}_{c,t}$ represents the size of the population at the time "t," in the age group "a" and for the country "c" ($N^{a}_{c,t} = \sum_{i-1}^{n} n^{a}_{c,i,t}$). $y^{a}_{c,i,t}$, the number of years of schooling accumulated by group "a" in the country "c" to attain the educational level "i" at time "t."[8]

Gini Index of Education of Aggregated Group Using Disaggregated Data by Age

Instead of calculating the weighted average Gini index for world region or country group, we construct a structural formula that allows us to better harness the wealth of disaggregated data in order to calculate a Gini index of education of an aggregated group (group of age interval or group of countries = region) taking into consideration changes over time in the duration of educational stages in each country and for each age group.

(a) *Gini index of a broad age group*[9]

$$\mathrm{Gini}^{G}_{c,t} = \frac{\sum_{a\in G}\sum_{a'\in G}\sum_{i=1}^{n}\sum_{j=1}^{n} n^{a}_{c,i,t}\left|y^{a}_{c,i,t} - y^{a'}_{c,j,t}\right| n^{a'}_{c,j,t}}{2\ N^{G}_{c,t}\left[\sum_{a\in G}\sum_{i=1}^{n} n^{a}_{c,i,t}\ y^{a}_{c,i,t}\right]} \tag{5}$$

where $\text{Gini}_{c,t}^{G}$, the Gini index of education of the broad age group "G" for the country "c," at the time "t."[10] Age group "a" corresponds to the following : $a=1$ ($a'=1$) to 15–19 age group, $a=2$ ($a'=2$) to 20–24 age group, …, and $a=13$ ($a'=13$) to 75 and above. $N_{c,t}^{G}$ represents the size of the population at the time "t", in the broad age group "G," and for the country "c." ($N_{c,t}^{G} = \sum_{a \in G} \sum_{i=1}^{n} n_{c,i,t}^{a} = \sum_{a \in G} N_{c,t}^{a}$).

(b) *Gini index of a broad group of countries*[11]

$$\text{Gini}_{R,t}^{a} = \frac{\sum_{c \in R} \sum_{c' \in R} \sum_{i=1}^{n} \sum_{j=1}^{n} n_{c,i,t}^{a} \left| y_{c,i,t}^{a} - y_{c',j,t}^{a} \right| n_{c',j,t}^{a}}{2 \; N_{R,t}^{a} \left[\sum_{c \in R} \sum_{i=1}^{n} n_{c,i,t}^{a} \; y_{c,i,t}^{a} \right]} \tag{6}$$

$\text{Gini}_{R,t}^{a}$, the Gini index of education of age group "a" for the region "R" at the time "t." c (c') represents a country in the region "R."

(c) *Gini index of a broad group of countries (or region "R") and a broad age group*

$$\text{Gini}_{R,t}^{G} = \frac{\sum_{c \in R} \sum_{c' \in R} \sum_{a \in G} \sum_{a' \in G} \sum_{i=1}^{n} \sum_{j=1}^{n} n_{c,i,t}^{a} \left| y_{c,i,t}^{a} - y_{c',j,t}^{a'} \right| n_{c',j,t}^{a'}}{2 \; N_{R,t}^{G} \left[\sum_{c \in R} \sum_{a \in G} \sum_{i=1}^{n} n_{c,i,t}^{a} \; y_{c,i,t}^{a} \right]} \tag{7}$$

Calculation of Durations of Schooling for Each Level of Education $y_{c,i,t}^{a}$

The corresponding durations of schooling for each stage $y_{c,i,t}^{a}$ are not explicitly available in Barro and Lee's (2010) dataset. The approach followed to find $y_{c,i,t}^{a}$ is to merge the two Barro and Lee (2010) datasets of total and female populations and to use average years of schooling of each stage for both total and female populations.

The average years of schooling of the primary stage can be defined as the weighted average number of years of education received by individuals who completed and those who have not completed the primary stage of schooling. Indeed, as we mentioned before, we consider seven educational levels. So, in computing the average years of schooling of the primary stage, we take into account only individuals who have a primary education whether they have finished or not ($i > 1$). In fact, the proportion of individuals who have not completed primary education would be equal to those who have reached level 2 ($i = 2$). However, for those who have completed it, we take into consideration the population with at least a primary school degree ($i \geq 3$).

$$\mathrm{aysp}^a_{c,t} = \underbrace{p^a_{c,2,t}[y^a_{c,2,t} - y^a_{c,1,t}]}_{\text{Incomplete primary cycle}} + \underbrace{\left(\sum_{j=3}^{7} p^a_{c,j,t}\right)[y^a_{c,3,t} - y^a_{c,1,t}]}_{\text{Complete primary cycle}} \tag{8}$$

where $p^a_{c,i,t}$, the fraction of group "a" in the country "c" having attained the educational level "i" at time "t."

The average years of schooling for secondary and higher stages can be obtained by following the same reasoning.

$$\mathrm{ayss}^a_{c,t} = \underbrace{p^a_{c,4,t}[y^a_{c,4,t} - y^a_{c,3,t}]}_{\text{Incomplete secondary cycle}} + \underbrace{\left(\sum_{j=5}^{7} p^a_{c,j,t}\right)[y^a_{c,5,t} - y^a_{c,3,t}]}_{\text{Complete secondary cycle}} \tag{9}$$

$$\mathrm{ayst}^a_{c,t} = \underbrace{p^a_{c,6,t}[y^a_{c,6,t} - y^a_{c,5,t}]}_{\text{Incomplete tertiary cycle}} + \underbrace{p^a_{c,7,t}[y^a_{c,7,t} - y^a_{c,5,t}]}_{\text{Complete tertiary cycle}} \tag{10}$$

We must calculate $y^a_{c,j,t}$ for each country "c", for each age group "a," and for each time period "t." This results in finding seven unknowns. In order to perform our calculations, we must build a system of seven equations.

As the $y^a_{c,j,t}$ is the same for males and females:

$$y_{(mf)}{}^a_{c,j,t} = y_{(m)}{}^a_{c,j,t} = y_{(f)}{}^a_{c,j,t} \tag{11}$$

We replicated the three equations for the average years of schooling of three stages {(1), (2), and (3)} for the total and female populations. In addition to this, the number of years of schooling accumulated by the illiterate population is equal to zero ($\forall a \in [1, 13]$; $y^a_{c,1,t} = 0$).

In total, we obtained for each age group of a given country at a given time a system of equations that corresponds to 24,674 systems of equations of seven equations and seven unknowns.[12]

$$\begin{cases} \text{aysp}_{(mf)}{}^{a}_{c,t} = p_{(mf)}{}^{a}_{c,2,t}[y^{a}_{c,2,t} - y^{a}_{c,1,t}] + \left(\sum_{j=3}^{7} p_{(mf)}{}^{a}_{c,j,t}\right)[y^{a}_{c,3,t} - y^{a}_{c,1,t}] \\ \text{aysp}_{(f)}{}^{a}_{c,t} = p_{(f)}{}^{a}_{c,2,t}[y^{a}_{c,2,t} - y^{a}_{c,1,t}] + \left(\sum_{j=3}^{7} p_{(f)}{}^{a}_{c,j,t}\right)[y^{a}_{c,3,t} - y^{a}_{c,1,t}] \\ \text{ayss}_{(mf)}{}^{a}_{c,t} = p_{(mf)}{}^{a}_{c,4,t}[y^{a}_{c,4,t} - y^{a}_{c,3,t}] + \left(\sum_{j=5}^{7} p_{(mf)}{}^{a}_{c,j,t}\right)[y^{a}_{c,5,t} - y^{a}_{c,3,t}] \\ \text{ayss}_{(f)}{}^{a}_{c,t} = p_{(f)}{}^{a}_{c,4,t}[y^{a}_{c,4,t} - y^{a}_{c,3,t}] + \left(\sum_{j=5}^{7} p_{(f)}{}^{a}_{c,j,t}\right)[y^{a}_{c,5,t} - y^{a}_{c,3,t}] \\ \text{ayst}_{(mf)}{}^{a}_{c,t} = p_{(mf)}{}^{a}_{c,6,t}[y^{a}_{c,6,t} - y^{a}_{c,5,t}] + p_{(mf)}{}^{a}_{c,7,t}[y^{a}_{c,7,t} - y^{a}_{c,5,t}] \\ \text{ayst}_{(f)}{}^{a}_{c,t} = p_{(f)}{}^{a}_{c,6,t}[y^{a}_{c,6,t} - y^{a}_{c,5,t}] + p_{(f)}{}^{a}_{c,7,t}[y^{a}_{c,7,t} - y^{a}_{c,5,t}] \\ y^{a}_{c,1,t} = 0 \end{cases}$$

where $\text{aysp}_{(mf)}{}^{a}_{c,t}$, average years of schooling of primary stage of the age group "*a*" of the country "*c*" in the total population at time "*t*." $\text{ayss}_{(mf)}{}^{a}_{c,t}$, average years of schooling of secondary stage of the age group "*a*" of the country "*c*" in the total population at time "*t*." $\text{ayst}_{(mf)}{}^{a}_{c,t}$, average years of schooling of tertiary stage of the age group "*a*" of the country "*c*" in the total population at time "*t*." $\text{aysp}_{(f)}{}^{a}_{c,t}$, average years of schooling of primary stage of the age group "*a*" of the country "*c*" in the population of females at time "*t*." $\text{ayss}_{(f)}{}^{a}_{c,t}$, average years of schooling of secondary stage of the age group "*a*" of the country "*c*" in the population of females at time "*t*." $\text{ayst}_{(f)}{}^{a}_{c,t}$, average years of schooling of tertiary stage of the age group "*a*" of the country "*c*" in the population of females at time "*t*." $p_{(mf)}{}^{a}_{c,j,t}$, the fraction of the age group "*a*" of the country "*c*" in the total population having attained the educational level "*j*" at time "*t*." $p_{(f)}{}^{a}_{c,j,t}$, the fraction of the age group "*a*" of the country "*c*" in the population of females having attained the educational level "*j*" at time "*t*."

The system of equations can be solved using the substitution method:

$$\begin{cases} y^a_{c,1,t} = 0 \\ y^a_{c,2,t} = \dfrac{\left(\sum_{j=3}^{7} p(f)^a_{c,j,t}\right)\left(\text{aysp}(mf)^a_{c,t}\right) - \left(\sum_{j=3}^{7} p(mf)^a_{c,j,t}\right)\left(\text{aysp}(f)^a_{c,t}\right)}{p(mf)^a_{c,2,t}\left(\sum_{j=3}^{7} p(f)^a_{c,j,t}\right) - p(f)^a_{c,2,t}\left(\sum_{j=3}^{7} p(mf)^a_{c,j,t}\right)} \\ y^a_{c,3,t} = \dfrac{p(mf)^a_{c,2,t}\left(\text{aysp}(f)^a_{c,t}\right) - p(f)^a_{c,2,t}\left(\text{aysp}(mf)^a_{c,t}\right)}{p(mf)^a_{c,2,t}\left(\sum_{j=3}^{7} p(f)^a_{c,j,t}\right) - p(f)^a_{c,2,t}\left(\sum_{j=3}^{7} p(mf)^a_{c,j,t}\right)} \\ y^a_{c,4,t} = y^a_{c,3,t} + \dfrac{\left(\sum_{j=5}^{7} p(f)^a_{c,j,t}\right)\left(\text{ayss}(mf)^a_{c,t}\right) - \left(\sum_{j=5}^{7} p(mf)^a_{c,j,t}\right)\left(\text{ayss}(f)^a_{c,t}\right)}{p(mf)^a_{c,4,t}\left(\sum_{j=5}^{7} p(f)^a_{c,j,t}\right) - p(f)^a_{c,4,t}\left(\sum_{j=5}^{7} p(mf)^a_{c,j,t}\right)} \\ y^a_{c,5,t} = y^a_{c,3,t} + \dfrac{p(mf)^a_{c,4,t}\left(\text{ayss}(f)^a_{c,t}\right) - p(f)^a_{c,4,t}\left(\text{ayss}(mf)^a_{c,t}\right)}{p(mf)^a_{c,4,t}\left(\sum_{j=5}^{7} p(f)^a_{c,j,t}\right) - p(f)^a_{c,4,t}\left(\sum_{j=5}^{7} p(mf)^a_{c,j,t}\right)} \\ y^a_{c,6,t} = y^a_{c,5,t} + \dfrac{p(f)^a_{c,7,t}\left(\text{ayst}(mf)^a_{c,t}\right) - p(mf)^a_{c,7,t}\left(\text{ayst}(f)^a_{c,t}\right)}{p(mf)^a_{c,6,t}\, p(f)^a_{c,7,t} - p(f)^a_{c,6,t}\, p(mf)^a_{c,7,t}} \\ y^a_{c,7,t} = y^a_{c,5,t} + \dfrac{p(mf)^a_{c,6,t}\left(\text{ayst}(f)^a_{c,t}\right) - p(f)^a_{c,6,t}\left(\text{ayst}(mf)^a_{c,t}\right)}{p(mf)^a_{c,6,t}\, p(f)^a_{c,7,t} - p(f)^a_{c,6,t}\, p(mf)^a_{c,7,t}} \end{cases}$$

It should be noted that when the denominator is equal to zero we can obtain the value of $y^a_{j,t}$ by the following equation: $(y^{a-1}_{j,t-5} = y^a_{j,t} = y^{a+1}_{j,t+5})$, because it is the same cohort that went through the same educational system.

GLOBAL TRENDS IN INEQUALITY IN EDUCATIONAL ATTAINMENT

The data show that educational inequality has been declining for all regions and for all age groups during the last six decades (see Table 3). However, it did not occur in a uniform manner because it depends on age groups and development levels. The world Gini index of education decreased from 0.64 in 1950 to 0.34 in 2010 among the population aged 15 years and above. For advanced countries, the Gini index of education for the population aged 15 years and above decreased from 0.38 to 0.19, whereas for developing

Table 3. Education Gini by Development Level and Age Group, 1950, 1970, 1990, 2010.

Region/Age Group	1950	1970	1990	2010
World (146)				
15–24	0.56	0.44	0.34	0.24
25–34	0.66	0.51	0.40	0.29
35–44	0.67	0.58	0.45	0.33
45–54	0.67	0.64	0.52	0.37
55–64	0.68	0.65	0.59	0.41
65–74	0.66	0.64	0.63	0.47
75 and over	0.61	0.61	0.57	0.51
15+	0.64	0.55	0.45	0.34
Advanced countries (24)				
15–24	0.34	0.27	0.22	0.16
25–34	0.35	0.30	0.21	0.15
35–44	0.37	0.34	0.24	0.17
45–54	0.38	0.34	0.29	0.18
55–64	0.40	0.36	0.34	0.20
65–74	0.40	0.39	0.37	0.25
75 and over	0.40	0.38	0.37	0.27
15+	0.38	0.33	0.28	0.19
Developing countries (122)				
15–24	0.61	0.47	0.35	0.25
25–34	0.75	0.56	0.42	0.31
35–44	0.78	0.64	0.49	0.35
45–54	0.79	0.74	0.57	0.40
55–64	0.81	0.76	0.66	0.45
65–74	0.80	0.77	0.73	0.53
75 and over	0.77	0.76	0.70	0.63
15+	0.73	0.61	0.48	0.36

Source: Author's calculations based on Barro and Lee Data (2010).

$$\text{Gini}_{R,t}^{G} = \frac{\sum_{c\in R}\sum_{c'\in R}\sum_{a\in G}\sum_{a'\in G}\sum_{i=1}^{n}\sum_{j=1}^{n} n_{c,i,t}^{a}\left|y_{c,i,t}^{a} - y_{c',j,t}^{a'}\right| n_{c',j,t}^{a'}}{2\,N_{R,t}^{G}\left[\sum_{c\in R}\sum_{a\in G}\sum_{i=1}^{n} n_{c,i,t}^{a}\,y_{c,i,t}^{a}\right]}$$

with "a" age group; "c" country; "t" time. Age group "a" corresponds for $a=1$ to 15–19 age group, $a=2$ to 20–24 age group, $a=13$–75 and above. n is the number of levels of education, which is equal in our study to 7 levels. i and j are educational levels. *$j=1$ for no formal education, $j=2$ for incomplete primary, $j=3$ for complete primary, $j=4$ for incomplete secondary, $j=5$ for complete secondary, $j=6$ for incomplete tertiary, and $j=7$ for complete tertiary.* $n_{c,i,t}^{a}$ represents the size of the population at the time "t," in the age group "a" and for the country "c" having attained the educational level "i." $y_{j,t}^{a}$ is the number of years of schooling accumulated by group "a" to attain the educational level "j" at time "t."

countries it declined from 0.73 to 0.36. Thus, among the population aged 15 years and above, the level of educational inequality for advanced countries, registered in 1950, is comparable to the level for developing countries in 2010. This results in a difference of six decades in terms of efforts allocated to reduce the educational inequality. The level of inequality was more pronounced in less developed countries in the 1950s, but it greatly lowered over the period, although the 2010 level still remains higher than in developed countries.

Education inequality declined for all age groups, but the decline has been particularly strong for young people aged between 15 and 24 years old who have the most egalitarian distribution of education in 2010. The world Gini index of education for this age group decreased from 0.56 to 0.24 between 1950 and 2010. In dynamics, however, the degree of inequality decreases with age. Note that the decline in inequality in developing countries has been the highest among the 15–24 years. They benefited from the quantitative progress related to the development of basic education in last century in these countries. These improvements in attainment among younger cohorts in every generation contribute to rising average years of schooling continually over time and to lower educational inequality. The gap between developed and developing countries has narrowed by 20 years over the young population aged 15–24 (see Fig. 1).

The distribution of education as measured by Gini coefficients is very sensitive to the improvement of access to basic education and especially to the changes in the proportion of population with no schooling. This can be indicated by an education Lorenz curve (Fig. 2). The shifting of a country's education Lorenz curve closer to the egalitarian line indicates some improvement of education equality. An examination of the education Lorenz curves of developing and advanced countries shows that advanced countries have a more equitable distribution of education than developing countries, as they have a flatter Lorenz curve, virtually connected to the origin of the graph. In fact, they expanded basic education rapidly and eliminated illiteracy successfully in the early 1950s (the proportion of population aged 15 and older with no schooling declines from 9.2% in 1950 to 2.3% in 2010) and achieved higher educational attainment (5.7% of population aged 15 and above attained the tertiary stage in 1950, and this proportion rose to 25.6% in 2010). Despite progress in expanding basic education in developing countries, more than 17% of the population (aged 15 years old and over) did not receive any education in 2010 (61.2% in 1950) and only 9.2% have attained the tertiary stage in 2010.

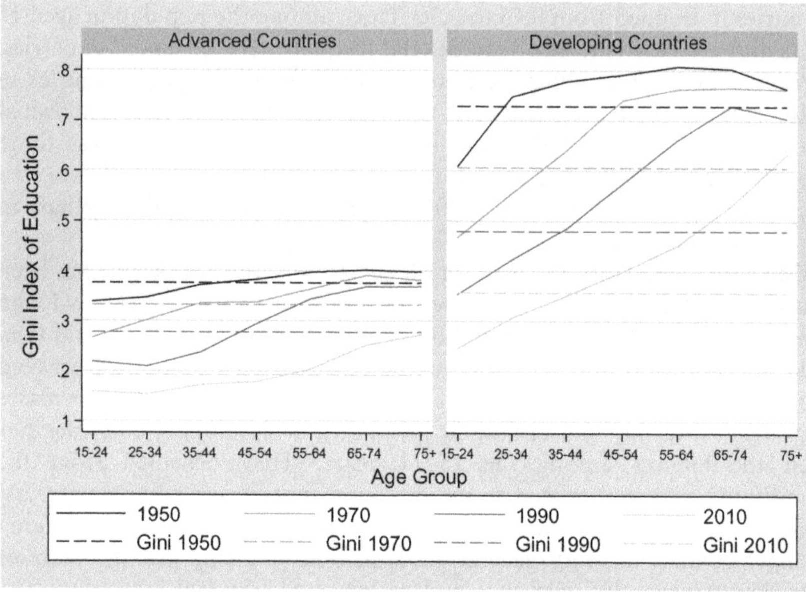

Fig. 1. Education Gini by Development Level and Age Group, 1950, 1970, 1990, 2010.

Table 4 summarizes the educational inequality among males and females during the last six decades by development level and region. It shows a clear downward trend for both genders of the world population aged 15 and above. However, educational inequality depends on the development level and the geographical zone. In 2010, the gender gap – measured by calculating the absolute difference between Gini coefficients for males and females – is considerably smaller for advanced countries, while it remains persistent and substantial for developing countries. The education gender gap in Latin America and the Caribbean, along with Europe and Central Asia, is gradually disappearing, but it remains relatively large for East Asia and the Pacific. Although the Middle East and North Africa, Sub-Saharan Africa, and South Asia have even larger gaps (11%, 11%, and 20%, respectively), these regions have achieved substantial progress in reducing the Gini coefficients for males and females. For example, the Middle East and North Africa begin at very high levels, but fall from 0.95 to 0.49 for females and from 0.89 to 0.38 for males. Nevertheless, a significant reduction in inequality is observed

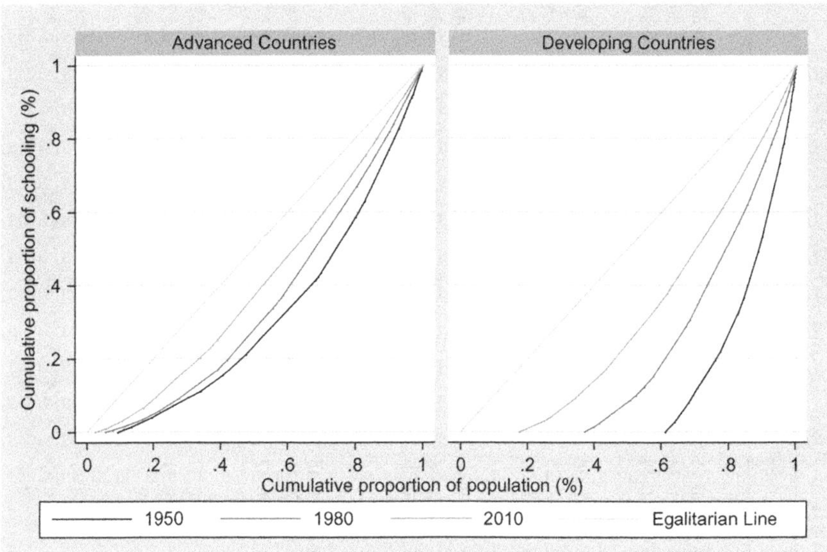

Fig. 2. Education Lorenz Curve by Development Level (population aged 15 or older), 1950, 1980, 2010.

for young people between 15 and 24 years old, mainly due to generalization of basic schooling during the last decades (Table 5).

In Fig. 3, we plotted the Education Lorenz curves of developed and developing countries by age. A horizontal reading of the curves gives the evolution of educational inequality in the same age through time. A vertical reading of the curves shows cross-section differences in educational inequality across age groups. A diagonal reading allows us to see the evolution of inequality within the same cohort through time. We can note, for example, that the level of inequality in the age group 15–24 has declined between 1950 and 2000, moving closer to that of developed countries. This reflects the advances in basic education for young people, especially during the last decades. As been said before, the degree of inequality is higher for upper age group. Indeed, the trend is downward over the period 1950–2010, while maintaining inter-generational differences.

Fig. 4 shows that the Gini index of education declines with the increase of the average levels of education. Countries with a high average of years of schooling are likely to have weak levels of inequality. This trend is confirmed, as is the case in most of the empirical work, in our sample

Table 4. Education Gini by Region and Gender (Population Aged 15 and Above), 1950–2010.

Year	1950	1955	1960	1965	1970	1975	1980	1985	1990	1995	2000	2005	2010
World (146)													
Female	0.68	0.66	0.64	0.62	0.59	0.57	0.54	0.51	0.48	0.46	0.43	0.40	0.38
Male	0.60	0.58	0.57	0.54	0.51	0.48	0.45	0.43	0.41	0.37	0.34	0.31	0.30
Total	0.64	0.62	0.60	0.58	0.55	0.53	0.49	0.47	0.45	0.42	0.39	0.36	0.34
Advanced countries (24)													
Female	0.38	0.38	0.37	0.35	0.34	0.33	0.31	0.30	0.29	0.27	0.24	0.21	0.20
Male	0.37	0.36	0.36	0.34	0.32	0.31	0.29	0.28	0.27	0.24	0.21	0.19	0.18
Total	0.38	0.37	0.36	0.35	0.33	0.32	0.30	0.29	0.28	0.25	0.23	0.20	0.19
Developing countries (122)													
Female	0.78	0.76	0.74	0.70	0.66	0.63	0.59	0.56	0.52	0.49	0.47	0.43	0.41
Male	0.67	0.65	0.63	0.60	0.55	0.52	0.48	0.45	0.43	0.39	0.35	0.33	0.31
Total	0.73	0.71	0.68	0.65	0.61	0.58	0.54	0.50	0.48	0.44	0.41	0.38	0.36
By region													
East Asia and the Pacific (19)													
Female	0.83	0.79	0.74	0.68	0.60	0.54	0.49	0.45	0.43	0.40	0.37	0.34	0.31
Male	0.69	0.65	0.61	0.56	0.49	0.45	0.39	0.38	0.39	0.33	0.27	0.25	0.24
Total	0.76	0.72	0.68	0.62	0.55	0.50	0.44	0.42	0.41	0.36	0.32	0.29	0.27
Europe and Central Asia (20)													
Female	0.44	0.43	0.41	0.38	0.35	0.32	0.30	0.27	0.25	0.22	0.20	0.18	0.17
Male	0.38	0.36	0.34	0.32	0.28	0.26	0.22	0.21	0.19	0.18	0.16	0.15	0.15
Total	0.42	0.40	0.38	0.36	0.32	0.30	0.26	0.24	0.22	0.20	0.18	0.16	0.16
Latin America and the Caribbean (25)													
Female	0.65	0.63	0.60	0.58	0.55	0.54	0.52	0.47	0.44	0.40	0.37	0.33	0.31
Male	0.60	0.59	0.57	0.55	0.51	0.51	0.50	0.46	0.43	0.40	0.36	0.31	0.30
Total	0.62	0.61	0.59	0.56	0.53	0.53	0.51	0.46	0.43	0.40	0.36	0.32	0.31

Middle East and North Africa (18)													
Female	0.95	0.94	0.93	0.92	0.89	0.86	0.81	0.75	0.69	0.64	0.58	0.53	0.49
Male	0.89	0.87	0.85	0.81	0.77	0.72	0.65	0.57	0.52	0.49	0.45	0.42	0.38
Total	0.92	0.91	0.89	0.86	0.83	0.79	0.73	0.66	0.61	0.56	0.51	0.47	0.43
South Asia (7)													
Female	0.93	0.92	0.91	0.89	0.87	0.86	0.84	0.79	0.75	0.71	0.67	0.61	0.57
Male	0.74	0.73	0.72	0.72	0.68	0.66	0.64	0.58	0.52	0.49	0.45	0.41	0.37
Total	0.83	0.82	0.81	0.81	0.77	0.76	0.74	0.68	0.63	0.60	0.56	0.50	0.46
Sub-Saharan Africa (33)													
Female	0.89	0.88	0.87	0.85	0.82	0.79	0.75	0.71	0.66	0.61	0.60	0.57	0.54
Male	0.79	0.77	0.74	0.71	0.68	0.65	0.61	0.57	0.52	0.49	0.47	0.45	0.43
Total	0.84	0.83	0.81	0.78	0.76	0.72	0.68	0.64	0.59	0.55	0.54	0.51	0.49

Source: Author's calculations based on Barro and Lee Data (2010)

$$\text{Gini}_{R,t}^{G} = \frac{\sum_{c\in R}\sum_{c'\in R}\sum_{a\in G}\sum_{a'\in G}\sum_{i=1}^{n}\sum_{j=1}^{n} n_{c,i,t}^{a}\left|y_{c,i,t}^{a}-y_{c'j,t}^{a'}\right| n_{c'j,t}^{a'}}{2\ N_{R,t}^{G}\left[\sum_{c\in R}\sum_{a\in G}\sum_{i=1}^{n} n_{c,i,t}^{a}\, y_{c,i,t}^{a}\right]}$$

with "a" age group; "c" country; "t" time. Age group "a" corresponds for $a=1$ to 15–19 age group, $a=2$ to 20–24 age group, $a=13$–75 and above. n is the number of levels of education, which is equal in our study to 7 levels. i and j are educational levels. *$j=1$ for no formal education, $j=2$ for incomplete primary, $j=3$ for complete primary, $j=4$ for incomplete secondary, $j=5$ for complete secondary, $j=6$ for incomplete tertiary, and $j=7$ for complete tertiary.* $n_{c,i,t}^{a}$ represents the size of the population at the time "t," in the age group "a" and for the country "c" having attained the educational level "i." $y_{j,t}^{a}$ is the number of years of schooling accumulated by group "a" to attain the educational level "j" at time "t."

Table 5. Education Gini by Region, Gender, and Age Group, 1950–2010.

Year	1950			1970			1990			2010		
Gender	Females	Males	Total	Females	Males	Total	Females	Males	Total	Females	Males	Total
World (146)												
15–19	0.54	0.51	0.53	0.44	0.41	0.42	0.35	0.30	0.32	0.24	0.21	0.23
20–24	0.64	0.54	0.59	0.50	0.41	0.46	0.38	0.32	0.35	0.27	0.22	0.25
25–29	0.69	0.59	0.64	0.55	0.47	0.51	0.42	0.37	0.39	0.31	0.25	0.28
30–34	0.72	0.63	0.68	0.56	0.47	0.51	0.45	0.36	0.41	0.34	0.27	0.31
35–39	0.71	0.64	0.68	0.62	0.54	0.58	0.48	0.42	0.45	0.37	0.30	0.33
40–44	0.70	0.63	0.67	0.63	0.53	0.58	0.50	0.42	0.46	0.38	0.30	0.34
45–49	0.71	0.64	0.67	0.67	0.57	0.62	0.55	0.49	0.52	0.40	0.31	0.35
50–54	0.70	0.64	0.67	0.70	0.62	0.66	0.57	0.48	0.52	0.43	0.34	0.39
55–59	0.71	0.65	0.68	0.68	0.61	0.65	0.63	0.54	0.59	0.45	0.35	0.40
60–64	0.71	0.64	0.68	0.68	0.60	0.64	0.63	0.57	0.60	0.48	0.37	0.43
65–69	0.70	0.62	0.67	0.67	0.61	0.64	0.65	0.59	0.63	0.52	0.40	0.46
70–74	0.68	0.60	0.65	0.65	0.59	0.62	0.66	0.59	0.63	0.54	0.42	0.48
75 and over	0.64	0.56	0.61	0.62	0.59	0.61	0.59	0.54	0.57	0.56	0.45	0.51
Advanced countries (24)												
15–19	0.35	0.32	0.33	0.25	0.25	0.25	0.21	0.23	0.22	0.16	0.16	0.16
20–24	0.34	0.34	0.34	0.27	0.26	0.27	0.19	0.18	0.19	0.13	0.12	0.13
25–29	0.36	0.34	0.35	0.30	0.29	0.29	0.21	0.20	0.20	0.15	0.14	0.14
30–34	0.35	0.34	0.34	0.31	0.30	0.31	0.21	0.21	0.21	0.16	0.16	0.16
35–39	0.37	0.37	0.37	0.34	0.33	0.34	0.24	0.23	0.23	0.17	0.17	0.17
40–44	0.38	0.37	0.37	0.34	0.33	0.33	0.25	0.24	0.24	0.18	0.17	0.17
45–49	0.39	0.38	0.38	0.35	0.33	0.34	0.29	0.27	0.28	0.17	0.17	0.17
50–54	0.39	0.38	0.38	0.33	0.32	0.33	0.32	0.30	0.31	0.19	0.18	0.19
55–59	0.41	0.38	0.40	0.37	0.35	0.36	0.35	0.33	0.34	0.20	0.18	0.19
60–64	0.41	0.38	0.40	0.37	0.36	0.36	0.35	0.34	0.35	0.23	0.21	0.22
65–69	0.41	0.39	0.40	0.40	0.39	0.39	0.37	0.37	0.37	0.24	0.22	0.24

70–74	0.41	0.39	0.40	0.39	0.38	0.39	0.36	0.36	0.36	0.28	0.25	0.27
75 and over	0.41	0.39	0.40	0.38	0.37	0.38	0.37	0.37	0.37	0.28	0.26	0.27
Developing countries (122)												
15–19	0.58	0.56	0.57	0.47	0.44	0.45	0.37	0.30	0.33	0.25	0.22	0.23
20–24	0.72	0.53	0.65	0.54	0.43	0.49	0.40	0.34	0.37	0.29	0.23	0.25
25–29	0.80	0.65	0.73	0.60	0.50	0.55	0.45	0.39	0.42	0.33	0.26	0.29
30–34	0.84	0.71	0.77	0.62	0.50	0.56	0.48	0.38	0.43	0.36	0.28	0.32
35–39	0.83	0.73	0.78	0.69	0.58	0.64	0.51	0.44	0.48	0.39	0.31	0.35
40–44	0.83	0.73	0.78	0.71	0.58	0.64	0.55	0.45	0.50	0.41	0.31	0.36
45–49	0.83	0.74	0.79	0.79	0.64	0.72	0.61	0.54	0.58	0.43	0.33	0.38
50–54	0.85	0.75	0.80	0.83	0.70	0.77	0.63	0.51	0.57	0.47	0.36	0.42
55–59	0.86	0.76	0.81	0.81	0.71	0.76	0.70	0.59	0.65	0.50	0.37	0.43
60–64	0.86	0.76	0.81	0.81	0.71	0.76	0.72	0.63	0.68	0.54	0.40	0.47
65–69	0.86	0.75	0.81	0.81	0.71	0.77	0.76	0.67	0.72	0.59	0.43	0.52
70–74	0.84	0.74	0.80	0.81	0.70	0.76	0.80	0.67	0.74	0.62	0.46	0.55
75 and over	0.80	0.70	0.77	0.80	0.71	0.76	0.75	0.63	0.70	0.71	0.52	0.63
East Asia and the Pacific (19)												
15–19	0.39	0.44	0.43	0.29	0.37	0.33	0.24	0.24	0.24	0.13	0.14	0.13
20–24	0.70	0.52	0.61	0.36	0.28	0.33	0.26	0.27	0.27	0.15	0.16	0.15
25–29	0.88	0.63	0.75	0.42	0.38	0.41	0.29	0.31	0.30	0.18	0.16	0.17
30–34	0.93	0.73	0.83	0.49	0.37	0.43	0.34	0.28	0.31	0.23	0.20	0.21
35–39	0.95	0.30	0.87	0.60	0.52	0.57	0.38	0.39	0.39	0.25	0.20	0.23
40–44	0.95	0.80	0.87	0.69	0.51	0.60	0.40	0.37	0.39	0.27	0.21	0.24
45–49	0.95	0.81	0.88	0.88	0.62	0.75	0.48	0.53	0.51	0.29	0.22	0.26
50–54	0.95	0.81	0.88	0.92	0.72	0.82	0.55	0.47	0.52	0.34	0.25	0.29
55–59	0.96	0.82	0.89	0.94	0.78	0.86	0.68	0.61	0.66	0.38	0.26	0.32
60–64	0.96	0.82	0.89	0.95	0.78	0.87	0.75	0.67	0.72	0.41	0.28	0.35
65–69	0.97	0.81	0.90	0.96	0.79	0.88	0.86	0.73	0.79	0.48	0.31	0.41
70–74	0.97	0.80	0.90	0.95	0.78	0.88	0.88	0.70	0.80	0.57	0.36	0.47
75 and over	0.97	0.78	0.90	0.96	0.79	0.89	0.88	0.66	0.79	0.77	0.48	0.65

Table 5. (*Continued*)

Year	1950			1970			1990			2010		
Gender	Females	Males	Total	Females	Males	Total	Females	Males	Total	Females	Males	Total
Europe and Central Asia (20)												
15–19	0.33	0.33	0.33	0.15	0.18	0.17	0.15	0.15	0.15	0.21	0.21	0.21
20–24	0.33	0.30	0.31	0.16	0.16	0.16	0.10	0.09	0.09	0.16	0.15	0.15
25–29	0.39	0.33	0.36	0.20	0.19	0.19	0.11	0.10	0.10	0.14	0.12	0.13
30–34	0.45	0.37	0.42	0.26	0.25	0.26	0.13	0.12	0.13	0.12	0.11	0.11
35–39	0.46	0.39	0.44	0.30	0.28	0.29	0.15	0.14	0.15	0.12	0.11	0.11
40–44	0.46	0.39	0.44	0.33	0.30	0.32	0.15	0.15	0.15	0.11	0.10	0.10
45–49	0.47	0.40	0.44	0.37	0.33	0.35	0.22	0.21	0.22	0.10	0.10	0.10
50–54	0.48	0.41	0.46	0.45	0.35	0.41	0.23	0.21	0.22	0.13	0.12	0.13
55–59	0.48	0.41	0.45	0.47	0.38	0.44	0.32	0.28	0.30	0.14	0.14	0.14
60–64	0.51	0.42	0.48	0.46	0.39	0.44	0.34	0.30	0.32	0.14	0.14	0.14
65–69	0.50	0.41	0.47	0.48	0.39	0.45	0.42	0.34	0.39	0.20	0.19	0.20
70–74	0.50	0.40	0.47	0.48	0.39	0.45	0.47	0.36	0.44	0.21	0.19	0.21
75 and over	0.50	0.39	0.47	0.49	0.39	0.47	0.47	0.34	0.44	0.34	0.25	0.31
Latin America and the Caribbean (25)												
15–19	0.60	0.58	0.59	0.46	0.42	0.44	0.11	0.26	0.27	0.21	0.23	0.22
20–24	0.62	0.59	0.60	0.50	0.48	0.49	0.16	0.34	0.32	0.17	0.18	0.18
25–29	0.64	0.60	0.62	0.54	0.50	0.52	0.27	0.45	0.42	0.21	0.20	0.21
30–34	0.63	0.60	0.62	0.54	0.52	0.53	0.28	0.42	0.42	0.24	0.24	0.24
35–39	0.64	0.60	0.62	0.57	0.53	0.55	0.33	0.44	0.45	0.27	0.27	0.27
40–44	0.66	0.60	0.63	0.59	0.54	0.57	0.37	0.46	0.47	0.30	0.29	0.29
45–49	0.67	0.61	0.64	0.61	0.56	0.58	0.45	0.49	0.51	0.35	0.34	0.34
50–54	0.69	0.62	0.66	0.61	0.56	0.58	0.48	0.51	0.53	0.41	0.39	0.40
55–59	0.70	0.63	0.67	0.63	0.58	0.60	0.53	0.52	0.54	0.41	0.39	0.40
60–64	0.71	0.63	0.67	0.63	0.58	0.60	0.59	0.55	0.57	0.49	0.46	0.48
65–69	0.71	0.65	0.68	0.65	0.60	0.63	0.66	0.58	0.59	0.50	0.46	0.48

70–74	0.72	0.66	0.69	0.65	0.60	0.63	0.64	0.57	0.59	0.54	0.51	0.52
75 and over	0.71	0.65	0.68	0.65	0.60	0.62	0.66	0.58	0.59	0.57	0.54	0.56
Middle East and North Africa (18)												
15–19	0.91	0.85	0.88	0.76	0.61	0.68	0.47	0.35	0.40	0.28	0.28	0.28
20–24	0.95	0.87	0.91	0.85	0.67	0.76	0.55	0.38	0.45	0.34	0.30	0.32
25–29	0.95	0.87	0.91	0.89	0.73	0.81	0.62	0.43	0.52	0.36	0.31	0.33
30–34	0.96	0.89	0.92	0.92	0.79	0.86	0.71	0.52	0.61	0.41	0.34	0.36
35–39	0.95	0.89	0.92	0.94	0.82	0.88	0.76	0.55	0.65	0.47	0.36	0.41
40–44	0.96	0.90	0.93	0.95	0.85	0.90	0.83	0.63	0.73	0.55	0.38	0.46
45–49	0.96	0.91	0.94	0.95	0.86	0.90	0.87	0.69	0.78	0.61	0.43	0.52
50–54	0.96	0.92	0.94	0.96	0.88	0.92	0.91	0.74	0.83	0.71	0.51	0.61
55–59	0.96	0.92	0.94	0.95	0.88	0.91	0.92	0.77	0.84	0.75	0.54	0.65
60–64	0.96	0.93	0.94	0.96	0.90	0.93	0.93	0.80	0.86	0.82	0.61	0.72
65–69	0.96	0.93	0.95	0.96	0.91	0.94	0.92	0.80	0.86	0.86	0.67	0.77
70–74	0.96	0.93	0.94	0.97	0.91	0.94	0.93	0.83	0.88	0.90	0.71	0.81
75 and over	0.96	0.93	0.95	0.96	0.91	0.94	0.91	0.81	0.87	0.89	0.72	0.81
South Asia (7)												
15–19	0.86	0.67	0.76	0.74	0.53	0.63	0.55	0.37	0.45	0.26	0.15	0.20
20–24	0.91	0.72	0.81	0.82	0.60	0.71	0.66	0.43	0.54	0.38	0.21	0.29
25–29	0.93	0.73	0.83	0.88	0.68	0.78	0.72	0.49	0.60	0.49	0.31	0.39
30–34	0.93	0.73	0.83	0.88	0.69	0.78	0.75	0.52	0.63	0.55	0.34	0.44
35–39	0.95	0.76	0.85	0.93	0.75	0.84	0.77	0.54	0.65	0.62	0.43	0.52
40–44	0.95	0.76	0.85	0.93	0.75	0.84	0.81	0.57	0.69	0.66	0.43	0.54
45–49	0.95	0.76	0.85	0.93	0.75	0.84	0.85	0.60	0.72	0.71	0.48	0.59
50–54	0.96	0.80	0.88	0.93	0.75	0.84	0.87	0.64	0.76	0.74	0.50	0.62
55–59	0.96	0.80	0.88	0.93	0.76	0.84	0.88	0.66	0.77	0.76	0.52	0.64
60–64	0.96	0.80	0.88	0.93	0.76	0.84	0.91	0.72	0.81	0.80	0.55	0.67
65–69	0.96	0.78	0.88	0.93	0.76	0.84	0.90	0.70	0.80	0.83	0.57	0.71
70–74	0.96	0.79	0.88	0.93	0.75	0.84	0.91	0.72	0.82	0.85	0.61	0.74
75 and over	0.96	0.79	0.88	0.93	0.76	0.84	0.91	0.71	0.81	0.86	0.61	0.75

Table 5. *(Continued)*

Year	1950			1970			1990			2010		
Gender	Females	Males	Total	Females	Males	Total	Females	Males	Total	Females	Males	Total
Sub-Saharan Africa (33)												
15–19	0.83	0.72	0.78	0.69	0.55	0.62	0.50	0.41	0.45	0.40	0.35	0.38
20–24	0.88	0.74	0.81	0.78	0.63	0.70	0.54	0.42	0.48	0.47	0.38	0.42
25–29	0.89	0.78	0.83	0.82	0.66	0.74	0.60	0.46	0.53	0.50	0.40	0.45
30–34	0.89	0.79	0.84	0.83	0.68	0.76	0.64	0.51	0.58	0.52	0.42	0.47
35–39	0.90	0.81	0.86	0.87	0.71	0.79	0.71	0.56	0.64	0.54	0.42	0.48
40–44	0.90	0.83	0.87	0.88	0.74	0.81	0.76	0.60	0.68	0.56	0.42	0.49
45–49	0.91	0.84	0.88	0.89	0.78	0.84	0.81	0.64	0.73	0.62	0.47	0.55
50–54	0.91	0.85	0.88	0.90	0.80	0.85	0.82	0.66	0.74	0.65	0.51	0.58
55–59	0.92	0.85	0.89	0.90	0.81	0.86	0.85	0.69	0.77	0.72	0.57	0.65
60–64	0.92	0.85	0.89	0.90	0.83	0.87	0.87	0.72	0.80	0.76	0.60	0.69
65–69	0.92	0.85	0.89	0.92	0.84	0.88	0.87	0.75	0.82	0.81	0.65	0.74
70–74	0.92	0.85	0.89	0.91	0.85	0.88	0.88	0.77	0.83	0.82	0.66	0.75
75 and over	0.93	0.86	0.90	0.90	0.84	0.88	0.87	0.77	0.83	0.83	0.69	0.77

Source: Author's calculations based on Barro and Lee Data (2010)

$$\text{Gini}^a_{R,t} = \frac{\sum_{c\in R}\sum_{c\prime\in R}\sum_{i=1}^{n}\sum_{j=1}^{n} n^a_{c,i,t}\left|y^a_{c,i,t} - y^a_{c\prime,j,t}\right| n^a_{c\prime,j,t}}{2\,N^a_{R,t}\left[\sum_{c\in R}\sum_{i=1}^{n} n^a_{c,i,t}\,y^a_{c,i,t}\right]}$$

with "a" age group; "c" country; "t" time. Age group "a" corresponds for $a=1$ to 15–19 age group, $a=2$ to 20–24 age group, $a=13$–75 and above. n is the number of levels of education, which is equal in our study to 7 levels. i and j are educational levels. $j=1$ *for no formal education,* $j=2$ *for incomplete primary,* $j=3$ *for complete primary,* $j=4$ *for incomplete secondary,* $j=5$ *for complete secondary,* $j=6$ *for incomplete tertiary , and* $j=7$ *for complete tertiary.* $n^a_{c,i,t}$ represents the size of the population at the time "t," in the age group "a" and for the country "c" having attained the educational level "i." $y^a_{j,t}$ is the number of years of schooling accumulated by group "a" to attain the educational level "j" at time "t."

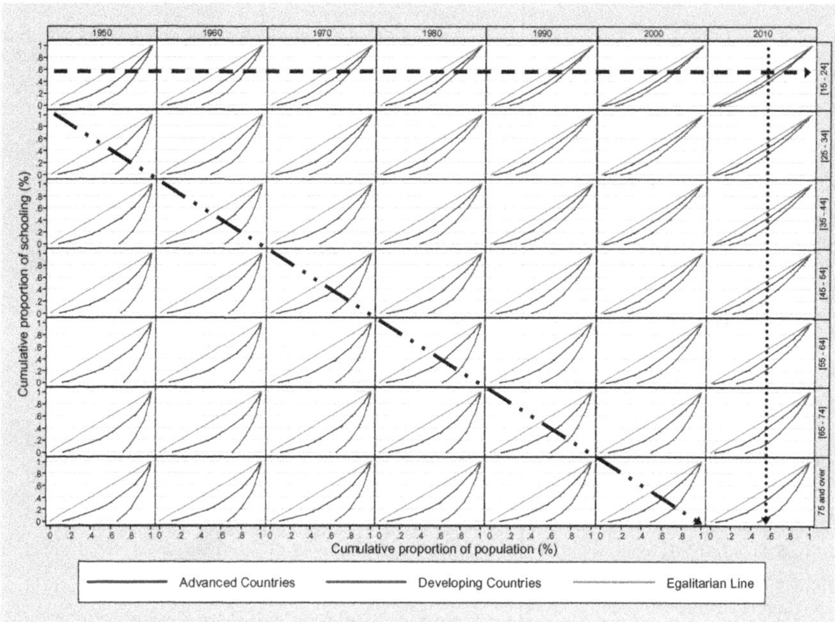

Fig. 3. Education Lorenz Curve by Age Group and Development Level from 1950 to 2010. (– – – – →) The Evolution over Time of the Education Lorenz Curve of the Same Age Group. (— · · — ·›) The Evolution over Time of Education Lorenz Curve of the Same Cohort. (················›) A Cross-Section Education Lorenz Curve over Age Group.

regardless of the region of the world. Thomas et al. (2001) find a strong negative association on cross-country data between Gini index of education and average years of schooling. This suggests that countries that spend more resources for education are also those where the distribution of enrollment between individuals is the most equitable. Moving any person out of illiteracy should improve the distribution of education and at the same time the level of educational attainment.

Our data show that the relation between inequality in education, measured by a standard deviation of schooling, and the level of schooling measured by the average years of schooling follows a bell-shaped curve for the case of all selected regions (Fig. 5). It means that during the development of education, the variance measured by standard deviation of schooling increases to reach a certain peak and then decreases. As in previous

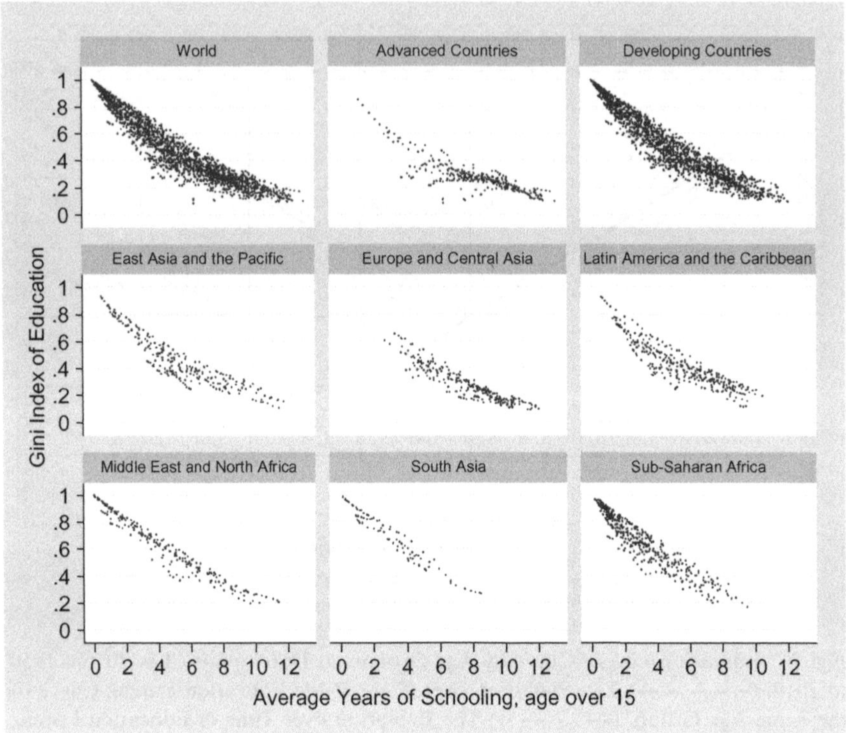

Fig. 4. Relationship between Education Gini and Average Years of Schooling by Region.

empirical work (Londoño, 1990; Ram, 1990; Thomas et al., 2001), the turning point is about 7 years, after which, the dispersion between individuals in education declines. Note that the higher is the level of development, the higher is the turning point.

CONCLUSION

This work presents extensive research on the measurement of inequality in education. We propose a new dataset on educational inequality by the estimation of a Gini index specific to education covering the period 1950–2010, the first attempt to present estimates by 5-year intervals and by

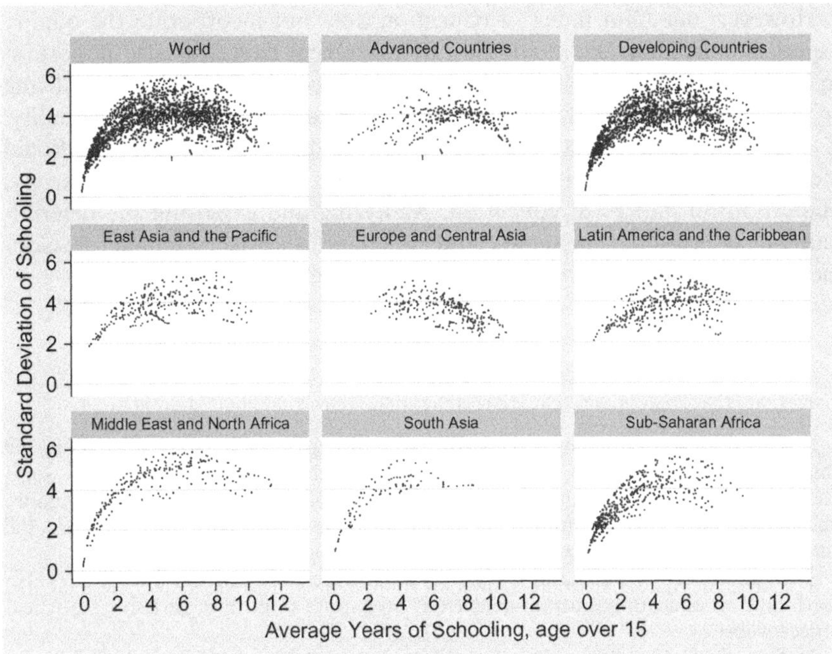

Fig. 5. Relationship between Standard Deviation of Schooling and Average Years of Schooling (Education Kuznets Curve by Region). Standard Deviation of Schooling (SDS) $= \sqrt{\sum_{i=1}^{n} p_i(y_i - \mu)^2}$.

gender for a broad panel. These estimates improve the measurement of inequality in education compared to the existing datasets by utilizing better estimation methodology, that is, disaggregating by age group and paying more attention to the duration of schooling stages than in previous studies. The data reveal a decrease in inequality in the world for the whole period. We find contrasting trends, depending on the level of development and age group. Education inequality, more manifest in developing countries in the 1950s, is strongly lowered over the period. Still, in 2010, the level remains higher than in advanced countries. In terms of educational policy in these countries, more attention is needed to improving basic education and to reducing dropout rates in primary and secondary schools, which leads to greater school achievement in a quantitative sense.

However, our Gini index of education does not incorporate the quality aspect of education. So, in addition to attainment data, it is also important to analyze educational inequality with a more complete picture by utilizing cognitive achievement data. To deepen our understanding of inequality, it will be helpful to expand the current dataset to include additional measures of human capital inequality, such as Theil, generalized entropy, and Atkinson indices of education. Analyzing and exploring the determinants of educational inequality and its relationship to economic development is also an important issue for future research.

NOTES

1. Educational attainment is the most frequently used human capital proxy in the empirical literature. Indeed, average years of schooling gained popularity as adult literacy rates capture only the first stages of human capital accumulation and ignore knowledge and skills acquired beyond basic levels. Enrolment ratios ignore the cumulative benefits of completing additional years of schooling.
2. In addition to OECD and UNESCO data sources, Cohen and Soto (2007) also used data on educational attainment from Singapore's and Bangladesh's statistical offices websites.
3. The Socio-Economic Database for Latin America and the Caribbean {CEDLAS and The World Bank: SEDLAC (2011)} presents information on Gini coefficient for the distribution of years of education by age group. However, using household survey data, it concerns only countries of Latin America and the Caribbean for discontinuous periods.
4. No formal education, incomplete primary, complete primary, lower secondary, upper secondary, incomplete tertiary, and complete tertiary.
5. Three fundamental educational stages are considered: primary, secondary, and tertiary.
6. Data on duration of educational stages can be obtained from the authors upon request.
7. The developing group is further broken down into six regions: Middle East/North Africa (18 countries), Sub-Saharan Africa (33), Latin America/Caribbean (25), East Asia/Pacific (19), South Asia (7), and Europe and Central Asia (20).
8. $y^a_{c,j,t}$ is not explicitly available in Barro and Lee's (2010) data set. We calculated $y^a_{j,t}$ by merging the two Barro and Lee's (2010) datasets corresponding to the total population and female {MF & F}(see IV.3).
9. 15+, 25+, [15, 65], [15, 24], [25, 34], …
10. For example *G* can be the population aged between [25–65], [15–24], or the 15 and over, 25 and over …
11. The world, Advanced Countries, Developing Countries, Middle East and North Africa, Sub-Saharan Africa, Latin America and the Caribbean, East Asia and the Pacific, South Asia, and Europe and Central Asia.

12. One hundred forty-six countries for 13 age groups at 13 moments between 1950 and 2010: 146 × 13 × 13 = 24,674.

ACKNOWLEDGMENTS

The authors would like to thank Lester Zeager for a careful reading and many helpful suggestions.

REFERENCES

Araujo, C., Ferreira, F., & Schady, N. (2004). *Is the world becoming more unequal? Changes in the world distribution of schooling*. Washington, DC: World Bank.

Barro, R. J., & Lee, J. W. (1993). International comparisons of educational attainment. *Journal of Monetary Economics*, *32*(3), 363–394.

Barro, R. J., & Lee, J. W. (1996). International measures of schooling years and schooling quality. *American Economic Review*, *86*(2), 218–223.

Barro, R., & Lee, J. W. (2001). International data on educational attainment: Updates and implications. *Oxford Economic Papers*, *53*(3), 541–563.

Barro, R. J., & Lee, J. W. (2010). *A new data set of educational attainment in the world, 1950–2010*. NBER Working Paper No. 15902. Cambridge, MA.

Castelló, A. (2010). Inequality and growth in advanced economies: An empirical investigation. *Journal of Economic Inequality*, *8*(3), 293–321.

Castelló, A., & Doménech, R. (2002). Human capital inequality and economic growth: Some new evidence. *The Economic Journal*, *112*(478), 187–200.

Checchi, D. (2004). Does educational achievement help to explain income inequality? In A. Cornia (Ed.), *Inequality, growth and poverty in an era of liberalization and globalization (Ch. 4)*. New York: Oxford University Press.

Cohen, D., & Soto, M. (2007). Growth and human capital: Good data, good results. *Journal of Economic Growth*, *12*(1), 51–76.

Földvári, P., & Van Leeuwen, B. (2011). Should less inequality in education lead to a more equal income distribution? *Education Economics*, *19*(5), 537–554.

Krueger, A. B., & Lindahl, M. (2001). Education for growth: Why and for whom? *Journal of Economic Literature*, *39*(4), 1101–1136.

Lambert, P. J. (2001). *The distribution and redistribution of income* (3rd ed.). Manchester: Manchester University Press.

Lim, A. S. K., & Tang, K. K. (2008). Human capital inequality and the Kuznets curve. *The Developing Economies*, *46*(1), 26–51.

Londoño, J. L. (1990). *Kuznetsian tales with attention to human capital*. Seminar paper at the Third Inter-American Seminar in Economics, Rio de Janeiro, Brazil.

López, R., Thomas, V., & Wang, Y. (1998). *Addressing the education puzzle: The distribution of education and economic reforms*. World Bank Working Paper Series No. 2031, World Bank, Washington, DC.

Meschi, E., & Scervini, F. (2010). *A new dataset on educational inequality*. GINI Discussion Paper No. 3, AIAS, Amsterdam.

Morrisson, C., & Murtin, F. (2009). The century of education. *Journal of Humain Capital*, *3*(1), 1–42.

Morrisson, C., & Murtin, F. (2010). *The Kuznets curve of education: A global perspective on education inequalities*. CEE Discussion Papers 0116, Centre for the Economics of Education, London School of Economics.

Psacharopoulos, G., & Arriagada, A. M. (1986). The educational composition of the labour force: An international comparison. *International Labour Review*, *125*(5), 561–574.

Ram, R. (1990). Educational expansion and schooling inequality: International evidence and some implications. *Review of Economics and Statistics*, *72*(2), 266–274.

The World Bank. (2006). *World development report 2006: Equity and development*. New York, NY: Oxford University Press.

Thomas, V., Wang, Y., & Fan, X. (2001). *Measuring education inequality: Gini coefficients of education*. Policy Research Working Paper No. 2525. Washington DC: The World Bank.

Thomas, V., Wang, Y., & Fan, X. (2003). Measuring education inequality: Gini coefficients of education for 140 countries (1960–2000). *Journal of Education Planning and Administration*, *17*(1), 5–33.

CHAPTER 14

UNDERSTANDING THE DRIVERS OF LOW-INCOME TRANSITIONS IN LUXEMBOURG

Alessio Fusco and Nizamul Islam

ABSTRACT

We analyse the determinants of poverty transitions, defined as movements across a low-income threshold, in Luxembourg. Data used are those from the Luxembourg socio-economic panel 'Liewen zu Lëtzebuerg' (PSELL3) running from 2003 to 2009. Using an endogenous switching first-order Markov model, we control for potential endogeneity to low-income transitions due to both initial conditions and non-random attrition. We find that employment protects from both remaining poor and entering poverty while several characteristics of the head of the household, such as low education or citizenship, and also household composition and housing tenure status are correlated to poverty entry but not to poverty persistence. In addition, attrition and initial low income are found to be endogenous processes with respect to low-income transitions. Finally, genuine state dependence accounts for a substantial level of aggregate state dependence.

Keywords: Poverty dynamics; Luxembourg; Markov transitions models; attrition; initial condition; state dependence

JEL classification: I32

Inequality, Mobility and Segregation: Essays in Honor of Jacques Silber
Research on Economic Inequality, Volume 20, 367–391

ISSN: 1049-2585/doi:10.1108/S1049-2585(2012)0000020017

"It might well be argued that concern with poverty in advanced countries, at a time when other countries face disaster, is unjustified and that the term 'poverty' cannot legitimately be applied. The parallel may be drawn with rearranging the deckchairs on the Titanic as the ship goes down. This does not, however, seem fully apposite. A closer parallel is with the position of those on ships steaming to the aid of the stricken vessel. The overriding objective should be to get to the rescue as rapidly as possible, but those on the rescuing ships should also be concerned that their steerage passengers do not die of exposure on the way. The relief of famine, and the redistribution of income to alleviate poverty on a world scale, should have priority, but the problem of poverty in advanced countries, defined in their terms, may legitimately come next on the list of concerns." (Atkinson, 2008)

INTRODUCTION

Luxembourg is known to be a small country; yet, a wealthy one. Indeed, as emphasised by Allegrezza, Heinrich, and Jesuit (2004), the economic power of Luxembourg has no common measure with the small size of the country in terms of surface and population. Is studying poverty in such a rich country worth the effort? In addition to the argument made above by Atkinson (2008), both normative and consequentialist arguments support a positive answer to that question. From a normative point of view, a minimum rights approach to poverty suggests that a certain level of income is a right for each citizen (Atkinson, 1989). If the average standard of living in a country like Luxembourg is high, some individuals do lag behind this average. Hence, the government should take care of the economic well-being of the disadvantaged and protect individuals from the consequences of adverse life-cycle events such as job loss or disability (Duncan et al., 1993). Consequentialist arguments are based on the negative externalities due to poverty. The evidence about the negative macro-level consequences of poverty on total economic output (see e.g. Bertola, 2000) as well as the negative impact of poverty on individual outcomes such as health or education (Grusky & Kanbur, 2006) pleads in favour of the usefulness of studying poverty in wealthier countries. Luxembourg is not an exception to this situation, especially in the face of the recent financial and economic crisis Luxembourg was confronted with and which is reflected in the recent decline of the annual GDP growth: between 2000 and 2007, the average annual growth rate was 4.7%; in 2008, the growth was very low (0.8%) and in 2009 it became negative at a level of −5.3%.[1]

These arguments certainly contribute to explain why, over the last three decades, a number of studies have been carried out on the topic of both income and non-income poverty in Luxembourg with the aim of determining its extent and forms (e.g. Berger, 2004). In our paper, poverty is defined as being in the bottom end of the income distribution, below a low-income threshold.[2] A salient feature of the Luxembourg income poverty profile is that children have a higher risk to be income poor (22.3% in 2009) than the overall population (14.9%), whereas the elderly have a lower risk (6%).[3] This age-related characteristic suggests that family-related transfers, despite being generous (Bradshaw & Chzhen, 2009), are less efficient in helping low-income people than are pension benefits (Allegrezza et al., 2004; Berger, Fusco, Jeandidier, & Reinstadler, 2009). Another specificity of Luxembourg is the heterogeneity of its population as a result of a high level of immigration. In 2010, more than four residents out of ten are foreigners (42.6%, Eurostat, 2010). In 2008, 23% of the immigrants were poor compared to 6% of the natives. These elements suggest that Luxembourg is a country with a very specific situation which makes it an interesting case study.[4]

The importance of adopting a longitudinal perspective when analysing poverty is well acknowledged (Bradbury, Jenkins, & Mickelwright, 2001; Jenkins, 2011). Following the low-income status of individuals over time provides at least two advantages. First, it allows us to capture the dynamic aspect of poverty. Poverty in a given period is certainly a problem but the persistence of poverty over time is much worse. Second, distinguishing between permanent and transitory poverty is important from an anti-poverty policy point of view. Knowing whether the same individuals are always poor or whether there is much mobility into and out of low income, implying that many individuals experience short poverty spells, helps to determine whether priority should be given to training and labour market policies or to transfers. Despite the importance of this longitudinal perspective and the availability of panel data, little is known about the turnover at the bottom end of the Luxembourg income distribution.

A notable exception is a study of STATEC (2010) analysing the determinants of poverty entry and exit in Luxembourg. This valuable study does not, however, account for several issues that can potentially bias the estimates, such as the initial conditions problem or non-random attrition. When modelling low-income transitions between two points in time, the initial conditions problem arises if the individuals at risk of being poor in the initial period are a non-random sample of the population (Heckman, 1981a). Attrition can also affect the estimates of low-income dynamics in the case where individuals leaving the panel are a selected group of the population. The aim of this paper is to analyse the drivers of low-income transitions in Luxembourg using the first-order Markov model of poverty transitions proposed by Cappellari and Jenkins (2004), which allows us to tackle these two potential sources of endogenous selection.

In addition, this model allows the analysis of the question of state dependence, which has not been done before in Luxembourg. State dependence in low income occurs when experiencing low income today increases the probability of experiencing low income tomorrow (Heckman, 1981b, 2001). State dependence can be spurious when it is the result of individual heterogeneity: the poor today might possess adverse observed or unobserved characteristics that will increase their probability of being poor tomorrow. In that case, the persistence into low income is due to the persistence of those adverse characteristics and not to the previous experience of poverty. Policies aiming at changing these individual characteristics, like training, might then be favoured. State dependence in low income might also be genuine when today's low income increases per se the risk of tomorrow low income. Biewen (2009) proposes several mechanisms to explain such a genuine effect: (i) adverse incentives in countries with a minimum-income guarantee, (ii) demoralisation or depreciation of human capital, (iii) potential health, drug or alcohol problems, (iv) bad networking or (v) household split. In the case of genuine state dependence (GSD), it is less straightforward to find tailored policies; however, short-term transfers aiming at reducing current poverty might be efficient in the long run. In the words of Poggi (2007), we need to break the 'vicious circle' of poverty. Assessing whether persistence into poverty is due to GSD or to observed and unobserved heterogeneity has important policy implications (see e.g. Stewart & Swaffield, 1999).

This paper is the first longitudinal analysis of low income in Luxembourg analysing the drivers of low-income entry and permanence while tackling the issues of state dependence, non-random attrition and initial conditions. The data used are those from the *Panel Socio-Economique 'Liewen zu Lëtzebuerg'* (PSELL3) from 2003 to 2009; they will be presented in Section 'Data and definitions' together with some methodological choices. Section 'Literature review and descriptive results' provides a literature review on Luxembourg and some descriptive results, while Section 'Econometric model' presents the econometric model used to analyse poverty entry and permanence, and Sections 'Results' discusses the results. Section 'Conclusion' finally concludes.

DATA AND DEFINITIONS

The main source to analyse poverty in Luxembourg is the *Socio-Economic Panel 'Liewen zu Lëtzebuerg'* (PSELL3) which is the Luxembourgish component of the European Union-*Statistics on Income and Living*

Conditions (EU-SILC). PSELL3 was launched in 2003, with an initial sample of around 3,500 households and around 10,000 individuals that were representative of the population living in private households. All households' members aged more than 16 answer a personal questionnaire and the reference person answers the household questionnaire. Original sample members are followed over time and interviewed at intervals of approximately one year. In case of split-off, new households are followed as well as all new co-residents. When children turn 16 they are asked to answer the personal questionnaire. Luxembourg is a country with a high level of immigration and of turnover in the resident population. To account for the evolving characteristics of the population, every year new individuals are included in the sample. Interviewed people provide information about their incomes, living conditions and other personal and household characteristics. PSELL3 is a suitable dataset for our analysis as it provides repeated annual observations since 2003 on the same individuals which allows us to link changes in poverty status with changes in household circumstances such as family arrangements or labour market situations. In this paper, we use the seven waves of the PSELL3 data covering the years 2003–2009.

Equivalent income, the main variable used to determine the status of poverty, is constructed by dividing the household total net income by an equivalence scale which allows us to compare households of different size and composition. The concept of income used in this paper is quite broad as it comprises earnings from work including company cars, all social benefits received in cash, income from investment and property and inter-household payments. Regarding the equivalence scale, we use the modified OECD equivalence scale, which assigns a value of 1 to the first adult in the household, 0.5 to each other adult and 0.3 to each child under 14 (Atkinson, Cantillon, Marlier, & Nolan, 2002). The use of equivalent income implies that income and demographic events will mechanically impact poverty (see Jenkins, 2000). More precisely, in a longitudinal perspective, income events reflecting changes in labour market situation or changes in the amount of non-labour income received and demographic events resulting from a joining event (e.g. birth or marriage) or a leaving event (e.g. death or divorce) will have an impact on poverty transitions and permanence (Cantó, 2003). The equivalent income variable, and hence the low-income status, is defined at the household level – so that all household members are assumed to share the same status. The unit of analysis is the individual as individuals can be followed over time, even in the case of household split-off.

In the European Union, poverty is defined in relation to the general level of prosperity in a country. The official definition of poverty in the European

Union is based on a *relative* poverty line equal to 60% of the equivalent median income. When measured on the basis of relative thresholds, poverty can decrease only if below low-income threshold individuals benefit more from economic progress than above low-income threshold individuals. Hence, this approach can be considered to be a reflection of inequality measuring the proportion of individuals who are left behind in rich countries. In the next section we provide a literature review as well as descriptive results of poverty in Luxembourg.

LITERATURE REVIEW AND DESCRIPTIVE RESULTS

According to the official definition of *relative* income poverty of the European Union, 12% of the residents of Luxembourg were at risk of income poverty in 2003. From 2003 to 2008, the poverty rate remained stable between 12% and 14% and significantly increased up to 14.9% in 2009 which coincided with the net decline in GDP growth that occurred that year (see Section 'Introduction'). These values are lower than the EU27 income poverty rate which was around 16.5% from 2005 to 2009 but higher than in some other European countries such as the Netherlands (11.1% in 2009) or the Czech Republic (8.6%). In 2009, the poverty rate of neighbouring countries was 12.9% in France, 15.5% in Germany and 14.6% in Belgium.

As mentioned previously, despite the availability of longitudinal data, little is known about the dynamics of poverty in Luxembourg.[5] To our knowledge, STATEC (2010) is the only source that provided a portrait of longitudinal poverty, documented the triggering events associated with poverty entry and exit and analysed their determinants for the period 2003–2008.[6] Out of this six-year window, they find that close to one individual out of four (23.5%) has experienced at least one year of poverty. Hence, the proportion of the population ever affected by low income is higher than what the annual poverty rates suggest. The group of individuals who have been poor at least once is quite heterogeneous. Indeed, 7.7% of Luxembourg residents have been poor for only one year – a transitory poverty experience; 9.2% have been poor for two, three or four years – a recurrent experience of poverty and finally, 6.6% of individuals have been poor for five or six years – a persistent experience of poverty. Even though these results do not account for censoring issues, they are in line with the overall paradox suggested by the OECD (2001) and, according to which, poverty is simultaneously fluid, many individuals being confronted at least once with it, and characterised by long-term traps. In addition, similarly to the cross-sectional poverty profile, the risk of being poor at least once over the period decreases with age (31% of the 0–14 years old compared with 16.1% of the over 55) and is higher for individuals with a precarious situation on the labour market (60.3% of the unemployed compared with 19.1% for full-time workers), immigrants (34.8% of Italians and 47.4% of Portuguese compared with 15.1% of Luxembourgish) and individuals living in childbearing households.

Another aspect of their study is the analysis of the events associated with poverty entry. The main trigger event into poverty is a decrease in household income which explains 92% of the transitions into poverty. In addition, a change in family structure accounts for only 8.6% of poverty entries and the type of income that decreases is important: 50.1% of the entries in poverty are linked to a decrease in income from work and 12.8% to a decrease of family allowances. Finally, they analyse the determinants of poverty entries using a logistic regression. The risk of entering poverty increases with the size of the household and with some events such as a divorce/separation or job loss and decreases during the transition from work to pension.[7] This study provides useful evidence about poverty dynamics in Luxembourg. However, it does not account for important issues that might affect the results: state dependence, initial conditions and non-random attrition.

These issues are illustrated in Table 1. The upper panel of Table 1 reports the pooled poverty transition matrix of individuals present in consecutive pairs of waves, $t-1$ and t. The probability of being in low income at time t is of 70.6% for individuals who were already low income the previous year (this corresponds to the probability of remaining poor), whereas it is equal to 4.2% for those who were not in low income the previous year (this corresponds to the probability of entering poverty) – a difference higher than 65%. This rough measure of aggregate state dependence (ASD) illustrates that the probability of being poor varies greatly according to the state of poverty in the previous year. In the case of Table 1, observed and unobserved determinants of initial poverty are not controlled for, so that the high state dependence might be due to an endogenous selection mechanism in the case of an overrepresentation of individuals likely to stay poor (resp. non-poor) among the group of poor individuals (resp. non-poor) at $t-1$.

The lower panel of Table 1 reports the poverty transition matrix of all individuals, that is, those present in both $t-1$ and t, and also those who were present in $t-1$ and exited the panel. It appears that 14.1% of the non-poor at time $t-1$ and 17.6% of the poor at time $t-1$ exited the panel at time t. This difference in terms of attrition rates according to the previous year's

Table 1. Poverty Transitions Matrix (in %).

	t			
$t-1$	Non Poor	Poor	Missing	Total
Individuals with non-missing poverty status at t (N = 47,211)				
Non- poor	95.8	4.2		100
Poor	29.4	70.6		100
All	87.6	12.4		100
All individuals (N = 55,226)				
Non-poor	82.2	3.7	14.1	100
Poor	24.2	58.2	17.6	100
All	74.9	10.6	14.5	100

Source: PSELL3, 2003–2009; authors' computation. Sample restricted to individuals with no missing values in the covariates used in following sections. Sample weights used.

poverty status illustrates the potential issue of endogeneity of sample retention. If attrition is non-random and depends on the poverty status, it might affect our estimates of poverty transitions. This issue is particularly relevant in our case as the PSELL3 presents a non-negligible level of attrition, even though it might be counterbalanced by the new sample added yearly (see Section 'Data and definitions').

When analysing the determinants of poverty dynamics and persistence, the issue of attrition and state dependence needs to be tackled. This is why we present in the next section the model proposed by Cappellari and Jenkins (2002a, 2002b, 2004) which is based on a simultaneous modelling of retention, initial poverty and current poverty.

ECONOMETRIC MODEL

Since the seminal work by Bane and Ellwood (1986), many econometric models have been proposed to assess the determinants of poverty dynamics – see for example Aassve, Burgess, Dickson, and Propper (2006) or Jenkins (2000, 2011) for a review. In this paper, we use the methodology proposed by Cappellari and Jenkins (2004) and based on a first-order Markov model of poverty transitions controlling for potential endogeneity to poverty transitions due to both initial conditions and (potential non-random) attrition (see also Ayllón, 2008; Buddelmeyer & Verick, 2008; Faye, Islam, & Zulu, 2011; Van Kerm, 2004, applies a variant of this methodology).

The main alternative approach to analyse the question of state dependence would be the use of non-linear dynamic random effects models – see Arulampalam, Booth, and Taylor (2000) and Stewart (2007) on unemployment, Poggi (2007) on social exclusion and Islam and Shimeles (2007), Biewen (2009) or Gradín and Cantó (2012) on poverty. This other type of transition model is based on a consistent estimation of the poverty status as a function of the previous poverty status and requires careful modelling of the initial conditions (see Wooldridge, 2005). Within this approach, a formal test of absence of true state dependence consists in assessing whether the regression coefficient of the lagged poverty status is equal to zero. Two elements related to the data should be noted here. First, the papers following non-linear dynamic random effects models usually do not model attrition. Second, they require for each individual a sequence of observations starting from the initial wave of the panel leading to the exclusion of individuals leaving temporarily the panel or joining the panel after the first year (Cappellari & Jenkins, 2008). By contrast, the Markovian model proposed by Cappellari and Jenkins (2004) allows us to analyse attrition (an important issue in our data) in a straightforward way and to use the annual refreshment samples of PSELL3 as well as incomplete data (see Section 'Data and definitions'). This explains our choice to favour this model.

An important result in the literature on poverty dynamics is that both the time spent in poverty and the recurrence of poverty spells impact on the probability of making a transition (e.g. Stevens, 1999; Devicienti, 2011). The main disadvantage of Cappellari and Jenkins modelling strategy is that these elements cannot be taken into account. This can be partially compensated by the fact that unobserved heterogeneity is accounted for: part of the elements covered by the duration and recurrence aspects of poverty spells are then likely to be accounted for too (Devicienti, 2011). However, it should be clear that the transition model used here should be seen as a complement to duration models (Jenkins, 2011).

We now turn to the presentation of the trivariate probit model used by Cappellari and Jenkins (2004) drawing heavily on the papers mentioned at the beginning of this section. Individuals are indexed from $i = 1 \ldots N$ and periods from $t = 1 \ldots T$. Let (1) p^*_{it-1} be the latent propensity of being poor for individual i at time $t-1$, (2) r^*_{it} the latent propensity of being retained in the sample for individual i between periods $t-1$ and t (i.e. the propensity for an individual with an observed income in $t-1$ to have an observed income in t)

and (3) p_{it}^* the latent propensity of being poor for individual i at time t. Each process is estimated simultaneously using the following model:

$$\begin{cases} p_{it-1}^* = \beta' x_{it-1} + u_{it-1} & (1) \\ r_{it}^* = \varphi' w_{it-1} + \mu_{it} & (2) \\ p_{it}^* = [\gamma_1' P_{it-1} + \gamma_2'(1 - P_{it-1})] z_{it-1} + \omega_{it} & (3) \end{cases}$$

x_{it-1}, w_{it-1} and z_{it-1} are vectors of explanatory variables related to individual and household characteristics. The variables included in x_{it-1} (resp. w_{it-1}) are the same as those included in z_{it-1} except that additional exclusion restrictions, which are necessary for model identification, are included. These exclusion restrictions are variables supposed to impact on initial low income (resp. retention) but not on low-income transitions. In the words of Ayllón (2008, p. 10), we need 'variables that affect the *level* of household equivalent income but not the *change* (see Stewart & Swaffield, 1999)'. The exclusion restrictions used are described in Section 'Results'.

Each error term (u_{it-1}, μ_{it}, ω_{it-1}) is assumed to follow a standard normal distribution and is the sum of a normal individual-specific unobserved (and time invariant) effect (η_i, ψ_i, ς_i) plus a normal orthogonal white noise (v_{it-1}, λ_{it}, τ_{it}). The joint distribution of the error terms (u_{it-1}, μ_{it}, ω_{it-1}) is trivariate normal. If the latent propensity of each process for an individual exceeds a certain value, then the individual realizes the outcome. Hence, we can define three binary variables of initial poverty ($P_{it-1} = 1$ if $p_{it-1}^* > 0$ and zero otherwise), retention ($R_{it-1} = 1$ if $r_{it}^* > 0$ and zero otherwise) and current poverty ($P_{it} = 1$ if $p_{it}^* > 0$ and zero otherwise).

The third equation is an equation of conditional current poverty as each explanatory variable of z_{it-1} can impact differently on the poverty status at t depending on poverty status at $t-1$. If $P_{it-1} = 1$ (resp. $P_{it-1} = 0$) the column vector γ_1' (resp. γ_2') is relevant and corresponds to the estimates of the determinants of persistence into (resp. entry in) poverty. As we will see below, these two sets of parameters can be used to provide a formal test of the absence of GSD. Hence, contrary to the dynamic non-linear approach presented above, the presence of state dependence is not measured here through the examination of the single coefficient of the lagged poverty status but through the differentiated impact of the set of covariates according to the lagged poverty status (Jenkins, 2011).

In addition to these three equations, and conditional on the existence of valid exclusion restrictions, a fourth part of the model is constituted by three unconstrained cross-equation correlation coefficients that are at the core of the tests of endogeneity of initial conditions and retention proposed by

Cappellari and Jenkins (2004). ρ_1, ρ_2 and ρ_3 refer to the correlation between the unobservable individual-specific factor affecting, respectively, sample retention and initial poverty; initial poverty and conditional current poverty; and conditional current poverty and sample retention. A positive value (resp. negative) for each of these correlation coefficients implies that individuals more likely to experiment one outcome are also more (resp. less) likely to experiment the other. For example, if ρ_1 is positive (resp. negative), individuals who were more likely to be poor in the previous year are more (resp. less) likely to remain in the panel, compared to those who were more likely not to be poor in the previous year. The test of exogeneity or ignorability of sample retention and initial conditions can be formulated as follows. If the null hypothesis $\rho_1 = \rho_3 = 0$ cannot be rejected, then the sample retention process is exogenous and it is not necessary to model attrition in order to have unbiased estimates (see an example of such a bivariate model in Stewart & Swaffield, 1999). If the null hypothesis $\rho_1 = \rho_2 = 0$ cannot be rejected, then the initial poverty status is exogenous. If the null hypothesis $\rho_1 = \rho_2 = \rho_3 = 0$ is not rejected, then a probit model can be applied to each process separately.[8]

After estimation of the model by simulated maximum likelihood, and taking into account the presence of repeated observations for each household at each point in time and for each individual across time (see Cappellari & Jenkins, 2004; 2006 for details), poverty transition probabilities can be derived. The probability of staying poor (Eq. (4)) and the probability of entering poverty (Eq. (5)) can be written as follows:

$$s_{it} = \Pr(P_{it} = 1 | P_{it-1} = 1) = \frac{\Phi_2(\gamma_1' z_{it-1}, \beta' x_{it-1}; \rho_2)}{\Phi(\beta' x_{it-1})} \tag{4}$$

$$e_{it} = \Pr(P_{it} = 1 | P_{it-1} = 0) = \frac{\Phi_2(\gamma_2' z_{it-1}, -\beta' x_{it-1}; -\rho_2)}{\Phi(-\beta' x_{it-1})} \tag{5}$$

Φ and Φ_2 stand for the cumulative density functions of the uni- and bi-variate normal distribution, respectively. It is worth noting that one advantage of the model is that the predicted transition probabilities are robust to attrition. Indeed, the predictions can be computed for all individuals present in $t-1$, even those who are not anymore in the panel in t, as the covariates are measured at this time point.

Finally, the model is built in a way that allows us to investigate the question of state dependence, that is the extent to which experiencing low income today increases the probability of experiencing low income tomorrow. Cappellari and Jenkins propose measures of ASD and GSD in low income. ASD is the difference between the aggregate persistence rate and the aggregate entry rate:

$$\mathrm{ASD} = \left(\frac{\sum\limits_{i \in \{P_{it-1}=1\}} \Pr(P_{it}=1|P_{it-1}=1)}{\sum\limits_{i} P_{it-1}} \right) - \left(\frac{\sum\limits_{i \in \{P_{it-1}=0\}} \Pr(P_{it}=1|P_{it-1}=0)}{\sum\limits_{i} (1-P_{it-1})} \right) \tag{6}$$

ASD does not allow differentiating between state dependence resulting from individual heterogeneity and GSD. Cappellari and Jenkins suggest a formal test for the absence of GSD where the null hypothesis is:

$$\mathrm{H}_0 : \gamma_1 = \gamma_2 \tag{7}$$

If this null hypothesis cannot be rejected, then the covariates have the same impact on poverty transitions, independently of the initial status of poverty. This means that knowing whether someone is poor in the previous year does not bring additional information regarding the impact of the explanatory variables. The measure of GSD proposed by Cappellari and Jenkins (2004) allows us to estimate the proportion of ASD that is non-spurious given the fact that individual heterogeneity (observed or unobserved) is controlled for (see Biewen, 2009). It consists of the average of the individual difference between the predicted probability of low-income permanence and low-income entry, which allows us to difference out the individual unobserved effects:

$$\mathrm{GSD} = \frac{1}{N} \sum_{i=1}^{N} [\Pr(P_{it}=1|P_{it-1}=1) - \Pr(P_{it}=1|P_{it-1}=0)] \tag{8}$$

Similarly to the poverty transitions predictions, the measures of aggregate and genuine state dependence can be obtained for all the individuals present in $t-1$, whether they are retained or not in the panel.

RESULTS

Our empirical application is based on the data and definitions presented in Section 'Data and definitions'. The dataset comprises pooled transitions identified through pairs of subsequent waves. The unit of analysis is the individual and the covariates reflect the demographic and working characteristics of the household an individual lives in.[9] The covariates refer to the individual, the head of the household and the household and are measured at the beginning of each potential transition (in $t-1$) which presents three advantages (Jenkins, 2000, 2011). First, it allows us to avoid a simultaneous change between poverty status and covariate. Second, it provides insight about who is more likely to make a transition on the basis of predetermined covariates which are observable by policymakers before the poverty problem arises. Third, as presented in the previous section, it allows computing post-estimation results, for all individuals present in $t-1$, even those who are not anymore in the panel in t, using estimates robust to non-random attrition.

At the individual level, age, age square and gender are controlled for. The household-level variables of our model refer to household composition (as measured by number of children aged less than 6, between 6 and 11 and between 12 and 17, number of adults and a dummy for lone parents), the attachment to the labour market (number of household's members at work other than the household head) and the tenure status of the accommodation (outright owner, acceding to property, tenant or rent free). The set of covariates used to describe the head of the household includes its citizenship, employment status, health status, marital status, education, age, age square and gender.[10] We also include dummy variables for each year. Our working sample is an unbalanced panel which consists of 15,677 individuals from 5,320 original households providing 55,226 person-wave observations. Table A.1 provides the mean value of the covariates for the whole population and by low-income status.

As mentioned in the previous section, a set of exclusion restrictions is needed for identification of the model. We are looking for variables affecting initial poverty and retention but not poverty transitions (conditional on previous poverty and retention) (see Stewart & Swaffield, 1999). For sample retention, we chose a dummy variable indicating whether the interviewer has changed between $t-2$ and $t-1$. A change in interviewer is expected to reduce the probability of staying in the sample and not to impact low-income transitions.[11] The exclusion restriction used for initial poverty status is a dummy variable indicating whether the head of the household's father was in a high-skilled job when the head of the household was between 12 and 16 years old. Individuals in that case are expected to have a lower likelihood of being initially low income than their counterpart, and this should not affect current poverty transition.[12] We tested the validity of these exclusion restrictions by checking whether they had a significant impact on the process

Table 2. Estimates of Model Correlations and Tests.

Correlation Coefficients Between Unobservables Affecting		*p*-Value
Initial poverty and retention (ρ_1)	−0.071*	0.036
Initial poverty and conditional current poverty (ρ_2)	−0.491***	0.000
Retention and conditional current poverty (ρ_3)	0.230	0.190
Test for exogeneity of initial conditions and retention		
Initial poverty: H0: $\rho_1=\rho_2=0$	22.31***	0.000
Retention: H0: $\rho_1=\rho_3=0$	5.87*	0.050
$\rho_1=\rho_2=\rho_3=0$	23.73***	0.000
Test for exclusion restriction		
Effect of hoh's father's job on initial poverty	8.74**	0.003
Effect of change of interviewer on retention	6.97**	0.008
Effect of hoh's father's job on transition	3.99	0.136
Effect of change of interviewer on transition	0.09	0.954
Effect of hoh's father's job and change of interviewer on transition	3.64	0.457
State dependence		
Absence of state dependence. H0: $\gamma_1=\gamma_2$	387.62***	0.000
Aggregate state dependence	0.65	
Genuine state dependence	0.39	

Source: PSELL3, 2003–2009; authors' computation. Sample restricted to individuals with no missing values in the covariates. hoh, head of the household. *$p<0.05$; **$p<0.01$; ***$p<0.001$, sample weights used.

they were referring to and a non-significant impact on the poverty transition equations (see Table 2).

The fit of our model to the data is quite good. Indeed, the predicted probabilities obtained from our estimation yielded comparable values as the sample means for each process, namely sample retention (85.41% compared to 85.40%), initial poverty status (12.75% and 12.68%), poverty persistence excluding the attrited individuals (68.1% compared to 70.6%) and poverty entry excluding the attrited individuals (3.87% compared to 4.2%). Table 2 presents the estimates of model correlations between unobservables. Individuals more likely to be initially in low income are less likely to be retained in the sample the following year (ρ_1 is negative and significant at $p<0.05$). In addition, individuals more likely to be initially in low income are less likely to stay in low income (ρ_2 is negative and significant at $p<0.001$). This result, similar to that obtained by Cappellari and Jenkins (2004) or Ayllón (2008), can be interpreted as a Galtonian regression to the mean – individuals with extreme results, very high or very low, are more likely to converge toward the mean in the subsequent year. Not taking the results about ρ_1 and ρ_2 into account might lead to an underestimation of the estimates of poverty persistence and entry. Finally, ρ_3, the correlation between poverty transition and retention is not measured precisely.

The Wald tests of exogeneity of initial conditions ($\rho_1 = \rho_2 = 0$) and of exogeneity of income retention ($\rho_1 = \rho_3 = 0$) are both rejected (at $p<0.001$ and $p<0.05$). When the three coefficients were tested jointly, the null hypothesis was strongly rejected ($p<0.001$). These results indicate that income retention and initial conditions are endogenous processes. They are similar to those obtained by Cappellari and Jenkins (2004) using British data but different from those obtained by Buddelmeyer and Verick (2008) who find that attrition is exogenous in Australia (and were not able to test for ignorability of initial conditions because of a lack of valid exclusion restriction). Ayllón (2008) obtains similar results when using a 50% poverty line, but finds that both initial condition and attrition are exogenous in Spain for a 60% poverty line.

The validity of the exclusion restrictions is tested by checking whether they had a significant impact on the process they were referring to and a non-significant impact on the poverty transition equations (see Table 2). The null hypothesis of a null impact of the head of the household's father's job and of the change in interviewer on poverty transition could not be rejected by the Wald tests, both when tested separately (p-values of 0.136 and 0.956) and when tested jointly (p-value of 0.457). In addition, the head of the household's father's job variable was found to have a statistically significant impact on initial poverty; the same result was found regarding the impact of interviewer change on sample retention. These results suggest that the exclusion restrictions we use are valid.

Table 2 also displays the statistics relative to aggregate and genuine state dependence. As mentioned in the previous section a formal test of the absence of genuine state dependence is the null hypothesis that $\gamma_1 = \gamma_2$. We obtained a test of 387.62 with 34 degrees of freedom and a p-value<0.0001 that led us to reject the null hypothesis of the absence of GSD. This result implies that the covariates have a differentiated impact on current poverty status conditional on previous year poverty status, as will be confirmed in Table 3 (and as could be expected from the descriptive statistics in Table A1). In Table 1, we reported that a rough measure of ASD, measured only on the non-attrited individuals, was slightly higher than 65%. After estimating our model, ASD, measured on both attrited and non-attrited

Table 3. Estimates of Conditional Current Poverty Status.

	Poor at t			
	Poor at $t-1$		Non-Poor at $t-1$	
	Coefficient	t	Coefficient	t
Individual characteristics				
Female	0.0367	(0.82)	0.0607*	(2.38)
Age	−0.00689*	(−2.01)	0.00565**	(2.62)
Age squared	0.000134*	(1.98)	−0.000149***	(−3.53)
Head of household characteristics				
Female	−0.0634	(−0.43)	0.0539	(0.69)
Age	0.0388*	(2.10)	0.00613	(0.43)
Age squared	−0.000442*	(−2.24)	0.0000409	(0.30)
Bad health	−0.0516	(−0.34)	0.356**	(3.28)
Portuguese	0.0383	(0.24)	0.716***	(7.08)
Other EU15	−0.0551	(−0.40)	0.189*	(2.17)
Non-EU15	0.189	(0.86)	0.902***	(6.75)
Single	−0.0570	(−0.41)	0.235*	(2.03)
Divorced	−0.115	(−0.67)	0.258*	(2.13)
Widow	−0.272	(−0.82)	−0.490**	(−3.23)
Lower education	0.138	(0.78)	0.542***	(5.68)
Secondary education	0.0895	(0.54)	0.387***	(4.06)
Part time	−0.175	(−0.44)	0.861**	(2.67)
Unemployed	0.288	(1.33)	0.444*	(2.16)
Self-employed	−0.252	(−1.37)	0.781***	(7.12)
Retired	−0.0502	(−0.22)	0.00547	(0.04)
Other	0.290	(1.78)	0.209	(1.55)
Household characteristics				
Number of children less than 6	−0.0749	(−0.94)	0.257***	(4.94)
Number of children between 6 and 11	−0.0164	(−0.19)	0.0858	(1.43)
Number of children between 12 and 17	0.0658	(0.73)	0.238***	(4.02)
Number of adults	0.105	(1.42)	0.0426	(0.87)
Lone parent	0.0961	(0.51)	−0.0565	(−0.35)
Number of individuals at work except hoh	−0.504***	(−3.49)	−0.364***	(−5.51)
Acceding to property	0.210	(1.36)	−0.182*	(−2.01)
Tenant or rent free	0.0910	(0.55)	0.184*	(2.01)
Wave 2	0.405*	(2.43)	−0.0465	(−0.46)
Wave 3	0.279	(1.90)	0.0157	(0.17)
Wave 4	0.0821	(0.64)	−0.145	(−1.48)
Wave 5	0.330*	(2.14)	−0.150	(−1.47)
Wave 6	0.0871	(0.65)	−0.309**	(−3.04)
Constant	−0.203	(−0.35)	−2.953***	(−7.29)
Log Likelihood	−47299.1			
N	55526			

Source: PSELL3, 2003–2009; authors' computation. Sample weights used. The reference person is a man living in a household whose head is a Luxembourgish well-educated married man, working full time and who owns its accommodation. hoh, head of the household. *$p<0.05$; **$p<0.01$; ***$p<0.001$.

individuals, was found to be equal to 0.65 and GSD to 0.39. GSD is equal to 60% of ASD. Hence, more than half of ASD is accounted for by GSD; however, the part of state dependence attributable to (un)observed heterogeneity is non-negligible. These results suggest that both policies aiming at reducing GSD – breaking the vicious circle of poverty (through means-tested transfers given the relative definition of poverty followed here) – and at changing the characteristics that make some individuals more prone to reproduce the state of poverty may be needed. In what follows we try to identify these characteristics upon which a policy can be applied.

Table 3 reports the estimates of the conditional current poverty status. Column 2 displays the estimates of current poverty if the individual was already poor in $t-1$ (γ_1) and Column 4 displays the estimates of current poverty if the individual was not poor in $t-1$ (γ_2). Regarding the determinants of remaining poor, only few coefficients of covariates are found to be statistically significant. The probability of remaining poor increases with the age of the head of the household, but at a decreasing rate – the maximum is reached when the head of the household is 44 years old. At the household level, as could be expected, an additional individual at work in the household strongly decreases the risk of staying poor. Hence, these results confirm the fact that in Luxembourg, as was already illustrated in the cross-sectional poverty profile and by STATEC (2010), employment seems to be efficient in protecting individuals from staying poor.

More covariates coefficients are found to have a statistically significant impact on the risk of entering poverty, which seems to indicate that there is more heterogeneity in poverty entry than permanence. Living in a household where the head is in bad health, single or divorced increases the risk of entering poverty. Similar to STATEC (2010), we find that good education of the head of the household protects from falling into poverty. Luxembourg is a country with high immigration so that citizenship is often an important covariate. Living in a household where the head is a non-EU15 or Portuguese, and to a lesser extent an EU15, strongly increases the risk of entering poverty compared to living in a household where the head is Luxembourgish. The status on the labour market of the household's head is also a strong determinant of entering poverty: households where the head is unemployed, part-time worker or self-employed are at a higher risk of entering poverty compared to when the head is a full-time worker. At the household level, as could be expected, an additional individual at work in the household strongly decreases the risk of entering poverty. Conversely to the persistence into poverty, household composition is

Table 4. Estimates of Initial Poverty Status and Retention Equations.

	Initial Poverty Status		Retention	
	Coefficient	t	Coefficient	t
Individual characteristics				
Female	0.0623	(1.85)	0.0329*	(2.12)
Age	0.00559**	(2.71)	0.000516	(0.36)
Age squared	−0.000151***	(−4.02)	0.0000158	(0.62)
Head of household characteristics				
Female	0.153	(1.86)	−0.0345	(−0.70)
Age	−0.0223	(−1.49)	0.0237**	(2.81)
Age squared	0.000274	(1.89)	−0.000292***	(−3.59)
Bad health	0.192*	(2.27)	−0.136*	(−2.37)
Portuguese	0.894***	(6.92)	0.0451	(0.66)
Other EU15	0.363***	(3.43)	−0.0950*	(−2.04)
Non-EU15	1.361***	(9.90)	−0.387***	(−3.47)
Single	0.191	(1.60)	−0.0414	(−0.68)
Divorced	0.148	(1.38)	−0.0479	(−0.76)
Widow	−1.082***	(−5.09)	−0.0523	(−0.78)
Lower education	0.779***	(6.19)	−0.0193	(−0.39)
Secondary education	0.478***	(4.01)	0.0156	(0.33)
Part time	0.755**	(2.85)	0.276	(1.08)
Unemployed	0.882***	(5.42)	0.119	(0.97)
Self-employed	0.811***	(6.98)	−0.0853	(−1.20)
Retired	0.0700	(0.46)	0.0521	(0.82)
Other	0.887***	(6.94)	0.0524	(0.81)
Household characteristics				
Number of children less than 6	0.193**	(3.23)	0.0469	(1.27)
Number of children between 6 and 11	0.167**	(3.13)	−0.0580	(−1.65)
Number of children between 12 and 17	0.354***	(6.21)	−0.0235	(−0.64)
Number of adults	0.113	(1.72)	−0.0882***	(−3.42)
Lone parent	0.339*	(1.96)	−0.105	(−1.14)
Number of individuals at work except hoh	−0.696***	(−7.72)	−0.0757*	(−2.27)
Acceding to property	−0.111	(−0.93)	−0.00594	(−0.12)
Tenant or rent free	0.397***	(3.59)	−0.108*	(−1.98)
Wave 2	0.0978	(1.51)	0.127*	(2.24)
Wave 3	0.161*	(2.46)	0.244***	(4.13)
Wave 4	0.197**	(3.01)	0.292***	(5.17)
Wave 5	0.140*	(2.06)	0.328***	(5.44)
Wave 6	0.159*	(2.34)	0.132*	(2.25)

Table 4. (*Continued*)

	Initial Poverty Status		Retention	
	Coefficient	*t*	Coefficient	*t*
Exclusion restrictions				
Father of household head in skilled job	−0.282**	(−2.85)		
Change of interviewer			−0.148**	(−2.64)
Constant	−2.152***	(−4.92)	0.769**	(3.29)
Log likelihood	−47299.1			
N	55,526			

Source: PSELL3, 2003–2009; authors' computation. Sample weights used. The reference person is a man living in a household whose head is a Luxembourgish well-educated married man, working full time and who owns its accommodation. hoh, head of the household. *$p<0.05$; **$p<0.01$; ***$p<0.001$.

correlated with the likelihood of entering poverty: an additional child aged less than 6 or between 12 and 17 increases the probability of entering poverty, whereas the coefficient related to the number of children aged between 6 and 11 is not significant. It can be seen as surprising that lone parents do not have a higher risk of staying in or entering poverty. This might be due to low sample size but it might also mean that living in lone parent families increases the risk of being poor, as shown by the determinants of initial poverty in Table 4 and at the cross-sectional level, but not the transitions into poverty (Ayllón, 2008). Being a tenant increases the risk of entering poverty.

As explained in Section 'Econometric model', the methodology allows us to analyse the determinants of initial poverty and attrition. Estimates are reported in Table 4. Most of the correlates of initial poverty are similar to those of poverty entry presented in Table 3. An additional effect is the positive impact of living in a lone parent household and of the presence of children aged between 6 and 11. Finally, as required for model identification, the exclusion restriction variable has a significant impact on initial poverty. If the father of the head of the household was in a skilled job, the probability of being initially poor is higher.

The probability of being retained in the panel is associated with age, the citizenship and health of the household head, the number of adults and the tenure status. Note that a change in interviewer, the exclusion restriction of the attrition, strongly negatively impacts the probability of staying in the panel.

CONCLUSION

The aim of this paper was to provide an analysis of the drivers of low-income transitions in Luxembourg, accounting for potential endogeneity due to initial condition or non-random attritions. Both processes were found to be endogenous so that not taking this into account would provide biased estimates of poverty transitions in Luxembourg.

A high proportion of aggregate state dependence was found, around 65%. Genuine state dependence accounts for 60% of aggregate state dependence. Hence, more than half of aggregate state dependence is accounted for by genuine state dependence; however, the part of state dependence attributable to (un)observed heterogeneity is non-negligible.

The econometric model highlights the individual and household characteristics associated with poverty entry and permanence. These results usefully complement the Luxembourg cross-sectional poverty profile. Employment protects from both remaining in low income and entering poverty. In addition, several characteristics of the head of the household significantly affect the risk of entering poverty but not of permanence into poverty: employment status, lower education, citizenship, bad health and marital status. Household composition and tenure status also impact poverty entry.

The conclusions about the characteristics of state dependence in Luxembourg suggest that both policies aiming at reducing genuine state dependence – breaking the vicious circle of poverty through means-tested transfers – and at changing the above highlighted characteristics that make some individuals more prone to reproduce the state of poverty may be needed.

NOTES

1. Figures available from the Luxembourg official statistics office website (STATEC) (last consulted October 11 2011): http://www.statistiques.public.lu/stat/TableViewer/tableView.aspx?ReportId=1436&IF_Language=fra&MainTheme=5&FldrName=2&RFPath=22. In 2010, the GDP growth increased again to a value of 2.7%. But this year is not covered in our data.

2. This income definition of poverty is the most commonly used in European countries (see Atkinson et al., 2002). In this paper, we use the terms poverty and low-income interchangeably.

3. An interesting point to highlight is that the current poverty profile is quite different from the one of thirty five years ago, in the mid-eighties, when child poverty was quite low and elderly poverty quite high (Allegrezza et al., 2004).

4. Another element of this specificity is the high level of cross-borders workers among the Luxembourg labour force. Cross-borders workers are however not covered by our data.

5. Regarding related topics, Reinstadler and Berger (2007) analysed the intergenerational transmission of poverty and Van Kerm and Fusco (2008) showed that there is some significant mobility in the income distribution in Luxembourg.

6. In fact, Duncan et al. (1993) and OECD (2001) already analysed poverty dynamic in Luxembourg in a comparative perspective using first three waves of the first and second *Socio-Economic Panel 'Liewen zu Lëtzebuerg'* (PSELL1 1984–1986 and PSELL2 – 1994–1997). However, these two studies faced a common problem of small sample size for Luxembourg which prevented them from drawing robust conclusions. Still, Duncan et al. (1993) presented Luxembourg as a successful example of poverty fighting as almost no short-term or long-term poverty was identified: "in fact the Luxembourg panel data were not very useful in our poverty transitions analysis because very few families in Luxembourg met any of our definitions of poverty. Despite a considerable influx of foreign workers from poorer EC countries, Luxembourg has combined extremely favorable employment conditions and a safety net of social insurance and assistance programs to reduce (although not eliminate) poverty among its residents. It should serve to remind us of what might be possible in [other countries]".

7. The determinants of poverty exit, also analysed by STATEC (2010), are not reported here.

8. In the absence of valid exclusion restriction, another possibility is to impose restrictions on a coefficient of correlation. For example, Buddelmeyer and Verick (2008) did not have valid exclusion restriction for initial poverty so that they had to constrain to 0 the correlation coefficients involving the initial poverty status. This prevented them from testing for the endogeneity of initial condition but they were, however, able to estimate the correlation coefficient between attrition and current poverty so that they could test for the endogeneity of retention.

9. Robust standard errors of the estimates are computed to account for the fact that there are repeated observations within each household but also that there are repeated observations for individuals across time. The original household from which the individual was sampled in its first appearance is used as the cluster.

10. In the PSELL3 data, the head of the household is defined as the person in charge of the accommodation. If two individuals are co-responsible (e.g. a couple co-owning a house), the head of the household is the older. We modified this last case and when two persons are in charge of the accommodation, we considered that the main income recipient among them is the head of the household. The hypothesis is that the household member with the highest personal income among the responsible of the accommodation has the highest influence on the household's standard of living. If they both have the same personal income, the older is designed as the head of the household.

11. Two other variables were tested as exclusion restriction for sample retention: whether an individual was an original sample member, that is, whether he is in the sample since the first year of apparition of its household (individuals who joined a household after the first year of apparition of this household are not considered as original sample members, e.g. new partners) and whether the households' answers

were considered 'very reliable' by the interviewer. Both variables were not found to be valid exclusion restrictions.

12. Other exclusion restrictions for initial conditions were tested. Using a module on intergenerational transmission of poverty present only in the third wave referring to the year 2005, interviewees were asked whether when aged between 12 and 16, the household they were living in was confronted to financial difficulties. We attributed the answer of the main income recipient to all the household members and then attributed this answer to all the waves. This inevitably implied a high loss of observations. In addition, following Ayllón (2008), we included the variable as to whether the head of the household suffers from a chronic disease.

ACKNOWLEDGMENTS

This research is part of the *PersiPov* project ('The dynamics and Persistence of Poverty in Luxembourg') supported by the Luxembourg Fonds National de la Recherche (contract C10/LM/783502) and by core funding for CEPS/INSTEAD from the Ministry of Higher Education and Research of Luxembourg. Comments by two anonymous referees, Sara Ayllón, Jacques Brosius, Karina Doorley, Anne Reinstadler, Jacques Silber, Philippe Van Kerm, Bogdan Voicu and participants to the 2011 OECD New Directions in Welfare congress, 2011 ECINEQ conference and CEPS/INSTEAD 'ateliers de recherche' are gratefully acknowledged. In addition, we would like to thank Sara Ayllón and Stephen P. Jenkins who provided us with additional details of their work that were helpful when conducting our research. The usual disclaimer applies.

REFERENCES

Aassve, A., Burgess, S., Dickson, M., & Propper, C. (2006). *Modelling poverty by not modelling poverty: An application of a simultaneous hazards approach to the UK*. Working Paper No. 106. Center for Analysis of Social Exclusion, London School of Economics, London.

Allegrezza, S., Heinrich, G., & Jesuit, D. (2004). Poverty and income inequality in Luxembourg and the Grande Région in comparative perspective. *Socio-Economic Review*, *2*, 263–283.

Arulampalam, W., Booth, A. L., & Taylor, M. P. (2000). Unemployment persistence. *Oxford Economic Papers*, *52*, 24–50.

Atkinson, A. B. (1989). *Poverty and social security*. London: harvester Wheatsheaf.

Atkinson, A. B. (2008). Poverty. In S. N. Durlauf & L. E. Blume (Eds.), *The new Palgrave Dictionary of economics* (2nd ed.). Palgrave Macmillan, 2008. The New Palgrave Dictionary of Economics Online. Palgrave Macmillan. Retrieved from http://www.dictionaryofeconomics.com.proxy.bnl.lu/article?id = pde2008_P000138. Accessed on 12 July 2012. doi:10.1057/9780230226203.1317

Atkinson, A. B., Cantillon, B., Marlier, E., & Nolan, B. (2002). *Social indicators: The EU and social inclusion*. Oxford: Oxford University Press.

Ayllón, S. (2008). *Modelling poverty transitions in Spain: Do attrition and initial conditions really matter*? IRISS Working Paper No. 2008-08, CEPS/INSTEAD, Differdange.

Bane, M. J., & Ellwood, D. (1986). Slipping into and out of poverty: The dynamics of spells. *Journal of Human Resources*, *21*, 1–23.

Berger, F. (2004). *Approche Monétaire et Approches Alternatives de la Pauvreté : Situation en 2003*. Population et Emploi n 6, décembre, CEPS/INSTEAD.

Berger, F., Fusco, A., Jeandidier, B., & Reinstadler, A. (2009). *La pauvreté des enfants au Luxembourg*. rapport pour le Ministère de la Famille et de l'Intégration du Luxembourg, Mai.

Bertola, G. (2000). Macroeconomics of distribution and growth. In A. B. Atkinson & F. Bourguignon (Eds), *Handbook of income distribution* (Ch. 9, pp. 605–675). Amsterdam: North Holland-Elsevier.

Biewen, M. (2009). Measuring state dependence in individual poverty histories when there is feedback to employment status and household composition. *Journal of Applied Econometrics*, *24*, 1095–1116.

Bradbury, B., Jenkins, S. P., & Mickelwright, J. (2001). *The dynamics of child poverty in industrialised countries*. Cambridge: Cambridge University Press.

Bradshaw, J., & Chzhen, Y. (2009). Child Poverty Policies across Europe. *Zeitschrift für Familienforschung*, *21*(2), S128–S149.

Buddelmeyer, H., & Verick, S. (2008). Understanding the drivers of poverty dynamics in Australian households. *The Economic Record*, *84*(266), 310–321.

Cantó, O. (2003). Finding out the routes to escape poverty: The relevance of demographic vs. labor market events in Spain. *Review of Income and Wealth*, *49*(4), 569–588.

Cappellari, L., & Jenkins, S. P. (2002a). Who stays poor? Who becomes poor? Evidence from the British Household Panel Survey. *The Economic Journal*, *112*(March), C60–C67.

Cappellari, L., & Jenkins, S. P. (2002b). *Modelling low income transitions*. Working Paper No. 2002-8. Institute for Social and Economic Research, University of Essex, Colchester.

Cappellari, L., & Jenkins, S. P. (2004). Modelling low income transitions. *Journal of Applied Econometrics*, *19*(5), 593–610.

Cappellari, L., & Jenkins, S. P. (2006). Calculation of multivariate normal probabilities by simulation, with applications to maximum simulated likelihood estimation. *The Stata Journal*, *6*(2), 156–189.

Cappellari, L., & Jenkins, S. P. (2008). Estimating low pay transition probabilities. *Journal of the Royal Statistical Society, Applied Statistics*, *57*(Part 2), 165–186.

Devicienti, F. (2011). Estimating poverty persistence in Britain. *Empirical Economics*, *40*(3), 657–687.

Duncan, G. J., Gustafsson, B., Hauser, R., Schmauss, G., Messinger, H., Muffels, R., … Ray, J.-C. (1993). Poverty dynamics in eight countries. *Journal of Population Economics*, *6*, 215–234.

Eurostat. (2010). *Europe in figures: Eurostat yearbook 2010*. Luxembourg: Publications Office of the European Union.

Faye, O., Islam N., & Zulu, E. (2011). *Poverty dynamics in Nairobi's slums. Testing for true state dependence and heterogeneity effects*. CEPS/INSTEAD Working Paper No. 2011/56, CEPS/INSTEAD, Esch sur Alzette.

Gradín, C., & Cantó, O. (2012). Why are child poverty rates so persistently high in Spain? *The Manchester School*, *80*(1), 117–143.

Grusky, D. B., & Kanbur, R. (2006). The conceptual foundation of poverty and inequality measurement. In D. B. Grusky & R. Kanbur (Eds), *Poverty and Inequality* (pp. 1–29). Stanford: Stanford University Press. Chapter 1.

Heckman, J. (1981a). The incidental parameters problem and the problem of initial conditions in estimating a discrete time-discrete data stochastic process. In C. F. Manski & D. McFadden (Eds), *Structural analysis of discrete data with econometric applications* (pp. 179–195). Cambridge: MIT Press.

Heckman, J. (1981b). Heterogeneity and state dependence. In S. Rosen (Ed.), *Studies in labor markets* (pp. 91–139). Chicago: University of Chicago Press.

Heckman, J. (2001). Micro data, heterogeneity and the evaluation of public policy: Nobel lecture. *Journal of Political Economy*, *109*(4), 673–748.

Islam, N., & Shimeles, A. (2007). *Poverty dynamics in Ethiopia: State dependence and transitory shocks*. Working Papers in Economics 260, Göteborg University, Göteborg.

Jenkins, S. P. (2000). Modelling household income dynamics. *Journal of Population Economics*, *13*, 529–567.

Jenkins, S. P. (2011). *Changing fortunes. Income mobility and poverty dynamics in Britain*. Oxford: Oxford University Press.

OECD. (2001). When money is tight: poverty dynamics in OECD countries. *Employment outlook* (Chapter 2). Retrieved from http://www.oecd.org/dataoecd/29/55/2079296.pdf

Poggi, A. (2007). Does persistence in social exclusion exist in Spain. *Journal of Economic Inequality*, *5*, 53–72.

Reinstadler, A., & Berger, F. (2007). Quelle analyse de la transmission intergénérationnelle de la pauvreté dans un pays à forte immigration comme le Luxembourg? CEPS/INSTEAD, Document de recherche Psell n 2007-13, 21 p.

STATEC. (2010). Rapport Travail et Cohésion Sociale, Cahiers Economiques number 111.

Stevens, A. H. (1999). Climbing out of poverty, falling back in: Measuring the persistence of poverty over multiple spells. *Journal of Human Resources*, *34*, 557–588.

Stewart, M. B. (2007). The interrelated dynamics of unemployment and low-wage employment. *Journal of Applied Econometrics*, *22*, 511–531.

Stewart, M. B., & Swaffield, J. (1999). Low pay dynamics and transition probabilities. *Economica*, *66*, 23–42.

Van Kerm, P. (2004). Une évaluation économétrique des flux vers et hors de la pauvreté en Belgique. In R. Doutrelepont, D. Mortelmans & M.-T. Casman (Eds), *Onze ans de vie en Belgique. Analyses socioéconomiques à partir du Panel Démographique Familiale* (pp. 251–272). Gent: Academia Press, Série Science et Société, Politique Scientifique Fédérale.

Van Kerm, P., & Fusco, A. (2008). La Progression du niveau de vie entre 2003 et 2006. Vivre au Luxembourg. Chronique de l'enquête PSELL-3/2006. CEPS/INSTEAD, 2 p.

Wooldridge, J. M. (2005). Simple solutions to the initial conditions problem for dynamic, nonlinear panel data with unobserved heterogeneity. *Journal of Applied Econometrics*, *20*, 39–54.

APPENDIX

Table A.1. Descriptive Statistics.

	All	Poor	Non-Poor
Individual characteristics			
Female	0.51	0.53	0.50
Age	38.09	31.31	39.07
Head of the household characteristics			
Female	0.23	0.30	0.22
Age	48.66	44.50	49.27
Bad or very bad health	0.08	0.14	0.07
Luxembourgish	0.61	0.30	0.66
Portuguese	0.15	0.35	0.12
Other EU15	0.20	0.20	0.20
Non-EU15	0.04	0.14	0.02
Married	0.74	0.69	0.75
Single	0.11	0.14	0.10
Divorced	0.08	0.14	0.08
Widow	0.06	0.03	0.07
Tertiary education	0.27	0.10	0.30
Lower education	0.37	0.60	0.33
Secondary education	0.36	0.31	0.37
Full time	0.67	0.63	0.68
Part time	0.00	0.01	0.00
Unemployed	0.02	0.07	0.01
Self-employed	0.06	0.06	0.05
Retired	0.18	0.09	0.19
Other	0.08	0.14	0.07
Father of household head in skilled job	0.29	0.14	0.31
Household characteristics			
Number of children less than 6	0.30	0.47	0.28
Number of children between 6 and 11	0.32	0.47	0.30
Number of children between 12 and 17	0.29	0.47	0.26
Number of adults	2.30	2.12	2.32
Lone parent	0.04	0.11	0.03
Number of individuals at work except household head	0.59	0.34	0.63
Outright owner	0.31	0.16	0.33
Acceding to property	0.43	0.33	0.45
Tenant or rent free	0.25	0.51	0.22
Change of interviewer	0.11	0.11	0.11

Source: PSELL3; authors' computation. Based on the 55,226 person waves observations with no missing values in the covariates. Sample weights used.

CHAPTER 15

WELFARE REFORM AND POVERTY: A LATENT TRAJECTORY MODEL ANALYSIS

Michael J. Camasso and Radha Jagannathan

ABSTRACT

This paper examines the effect of welfare reform policies on changes in poverty in the United States during 1992–2005. Using state-level panel data we estimate latent trajectory models to determine if welfare reform has contributed to changes in the trajectories of poverty growth (decline) beyond what would have naturally occurred through the passage of time. Our results show that (a) states vary considerably in both their mean initial level as well as trajectories of poverty; (b) welfare reform was responsible for nearly 27% of the decline in poverty during the study period; (c) the economy played a secondary role, responsible for a 10% reduction in poverty; and (d) income support policies like minimum wage and child support collection also had an important role to play, with the latter contributing as much as welfare reform to poverty reduction. Our estimates remain robust against changes in modeling strategies and methods.

Keywords: Latent trajectory model; poverty; random coefficient model; welfare reform

Inequality, Mobility and Segregation: Essays in Honor of Jacques Silber
Research on Economic Inequality, Volume 20, 393–422

ISSN: 1049-2585/doi:10.1108/S1049-2585(2012)0000020018

INTRODUCTION

Although the 1996 welfare reform legislation Personal Responsibility and Work Opportunity Reconciliation Act (PRWORA) did not promulgate poverty reduction as its goal, it sought to change the "culture of poverty" characterized by high rates of non-marriages, nonmarital childbearing, male joblessness and dependence on public assistance, to a "culture of work" through increasing investments in human capital and attendant opportunity costs (Haskins, 2009; Besharov, 2008). The law gave birth to Temporary Assistance to Needy Families (TANF) and instituted sweeping structural changes to TANF's predecessor, Aid to Families with Dependent Children (AFDC). The overarching themes of the new program were inculcation of individual responsibility and promotion of economic self-sufficiency. Recipients were to treat welfare assistance as temporary and time limited and to show reciprocal responsibility to the state by "working" for their benefits.

With the reauthorization of PRWORA expected to occur this year,[1] we can expect welfare reform to once again take its place at the center of domestic policy debate. Poverty rates declined substantially over the 1990s, from a 25-year high of 15% in 1993 to 10.9% in 2000. They have steadily climbed back up since 2000, reaching 12.3% in 2005 (U.S. Census Bureau). Concurrent with this trend are increases in the labor force participation rates of single mothers from 35% in 1990 to about 50% in 2005 (Besharov, 2008). Studies of trends in the poverty rate and employment rate among low-skilled women have stimulated discussions about the role of welfare reform in either alleviating or exacerbating poverty. Proponents of welfare reform claim that despite dire warnings from opponents, PRWORA has had a beneficial effect on poverty (Haskins, 2009). Of course, the implementation of welfare reform was coincident with flourishing economic times, but nonetheless there is now a general consensus that welfare reform has also had an incremental hand in reducing welfare caseloads and increasing women's employment and earnings (Blank, 2002; Blank & Schmidt, 2001).

In this paper, we examine the effect of four policies identified as the most salient and controversial components of welfare reform (Leiberman & Shaw, 2000; Soss, Schram, Vartanian, & O'Brien, 2001) on poverty rates, viz., (a) work requirements, which focus on imposing obligations to work in exchange for assistance; (b) time limits that impose a life time cap on welfare benefits; (c) the family cap, which denies cash benefits to families for children born while the mother is receiving public assistance; and (d) sanction policy that penalizes recipients for program rule infractions.

The principal objectives of this paper are (1) to determine if welfare reform has led to changes in the trajectories of poverty rate beyond what would have naturally occurred through the passage of time; (2) to update the literature on poverty changes by using a longer and more current time series, with 4 years of pre-PRWORA era data and a decade of PRWORA-era data; and (3) to measure the relative impact of poverty change attributable to welfare reform, macroeconomic performance, and other state and federal income support policies. We use state-level panel data on welfare reform and poverty changes for the years 1992–2005 and employ latent trajectory models to make our empirical tests.

REVIEW OF THE LITERATURE

Welfare reform has become one of the most studied topics in recent history. A number of studies have concluded that welfare reform has led to large declines in caseloads (e.g., Council of Economic Advisers, 1999; Grogger, 2004) as well as increases in employment, earnings, and income (e.g., Grogger, 2003; Grogger & Karoly, 2005). Experimental evidence from MDRC evaluations of waivers suggest that welfare reform initiatives that "included only mandatory employment services usually left families no better off financially than they would have been without the programs" (Bloom & Michalopoulos, 2001, p. ES-2). On the other hand, when these mandatory work requirements were supplemented by earnings, they reduced poverty anywhere from 10% to 17% (Grogger & Karoly, 2005). However, Bloom and Michalopoulos (2001) report that a majority of program participants remained in poverty at the end of the study period. While such experimental evidence from random assignment waiver-period studies can be persuasive, it does not capture the diversity of PRWORA reforms and can lack external validity (Duncan & Chase-Lansdale, 2001).

Findings from nationally representative econometric studies that use state-level aggregated micro data and fixed effects specifications show mixed results. Shoeni and Blank (2000) model welfare reform using a waiver dummy and a TANF dummy and find an 8% decline in poverty post-waiver and post-TANF among women with less than high school education. Bitler, Gelbach, and Hoynes (2002) similarly find that TANF accompanied by waivers significantly reduces poverty for female high school dropouts. Bavier (2002) also reports similar reductions in poverty due to TANF.

Gundersen and Ziliak (2004), find "limited and mixed evidence" of welfare reform effect on poverty. They report significant reductions in both the number of families living in poverty and the severity of poverty, but attribute the reductions largely to economic growth and Earned Income Tax Credit (EITC) support. Similarly, Weber, Bruce, Mark Edwards, and Greg Duncan (2003) report that while welfare reform has contributed to increased probabilities of employment, it did not reduce poverty among single mothers.

McKernan and Ratcliffe (2006) model welfare reform with a comprehensive set of 19 policy initiatives using fixed effects regression. For comparative purposes, they also model welfare reform using waiver and TANF dummies. While the black box approach does not yield significant welfare reform effects on poverty, these authors find that family caps increase poverty by 6% while severe sanctions increase poverty by 11.5% and some forms of time limit may reduce poverty rates among never married mothers.

CONCEPTUAL BACKGROUND – *DETERMINANTS OF POVERTY*

Welfare Reform

Four types of waivers were commonly enacted under and Section 1115 of the Social Security Act (49 *Stat.* 620 [1935]; 42 USC 1315(a) [2006]). Changes to traditional (AFDC) *work requirements* under the waiver program took the form of less generous child exemptions for participation in the Job Opportunities and Basic Skills Training (JOBS) program and required welfare recipients to engage in work or work-related activities sooner in terms of the age of their youngest child. Under PRWORA, a state had the choice of adopting federally recommended work requirements or making their requirement more stringent than the federal standards. Twenty-six states implemented a work requirement that was stricter than the federal requirement (American Public Welfare Association, 1997; Soss et al., 2001).

Welfare reform also put restrictions on the amount of time (*time limits*) a family could receive welfare benefits. Twenty-four states received waivers to experiment with this reform element prior to the federal passage of PRWORA which limited benefit receipt to a term of 5 years (Harvey, Camasso, & Jagannathan, 2000). Under PRWORA, a state could also establish time limits shorter than the prescribed 5 years, and 21 states did so (American Public Welfare Association, 1997; Soss et al., 2001). Time limits have the potential to affect welfare receipt decisions by signaling the temporary nature of benefit receipt. It is expected that in addition to perfunctory or mechanical effects that may unfold over time when families start reaching the limit of their welfare stay, time limits may also exert behavioral effects that are conditioned by the age of the youngest child in the family. Through their effect on welfare recipiency decision, time limits are hypothesized to have an ambiguous effect on poverty. Loss of welfare benefits may lead some women to increase their labor supply and earn enough to offset or exceed benefit loss (Moffitt & Pavetti, 2000) and other women to seek other compensating sources of unearned income, for example, private transfers from other family members or friends (McKernan & Ratcliffe, 2006). In either of these scenarios, time limits may decrease poverty. If, however, neither scenario obtains, time limits will have the effect of increasing poverty.

The *family cap* is widely considered to be a measure that is expressly designed to reduce nonmarital birth rates (U.S. General Accounting Office, 2001). The amount of benefit loss varies by state, as do the initiatives put in place to cushion the financial loss. Although family caps are not required under PRWORA states have the option to adopt them under the voluntary provisions section of the original act (PRWORA; 110 *Stat.* 2105). To date, 23 states have done so. Of these, 17 states adopted them before the passage of PRWORA under Section 1115 waiver program. While this policy's specific intent was to reduce nonmarital births, it is also possible that by reducing the incentive to stay on welfare it may encourage families to exit the rolls for other reasons. For example, if women were to "game" the system, they could leave the rolls while pregnant and return after the baby is born, which would effectively reduce the caseload, at least in the short term and in turn lead to higher poverty rates. However, in the long run, if such women were to make behavioral changes and choose to substitute work for welfare, the poverty rate may be lower.

The *sanction policy* entails reducing the welfare grant amount for a length of time when welfare recipients do not comply with program rules. Sanctioning also varies widely across states. Under AFDC, a worst-case scenario saw the elimination of the adult portion of the benefit for 6 months or until compliance. While the federal government required that all states sanction recipients for noncompliance under TANF, states were allowed to determine the severity of the sanction. Sanction policies are typically classified as weak, moderate, or severe depending on the amount, timing, and length of benefit reduction (Rector & Youssef, 1999; Soss et al., 2001). As of 2005, 14 states enforce the most severe sanction of full family benefit reduction until compliance. Sixteen states maintain the sanction for 1–3 months, 11 states for 6 months, and 2 states for 1–3 years. In eight states, the sanction is permanent (Urban Institute, 2005). Severe sanctioning policies are expected to have an ambiguous effect on poverty. On the one hand, withholding of grant amounts through sanctioning can have the mechanical effect of increasing poverty, while on the other hand, sanctioning may either hasten the recipients' compliance with program rules thus restoring lost family (unearned) income, or it may behaviorally reduce poverty if recipients choose to stay off the welfare rolls and engage in the labor market, thus increasing their (earned) income.

In this paper we focus on work requirements, time limits, family cap, and sanctions inasmuch as these four policies have been identified as the most salient in both public debates of welfare reform and state adoption of get tough policy options (Soss et al., 2001).

Economy

Because welfare reform was implemented during a period of strong and widely distributed growth, any analysis of change in poverty rates must also take into account the role of the economy. The national *unemployment* rate fell by nearly 2–1/2 percentage points in the 1990s and the number of employed Americans increased by about 20 million. Demand for low-wage workers was especially high and real wages for low-wage workers grew from $6.54 in 1994 to $7.35 in 2000 (Congressional Budget Office, 2006). However, the early years of the new century witnessed an economic slow-down, with unemployment rising by a full percentage point and employment growth slowing down by 0.36 between 2000 and 2005. While research on the link between poverty and economic growth has traditionally shown a strong inverse association in the 1960s, 1970s, 1990s, and later (Blank, 1993; Haveman & Schwabish, 2000; Iceland, 2003), the relationship weakened in the 1980s when poverty rates failed to closely track economic growth. Some researchers attribute this weakened correlation to rising income inequalities (Blank & Card, 1993; Iceland, 2003), while others propose that the attenuation was spurious and possibly due to analyses of aggregate national data that may mask considerable heterogeneity at the subnational level (Gundersen & Ziliak, 2004).

Other Relevant State and Federal Policies of Income Support

Welfare Benefits

Benefit levels have always varied across states both under AFDC and TANF. For example, Alaska provides the most generous benefit of $923 for a family of three while the most a family is entitled to in Mississippi is $170. While benefits have changed relatively infrequently over time, the period

1992–2005 witnessed a 25% decline in real welfare benefits. Benefit generosity by itself is not expected to make a difference in poverty rates since no state offers benefits that exceed poverty thresholds. But combined with earned income, higher benefits have the potential to lower poverty rates. However, higher benefits, in the absence of labor supply and earned income, may increase poverty.

Earned Income Tax Credit

The EITC policy was established in the tax code in 1975 and provides cash assistance to lower income working parents and individuals through the tax system. The program became a central part of the federal government's antipoverty strategy and took on a transformative role for low income families after major expansions in 1990 and 1993 and adopted a "make work pay" philosophy, coincident with welfare reform. Because EITC increases work incentives for low wageworkers, it is expected to lower poverty. However, such a prediction may be too simplistic because (a) official poverty rates are measured pretax and therefore do not count the EITC, and therefore (b) the effects of EITC on poverty are realized only through its effect on labor supply and earnings.

Minimum Wage

There were five increases in the federal minimum wage during the 1990s, the decade of welfare reform, when it increased from $3.35 in 1990 to $5.15 in 1998, and stayed at that level until 2008. From the supply side perspective, by increasing the return to work and making work more attractive, the minimum wage has the potential to reduce poverty. From the demand side however, if increases in minimum wage have disemployment effects in the low-wage labor market, such potential may not be realized, and may actually increase poverty. There isn't a strong consensus in the economic literature on the disemployment effects of minimum wage increases. Some studies find such an effect (review by Brown, Gilroy, & Kohen, 1982) while others do not (Bernstein & Schmitt, 1998).

Child Support Collection

Child support payments collected by the Office of Child Support Enforcement (OCSE) from noncustodial fathers and distributed to families have increased a good deal over the years and have made a real difference in alleviating poverty, especially among low income families. In 2007, the program collected a total of $25 billion for an average of $1,582 per case, at a cost of $5.6 billion. Over the study period, collections per case have increased in real dollars from \$740.62 per case in 1992 to \$1,274.80 per case in 2005, an increase of 72%.[2] Child support dollars received by families are expected to reduce poverty.

In summary, we expect work requirements, the economy, and child support collection to reduce poverty. However, the effect of time limit, family cap, sanctions, welfare benefits, EITC, and minimum wage cannot be unambiguously predicted.

EMPIRICAL FRAMEWORK – DATA AND EMPIRICAL MODEL

Our data set contains state- and year-specific information from 1992 through 2005 on all 50 states and the District of Columbia on key welfare reform policies, economy, other relevant state policies, and poverty rate. The number of state-year observations total 714 ($=51 \times 14$). Our study period includes 4 years of welfare reform (1992–1995) through the Section 1115 waiver program and 10 years of PRWORA-era which also includes a complete economic cycle with an expansion and a contraction.

We rely on state-level data rather than micro-level survey data such as the Survey of Income and Program Participation (SIPP), since many of the policies vary across states, and not individuals. Our use of state-level data also increases the efficiency of our estimates since most survey data often provide insufficient numbers of observations to estimate many variables, especially for small states.

Dependent Variable

Following much of the literature, we use the official poverty rate published by the U.S. Census Bureau[3] as the dependent variable. The Census Bureau classifies a person or family to be poor if their economic resources do not meet a particular threshold level. The official definition takes the total pretax money income (earned and unearned) for a family and compares this amount to a threshold which varies by family size and age composition. The Census Bureau bases its poverty rate computation on the March Current Population Survey (CPS) which gathers information from over 50,000 U.S. households. The poverty threshold is indexed to changes in prices through the consumer price index (CPI-U). Fig. 1 portrays the trend in the national poverty rate over the study period and shows a nonlinear trend where

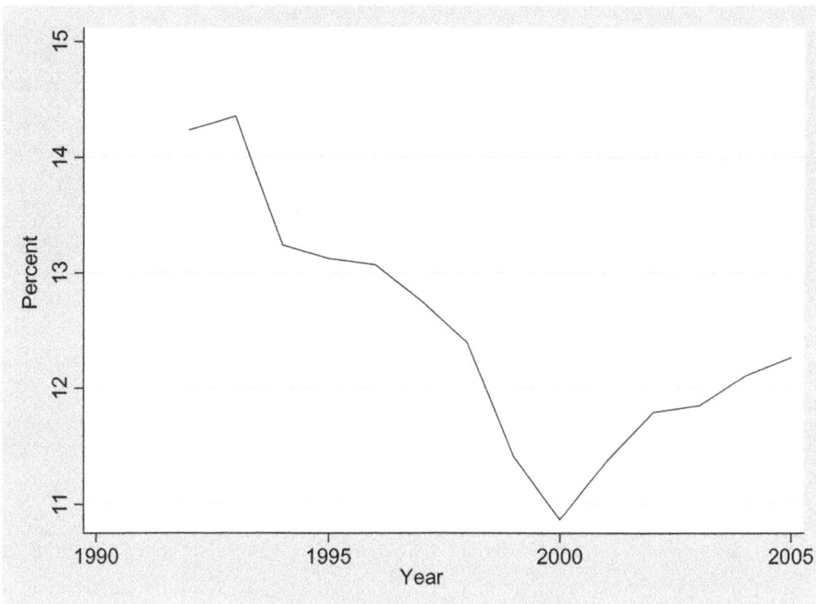

Fig. 1. U.S. Poverty Rate 1992–2005.

poverty steadily decreased until 2000 and has since begun to increase. Fig. 2 shows state-specific trends in poverty rates that closely mirror the national trend.

Focal Independent Variable – Welfare Reform

We model welfare reform using four specific policies. The two dummy variables that represent *work requirements* and *time limits* distinguish states with PRWORA-era rules that have more rigorous work requirements than the federal standard or time limits that are shorter than the 5 year limit imposed by PRWORA, and/or stricter work requirements or time limits under the Section 1115 waiver program.[4] The variables are coded as 1 when such is the case, following the coding protocol used by Fording (2003) and Soss and colleagues (2001).

The *family cap* variable is measured as a dummy variable with 1 indicating states with a cap in a given year and 0 otherwise. Information on operating family caps was obtained from the Urban Institute's Welfare

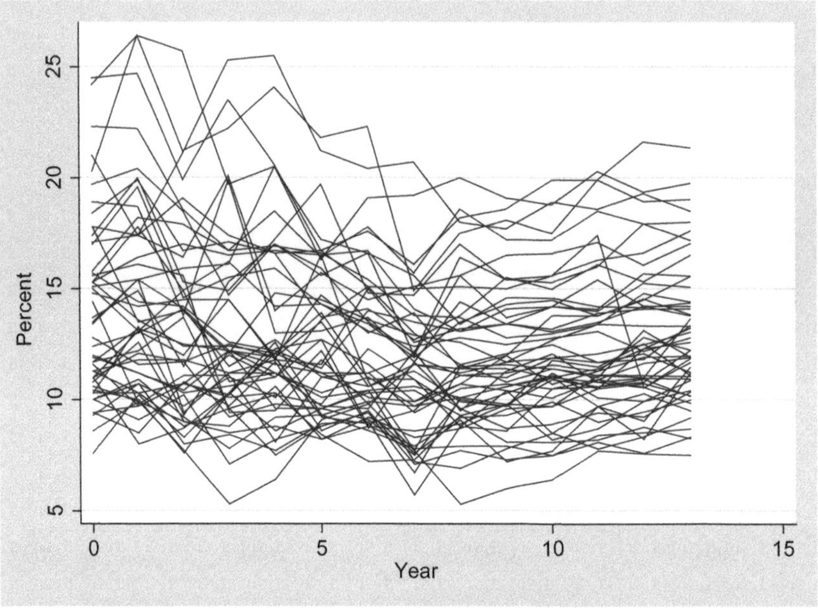

Fig. 2. Poverty Rate by State 1992–2005.

Rules Databook. While many studies have classified *sanctioning* policies as weak, moderate or severe, results consistently show that stronger sanctions (Council of Economic Advisors (CEA), 1997, 1999; Soss et al., 2001) have more significant impacts on welfare exits relative to weak sanctions. In this study, we use a dummy variable that is coded as "1" when most severe sanctions such as imposition of loss of full benefits immediately or in a delayed fashion or closing of the case as a punishment for noncompliance. Information on the most severe sanctions is obtained from Urban Institute's Welfare Rules Databook.

Economy

Our study period captures 8 years of booming economic expansion (1992–2000) as well as 5 years of much-below normal economic expansion characterized by weak private sector growth (2001–2005). We use two measures of the business cycle to capture the state of the economy: the annual state-level *unemployment* rate and the employment growth rate, both gathered from the Bureau of Labor Statistics. While both measures comprise important features of the low-wage labor market opportunities, employment growth rates serve as better indicators of demand-side shocks to the labor market as they portray the evolution of job vacancies over the business cycle (Blanchard & Katz, 1992; Gundersen & Ziliak, 2004). We also include interactions of these two variables with time to measure their time path effect over the study period. The *unemployment* rate is expected to have a positive effect on poverty while *employment growth* rate is hypothesized to reduce poverty.

Other Relevant Federal and State Policies

We include three other relevant state policies: monthly AFDC/TANF cash benefits, EITC, and state minimum wage. *Monthly welfare benefits* are gathered from the Urban Institute's Welfare Rules Databook and represent the maximum monthly cash benefits allotted to a family of three. We utilize the average amount of EITC claimed by each state in each year as our EITC policy variable.[5] The EITC information comes from the Individual Master File System maintained by the Internal Revenue Service's (IRS) Statistics of Income Division. The minimum wage represents the value of state-specific minimum wage converted to a monthly basis in order to express it on the same scale as the *monthly welfare benefits*. Following Council of Economic Advisors (CEA) (1999) and others, we assume 30 hours of work per week for 4.33 weeks. We use the CPI-U to adjust all monetary variables to 2005 dollars.

Control Variables

Demographic Controls

The analyses include two demographic controls: variables measuring the respective percentages of black and Hispanic women aged 15–44 in a state's general population. Data from the Census and the Census Bureau's intercensal population estimates provide information on the state population by race/ethnicity.

Political Climate

For a given year, the analysis includes the political party affiliation, Republican or Democrat, of the state governor, whether the state senate is controlled by Republicans or Democrats, and whether the state house (assembly) is controlled by Republicans or Democrats. Each of the three variables is coded as a 1 for Republican majority. The primary source of these data is the Council of State Governments (CSG, various years). Political variables are a mainstay in models seeking to explain the adoption of stringent welfare reforms (see, e.g., Fording, 2003; Soss et al., 2001). They are used in model specifications for welfare reform outcomes to gauge the rigor with which reforms are monitored and enforced. Republican regimes are generally viewed as more efficient on both counts (Sabia, 2008).

ANALYTIC METHOD AND EMPIRICAL ESTIMATION

We model trajectories of poverty rates using latent trajectory or random coefficient models by the method of maximum likelihood using Stata's xtmixed command. These models permit straightforward examination of both *intra*-unit (within state) change over time and *inter*-unit (between states) variability in intra-unit change. The basic premise of the LTM is that the observed data can be used to uncover an unobserved or latent trajectory for each unit that gives rise to that unit's observed repeated measures (Bollen & Curran, 2006; Curran & Hussong, 2003). Further, this trajectory process can be conditioned on one or more predictor variables. We investigate (a) differences in state-specific trajectories across states and allow each state to deviate in its initial status (intercept) and rate of change (slope) in its poverty rate from the overall mean intercept and slope; and if (b) welfare reform, after controlling for the economy, other state and federal income support policies, political climate and demographic composition, has contributed to changes in the poverty trajectories.

We estimate six different specifications, starting with a simple random intercept model. In each specification, given the nonlinearity in the growth trajectory of poverty shown in Figs. 1 and 2 where growth is initially negative and then becomes positive, we also include a fixed quadratic term for the time trajectory.[6] Model 1 is the unconditional random intercept model which examines just the state-specific trajectories over time. We specify this model in the HLM tradition as containing two levels:

$$\text{Level 1}: \; Y_{ij} = \eta_{1j} + \beta_2 \times time_{ij} + \beta_3 \times time_{ij}^2 + \varepsilon_{ij} \qquad (1.1)$$

$$\text{Level 2}: \; \eta_{1j} = \beta_1 + \zeta_{1j} \qquad (1.2)$$

where Y_{ij} is official poverty rate at time i for state j; η_{1j} is the intercept of the underlying trajectory for state j which becomes the response variable in the Level 2 equation; β_2 is the fixed slope coefficient for time or the mean state growth rate over time; Time is a linear trend variable scaled to have a value of 0 in 1992, the beginning of the study period when states began to be active in welfare reform; β_3 is the slope coefficient for quadratic time trend; ε_{ij} is the residual at time i for state j and *iid* normal with mean 0 and variance θ^2; β_1 is the overall mean intercept pooled across all states; and ζ_{1j} is the deviation of each state from the overall mean and normal with mean 0 and unstructured (to be estimated) variance.

Since the Level 2 equation cannot be estimated directly because the random intercepts η_{1j} are not observed, we substitute (1.2) into (1.1) to obtain the reduced-form model for the observed responses Y_{ij}, as follows:

$$Y_{ij} = (\beta_1 + \beta_2 \times time_{ij} + \beta_3 \times time_{ij}^2) + (\zeta_{1j} + \varepsilon_{ij}) \tag{1.3}$$

In the reduced form the fixed parameters are β_1, β_2, and β_3, and the random parameters are ζ_{1j} and ε_{ij}. In rather poetic terms, Crowder and Hand (1996) refer to the fixed part as the "immutable constant of the universe," to ζ_{1j} as the "lasting characteristic of the individual" and to ε_{ij} as the "fleeting aberration of the moment." In this simple random intercept model, we estimate the mean starting point β_1, that is, the mean poverty rate in time 0 (1992), the fixed slope on the time variable β_2, the fixed slope β_3 for the quadratic term, the variance in the starting point, and time-specific residual variances.

Model 2 is a random coefficient model where we allow each state to have a distinct poverty growth rate or trajectory η_{2j} in addition to intercept, and specify the Level 1, Level 2, and the reduced-form equations as follows:

$$\text{Level 1}: \ Y_{ij} = \eta_{1j} + \eta_{2j} \times time_{ij} + \beta_3 \times time_{ij}^2 + \varepsilon_{ij} \tag{2.1}$$

$$\text{Level 2}: \ \eta_{1j} = \beta_1 + \zeta_{1j} \tag{2.2a}$$

$$\eta_{2j} = \beta_2 + \zeta_{2j} \tag{2.2b}$$

$$\begin{aligned}\text{Reduced-form}: \ Y_{ij} &= (\beta_1 + \beta_2 \times time_{ij} + \beta_3 \times time_{ij}^2) \\ &\quad + (\zeta_{1j} + \zeta_{2j} \times time_{ij} + \varepsilon_{ij})\end{aligned} \tag{2.3}$$

where β_1 and β_2, the mean intercept and slope, respectively; β_3 is as before, and ζ_{1j} and ζ_{2j} are the deviations of each state from the group mean with ζ_{1j}

and ζ_{2j} now bivariate normal with mean 0 and unstructured variance. As before, the fixed component contains β_1, β_2, and β_3 and the random parameters are ζ_{1j}, ζ_{2j}, and ε_{ij}.

Two additional parameters are estimated in this model: the variance in slopes ζ_{2j}, which tells us the amount of state-level variability in the growth rate of poverty around the national mean, and the covariance between ζ_{1j} and ζ_{2j}. Also note that Model 2 is still an unconditional model inasmuch as no covariates are used to predict the random intercepts and slopes.

In Models 1 and 2, we have made the assumption that the time and state-specific values of poverty rate (Y_{ij}) are completely governed by the underlying trajectory process and any deviations of these values from the trajectory are treated as error. We now extend these models to capture situations in which we do not necessarily anticipate that poverty rates are completely determined by the underlying trajectory process; rather they are related only partly to the trajectory process but may also be influenced by other time-specific variables, especially the implementation of welfare reform measures.

We estimate four models that assess the simultaneous effects of the welfare reform measure(s) *and* the underlying random trajectory components in predicting poverty rates at time *i* for state *j*, while also sequentially controlling for the economy, other relevant policies, demographic and political climate variables. The first, (Model 3) includes only measures of welfare reform; the second (Model 4) adds economic variables to the previous model; the third (Model 5) adds other state and federal income support policies; and the last (Model 6) includes variables from all the preceding models and adds political and demographic controls. It is important to note that in Models 3–6, a trajectory process is not estimated for either the focal welfare policy variables or the control variables.[7] The final model, Model 6 is represented in the following reduced-form equation:

$$\begin{aligned}Y_{ij} = (&\beta_1 + \beta_2 \times time_{ij} + \beta_3 \times time^2_{ij} + \lambda_1 \times \mathbf{Welfare\ Reform}_{ij} + \gamma_1 \times Unemployment_{ij}\\ &+ \gamma_2 \times Employment\ Growth_{ij} + \beta_4 \times Monthly\ Welfare\ Benefit_{ij} + \beta_5 \times EITC_{ij}\\ &+ \beta_6 \times Monthly\ Minimum\ Wage_{ij} + \beta_7 \times Child\ Support_{ij} + \beta_8 \times \%Fem.\ Popn.\ Black_{ij}\\ &+ \beta_9 \times \%Fem.\ Popn.\ Hispanic_{ij} + \beta_{10} \times Republican\ Senate_{ij} + \beta_{11} \times Republican\ House_{ij}\\ &+ \beta_{12} \times Republican\ Governor_{ij}) + (\zeta_{1j} + \zeta_{2j} \times time_{ij} + \varepsilon_{ij}) \qquad (3.3)\end{aligned}$$

Welfare Reform here represents a vector of four policy initiatives. In each model, the economic variables – *unemployment* rate and employment growth rate – are also interacted with time to allow for the economic slowdown over time.

In Models 1–6, it is assumed that the ζ_j and ε_{ij} are uncorrelated and in Models 3–6 it is also assumed that they are also uncorrelated with each of the covariates (the exogeneity assumption). The exogeneity assumption with respect to the ζ_j is empirically untenable in most cases inasmuch as it implies that unobserved state-level characteristics that are time invariant (ζ_j), for example, the state culture or overall inclinations toward the poor, not be correlated with other included variables in the model, for example, the political or economic climate. If such correlations exist, estimated effects may be subject to state-level confounding or omitted variables bias. It should be noted that in our analyses we find such correlations to be low.[8] One way to remove this residual correlation is to include cluster means of covariates (in addition to the covariates) in the Level 1 equation and thus allow for the within and between effect of a covariate to be different (Rabe-Hesketh & Skrondal, 2008). However, a more often adopted modeling alternative to overcoming the endogeneity problem is the fixed effects models, where the ζs are not treated as random variables but as fixed covariates much like any other covariates in the model.

A major advantage of the random effects models is the ease and parsimony with which growth rate trajectories can be estimated. For example, in a simple model with no covariates excepting time, the fixed effects estimation requires for each state, one parameter for the intercept and an another parameter (state $\times$ time) to capture the change in slope – a specification that can be very demanding of the data and use up many degrees of freedom. The corresponding random effects model on the other hand, estimates a mean intercept and a mean slope (the fixed part of the model) and three other parameters that contain the variability around these two group means and their covariance (the random part of the model). Also, if the number of repeated measures (group size) for each state is small and therefore does not contain much information, the state fixed effects may be estimated with large standard errors. This problem is avoided in the random effects models since these intercepts are not estimated.

While methodological considerations should play a role in the selection of random effects modeling, the principal motivation for their use in this paper is our conceptualization of poverty as following an underlying growth trajectory stemming from bust and boom cycles of the economy and how welfare reform and other income support policies have sought to alter this trajectory.

Distribution of Study Variables

Table 1 provides the distribution of the study variables for the 50 states and the District of Columbia over the 14-year study period. The means for the

Table 1. Distribution of Study Variables.

Variable		Mean	Standard Deviation	Min	Max	Observations
Poverty rate	Overall	12.48824	3.725772	5.2	26.4	$N=714$
	Between		3.275348	7.071429	19.88571	$n=51$
	Within		1.830047	6.166806	19.28109	$T=14$
Work requirement	Overall	0.42577	0.494806	0	1	$N=714$
	Between		0.348747	0	0.928571	$n=51$
	Within		0.354155	−0.5028	1.354342	$T=14$
Time limit	Overall	0.340336	0.474154	0	1	$N=714$
	Between		0.343923	0	0.857143	$n=51$
	Within		0.32969	−0.51681	1.268908	$T=14$
Family cap	Overall	0.338936	0.47368	0	1	$N=714$
	Between		0.375212	0	1	$n=51$
	Within		0.293522	−0.51821	1.12465	$T=14$
Sanction	Overall	0.512605	0.500192	0	1	$N=714$
	Between		0.266384	0	1	$n=51$
	Within		0.424882	−0.20168	1.441176	$T=14$
Unemployment rate	Overall	5.321849	1.689186	2.3	12.5	$N=714$
	Between		0.485326	4.264286	6.478571	$n=51$
	Within		1.619291	2.114706	12.67185	$T=14$
Employment growth rate	Overall	1.666667	1.663858	−3.1	9.9	$N=714$
	Between		0.843953	0.071429	4.907143	$n=51$
	Within		1.438456	−3.14048	6.659523	$T=14$
Maximum welfare benefits	Overall	472.3229	203.0366	0	1294.251	$N=714$
	Between		198.1478	0	1098.864	$n=51$
	Within		51.74143	268.8307	683.7397	$T=14$

Average *EITC* amount	Overall	1657.353	334.4347	0	2234.671	$N=714$
	Between		267.9409	0	2028.752	$n=51$
	Within		203.3794	871.9616	1885.745	$T=14$
Minimum wage (monthly)	Overall	716.2742	153.1526	0	994.3234	$N=714$
	Between		141.4519	0	896.266	$n=51$
	Within		61.74053	548.9249	1052.18	$T=14$
Child support collection	Overall	1034.054	489.0407	0	2534.478	$N=714$
	Between		395.9756	0	1946.626	$n=51$
	Within		291.9298	202.2563	1814.496	$T=14$
% Female population black	Overall	11.13762	11.83669	0.28446	64.096	$N=714$
	Between		11.88313	0.307871	58.34616	$n=51$
	Within		1.213716	2.730256	16.88746	$T=14$
% Female population Hispanic	Overall	7.735291	8.965602	0.518661	47.54353	$N=714$
	Between		8.88056	0.709063	42.78829	$n=51$
	Within		1.719181	0.954417	14.70078	$T=14$
Republican Senate	Overall	0.435574	0.49618	0	1	$N=714$
	Between		0.387102	0	1	$n=51$
	Within		0.314767	−0.493	1.364146	$T=14$
Republican House	Overall	0.408964	0.491987	0	1	$N=714$
	Between		0.409848	0	1	$n=51$
	Within		0.277739	−0.51961	1.337535	$T=14$
Republican Governor	Overall	0.532213	0.497905	0	1	$N=714$
	Between		0.295826	0	1	$n=51$
	Within		0.402482	−0.39636	1.460784	$T=14$

modified dummy policy variables like work requirements, time limits, family cap, and sanctions represent the proportion of state-years in which a policy is observed.

The table shows that there is much more variability in poverty rates between states than there is within each state over time providing further support for our choice of random effects over fixed effects models. The same is true of virtually all of the policy variables and demographic/political controls.

RESULTS

Table 2 presents the results of regressions from the linear trajectory models. The table presents coefficients for the fixed portion of the reduced-form equations in the top, followed by the variance (standard deviation) estimates of the random effects and the intervals within which 95% of the states' random intercepts and slopes are expected to lie.[9] Forming these intervals is particularly important for slopes since it is useful to know whether the slopes (of the trajectories) are likely to have different signs for different states. Also presented are the estimated correlation between intercepts and slopes. Log likelihood statistics are presented at the bottom along with the p-value for a likelihood ratio test of each model against an ordinary linear regression model, or equivalently that there are no random effects, that is, ζ_j are 0. If this is true then a multilevel model is not required. This p-value for all the models for each of the outcomes is highly significant indicating that the random effects are appropriate, that states did vary significantly in their poverty rate at the beginning of the study period (1992) and that there was significant variability in the state trajectories of this outcome.

Model 1 is the baseline model corresponding to reduced-form Eq. (1.3) where only the intercepts are allowed to vary randomly. The fixed portion of the model ($\beta_1 + \beta_2 \times time_{ij}$) simply states that we are estimating one overall regression line representing the population average. The random effect ζ_{1j} serves to shift this regression line up or down according to each state. In this model the common slope of "time" shared by all states is estimated at −0.66 and is statistically significant, meaning that on average the poverty rate was declining by about two-thirds of a percentage point over the study period, but the coefficient for the quadratic term is positive and significant, indicating that poverty rates increased after a time. The estimated mean intercept is 14.66 which represents the average national poverty rate at

Table 2. Latent Trajectory Regression of Poverty on Separate Reform, Economy, Other State Policies, and Demographic/Political Controls.

Fixed effects	Model 1 Coefficient (Std. Error)	Model 2 Coefficient (Std. Error)	Model 3 Coefficient (Std. Error)	Model 4 Coefficient (Std. Error)	Model 5 Coefficient (Std. Error)	Model 6 Coefficient (Std. Error)
Mean initial status (β_1)	14.66 (0.48)**	14.66 (0.57)**	14.62 (0.57)**	16.26 (0.69)**	16.59 (1.30)**	38.47 (3.57)**
Mean growth rate (β_2)	−0.66 (0.06)**	−0.66 (0.06)**	−0.63 (0.07)**	−1.01 (0.09)**	−1.09 (0.12)**	−0.74 (0.13)**
Growth rate squared (β_3)	0.04 (0.004)**	0.04 (0.004)**	0.04 (0.004)**	0.04 (0.004)**	0.05 (0.006)**	0.04 (0.01)**
Work requirement (λ_1)			0.14 (0.20)	0.07 (0.20)	0.05 (0.20)	0.16 (0.20)
Time limit (λ_2)			0.50 (0.21)**	0.47 (0.22)**	0.34 (0.21)	0.18 (0.21)
Family cap (λ_3)			−0.22 (0.25)	−0.12 (0.25)	−0.24 (0.24)	−0.25 (0.23)
Sanction (λ_4)			−0.69 (0.21)**	−0.62 (0.21)	−0.63 (0.21)**	−0.66 (0.21)**
Unemployment (γ_1)				−0.28 (0.06)**	−0.29 (0.06)**	−0.25 (0.06)**
Unemployment* time (γ_2)				0.07 (0.01)**	0.07 (0.01)**	0.06 (0.01)**
Employment growth (γ_3)				−0.03 (0.05)	−0.095 (0.047)**	−0.09 (0.047)**
Welfare benefit (β_3)					−0.0005 (0.001)	0.0004 (0.001)
Average EITC amount (β_4)					0.001 (0.001)	0.001 (0.001)
Minimum wage (β_5)					−0.001 (0.001)	−0.002 (0.001)**
Child support collection (β_6)					−0.001 (0.0003)**	−0.001 (0.0003)**
Demographic and political controls			No	No	No	Yes

Table 2. *(Continued)*

Fixed effects	Model 1 Coefficient (Std. Error)	Model 2 Coefficient (Std. Error)	Model 3 Coefficient (Std. Error)	Model 4 Coefficient (Std. Error)	Model 5 Coefficient (Std. Error)	Model 6 Coefficient (Std. Error)
Random effects	Estimate 95% C.I.	Estimate 95% C.I.	Estimate 95% C.I.	Estimate 95% C.I.	Estimate 95% C.I.	Estimate 95% C.I.
Standard deviation of initial status (ζ_{1j})	3.21 [8.4, 20.9]	3.91 [7.0, 22.3]	3.91 [7.0, 22.3]	3.97 [8.5, 24.0]	3.64 [9.5, 23.7]	2.93 [32.7, 44.2]
Standard deviation of growth rate (ζ_{2j})		0.12 [−0.9, −0.4]	0.13 [−0.9, −0.4]	0.16 [−1.3, −0.7]	0.17 [−1.4, −0.8]	0.14 [−1.0, −0.5]
Correlation (ζ_1, ζ_2)		−0.88	−0.89	−0.89	−0.93	−0.92
Standard deviation of Level 1 error (ε_{ij})	1.64	1.55	1.53	1.48	1.47	1.46
Log likelihood	−1466.51	−1441.36	−1430.83	−1413.56	−1403.59	−1381.51
P ($\bar{\chi}^2$)	0.00	0.00	0.00	0.00	0.00	0.00

*p-value < 0.10.
**p-value < 0.05.

the start of the study period, in 1992. States vary in their initial level of poverty rate on average by 3.2 points (standard deviation of ζ_{1j}), and within the states, the estimated standard deviation around the state-specific regression lines is 1.6 (standard deviation of the residuals ε_{ij}).

Model 2 extends Model 1 and allows the state slopes to vary also (see Eq. (2.3)). The mean intercept (14.66) and slope (−0.66 and 0.04) are identical to Model 1. Given the estimated standard deviation of the random slopes of 0.12, we can say that a state whose poverty rate reduction is one standard deviation above average is expected to decline at the rate of $0.12 + (-0.66 + 0.04) = -0.5$ or half a percentage point per year. Indications of improvement in fit from the random intercept model are provided by a significant increase in the log likelihood value as well as the reduction in the Level 1 residual standard deviation from 1.64 to 1.55. The estimated correlation of −0.88 between the intercept and the slope indicates that states with an initially higher poverty rate tended to experience declines at a slightly slower rate.

Welfare Reform

Results from linear trajectory regressions of poverty on welfare reform modeled as four distinct policies are shown in columns 3–6 of Table 2. Model 3, with only the reform policies, shows that of the four reform policies, only two show statistically significant effects. Consistent with expectation, time limits increase poverty by half a point. Severe sanctioning on the other hand serves to reduce poverty by a little over two-thirds of a point. With addition of control variables, only sanctioning policy maintains its direction, magnitude, and statistical significance throughout the modeling sequence.

The final model (Model 6, Eq. (3.3)) shows the effect of *unemployment* rate to be a 0.14 point increase in poverty while each point increase in employment growth reduces poverty by almost a tenth of a point. The estimated effects of minimum wage and child support dollars are also statistically significant.

The random effects (ζ_{1j}, ζ_{2j} and ε_{ij}) are of slightly lower magnitude in the final model relative to previous conditional models. Model fit also gets better as more control variables are added. The correlation between the random intercepts and slopes are strong and negative. In all instances the mean intercept, the mean slope and the mean quadratic term are significant indicating that all three parameters are necessary for describing the mean trajectory.

SENSITIVITY ANALYSES – ALTERNATIVE SPECIFICATIONS

To check the robustness of the welfare policy effect we have uncovered here, we undertook two sensitivity checks: (1) To remove any possible correlation between ζ_j and independent/control variables, we added the state level means of all independent/control variables to Models 3–6 and find that our results are substantively unaltered (results are available from authors). (2) We also undertook estimation of the final model using (a) lagged welfare reform measures, (b) modeling welfare reform as a single black box dummy variable, (c) the more traditional econometric approach with state fixed effects and state-specific linear time trend, and a national quadratic trend with levels and changes in poverty rates, (d) 125% poverty rate as the dependent variable, and (e) poverty rate of female-headed families as the dependent variable. Results from this exercise are shown in Table 3, which indicate that the significant effects we have reported in Table 2 (Model 6) are largely similar despite varying modeling assumptions (e.g., fixed vs. random effects) and measures of poverty. The magnitude of some of the effects do vary (e.g., the sanctioning effect varies from −0.42 to −1.54), however, our Model 6 results from LTM provide the most conservative effects for the most part. It is also noteworthy that when welfare reform is modeled as a black box dummy, we find no significant reform effects.

DISCUSSION AND CONCLUSION

In this paper we find evidence supporting an independent welfare reform effect on poverty even after accounting for state-specific growth trajectories, the economy, other state and federal policies, and demographic and political influences. Based on Model 6, our key findings can be summarized as follows:

- There is considerable variability across states in both their mean initial level and linear trajectories of poverty rates, providing support for our conceptualization and estimation of random coefficient models.

Table 3. Comparison of Model 6 Estimates to Other Modeling Strategies, Methods, and Dependent Variables.

	LTM Estimate from Table 3, Model 6	LTM Estimate – Lagged Welfare Reform	LTM Estimate – Welfare Reform Dummy	Fixed Effects Estimate Poverty Rate (level)	Fixed Effects Estimate Poverty Rate (change)	LTM Estimate – Dep. Var: 125% Poverty	LTM Estimate – Dep. Var: Poverty in Female-Headed Household
Variable							
Welfare Reform							
Reform dummy	–	–	–	–	–	–	–
Work requirement	0.16	−0.04	–	−0.17	−0.06	0.13	0.88
Time limit	0.18	0.43	–	0.38	0.02	0.22	−0.18
Family cap	−0.25	−0.30	–	0.20	0.10	−0.11	−1.70**
Sanction	−0.66**	−0.42**	–	−0.74**	−0.68**	−0.73**	−1.54**
Economy							
Unemployment rate	0.14**	0.08**	0.16**	0.10**	−0.08**	0.17**	−0.03
Employment growth rate	−0.09**	−0.11**	−0.09*	−0.14**	0.003	−0.08*	−0.12
Other Policies							
Welfare benefits	0.0004	0.001	0.001	0.009**	0.006	0.0001	−0.0001
EITC	0.001	0.001	0.001	−0.001	−0.002	0.001	−0.005**
Minimum wage	−0.002**	−0.002**	−0.002**	−0.003**	−0.0002	−0.003**	−0.005**
Child support	−0.001**	−0.001**	−0.001**	0.001	0.0003	−0.001**	−0.003**

Note: All models include demographic and political controls.
*$p<0.1$.
**$p<0.05$.

- Magnitude and statistical significance of welfare policy effects are sensitive to how welfare reform is operationalized.
- Welfare reform leads to reductions in poverty rate. Specifically, welfare reform leads to a two-thirds of a point decline in poverty rate through severe sanctioning policies.
- The economy also contributed to changes in poverty rates, but to a far lesser extent. A one percentage point increase in unemployment results in

Table 4. Summary of Significant LTM Findings: Percentage of Change in Poverty Attributable to Welfare Reform, the Economy and Other Income Support Policies.

(a) Mean and changes in poverty

Year	Mean	Change, 1992–2000	Change, 2000–2005	Change, 1992–2005
1992	14.233			
2000	10.863			
2005	12.271	−3.37	1.41	−1.96

(b) Change in poverty explained by welfare reform, economy, and other income support policies

Expressed:	As Coefficient	Average Change in Variable			As % of Change in Poverty in[a]:		
		1992–2000	2000–2005	1992–2005	1992–2000	2000–2005	1992–2005
Attributable to							
Welfare reform							
Sanctions	−0.66	0.66	0.12	0.78	13.0	−6.0	26.3
Economy							
Unemployment rate	0.14	−1.963	1.026	−0.937	8.0	10.0	7.0
Employment growth	−0.09	0.90	−0.365	0.535	2.0	2.0	2.5
Income support							
Minimum wage	−0.002	$17.87	−$30.14	−$12.27	1.0	4.0	1.0
Child support	−0.001	$437.07	$98.11	$534.18	13.0	−7.0	27.0

[a]Calculation is: (coefficient * average change in variable)/change in poverty during period.

0.14 point increase in poverty and a percentage point increase in employment growth reduces poverty by about a tenth of a point.
- An average increase of $534 in child support collections helped accelerate poverty declines by half a point.
- A $12 decline in the real value of *monthly minimum wage* led to two-hundredths of a point increase in poverty.

In Table 4 we present a summary of our significant findings in terms of how much of the share in the poverty decline of 1.96 percentage points (from 1992 to 2005) can be attributed to welfare reform (sanctions), the economy, and the other state policies. The decomposition is also performed for two blocks of time periods, from 1992 to 2000 during which there was considerable economic growth and from 2000 to 2005 when the economy slowed down and poverty rates increased. The table shows that during 1992–2000 and over the entire study period 1992–2005, increased incidence of severe sanctioning policies and increased child support collections both contributed to about the same share of the poverty decline, which is 13% in 1992–2000 and about 27% in 1992–2005. The combined economic effect of *unemployment* and *employment growth* rates account for about 10% of poverty decline, while increases in the minimum wage can be credited with about 1% of the decline. We also see that during the period of economic slump (2000–2005), the economy's share of increased poverty was much higher (at 10%) relative to the reductions in poverty brought about by welfare reform or child support dollars.

Our analyses lead us to conclude that welfare reform has been a significant driver of poverty reductions over the period 1992–2005. Severe sanctioning policies that eliminate all or a portion of welfare benefits for some length of time or permanently for nonconformance with program rules appears to lower poverty. Research by McKernan and Ratcliffe (2006), the only other work that examines specific welfare reform policies, however, finds a marginally significant *increase* in poverty.

We believe that the behavioral mechanism by which sanctioning affects poverty is through welfare entry and exits. Sanctions may serve as a general threat factor to potential welfare recipients, thereby encouraging them to substitute work for welfare. Poverty reducing effects of sanctions also become possible if welfare exits of current recipients result in employment and subsequent rise in earnings. It is possible that severe sanctions lead recipients to prefer engaging in the actual labor market to the "hassles" of complying with mandatory participation in busy work or work-related training. Since most of the recipients will still be able to avail themselves of the other in-kind benefits such as Medicaid, child care, etc., it is also possible that they find their formal labor supply to be more rewarding both economically and psychologically. Several studies suggest that recipients indeed leave the rolls for work and remain on the labor force (Acs & Loprest, 2001; Loprest, 1999).

Our analyses also point up the difficulty in identifying welfare reform effect using a black box approach where "sticks" and "carrots" can produce offsetting effects leading to a overall non-effect. We find a negative but nonsignificant relationship between welfare reform and poverty when we model welfare reform more generally as a dummy variable representing waivers or TANF. Similar negative, nonsignificant effects are also reported by McKernan and Ratcliffe (2006), Weber et al. (2003), and Gundersen and Ziliak (2004). However, Shoeni and Blank (2000) do report significant waiver and TANF dummy effects on poverty.

With respect to other state and federal income support policies, we find that increases in minimum wage and child support collection alleviate poverty. Our results on both of these policies are consistent with those reported by McKernan and Ratcliffe (2006) and the minimum wage results also agree with Gundersen and Ziliak (2004). We show that child support dollars are at least as effective in reducing poverty as is the sanctioning policy.

We find the macroeconomy to have significantly influenced changes in poverty rates over the study period. The economic expansion of the 1990s and the subsequent slowdown in the 2000s have had anticipated effects on poverty. This finding is consistent with Gundersen and Ziliak (2004) analyses, although they attribute a much more significant role to the macroeconomic performance of the 1990s in poverty reduction while finding no welfare reform effects. The EITC policy, while generally believed to be an anti-poverty device, does not emerge as a significant factor in our analyses. This finding is also consistent with other research (Gundersen & Ziliak, 2004; McKernan & Ratcliffe, 2006) that shows either no or positive EITC impact on poverty or deep poverty, measures that are based on before-tax income.

Finally, our results show remarkable robustness in the face of different analytical methods and rigorous sensitivity analyses. We have integrated the econometric and statistical traditions of fixed effects modeling and latent trajectory modeling in answering the welfare effect question, and report findings that are largely consonant with existing fixed-effect modeling specifications.

In this paper we find that welfare reform has played a role in the reduction of poverty. Our work, however, leaves a number of important questions unanswered. For example, have former recipients become self-sufficient?

Has this reduction in welfare utilization led to greater work activity and increased economic resources for the welfare leavers? What will be the long run effects of welfare reform? Will the lack luster economy of the early/middle 2000s and the more recent economic downturn drive more poor women and their children into deeper poverty? These are some of the questions that will undoubtedly be addressed when welfare reform is revisited in 2012 for reauthorization.

NOTES

1. The TANF reauthorization is pending in Congress. The originally scheduled reauthorization in 2010 did not take place; instead Congress extended the block grant at first to September 2011 and then again to December 2011 (CLASP, 2011).
2. We thank our colleague Jocelyn Crowley at Rutgers University for providing us with data on child support collections over the study period.
3. These data are downloaded from http://www.census.gov/hhes/www/poverty/detailedpovtabs.html
4. The following states were classified as having stringent work requirements: AZ, AR, CO, CT, DE, FL, GA, ID, IL, IN, IA, KS, MD, MA, MI, MN, MS, MO, MT, NE, NH, NJ, NM, NY, NC, ND, OH, OK, OR, SC, SD, TN, TX, UT, VT, VA, WA, WV, WI, WY. States that had stringent time limits were: AZ, AR, CA, CO, CT, DE, FL, GA, HI, ID, IL, IN, IA, LA, MA, MI, MO, MT, NE, NH, NC, ND, OH, OK, OR, SC, SD, TN, TX, UT, VT, VA, WA.
5. We also tried percentage of total tax returns that were EITC returns claimed by each state in some of the specifications and did not find the effects to be different.
6. We only estimate an average quadratic term across all states and do not allow it to vary randomly by state. Given the number of observations per state, allowing too many random effects leads to over-fitting and an inability to calculate standard errors. As Rabe-Hesketh and Skrondal (2008) point out, "it is perfectly reasonable to allow only the lower-order terms of the polynomial used in the fixed part of the model to vary randomly between subjects" (p. 219).
7. In other words, we do not allow each state's own slope to vary randomly with respect to these variables. Doing so quickly increases the number of parameters estimated, leading to over-fitting and an inability to calculate standard errors. If there are k random slopes (plus 1 random intercept), then the number of parameters in the random portion becomes $(k+2)(k+1)/2+1$ (Rabe-Hesketh & Skrondal, 2008). For example, allowing each of the four separate policy variables to also have random slopes will result in 22 random parameters.
8. The highest correlation we find between the ζ_j and the independent variables is 0.4, which occurs in the case of one of the demographic controls, the percentage of *female population black* or *Hispanic*.
9. It is important to note here that these intervals represent ranges which contain 95% of the realizations of the *random variable*, and are different from confidence

intervals used in a the usual statistical sense which represent ranges that contain the unknown *parameter* (Rabe-Hesketh & Skrondal, 2008).

ACKNOWLEDGMENTS

The authors would like to thank German Rodriguez of Princeton University, Peter Selb of University of Konstanz, Germany, participants at the Fourth Annual Meeting of the Study of Economic Inequality (ECINEQ), and an REI anonymous reviewer for their excellent feedback.

REFERENCES

Acs, G., & Loprest, P. (2001). *Initial synthesis report of the findings from ASPE's 'leavers' grants*. Washington, DC: U.S. Department of Health and Human Services.

American Public Welfare Association. (1997). Welfare reform management, service delivery, and policy decisions. *Survey Notes*, *1*, 7–8.

Bavier, R. (2002). *The impact of welfare reform on families in data from the survey of income and program participation*. Washington, DC: Office of Management and Budget.

Bernstein, J., & Schmitt, J. (1998). *Making work pay: The impact of the 1996–97 minimum wage increase*. Washington, DC: Economic Policy Institute.

Besharov, D. J. (2008). Two cheers for American welfare reform – Lessons learned, questions raised, next steps. *Policy Exchange*. Welfare Reform Academy. Available at http://www.welfareacademy.org/pubs/

Bitler, M. P., Gelbach, J. B., & Hoynes, H. W. (2002). *The impact of welfare reform on living arrangements*. Unpublished manuscript. Economics Department, University of California, Davis, CA.

Blanchard, O., & Katz, V. (1992). Regional evolutions. *Brookings Papers on Economic Activity*, *1*, 1–75.

Blank, R. (1993). Why were poverty rates so high in the 1980s? In D. Papadimitriou & E. Wolff (Eds), *Poverty and prosperity in the USA in the late twentieth century* (pp. 21–55). New York, NY: St. Martin's Press.

Blank, R., & Card, D. (1993). Poverty, income distribution, and growth: Are they still connected? *Brookings Papers on Economic Activity*, *2*, 285–339.

Blank, R. M. (2002). Evaluating welfare reform in the United States. *Journal of Economic Literature*, *40*(4), 1105–1166.

Blank, R. M., & Schmidt, L. (2001). Work, wages, and welfare. In R. M. Blank & R. Haskins (Eds), *The new world of welfare* (pp. 70–96). Washington, DC: The Brookings Institution.

Bloom, D., & Michalopoulos, C. (2001). *How welfare and work policies affect employment and income: A synthesis of research*. New York, NY: MDRC.

Bollen, K. A., & Curran, P. J. (2006). *Latent curve models: A structural equation perspective*. Hoboken, NJ: Wiley.

Brown, C., Gilroy, C., & Kohen, A. (1982). The effects of the minimum wage on employment and unemployment. *Journal of Economic Literature*, *20*(June), 487–528.
Center for Law and Social Policy (CLASP). (2011). *TANF policy brief*. Washington, DC. Retrieved from http://www.clasp.org/federal_policy/pages?id=0021
Congressional Budget Office. (2006). *Changes in low-wage labor markets between 1979 and 2005*. Washington, DC: Congressional Budget Office.
Council of Economic Advisors (CEA). (1997). *Technical report: Explaining the decline in welfare receipt, 1993–1996*. Washington, DC: The White House.
Council of Economic Advisors (CEA). (1999). *Technical report: The effects of welfare policy and the economic expansion on welfare caseloads: An update*. Washington, DC: The White House.
Council of State Governments (CSG). (Various Years). *The book of the States, 1978–1979* (Vol. 22). Lexington, KY: CSG.
Crowder, M. J., & Hand, D. J. (1996). *Practical longitudinal data analysis*. London: Chapman and Hall.
Curran, P. J., & Hussong, A. M. (2003). The use of latent trajectory models in psychopathology research. *Journal of Abnormal Psychology*, *112*(4), 526–544.
Duncan, G. J., & Chase-Lansdale, P. L. (2001). Welfare reform and children's well-being. In R. M. Blank & R. Haskins (Eds), *The new world of welfare* (pp. 391–417). Washington, DC: Brookings Institution Press.
Fording, R. C. (2003). Laboratories of democracy or symbol politics? The racial origins of welfare reform. In S. F. Schram, J. Soss & R. C. Fording (Eds), *Race and the politics of welfare reform* (pp. 72–97). Ann Arbor, MI: University of Michigan Press.
Grogger, J. (2003). The effects of time limits, the EITC, and other policy changes on welfare use, work, and income among female-headed families. *The Review of Economics and Statistics*, *85*(2), 394–408.
Grogger, J. (2004). Time limits and welfare use. *Journal of Human Resources*, *39*(2), 405–424.
Grogger, J., & Karoly, L. A. (2005). *Welfare reform: Effects of a decade of change*. Cambridge, MA: Harvard University Press.
Gundersen, C., & Ziliak, J. P. (2004). Poverty and macroeconomic performance across space, race, and family structure. *Demography*, *41*(1), 61–86.
Harvey, C., Camasso, M. J., & Jagannathan, R. (2000) Evaluating welfare reform waivers under Section 1115. *Journal of Economic Perspectives*, *14*(4), 165–188.
Haskins, R. (2009). *Ten years of welfare reform*. Washington, DC: Brookings Institution.
Haveman, R., & Schwabish, J. (2000). Has macroeconomic performance regained its antipoverty bite? *Contemporary Economic Policy*, *18*, 415–427.
Iceland, J. (2003). Why poverty remains high: The role of income growth, economic inequality, and changes in family structure, 1949–1999. *Demography*, *40*, 499–519.
Leiberman, R. C., & Shaw, G. M. (2000). Looking inward, looking outward: The politics of state welfare innovation under devolution. *Political Research Quarterly*, *53*, 215–240.
Loprest, P. (1999). *Families who left welfare: Who are they and how are they doing?* Discussion Paper No. 99-02. Assessing the New Federalism – The Urban Institute, Washington, DC.
McKernan, S.-M., & Ratcliffe, C. (2006). *The effect of specific welfare policies on poverty*. Washington, DC: The Urban Institute.
Moffitt, R. A., & Pavetti, L. A. (2000). Time limits. In D. E. Card & R. M. Blank (Eds), *Finding jobs: Work and welfare reform* (pp. 507–535). New York, NY: Russell Sage Foundation.

Rabe-Hesketh, S., & Skrondal, A. (2008). *Multilevel and longitudinal modeling using Stata* (2nd ed.). College Station, TX: StataCorp LP.

Rector, R. E., & Youssef, S. E. (1999). *The determinants of welfare caseload decline*. Report No. 99-04. Heritage Foundation, Center for Data Analysis, Washington, DC.

Sabia, J. J. (2008). Blacks and the family cap: Pregnancy, abortion, and spillovers. *Journal of Population Economics*, *21*(1), 111–134.

Shoeni, R. F., & Blank, R.M. (2000). *What has welfare reform accomplished? Impacts on Welfare participation, employment, income, poverty, and family structure*. National Bureau of Economic Research Working Paper No. 7627. National Bureau of Economic Research, Cambridge, MA.

Soss, J., Schram, S. F., Vartanian, T. P., & O'Brien, E. (2001). Setting the terms of relief: explaining state policy choices in the devolution revolution. *American Journal of Political Science*, *45*(2), 378–395.

Urban Institute. (2005). *Fast facts – Worst case sanctions*. Washington, DC: The Urban Institute.

U.S. General Accounting Office. (2001). *Welfare reform: More research needed on TANF family caps and other policies for reducing out-of-wedlock births*. Report to Congressional Requesters, No. GAO-01-924. U.S. General Accounting Office, Washington, DC.

Weber, Bruce, Mark Edwards, and Greg Duncan. (2003). *Single mother work and poverty under welfare reform: Are policy impacts different in rural areas?* National Poverty Center Working Paper 03-7. National Poverty Center, Ann Arbor, MI.